N

Arctic Ocean

9

0   1   2   3   4   500 KM
0   2   4   6   800 Miles

5

15   19

11

17

North Sea

10

4

3

USSR

Atlantic Ocean

14

2

7

13

6

20

1

16   18

12

21

8

Mediterranean

AFRICA

1	Austria		
2	Belgium		
3	Denmark	10	Irish Republic		
4	England & Wales	11	Northern Ireland		
5	Finland	12	Italy	17	Scotland
6	France	13	Luxembourg	18	Spain
7	Germany	14	Netherlands	19	Sweden
8	Greece	15	Norway	20	Switzerland
9	Iceland	16	Portugal	21	Yugoslavia

EXPLORING EUROPE

Edited by
Richard Quilter

MPC

British Library Cataloguing in Publication Data
Quilter, Richard
  Exploring Europe. — 2nd ed.
  1. Europe — visitors' guides
  I. Title
914'.04448

ISBN 0 86190 357 9

Published by:
Moorland Publishing Co Ltd,
Moor Farm Road West, Ashbourne,
Derbyshire, England, DE6 1HD

Printed in the UK by:
Richard Clay Ltd,
Bungay, Suffolk

Contents

List of Maps and Plans

Preface

Everyone who visits Europe wishes to make the most of their holidays there and many prefer to select the less-frequented routes, while at the same time enjoying the best that each country has to offer.

Exploring Europe is a book which meets such a wish by offering detailed itineraries along these lesser-known routes, suggesting what to see on the way, noting necessary practical information and making a feature of providing background knowledge for each country. It is based on the *YHA Pocket Guide to Europe*, which first appeared in 1952, was enlarged as the *Youth Hostellers' Guide to Europe* and ran to nine editions. It keeps pace with the increasing popularity of touring Europe and its purpose conforms to the original work; the surprising diversity of places of scenic and cultural interest to be found in touring European countries is evident in the recommended itineraries. Much of the text has been re-written; it has been completely revised, updated and re-set.

We are indebted to John Booker, Maurice Collet, Robert Crawford, Charles Dawson, John Grier, Margaret Griffen, Graham Heath, Marion Hume, John Morley, Norman Nesbitt, John Parfitt, K.J. Penning, R.M. Stuttart, Maurice Tomlin, E.M. Wheeler, Henry Wilkes and Rollo Woods for their work in selecting the itineraries and writing the chapters. We are grateful, too, for the first-hand advice we have had from national tourist associations on the Continent and from individual readers.

We have tried to ensure the accuracy of all the information given, but in a work of this nature omissions and errors are almost inevitable and we ask our readers to send us comments and suggestions which may be useful in the preparation of a future edition.

Notes for Users

Arrangement
A general description of the country, its people and its culture comes first, followed by special information for the tourist. Then comes a detailed description of all the most important areas, arranged in the form of Routes (**R1, R2**, etc), with side-routes to more out of the way places (**R1(i)**, **R1(ii)**, etc), printed in smaller type.

Routes
The routes are not intended to be exclusive; in many cases, in fact, they are too long to be covered in the course of a single holiday; they indicate the main lines of communication and provide a means of linking the various towns and other places which the traveller may wish to visit.

Places which are specially worth seeing or which are important centres of communication are printed in the text in bold type (eg **Bregenz**); all other place names and places of interest are printed in italics. The index lists all place names except those which are mentioned only in passing.

Maps
The outline maps in the text must be supplemented by good cyclists' or walkers' maps, as mentioned under each country. In most cases these can be supplied from stock by YHA Adventure Shops at their stores throughout Britain or can be obtained by them to order.

Plans
Plans of many of the principal towns are included at their appropriate place in the text. They are diagrams only, to indicate the location of the main sights.

Youth Hostels
Youth hostels are indicated Δ following place names (eg *Bruges* Δ). In *all* cases their continued existence and location should by checked from an *annual* publication, ie the *International Youth Hostel Handbook* or the national youth hostel handbook of the country concerned.

Rail, Bus and Steamer Services
Where these are stated to be seasonal, care should by taken to check availability. The tourist season for some services (eg certain steamer routes in Norway) is short. In all cases departure times should be checked from current sources.

AUSTRIA

Geographical Outline

Land

Austria, land-locked in Central Europe and bounded by six countries, is 350 miles (560km) long and barely 25 miles (40km) broad at some points. The western provinces of *Vorarlberg, Tirol* and *Salzburg* consist entirely of high mountain ranges which extend eastwards through *Carinthia* and *Styria* towards *Vienna*, leaving only a narrow plain along the Czech and Hungarian frontiers.

The main mountain chains run from west to east. There is a central line of very high peaks of ancient rock (10,000-12,400ft, 3,000-3,800m) consisting largely of granite in the *Ötztaler, Stubaier* and *Zillertaler Alps*, the *High Tauern* and the *Lower Tauern*. To the north and south of this line lie chains of younger rock, principally limestone, with peaks ranging from 7,000ft to 9,000ft (2,100m to 2,700m); the southern chain forming the border with Italy and Yugoslavia, but the northern chain (along the German frontier) extends through the *Lechtaler Alps*, the *North Tirol Limestone Alps*, the *Salzburg Limestone Alps* to the *Salzkammergut* and the *Vienna Forest*.

The main river is the Danube (*Donau*) which crosses the north-eastern part of the country from *Passau* to *Vienna*. Into it flow a number of alpine rivers, including the *Inn* (originating in the Swiss *Engadine* and passing through *Innsbruck*), the *Salzach* (on which *Salzburg* lies) and the *Traun*, which drains part of the *Salzkammergut*.

The *Salzkammergut* lakes, within easy reach of *Salzburg*, and the *Carinthian* lakes, near *Klagenfurt* and notable for their warm temperature, comprise the two groups of Austria's mountain lakes.

Climate

The climate of most of Austria is alpine. Snow generally covers the whole country during January, lasting until the end of March in the mountain areas and until the end of April on the higher slopes (6,000ft, 1,800m, and above). The permanent snowline occurs at about 8,500ft (2,590m). The föhn wind, dry and warm, is most apparent in spring, melting the snows and affording early access to alpine pastures in the *Inn*, *Ötztal* and *Salzach* valleys. Mountain torrents are then in spate and avalanches frequently occur. Rainfall is higher in the west (*Tirol* and *Salzburg*) than in the south and east (*Carinthia* and *Vienna*) and the latter areas also enjoy more sunshine.

The best months for a visit are from January to March or April for winter sports, May and June for spring flowers and July to September for walking or climbing at high altitudes.

Plants and Animals

The mountain slopes are frequently covered up to about 6,500ft (2,000m) with spruce and pine forests, whose dark green is broken by the emerald of alpine meadows. Amongst the many alpine flowers are several varieties of gentian and saxifrage and, close to the snowline, the edelweiss. Most of the rarer flowers are protected by law and should not be picked.

Animals likely to be seen include the chamois, wild goat, mountain hare and marmot.

The People

Population

Austria's population is about 7,500,000; a fifth of this figure is ascribed to *Vienna,* another fifth accounts for the populations of the provincial capitals.

Language

The language is German, spoken in varying dialects. Despite the bond of language, the majority of Austrians regard themselves as an independent people, with separate traditions; this is particularly the case in *Vienna.*

Religion

Austria is predominantly Catholic and, especially in the country districts, religion is a vital force in the lives of the people.

History

The Austrian Republic of today is all that remains of the vast Habsburg Empire which embraced Austria, Hungary and parts of Czechoslovakia, Yugoslavia, Italy and Poland.

Exposed to the east, overrun in the Dark Ages by Vandals, Visigoths, Huns,

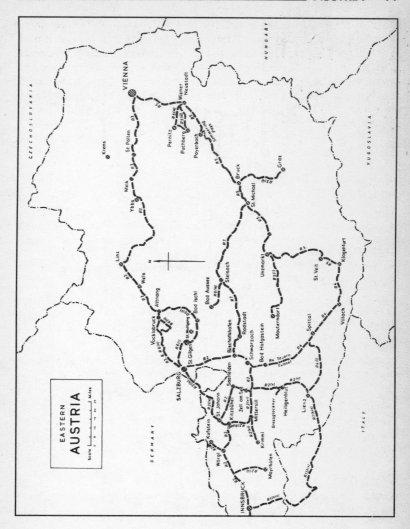

Avars and Slavs, Austria found temporary respite in the eighth century under Charlemagne and was Christianized by the Irish monk St Columba and the English St Boniface. Its position in the heart of Europe required and encouraged strong leaders, such as the Habsburgs provided for nearly seven centuries from 1272. They gave peace to the Danube basin, and were a bulwark for the rest of the

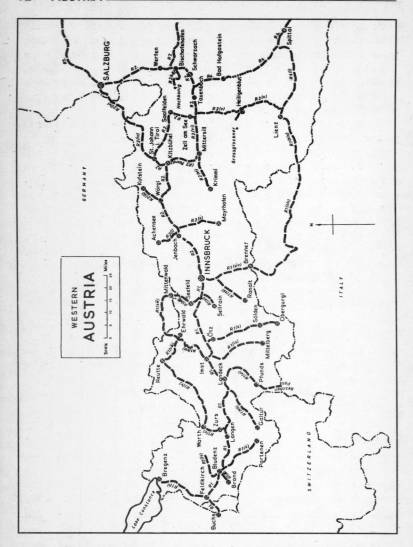

continent against Turkish expansion of their conquests in Hungary and south-east Europe. Vienna was besieged in 1529 and again in 1683. But the defeat of the Turks at Mohács (1687) removed the danger and allowed Habsburg power to be extended over Hungary.

Besides ruling in their own territories the Habsburgs, consistent champions of Catholicism, were also, for nearly four centuries, emperors of the 'Holy Roman Empire'. This dispersal of interests and strength was little help to Austria: it embroiled her in the Thirty Years' War (1618-48) and in irrelevant struggles to defend remote parts of the Empire. Not until the eighteenth century, under Maria Theresa and her son Joseph II, was attention given to the condition of the people, and long-needed reforms carried out.

Decisively defeated by Napoleon at Austerlitz in 1806, the Habsburgs had to renounce the Holy Roman Empire as it was formally abolished, but emerged purged and strengthened in their own re-shaped dominions. The young and brilliant Metternich, the supreme diplomat of the age, achieved in the Congress of Vienna a balance of European alliances favourable to Austria and to the maintenance of peace. Until his fall in 1848 he remained the chief arbiter of Europe's affairs, but insensitive to popular and national movements. The popular rising in Vienna in 1848 was put down, but renewed pressure for reform gained Austria a liberal constitution in 1867. Francis Joseph II, the last great Habsburg (reigned 1848-1916), had some success in meeting the varied wishes of the many nationalities of his realms, but World War I finished the empire and a large number of small, independent states emerged, including Austria. In 1938 the Nazis forcibly incorporated Austria into Germany, but at the end of World War II it resumed its existence as an independent state.

Government

Austria is a democratic federal republic of nine provinces (*Länder*) including the Province of Vienna. The two-chamber government consists of a national diet of 165 members elected by direct vote and a federal diet elected according to the proportionate strength of parties in each of the *Länder*. The president is elected for six years. The *Länder* have a considerable measure of self-government.

Resources

Austria is a poor country. A high proportion of its land is uncultivable mountain and there are few natural resources except oil and some iron. But the peasant population makes full use of every square foot of cultivable land, and crops of grass for fodder are grown on the most precipitous hillsides. Timber is a major product of the alpine areas and hydro-electric power is being developed. The major industrial areas are in the eastern part of the country, particularly in and around *Vienna*.

Customs

The Austrians are a light-hearted and carefree people; the Viennese, in particular, have a reputation for good-natured wit and gaiety.

Austrian manners are courteous; it is usual to shake hands on meeting and parting and, amongst city-dwellers, a man will often kiss a woman's hand in greeting. A frequent greeting, particularly in the countryside, is *Grüss Gott* (God greet you).

In country districts, particularly in the *Tirol*, picturesque national costumes of various types are still worn, at least on Sundays and holidays. Short leather trousers are often worn by men of all ages as workaday attire, with green-lapelled jackets and green hats, sometimes with a tuft of chamois hair. National dances and yodelling are popular in many villages, and saints' days (of which there are many) provide the opportunity for all kinds of local celebrations.

Small shrines (or calvaries) often piously decked with fresh flowers, are a frequent feature on the roadside or on mountain paths.

Culture

Music

Music is the predominant art of Austria. *Vienna* was the home of the great classical musicians of the eighteenth and nineteenth century — Haydn, Mozart, Beethoven and Schubert — and of many masters of light music such as Johann Strauss (father and son) and Lehar; also, in the twentieth century, of Schönberg, whose twelve-tone system — a major break with tradition — makes him one of the great innovators among composers. The *Staatsoper* (National Opera), Vienna Philharmonic Orchestra, Vienna Symphonic Orchestra and the *Salzburg* Festival have won international fame. Festivals are also held at *Vienna* (May/June) at *Bregenz* and at *Salzburg* (July/August).

Architecture

Architecture has played a role second only to music in Austria's cultural history. Gothic style is represented in Vienna by the *Stefansdom* (St Stephen's Cathedral) and the Church of *Maria am Gestade*, and in the choir of the *Franziskaner* Church in *Salzburg*. Among the landmarks of the Renaissance style is the tomb of Kaiser Maximilian in the *Hofkirche* in *Innsbruck*. But it was in the seventeenth and eighteenth centuries that Austrian architecture reached its finest flower. *Salzburg* Cathedral (1630) is a notable example of early Baroque style, under strong Italian influence; early in the eighteenth century came a series of magnificent buildings in Vienna designed by Fischer von Erlach (father and son): the National Library, the Winter Palace of Prince Eugene; and by Lukas von Hildebrandt: the Belvedere Palace and the Schönbrunn Palace.

Painting

Modern Austrian painters, with the exception of Kokoschka, are little known outside their own country, because their work is in localized styles in isolation from the rest of Europe.

Literature

The works of a number of twentieth-century authors have been translated into English, amongst them von Hoffmannsthal, Schnitzler, Kafka and Zweig. The stories of Kafka, in particular, haunt the mind as disturbing modern parables.

Science

In two fields — psychology and philosophy — Austrian (or, more strictly, Viennese) contributions have had a profound effect on the modern world. Freud (1856-1939) is the founder of psycho-analysis. Wittgenstein, the leading member of the 'Vienna Circle' of philosophers, has been the most original thinker in the now dominant school of linguistic philosophy. In economics, also, an 'Austrian School' led by Böhm-Bawerk, has influenced theory.

Touring Information

Touring Areas

Austria's fame as a tourist country rests on its mountains, and it is the mountain provinces of Western Austria which are most popular — *Vorarlberg, Tirol* and *Salzburg*. The southern province of *Carinthia (Kärnten)* is popular too, because of its particularly dry and sunny climate and its warm lakes. *Upper Austria* is less mountainous, except at its south-eastern extremity, which contains the famous *Salzkammergut* lakes. *Styria (Steiermark)* contains many mountains of 7,000ft (2,100m) or more but is less well known; it is an admirable region for travellers who wish to get off the beaten track. Finally, there is *Vienna*, which has its own attractions: architecture, music, modern social developments (kindergartens, well-planned municipal housing) alongside the carefree life of cafés and wine-taverns.

As in most countries, the famous tourist centres are generally more crowded and more expensive than the less-known areas. *Salzburg* (particularly during the Festival month of August), *Innsbruck, Kitzbühel, Zell-am-See, St Anton-am-Arlberg, Pertisau, Velden, Seefeld, Pörtschach/Wörthersee* — are fashionable centres at which those with a modest purse will not find such a warm welcome. But elsewhere, particularly in small towns and villages, living is inexpensive; where there is no youth hostel or mountain hut a bed at a small inn or in a private house can often be had for less than a room in a local one-star hotel. What is more, there is a tradition of economical touring in the mountains of Austria and the traveller who has little money to spend is nevertheless welcome.

Access

The three railway routes to Austria are through France and Switzerland arriving in *Vorarlberg*, or through Belgium and Germany to *Salzburg* and to *Passau*; daily service on each route, 20-hours' journey London to Austrian frontier. Daily flights to *Vienna*, several times weekly to *Salzburg*.

Transport

The railways provide the only satisfactory means of long distance transport. Owing to the difficult terrain, trains cannot travel at high speeds although most of the lines are electrified. Second class carriages on expresses and some other services are quite comfortable, but local trains are often crowded, particularly in summer; long stops at main stations give time to purchase refreshments from the platform buffets. Run-about tickets, issued by Austrian Federal Railways to visitors under 26 years, are valid for 9 or 16 days on all state and private railways, Postkraftwagen and some lake steamers.

There are few long-distance motor-coaches, but for shorter distances, particularly in mountain districts, the motor-buses operated by the Post Office (*Postkraftwagen*) offer the best and sometimes the only means of transport.

Many cable railways (*Seilschwebebahn*), chair-lifts (*Sessellift*) and ski-lifts connect the main tourist centres to peaks and viewpoints. Downward journeys are often cheaper; so too are return fares.

Steamboats or motor-boats ply on most of the lakes and on the River *Danube*, providing a pleasant, but usually more expensive, means of transport.

Clothing

As in all mountain countries, the rule for summer attire is: as light as possible by day, particularly in the valleys and in towns, but with a reserve of warm clothing for the evenings and for high altitudes. A raincoat is necessary, even in the height of summer, as sudden heavy rainstorms occur from time to time. For walking on mountain paths boots are essential.

Restaurants

Eating out can be rather expensive, but a cheap and simple meal can often be had at bakeries, fish shops or butchers where tables and chairs are set out during shop hours. In restaurants, green salad is frequently served with meat, but cooked vegetables are less frequent and potatoes are often replaced by macaroni. Tea, to English taste, can seldom be had except in large towns, and coffee is expensive, particularly if ordered with whipped cream — known as *Schlagobers*. Unfermented apple-juice (*Apfelsaft*) is an excellent drink obtainable everywhere. Soups are always excellent, particularly those containing small dumplings

(*Nockerl* or *Knödel*). *Jause* is the local Austrian name for light refreshments, particularly in the afternoon.

The principal types of meat which you will find on a menu are *Rind* (beef), *Schwein* (pork), *Kalb* (veal), *Wurst* (sausage), *Schinken* (ham), *Speck* (bacon). Other useful words are: *Eier* (eggs), *Käse* (cheese), *Gemüse* (vegetables), *Kartoffel* (potatoes).

Public Holidays

1 and 6 January, Easter Monday, 1 May, Ascension Day, Whit Monday, Corpus Christi, 15 August, 26 October, 1 November, 8 December, Christmas and Boxing Days.

Shops are closed on Saturday afternoons, except food shops, and some others are closed on Wednesday afternoons.

Maps

Kummerley and Frey's relief-shaded map of Austria on a scale of 1:500,000 is recommended; so too is Mair's series of eight maps on a scale of 1:200,000. The most popular maps for walking tours are Freytag & Berndt's 1:100,000 series; each of the forty-five sheets covers an area of about 600sq miles (1,500sq km). The best details for climbers are in the magnificent maps of the most important massifs published by the Austrian Alpine Club on a scale of 1:25,000.

Walking and Climbing

Austria is an ideal country for walking and climbing. All the mountain ranges are traversed by paths, inconspicuously but adequately marked by occasional coloured signs on trees or rocks; these coloured markings are reproduced on all the large scale maps. Such maps also indicate the location of the many alpine huts, maintained by the Austrian Alpine Club and other organisations, which provide inexpensive accommodation for all walkers and climbers and supplement the Austrian youth hostel network. The huts are generally substantial stone or timber buildings, situated at altitudes of 3,000ft (900m) to 9,000ft (2,700m) with a resident warden (at least during the summer months). Some provide meals and although cooking facilities are seldom available, boiling water for tea-making is provided at a nominal charge. Accommodation cannot be booked in advance but the huts are rarely full to capacity and visitors are never turned away; members of the Alpine Club do, however, receive priority in the allocation of sleeping accommodation.

The Austrian Alpine Club (the largest of the organisations owning mountain huts) maintains an office in the UK at Longcroft House, Fretherne Road, Welwyn Garden City, Herts. Membership of the Club costs £15 per year, with an entrance fee of £1. There are reductions for those under 25 years, and for those who are married to members. A handbook giving a full list of huts is published, printed in German, with an English key.

For the serious rock and mountain climber Austria offers almost unlimited opportunities. There are superb rock-faces in the limestone mountains of northern *Tirol* (eg *Karwendel* and *Kaisergebirge*), whilst all types of glacier and snow work can be undertaken among the peaks of the central mountain chain (*Ötztaler Alps, Silvretta Group, High Tauern*). The *Wildspitze* (*Ötztaler Alps*) can be specially recommended. Guides can be hired in all the higher mountain villages to assist less experienced climbers.

Skiing

Austria is an ideal country for skiing, both for learners and experts. Snow conditions are usually at their best in January, February and March, but above 5,000ft (1,500m) or so, good skiing can often be enjoyed at Christmas and Easter. The Western provinces (*Vorarlberg* and *Tirol*) are rather more fashionable, and hence more expensive, than *Salzburg, Upper Austria* and *Carinthia*. Skis and sticks can be hired, but the hiring of boots is not possible at all resorts.

Motoring

Motorists should seek detailed advice from their own motoring organisation, should carry their driving licence, insurance and registration certificates, red warning triangle and display their country of origin sticker. There is an almost complete motorway system (some are toll roads) with many examples of daring engineering.

Traffic coming from right has priority, except on major roads; trams have priority over cars, so too do Postbuses on mountain roads. Traffic going up has priority over traffic (except buses) coming down.

Cycling

The main roads, metalled and well engineered, generally follow the river valleys. Minor roads can sometimes be rough-surfaced, steep and sharply curved. Cyclists who enjoy riding rough will find plenty of opportunities to test their skill. Bicycles are carried cheaply if they go on the train with the passenger.

Touring Routes

R1 Swiss Frontier to Brenner Pass, via Arlberg Pass and Innsbruck (134 miles, 215km)

This is the customary approach to Western Austria, following the railway route of the *Arlberg Express*, through the *Vorarlberg* province into *Tirol*. Fine mountain scenery on almost the entire journey.

Buchs (Swiss and Austrian Customs) thence 12 miles (19km) to *Feldkirch*Δ, 1,506ft (459m), a little fortified town partly medieval; arcaded *Marktgasse* in old town and *Schattenburg Castle* are twelfth century; fifteenth-century parish church.

R1 (i) From *Feldkirch* (24 miles, 38km) to **Bregenz** Δ, capital of **Vorarlberg**, picturesque medieval town beautifully situated on *Lake Constance (Bodensee)*. *Landesmuseum* (Provincial Museum) containing medieval altars.

EXCURSIONS: (a) cable railway to *Pfänder* (3,350ft, 1,021m). (b) *Bregenzer Forest*: rail to *Bezau*, 22 miles (35km) thence bus through magnificent wooded mountains to *Schröcken*, 19 miles (30km) good centre for mountain tours. (c) steamers on *Lake Constance* to Swiss and German resorts.

On for 14 miles (22km) to **Bludenz** (1,919ft, 585m), an old-fashioned town where *Kloster* and *Montafon valleys* meet.

R1 (ii) *Bludenz* to *Partenen*, via attractive mountain valley of *Montafon*, leading to *Rhätikon* and *Silvretta* mountain groups on Swiss frontier. Picturesque houses, stone and wood, gabled front, half brown, half white; attractive local costumes ('Maidens' Crowns' worn by girls on Corpus Christi day — eleven days after Whit Sunday). Rail to *Schruns*, 8 miles (13km) and (2,260ft, 688m) good mountain touring centre, chair lifts. On foot to *Sulzfluh* (9,300ft, 2,834m) via *Tilisuna Hut*. By bus further up *Montafon Valley* for 11 miles (18km) to *Partenen*, winter sports centre (3,380ft, 1,030m).

R1 (iii) Bus *Bludenz* to *Brandner Valley*. *Brand* 8 miles (13km) (3,465ft, 1,053m), popular summer and winter resort at foot of *Schesaplana* (9,735ft, 2,967m), cable railway to *Niggenkopf* (5,500ft, 1,676m).

EXCURSIONS: *Lünersee* (6,375ft, 1,943m) largest alpine lake in *Vorarlberg*, 3 hours to *Douglas Hut*. Thence in 3 hours to the *Schesaplana*.

R1 (iv) Bus *Bludenz* to beautiful **Walser Valley**: 12 miles (19km) to *Sonntag*, thence to *Fontanella* and *Faschinajoch Pass* 4,800ft (1,488m). Fine views en route.

Continue up picturesque *Kloster Valley* 15 miles (24km) to *Langen* (3,995ft, 1,218m) junction for route to *Lech Valley*.

R1 (v) Bus via *Flexen Pass* to *Zurs* (5,642ft, 1,720m) famous winter sports centre, along magnificently engineered road with superb views, to *Lech* (4,746ft, 1,446m) summer and winter resort with cable railway to *Oberlech* (5,626ft, 1,714m). Continue to *Warth*, and down gently sloping *Lech Valley* to *Reutte*Δ (see **R1(viii)**).

Continue by railway through *Arlberg* tunnel or by road via *St Christoph* and the **Arlberg Pass** (5,911ft, 1,801m), second highest in Austria. It is 7 miles (11km) to **St Anton** (4,277ft, 1,304m) fashionable winter sports centre, just in the **Tirol**. Road and rail continue down *Stanzer Valley*, between *Lechtaler Alps* and *Ferwall Group* for 4 miles (6km) to *Pettneu* (4,010ft, 1,222m) with easy climb in 6 hours to *Hoher Riffler* 10,400ft (3,169m), thence 12 miles (19km) to **Landeck** (2,676ft, 815m), important centre of communications on River *Inn*; picturesque castle and parish church. Cable car up to the *Venetberg* (8,344ft, 2,513m).

R1 (vi) Bus up upper *Inn Valley*, past series of mountain villages for 31 miles (50km) to **Reschen Pass** (5,030ft, 1,533m) on Italian frontier.

R1 (vii) Bus up **Paznaun Valley**, 25 miles (40km) to *Galtür* (5,192ft, 1,583m), centre for tours in *Silvretta* mountains.

On down *Inn Valley* for 12 miles (19km) to *Imst* (2,716ft, 827m) junction for principal road connection to *Reutte* and the *Zugspitze*.

R1 (viii) Bus *Imst*-**Reutte**, 34 miles (55km) via *Fern Pass* (3,993ft, 1,217m) and *Lermoos* (3,264ft, 995m) tourist centre with fine views on to *Wetterstein* mountains. *Reutte*Δ is an old market town close to the German frontier, and a good centre for excursions by bus via *Füssen* to the castles of *Hochenschwangau* and *Neuschwanstein*.

EXCURSIONS: (a) on foot via *Stuiben* waterfalls to the *Plansee*. (b) via the tiny *Frauensee* to the *Otto Mayr Hut*, in the *Tannheim* mountain group.

R1 (ix) *Imst* is also junction for **Pitz Valley**, a beautiful unspoilt valley with fine glacier scenery. Bus from *Imst* to *Plangeross*, 24 miles (38km); walk to *Mittelberg* (2$^1/_2$ miles, 4km).

EXCURSIONS: glaciers 1 hour, *Riffelsee* (lake and hut, 7,360ft, 2,243m) 2 hours.

Continue for 7 miles (11km) to *Ötztal.*

R1 (x) From *Ötztal* station up the **Ötz Valley**, one of the loveliest in Austria, 35 miles (56km) long (bus from *Ötztal* station to *Obergurgl*, nearly 3 hours), 3 miles (5km) to *Schlatt*. Four miles (6km) to **Ötz** for *Gasthof Stern* — Gothic paintings; bathing at *Lake Piburger*, 40 minutes' walk.

EXCURSIONS: (a) *Bielefelder Hut* on the *Acherkogel* (7,111ft, 2,167m), 4 hours (b) bus to *Kühtai* with bus connection on to *Gries im Sellrain* (**R1(xi)**). Or on foot *Ötz* to *Gries*, 9-10 hours.

Continue up *Ötz Valley* to *Umhausen*, (5$^1/_2$ miles, 9km) (see fine *Stuiben* waterfall (500ft, 152m), $^3/_4$ hour walk. Not to be confused with *Stuiben* falls near *Reutte*). *Langenfeld*, 5$^1/_2$ miles (9km), birthplace of Franz Senn, founder of German and Austrian Alpine Club.

EXCURSION: to *Lake Winnebach* with Hut (7,827ft, 2,368m), via attractive village of *Gries im Sulztal*, 4$^1/_2$ hours.

Sölden, 9$^1/_2$ miles, 15km (4,405ft, 1,342m), main tourist centre for valley. (On foot in 2 hours, or by chair-lift in 16 minutes, to *Hochsölden*, (6,790ft, 2,069m) good for late skiing). At *Zwielselstein* (2$^1/_2$ miles, 4km) the valley forks, one branch leading to

Obergurgl 8 miles (13km), highest parish in Europe (6,321ft, 1,927m), the other to *Vent* (6,270ft, 1,911m), at foot of the *Wildspitze* (12,309ft, 3,657m), highest peak in *Tirol*. Both *Obergurgl* and *Vent* are excellent centres for climbing to glaciers, mountain huts and peaks in *Ötztaler Alps*; from *Vent* the *Wildspitze* can be climbed in 6 hours (guide necessary).

From *Ötztal* continue 6 miles (10km) to *Stams*; Cistercian monastery with fine carved altar and 'Rose Railing' (1716), thence along broadening *Inn Valley* with *Mieminger Chain* to the north (charming mountains rising to 8,000ft (2,400m), best approach from *Telfs*) and *Stubaier Alps* to the south. After 22 miles (35km) comes *Kematen*, important only as junction for **Sellrain Valley**.

R1 (xi) Bus to *Gries im Sellrain* (4,061ft, 1,237m), centre of attractive valley.

EXCURSIONS: on foot to *Kühtai*, small ski village with *Dortmunder Hut* at 6,487ft (1,977m), and by bus to *Praxmar* (5,579ft, 1,701m) for ascents to various mountain huts.

From *Kematen*, 7 miles (11km) to **Innsbruck**.

Innsbruck△

Cultural and tourist capital of the *Tirol*, one of the most beautifully situated towns in Europe, lying in *Inn Valley*, with towering peaks to north and south, snow-capped until April-May. From railway station turn right along *Südtiroler Platz*, left via *Brixner Strasse, Bozner Platz* (for buses), *Meraner Strasse* into *Maria Theresian Str*, main street of town with impressive mountain background and baroque buildings. In centre of street, *Annasäule*, pillar commemorating liberation from Bavaria in 1703. Turn right along *Maria Theresian Str*, which leads into *Herzog Friedrich Str*, centre of oldest part of town; where this street bears left, see *Goldenes Dachl* (Golden Roof), picturesque Gothic bay window, richly sculptured. Turn right down *Hofgasse* (sixteenth-century houses) to *Hofburg*, former imperial palace (1496, renovated eighteenth century); conducted tours of palace including *Hofkirche*, built in sixteenth century to hold *Tomb of Emperor Maximilian*. Finest Renaissance sculpture in Austria; two of statues designed by Albrecht Dürer. Next to church is *Tiroler Volkskunst Museum*, largest collection of peasant costumes and furniture in Austria or Germany. Behind *Hofburg* is *Hofgarten*, palace garden of shady lakes and great willows.

EXCURSIONS: (a) cable railway from *Mühlauer* bridge, on north side of city to *Hungerburg* (2,860ft, 921m) fine view; further railways to *Hafelekar* (7,419ft, 2,261m) fine path along ridge. (b) bus to *Ambras* (castle, with fine interior, and view over city) and *Igls* (8 miles, 13km), smart resort. Thence cable railway ascends to *Patscherkofel* mountain (6,500ft, 1,990m), hour walk to summit (7,450ft, 2,179m).

R1 (xii) Railway from *Innsbruck* up **Stubaital** to *Fulpmes* 11 miles (18km), thence bus to *Neustift*Δ,(3,237ft, 987m) and *Ranalt* (4,150ft, 1,265m), both good centres for exploring *Stubaital Alps.*

R1 (xiii) By railway from *Innsbruck* to *Seefeld* (3,870ft, 1,179m), fashionable mountain resort, and *Scharnitz*, good centre for tours in *Karwendel Mountains*, in particular, magnificent four-day walk up **Karwendel Valley** via *Karwendel, Falken*

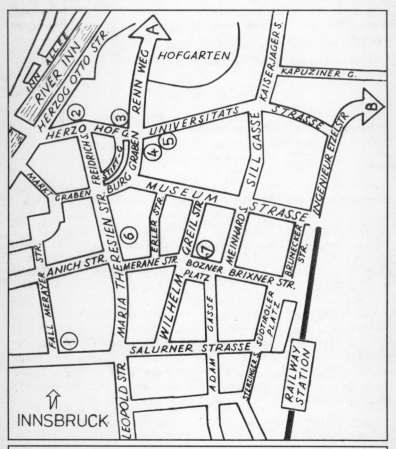

1 General Post Office. 2 'Goldenes Dachl'. 3 Hofburg. 4 Hofkirche.
5 Tiroler Volkskunst Museum. 6 Annasäule. 7 Trolleybus to youth hostel.
A to Kufstein, Salzburg, Vienna. B to youth hostel

and *Lamsenjoch* huts to *Achensee*. Train continues across German territory via *Mittenwald* and re-enters Austria at *Ehrwald* (3,267ft, 996m) resort at foot of **Zugspitze** (9,725ft, 2,964m) impressive mountain, with peak forming Austrian-German frontier. Cable railway from *Ehrwald* to summit.

R1 (xiv) Rail or road up the *Wipptal* to the **Brenner Pass** (23 miles, 37km) via *Steinach* (3,447ft, 1,050m) and *Gries am Brenner* (4,116ft, 1,255m), both popular small resorts. The *Brenner Pass* (4,494ft, 1,370m) is the lowest north-south crossing over the Alps, formerly a Roman road. Through train across Italian territory to *Lienz*Δ in *East Tirol* (see **R4(i)**).

R2 Innsbruck to Salzburg via Kitzbühel (160 miles, 257km)

A continuation of the *Arlberg Express* route by following the *Inn Valley* down to *Wörgl* and climbing the watershed between *Kitzbühel* and *Zell* into the upper *Salzach Valley*. Scenery is superb all the way, but the journey is slow and takes 4 hours, even by express train.

Innsbruck to *Solbad Hall*, 6 miles (10km) old town with fine parish church; on for further 11 miles (18km) to *Schwaz*, with many old houses, and fine fourteenth-century church; once most important town in the *Tirol*.

EXCURSION: on foot to *Kellerjoch* (7,700ft, 2,346m), easy ascent, wonderful view.

Continue 5 miles (8km) to *Jenbach*. *Tratzberg Castle*, containing frescoed Habsburg family tree (1507) and many notable paintings.

R2 (i) Rack railway *Jenbach-Achensee* summer only (4 miles, 6km). **Achensee** (3,045ft, 928km) is largest and loveliest lake in *Tirol* (6 miles, 10km, long). Steamer from rail terminus to *Pertisau*, fashionable lakeside resort.

R2 (ii) Narrow gauge steam railway from *Jenbach*, 20 miles (32km) up the beautiful **Zillertal**, through *Stummerberg*Δ to *Mayrhofen* (2,066ft, 630m), starting point for tours into the *Zillertal Alps*.

EXCURSIONS: (a) *Ahornspitze* (9,900ft, 3,017m) 6¹/₂ hours (not difficult climb). (b) *Tuxer Valley*, leading to big glacier of *Gefrorene Wand* (Frozen Wall) and magnificent *Tuxer* waterfalls. (c) *Zemmtal Valley* to *Berliner Hut* (6,750ft, 2,057m). (d) *Zillergrund*, a full day's walk to *Plauener Hut* (7,700ft, 2,346m).

From *Jenbach*, 6 miles (10km) to *Brixlegg*, pleasant village with several castles nearby (*Matzen, Kropsberg*) and *Rattenberg*, an extremely picturesque town (Gothic *Hofer Chapel*).

EXCURSION: to lovely *Reintaler* lakes, 40 minutes' walk; bathing.

Continue 9 miles (14km) to **Wörgl**, junction for rail and road to *Kufstein* and *Munich*.

R2 (iii) Following *Inn Valley* 8 miles (13km) to **Kufstein**Δ, important summer and winter centre with good approach to *Kaiser Mountains*, wild and picturesque walking country, with huge rock walls, favourite ground for climbers. *Hintersteinersee*, a lake at western end of range, and views from *Stripsenjoch Hut*.

Railway continues 6 miles (10km) to *Hopfgarten*.

EXCURSION: to the *Höhe Salve* (5,030ft, 1,533m), popular and fine viewpoint (3 hours on foot, or by ski-lift, longest in Europe).

On for another 6 miles (10km) to *Westendorf*, pleasant summer and winter resort, chairlift to *Alpenrosenhaus* (5,250ft, 1,600m) starting point for many mountain walks.

Thence to **Kitzbühel**, after 10$^1/_2$ miles (17km), fashionable winter-sports and summer resort (2,503ft, 762m). Many suspension railways and ski-lifts to surrounding heights.

EXCURSIONS: (a) cable railway to *Hahnenkamm* (5,450ft, 1,661m), from here 1$^1/_2$ hours to *Ehrenbachhöhe* (5,955ft, 1,815m) magnificent view. (b) cable railways, in three stages from *Kitzbühel* to *Kitzbüheler Horn*, exceptionally fine view from summit of *Horn*, $^1/_2$ hour walk; ascent on foot from *Kitzbühel* to *Horn* takes 3 hours. (c) bus or rail to *Schwarzsee*, warm-water lake, good bathing.

Railway and road continue, 5 miles (8km) to *St Johann-im-Tirol*, attractive small town at confluence of several valleys. Here main road to *Salzburg* leaves the railway line.

R2 (iv) Motor road **St Johann-Salzburg** via *Lofer*. Across German territory via *Bad Reichenhall* or *Berchtesgaden*; greatly shortens the normal route via *Zell-am-See* and *Bischofshofen*. Buses operate.

Railway continues via *Hochfilzen* and the *Griesenpass* (3,136ft, 955m) into the **Province of Salzburg**, descending through 23 miles (37km) to *Saalfelden* (2,240ft, 683m) a good centre for walking tours.

EXCURSIONS: (a) *Steinernes Meer* — Sea of Stone — a strange wilderness of boulders lying along German frontier; access (with night's halt at the *Riemann Hut*) to beautiful *Königssee* in Bavaria. (b) via *Urschlaub* valley and *Hintertal* to climb the *Hochkönig* (9,690ft, 2,953m) not for inexperienced climbers; for an easier approach see under *Bischofshofen* (**R2 (vii)**).

After 8 miles (13km) the train reaches **Zell-am-See△** (2,486ft, 758m), fashionable resort on *Lake Zeller*, centre for *Grossglockner* and *Pinzgau*.

EXCURSIONS: (a) by motorboat across lake to summer resort of *Thumersbach*. (b) on foot in 3 hours or by cable railway in 8 minutes to *Schmittenhöhe* (6,457ft, 1,968m), with magnificent views, including thirty-one peaks over 9,000ft (2,700m) high, and starting point of superb high-level footpath, the **Pinzgauer Path**, 15 miles (24km) at 6,000ft (1,800m) above sea level, with fine views to the glacier-crowned mountains of the *High Tauern* across the valley. (c) to *Kaprun*Δ 6 miles (10km), huge Tauern hydro-electric station.

R2 (v) Motor-coach from *Zell-am-See* to *Heiligenblut* 30 miles (48km) via **Grossglockner mountain road**. A spectacular journey through wild alpine scenery, along one of the highest roads in Europe. Open June-October only. The road climbs with many bends and tunnels, to nearly 9,000ft (2,700m) with a branch road (*Gletscherstrasse*) leading to *Franz Josef's Höhe* (7,900ft, 2,408m) looking out over the vast *Pasterze* glacier, with *Grossglockner* (12,457ft, 3,796m), Austria's highest mountain, in background. From *Heiligenblut*Δ there is a road to *Lienz*Δ and *Carinthia* (see **R4 (i)**). Bus from *Zell* to *Lienz* (6 hours), twice daily in summer.

R2 (vi) From *Zell-am-See* by narrow gauge railway through **Pinzgau** (valley of the *Salzach*) 33 miles (53km) to *Krimml*. *Mittersill* 18 miles (29km) is junction for main road via *Pass Thurn*, to *Kitzbühel* (fine views of *Tauern* mountains from road); also nearest point to *Amer Valley* nature reserve. *Neukirchen* 28 miles (48km) from *Zell* is centre for climbers ascending the *Grossvenediger* (12,000ft, 3,657m). *Krimml* has famous waterfalls, largest in eastern Alps.

Railway continues 10 miles (16km) to *Taxenbach*, station for *Rauris Valley* (bus to *Kolm-Saigurn*, lovely mountain centre at foot of *Höher Sonnblick*, 10,200 ft, 3,109m peak). Thence 11 miles (18km) to *Schwarzach St Veit*, junction for *Tauern Railway* to *Carinthia* (see **R4**). Continue 3 miles (5km) to *St Johann im Pongau*Δ, station for the *Leichtensteinklamm* (1 hour on foot) an attractive gorge, with waterfall (admission charge). Train continues 5 miles (8km) to *Bischofshofen* (1,785ft, 544m), junction for railway to *Selzthal* and *Vienna* (see **R7**).

R2 (vii) to the **Hochkönig** (9,600ft, 2,926m). *Bischofshofen* is an excellent starting point for visiting the *Salzburg Limestone Alps*, good walking country giving an impression of greater height than it actually possesses. *Bischofshofen — Mühlbach — Arthurhaus* by bus (or direct on foot, choice of two paths, in 3 hours): on foot 1$^3/_4$ hours to *Mitterbergalpe*, thence in 5 hours to the *Ubergossene Alm* ('Iced Meadow'), a broad mountain-ridge under permanent snow; in one further hour to summit of *Hochkönig* ('Tall King'), magnificent view, alpine hut.

On from *Bischofshofen* for 5 miles (8km) to *Werfen*, *Burg Hohenwerfen*, built in eleventh century for Archbishop of *Salzburg*.

EXCURSION: **Giant Ice Caves**, well worth a visit. Largest known caves in Europe containing extraordinarily beautiful natural ice formations, electrically illuminated; open summer only, warm clothing and boots advised. Conducted tour takes 2 hours. (Ascent from Werfen 3$^1/_2$ hours on foot.)

Train continues 11 miles (18km) to *Golling*.

EXCURSIONS: Waterfall at *Schwarzbachfall*, 1 hour, *Lueg Pass*, $^3/_4$ hour, *Höher Göll* (8,310ft, 2,533m), 6$^1/_2$ hours climb, so-called 'Salzburg Dolomite Road', 20 miles (32km) long, via *Abtenau* to *Annaberg*Δ skirting *Tennengebirge*; superb views; bus service.

On for 6 miles (10km) to *Hallein*Δ seventeenth-century old town of narrow streets and tiny squares and *Dürrnberg* salt-mines, worked since Neolithic times, but now little more than electrically illuminated caves for tourists. Thence 12 miles (19km) to **Salzburg.**

Salzburg△

A town with many ecclesiastical, artistic and musical associations, beautifully situated on River *Salzach* against a background of mountains and dominated by the citadel (*Hohensalzburg*). Picturesque streets and many examples of noble architecture, palaces and spacious squares.

The old town lies to the west of river. Trolley bus from station to *Staatsbrücke* for view of river; follow trolleybus line beyond bridge as far as *Alter Markt*, then bear left into large *Residenzplatz*, splendid seventeenth-century fountain. On south side of square is the *Residenz*, built in seventeenth century, formerly an archbishop's palace. Opposite is *Glockenspiel*, with fine set of thirty-five bells playing daily. Leading off the square is *Mozartplatz* with statue of *Mozart* (nineteenth century). Cross *Residenzplatz* diagonally and pass via arcade into quiet *Domplatz* (Cathedral Square), where miracle play *Jedermann* (*Everyman*) is performed during August. The *Cathedral*, fine early baroque building, dates from 1614-28 (painted ceilings and high altar). On opposite side of *Domplatz* is Franciscan church (Romanesque nave and Gothic choir), and to the left is the Benedictine *Abbey of St Peter*, Austria's oldest monastery (seventeenth century or earlier); *St Peter's Church*, with fifteenth-century Madonna and monument to Mozart's sister, and the *St Peter-Stifskeller*, a popular restaurant in genuine medieval setting. Through the *St Peter-Friedhof* (cemetery) to cable railway leading up to the citadel of *Hohensalzburg* (1,780ft, 542m), founded in the eleventh century but present buildings date from early sixteenth century; formerly home of archbishops; excellent view from tower of *Reckturm*; mechanical organ, built in 1502, plays daily. Return to *Domplatz*, then via *Franziskaner Gasse* across *Max Reinhardt Platz* to *Hofstallgasse* and see on left the *Festspielhaus* (festival theatre and concert hall). Continue via *Sigmundsplatz* (on left is *Neutor*, a road tunnel built in eighteenth century) to *Gstättergasse*; at No 13 is a lift on to the *Mönschsberg* (1,650ft, 503m) with café and fine view. Return along *Gstättergasse*, but bear left down *Getreidegasse*. At No 9 is *Mozart's Birthplace*, with museum. Return via *Rathausplatz* to *Staatsbrücke*.

> EXCURSIONS: (a) *Gaisberg* (4,200ft, 1,280m), mountain lying 3 miles (5km) east of the town, with superb view. Bus service, or on foot in 3 hours. (b) *Hellbrunn* Palace, seventeenth-century summer residence, with fine park and interesting water-toys (local bus from *Salzburg*).

1 Cathedral. 2 Abbey of St Peter. 3 Mozart's Birthplace. 4 Town
Museum. 5 Mozarteum. A to Innsbruck. B to Station. C to Vienna.

R3 Salzburg — Linz — Vienna (199 miles, 320km)

Arlberg Express railway route keeps to the uneventful lowland country north of
the *Salzkammergut*. *Vöcklabruck* comes after 41 miles (66km), a friendly little
town with many old buildings and town walls. *Attnang-Puchheim*, 3 miles (5km)
further on, is the junction for *Salzkammergut* line (see **R6(ii)**), then, after 19 miles
(30km) is *Wels*, another old town, with a fine parish church. On for 16 miles
(26km) to *Linz* Δ on the *Danube*, Austria's third largest town, with big steelworks.

The journey from *Linz* to *Vienna* may be undertaken by road, rail or river
steamer ($2^1/_2$ hours by express train, 6 hours by steamer). The countryside is
unremarkable as far as *Ybbs* where begins the *Wachau*, a beautiful area of wooded
hills with many castles, vineyards and fine churches. At *Melk* Δ 65 miles (105km)
from *Linz*, is a Benedictine abbey, one of the finest baroque buildings in Europe,
on rocky cliff above the *Danube*. The *Wachau* ends at *Krems* Δ, off the main
railway line; ancient town with many fine buildings. Then through flat and
uninteresting landscape until the *Wienerwald*, a wooded hill country immortalised by Strauss, is reached. From the southern slopes of these hills there is a fine

view of *Vienna*, particularly at night from the *Kahlenberg* (1,590ft, 485m).

R4 Innsbruck — Schwarzach — Klagenfurt, via Tauern Tunnel (209 miles, 336km)

For *Innsbruck — Schwarzach*, see **R2**. At *Schwarzach St Veit* the *Tauern Railway* leaves the main line; a single track which crosses the high Alps from north to south between the *Brenner Pass* and *Graz*. It climbs steeply and offers fine views, principally on the right-hand side.

After 13 miles (21km) comes *Bad Hofgastein* (2,800ft, 853m) popular resort and spa; then on to ridge path for 5 miles (8km) and by Kaiser Wilhelm Promenade into *Bad Gastein* Δ (3,562ft, 1,085m), fashionable spa which has retained much of its eighteenth-century elegance; cable railway on to the *Stubnerkogel* (7,400ft, 2,255m), magnificent views. Continue for 5 miles (8km) to *Böckstein* (3,700ft, 1,127m) a smaller and more modest resort, good centre for mountain tours.

EXCURSIONS: (a) on foot to *Nassfeld* (2 hours, 5,240ft, 1,597m) a mountain and ski village in beautiful surroundings; electric underground railway to *Kolm-Saigurn* (see **R2**, under *Taxenbach*). (b) ascent of the *Ankogel* (10,700ft, 3,261m).

The *Tauern Tunnel* (5$^1/_2$ miles) 9km long, emerges in *Carinthia* at *Mallnitz* (3,887ft, 1,185m) a mountain resort enjoying increasing popularity. Fine situation and shares generally good weather of *Carinthia*.

EXCURSIONS: (a) via the *Hannoverhaus* (Alpine Club Hut) to the *Ankogel* (10,700ft, 3,261m) or *Hochalmspitze* (11,000ft, 3,352m). (b) chair-lift to *Hausleralm* (6,270ft, 1,911m).

The railway descends, offering further superb views, clinging to the side of the *Möll Valley*, through *Obervellach* (cable railway from station to village (1,155ft, 352m below). Then 22 miles (35km) to *Spittal*Δ, centre for *Lake Millstätter*. Buses to *Seeboden* and *Millstatt*, favourite summer resorts on beautiful warm lake.

R4 (i) From *Spittal* a branch line leads into **East Tirol**, an isolated, little known, but very attractive region, bordering on the Italian Dolomites. After 21 miles (34km) comes *Greifenburg-Weissensee*, station for resorts on *Weissensee*, highest warm-water lake in Alps (3,050ft, 930m), quiet and unsophisticated. Eighteen miles (29km) to *Lengberg*, and a further 4 miles (6km) to **Lienz** Δ (2,200ft, 670m) principal town of east *Tirol*, pleasant and unspoilt, at junction of *Drau* and *Isel* valleys.

EXCURSIONS: (a) by bus to *Heiligenblut*Δ (25 miles, 40km, 2 hours) well-known mountain village at southern end of *Grossglockner Road* (continuation by bus over *Grossglockner* to *Zell-am-See*, see **R2 (v)**) with fine parish church, contains receptacle of the Holy Blood (whence the name *Heiligenblut*). (b) by bus to *Matrei-am-Venediger*, and *Hinterbichl* (4,300ft, 1,310m) highest point in *Virgental*, summer home of Vienna Boys' Choir, good centre for climbs in *Sud Venediger Group*. (c) via *Huben* 13 miles (21km) to the *Kalser or Defereggen Valleys* (bus services) offering fine views of *Glockner Group*. (d) up *Drau* valley 20 miles (32km) to *Sillian*Δ small climbing centre. (e) bathing at *Lake Tristacher* (2 miles, 3km). From *Lienz*, railway continues via *San Candido* into Italy. Through trains run *Lienz-Brenner-Innsbruck*, across Italian territory (see **R1(xiv)**).

Main railway contiues from *Spittal* for 23 miles (35km) to **Villach** Δ (1,607ft, 509m) communications and trading centre, junction for railways to Yugoslavia and Italy.

EXCURSIONS: (a) *Villacher Alpe (Dobratsch)*, 7,100ft, 2,163m, $2^1/_2$ hours' walk, superb view. (b) by train or bus to the *Ossiacher See*, pleasant lake, 7 miles (11km) long, with numerous small resorts; less crowded and fashionable than *Wörther See*; cable railway from *Annenheim*, on *Ossiacher See* to *Kanzelhöhe* (4,900ft, 1,493m). (c) by rail up the *Gailtal* to *Hermagor* and *Koeschach*; isolated valley little known to foreign tourists. From *Hermagor*, ascent to the *Gartnerkofel* (7,200ft, 2,195m), the only place outside the Himalayas in which the blue flower, wulfenia, grows. (b) into the *Karawanken Mountains*, wild country skirting Yugoslav frontier; best centre is *Feistritz*, east of *Rosenbach*. (e) by rail (8 miles, 13km, on line to *Rosenbach*) to *Faak* for delightful *Faaker See*, surrounded by forest.

From *Villach* it is 10 miles (16km) to *Velden*, expensive and fashionable resort on the warm *Wörthersee* and a further 5 miles (8km) to *Pörtschach*, a similar resort; thence 9 miles (14km) *Klagenfurt*.

Klagenfurt Δ, capital of *Carinthia*, attractive town, bounded by hills. See the *Landhaus* with its arcaded courtyard, the *Landesmuseum* and explore the narrow streets off the *Alter Platz*, especially the *Herrengasse*.

R5 Klagenfurt — Semmering — Vienna (209 miles, 336km)

This is the southern, and longer, approach to *Vienna*; much fine mountain country en route, where few foreign tourists will be found. To left of railway lie the *Gurktaler Alps*, the *Lower Tauern*, and the *Styrian Limestone Alps*; to right are the *Seetaler Alps*, and the *Glein Alps*.

Klagenfurt to *St-Veit-an-der-Glan* 11 miles (18km) and on to *Launsdorf* 5 miles (8km).

EXCURSIONS: on foot in 1 hour to *Hochosterwitz Castle*, sixteenth-century construction, contains weapons and armour; magnificently situated on chalk spur at 2,400ft (732m).

Treibach-Althofen, 10 miles (16km), junction for railway to *Gurk*, reached after another 10 miles (16km), has fine twelfth-century cathedral; then 9 miles (14km) to *Friesach* and 18 miles (29km) to *Unzmarkt*, junction for railway to *Mauterndorf*.

R5 (i) From *Unzmarkt* to *Mauterndorf* by rail, 47 miles (76km). This route follows the *Mur Valley* along southern slope of *Lower Tauern Mountains*, 17 miles (27km), to

Murau Δ, summer and winter resort; 14 miles (23km) to *Preillitz* (bus to *Turracher Höhe*), 5,800ft (1,767m), steepest road in Austria, winter sports centre; 10 miles (16km), *Tamsweg* (3,349ft, 1,020m) good centre for the *Lurgau* (upper *Mur* valley) 7 miles (11km), *Mauterndorf*, market town and resort. Railway ends here but road crosses *Radstädter Tauern Pass* (5,702ft, 1,138m) through *Obertauern* (5,400ft, 1,646m) (ski centre) to *Radstadt* (see **R7**).

On for 12 miles (19km) to *Judenburg* and a further 4 miles (6km) to *Zeltweg*, junction for branch railway through *Lavant* valley to Yugoslav frontier. After 20 miles (32km) comes *St Michael*, junction for railway to *Selzthal* (see **R7**) then 4 miles (6km) to *Leoben* and 13 miles (21km) to *Bruck an der Mur*Δ with its *Rathaus*, fine seventeenth-century fountain and early sixteenth-century Gothic *Kornmesserhaus* with arcades. Junction for railway to *Graz*.

R5 (ii) *Bruck an der Mur* to *Graz* 34 miles (55km). Following the *Mur Valley* via *Peggau* (see the *Lurgrotte*, largest stalactite caves in Austria) to **Graz** Δ, capital of **Styria**, second largest city in Austria; university, theatres, museums, etc. Although an industrial centre, it is attractively laid out, with plenty of open spaces. *Schlossberg* at 500ft (152m) dominates city, fine view; on top is a sixteenth-century clock-tower, with 7-ton bell (1587). Other sights: spiral staircase in castle (fifteenth century), thirteenth-century Madonna in *Leechkirche (Rittergasse),* altar-piece in fifteenth-century cathedral.

From *Bruck*, main line continues 18 miles (29km) to *Krieglach* and a further 18 miles (29km) to *Semmering* on border between *Steiermark (Styria)* and *Lower Austria*; train descends in spectacular curves, with many viaducts and tunnels to *Payerbach-Reichenau*, good approach to limestone Alps to north.

EXCURSIONS: (a) bus (4 miles, 6km) to *Hirschwang*, then by cable railway to edge of plateau (5,072ft, 1,546m), thence on foot to summit of *Raxalpe* (6,029ft, 1,837m), very fine views. (b) by bus to *Preiner Gscheid* (10 miles, 16km) then on foot in 3 hours to summit of *Raxalpe*.

Railway line continues over plain via *Neunkirchen* and *Wiener Neustadt* to *Vienna*.

R5 (iii) *Wiener Neustadt* by branch line and cog railway (16 miles, 26km) to *Puchberg am Schneeberg* and thence by narrow-gauge steam locomotive (6 miles, 9km) up to **Hochschneeberg** (6,806ft, 2,075m) highest peak in *Lower Austria*, fine view; also rock walls, *Höhe Wand* and *Dürre Wand*. On foot (13 miles, 21km) to *Pernitz*Δ. Bus to *Wiener Neustadt* or train to *Vienna*.

R6 The Salzkammergut

The *Salzkammergut* consists of two chains of lakes set among the limestone mountains north of main line of the Alps. The eastern chain, along the River *Traun*, starts at southern end with two small and secluded lakes, the *Grundlsee* and the *Altaussee* (both 2,000ft, 700m) and descends through the *Hallstätter See* (1,670ft, 509m) to the *Traun See* (or *Gmunder See*) (1,384ft, 421m).

The western chain consists of the *Wolfgang See* (1,770ft, 539m) which actually drains into the *Traun* via a tributary, the *Mond See* (1,580ft, 482m), and the *Atter* (or *Kammer*) *See* (1,530ft, 466m), both of which drain into the *Ager.*

The *Wolfgang See*, which has a beautiful setting, has acquired a worldwide reputation from the operetta *White Horse Inn* and is more crowded and expensive than the other lakes. *St Gilgen*Δ is a lakeside resort. *St Wolfgang* on north shore of lake has steam railway (summer only) to summit of *Schafberg* (1,783ft, 543m).

The *Hallstätter See*, less easy of access and quieter, is probably the most beautiful, being almost completely surrounded by lofty mountains; wooded banks drop steeply near to the water's edge. *Hallstatt-Lahn*Δ is on south-west shore where aerial cableway connects to salt-mine.

The *Atter See,* the largest of the mountain lakes, has a youth hostel at *Weissenbach*. The *Traun See* is the second largest, but the surroundings are less striking, although the *Traun See* reflects the peak of the *Traunstein* (5,580ft, 1,701m) on its eastern shore. *Ebensee*Δ is at south-western end of lake, at the influx of the *Traun.*

The *Salzkammergut* has a somewhat higher rainfall than other parts of Austria but its great natural beauty outweighs this disadvantage.

There are three main mountain ranges in the area. The highest is the *Dachstein* group, to the south of the *Hallstätter See*. The *High Dachstein* itself (9,800ft, 2,986m) can only be tackled by experienced climbers with a guide (9 hours from *Hallstatt*), but the *Dachstein caves* (4,400ft, 1,340m), huge chambers of bare rock, tunnels and ice caves, can be reached in $2^1/_2$ hours by footpath from *Obertraun* Δ or by cable railway.

The second group is the *Totes Gebirge* to the north of *Altaussee* and *Grundlsee* at about 6,000ft (1,800m), forming a plateau, from the edges of which are very fine views. Vegetation is scanty, mountain huts are numerous. *Hinterstoder*Δ and *Bad Aussee*Δ are summer resorts.

The third group is the *Höllengebirge*, a small range between the *Atter See* and *Traun See*, approached from *Ebensee*. Cable railway from *Ebensee* to the *Feuerkogel* (5,330ft, 1,626m).

R6 (i) By rail in 30 minutes from *Salzburg* to *Steindorf*, thence by bus through attractive scenery, to *Bad Ischl*Δ via *Mond See*Δ and *Wolfgang See*.

R6 (ii) By rail in $2^1/_2$ hours *Salzburg-Attnang-Bad Ischl* via *Traun See*. This line continues via *Hallstätter See* to *Bad Aussee* (whence buses to *Altaussee* and *Grundlsee*). There are through trains *Salzburg-Bad Aussee*.

R6 (iii) Approach from the south by rail from *Stainach-Irdning*, on line *Bischofshofen-Selzthal* (see **R7**), to *Bad Aussee*.

R6 (iv) Branch railways from *Vöcklabruck* or *Vöcklamarkt* (both on line *Salzburg-Attnang*) to stations on the *Atter See*.

Steamers and motor-boats ply on all the lakes, and buses connect the majority of centres.

R7 Bischofshofen — Selzthal — St Michael (104 miles, 167km)

This is an alternative route to *Vienna*; although longer by about 50 miles (80km) than the direct route via *Linz* it passes through more attractive scenery. Diesel trains run from *Salzburg* to *St Michael* and on via *Semmering* into *Vienna*.

From *Bischofshofen* (see **R2**), the train climbs more than 1,000ft (300m) in 15 miles (24km) to *Radstadt*, a village still surrounded by its wall, the junction for the road via the *Tauern Pass* into *Carinthia* (see **R5(i)**).

On for 12 miles (19km) to *Schladming*Δ (2,427ft, 740m), excellent centre for mountain tours.

> EXCURSIONS: (a) *High Dachstein* (9,800ft, 2,986m) very rewarding, but only for good climbers, with guide. (b) *Ramsau*, a lovely mountain plateau, about 3,000ft (900m), 2 hours on foot. (c) *Hochgolling* (9,500ft, 2,895m), highest peak in *Lower Tauern*; very fine view, only with guide.

Continue for 24 miles (39km) to *Stainach-Irdning*, junction for line to *Salzkammergut* (see **R6(iii)**) and on for 17 miles (27km) to *Selzthal*, 2,100ft (640km) important railway junction, with connections to *Linz*. Railway climbs to cross watershed between *Enns* and *Mur* valleys at *Schoben Pass* (2,790ft, 850m), with *Lower Tauern* range to the south-west and *Eisenerzen Alps* to the north-east. It then descends 820ft (250m) on the 39 miles (63km) journey to *St Michael*, on main line *Klagenfurt-Vienna*. (For continuation of journey to *Vienna*, see **R5**.)

Vienna

Vienna Δ is quite different from the rest of Austria, a city with traditions of imperial grandeur, music, noble architecture and wealth. From 1945 to 1955 it was under four-power occupation but since then the city has regained its poise and reputation as the capital of an independent Austria.

The old city is bounded on the north-east by the *Danube Canal*, and surrounded on the remaining sides by the *Ring*, a vast boulevard, which changes its name from section to section (*Schubert Ring, Kärntner Ring, Opern Ring*, etc); on either side of it are state buildings, theatres and museums, and beneath it is a fine shopping centre, nicknamed the *Jonas Grotto*. The modern industrial and shopping area, together with the railway terminals, lie further out, then the residential zone comes to the edge of the *Vienna Woods* on the north-west.

Central Vienna was badly damaged in the war, particularly along the *Danube Canal*, but its buildings and monuments have been meticulously restored and new amenities have been added.

The heart of the city is *St Stephen's Cathedral (Stefansdom)* in *St Stephen's*

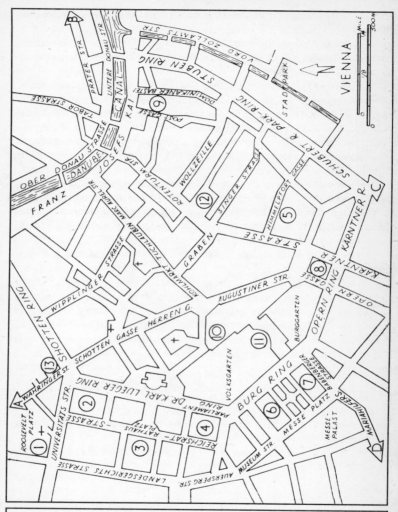

1 Votive Church. 2 University. 3 Town Hall. 4 Parliament House.
5 Winter Palace. 6 Natural History Museum. 7 Fine Arts Museum.
8 State Opera. 9 General Post Office. 10 Hofburg. 11 New Hofburg.
12 St Stephen's Cathedral. 13 Tram Terminus.
A to Vienna Woods. B to Prater. C to South Railway Station. D to West
Railway Station.

Square. It dates in part from the thirteenth century; the tower, which can be climbed to about 300ft (90m) (fine view) is fourteenth century.

To the west, beyond *Graben* and *Kohlmarkt*, is the *Hofburg* (Imperial Palace); mixture of styles, dating from 1530 to the nineteenth century. The *Josefsplatz*, on the east side, is particularly attractive.

Turn south-east via *Stallburggasse* and *Plankengasse* into *Neuer Markt*, where there is a fine fountain, the *Donnerbrunnen* (early eighteenth century).

Cross *Kärntnerstrasse* into *Himmelpfortstrasse*; on right is former *Winter Palace of Prince Eugene*, magnificent baroque building begun by Fischer von Erlach the Elder in 1695.

Return to *Kärntnerstrasse*, turn left, walk to the *Ring*, turning right into the *Opern Ring*. The first building on the right is the *State Opera*. Coming into *Burg Ring*, the west front of the *Hofburg* is on right and the *Museum of Natural History* and *Museum of Art History* on left. Both have fine collections, particularly the Art Museum (sixteenth- and seventeenth-century paintings, Egyptian, Greek and Roman antiquities). In the *Burg Ring*, Parliament House is on left, whilst in the *Karl Leuger Ring* the *Burg Theatre* is on right, with Town Hall (set back behind the park) and University on left. Most of these are of heavy nineteenth-century design.

Among other sights are the *Belvedere*, a magnificent baroque palace (1700-23), with fine gardens, situated due south of *Schubert Ring*, and, on outskirts of the city, south-west from the west railway station, is the *Imperial Palace of Schönbrunn* (1694-1749) containing 1,400 rooms, with a superb park; see too, the *Prater*, Vienna's 'Hyde Park', with fun-fair attached, in south-east of town near *Danube Canal*.

EXCURSIONS: (a) *Grinzing*, the wine-growing village on the northern edge of the city; many taverns, known as *Heurigen*, where wine is drunk and music played by a *Schrammel* quartet (violins, guitar and accordion): when a tavern is selling *Heuriger* (ie new wine) a green wreath is hung over the door. (b) the *Kahlenberg* (1,590ft, 485m) and *Leopoldsberg* (1,390ft, 423m) two small peaks of the *Vienna Woods*, offering delightful views over the city and the *Danube* valley.

BELGIUM

Geographical Outline

Land

Belgium is a compact country with an area of only 11,775 sq miles (30,497 sq km). Its coastal provinces, *West* and *East Flanders*,comprise the historically tragic plain ravaged by battles throughout the centuries, fronted by a strip of reclaimed low-lying land several miles wide, and protected from the sea by sand dunes and dykes. The north-east extension of the plain, in the provinces of *Antwerp* and *Limburg*, is the *Kempen*, which largely consists of heathland and bog. Southwards, between the Rivers *Scheldt* and *Sambre*, and comprising the provinces of *Hainaut* and *Brabant*, the land is a low plateau rising gently to about 600ft (180m). South again beyond the mineral-rich *Sambre-Meuse* region, lies the hilly, wooded country of the *Ardennes*, reaching over 2,000ft (600m) in the *Hautes Fagnes*.

Climate

The climate is similar to that of southern England, though a little colder in winter and warmer in summer. The average rainfall, rather less near the coast than in London, increases towards the south-east as the land rises. Fogs are frequent in the west.

Plants

About one-fifth of the country is wooded, mixed deciduous, except the pine woods in the *Kempen* and spruce forests in the *Ardennes*. White poplar is common along the coast; hedgerows border the fields and roads. Pig-wort, sea-lavender and juniper berry are found among the sand-dunes, and the *Kempen* is at its most attractive in late summer when the heather is in bloom.

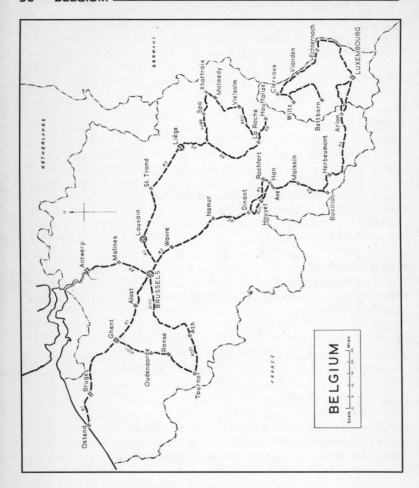

The People

Population

With a population of more than 10 million, average density is the second highest in Europe. This is not entirely attributable to the existence of many towns or to highly developed industry; some rural parts, particularly the plain of *Flanders*, are intensively cultivated and closely settled.

The people form two major groups of different ancestry. The Flemings of the north and west, slightly in the majority, are of the Salian Frankish (Germanic) stock which entered the country in the fourth and fifth centuries. The Walloons represent the older Celto-Roman people who were settled there before the Frankish invasions. Nordic and alpine physical types have largely merged throughout the centuries of mixing, but there remains a tendency for the Flemings to be taller and fairer.

Language

Language is today the chief distinction between the two groups. The Flemings speak Dutch; the Walloons speak French and their own three dialects of it. Both languages are official and of equal standing and such people as railway and post-office clerks, bank officials and tram-conductors are normally required to speak both. It is quite common, near the border between *Flanders* and *Wallonie*, to see the street names in both languages.

A German-speaking minority of about 60,000 live in the *Eupen* and *Malmedy* area near the eastern frontier.

Religion

The majority of the people belong to the Roman Catholic Church. Practising Catholics are more numerous among the Flemings and, generally, in rural areas rather than in the towns.

History

The country enters history as the territory of the Belgae, the Celtic Iron Age tribes who gave Caesar so much trouble. After the collapse of Roman rule the Franks came in from the east and, a century later, their leader Clovis of Tournai led the further expansion which made them masters of what is now France. Under his dynasty and that of Charlemagne, Belgium had no separate history but was a prosperous part of the Frankish Kingdom. Flemish cloth was valued abroad until trade was brought to an end by the Viking raids. These, and the partitioning of the country at the death of Charlemagne, led to the rise of powerful local lords (eg the counts of Flanders) as each region sought security.

Trade and industry grew again from the tenth century, and with them a rich town life matched only in Italy. Two centuries of bustling individualism were marked by the rise of merchant classes, the winning of charter privileges by each town, and the growth of exclusive craft guilds. Rivalries and class war were intensely local.

Such vigorous independence contrasts sharply with what was to happen to these 'southern Netherlands' during the next five centuries, during which authority was imposed from outside and they became caught up into the main-stream of European affairs through dynastic marriages and alliances. Successively they became subject to the French Crown (1226), to the dukes of Burgundy, and to the Spanish and Austrian Habsburgs. Under the Burgundians, Philip the Bold and Philip the Good, in the fifteenth century, they were linked with the Dutch provinces to form a United Netherlands and in this form they passed by marriage into the fateful union with Spain. Being by far the best developed economically, the Belgian provinces benefited greatly from this association with a world empire; *Antwerp* in the sixteenth century, handling the products of the Spanish and Portuguese colonies, became the great centre of international trade, banking and exchange, and *Brussels* was the political capital of the emperor Charles V, who was a Belgian by birth.

In religious matters Charles's reign was less happy. The Reformation was put down only to revive in the reaction against his son, the unpopular Philip II of Spain. His bigotry, and the clumsiness of the governor, the duke of Alba, led to the famous Revolt of the Netherlands, successful in the north but defeated in Belgium. The Dutch Republic became separated from modern Belgium, in which Habsburg rule and the Catholic religion were re-established. The Dutch went forward to empire and prosperity. Belgium became, in the seventeenth and eighteenth centuries, a battleground of warring powers where Marlborough marched and Bourbons and Habsburgs contended.

A period of French rule, followed by a brief reunion with Holland (1815-30), led to a demand for independence. This was gained by the revolution of 1830, and the adoption of a liberal constitution and a guarantee of neutrality by the powers. Belgium turned to the solution of internal problems — the 'schools' question on religious instruction and the 'language' question — and to development as a modern industrial state. But the two World Wars again emphasised her strategic position and essentially international interests, now shown in her full participation in economic and political groupings in western Europe.

Government

Belgium is governed by a parliamentary democracy under a limited monarchy. The Parliament has two houses — the Chamber of Representatives and the Senate. The people's representatives are elected every 4 years, men and women of 21 years and over having the vote.

Resources

Belgium is intensively cultivated, *Hainaut, Brabant, Flanders* and the *Kempen* being the main farming areas, although only about 5 per cent of the working population are employed in agriculture. The soil — not naturally rich — is made to produce high yields per acre. For its size Belgium produces more grain than any other country in the world. Forestry is important in the *Ardennes*, but much timber is also imported.

Mineral resources consist of coal, iron, copper, lead and zinc. Many coal mines have been closed, but new industry based on oil has been set up around the ports of *Antwerp* and *Ghent*. Heavy industry is established along the River *Sambre*, and along the River *Meuse* from *Namur* to *Liège*. *Charleroi* and *Liège* are particularly important for steel, iron and glass products and machinery of all kinds. *Liège* and nearby *Verviers* are centres of the woollen industry. Linen, cotton and silk goods are manufactured in *Antwerp* and *Ghent*. Other important products are lace (*Brussels, Mechelen, Bruges*), carpets (*Tournai*), beet sugar (*Hainaut*), and beer (*Louvain*). Fishing is relatively unimportant, the main fishing port being *Ostend*. In spite of an extensive international trade, Belgium has only a small merchant navy. The most important ports are *Antwerp, Ghent* and *Zeebrugge*. *Antwerp* is a world centre for the cutting of diamonds.

Customs

Although the Belgians consist of two races, the Flemings and the Walloons, who each jealously guard their language and their customs, they are yet united as a nation and take great pride in their history and free institutions. The old costumes are no longer seen, but many festivals, parades and village fairs (*Kermesses*) are still kept up in all parts of the country. Of particular interest are: the Procession of the Penitents of *Veurne* (last Sunday in July), its resemblance to Spanish ceremonies is a reminder of the Spanish rulers of the Low Countries; the colourful Procession of the Holy Blood at *Bruges* on Ascension Day; the Carnival of *Binche*, three days of processions and festivities culminating with Shrove Tuesday, and the Trinity Sunday celebrations at *Mons*, including a fight between St George and the Dragon.

The playing of carillons originated in Belgium and hymn tunes are still commonly heard coming from the belfries of Belgian churches. Originally played on a keyboard, they are now often mechanically controlled.

Culture

Architecture

At the beginning of the eleventh century the first Romanesque architecture made its appearance in the church of *St Jean* at *Liège*; this owes much to Rhenish influences; some of the original building is still in existence. This style, which is characterised by a large chancel, is found in many churches in *Limburg* and *Brabant*. The western part of the country, however, came under French influence during the Romanesque period. A wonderful example of this is *Tournai* cathedral, begun in 1110, which shows in the choir the transition from Romanesque to Gothic. The influence of this cathedral can be seen in buildings throughout *Flanders* and *Brabant*.

During the Gothic period, in the thirteenth century, there was little difference between the styles of the *Meuse* and the *Scheldt* regions. One of the best examples of this period is the church of *Notre Dame de Pamele* at *Oudenaarde*. In *Brussels* a more florid style developed and examples of this can be found in churches in all parts of the country. Fine Gothic market halls and town halls are to be seen in many Belgian towns.

In the Gothic architecture of the sixteenth century, an Italian influence is apparent but in the following century a new trend began to appear and richer ornamentation was used. This was the Belgian baroque period, examples of which may be seen not only in churches all over Belgium but in many town houses, particularly in *Antwerp, Ghent* and *Mechelen*. The *Grand' Place* in *Brussels* consists, apart from the King's House and the Town Hall, entirely of baroque buildings.

The eighteenth century produced a great deal of domestic architecture in the Louis XV and Louis XVI styles. In the nineteenth century styles were imitative and it was not until the end of the century that new life was infused into architecture with the appearance of the first buildings in modern style, designed by Victor Horta and Henri van de Velde. Much good work has been done since then and well-designed modern buildings of all kinds can be found in every Belgian town today.

Painting

Painting is the characteristic art-form of Belgium, and of Flanders in particular. The first great name in Flemish art, Jan van Eyck, appeared in the early fifteenth century. His knowledge of perspective and capacity for precise and realistic details gave a lead to the Flemish School.

The early sixteenth century produced Pieter Breughel, a master of peasant portraiture, but his fame is outclassed by the great artist Pieter Paul Rubens (1577-1640) who showed in his work the influence both of his Flemish teacher and of the colour and beauty of the paintings of Italy, where he spent eight years of his life. Anthony van Dyck (1599-1641) came under the influence of Rubens, in whose studio he worked for several years; he is famous for his portraits, painted in mellow tones.

The largest art collections in Belgium are in the museums of *Brussels, Bruges* and *Antwerp*, where examples of the work of most of Belgium's painters may be seen.

Museums

The three principal museums of *Brussels* are the Museum of Antique Paintings (for the study of the Flemish School), the Museum of Modern Painting, and the Royal Museums of Art and History. The most important museums of *Antwerp* are the Rubens House, Steen Maritime Museum, the Plantin Printing Museum, the Museum of Fine Arts and the Mayer van den Bergh Museum; in *Bruges*, the Gruuthuse Museum and the Groeninge Museum.

Music

The Belgians are a musical nation; orchestral societies and choral societies flourish in all parts of the country. Musical education is provided in the Royal Conservatoires of *Brussels, Antwerp, Liège* and *Ghent*. Belgium has produced a great number of composers but César Franck is the really outstanding one.

The principal opera houses are in *Brussels, Antwerp* and *Ghent*. In *Brussels* opera and ballet are produced at the *Théâtre Royal de la Monnaie*, concerts and plays at the *Palais des Beaux-Arts*, and plays at the *Théâtre Royal du Parc*, and there are other theatres and concert halls. Foremost in *Antwerp* are the *Elizabethzaal* (concerts), the *Royal Theatre* and the *Flemish Opera House*. There are theatres and concert halls in most of the larger towns.

Literature

Maeterlinck and Cammaerts and the historian Pirenne are writers best known in translation. Pirenne's works on the origins and sitings of towns will be of particular interest to historically-minded travellers.

Touring Information

Touring Areas

The most attractive scenery in Belgium, and the best walking country, is the hilly, wooded area of the *Ardennes*, where it is wild and practically untouched by industry or cultivation. There is some very pleasant, though flatter, countryside to the north-west of the *Ardennes*, and in the Flemish part of the country there is a wealth of architecturally-interesting old towns. Along the sea coast the resorts make an all-but-unbroken esplanade, facing broad sandy beaches.

Access

The most direct route to Belgium is from Dover to *Ostend*, a $3^1/_2$ hour ferry crossing. RTM (Régie Belges des Transports Maritimes) run two services by day and one by night with connecting boat trains from London and to *Antwerp* and *Brussels* and beyond — as well as vehicle ferries, six to eight times daily in each direction. Jetfoil run up to five services daily (crossing time $1^3/_4$ hours; supplement payable), also with rail connections. Hoverspeed have a hovercraft service between Dover and *Calais* (crossing time 35 minutes) with connecting coach services from London to *Antwerp*, *Mons* and *Brussels* making overall journey times of $6^3/_4$ hours to *Antwerp*, $6^1/_4$ hours to *Mons* and $7^1/_4$ hours to *Brussels*. P&O

Ferries run a total of eight crossings between Dover/Felixstowe and *Zeebrugge* (crossing times of $4^1/_2$ hours Dover to *Zeebrugge*, $5^1/_2$ hours Felixstowe to *Zeebrugge* by day, 8 hours by night).

There are direct scheduled air services between London and *Antwerp, Brussels* and *Ostend* by British Airways, Air UK, British Air Ferries and Sabena.

Transport

Belgium is a small country with a dense railway network and an efficient service of trains, largely electrified. Sixteen-day season tickets for the entire network are available; so too are tickets for use on any five days within a seventeen-day period. Also, a Fixed-rate Reduction Card can be purchased; the holder can then buy ordinary tickets at half-price for one month. In addition to the state railways several bus routes link towns and villages and tramways run the whole length of the coast; cheaper than rail for short journeys.

A pleasure steamer operates between *Namur* and *Dinant* during the summer and there are boat trips along the *Scheldt* from *Antwerp*.

Money

The unit of currency is the *franc*, divided into 100 *centimes*, but the smallest coin in general use is 50 *centimes*.

Food and Drink

The national beverages are coffee and beer. Breakfast usually consists of coffee, roll and butter, and jam. The main meal is at midday and supper is at about 7pm. Coffee is often taken about 4pm. There is a high standard of cooking throughout the country and meals are ample. Cakes, pastries and coffee are served by many *pâtisseries*. There are no licensing hours but the sale of spirits is prohibited in restaurants and cafés.

Holidays and Closing Days

Public holidays (on which banks and most shops are closed) are: New Year's Day, Easter Monday, Labour Day (1 May), Ascension Day, Whit-Monday, National Festival (21 July), Assumption (15 August), All Saints (1 November), Armistice Day (11 November), Christmas Day. Banks are usually also closed between 12 noon and 2pm on ordinary working days.

Maps

Michelin map No 409, depicting Belgium and Luxembourg, scale 1:350,000 is recommended; Michelin maps Nos 2 and 4, showing almost the same coverage but in more detail, are on a scale of 1:200,000.

Youth Hostels

There are two youth hostel associations in Belgium: the Vlaamse Jeugdher-bergcentrale (VJHC) which operates in *Flanders*, and the Centrale Wallonne (CWAJ) operating in the French-speaking area. The hostels of the former are large, highly organised and much frequented by schools and youth groups; the hostels of the CWAJ are smaller and more informal, similar in some ways to those in France.

Motoring

Belgium's road network, the most compact in Europe, has motorways which connect most parts of the country. Access is free, speed limit 120km/h (75mph), elsewhere it is 60km/h (37mph) in built-up areas, 90 km/h (55mph) outside.

A driving licence and registration papers must be carried; an international green card is not obligatory, except for USA and Canadian visitors. All motorists must display their country of origin sticker and carry a red warning triangle for use in case of breakdown.

Driving is on the right, overtaking on left; traffic coming from the right has priority.

Touring Club de Belgique is at 44 Rue de la Loi, Brussels; Royal Automobile Club de Belgique is at 53 Rue d'Arlon, Brussels.

These notes apply equally to motoring in Luxembourg.

Touring Routes

R1 Ostend — Brussels (75 miles, 120km)
Ostend Δ important port, principal town on Belgian coast, popular and lively holiday resort with 5 miles (8km) of wide beaches. Take the road N10 from the east side of the town, across a flat agricultural plain, dotted with houses and farms and intersected by canals and dykes.

Continue 15 miles (24km) to **Bruges**Δ intersected by many canals, numerous bridges cross them and winding streets crowd between. Many medieval build-ings, notably the *Halles* (1248); the *Town Hall* (1376); and church of *Notre Dame* containing a sculpture by Michelangelo and some fine paintings; *St John's Hospital* (twelfth century); the Cathedral of *St Sauveur*, oldest brick church in Belgium, the famous *Belfry* with its fine view; the *Chapel of the Holy Blood* where a relic said to contain some drops of Christ's blood is treasured, and the picturesque *Béguinage* (1245). Several museums contain fine works of art.

Eastwards for 30 miles (48km) via *Maldegem* Δ to **Ghent**, built across many islands formed by confluence of River *Lys (Leie)* and the *Scheldt*. Industrial and horticultural centre; second most important port with canal for ocean-going ships to *Scheldt* estuary; many seventeenth- and eighteenth-century houses in French style; many historic buildings; *St Bavo's* Cathedral (Gothic, twelfth century onwards, richly decorated interior with famous van Eyck altarpiece *Adoration of the Mystic Lamb*); the *Cloth Hall* (*Lakenhalle*) with fine fourteenth-century belfry, 312ft (95m) and affording wonderful view; *St Nicholas* Church (begun in thirteenth century); *Town Hall*, sixteenth century, part Gothic, part Renaissance; *St Michael's* Church (begun 1440), the former Dominican monastery; the *Castle of the Counts of Flanders* (*Gravensteen*), parts of which date from ninth century; ruined Abbey of *St Bavo*.

Aalst, small town with large but unfinished fifteenth-century Gothic church, *Hekelgem*, ruins of Abbey of *Affligem*; *Asse*, interesting Gothic church, *Brussels* is entered from the north-west by the N10.

Brussels△

A city of modern buildings, wide avenues and many open spaces, though there are still numerous interesting old buildings and frequent examples of art nouveau architecture. The main part of the city is a pentagon, bounded by wide boulevards; these are at their most attractive in May when the chestnut trees are in bloom.

South of the *Nord* railway station are the fashionable shops, cafés and restaurants in the *Boulevard Adolphe Max, Place Brouckère* and *Rue Neuve*. To the south-east of the *Bourse* and in the heart of the Old Town, with its narrow streets, lies the **Grand' Place**, a square bounded on one side by the *Hôtel de Ville* and on the others by guild houses built in the Belgian baroque style. The *Maison du Roi* in late Gothic style, which has never in fact been occupied by the king and is now a museum, is also in this square. The *Hôtel de Ville*, dating from the fifteenth century, is one of the finest civic buildings in Gothic style in Belgium; certain rooms and the tower are open to visitors on weekdays. A flower market is held in the *Grand' Place* once a week.

The *Rue de l'Etuve*, south of the *Hôtel de Ville* leads to the well-known fountain statuette of the *Manneken Pis*.

East of the *Grand' Place*, in the Upper Town, is the *Palais des Beaux Arts* (1928), with halls for concerts, art exhibitions and lectures. Nearby are the *Museum of Modern Painting* and the *Museum of Antique Painting and Sculpture*. At the far end of the *Rue de la Régence* is the *Palais de Justice*, a building larger than St Peter's, Rome, built in Greco-Roman style towards the end of the last century.

The Royal Palace, rebuilt at the beginning of this century, stands at one end of the *Parc de Bruxelles*. At the other end, lies the *Palais de la Nation*, housing the Legislative Assembly. To the west is *St Michael's Cathedral*, a lovely Gothic building, part of which dates from the twelfth century; its façade has twin towers, a more common feature of French than of Belgian churches.

The King's Palace and Park of *Laeken* are closed to visitors; attractive public gardens adjoin. The favourite park of Brussels is the *Bois de la Cambre*, originally part of the Forest of *Soignes*, to the south-east beyond the fashionable residential quarter of the *Avenue Louise*.

> **R1 (i)** Detour from *Ghent* via *Tournai*. *Oudenaarde* 18 miles (29km), splendid town hall (1535), flamboyant Gothic churches of *St Walburga* and *Notre Dame*, thirteenth century; site of Marlborough's victory just north of town; *Ronse* 7 miles (11km) Roman crypt of *St Hermès* church, walks on wooded hills of *Kluisberg*, **Tournai**Δ 15 miles (24km) cathedral, Romanesque and Gothic, finest church in Belgium; *Ath*, 17 miles (27km), *St Julien's* church, Gothic, Town Hall seventeenth century; *Geraardsbergen* Δ 12 miles (19km) and *Ninove*, 8 miles (13km), industrial towns with character; *Brussels* 15 miles (24km).

R2 Brussels to Namur (40 miles, 64km)

Highway N4 leaves *Brussels* from south-east. Road passes through the Forest of *Soignes*, an area of woodland and lakes. Fifteen sq miles (39 sq km) in extent. South- west of forest, on road N5, is site of Battle of Waterloo; overlook battlefield from top of *Lion Mound*. Continue for 15 miles (24km) on N4 to *Wavre*, church of *St John the Baptist* (fifteenth century) and nearby *Louvain-la-Neuve*Δ. Soon the gently undulating countryside gives way to a more hilly and picturesque landscape. *Gembloux*, remains of old ramparts; nearby fine *Corroy-le-Château*. **Namur**Δ, in valley, at junction of River *Sambre* and River *Meuse*, dominated by citadel on rocky cliff (cable-car); cathedral of *Saint-Aubain* begun 1751, classical style, sombre interior; church of *St Loup*, in exuberant baroque; many museums.

R3 Brussels to Liège (62 miles, 100km)

Leave *Brussels* by *Avenue de Tervuren*, follow route N3, alongside Forest of *Soignes* and, along the valley of the *Voer*. Old church at *Bertem*, dating from ninth century, is an excellent example of Brabantine architecture.

Leuven on River *Dyle*, former capital of *Brabant*, gracious, Catholic university town; mostly traffic-free. Magnificent fifteenth-century Town Hall, flamboyant Gothic style, has scenes from the Old and New Testaments sculptured on the front. The *Halles*, lovely fourteenth- and fifteenth-century market-building, now houses the University and Library. The churches of *St Kwinten, St Jacob* and *St Pieter* are all historically interesting. A *Abbey of Park*, founded 1129, just south-east of the town, elaborate monastic buildings beautifully situated. Continue to *Boutersem* Δ on road to *Tienen*.

Tienen, small town, two churches dating from thirteenth century are *Notre Dame du Lac* and *St Germain*. *Hakendover* has been a centre for pilgrimages in January and on Easter Monday for more than twelve centuries. *St Truiden* is a district of cherry-orchards; *Béguinage* (frescoes and astronomical clock) and church of *St Leonard*.

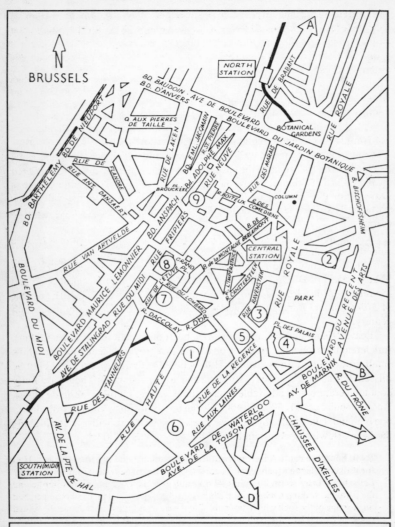

1 Youth Hostel. 2 Palais de la Nation. 3 Palais des Beaux Arts. 4 Royal Palace. 5 Museums. 6 Palais de Justice. 7 Pissing Boy Statue. 8 Town Hall. 9 Post Office.
A to Antwerp. B to Luxembourg Station. C to Namur. D to Charleroi, Nivelles

Liège△, handsome city, spacious street plan of boulevards and parks; at junction of River *Ourthe* and River *Meuse*. An excellent starting point for a tour of the *Ardennes*, following either the valley of the *Ourthe* or that of the River *Amblève*. Cathedral of *St Paul* (begun 968); church of *St Jacques*, outstanding example of flamboyant Gothic; *Palais de Justice* (sixteenth century and later); *Maison Curtius*, fine example of Renaissance mansion, now Archaeological Museum. *Museum of Walloon Life; D'Assembourg Museum*, rich eighteenth-century interiors; *Museum of Fine Arts* (Belgian masters).

R4 Namur to Luxembourg via Dinant (146 miles, 235km)

The most interesting route, well worth the extra miles, follows the *Meuse* as far as *Dinant*. The N47 road on the eastern bank is more picturesque. Leave *Namur* by the suburb of *Jambes*, follow the narrow river valley past the little village of *Dave*, with the its château. There are steep rocky sides to the valley and particularly striking are the Rochers de Frênes, towering over the river at *Lustin* (grottoes).

Houx, ruins of *Château de Poilvache* (eleventh century). Just past *Houx* a ruined tower marks the site of former Abbey of the *Gérousarts*.

Nineteen miles (30km) from *Namur*, at the foot of rocky heights, lies small holiday resort of **Dinant**; Church of *Notre Dame*, several times destroyed and rebuilt. Good view from *Montfort Tower* on hill behind town (chair-lift); grottoes of *Mont Fat* and *Rampeine*; town dominated by the *Citadel*, early nineteenth century.

Leave *Dinant* by N47, and soon branch left on to N48 for 14 miles (22km), fork left to little town of *Ciergnon*, on River *Lesse* (royal château). At *Rochefort*, small grotto, right turn is taken to **Han**, where the famed grotto should not be missed. It is about 2¹/₂ miles (3km) long and, as the visit takes 3 hours in a fairly cool temperature, it is advisable to take some warmer clothing. *Salle du Dôme*, is a spectacular cavern, 500ft by 460ft (150m by 140m), on two levels; in the lower one is a small lake formed by the River *Lesse*. The visit ends with a boat trip along the *Lesse*, flowing underground through lovely grottoes and labyrinths.

R4 (i) Footpath route Anseremme to Han. A recommended alternative route to **Han** for walkers is along a path of the Touring Club de Belgique, which follows the *River Lesse* from *Anseremme*, 2¹/₂ miles (4km) south of *Dinant*. After 2 miles (3km) along the path, the striking *Château de Walzin* is reached, a fortified manor-house perched on the edge of the rock which drops sheer to the river. A little farther on are the ruined tower of *Caverenne* also built on a rock, and the 150ft (45m) high rock formation of *Chaleux*, known as 'The Candle'. The *Château de Vêve* is also passed and the tower of the *Château d'Ardenne*, standing in a large park, can be seen. About 10 miles (16km) from *Anseremme*, the pleasant little village of *Houyet* stands on the bank of the River *Lesse* where it is joined by the River *Hilan*. At *Houyet* the road to *Han* can be rejoined or the path can be followed for the remaining 15 miles (24km).

From *Han,* via *Ave, Maissin* and *Paliseul,* cross the *Ardennes* to the picturesque valley of the River *Semois. Bouillon* Δ stands at the bend of the river,
beneath rocky heights topped by an interesting ruined castle. The attractive
twisting course of the river below *Bouillon* repays exploration, especially on foot.

Returning to *Sensenruth,* road to right should be taken, leading along *Semois*
valley to *Herbeumont*Δ, at foot of wooded hill with ruined twelfth-century
fortress. The river valley can be followed almost to *Florenville,* small market
town, thence road N50 to Abbey of *Orval,* where a new abbey has been built
beside twelfth- and thirteenth-century ruins of the original building. The road
through *Etalle* leads to *Arlon* and *Luxembourg.*

R5 Brussels — Antwerp — Dutch border (48 miles, 77km)
Leave *Brussels* by *Chaussée de Vilvoorde* following road N1 to *Vilvoorde,* with
the church of *Notre Dame* (partly fourteenth century).

Halfway between *Brussels* and *Antwerp* lies the interesting old town of
Mechelen, religious capital of Belgium since sixteenth century. Cathedral of *St
Rombout,* one of the finest examples of Gothic architecture in Flanders, has a

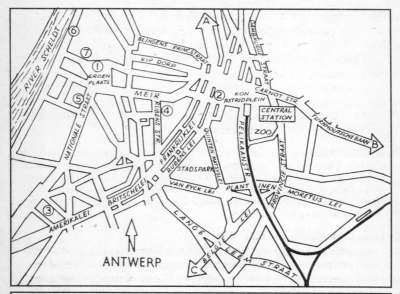

1 Cathedral. 2 Opera. 3 Museum of Fine Art. 4 Ruben's House. 5 Plantin
Printing Museum. 6 Steen Navigation Museum. 7 Town Hall.
A to Breda. B to Turnhout. C to youth hostel.

320ft (98m) tower, carillon of forty-nine bells and affords wide views. Town Hall (begun 1320); baroque church of the *Grand Béguinage*, fifteenth century; church of *St John; OL-Vrouw-over-de Dijle* (Gothic); *Brussels Gate; Palace of Justice* (Gothic and Renaissance); the restored sixteenth-century *Busleyden Mansion* (Museum of Local History, with section devoted to the carillon) and many lovely old houses, *Hofstade*Δ lies 2¹/₂ miles (4km) to south-east.

Antwerpʌ

Main port and second largest town of Belgium; many interesting old buildings, the capital of Flemish culture and art. Although 55 miles (88km) from the sea, on River *Scheldt*, it is one of the chief ports of the continent. City Tourist Office is opposite Central Station.

Head westwards from Central Station, along *De Keyserlei*, crossing *Frankrijlei* and along *Leysstraat* to the *Meir*.

A little farther, on the left, is *Wapperstraat* and the *House of Rubens*, a seventeenth-century mansion in which may be seen many of the master's original paintings. Reduced charge for hostellers. Returning to the *Meir*, the Royal Palace (Rococo, dating from 1745) is a few yards along on the left. Westward stands a block of flats, said to be highest in Europe, from the top of which is a fine view of the city. At the far end of the *Groenplaats*, a treeplanted square, is *Cathedral of Notre Dame*, one of the finest Gothic churches in Belgium, fourteenth to seventeenth century, with Rubens paintings. Just beyond, in the *Grote Markt*, is sixteenth-century *Town Hall*. Nearby are *Plantin Museum*, workshop of sixteenth-century printer, and *Steen Navigation Museum*, in castle.

Highway E10 continues from the north side of *Antwerp*, reaching the Dutch frontier after 17 miles (27km) and continuing to *Breda*.

EXCURSIONS from *Antwerp*: (a) to *Lier* 9 miles (14km) south-east; a quiet and delightful little town on River *Nete* with fine Gothic cathedral, *St Gommarus*, rich in works of art. *Nijlen*Δ is 5 miles (8km) eastwards with woodland, heath and riverside walks. (b) to *St Niklaas*, 13 miles (21km) industrial and commercial centre of *Waas* district, the 'Garden of Belgium', fine market place; museum has unique Mercator collection including his original globe.

R6 Liège to Houffalize (66 miles, 106km)

This route leads up the winding valley of the River *Ourthe*. Leave *Liège* by highway N31; just outside town N34 branches off to the right across River *Ourthe*. This road is taken, passing the industrial town of *Angleur* on right, soon after which the *Château de Colonstère* can be seen high up on the right and, on the other bank of the river, the *Château de Sainval*. *Tilff*Δ, small village with interesting grotto, is 7 miles (11km) from *Liège*. At *Poulseur* the old keep stands on a hill on one side of the river, with the ruined *Château de Montfort* opposite. At *Comblain-*

au-Pont are interesting grottoes in the limestone; visit takes over an hour. The road leaves the river at *Hamoir* — excursions on foot should be made along the lovely river valley — crosses a plateau, descends and recrosses the river just before *Durbuy*. On to *Hotton* and *Rendeux* then 3 miles (5km) to *Marcourt* where road runs close to left bank, making a sharp turn at rocky heights on which stand ruins of *Château de Laroche*. Little town of *Laroche* is favoured base for walkers; local pottery is well-known. Take road to *Nadrin*, for visit to *Rocher d' Hérou*, a wild and lovely spot near junction of East and West *Ourthe*. *Houffalize*, a pleasant town on East *Ourthe*; see tower and walls of thirteenth-century church.

R6 (i) The Ardennes. From *Comblain-au-Pont* eastwards along River *Amblève*, past ruins of *Château d' Amblève* to *Sougné-Remouchamps* and across plateau to *Spa* 15 miles (24km), at altitude of 1,000ft (300m) is faded reminder of eighteenth- and nineteenth-century elegance; its name added new word to dictionaries. *Xhoffraix* 13 miles (21km) for *Hautes Fagnes*, climbs to *Botrange* 2,277ft (694m) — highest point in the country — and *Baraque Michel* 2,215ft (675m), *Bévercé-Malmédy*△, 9 miles (14km), ravaged in Ardennes battles of 1944/5; now beautifully restored. See noble abbey and chapter house — now folklore museum, then via *Stavelot* and south along river to *Vielsalm* 15 miles (24km) (château, arboretum); road across hills south-west (*Baraque de Fraiture*, 2,140ft, 652m) to rejoin **R6** at *Laroche-en-Ardenne*, 23 miles (37km).

DENMARK

Geographical Outline

Land

Denmark is just over half the size of Scotland. Its coastline is over 4,500 miles (7,250km) long and though the country is low-lying, nowhere higher than 570ft (175m), it is hardly flat. Scenery is mostly gentle, a green and homely landscape with many small lakes and fjords, no place being far from the sea.

The peninsula of Jutland (*Jylland*), lying northwards from Germany, occupies about three-quarters of the total area. The remainder is made up of about 500 islands of which about 100 are inhabited. The most important are Zealand (*Sjælland*) on which stands Copenhagen (*København*), separated from South Sweden on the east by the narrow *Sound*, and Funen (*Fyn*) which lies between Jutland and Zealand, separated from these two by the Little Belt (*Lille Bælt*) and by the Great Belt (*Store Bælt*) respectively. Other larger islands to the south of Zealand are *Lolland* and *Falster*.

The Faeroe (*Færøerne*) Islands, lying between Scotland and Iceland, and Greenland (*Grønland*) are self-governing communities belonging to Denmark.

Bornholm in the Baltic Sea south-east of Sweden, seven hours by ferry from *Copenhagen*, belongs to Denmark, and has scenery of granite, rugged cliffs and ravines, although the highest point is only 530ft (162m).

Difficulties of transport are considerable, but these have been overcome by an extensive system of state-owned and private ferries, as well as by the construction of bridges, masterpieces of engineering skill. The nature of the country allows the continued existence of numbers of picturesque country and seaside villages where 'time seems to stand still'.

Climate

The maritime climate is tempered by cold winters; January and February mean temperatures are at freezing point and the months between October and April are

mostly dull and grey. The prevailing winds are westerly, and there is always a breeze. Annual rainfall averages 24in (600mm) with least in spring and most in late summer and autumn. The best holiday season is probably from May to early September, with July the warmest month. Spring comes in mid-April to early May with the beech trees breaking into leaf. Townspeople make excursions to the woods and bring home armfuls of the fresh green twigs for decoration in the home to symbolise the end of winter and the return of spring.

Plants and Animals

Woodland occupies about a tenth of the land area, the most important trees being beech and Norway spruce. The beech forests are famous for their beauty and are the subject of many Danish poems and songs; some of the trees in the *Dyrehaven*, north of *Copenhagen*, attain enormous size. Oak occurs in plenty but elm is comparatively rare. *Rold* forest, near *Ålborg*, is the largest in Denmark. Other forests occur near *Silkeborg* in Jutland, *Grib Skov* in North Zealand and *Almindingen* on *Bornholm*. Juniper flourishes on the chalky hillsides of the island of *Møn* off South Zealand.

In west Jutland there are extensive heather-clad hills and heaths and much of the country between *Esbjerg* and the frontier with Germany is marshland, drained by canals. The district of *Vendsyssel* north of the *Limfjord* in north Jutland is largely made up of sandhills. Much land has been reclaimed but there are considerable areas of drifting sand in which mare's-tail grass and gorse alone seem to flourish.

The skylark is the most common bird, but the stork is the bird which most interests visitors, and it is held in the same esteem by the Danes as by the Dutch. Unfortunately the stork is becoming a rare guest, but the marshlands of Jutland remain its especial haunt and cartwheels are set on the tops of houses to encourage it to nest there.

The People

Population

Denmark, with a population of nearly five million, is by far the most densely populated of the Scandinavian countries. Rather more than one and a quarter million people live in the *Copenhagen* area; nearly four million people live in towns.

Language

The Danish language is related to Swedish, Norwegian and Icelandic, together with some affinities with English, Dutch and German. The Danes have three letters in their alphabet which are not found in English — å (sometimes written aa) pronounced like 'or'; æ pronounced like 'air'; and ø pronounced like 'er'; these letters are placed at the end of alphabetical lists.

History

Behind today's uneventfully democratic prosperity lies a long and complex story of national struggle. Strategically well placed but with few natural resources, the Danes from the ninth to the twelfth century sought by conquest an outlet for their growing population. As Vikings ('sea-rovers') they, with the other Scandinavians, were feared from Russia to England and from northern France to Sicily. But, starting as mere raiders, they developed gifts as creators and rulers of states. They founded Normandy, and their descendants, in 1066, achieved the Norman Conquest of England. Earlier, Canute's empire had comprised Denmark, England and Norway — the first of many unions in which Denmark was involved.

From the twelfth century, when Absalon, the statesman-bishop of *Roskilde*, founded *Copenhagen* as one of several fortresses to defend the coast, the struggle for overlordship of the Baltic lands is a recurring theme in Danish history. Holding *Scania* (*Skåne*, now part of Sweden) Denmark commanded both sides of the *Sound* and all the channels at the outlet of the Baltic; thus the dues which she was able to exact from shipping were a source of revenue but an irritation to other states and to the Hanseatic League.

The Union of *Kalmar* (1397), an alliance under one king of the Crowns of Denmark, Norway and Sweden, in which Denmark was the dominant partner, was an attempt to counter the growth of German power. The link with Norway lasted for four centuries, but Sweden, more naturally a rival for power in the Baltic than an ally, seceded in 1448. Thereafter until 1720 the two countries were frequently at war, while other powers helped or hindered one side or the other to ensure that neither secured dominance in the Baltic. Denmark's strategic position made her at first the strongest of the Scandinavian states. But with the growth of powers with greater natural resources she was forced to give up her ambitions in the eastern Baltic and in Germany. Even *Bornholm* was lost, but was later recovered. *Skåne*, also, changed hands more than once and was finally lost in 1720.

Meanwhile, internal changes were marked by the acceptance of Luther's Reformation in 1536 and by the constitutional revolution of 1660 in which the Kongelov (Royal Law), drawn up in secret, made the king the most absolute sovereign in Europe for a century and a half. Under this rule commerce expanded and the arts and sciences flourished, but the state of agriculture and of the peasantry pointed to the need for reform. This came in 1786 through a group of able ministers and liberal landowners, led by Bernstorff and Count Reventlow, who were determined to change the Danish countryside. In a few years the economic and social system based on feudalism was broken up; the serfs became freemen practising advanced farming; education became widespread. The pattern of modern Denmark was created.

The nineteenth century brought travail in foreign affairs but further progress at home. In 1807 England, seeking to forestall Napoleon, seized the Danish fleet by the bombardment of *Copenhagen*. Norway was lost in 1814. The long-unsettled question of Schleswig-Holstein led to wars in 1848 and 1864 and the loss of these territories to Prussia and Austria. Not until the plebiscite of 1920 was the northern (Danish speaking) half of Schleswig returned.

Denmark was overrun by the Germans in 1940 but the Danes maintained active resistance throughout the latter years of occupation. Margrethe II, who, as Princess Margrethe, married a French commoner, became sovereign in 1972.

Government

Since 1849 Denmark has been a parlimentary democracy under a limited monarchy.

Parliament (*Folketinget*) consists of 179 members representing ten political parties, but largely Social Democrats, Conservatives, Liberals and Progressives.

Resources

Denmark was until quite recently an agricultural country; now only about nine per cent of the population are engaged in farming. Nearly thirty per cent are engaged in administration and services, twenty per cent in commerce and transport and twenty-five per cent in manfacturing, but many of the industries, such as dairy machinery and canned goods, are dependent on the farming community. Other products, some of which have a world-wide reputation are artistic porcelain, fine silverware, diesel engines, ships and chemicals.

There is little mineral wealth. On *Bornholm*, clay for porcelain and earthenware manufacture is worked extensively and granite is quarried. Several of Copenhagen's most important buildings are of *Bornholm* granite.

Denmark's agricultural revolution, using scientific methods and co-operative farming, dates from the 1870s and now consists of about 100,000 farms, almost all of which are quite small.

Customs

Danish people work and play hard. All the large towns have sports centres (Indrætsanlæg) with football pitches, tennis courts, running and cycling tracks and swimming baths. Yachting, rowing, swimming and all water sports are pursued with enthusiasm; at weekends there is a large exodus from the towns to the shore, the woods and countryside.

Danes are widely read, great readers of newspapers and well-informed in world affairs. Most of the young people from secondary schools have more than a working knowledge of other languages besides their own, especially English and German.

Danish people are open-minded and uninhibited; they have no censorship or licensing restrictions, their individual freedom is everywhere apparent, so, too, is their high standard of living and their patriotism.

Food and Drink

Breakfast, *morgen complet*, consists of egg, cheese, bread, butter and coffee or tea. Lunch (*frokost*) usually consists of open sandwiches (*smørrebrød*) made of many varieties and combinations of fish, shrimp, chicken, ham, pork, egg, cheese, eel and sausage. The principal meal of the day is dinner (*middag*) in the early evening and consists of a fish or meat course and a light sweet resembling a cake, or a cornflour mould with fruit juice and cream (*rødgrød med fløde*).

Coffee (*kaffe*) is the Danes' usual drink but the quality is variable. Milk (*mælk*) is drunk extensively, and is cheap and good. The orangeade (*appelsin-vand*), the non-alcholic cider (*æblemost*) and the temperance beer (*dobbeltøl*) are delicious. Danes are great beer drinkers and favour lager, such as Tuborg or Carlsberg. *Aqua vitae* is the Danish national drink, traditionally drunk at the beginning of a meal; a potent spirit, to be taken, if at all, with discretion.

Culture

Architecture

Brick, tiles, lime and timber are the traditional building materials. In earlier times the surface clays, red from the atmospheric oxidation of the iron they contained, were used to make bricks which fired to a pleasing red shade. Of recent years the deeper clays have had to be quarried and these, being less oxidised, fire to a less attractive pale yellow. The earliest houses were built of peat and clay and roofed with straw bound with seaweed or heather. They consisted of one long block — the same hipped roof covering both the farmer and his cattle. Such houses, now brick walled, may be found in western Jutland today. The conventional plan for the Danish farm of medieval times is, however, four-winged round a central yard or *gård*, the construction being half-timbered with a filling of brick. Similarly the churches were built of brick, with flint and granite incorporated in the outer walls. The interiors were often finished with plaster made from local lime, forming a suitable base for mural painting and design. The charm of the Danish country town or village today lies in its half-timbered houses, cobbled passages and flower-decked courtyards.

Copenhagen has suffered seriously from bombardment and fires, but the centre of the city still retains its ancient, characteristic half-timbered centuries-old houses and its narrow streets. In particular, the reign of Christian IV (1588-1648) has left some outstanding architectural gems — *Rosenborg Castle*, the *Bourse* and the *Round Tower* in *Copenhagen* and *Frederiksborg Castle* at *Hillerød* in north Zealand.

Outstanding examples of modern architecture in *Copenhagen* are Grundtvig's Memorial Church, the Radio House, the Aquarium, the new Police Headquarters and the SAS Royal Hotel; the Town Hall and the assembly hall of the university at *Århus* and the large dance hall and restaurant *Kilden* at *Ålborg*. Such examples of recent Danish architecture occasion comment, but the work of Danish architects is internationally famous.

Painting and Sculpture

There were local craftsmen in Denmark in medieval times, as shown by the mural paintings and wrought ironwork in many churches, but the larger works of art of this period, such as the altarpieces in *St Knud's* church at *Odense* and in *Roskilde* cathedral, are almost invariably the work of foreign artists. Denmark's best known artist is Thorvaldsen (1770-1844), the poor boy who became Europe's most famous sculptor. A museum is devoted wholly to his works. Danish painters have been largely inspired by the countryside — the peasant farms, the Jutland heathlands and, particularly of recent years, the sand dunes and the beaches at the *Skaw*.

Design

Denmark is world famous for its industrial art: the Royal Copenhagen porcelain and the porcelain of Bing and Grøndahl, the silverwork of Georg Jensen, wooden toys, furniture and electrical equipment.

Museums

Rosenborg Castle in *Copenhagen* (1606-17) was built by Christian IV in the Dutch Renaissance style, in the *Kongens Have* (the Royal Gardens) off *Gothersgade*. It was used as a royal residence during the seventeenth and eighteenth centuries; the Crown Jewels are kept here.

The National Museum is in *Prinsens* Palace at the back of *Christiansborg*, the Parliament House. The collections are rich, particularly those of the Stone, Bronze and Iron Ages, of Viking times, of coins and medals and of Eskimo ethnography. The national-historical collections at *Frederiksborg Castle, Hillerød*, and *Kronborg Castle, Elsinore*, are also part of the National Museum.

In *Charlottenlund*, about 3 miles (5km) north of the city centre by electric train, is the Danish Aquarium — one of the most modern and delightful aquariums in the world in which both salt and fresh water fish can be seen in huge tanks under conditions simulating their natural habitat.

The Zoological Museum, north-west of the city, is one of Europe's finest and most modern of its kind.

The open-air museum at *Sorgenfri* (outskirts of *Copenhagen*) is a collection of farm and peasant houses from Denmark and South Sweden, furnished according to period and distributed over a considerable area. There is a similar museum, showing town houses, in the town park at *Århus* (see under **R7**).

Literature

Hans Andersen's fairy tales are loved by children and parents in many lands, and Denmark shows its pride in him in many ways. His contemporary, Kierkegaard (1813-55), was a profound thinker, originator amongst other things of the philosophy of existentialism. Among other writers with more than national reputations and whose works can be read in English are the critic Brandes (1842-

1927), Jensen (1873-1950) and Blixen (1885-1962).

Music and Ballet

Music flourishes in Denmark with orchestras and concerts in many towns. Among Danish composers Carl Nielsen (1865-1931) is the best known, but Buxtehude (1637-1707) and Jacob Gade (1879-1963) are world-famous too.

The Royal Danish Ballet enjoys a unique reputation; its standards are extremely high and it possesses a repertory going back several hundred years.

Science

The astronomer Tycho Brahe (1546-1601) enjoyed the patronage of Frederick II who built an observatory for him on an island in the *Sound*. His systematic work set a new standard of accuracy in observation and did much to confirm the Copernican theory of the universe. Another early scientist was Niels Stensen (1638-86), famous as an anatomist for his study of glands and of muscular contraction, and as a geologist, being the first to appreciate the true origin of fossils.

Niels Bohr (1885-1962), the physicist, is known for his work on atomic structure and for his development of Planck's Quantum Theory. He was awarded a Nobel Prize in 1922.

Touring Information

Touring Areas

Denmark can be conveniently divided into three parts, for purposes of tourist travel.

The peninsula of **Jutland**, consists of an extensive tract of marshland, heath and sand-dunes in the west, and of low hills and valleys in the east, with a coastline of picturesque fjords. The towns and places of interest are relatively widely separated and *Jutland* can well be regarded as a separate region. Excellent beaches can be found on the west coast from *Blåvandshuk* to *Skagen* and in the islands of *Rømø* and *Fanø*.

Zealand and the islands constitute a convenient unit. Most of Denmark's tourist attractions are on *Zealand*, a country of pastoral beauty, of delightful beech woods and of large lakes and meres. *Copenhagen* and the other towns of *Zealand* teem with historical associations.

Bornholm lies in the Baltic, seven to eight hours sail from *Copenhagen*. All that is best in Denmark is to be found there in miniature and a long weekend, at least, should be spent there.

If only one holiday can be spent in Denmark and time is limited, a desirable circuit is across southern *Jutland*, through *Funen* to *Zealand* by the Little Belt Bridge and the Great Belt Ferry, and back either by ferry from *Kalundborg* in

Zealand to *Århus* on *Jutland*, a 5-hour sail, or again over the Great Belt Ferry, well worth doing twice, through south *Funen* and over the ferry from *Bøjden* to *Fynshav* on the island of *Als*.

Access

The best route to Denmark from Britain is by ferry directly across the North Sea from Harwich to *Esbjerg* in 19 hours; from Newcastle to *Esbjerg* in summer only. Other ferry routes are from Harwich to *Hamburg* in 20 hours and daily ferry and train services via *Hook of Holland* or *Ostend* to *Copenhagen* in 25 hours from London.

Express boat-train connections from London, from *Esbjerg* to *Copenhagen*, via *Fredericia* and *Odense* and from *Hamburg* to *Copenhagen*.

Transport

The principal railways are state-owned but a few local lines are owned privately or by the local communes. Fares are graded so that the price per kilometre becomes cheaper the longer the distance travelled. On many of the long distance trains seat reservations are compulsory. Refreshments are available on a few only of the long distance trains, but there are excellent restaurants on the Great Belt Ferry and Danish railway meals are always good. A one-month pass covering rail and ferry travel throughout Denmark costs £115.

Bus services connect most of towns and there is a network of local buses, but such journeys can be tedious for stops are often frequent and sometimes lengthy.

There is a useful ferry between *Hundested* in north *Zealand* and *Grenå* in mid-*Jutland*; other ferries ply between *Frederikshavn* and *Oslo* and *Gothenburg*. Night services between *Copenhagen* and *Rønne*, on the west coast of *Bornholm*, are operated by the 1866 Bornholm Steamship Company; there is a saloon, and a sleeping bag is a comfort here. Danish State Railways operate the ferry service from *Århus* to *Kalundborg*.

Restaurants

Danish food is excellent, but restaurant meals are expensive, although less costly meals can be enjoyed in *Copenhagen* in the cafeterias of the larger department stores. Food in the country inns is good and the portions are generous. Many Danish youth hostels are open at midday and serve lunch; *smørrebrod* lunch packet can be ordered too.

Public Holidays

1 January, Maundy Thursday, Good Friday, Easter Sunday, Easter Monday, Prayer Day (fourth Friday after Easter), Ascension Day, Whit Sunday, Whit Monday, Christmas Day and 26 December.

Maps

Lascelles map of Denmark on a scale of 1:300,000 is a useful general map of the country. The Danish Geodetic Institute publish more detailed maps on four sheets on a scale of 1:200,000.

Motoring

Roads in Denmark are unusually good, but often monotonous, especially motorways, although they are free; ferries, which are many, are not.

National driving licence, car registration certificate and evidence of third-party insurance must be carried. International green insurance card is not compulsory for visitors from EEC member countries.

Driving is on the right, giving way to traffic coming from the right. Speed limits, in towns 60km/h (37mph), 90km/h (56mph) elsewhere; on motorways 110km/h (69mph). On the spot fines are imposed.

Members of a national motoring organisation in their own country may take advantage of facilities offered by the FDM — Forenede Danske Motorejere, Blegdamsvej 124, 2100 Copenhagen Ø.

Cycling

Cycling is remarkably popular and during the rush-hours in Copenhagen, thousands of cyclists occupy the main roads of the city and suburbs. Use of cycle-tracks on busy roads is compulsory but elsewhere there is a close network of bicycle paths. Pedestrian crossings are marked with a blue circle containing the words '*For gående*'.

Cycles can be hired in *Copenhagen* from Københavns Cyklebørs, Gothersgade 159 and the head office of the Dansk Cyclist Forbund is at Kjeld Langes Gade 14.

Camping

Denmark has more than 500 camping sites approved and listed by Friluftsradet, Skjoldsgade 10, Copenhagen Ø, and their handbook is on sale at bookshops. Campers without an International Camping Carnet can buy a camping pass at the first camping site visited.

Canoeing

The largest river is the *Gudenå* in *Jutland*, which forms a series of delightful lakes in the *Silkeborg* district. Canoes may be hired and at the end of the journey returned by rail at an inclusive price. This is one of many holiday facilities organised by the Danish YHA through Dansk Vandrelaug Rejser, Kultorvet 7, Copenhagen K.

1 Trinity Church and Round Tower. 2 Royal Theatre. 3 National Museum.
4 Ships to Malmø. 5 Town Hall. 6 Amalienborg. 7 University. 8 Rosenborg Castle. 9 Ny Carlsberg Glyptotek. 10 Our Saviour's Church (Vor
Frelsers Kirke). 11 Knippelsbro. 12 to Carlsberg Brewery. 13 approach to
Christiansborg Castle. 14 Gammel Torv.

Copenhagenᐃ

The *Hovedbanegård* is the terminus for all main line trains; a particularly fine
railway station, with the platforms below ground. Suburban electric or 'S' trains
also pass through it, linking it with local stations within the city.

Road approaches are from the west along A1 highway, or E66 motorway,
from *Roskilde*, from the south along the coast from *Køge*, from the north along
the delightful '*Danish Riviera*' — the coastway from *Elsinore* — and from the
north-west by *Hillerød, Birkerød* and *Lyngby*.

Buses are the main means of transport in the city; all routes go through the city
centre and fares are cheap. It is, however, preferable to go sight-seeing on foot;
most of the places to visit are within easy walking distance of the Town Hall.

The continous stretch of narrow streets, a mile long, between *Rådhusplads*
(Town Hall Square) and *Kongens Nytorv* (the King's New Market) is a pedestrian
precinct, popularly known as *Strøget* but the name nowhere appears as a street

sign; a busy and varied shopping street; not to be missed a cheaper shopping centre is along *Vesterbrogade* beyond the railway station.

The City Centre and East of the City

Start opposite Railway Station on *Vesterbrogade* and visit the 'Den Permanente' showrooms of Danish handicrafts. In middle of road the *Pillar of Freedom* commemorates the emancipation of Danish peasants from bondage. Turn east along *Vesterbrogade*; on right is entrance to *Tivoli*.

Copenhagen's *Tivoli* is unique yet typically Danish. A great pleasure garden, it has many cafés, lawns and flower beds, fountains, dance halls, concert halls and side shows. You can have a wonderful evening very cheaply or spend a lot of money, according to your pocket. Amongst the things which are free after paying the modest admission charge to the gardens is the famous Pantomime Theatre featuring mime and ballet. Take care where you eat; there are both cheap and expensive restaurants in *Tivoli*.

Rådhusplads (Town Hall Square) is the centre of modern Copenhagen. Note the novel barometer on the roof at the corner of *Vesterbrogade*, also the statues in the square; the famous *Dragon Fountain,* which depicts a bull fighting a dragon, and a tall pillar carrying figures blowing Denmark's ancient musical instrument, the *lure*. Town Hall in *fin de siècle* architecture, is open to public; interesting interior; see Jens Olsen's astronomical clock. Statue of Bishop Absalon, founder of Copenhagen, over door; tower, at 370ft and highest viewpoint in city, affords wonderful view.

English books and papers on sale at *Boghallen* bookshop on the *Politiken* corner in the square. The famous *Ny Carlsberg Glyptotek* with its art treasures is in *H.C. Andersen's Boulevard* behind the *Tivoli*; fine collection of Etruscan, Egyptian and Roman art.

Frederiksberggade, at eastern side of square, and *Strøget* begins here with the *Gammel Torv* (the Old Market) 200m along on the left; *Ny Torv* (the New Market) on the right. Classical building in *Ny Torv* is *Law Courts*, connected by a 'bridge of sighs' with former prison. Little narrow streets in immediate neighbourhood contain many interesting antique shops.

See *Caritas Fountain* in *Gammel Torv*, where golden apples play in water on queen's birthday. Just off square is the cathedral, *Vor Frue-Kirke*, Church of Our Lady, re-erected 1811-29, after the bombardment of 1807; over entrance is a bas-relief of Christ preaching on the Mount, by Thorvaldsen; in vaulted interior are his famous and exquisite statues of Christ and the twelve Apostles.

North of the church lie old *University* buildings. Modern extensions are in north part of town beyond lakes. University, founded 1479, has 11,000 students. The *Zoological Museum*, notable for its collection of whales, is in the University Park.

Krystalgade leads to *Church of the Trinity* with Round Tower 118ft (36m) high, built by Christian IV as an observatory. Tower may be ascended by broad spiral roadway up which Peter the Great of Russia is supposed to have driven a carriage and pair. Excellent view from top. Return down *Købmagergade* rejoining *Strøget* in section known as *Amagertorv*.

Note beautiful *Stork Fountain* in roadway. At No 6 is shop of Royal Porcelain Factory and at No 4 that of Bing and Grøndahl. Facing end of *Købmagergade* is *Højbroplads* with *Copenhagen's* open-air flower market and fine statue of Bishop Absalon.

Gammelstrand is on immediate right; fishmarket, with some noted fish restaurants; also state pawnbrokers, for occasional bargains in jewellery. Cross canal to reach huge block of state buildings which cluster round *Christiansborg Palace* and *Thorvaldsen's* Museum.

This area, known as *Slotsholmen* (Castle Island) and enclosed by canals, marks marshy spot on which Absalon built his first fortress. In front of Palace is equestrian statue of Frederick VII who gave Denmark its Constitution. Castle burnt down many times, rebuilt in present form in 1907-28, Royal Reception Rooms particularly fine. *Christiansborg* also contains *Houses of Parliament*.

Pass over *Marble Bridge* to National Museum in *Prinsens Palace* with exceptionally fine prehistoric and arctic ethnographical collections.

In *Tøjhusgade*, almost facing entrance to Houses of Parliament is Royal Danish Arsenal Museum (*Tøjhusmuseet*) housed in the armoury erected by Christian IV 1598-1604; close by is garden entrance to Royal Library.

Returning to front of *Christiansborg*, the Exchange is close by, built 1619-40 in Dutch Renaissance style by Christian IV; note remarkable spire of twisted dragons' tails. Across river in *Christianshavn* is high spire of *Our Saviour's Church*, with figure of the saviour and external spiral staircase.

From *Knippelsbro* take boat to *Langelinie* (see below) or continue tour by crossing bridge over canal on left to *Holmens Church*, opposite Exchange, erected in 1619 by Christian IV. Notice Royal pew. On same side as church is *National Bank*, and beyond it are imposing offices of East Asiatic Company.

Return to *Amagertorv* and walk along portion of *Strøget* known as *Ostergade*, fashionable shopping quarter.

In *Kongens Nytorv* is equestrian statue of Christian V, on right are *Magasin du Nord*, Scandinavia's largest store, *Royal Theatre*, and *Charlottenborg*, the art academy. Some inexpensive restaurants are also to be found in *Kongens Nytorv*. *Nyhavn* (new harbour) makes a pleasing picture with waterway extending up to the town and old houses flanking waterside; many are restaurants and cafés but this is a tough sailors' quarter, to be avoided at night. Hans Andersen lived, on and off, at No 67, during 1849-65. Ferry from *Nyhavn* to *Christianshavn*.

Follow *Gothersgade* to *Kongens Have* (the King's Garden) where, on right hand are well-known statues of *Hans Andersen*, '*Boy with a Swan*' and '*Well with Dancing Girls*'. Cross park diagonally to *Rosenborg Castle*, built by Christian IV

1606-17, in *Østervoldgade; Museum of Royal Family*, Crown Jewels and regalia, outstanding collection of porcelain, silver and paintings. On opposite side of *Østervoldgade*, built on old ramparts and not to be missed are the city's prestigious *Botanical Gardens*, with Royal Observatory, *Botanical Laboratory* and *Geological Museum*.

Return to *Kongens Nytorv* and follow *Bredgade*, with superior shops, many in premises converted from town houses of the nobility. On left at end of *Frederiksgade* is the *Marble Church*, with dome over 200ft (60m) high and only a little less in diameter than St Peter's, Rome; fine altar.

On opposite side of *Bredgade* lies *Amalienborg Palace*, actually four palaces, mid-eighteenth century, rococo style, originally houses of noblemen, but came to be occupied by Royal Family after fire at *Christiansborg* in 1794. Note fine Ionic colonnade which, owing to lack of funds, was constructed in wood. In centre of square is equestrian statue of Frederick V by Saly, considered most beautiful statue in Copenhagen. Observe picturesque uniforms of Life Guards and, when Queen is in residence, see Changing of the Guard, accompanied by military band, at 12 noon.

Proceed along *Bredgade* to *Alexander Newsky Church*, Greek Catholic church, on left; built 1883, Byzantine style with three large gilt cupolas. At corner of *Bredgade* and *Toldbodvej* is *'Grønningen'*, inexpensive restaurant. Continue along *Toldbodvej* past *Kastellet* to *English Church*, St Albans, with graceful spire in typical English setting. By side of church is enormous statuary group and fountain by Bundgråd which represents Gefion and her sons, whom she had changed into bulls, ploughing Zealand out of Sweden.

Continue northwards to famous promenade of *Langelinie*, with harbour and waters of *Sound* on right and beautifully planted shrubberies and flowerbeds on left. Interesting sculptures, including on rock on shore, famous statue by Eriksen of *'Little Mermaid'*, one of Hans Andersen's characters, and fine statue, *'The Swimmer'*, by Swedish sculptor, Børjeson. Northward along the *Linie* lies pleasure boat harbour and extensive *Free Port*, largest harbour in Baltic, with enormous international trade.

From *Langelinie* return to city centre by train or bus from *Osterport* station or by boat.

A Tour West of the City

Take bus from *Vesterbrodgade* to *Rahbeks Allé* for New Carlsberg Brewery, largest in the world. Expert guide in attendance; opportunity to taste the products, both alcoholic and non-alcoholic.

From Carlsberg proceed along *Pile Allé* and left into *Raskildevej* to *Zoological Gardens* among largest in Europe, recently modernised. Near at hand is *Frederiksberg Palace* built by Frederick IV in early eighteenth century; Palace is not open to visitors but in adjoining park are fine avenues of enormous trees, with canals built for a king's pleasure.

Return to town by bus down *Frederiksberg Allé*.

Touring Routes

Each of these routes is limited to one main island, except **R4** which crosses Denmark from east to west. Further tours can be made by combining parts of the various routes and linking them by the internal boat and ferry services.

R1 Copenhagen — Elsinore — Copenhagen (65 miles, 104km)

Northwards from *Copenhagen* for 6 miles (10km) comes *Klampenborg* a popular summer resort on the shores of the tideless *Sound*; delightful setting.

Dyrehaven (Deer Park) entered by Red Gate, near *Klampenborg* station; over 2,000 acres in extent, enclosed by Christian V in 1670. Magnificent trees, principally beeches; large herd of deer. Close by is *Bakken*, a vast funfair. Numerous footpaths and cycle tracks. Favourite point is *Eremitagen*, early eighteenth century, in pale yellow baroque, a royal shooting box with wonderful view over *Sound* to Sweden. *Rådvad*Δ is nearby.

Continue northwards along the so-called '*Danish Riviera*' continuously fringed with gardens and villas. From *Nivå* see island of *Hveen* where famous Danish astronomer, Tycho Brahe, had his observatory. There is a fine new exhibition centre for contemporary painting and sculpture in Humlebæk. Swedish coast and town of *Hälsingborg* now clearly in sight.

On for 5 miles (3km) to **Elsinore**Δ (*Helsingør*). Principal feature is castle, *Kronborg*, commanding the *Sound*, here less than 3 miles (5km) wide, fine Renaissance building on site of earlier fortress, surrounded by moats and ramparts. Shakespeare's *Hamlet* is sometimes acted in courtyard and Maritime Museum is housed here. King's Tower affords view across the *Sound*; Queen's Tower is used as a lighthouse. Visit *St Maria's Church* for medieval mural paintings; Carmelite monastery, fifteenth-century *St Olaf's Church*, many beautiful old houses in *Strandgade* and *Stengade*, and sixteenth-century *Marienlyst Palace*. Ferry across the *Sound* to *Hälsingborg* in Sweden, worth taking if only for view of *Kronborg* from the sea.

North from *Elsinore* are many holiday resorts with splendid sands for bathing; inland for 9 miles (14km) to *Fredensborg* and its castle, one of the summer residences of Royal Family, built 1719-26 in Italian style, beautifully situated close to lake *Esrum Sø* in delightful park containing much sandstone and marble statuary.

South-west for 6 miles (10km) to *Hillerød* for *Frederiksborg* palace, in red brick and ornately decorated; built by Christian IV (1602-20) restored in nineteenth century; Museum of National History housed here. Chapel, richly decorated, contains arms of the knights of Order of the Elephant, and those of the

British Queen Elizabeth, and Duke of Edinburgh; famous organ, built 1610, with 1,001 wooden pipes.

From *Hillerød* to *Copenhagen* is 23 miles (37km) via *Farum*, beautifully situated town by lakes and near nature park.

R2 Copenhagen to Slagelse via Vordingborg and Møn (160 miles, 257km)

South Zealand is pleasantly pastoral but does not contain as much of interest as north Zealand. *Møn*, however, is said to be the most attractive of the Danish islands.

Køge△ is 23 miles (37km) south from *Copenhagen*; has sandy beaches along wide bay, interesting church, the tower of which was used as lighthouse and height from which pirates were hung. Much half-timbering, many ancient houses.

Continue southwards for 34 miles (55km) on E4 to *Vordingborg*△ where fourteenth-century castle has *Goose Tower*, topped by golden goose set up to annoy Hanseatic towns, which Danes dubbed as a flock of geese. Impressive ramparts and interesting botanical gardens. View from top of tower over south Zealand and the famous *Storstrøm* bridge, 2 miles (3km) long, leading to island of *Falster*.

Continue 17 miles (27km) via *Kalvehave* to *Stege* over Queen Alexandrine's bridge to island of *Møn* and head eastwards for 12 miles (19km) to **Møns Klint** △, a stretch of 5 miles (8km) chalk cliffs, approached by easy climb terminating in beech forest perched 400ft (120m) above sea. Cliffs, full of fossils and distorted into fanciful shapes during the last Ice Age, make a startling coastline. Nearby is *Liselund* — pretty park with thatched mansion, Norwegian house, Swiss cottage and Chinese summer house. Many churches in neighbourhood richly ornamented with thirteenth- and fourteenth-century frescoes.

Return via *Vordingborg* and proceed north-westwards for 69 miles (110km) to *Slagelse*△ on main route to Jutland (see **R4**).

R3 Circuit of Bornholm (56 miles, 90km)

An island of granite cliffs, beech woods and sandy beaches; runic stones and prehistoric remains abound. *Rønne*△ at westernmost point of island and *Bornholm's* port and chief town, picturesque setting and old houses expertly repaired after destruction caused by Russian bombing in 1945.

Round fortress-churches of *Bornholm* are famous and those at *Nylars* and *Nyker* are within easy reach of *Rønne*. *Ols Kirke* is close to *Tejn* and *Osterlars Kirke* near to *Gudhjem* △.

A week's tour of *Bornholm* on foot could be accomplished by making a round-trip of its circumference. *Rønne* to *Dueodde*△, by footpaths or coast road for 14 miles (23km), the most southerly point, has lighthouse (view) and beaches of fine white sand, thence northwards following coast through beech woods for 9 miles (14km) via *Neksø* to *Svaneke*△, little harbour cut out of rock; curious smoke-houses where herrings are cured. Motor-boats from here to *Christiansø*, most easterly of Danish islands, and seal and bird sanctuary of *Græsholm*. Between *Neksø* and *Svaneke*Δ, rock changes from sandstone to granite, and rugged coastline extending to extreme north of island becomes most picturesque. Take cliff and shore paths for 8 miles (13km) to *Gudhjem*Δ and on along cliffs for 9 miles (14km) to *Sandvig*Δ nearest village to northern corner, rocky, with tracts of heather, birch and pine. Walk the 4 miles (6km) around promontory, said to be finest cliff walk in Denmark, to cliff-top *Hammershus*, Denmark's largest castle ruin. From here a 6 mile (4km) cliff path connects with *Hasle*Δ, thence by woodland footpath for another 6 miles (10km) to *Rønne*.

R4 Copenhagen to Esbjerg via Odense (170 miles, 274km)

This is principal route across the country, following main road; some interesting sightseeing alternating with rather monotonous stretches of countryside.

By motorway for 19 miles (30km) to *Roskilde*Δ, beautifully situated on fjord, famous for twelfth-century cathedral, with graceful spires added in 1635. Most Danish kings are buried here. Fine Renaissance reredos and sixteenth-century clock with moving figures. In Christian I's chapel is pillar recording heights of many kings, including Peter the Great of Russia and Edward VIII.

Continue for 16 miles (26km) by road A14 to *Ringsted*Δ in centre of Zealand, was capital in Viking times; *St Benats Kirke*, notable Romanesque-style church, with royal tombs. Next after 10 miles (16km) on E66 comes *Sorø*, which has Denmark's leading public school, the Academy — founded 1586. Church is part of old abbey established by Bishop Absalon, founder of *Copenhagen*.

*Slagelse*Δ is 9 miles (14km) further on. Alternatively, take road southwards to rail junction for *Kalundborg*, thence ferry northwards to *Århus*Δ, *Næstved*Δ and *Vordingborg*Δ — an old-established town but little of antiquity remains, owing to many fires. *Korsør*Δ 11 miles (18km) beyond *Slagelse* is Zealand terminus for Great Belt Ferry, a pleasing interlude in cross-country journey. The express trains, which are carried on ferry, move off immediately on reaching harbour. *Nyborg*Δ is terminus of ferry on *Funen* and junction for *Svendborg*Δ (see **R5**).

*Odense*Δ, 18 miles (29km) from *Nyborg* is capital of *Funen* and Denmark's third largest town; ancient origin, rich in historical and cultural associations but somewhat industrialised, connected to fjord by canal and trading as a port. *St Knud's* church, thirteenth-century Gothic; in crypt are bones of holy King Canute, murdered by pagans in 1086. Hans Andersen's birthplace and childhood home is in *Munkemøllestræde*, museum in *Hans Jensens Stræde*; several parks, open-air museum and DSB railway museum. Opposite station is *Kongens Have*, extensive gardens with many fine fruit trees and lily-pond adjoining Royal Palace built in 1721.

Branch railway from *Odense* runs southwards to *Fåborg* (see **R5**).

On for 29 miles (46km) to *Middelfart* (meaning middle-ferry) and Little Belt Bridge, almost three-quarters of a mile long, which carries both railway and highway. See the Folk Museum and explore narrow streets around harbour.

Fredericia Δ is 6 miles (10km) further; a railway junction, and a town built within ramparts. Church contains graves of Danish soldiers killed during the Prussian-Danish War of 1848-50, and memorial statue *The Brave Soldier* near the Prince's Gate.

*Kolding*Δ, reached after 14 miles (22km), is at intersection of east-west and north-south highways. Visit the *Koldinghus*, all that remains of medieval fortress, now museum of art and history; Botanical Gardens should not be missed. *Esbjerg*Δ, 45 miles (72km) beyond *Kolding*, is modern port which has extensive trade with Britain.

Island of *Fano*, reached in 20 minutes by ferry, is famous for bathing beaches, peasant costumes and old houses at *Nordby* and *Sønderho*; well worth visiting.

R5 Nyborg to Odense via South Funen (61 miles, 98km)

North Funen has little interest for tourists but southern and central parts of island are attractive. Road from *Nyborg*Δ goes through fruit-growing country for 21 miles (34km) to *Svendborg*Δ, situated on sound separating *Funen* from small island of *Taasinge*. Harbour is full of interest; much half-timbering and many cobbled streets in old town, numerous walks along the sound and excursions by local ferry to *Taasinge*. Ferries also connect with islands of *Langeland*Δ, *Lolland*Δ and *Aerø*Δ.

Continue westwards through undulating country, aptly named 'Garden of Denmark', for 16 miles (26km) to *Fåborg*Δ quaint town with numerous lanes and courtyards containing cottages with small gardens; known as artists' paradise. See the Bell Tower, only remaining part of medieval St Nicholas Church, and the museum's fine collection of *Funen* painters.

Road from *Fåborg* to *Odense*Δ goes across quite hilly country, the so-called *Funen Alps*, for 24 miles (39km); alternatively take road A8 for 14 miles (23km) to *Kværndrup*, visiting lovely fortified manor house of *Egeskov* (sixteenth century), built on piles in lake, with fine park and French garden and veteran car museum; thence on A9 for 5 miles (8km) to *Ringe*Δ and 13 miles (21km) northwards to *Odense*.

R6 Esbjerg to Kolding via South Jutland (147 miles, 236km)

*Ribe*Δ is 22 miles (35km) south of *Esbjerg* — a wonderful town in which to spend first night in Denmark. First mentioned as early as 850, episcopal residence since 948; one of the oldest cathedrals in Scandinavia (1130), wonderful view from top of tower; many red brick and half-timbered houses.

A11 to *Tønder* continues southwards for 36 miles (58km) across marsh country, in places only a yard above the sea, with dykes to prevent flooding. A trip

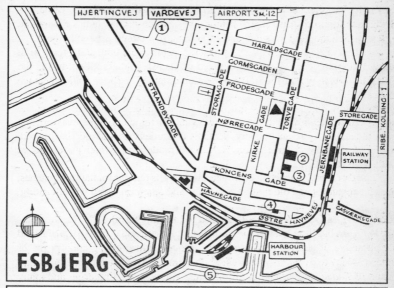

1 Youth Hostel. 2 Bus Station. 3 Town Hall. 4 Water Towers. 5 Arrival quay for ferries from England.

to *Rømø*Δ, an island of rough heathland and desolate sand dunes can be made; by 5 mile (8km) causeway from *Skærbæk*. Motorists and cyclists may wish to miss *Tønder* and travel across country to *Åbenrå*Δ or *Sønderborg*Δ but *Tønder* is on railway line from Esbjerg via Ribe.

*Tønder*Δ, close to German border, is home of Tønder lace, cottage industry, recently revived. Old houses and quaint doorways are worth seeing, so too is town museum.

Eastwards on A8 for 50 miles (80km) to *Sønderborg* or by bus to *Tinglev* (*Store Jyndevad*Δ nearby) and thence by train. *Sønderborg*Δ is on *Als Sound* which separates island of *Als* from mainland. Fine situation, popular yachting centre. Castle, now used in part as museum, contains relics of Danish-Prussian wars and of German occupation.

On for 11 miles (18km) to *Fynshav* connected by ferry to *Bøjen*, near *Fåborg* in South Funen (see **R5**). Our route is northwards to *Åbenrå*, either direct by road or rail via *Tinglev* and *Rødekro*.

Åbenrå Δ is 21 miles (34km) by road from *Sønderborg*; pleasing town on pretty fjord, with some interesting old houses. From *Åbenrå*, continue for 32 miles (51miles) through *Haderslev*Δ, with newly restored cathedral, to *Kolding*Δ.

R7 Esbjerg to the Skaw via North Jutland (315 miles, 507km)

This area cannot easily be included in a circular tour. Almost all places of interest are on the more fertile eastern side of peninsula along main road from *Kolding* to the *Skaw* in extreme north. Those with limited time should, on arrival at *Esbjerg*, make for *Silkeborg*Δ via *Grindsted*, explore the lakes, continue to *Århus*, and cross by boat to Zealand. North Jutland, however, has a charm of its own, and the following itinerary takes the east coast route to the extreme north.

Take main road ¡ ʾ68 for 45 miles (72km) from *Esbjerg*Δ to *Kolding*Δ and thence northwards for 17 miles (27km) to *Vejle*Δ prettily situated on a fjord, up attractive *Grejsdal* valley to *Jelling*; here are burial mounds of Gorm and Thyra, the first known Danish king and queen and great grand-parents of King Canute. Two large runic stones in churchyard, with remarkable carvings, one erected by Gorm to Thyra, the other by King Harald Bluetooth commemorates Denmark's conversion to Christianity. Norman church contains interesting mural paintings. *Horsens*Δ is 16 miles (26km) from *Vejle*.

*Skanderborg*Δ 14 miles (23km) from *Horsens*, is tourist centre and approach to *Denmark's Lakeland*, of which principal town is *Silkeborg*Δ 20 miles (32km) from *Skanderborg*. Railway and road skirt lakes, backed by range of beautiful tree- and heather-covered hills. Good walking, canoeing and fishing in the neighbourhood but water weed restricts bathing. Hill with tower on opposite side of lake to railway is *Himmelbjerget*, 482ft (147m), Denmark's second highest. Paddle steamers ply on the lakes. Diversion is to leave train from *Skanderborg* at *Laven*, cross by steamer to *Himmelbjerget*, climb hill, and complete journey to *Silkeborg* by steamer.

Return to *Skanderborg*, thence north-eastwards for 16 miles (26km) to **Århus**Δ, second largest town and terminus of boat services to *Copenhagen* and *Kalundborg*. Old Town (*Den Gamle By*), in Botanical Gardens off *Vesterbrogade*, has remarkable collection of old houses, grouped together on banks of stream to form village, complete with mayor's house, shops and windmill. Redbrick cathedral is twelfth-century Romanesque, partly rebuilt in Gothic style in the fifteenth century, and has longest nave in the country. Note wrought-iron doors, medieval reredos and frescoes. *Århus* is famous also for modern architecture, the Town Hall with 200ft (60m) tower, imposing exterior and still more impressive interior; several conducted tours every day.

From *Århus* continue north-west, leaving main line and highway on right, and, after 40 miles (64km) come to *Viborg*Δ, an ancient town on *Lake Hald*. Granite cathedral, nineteenth century, on site of earlier churches has twin towers; wonderful series of frescoes by Joakim Skovgård decorate the nave and chancel. From *Viborg* turn north-eastwards through pretty lake country for 29 miles (47km) to *Hobro*Δ, then 15 miles (24km) due north to *Rebild*Δ in national park of heather-clad hills and largest area of woodland in Denmark.

*Ålborg*Δ on *Limfjord*, is 15 miles (24km) farther north; has many beautiful parks, modern domestic architecture and several examples of modernistic sculpture in streets and gardens. See *Jens Bang's* house (1624) and North Jutland Museum of Art. A pleasant excursion from *Ålborg* is by bus to *Blokhus*△ on west coast; some of finest sands in Europe.

Continue via *Sæby*△ to *Frederikshavn*△ 39 miles (63km) (boat service to *Larvik, Oslo* and *Gothenburg*) and the *Skaw*, past island of *Læsø*. Beyond *Frederikshavn* the country becomes increasingly sandy and barren. On left before *Skagen* is *Råbjerg Mile*, square mile of drifting sand, and on right, near *Skagen* is church of which only the tower can be seen above sand. *Skagen*△, 25 miles (40km) from *Frederikshavn*, is pretty village with fishermen's cottages and gardens, home or summer residence of many writers or artists. Fine beach and rolling sandhills. Beyond lighthouse and German gun emplacements comes *Grenen*, extreme tip of Europe's only northwards-pointing peninsula, where ridge of shingle sticks hook-wise out into sea, always lashed in foam, between waters of *Skagerrak* and *Kattegat*.

ENGLAND AND WALES

Geographical Outline

The British Isles

Lying north-west of the European mainland, in the shallow seas of the 'continental shelf', the British Isles include two principal islands, Great Britain and Ireland, together with numerous small islands either standing alone such as *Man* and *Arran*, or forming groups, such as the *Shetlands*, *Orkneys*, *Hebrides*, *Scilly Isles* and *Channel Islands*. Even considering only those which are inhabited, it is unlikely that anyone has ever visited them all.

This diversity is much enhanced by the complexity of their structure — the unexpected fact that in this small section of the earth's surface almost every part of the geological succession is present. The effect is seen not only in dramatic contrasts of scenery and ways of life, but also in subtle variations over small areas, within a single parish or even a single farm.

Diversity also comes from the many settlers and invaders who have contributed to the islands' story, whose subsequent history includes their transition from poor and remote outposts of the inhabited world to a strategic position in world communications and trade, vigorous centres of dispersal of men and ideas whose influence is still at work in every continent.

The present political division is an example of history overriding geographical considerations. The largest political unit does not include the whole of the British Isles though it comprises more than the principal island. It is the *United Kingdom (UK) of Great Britain and Northern Ireland*, and includes, in effect, all the British Isles with the exception of the independent *Republic of Ireland*. The two countries of *England* and *Wales* comprise the southern and larger part of Great Britain.

Land

The basic division is between *Lowland Britain*, lying roughly south and east of a line from the mouth of the *Exe* to the mouth of the *Tees*, and *Highland Britain*

to the north and west.

The lowland zone is rarely a plain but is a region of broad river valleys, low undulating hills, and a fairly regular succession of scarplands exposing comparatively young rocks. Its better soils, from light chalklands to heavy clays, permit good arable farming, but there are many areas of woodland and open heath. Easy to settle, and with few extremes, its villages and towns closely succeed one another. The River *Thames* spans it from west to east and communication between *London* and other parts is relatively easy.

Highland Britain provides a sharp contrast. It is built of older rocks, lower in succession than the Coal Measures; many are immensely ancient and there has been far more time than in the lowlands for them to be affected by earth movements and weathering. They were high mountains before the great chains of Europe and Asia, the *Alps* and the *Himalayas*, were upfolded, and, as seen today, are only the worn-down stumps of the great ranges of early times. What remains is a dramatic, extremely varied upland region, mostly above a thousand feet, and rising higher in, for example, the granite mass of *Dartmoor*, the sandstones of the *Black Mountains*, the rugged igneous mountains of *Snowdonia* and the *Lake District*, and the Carboniferous rocks of the *Pennines*. On the fringe of the region, where the Coal Measures tend to occur, mining and heavy industry support dense populations. But as a whole it is sparsely peopled, settlement being confined either to the coasts or to isolated hill farms, or villages in the narrow valleys between which, as in the region as a whole, communication is difficult. With its generally thin soils and higher rainfall, grassland and rough pasture predominate, supporting a pastoral, dairying and stock-rearing type of farming.

The first of many contrasts between *England* and *Wales* is that *Wales* is part of the highland zone, while *England* comprises the whole lowland zone together with parts of the highland zone — the *Pennines*, the *Lake District* and the peninsula of *Devon* and *Cornwall*.

Working outwards from *London*, the *London Basin* is bounded north and south by chalk uplands, the *Chilterns* on the north, the *North Downs* on the south — a name which contrasts them with the *South Downs*, also of chalk, forming billowing rounded hills behind the coast of *Sussex*. It is this chalk, appearing again in Northern France, which was breached by the sea when it rose with the melt waters at the end of the Ice Age, separating Britain from the Continent. Similarly the *North Downs* extend eastwards through *Kent* to break on the coast in the white cliffs of *Dover*. The two lines of downs are the supporting sides of what was once a dome of chalk, the top of which has been eroded away to expose the clays and sands of the *Weald*, an intimately varied country crowned by *Leith Hill*.

The chalklands reach furthest north at *Flamborough Head* in *Yorkshire* but all converge on *Salisbury Plain* — a fact which made it the hub of the country in prehistoric times, as they were free from the oak forests with their dense, almost impassable, undergrowth which then covered the heavier soils.

Moving across lowland England from south-east to north-west the cyclist especially will become aware of a succession of scarplands. After the gentle climb out of the *London Basin*, comes the *Chiltern* edge and the sharp drop to a clay vale. The process is repeated in a further gentle rise across the oolitic limestone which crosses the country from the *Dorset* coast to the moors of north-east *Yorkshire*, forming everywhere striking scenery, enriched by churches and villages of outstanding beauty built from local stone. This is well seen in the *Cotswolds* from which there is an impressive drop over the western scarp into the *Vale of Severn*.

Such scarps may be thought of as providing a framework for the lowland country, within which are many other features such as the reclaimed levels of the *Fens*; the *Broads*, rivers and estuaries of *East Anglia*; the extensive sandy heaths of *Surrey* and *Hampshire*; the *Isle of Wight*; and finally, the course of the *Thames* itself which after a leisurely passage across the broad clays of *Oxfordshire*, breaks through the *Chilterns* at *Goring* to enter the *London Basin*.

Nearly equal to the lowland of the scarps is the other lowland that lies between it and the highland zone, like an inverted triangle whose apex is the *Vale of Severn* and which broadens out to form the *Midlands* and the *Cheshire Plain*, with extensions northward on both sides of the *Pennines* in the *Lancashire Plain* and the *Vale of York*. Projecting through its clays and rich red sandstones are isolated inliers of the ancient rocks — *Charnwood Forest*, the *Malvern Hills* and the *Wrekin of Shropshire*. In *Herefordshire* and *Shropshire* the lowlands lap against the border hills of *Wales*.

In the north country, beyond the *Yorkshire Wolds* and *North York Moors*, a fine coast runs north from *Bridlington* to *Saltburn*, and again in *Northumberland* past the *Farne Islands* and *Holy Island* to *Berwick*.

Inland, the *Pennines*, running north for about 200miles (320km) from the *Peak District* of *Derbyshire* to the *Cheviots* and the Scottish Border, are well called the 'backbone of England'. Their bleak gritstone and limestone tablelands, reaching (2,930ft, 893m) in *Cross Fell*, form a barrier between the populous lowlands on either side. But their dales (a northern name for valleys) have much fine scenery, and the areas of Carboniferous Limestone are remarkable for their cliffs, caves, pot-holes and underground streams, particularly in the *Craven* area around *Ingleborough*.

The other chief hill mass of the north contains the famous *Lake District*, with many lake-filled dales radiating from a dome of mountains, of which *Scafell Pike* 3,210ft (978m) is the highest point in England. The more rugged and precipitous central part, formed of volcanic rocks, is flanked on the north by older slates, and on the south by younger (but still ancient) slates, giving rise to smoother and softer scenery north of *Derwentwater* and around *Coniston* and *Windermere*.

Combinations of volcanics and slates are seen in *North Wales* in the *Berwyn Mountains* and more spectacularly in the mountain and coastal scenery of *Snowdonia* (*Snowdon* 3,560ft, 1,085m). The latter are composed in part of the yet older Cambrian series, while across the *Menai Strait* is *Anglesey*, much of which is structurally the most ancient part of south Britain.

Mid-Wales is a comparatively smooth upland whose chief beauty is in its rivers and valleys. The *Severn*, *Wye* and many more flow out to the English lowland, whilst others, such as the *Rhiedol* and *Dyfi* (*Dovey*), reach the sea direct.

South of the *Wye* the scarp face of the *Brecon Beacons*, cut in Old Red Sandstone, is a prelude to the varied and colourful landscape of *South Wales*. Away from the mining valleys (not uninteresting in themselves) the *Vales* of *Neath* and *Glamorgan*, the coasts of *Gower* and *Pembrokeshire*, the *Prescelly*

Hills and the little-known hills of *Carmarthenshire* — from *Carmarthen Van* to those around the River *Cothi* — present a rich diversity of scene.

Moving back into England through the *Forest of Dean*, the same is true of the south-west peninsula. Out of its warm and mellow farmlands rise scenically varied hills; the *Mendips*, *Quantocks*, *Exmoor* and *Dartmoor*. And its famous coasts from *Minehead* on the north, from *Portland Bill* on the south, converge south-west through *Devon* and *Cornwall* to meet at *Land's End*.

Climate

The prevalent south-westerly winds from the Atlantic account for the general mildness and humidity of the climate. Its variability is due partly to the alternating sunny and showery conditions produced by oceanic influences, partly to occasional winds from eastern Europe bringing more extreme conditions of cold in winter and heat in summer.

The wettest parts are the hill districts, especially in the west (over 60in, 150cm), and rainfall decreases to under 30in (75cm) in the east. The extreme cases are over 200in (500cm) in the centre of the *Lake District* and under 20in (50cm) in the *Thames* estuary.

Temperature decreases from west to east in winter and from south to north in summer. But nowhere is it ever very hot or ever very cold. Winters in the British Isles are warmer than in any other country in the same latitudes.

Spring and early autumn are delightful seasons for touring. Of the summer months, June and September tend to be more settled than July and August.

Plants and Animals

Only a few species of plants survived the Ice Age, during which most of the country north of the *Thames* was covered by ice sheets. At their retreat the country was re-colonized by vegetation from the Continent, but this was interrupted by the cutting of the Channel so that many plants common in Europe are absent. The Scots pine is the only native conifer.

The natural cover on heavy soils is oak forest, with alder along river banks, giving way to marsh and fen where subject to floods; on chalk and limestone it is birch, ash and beech; on sandy soils, Scots pine and heathland flora.

Little of the natural forest survives. From Anglo-Saxon times heavy soils were gradually put to the plough or converted to meadow; later the chalk downs and limestone uplands were turned to close-cropped pasture by the sheep rearing industry to supply the great export market in English wool. And further inroads were made by the demand for charcoal for iron smelting prior to the development of coal-mining. Much of this was necessary to secure improved land use, but in some of the wetter parts loss of the forest has produced a bog vegetation of little practical value.

Despite such changes the diversity of natural and semi-natural vegetation is considerable on account of the varied soils, the survival of uncultivated common lands and the great range of habitats on the 2,750 miles (4,425km) of coast. Finally, in the uplands, there are large areas of cotton grass and heather moors with, in the higher parts, a tundra vegetation of lichens, mosses and bilberry.

Introduced species, in a country whose plant collectors have explored the most remote parts of the world, are numerous.

Wild animals have suffered even more than plants from the claims of man. But red deer flourish in the combes of *Exmoor* and on the *Quantocks*, and other deer are increasing in the plantations of the Forestry Commission; semi-wild ponies are to be seen in *Central* and *South Wales* and the *New Forest*; the fox, badger, stoat, weasel, hare and rabbit occur everywhere; the red squirrel competes for territory with the introduced grey squirrel; the pine marten is being seen again in the *Lake District*. The grey seal and the common seal are frequently seen on the Atlantic coasts, and there is a large colony of grey seals on the *Farne Islands* off the coast of *Northumberland*. Only two snakes occur: the harmless grass snake and the poisonous viper, or adder, which is widely distributed, chiefly on pine and heath lands.

Bird life is remarkably rich. It includes game birds, such as grouse, pheasant and partridge: many species of hawk and owl; waders and wildfowl, especially on the many estuaries; the raven, starling, magpie, cuckoo, swallow, swift, and many smaller birds of field, wood, stream and hedgerow. The sea-cliffs and offshore islands are breeding places of large colonies of sea-birds, including the puffin, razorbill, gannet, guillemot, cormorant, shearwater and various species of tern and gull.

The People

Population

Of the population of about 50 million, about 2,800,000 live in *Wales*. In both countries about four out of five live in towns or built-up areas, the main concentrations being *Greater London* (9 million) and the traditional industrial areas (often associated with coalfields) — including *Tyneside*, parts of *Lancashire* and the *West Riding of Yorkshire*, the *Birmingham* region and the *South Wales* coalfields. *Birmingham* has a population of more than a million, while *Liverpool*, *Manchester*, *Leeds* and *Sheffield* are cities with half a million or more people. But these and others are regional centres for the clusters of smaller industrial towns in which the majority of the people live.

This extreme concentration in a few areas, occupying only about a tenth of the area of the country accounts for the preservation of so much good farm land and comparatively wild countryside which may surprise the visitor who knows this to be one of the most densely populated countries in the world.

Language

It might be thought that English, the most widely used language in the world, would be spoken to a standard form by the people of its homeland. But, as a little experience will show, there are intriguing differences of vocabulary and intonation. The almost Scots lilt of *Northumberland* contrasts with the slow burr of the *West Country*; the suppressed consonants of the *London 'Cockney'* and of rural *Hertfordshire* contrast with their careful over-emphasis in *Lancashire* and *Yorkshire*. Vowels undergo every possible change between light and heavy as one travels the English shires.

Such differences go back far in history, surviving the many changes in the language since the tribes of the English settlement brought the dialects of their West Germanic tongue; since then Scandinavian and Norman invaders have added much from Norse and French.

Welsh, spoken by nearly a million people in *Wales*, is one of the surviving Celtic languages, once widespread in Western Europe but now confined to a few parts of the Atlantic seaboard. The other living Celtic tongues are Irish, Gaelic (in parts of Scotland) and Breton (in Brittany). Others which have become very nearly extinct are Cornish and Manx. In Wales the native tongue is sustained by a rich ancient literature and kept vigorous and receptive by the annual Eisteddfod — a competitive festival of poetry and song. But nearly all who speak it are bilingual and English is understood almost everywhere.

Religion

Protestantism in England and Wales has not stopped at one movement of reformation producing the break with Rome. Chapels of various sects, Wesleyan Methodist, Baptist, United Reformed and many more are as familiar a sight in town and village as is the ancient church of the established religion — the protestant Church of England — whose head is the Queen, with a hierarchy of archbishops, bishops and clergy. The historical reasons for these differences may appear remote today in a country where only a minority now adhere (other than nominally) to any religious organization. Yet such loyalties still greatly enrich the national life: *Wales* remembers how it was revitalised by its Methodist revival; the Society of Friends ('Quakers'), always small in numbers, is large in influence and example; two-thirds of those born in England are baptised in church; and it is still the case that much varied social life and social service is centred on churches, chapels and such bodies as the Salvation Army. Roman Catholics number more than 3 million. There is a considerable Jewish community and a growing number of Muslims.

History

Britain was for 400 years the Roman province of *Britannia*. The lowland zone was brought under control, with towns for the natives in each tribal area, villas and farms in the countryside, and advanced military bases at *York*, *Chester* and *Caerleon* for the intended conquest of the highland zone. Here only forts were built, but road-making was as persistent as in the lowlands. The emperor Hadrian's wall from the *Solway* to the *Tyne* was built in AD122 and the decision in AD211 to make it the northern frontier of the province marks the abandonment of the attempt to conquer the north of the island.

In 410 the Roman legions were withdrawn, although even earlier the province had been suffering raids from all quarters; now it was defenceless. The attempt to keep out the Picts of the north by inviting over the Angles — a Germanic people from Schleswig — led only to a long and bloody struggle. Waves of invaders from across the North Sea — Angles, Jutes and Saxons — exterminated the people of south-east Britain, establishing their own tribal areas, still remembered in the names of districts and counties such as *East Anglia*, *Wessex*, *Essex* and *Sussex* (the kingdoms of the Angles and of the West, East, and South Saxons).

The highlands of the west were a refuge. Elsewhere, the Anglo-Saxons, settling in countless village communities and making clearings in the forest for beast and plough, laid down the basic pattern of what was to become England. Dominion lay first with *Northumbria* (seventh century), then with *Mercia*, a midland kingdom (eighth century) and with *Wessex* (ninth century). Christianity was re-introduced by the missions of St Columba from Ireland and of St Augustine from Rome. Despite the times there was progress in arts and learning. Bede of *Jarrow*, the first English historian, was one of the greatest Europeans of the Dark Ages. Alfred the Great, king of Wessex, was educator and law-giver as well as warrior against the Danes.

The fearful Danish raids introduced another element still noticeable in place-name and dialect in the north, and it was a Danish king, Canute, who first ruled unquestionably over all England.

The civilization which sprang from this tribalism was a matter of pride to the English. They were freemen living under their local laws. But all this was changed in the fatal year of 1066 when Harold, having defeated a Norwegian invasion in the north, marched south to heroic defeat against Duke William of Normandy and England came quickly under the iron hand of the Conqueror. The feudal system was imposed. Great castles dominated the land. Norman authority was made visible in Church and State and the Domesday survey provided an inventory of the wealth of each locality for effective central control.

Under Henry II the justice of the king's courts became accessible to all and gave protection against local tyranny. From these reforms stems the English legal system and its clear concept of the rule of law.

Trade expanded, with wool as the staple export. Craft guilds and merchant guilds were formed in the towns. It was the city of London as well as the barons which compelled the autocratic King John to sign *Magna Carta*, in 1215, to ensure the rights and liberties of the people and to provide the basis of the English constitution. Out of the practice of the kings in calling knights and representatives of the towns to take part in council along with the barons grew Parliament. And out of its insistence on redress of grievances before providing money for campaigns and other royal needs grew its capacity to submit bills for the making of new laws.

Persistent efforts to unify the islands brought success in Ireland under Henry II, in Wales under Edward I, but disaster at Bannockburn (1314) against the Scots. The large territories in southern and western France of which the kings were lords involved the country in constant war. The Hundred Years' War with France filled the period with sound and fury, but signified nothing unless it was, with the Wars of the Roses, fought entirely on home ground, the demise of the notion of medieval chivalry. Feudalism faded, together with its subsistence economy and labourers tied to the manor; prosperity which came from trade and high wages were offered in competition when labour became scarce after the Black Death (1349).

The Welsh Tudors came to the throne in 1485. Everything was astir, and the Church went down under the despotism of Henry VIII and his minister Thomas Cromwell. Many of the best Englishmen were beheaded and abbeys in England today are thought of most naturally as ruins.

Under Elizabeth I (1558-1603) Protestantism was established, a threat from Catholic Spain receded after the Armada (1588), and a great flowering of learning and expression took place, reaching its peak with Shakespeare and his contemporaries.

The Scottish Stuarts, ruled as kings of England and Scotland separately and wished to reimpose absolutism in England. Charles I tried to rule without Parliament. The clash brought civil war, the execution of the king (1649) and Parliament's declaration of its own supremacy. The latter part of Oliver Cromwell's rule was a dictatorship; the last of the restored Stuarts, James II, forced his own ideas against the will of the nation, but had to flee when William of Orange was invited from the Continent to secure a free and legal Parliament (1689). A Bill of Rights defined the liberties of the subject and England entered the eighteenth century as a land of security for men of property in an age of increasing plenty.

At home, Scotland and England were united in a joint Parliament (1707); the beginning of party politics came with the grouping of opinion into Whig and Tory; Cabinet government, headed by a Prime Minister, emerged; scientific crop rotation and stock breeding worked a revolution on the land; and the famous Industrial Revolution in the eighteenth and nineteenth centuries brought a movement from cottage industry to factory and from countryside to town.

Abroad, England had developed two main interests. First, the colonies, the results of sea-power, exploration and trade. The American Colonies were lost by 1783, but great acts of nation-making were still to be done in new and almost empty lands and in the teeming sub-continent of India. Secondly, there was the need to ensure that no one power became dominant on the Continent. This was the basis of the many wars from Marlborough's campaigns through the struggle against Napoleon culminating in Trafalgar and Waterloo to World War II.

The nineteenth century settled into the long Victorian prosperity with Britain the workshop of the world, centre of a wide empire, and a profound believer in free trade. The new industrial classes developed trade unionism; extensions of the vote were won and were followed by much-needed reforms of labour and social conditions and of the harsh criminal code.

In the twentieth century Britain has adapted itself to conditions in which many nations compete as industrial powers, and in which sea-power is no longer an island's secure defence, by means of membership of the European Economic Community and the North Atlantic Treaty Organization. Consitutionally it has evolved further towards effective democracy: at home, in the curtailing of the power of veto of the House of Lords and in the establishment of women's rights after a long and bitter campaign; abroad, in the emergence of self-governing Dominions, a change in fact and spirit from Empire to Commonwealth.

Government

Britain is a parliamentary democracy under a limited monarchy. The sovereign is also head of the Commonwealth. Parliament, the legislative body, consists of two Houses, the House of Lords, composed of hereditary peers, life peers, archbishops and bishops, and the House of Commons made up of 650 members of Parliament, elected by direct universal suffrage to represent constituencies in Great Britain and Northern Ireland.

The executive is nominally the Crown, but in practice it is a Cabinet of Ministers headed and chosen by the Prime Minister who is dependent on the support of a majority in the House of Commons.

Resources

The industrial strength of the nation depends far more on research, inventiveness, a wide range of traditional but adaptable skills and heavy accumulation of capital equipment than on natural resources. But the country is fortunate in the distribution, quality and variety of its coal measures and their ample reserves. The coal industry produces about 120 million tons a year. Iron ore (chiefly low grade from open-cast sites) is worked in the *East Midlands* and the *Cleveland* district of *Yorkshire*, but a large import is also necessary. Oil fields in the North Sea are now on stream; thus Britain has become a major oil-producing country.

Success in foreign trading is a necessity for a country whose people depend on imports for a third of their food. Manufacturing industry is therefore concerned as much with exports as with home demand. Many industries remain localized on or near the coalfields where they grew at the time of the Industrial Revolution — cotton textiles in *Lancashire*, woollens in the *West Riding of Yorkshire*, cutlery in *Sheffield*, the *'Potteries'* around *Stoke-on-Trent*. But newer industries, using electric power, have tended to settle near markets or ports — the ancient university city of *Oxford*, conveniently near to *London*, has become one of the centres of the motor vehicle industry. And *London* itself, once largely administrative and commercial, is now also the most important centre for many light industries. Among heavy industries, steel production remains significant. There is a considerable export of atomic fuels and Britain is now a leading European nation in the use of nuclear energy for peaceful purposes.

Agriculture is highly mechanised in the arable areas in the east where farms average 100 acres. Permanent grass predominates in the Midlands and the west. Wheat, barley, oats, potatoes and sugar beet are the chief crops. Regional specialities include hops, apples and pears in *Kent*, plums in the *Vale of Evesham*, bulbs in south *Lincolnshire*, cut flowers around *Penzance* and early potatoes on the *Pembrokeshire* coast.

British stock rearing is famous and its products have improved the herds of Commonwealth and other countries. There is a 200-year-old tradition of scientific breeding and many types of cattle and sheep are to be seen. Among cattle the black and white British Friesian (the highest milk yielder) and the red and white Shorthorn (reared both for milk and beef) predominate. The Ayrshire, white with red markings, is a good yielder on poorer land. The sable-coloured Jersey and the light brown and white Guernsey are prized for the richness of their milk. The chief English beef breed is the handsome rugged Hereford. In *Wales* the Welsh Black is valued as a dual purpose animal.

Forestry employs comparatively few people but the Foresty Commission is working great changes in the landscape, particularly on marginal land.

Fishing is no longer so important, but is still carried out from the trawling ports of *Fleetwood*, *Hull*, *Grimsby* and *Great Yarmouth* and from countless villages around the coast.

Food and Drink

The traditional English breakfast consists of porridge or dry cereal with milk, a cooked course of bacon and egg, followed by toast with marmalade, coffee or tea, although the majority are now adopting the lighter 'continental' style breakfast.

The midday meal is called 'dinner' when it is the main meal of the day, or 'lunch' by those who take their main meal in the evening. In either case it will generally be meat or fish with vegetables, followed by a sweet course or cheese or fruit and coffee.

English cooking is at its most reliable in standard dishes such as roast beef and Yorkshire pudding, or roast lamb and mint sauce which can be excellent because of the generally high quality of the meat available. Fish too, is of high quality; plaice is a popular fish delicacy, smoked herrings, called kippers, are served as a less expensive and nourishing dish except at main meals. Other good examples of English fare are fruit pies, such as apple, blackberry, bilberry and gooseberry, and steamed puddings served as a sweet, while English cheeses are renowned for their variety and flavour.

Tea is the universal drink, although coffee is widely drunk. Beer is the most popular alcoholic drink, except in the cider country of the south-west. Cider, made from fermented apples, is pleasant, refreshing and cheap, but unexpectedly potent. Wines and spirits being heavily taxed, are expensive.

Alcoholic drinks of all kinds are only obtainable during certain hours and from licensed premises (which include railway buffets, inns, wine bars, the majority of hotels and some restaurants).

Sport

Cricket, the traditional summer game, has endearing qualities even for those who do not pretend to understand its finer points. Not even the giant tussles of Commonwealth Test Matches have quite gone to its head and it is still played for its own sake in its original setting on village greens.

Cup Tie or international games in Association football or Rugby football are great popular occasions, as also are the Oxford and Cambridge Boat Race and some of the 'classic' horse races — the Derby, Oaks and St Leger in the flat season, and the Grand National which is raced over obstacles. Wimbledon tennis tournament is also extremely popular.

Field sports are still part of the life of the countryside and they include fox hunting (huntsmen mounted on horseback, but the field follows on foot in the *Lakeland* mountains); stag hunting on *Exmoor* and hare hunting by harriers or beagles. These are chiefly supported by regular country-dwelling followers, whereas grouse shooting lends itself to moorland excursions by well-to-do townsmen. At the other extreme, fishing claims a larger number of participants than any other sport.

The many creeks and estuaries provide good anchorages and a wide range of inshore sailing. *Cowes* on the *Isle of Wight* and *Burnham-on-Crouch* in *Essex* are the principal yachting resorts, but many others meet the less fashionable preferences of weekend yachtsmen.

Culture

Architecture

The few churches surviving from the Saxon period show Romanesque influence but have characteristic features in a narrow nave, long and short stonework and a massive tower divided into stages by horizontal strips. Re-building of churches was taken up energetically by the Normans soon after the Conquest and within thirty years work had begun on most of the cathedrals. The style was the full Romanesque which in England is called Norman. *Durham* cathedral is its finest achievement, but there are many other examples.

Cistercian monks, coming from France in 1129, introduced the pointed arch. Its use in lancet widows, with other features such as clusters of shafts instead of massive piers, distinguishes the Early English style — the first of three styles of English Gothic. Salisbury cathedral shows it to perfection. The Decorated style (early fourteenth century) has wider windows, with flowing curves in the window tracery, as in the choir of *Ely* cathedral. It was soon followed by the even lighter and airier style known as Perpendicular — peculiar to Britain and representing a great technical advance, seen in the audacious slenderness of columns supporting the roof and the intricacy of the fan vaulting. Famous examples include *Henry VII's Chapel* in *Westminister Abbey* and *King's College Chapel, Cambridge*.

Renaissance influences were delayed by the Reformation. Instead, there was a Tudor style of domestic architecture, of native inspiration, seen in great houses, such as *Hardwick Hall*, created for the new aristocracy. Under the first two Stuarts Inigo Jones first looked to Italian and classic models and introduced the Palladian style in the *Banqueting House* of *Whitehall* and the *Queen's House* at *Greenwich*. After the Restoration (1660) classic models were universally favoured and the re-building of *St Paul's* cathedral and other London churches by Sir Christopher Wren after the Great Fire (1666) showed that Gothic was dead. Wren's work was further developed by Hawksmoor and Vanbrugh (early eighteenth century). But such grandiose architecture as Vanbrugh's *Blenheim Palace* in *Oxfordshire* and *Castle Howard* in *Yorkshire* is professionally admired rather than liked, for the Baroque style never gained popularity in Britain. The dominant style of the century, called Georgian, at first followed Palladio and Inigo Jones. Its early exponent, William Kent, was also originator of English landscape gardening. The style entered a richer, more ornate, phase in the second half of the century through the work of the Scottish brothers Adam, particularly Robert, whose art is best seen in exquisite interiors, including *Kenwood, Hampstead*.

Late Georgian included (from 1810) the flourish of the Regency period but was challenged by the Gothic Revival — a movement of taste which produced Barry's *Houses of Parliament* and *St Pancras* station, scattered mock ruins over the countryside in pursuit of the picturesque, and fostered Victorian excesses to be seen in almost every town in the country. Its champion was Ruskin, but he lived to regret it. Gothic detail, such as the leaves of the chapter house at *Southwell*, was the product of the individual response and devout labour of craftsmen. Its easy repetition in the new machine age was devoid of feeling and meaning.

The functional architecture appropriate to such an age, and which had been developed on the Continent, was late in gaining acceptance and has only been widely adopted by British architects since World War II. Their most influential contribution to it in individual buildings appears to be in the design of schools. But the post-war decision to build several new towns has led to experiments in planning the whole social environment; those near London are *Harlow*, *Hemel Hempstead*, *Milton Keynes* and *Crawley*.

Art

Illuminated manuscripts and stone crosses were the chief expressions of Anglo-Saxon art. Later, popular craftsmanship was concentrated upon the Gothic churches and cathedrals. The Reformation of the sixteenth century, followed by Puritanism in the seventeenth century, cast a blight over much of the work of the past and prevented native participation in the great contemporary achievements in the visual arts of the Continent. The Court employed foreign artists: Holbein, Rubens and van Dyck.

Change came with the wealth and confidence of eighteenth-century society. Hogarth captured the vitality of the age. Patronage at last produced a portrait painter of the first rank in Gainsborough. It also founded an Academy around the dominating figure of Reynolds. The annual exhibition of this Royal Academy remains a notable event in the London season. In the applied arts the demands of aristocratic society fostered exquisite craftsmanship, notably in silverware and in the furniture made by Chippendale and Sheraton.

Landscape painting, both in watercolour (a peculiarly English medium) and oil, developed particularly in *East Anglia*. Chrome, Cotman, Girtin and Richard Wilson are minor masters, Constable and Turner break the bonds of English provincialism.

The so-called Pre-Raphaelite movement of the early Victorian age was an attempt led by D.G. Rossetti to recapture the simplicity of the Italian primitives. Its influence, though considerable, was wholly local. Its results excited both admiration and disfavour at the time. Whistler, who had studied in Paris, livened the scene and founded a group in *Chelsea* on the misty bank of the Thames.

The twentieth century has seen work of real power in the haunting sculptured forms of Henry Moore, Epstein's allegorical and religious figures (at *Coventry* and *Llandaff* cathedrals) and in his portrait bronzes. Among painters, Paul Nash, Ivon Hitchens, Graham Sutherland and John Piper are only a few among those whose style is unmistakably their own.

Literature

The beginnings of English poetry and prose are found in the native British epics of Arthur — oral stories originating, perhaps in the sixth century, in *South Wales* and *Cornwall* which later incorporated the Christian ideas of medieval chivalry and entered into literature all over Europe. The Angles brought their own epic, *Beowulf*, from Scandinavia. English prose begins with the *Anglo-Saxon Chronicle* in which the terse style develops flexibility as the record unfolds but never loses the capacity to move the reader by economy of words and understatement.

From these beginnings a body of literature developed which for diversity, quality and richness has never been surpassed. Wherever you go in England or Wales poets, novelists, historians or commentators have been there before you. Chaucer's *Canterbury Tales* enliven a journey between *Southwark* and *Canterbury*; Shakespeare is for many the greatest playwright; and Johnson, Lamb and Dickens haunt *London*. Matthew Arnold broods over the middle *Thames* as does Dyer over *Grongar Hill*. You can be with Crabbe in *East Anglia*, Hardy in *Dorset*, Wordsworth over every yard of the *Lake District* and the Brontë sisters in Yorkshire. You can travel *Wales* with Giraldus, or Borrow, or be with Dylan Thomas *Under Milk Wood*. Defoe, Celia Fiennes and J.B. Priestley are factual and tireless predecessors almost wherever you may go.

Even this list does not begin to cover the immense range; Jane Austen, H.G. Wells, George Orwell, Somerset Maugham are the experts of this art form.

Science

This is the land of Newton (1642-1727) who first brought comprehensive understanding of the physical forces governing the universe; of Darwin (1809-82) whose theory of natural selection brought similar comprehension of evolution to explain the marvellous abundance of living things; and of Keynes (1883-1946) who, working in the less predictable field of human affairs, brought an understanding of economic forces which has contributed to well-being wherever governments have accepted its teaching.

These men were not alone. Each had contemporaries almost equally eminent. The foundation of the Royal Society in 1662 had quickened interest in experimental science. Harvey's discovery of the circulation of the blood and Dalton's atomic theory were early successes. By the nineteenth century every science was progressing and men such as Faraday were contributing to several branches. Nowhere is the greatness of the Victorian era better seen than in its scientists, and the line of research has gone forward into the specialisms of the twentieth century around such names as Fleming and Rutherford.

Art Galleries

Only *London* is comprehensive, but there are good collections in other cities, including *Birmingham*, *Leeds*, *Liverpool* and *Norwich*. A vast amount of artistic wealth is held privately in country houses, many open to the public for a fee at certain times. But, generally there is more satisfaction in visiting an historic house in the care of the National Trust or other public body.

Museums

Besides the great national collections in *London* there are numerous museums throughout the country. Outstanding are the *National Museum of Wales*, *Cardiff*; *Welsh Folk Museum*, *St Fagan's*; *Fitzwilliam Museum*, *Cambridge*; *Ashmolean Museum*, *Oxford*; *Bowes Museum*, *Barnard Castle*, *County Durham*; *Castle* and *Railway Museums*, *York*; *Castle Museum*, *Colchester*; *Museum of English Rural Life*, *Reading*; *Ironbridge Gorge Museum*, *Telford*, *Shropshire*; *Beamish Open-Air Museum*, *County Durham*, and the *National Motor Museum* (antique cars, bicycles, etc) at *Beaulieu*, *Hampshire*.

Music

The country was certainly musical in the 'merrie England' of Elizabethan times. Madrigal singing was its characteristic expression. A native tradition of composition led, despite Puritanism, to Purcell (1659-95) the greatest of English composers. But it is the German, Handel (1685-1759), whose main works were written in England, who has reigned in popular affection. It may be partly this and partly the lack of a substantial native composer over the next 150 years that caused the English to submit with docility to the charge that they were not a musical nation.

Belatedly, towards the end of the nineteenth century, came Elgar, in the line of the great Central European composers and at this time the light operas of Gilbert and Sullivan created a new popular theatrical tradition.

English musical life gained new vigour from diverse courses in the twentieth century. Holst turned to astrological and oriental mysticism, whereas Vaughan Williams and many lesser composers sought to illustrate the peculiar character of English folk song. Britten (1913-76) acquired a lasting international reputation for accuracy of musical expression, especially in the setting of words. British 'pop' musicians lead the way in the modern music world.

Touring Information

Travel in Britain

Rail: The rail network provides comfortable travel, particularly on expresses; trains usually run to time, but Sunday, when track maintenance is carried out, is sometimes an exception. Seats may be booked in advance on principal trains.

Reduced rates on Saver Return tickets, for journeys over 60 miles (96km).

Valid outwards only on day of travel, return within one month. Cheap Day tickets for journeys up to 50 miles (80km). Also Rail Rover tickets issued March-October allowing 7 days' unlimited travel in specified areas.

Bus and Coach Services: cover most parts of Britain and are often cheaper than rail but journeys usually take much longer. Coach stations act as terminals for long- distance services (for which advance booking is advisable) and are connected with local bus services. Reduced rates are often available for day or period return and, on some services, for mid-week travel. Britexpress travel cards for overseas visitors, valid 8, 15 or 21 days, give unlimited travel on express coach routes throughout Great Britain.

Money

The unit of currency is the Pound Sterling (£ — symbol derived from the Latin '*libra*'). It is divided into 100 pence. Coins are issued for 1p, 2p, 5p, 10p, 20p, 50p and £1. Bank of England notes are issued for £5, £10, £20, and £50.

Restaurants

Eating out particularly at restaurants, is not cheap, but pubs offer reasonably-priced snacks and cooked dishes at counter service. In the countryside away from motorways, many small establishments cater for travellers at reasonable prices.

Public Holidays

1 January, Good Friday, Easter Monday, first Monday in May, last Monday in May or first Monday in June, last Monday in August, Christmas Day and 26 December. Most shops are closed on public holidays and bus and railway services are restricted. Also every town has one early closing day (1pm) weekly. Most shops close by 6pm.

Maps and Guide Books

The official Ordnance Survey maps, scale 1:50,000, are standard for walkers; the 1:25,000 scale Pathfinder and Outdoor Leisure series provide for more detailed exploration. Bartholomew's 1:100,000 series are particularly useful for cycling. Ordnance Survey 1:250,000 series are excellent maps for motorists. YHA map of England & Wales, showing hostels, roads and railways, scale 1:1,350,000, is useful for planning purposes.

There are many country and local guide books, which vary greatly in quality. Admirable productions published by Her Majesty's Stationery Office (HMSO) for the Countryside Commission are the guides to the *Dartmoor, Exmoor, Northumberland, Lake District, Brecon Beacons, Snowdonia* and *Peak District National Parks*; also those published for the Forestry Commission on certain Forests and Forest Parks.

Accommodation

There are about 260 youth hostels, chiefly in the countryside but also in cathedral cities and other interesting towns. Advance booking is advisable mid-July to first week of September, also Easter and Spring Bank Holiday and on Saturday nights throughout the year; essential at all times for school parties and other groups.

Other reasonably priced accommodation is listed in the *Rambler's Yearbook* issued annually by the Ramblers' Association.

Camping

There are numerous camping sites in holiday areas. Membership of the Camping Club of Great Britain and Ireland, 11 Lower Grosvenor Place, London SW1 is advantageous. Permission of farmer or landowner should always first be obtained.

Walking

Footpaths abound in every parish as the Ordnance Survey 1:50,000 maps will show, but they are not all rights of way. Each National Park provides extensive and varied walking, often over open country; *Northumberland, Lake District, North York Moors, Yorkshire Dales, Peak District, Snowdonia, Pembrokeshire Coast, Brecon Beacons* and *Black Mountains, Exmoor, Dartmoor* and *New Forest*. There are many other lovely areas, including the *Surrey* commons, the *Chilterns*, the *Downs* of *Kent, Sussex, Surrey, Berkshire, Wiltshire* the *Isle of Wight, Dorset, Mendips, Quantocks, Wye Valley* and *Gower*.

Long-distance routes designated by the Countryside Commission are the *Pennine Way (Derbyshire* to *Scottish Border), Offa's Dyke* (along the *Welsh Border), South Downs Way, North Downs Way, Ridgeway Path* (from *Avebury* in *Wiltshire* to *Ivinghoe Beacon* in *Buckinghamshire). Cleveland Way* (around the *North York Moors) Pembrokeshire Coast* and around the *South-West Peninsula* (coast of *Somerset, Devon* and *Cornwall*).

Rock Climbing

Details of climbing clubs can be obtained from the British Mountaineering Council, Crawford House, Precinct Centre, Booth Street East, Manchester M13 9RZ. Courses are arranged by YHA, Trevelyan House, St Stephen's Hill, St Albans, Herts.

Rock climbing areas are in *Snowdonia*, the *Lake District* and to a lesser extent in *Cornwall*. Gritstone outcrops in some parts of the *Pennines* and a few sandstone outcrops in *Kent* and *Surrey* attract some climbers. Guide books are issued describing each climb in detail. In hill areas get local advice, remember that weather conditions can turn treacherous; leave word about your proposed route or climb.

Caving and Potholing

Only to be undertaken with an experienced party. Information can be obtained from the National Caving Association, 3 Valletort Road, Stoke, Plymouth, Devon, PL1 5PH.

Chief areas are the *Craven* district of *Yorkshire*, the *Mendips* near *Bristol*, *Derbyshire Peak District* and the limestone areas of *South Wales*. Same cautions as for rock climbing. Additional danger is underground flooding after rain which may come with unexpected suddenness. Guide books detailing underground routes and advice are published for many areas.

Cycling

England and Wales are ideal for cycle touring. The villages are close to one another, and accommodation is plentiful and moderate in price. All roads are tar-bound and are generally in good condition, but main roads are often too busy for cyclists. Except in Eastern England the country is hilly and a change speed gear is advisable.

Motoring

Prudent motorists visiting Britain will make themselves familiar with the information given in the Government publication *The Highway Code*, obtainable at ports of entry and at bookshops throughout the country. Visitors who are members of a motoring organisation in their own country should seek their advice; they can expect reciprocal facilities from counterpart British associations.

A current driving licence, car registration papers and an International Insurance Certificate with third-party cover, or an International Green Card of Insurance are necessary documents.

Tolls are payable at some bridges and tunnels; motorways (prefixed M on maps) are free; main roads (A), minor roads (B). Speed limit in built-up areas is 48km/h (30mph); motorways and roads with dual-carriageways 112km/h (70mph), other roads 96km/h (60mph), unless specified otherwise. All vehicles are driven on the left-hand side of the road.

Entrance Fees to Historic Buildings

English Heritage offer 12 month membership which gives admission to over 400 monuments and buildings in their care in England, including the *Tower of London* and *Hampton Court*. English Heritage can be contacted at PO Box 1BB, London W1A 1BB and at principal monuments. Membership of the National Trust, 36 Queen Anne's Gate, London SW1 1HS secures free admission to over 100 properties. Visitors from overseas can buy tickest from the London Tourist Board, Victoria Station, London SW1, which secures admission to both English Heritage and National Trust properties.

London

Practical Hints. Even the visitor's London covers a large area, and careful planning is needed if you are to make the most of your time. Diagrams of the public transport system, bus and Underground, are issued free at information offices at St James Park and Piccadilly Circus stations.

Shopping centres are numerous. *Oxford Street* is a popular thoroughfare with several large department stores; parallel is *Piccadilly*, and linking them are *Bond Street*, with many luxury shops, and the handsome curve of *Regent Street*. Among *West End* centres are *Knightsbridge* and *Kensington*.

Galleries and Museums are not open on Sundays until 2 or 2.30pm.

Cafés and restaurants. There is a wide choice, but look at the list outside, or a meal may cost you more than expected. Best value in the popular ranges is not in the tempting and rather flashy new snack bars but in the many small unpretentious places in the side streets.

Youth Hostels. Holland House (King George VI Memorial Youth Hostel); Earls Court; Hampstead Heath; Highgate; Carter Lane (near *St Paul's Cathedral*).

YHA, Adventure Shops, for outdoor clothing and equipment, books, maps, railway, air and boat tickets; in London at 14 Southampton Street, Covent Garden, WC2.

Modern London has grown around two cities. The first is old London, known as '*the City*', dating from Roman times, centre of business, finance and trade, governed by its Lord Mayor and Corporation. Its narrow streets are dominated by *St Paul's*, but towering offices challenge the steeples of its many ancient churches. It suffered the Great Fire of 1666 and also air raids in World War II. The second is the *City of Westminster*, a mile or so further up the *Thames*, which grew around its abbey and palace, the original royal residence, to become the centre of government of the country.

1 The City

From *Charing Cross* walk east along *Strand*. Second church is *St Clement Danes* (finest restored interior; RAF memorial church). Enter *City* at *Temple Bar, Fleet Street* (*Royal Courts of Justice* on left); passages, right, to *Temple* and lawyers' chambers around *Pump Court* and other courts; associations with Johnson, Goldsmith, Lamb, Dickens; *Middle Temple Hall* (*Twelfth Night* performed here 1602). Return to *Fleet Street*. In *Chancery Lane* is *Record Office Museum* (Domesday Book, Shakespeare's signature, Gunpowder Plot letter, log of Nelson's *Victory*).

Further along *Fleet Street*, left, through *Hind Court* to *Gough Square, No 17, Johnson's House* (his famous dictionary compiled here). *St Bride's* (Wren church restored). *Ludgate Hill* to **St Paul's Cathedral** (Wren's masterpiece; second largest church dome in the world; new *High Altar*, 1958; *American Memorial*

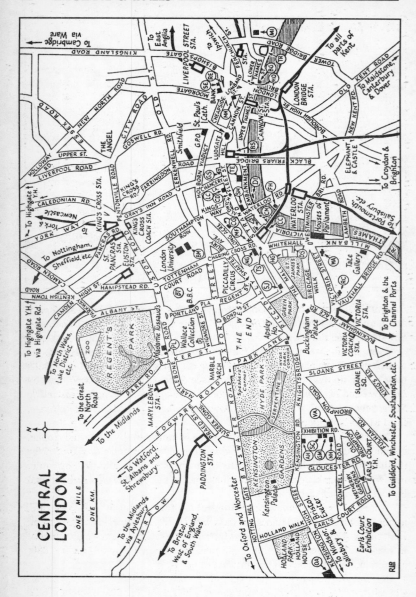

CENTRAL LONDON

Key to plan of Central London

AH	Royal Albert Hall	SC	Science Museum
MO	Monument	SE	Stock Exchange
BM	British Museum	FH	Royal Festival Hall
NG	National Gallery	SH	Somerset House
BS	Blackfriars Railway Station	GM	Geological Museum
BT	British Telecom Tower	SJ	St James' Palace
NH	Natural History Museum	GS	Gough Square (Dr Johnson's
CC	Charing Cross Railway Station		House)
OA	Olympia	TE	Temple
PL	Planetarium	TR	Tower
CD	St Clement Danes Church	HG	Horse Guards Parade
RC	Roman Catholic Cathedral,	TS	Trafalgar Square
	Westminster	LC	Law Courts
CG	Covent Garden Opera House	VA	Victoria and Albert Museum
CN	Cleopatra's Needle	MF	St Martin-in-the-Fields
RE	Royal Exchange	MH	Mansion House
DS	No 10 Downing Street	WA	Westminster Abbey

Chapel, 1958; statue of John Donne from Old St Paul's; Wren's grave in crypt; climb to famous *Whispering Gallery* and *Stone Gallery*, view over London, or 627 steps to the *Ball*.)

From north-eastern end of *St Paul's Churchyard* along *Cheapside*, once the market place (note names of streets running off). *St Mary-le-Bow* (of Bow Bells fame). Left, up *King Street* to *Guildhall* (see *Great Hall* and *Library*). East by *Lothbury* and *Throgmorton Street* to *Stock Exchange*. West along *Threadneedle Street* between *Bank of England* and *Royal Exchange*. Ahead is *Mansion House*, Lord Mayor's residence.

South-east by *King William Street* to **The Monument** (by Wren and Hooke, commemorates Great Fire 1666; good view of City from top). *London Bridge* (until 1750 only crossing of river); scene of much history, including Viking battle; near southern bank, upstream, stood Shakespeare's *Globe Theatre*; downstream is *Pool of London* and *Tower Bridge*.

Across bridge is *Southwark*. **Cathedral** has fine memorial to Shakespeare, tombs of John Gower and Lancelot Andrewes, *Harvard Chapel* in north transept; John Harvard baptised here, 1607; *Lady Chapel*; look also for amusing memorial to Lockyer, an eighteenth-century pill maker; wooden effigy of knight, 1280; collection of roof bosses, at western end of nave.

Re-cross *London Bridge*; turn right along *Eastcheap* and *Great Tower Street*, Church of *All Hallows, Barking* (associated with *Tower*, Toc H and shipping). To the *Tower* (dark memorial of despotism). Return by boat from *Tower Pier* to *Westminster*. Note *National Theatre* and *Royal Festival Hall* on south bank by *Waterloo Bridge* and, on north bank, *Cleopatra's Needle*.

2 Westminster to Trafalgar Square

Stand on *Westminster Bridge*, where Wordsworth wrote his famous sonnet; fine views along river in shadow of '*Big Ben*'. To *Parliament Square*, flanked by statues of statesmen. Enter by west door **Westminster Abbey**. *Tomb of Unknown Warrior* and, all around, the nation's history in tomb and monument; *Statesmen's Corner* transept; *Poets' Corner* transept; behind *High Altar* is *Edward the Confessor's Chapel* with tombs of early kings and queens; *Coronation Chair*; steps lead to **Henry VII's Chapel**. From south aisle through *Cloisters* is *Chapter House*, scene of early parliaments.

St Margaret's Church, just north of abbey, fifteenth-century Gothic; famous east window; memorials to Caxton and Raleigh; windows to Milton and to Raleigh and splendid new windows by Piper.

Houses of Parliament (still officially the *Palace of Westminster*). To attend debates you queue for a place in the Gallery. **House of Lords**, with Throne of Queen's Speech, and Woolsack; **House of Commons** (re-built 1948); *St Stephen's Hall*, used by Commons for 300 years, statues of kings, queens, statesmen, historical scenes on panels; **Westminster Hall** (1097) with famous fourteenth-century hammerbeam roof, scene of state trials including Sir Thomas More, Guy Fawkes, Charles I, Warren Hastings; *St Stephen's Crypt*.

Walk along *Parliament Street* past government offices and *Cenotaph; Downing Street*, left, with No 10. Further along, *Parliament Street* is called *Whitehall*, after *Whitehall Palace*, of which only Inigo Jones' *Banqueting House* remains; from an upper window Charles I stepped out to scaffold; continue along *Whitehall*; on left, *Horse Guards*. Pass statue (1635) of Charles I.

Trafalgar Square, with *Nelson's Column*, fountains; *St Martin-in-the-Fields* (by Gibbs, 1721-6). **National Gallery**, superb collection chief schools of painting; each room needs separate visit.

In *St Martin's Place*, by statue of Nurse Cavell, **National Portrait Gallery** (the great and famous in all spheres over 500 years of history).

3 Buckingham Palace, Parks and Squares

Trafalgar Square. Through *Admiralty Arch* to *St James' Park*, its lake, and *Mall* (processional way) to *Buckingham Palace*. London residence of the Queen; Changing of the Guard daily at 11.30am. Along *Constitution Hill*, by *Green Park* to *Hyde Park Corner*. *Apsley House (Wellington Museum*, with Adam drawing-room and fine paintings).

Walk along eastern side of *Hyde Park*, or bus along *Park Lane* to *Marble Arch*; along *Oxford Street*, left up *Duke Street* to *Manchester Square* for *Wallace*

Collection (treasury of paintings, furniture, arms, armour, objets d'art). Return down *Duke Street*, continue along it, crossing *Oxford Street*, to *Grosvenor Street* and turn right, into *New Bond Street* and *Old Bond Street* (luxury shops) to *Piccadilly*.

Some Other Major Sights
(Best undertaken by special visits. Nearest underground station in brackets.)

Westminster Cathedral: Roman Catholic, built 1895-1903 by Bentley in Byzantine style, splendid structure, interior still to be lined with marble and mosaics (Victoria).

St Bartholomew the Great: (1123), Norman priory church, finest church to survive the Great Fire (Barbican).

Museum of London, *London Wall*; history of London from Roman times (closed Mondays) (Moorgate).

British Museum: immensely rich; treasures include Elgin marbles, Rosetta Stone, Codex Sinaiticus, Portland Vase, Sutton Hoo Burial-ship. Visit at least the Edward VII Galleries (Tottenham Court Rd).

Courtauld Institute Galleries, *Somerset House*; distinguished addition to London's art collections (Temple).

South Kensington Museums: these include, in separate buildings, **Victoria and Albert Museum** (vast art collections, all countries; see especially the Raphael Cartoons); **Geological Museum, Natural History Museum, Science Museum** (South Kensington).

Soane Museum, *13 Lincoln's Inn Fields*; has Hogarth's *Rake's Progress* paintings, etc. in a pleasing house (closed Mondays and all August) (Holborn).

Tate Gallery, *Millbank*; chief collections of British paintings and sculpture, notably Hogarth, Blake, Constable, Turner; important also for modern foreign schools from French Impressionists onwards (Pimlico).

Regent's Park: pleasing in itself; contains also famous **Zoo** (cheaper on Mondays). Huge collection, feeding time 2pm winter, 3pm summer, and **Aquarium** (Gt Portland St).

Madam Tussaud's: waxworks, of the famous and infamous (Baker St).

Planetarium: projection of the skies, popularly explained; frequent showings lasting about an hour (Baker St).

Hampstead Heath and **Kenwood Hous**e. House has fine Adam room, furniture and paintings (Iveagh Bequest) (Hampstead).

Excursions around London

Accessible quickly by Underground or train. River steamers (summer) are a pleasant alternative for outward or homeward journey.

Greenwich. Royal Naval College (by Wren; *Great Hall* painted in baroque style by Thornhill); open afternoons only, closed Thursdays. **Queen's House** (by Inigo Jones, with *National Maritime Museum* and library). **Greenwich Park** with fine view of *London* and *Thames*, old Royal Observatory with interesting display; Greenwich meridian: longitude 0.

Kew, Royal Botanic Gardens. Spacious, delightful for stroll or study; the world's flora in open air or hot house. May be combined with visit to *Richmond*.

Richmond. Immediately south of *Kew*. From *Richmond Bridge* (eighteenth century) walk up *Hill Rise* to the **Terrace**, famous view of *Thames* valley, and *Richmond Hill*. In *Richmond Park*, deer roam freely.

Hampton Court. Wolsey's great house, enlarged by Henry VIII and Wren; largest royal palace. *Gatehouse, Tennis Court*, astronomical clock. *State Apartments, Galleries, Great Hall, Cellars, Kitchens*, fine formal gardens, *Maze*.

Windsor△. State rooms of **Castle** open when Court not in residence; great storehouse of art and craftsmanship. **St George's Chapel**, perfect example of Perpendicular style. *Windsor Great Park*, deer and ancient oaks. *Eton College Chapel*.

Touring Routes
South-East England

This is the chalkland of England, first seen by visitors from the Continent in the white cliffs of *Dover*. Between its three ranges of low hills — the *North* and *South Downs* and the *Chilterns* — are wide lowlands containing rich farming country and the great metropolis of *London*. Despite growth of population it is still a land of tidy farms and quiet villages.

R1 The Chilterns, London — Dunstable — St Albans — London (95 miles, 153km)

The chalk hills of the *Chilterns*, with their fine beech woods, rise gently from the *London Basin* to fall suddenly in a steep escarpment to the plains beyond. Nearly every town and village has good examples of English domestic architecture.

By road, or train from *Paddington* or *Marylebone*, to *Beaconsfield*, to get clear of *London* environs. *Beaconsfield* (many Georgian houses, home of Disraeli). *Chalfont St Giles*, where Milton, escaping from the plague in London, wrote *Paradise Lost* and *Paradise Regained*. Two miles (3km) south is *Jordans*△

associated with William Penn and American state that bears his name; his grave is in burial ground of Quaker Meeting House. *High Wycombe* (centre of furniture trade). *West Wycombe*, entire village of fifteenth- to eighteenth-century houses, belongs to National Trust. *Bradenham*Δ is nearby.

Dry valleys run up from south-east to scarp slope and roads tend to follow them, but footpaths and tracks follow line of hills. Scarp has scalloped edge; some headlands wooded, others covered with turf and scrub; a beautiful and peaceful landscape with fine views. Villages follow foot of scarp at points where spring water issues. At *Bledlow* and *Whiteleaf* are crosses of unknown origin cut in chalk hillside.

*Ivinghoe*Δ is close to start of *Ridgeway Path* at *Ivinghoe Beacon* 904ft, (275m); *Duncombe Terrace*; *Ashridge*. Nearby is *Whipsnade Zoo* where animals roam in large outdoor pens. From *Dunstable* return via **St Albans**; Roman *Verulanium*, remains of wall, tessellated pavement and theatre. Cathedral stands where St Alban, Britain's first Christian martyr, died AD305. Earliest Norman tower in England, largely built from Roman materials; eleventh-century wall paintings. Town has fifteenth-century clock tower and one of oldest inns in England — *The Fighting Cocks*. *Sandridge*Δ (summer only) is 2 miles (3km) to north. Road or train to *London*.

R2 The North Downs, South Downs and Weald, London — Canterbury — Chichester — London (250 miles, 402km)

By road, or train from *Victoria* or *Charing Cross*, to *Merstham* across south London suburbs. **North Downs** run east with *Pilgrims' Way* at their foot on edge of the *Weald* — a country of orchards and hop fields on clay soils, with much woodland including *Ashdown Forest*. Oast houses for drying hops are a feature. Many delightful villages.

*Crockham Hill*Δ overlooking *Weald*, *Kemsing*Δ on *Pilgrims' Way*. *Chilham*, perhaps prettiest village in Kent; houses grouped around church and castle.

CanterburyΔ; historic cathedral; archbishopric of Primate of all England; *Shrine of Becket* a place of pilgrimage for centuries. City has other ancient churches; see also *West Gate, Christ Church Gate, St Dunstan's Street* with *Falstaff Hotel, Butchery Lane*; town walls in *Broad Street*.

*Dover*Δ; its white cliffs almost a symbol of England; Roman lighthouse, Saxon tower, Norman keep.

Northwards along coast to *Deal*, where Julius Caesar first landed; *Sandwich*, oldest of *Cinque Ports*, with old gatehouse. Flemish and Dutch weavers settled in this area in fourteenth century; traces of their brickwork and gables add slightly foreign touch to villages.

From *Dover* the *Vale of Kent* is reached via *Folkestone*. Its notable villages include *Tenterden* (birthplace of Caxton), *Smarden, High Halden* and *Biddenden*. *Sissinghurst Castle*; gardens open in summer. *Bodiam*, impressive moated castle.

Coast road leads to *Rye* and *Winchelsea*, two more *Cinque Ports*, now silted, but with many relics of their former importance. *Hastings*, seaside resort with interesting old fishing town; *Guestling*△ is 3 miles (5km) north-east. The famous battle was fought 7 miles (11km) inland where *Battle Abbey*, built by William the Conqueror, stands to commemorate his victory.

Beachy Head △ 18 miles (29km) west of *Hastings*, great chalk cliff where **South Downs** reach the sea; start of *South Downs Way*. Their rounded whale-backed hills, cut by several small rivers, covered with short springy turf in east, wooded in west, provide good walking country, especially around *Alfriston* △ and cycling country west of *Lewes* (town clustering below its Norman keep). *Telscombe*△ and *Truleigh Hill*△ are on the route and *Brighton* △ lies nearby. Many other pleasing towns and villages. *Steyning*; *Amberley* (castle); *Arundel*△ (castle); *Bignor* (remains of Roman villa); *Petworth* (great mansion, *Petworth House*); *Midhurst (Cowdray Park*, entered from its High Street, is fine example of English parkland).

Chichester, dignified town; cathedral has spectacular stained-glass window by Marc Chagall with beautiful precincts; Roman remains; stately houses.

Northwards from *Midhurst*, road climbs to heathlands around *Hindhead*△ with natural ampitheatre of *Devil's Punch Bowl*. *Guildford* has notable modern cathedral; seventeenth-century Abbot's Hospital; St Mary's Church with pre-Norman tower; castle; Castle Arch House; much Georgian brickwork, tile-hung houses, pointed gables.

Between *Guildford* and *Reigate*, 15 miles (24km) to east, *Box Hill* and other chalk slopes contrast with sandy country around *Leith Hill* 965ft (294m) highest point in the south-east. Both hills have extensive views. Pleasant villages about here include *Albury, Shere, Friday Street* and *Abinger*, with *Holmbury St Mary*△ and *Tanners Hatch* △ nearby. From *Dorking* road or train to *London*.

East Anglia

This eastward-extending bulge of *Norfolk* and *Suffolk*, together with parts of adjacent counties, is driest part of England; its countryside, almost untouched by modern industry, is rich in domestic architecture, great houses, fine churches and prosperous farmlands.

R3 London — Cambridge — Norwich — Colchester (228 miles, 367km)
Road, or train from *Liverpool St* through east London suburbs, to *Audley End*; vast mansion, one of greatest sixteenth-century houses. *Saffron Walden* △ delightful market town with many Tudor buildings. **Cambridge**△, one of the two ancient university towns; great historical and architectural interest. Colleges usually admit visitors to courts all day and to other parts at certain times. Oldest is *Peterhouse* (1284). *Trinity College, King's College*, with famous chapel, and

Queen's are well known. The *Backs*, riverside lawns, give most characteristic view of main colleges.

North-west from *Cambridge* main road follows line of Roman road, *Via Devena*, to *Huntingdon* and delightful group of villages on River *Ouse*. Oliver Cromwell and Samuel Pepys were educated here. Eastwards *Ouse* flows past *Houghton Mill* through *Hemingford Abbots* and *Hemingford Gray* (with twelfth-century manor house) to *St Ives*; stone bridge with ancient chantry chapel.

This is the *Fen* country, flat and partly below sea level, extensively drained. Towns and villages stand where a slight rise gave drier setting. Cathedral at *Ely*Δ on such a hill, dominates countryside for miles around; Norman and Early Gothic with unique octagontal lantern tower. Eight miles (13km) southwards is *Wicken Fen*, one of few remaining pieces of natural fen, preserved by National Trust as ecological sanctuary. Reclaimed Fenland makes rich agricultural land, especially for wheat, sugar beet, fruit and flower production. River *Ouse* reaches sea by way of *Downham Market* (buildings of 'gingerbread stone') and *King's Lynn* Δ, busy market town and seaport; Guildhall, fifteenth century, has characteristic East Anglian flint flushwork; Renaissance Customs House, medieval merchants' houses; churches of *St Mary* (Early English chancel) and *St Nicholas* (tiebeam roof; beautiful south porch). *Sandringham*, country home of the Royal Family, is 8 miles (13km) to north-east. *Hunstanton* Δ, on Norfolk coastal path; quiet villages, many once ports, now separated from sea by salt marshes. *Burnham Thorpe* (15 miles, 24km east of *Hunstanton*) birthplace of Nelson, *Holkham Hall* nearby is masterpiece of eighteenth-century architect William Kent. *Wells-next-the-Sea* has narrow-gauge railway to *Walsingham*, which has a famous Roman Catholic shrine; annual pilgrimage. *Blakeney Point*, shingle spit, bird sanctuary. *Sheringham*Δ, *Cromer* and *Overstrand* have fine sandy beaches. North-eastwards from *Norwich* are the *Broads*, shallow, partly tidal, waters, popular for yachting and study of natural history. *Norwich*Δ, chief market centre of East Anglia: market square, with numerous stalls beneath distinguished modern *City Hall* and fine medieval church of *St Peter Mancroft*. Cathedral, eleventh to sixteenth century, cloisters, lofty spire; Norman castle has museum and art gallery; ancient *Maddermarket* with theatre; many other interesting buildings.

Southwards from *Norwich,* and through *Suffolk* and *North Essex* are many towns and villages, important centres of cloth trade in Tudor times with old houses, churches and guildhalls, *Wymondham*, has curious market cross (1616) standing on pillars. *Thetford* 25 miles (40km), has ancient Guildhall and, 5 miles (9km) north-west are prehistoric flint mines of *Grime's Graves*; *Brandon* Δ is nearby. Due south for 12 miles (19km) to *Bury St Edmunds*, burial place of Edmund, last king of East Ang*l*ia, martyed by Danes in 870, Abbey Gateway (1347), Norman tower, *St James' Church* and *St Mary's Church* with tomb of the Mary Tudor who married Louis XII of France. *Lavenham*, is 10 miles (16km) south, has street of unspoilt Tudor architecture; great fifteenth-century church, built when wool brought prosperity. *Alpheton* △ is 2¹/₂ miles (4km) north-west. *Long Melford* (5 miles) 8km south-west, rivals *Lavenham*; famous for stained glass. *Castle Hedingham* △, village of half-timbered houses overlooked by Norman castle keep, is 12 miles (19km) south-west.

R3 (i) *Castle Hedingham* to *Finchingfield* is 8 miles (13km) westwards, thence continuing in same direction for 7 miles (11km) to *Thaxted*, perfect unspoilt village of fifteenth-century houses, Perpendicular church; 11 miles (17km) *Bishop's Stortford*, road or train to London.

Blaxhall△ near upper reaches River *Alde*, 8 miles (13km) from old seaside town of *Aldeburgh*, associated with Benjamin Britten's opera *Peter Grimes* and festival of music and arts held annually in June.

Colchester△ 18 miles (29km) of *Long Melford* via *Sudbury*; many Roman remains, including town walls and gateway; Saxon, Norman and later buildings. Good museum in castle. Near *East Bergholt*, 10 miles (16km) north-east are *Willy Lott's Cottage* and *Flatford Mill*, associated with John Constable, born at *Bergholt*. From *Colchester* return to London by train.

The Cotswolds, Vale of Severn and Stratford-upon-Avon

The *Cotswold Hills*, lying north-eastwards from near *Bath* to the *Northampton-shire Uplands* form an upland area of farmland; small towns and villages of honey-coloured limestone famous for their mellow dignity. The escarpment faces west and north to the clay lands around the Rivers *Severn* and *Avon* — a fruit-growing and dairy-farming region with villages of timber and thatch, and historic towns such as *Gloucester* and *Stratford-upon-Avon*.

R4 The Cotswolds, Oxford to Gloucester (61 miles, 98km)

Oxford △ with its famous university, starting point for *Cotswold* tour but also a place to linger. Twenty-two colleges, many open to visitors on enquiry at lodges. *University* (oldest, 1249), *Merton* (library and chapel), *New* (almost unchanged since 1379; beautiful garden), *Magdalen* and *Christ Church* (whose chapel is also the cathedral). Also *Ashmolean* and *University* museums, *Bodleian Library*, *Radcliffe Camera* (view from dome) and *Sheldonian Theatre*.

Road to *Gloucester* joins valley of *Windrush*, a tributary of *Thames*. *Witney*, important for manufacture of blankets. Ancient town hall and butter cross in High Street. Eight miles (13km) west, is *Burford*, one of finest towns in *Cotswolds*. Steep main street lined with Tudor houses. See the *Tolsey* building in main street, church which housed prisoners of war in the Civil War, and adjacent almshouses.

The *Cotswolds* are so rich in beautiful villages, that it is hardly necessary to do more than suggest those specially worth visiting. From *Burford* choice of routes (a) south to *Lechlade* on Thames, with *Inglesham* Δ nearby, and via *Fairford* to *Cirencester*, pleasant town, wide, curving main street; museum; excellent display of Roman remains. Between *Cirencester* and *Gloucester* is one of the best stretches of *Cotswolds*; wooded valleys, innumerable tracks and lanes for walker and cyclist; ancient towns and villages of *Tetbury, Nailsworth, Minchinhampton, Bisley, Painswick*, the *Duntisbournes (Duntisbourne Abbots*Δ) and *Birdlip* (fine view on *Cotswolds* edge). *Chedworth* (Roman Villa). (b) North from *Burford* to *Stow-on-the-Wold* Δ ancient market town; lovely villages of *Upper* and *Lower Slaughter, Upper* and *Lower Swell, Bourton-on-the-Water*—whereRriver *Windrush* flows through village, spanned by series of bridges. Beyond *Stow* are other fine examples of local architecture in *Chipping Campden, Chipping Norton, Moreton-in-Marsh*. Near *Chipping Norton* are *Rollright Stones*, one of best ancient stone circles in Midlands, and *Great* and *Little Tew*, loveliest villages in *Oxfordshire*. Westwards from *Stow* ground rises steadily then drops in scarp slope to the *Severn* plain. Views north and west across hills of *Welsh Border* country. (c) West from *Burford* to *Northleach*, which like so many *Cotswold* towns owed its original prosperity to now departed wool trade. *Cleeve Hill*Δ, then down escarpment to *Cheltenham* (fashionable residential town) and *Gloucester*.

R5 Gloucester — Stratford-upon-Avon — Warwick — Kenilworth (48 miles, 77km)

Gloucester, on River *Severn*, pre-Roman foundation. Magnificent cathedral, massive cylindrical pillars make Norman origin evident, but choir and exterior are early Perpendicular; fan-vaulted cloisters. Fifteenth-century *New Inn* has galleried courtyard. Twelve miles (19km) up-river to *Tewkesbury*, half-timbered town, many medieval alleys; abbey church is one of finest examples of Norman architecture.

Evesham 14 miles (22km) centre of fruit farming area; few miles south-east is *Broadway*, a show village of *Cotswolds*. Eighteen miles (29km) to **Stratford-upon-Avon** Δ Shakespeare's birthplace, Guild House, Grammar School where he was educated, *Holy Trinity Church* with Shakespearian associations, *New Place Museum, Falcon Inn, Memorial Theatre, John Harvard's House, Anne Hathaway's Cottage* at *Shottery*.

Warwick has imposing fourteenth-century castle, overlooking River *Avon*, containing magnificent collection of paintings by Rubens and Van Dyck. Finest building in town is *Leycester Hospital*, by *West Gate*; many other half-timbered buildings. Nearby is *Royal Leamington Spa* where medicinal springs have been in use since the sixteenth century; see Walker Art Gallery and walk along the *Parade*, most graceful street in Midlands.

Kenilworth: Norman castle, priory gatehouse, and much old red brick architecture.

Western England and the South-West

The West of England is rich in prehistoric sites, and has, also, many old towns and cities. The peninsula of *Cornwall, Devon* and *North Somerset* has fine coastal scenery, quaint seaside villages and challenging open moorland country.

R6 Winchester — Salisbury — Swanage 91 miles (146km)

West Country begins with **Winchester**△, Roman foundation. Anglo-Saxon capital. Eleventh- to fifteenth-century cathedral, interior makes visual impact, largest nave in Europe, many chantry chapels and notable tombs. See twelfth-century *Hospital of St Cross*, oldest charitable institution, famous public school founded 1382 and *Castle Hall* where legendary King Arthur's Round Table is displayed.

On for 20 miles (32km) to **Salisbury**△ where medieval aspect is preserved within original gridiron street plan; cathedral, thirteenth century set in spacious lawns, is magnificent example of Early English style; see, especially, Lady chapel; 404ft (123m) spire, tallest in England. Walled close has notable houses, particularly *Mompesson House*.

R6 (i) Salisbury to Stonehenge, Marlborough and Avebury 2 miles (3km) north is *Old Sarum*, on conical hill, with remains of successive settlements by Celts, Romans and Normans, remains of Norman abbey within Iron Age fort. Site abandoned when *Salisbury* cathedral was built. On chalk expanse of *Salisbury Plain* 8 miles (13km) north is magnificent prehistoric group of **Stonehenge**. Carved into chalk hills of *Salisbury Plain* and *Berkshire Downs* are outlines of many white horses, some ancient. The horse at *Uffington*, on northern edge of *Berkshire Downs*, gives its name to *Vale of the White Horse*. *Marlborough*, 29miles (46km) north of *Stonehenge*, has spacious main street faced by Georgian buildings. Merlin, King Arthur's wizard, is supposedly buried here in grounds of famous public school. On for 5 miles (8km) to **Avebury**, largest stone circle in Europe, outer ditch encloses area of 28 acres and is Britain's most important survival from early Bronze Age. Many related tumuli and stone avenues in vicinity: *Silbury Hill,* largest and probably most mysterious artificial mound in Europe.

South-west from *Salisbury* on A354: at *Coombe Bissett* 4 miles (6km) turn westwards through *Broad Chalke* and along *Ridge Way* (fine views) north of *Cranborne Chase*. *Shaftesbury* 20 miles (32km) old market town, steep twisting streets. Seven miles (11km) south-west B3092 to *Sturminster* and south across *Dorset Downs* to *Milton Abbas* 16 miles, (26km) beautifully situated village and abbey. At *Cerne Abbas*, 10 miles (16km) west is giant prehistoric figure cut in chalk hillside.

The River *Piddle* flows through several delightful villages of which *Tolpuddle* is famous for the 'Martyrs' transported to Australia (1834) for forming a trade union.

Dorchester, county town of *Dorset*, the 'Casterbridge' of Thomas Hardy's novels. Pleasing town, tree-lined avenues, links with Pilgrim Fathers; *Maumbury Rings*, just south of the town, is site of Stone Age circle, adapted by the Romans to make an amphitheatre.

Maiden Castle 2 miles (3km) south-west, huge prehistoric site; fortified hill-top village, built 2,000BC, later abandoned, but used again in early Iron Age. Much later a Roman temple was built on the site. Traces of defensive ramparts, hut circles and other buildings.

East of *Dorchester*, *South Dorset Downs* reach sea near *Swanage*Δ 30 miles (48km). Hardy's 'Knollsea' lying between two headlands; ruins of *Corfe Castle*. 16 miles (26km) to the west is beautiful landlocked *Lulworth Cove*Δ, an almost circular bay.

R7 Salisbury — Exeter — Plymouth — Land's End — St Ives — Minehead — Bristol — Bath 445 miles (716km)
Many interesting towns and villages on road to *Exeter*. *Shaftesbury* (see **R6**), *Stalbridge, Sherborne*, 18 miles (29km); abbey with magnificent fan vaulting; ancient school, castle partly built by Sir Walter Raleigh. *Yeovil*, 15 miles (24km) church of St John the Baptist (1380); ancient inns; museum. Great house of *Montacute* (Tudor) is 4 miles (6km) west. *Chard* has ancient inns, fine houses. *Honiton*, 27 miles (43km). *Ottery St Mary* (birthplace of Coleridge).

*Exeter*Δ, 20 miles (32km) most westerly town in Roman Empire; now county town of *Devon*; traces of city wall remain. Fourteenth-century cathedral with magnificent Gothic vaulting, in calm close of medieval buildings.

R(i) Dartmoor National Park. Between *Exeter* and *Plymouth* is *Dartmoor*, an area of granite almost entirely covered by moorland, but here and there by treacherous bogs Granite tors top the heights among which *High Wilhays* reaches 2,039ft (622m). Abounds in stone circles, stone avenues and other prehistoric remains. Rivers have cut deep wooded valleys at the edge of the moorland, the *Teign, Bovey* and *Dart* making pretty scenery. *Postbridge* is site of ancient stone 'clapper' bridge. At *Buckfast* under south-east end of moor, is abbey almost entirely rebuilt during present century by its Benedictine monks. Standard gauge steam railway runs 7 miles (11km) *Buckfastleigh* to *Totnes*.

Totnes (Dartington Δ nearby) and *Dartmouth*, interesting old towns; between them River *Dart* broadens into estuary at *Maypool* Δ and, further on, is *Start Bay*Δ. Between *Exeter* and *Dartmouth* are many coastal towns and villages, crowded in summer. *Brixham* is, perhaps, the most attractive. South-west from *Dartmouth* is beautiful estuary of *Salcombe*Δ where stretch of cliffs between *Bolt Head* and *Bolt Tail* is gem of *South Devon* coastline; on for 11 miles (18km) to *Bigbury*Δ. To west and south of *Dartmouth* is rolling farmland, a patchwork of fields in red soil which combines with greenness of crops to form a colourful landscape.

Plymouth Δ, finely situated on Plymouth Sound; starting point of Elizabethan voyages of discovery; here Drake sailed to defeat Armada (1588) and

Mayflower put out with Pilgrim Fathers (1620).

From *Plymouth* to *Land's End* chief attraction is wonderful coastline: many picturesque ports and fishing villages, *Looe, Polperro, Fowey* with nearby *Golant*△, *Mevagissey* with *Boswinger*△ 4 miles (6km) to south-west, *Falmouth* with *Pendennis Castle*△, one of Henry VIII's coastal strongholds; *Coverack*△, *Helston, Marazion, Penzance*△, *Newlyn, Mousehole*; *Lizard Point* is most southerly point in England, as *Land's End* is most westerly. Climate sub-tropical, almost every garden has its palm tree. *St Michael's Mount*, with battlemented castle on site of Benedictine monastery.

From *Land's End* return by north coast; fine scenery, quaint villages: *St Ives, St Agnes, Perranporth* △, *Newquay*△ where *Bedruthan Steps*, great detached masses of rock lie on beach beneath towering cliffs. *Treyarnon Bay*△, *Tintagel*△ for *Tintagel Castle*, legendary birthplace of King Arthur. *Boscastle* △.

Clovelly, perhaps most visited village in England, has cobbled main street in a series of steps from harbour to village. Less crowded but no less worthwhile are great cliffs of *Hartland Point*, with *Elmscott*△ nearby; views over *Bristol Channel* to *Lundy Island*.

East from *Clovelly* lie valleys of Rivers *Torridge* and *Taw,* whose joint estuary reaches sea at *Appledore*; fishing village of Kingsley's *Westward Ho!*; *Bideford* on *Torridge (Instow*△ nearby) and *Barnstaple* on *Taw* retain a sense of past importance.

From *Barnstaple* roads lead north to *Ilfracombe*△, north-east to **Exmoor**, another National Park, astride *Devon-Somerset* border; wide expanse of rolling hills covered with coarse grass or heather and bracken, crossed by many minor roads and trackways; near centre of moor is *Exford*△. As on *Dartmoor*, rivers cut deeply, forming famous *Doone Valley* and wooded valleys of the *Barle, Exe* and *Horner Water. Dunkery Beacon* 1,707ft (520m) is highest point. Along north coast on edge of moor, are fine cliffs and old towns and villages; *Lynton*△, *Selworthy*, in steep river valley west of *Minehead*△ has some of best cob and thatch cottages in the south-west. *Dunster*; ancient Yarn Market and Butter Cross in main street.

Road east from *Minehead* skirts northern end of *Quantock Hills*, delightful small range of heather-clad hills; *Holford*△ and *Crowcombe*△, many footpaths. At *Bridgewater* one road runs directly to *Bristol* and another along line of *Polden Hills* to *Glastonbury*; 3 miles (5km) is *Street*△. On *Sedgemoor*, beyond *Polden Hills*, King Alfred hid and prepared to defeat the Danes, ending with signing of Treaty at *Wedmore* (878) near *Cheddar*△. At **Wells** the cathedral is a masterpiece of Early English and Decorated styles; famous west front has over 600 statues. Town stands at foot of *Mendip Hills*, a limestone tableland with spectacular gorges, the most famous being *Cheddar*, best approached from north-east. Several caves open to visitors both here and along line of hills.

Bristol △, seaport since tenth century, trade with America. Brunel's *Great*

Britain first iron-built ship, seen in yard where built in 1843; his *Clifton Suspension Bridge* gracefully spans *Avon Gorge*, affording spectacular views. *St Mary Redcliffe*, late Perpendicular, said to be finest parish church in England; cathedral beautifully spacious, especially splendid choir. *Theatre Royal*, 1766, oldest theatre in country, original decoration preserved.

Bath △ a Roman spa of hot water springs. Became fashionable resort under Beau Nash in eighteenth century, and a setting for many English novels; a town of elegant Georgian architecture distinguished and formal in square, circus and terrace. *Royal Crescent, Pump Room, Pulteney Bridge* and *Assembly Rooms* are notable examples. Festival of Arts, late May to early June.

Wales and the Welsh Border

The contrasts with England are many. The country is wilder and, except in the south-east, less populous. The gentle rhythms of the English landscape are replaced by dramatic changes of scene. The streams are often mountain torrents, but many descend to fertile lovely valleys. The Welsh people have their own distinctive culture and ancient language and look back to different origins.

Between Welsh highlands and English lowlands, the Border zone shares some of the features of each, but — as so often on frontiers — has an exhilarating atmosphere of its own.

R8 The Welsh Border. Chepstow to Shrewsbury (109 miles, 175km)
Approach direct from *Gloucester* or by *Severn Bridge*, 15 miles (24km) north of *Bristol*, to *Chepstow*△: fine castle above River *Wye* which follows beautiful and extraordinary course from *Monmouth*; deep wooded banks, high limestone cliffs. *Tintern Abbey* (Cistercian) 5 miles (8km) north, magnificent ruins. At *Bigsweir*, 4 miles (6km), cross river, 2 miles (3km) upstream to *St Briavels Castle*△ overlooking *Forest of Dean*, once a royal hunting ground.

Monmouth △, 8 miles (13km), at confluence of *Monnow* and *Wye* has only remaining fortified bridge (*Monnow Bridge*) in England. Five miles (8km) north-east to *Symonds Yat*, famous viewpoint, where *Wye* makes great loop. *Goodrich* village and castle; *Welsh Bicknor*△; *Ross-on-Wye* is small town with fine stone market hall. Northwards are many examples of half-timbered architecture of black and white appearance, best seen in *Ledbury* and *Hereford*. On for 7 miles (11km) to *Much Marcle*.

R8 (i) Hereford and Herefordshire villages. *Rushall* to *Woolhope* and *Fownhope*, among low hills geologically famous. **Hereford**, 12 miles (19km). County town, interesting houses and inns. Cathedral famous for unique map of the world *(Mappa Mundi*, 1313) and over 1,400 chained books, including Caxtons. *Weobley*, superb half-timbered village is 8 miles (13km) north-west of *Hereford*.

Main route continues 7 miles (11km) to *Ledbury* at southern end of **Malvern Hills**, 1,395ft (424m). Many paths along grass-covered hills, wide views, remains of early British camp on *Hereford Beacon*.

Great Malvern beautiful priory church spared by Henry VIII at Dissolution of Monasteries and most elaborate Victorian Gothic railway station in the country. *Malvern Wells*Δ is 1 mile (1¹/₂km) south. Five miles (8km) north to *Bransford* and north-west along *Teme* Valley to *Tenbury Wells* and on to **Ludlow**Δ, 23 miles (37km), one of the most attractive towns in England; wealth of old buildings, *Feathers Hotel*, castle; *St Lawrence's* is a noble guild church with beautiful glass. To south-west is lovely wooded country on *Powys* border; many half-timbered villages.

Seven miles (11km) north-west is *Stokesay Castle*, fine example of thirteenth-century moated fortified manor house; Tudor gatehouse; adjacent church has box pews. *Wenlock Edge*, limestone escarpment, runs 15 miles (24km) north-east-wards towards *Much Wenlock*. *Wilderhope Manor*Δ, is close by, a Tudor house set in lovely farmland.

Church Stretton, 8 miles (13km) west, for walks on surrounding hills of much geological interest, including *Long Mynd*, with steep dry valleys, and *Caer Caradoc* which has traces of ancient British settlement. The *Port Way* which runs its switchback way along *Long Mynd* is excellent route for walkers and cyclists; *Bridges*Δ on west side of hills. Four miles (6km) north of *Church Stretton*. Leave main road at *Leebotwood*. Five miles (8km) north-east to *Acton Burnell* castle, in park, reputed meeting place of first Parliament (1265). Continue 6 miles (10km) east to *Much Wenlock*, ancient market town. Turn north for 3 miles (5km) for fine Norman abbey at *Buildwas*, set beside River *Severn*. *Coalbrookdale* is an early centre of Industrial Revolution; at *Ironbridge*Δ is world's first iron bridge (1779); still in use. *Wroxeter* 6 miles (10km), has remains of Roman town, *Uriconium*. On for 6 miles (10km) to **Shrewsbury**Δ, historic town in bend of *Severn*; fine churches, groups of timbered houses, narrow lanes and passageways; statue of Charles Darwin who was educated at its famous school.

R9 South Wales. Monmouth — Brecon — Carmarthen — Tenby — St David's (145 miles, 233km)

From *Monmouth* (see **R8**) to *Rockfield*, 2 miles (3km), and north-west by minor road through *St Maughans Green* to *Skenfrith*, 5 miles (8km), castle; westwards for 7 miles (11km) to *Llanvetherine* (fine twelfth-century *White Castle*) and 5 miles (8km) to *Abergavenny*. *Crickhowell* is 6 miles (10km) to north-west; picturesque village with thirteen arch-stone bridge over River *Usk* which here passes between hills of *Brecon Beacons* and *Black Mountains*. Excellent walking country.

EXCURSION: *Sugar Loaf* (1,995ft, 608m), isolated hill 3 miles (5km) east, fine view.

R9 (i) *Crickhowell*, north-east up *Grwyne Fawr* valley to *Llanbedr*, *Pont Newydd* and *Partrishaw*, 5 miles (8km), tiny, lonely church in wild valley. Return 1 mile (1½km) and take lane east into famous **Vale of Ewyas**. *Llanthony*, 7 miles (11km), twelfth-century abbey (Transitional Norman). Continue 4 miles (6km) to *Capel-y-Ffin*Δ (King George VI Memorial Hostel) for high-level ridge walking and riding in *Black Mountains* — open breezy heights up to 2,600ft (800m) with huge and colourful views.

Main route continues up *Usk* valley; road and path on north bank and climb to *Bwlch*, 6 miles (10km), fine view. *Brecon*, 7 miles (11km), county town; cathedral built of red sandstone. *Ty'n-y-Caeau* Δ lies 2½ miles (4km) to east. *Pen-y-Crug* (1,088ft, 332m), 1½ miles (2½km) north-west for view over town and *Brecon Beacons* (highest point, *Pen-y-Fan*, 2,907ft, 886m).

R9 (ii) **Two-day walk**, each of 10 miles (16km), from *Brecon* over *Brecon Beacons* via *Cwm Cynwyn* and *Pen-y-Fan*, descend to *Llwyn-y-Celyn*Δ. Next day, south-west over *Fan Fawr* (2,409ft, 734m) to *Ystradfellte*Δ, centre for gorges and waterfalls of upper *Neath* and *Melte* valleys. On hills west is section of Roman road, *Sarn Helen*.

R9 (iii) **West of Swansea** is famous *Gower Peninsula*, the first designated *Area of Outstanding Natural Beauty*. South coast has limestone cliffs, caves, sandy bays and beaches, many wild flowers; inland are sandstone hills with extensive views; castles and small distinctive churches; *Port Eynon*Δ. Bus services from Swansea.

R9 (iv) **Cardiff**Δ. Metropolis of Wales, handsome group of public buildings, including *National Museum of Wales* (illustrating all aspects of Wales and Welsh life; also *Art Gallery* and *National Portrait Collection*). Castle, *Llandaff Cathedral*, 2½ miles (4km) north, twelfth century; unique feature is the statue of Christ, by Epstein, and arch bearing it. *St Fagan's Castle* 4 miles (6km), has *Welsh National Folk Museum*.

Main route continues westwards for 9 miles (14km) from *Brecon* to *Senny Bridge*, then on for 3 miles (5km) to *Trecastle*, whence take mountain road for 9 miles (14km), via *Llangadog* to *Llanddeusant*Δ.

EXCURSION: walk to source of River *Usk* and *Carmarthen Van* (2,632ft, 802m), very extensive view.

Llangadock, 7 miles (11km), picturesque small town in fertile *Towy* valley; on to *Llandeilo*, 7 miles (11km).

EXCURSION: *Careg Cennen*, 4 miles (6km) south-east, dramatically sited thirteenth-century castle.

At *Broadoak* 4 miles (6km), turn south to *Llangathen*; lane west out of village leads to *Grongar Hill* (410ft, 125m) in centre of *Towy* valley, subject of famous poem. Cross *Towy* to *Carmarthen*, 14 miles (23km), county and market town of narrow, busy, streets, St Peter's church, Guildhall, museum; coracles still in use on *Towy*.

EXCURSION: 10 miles (16km) south to *Kidwelly*. Huge eleventh-century castle, well preserved. Beautiful estuaries of *Towy* and *Gwendraeth*.

From *Carmarthen* for 12 miles (19km) to *Llanstephen*, attractive village, castle. West for 2 miles (3km) to ferry across River *Taf* to *Laugharne*, handsome small town with ancient charter (1307); associations with Dylan Thomas; harbour, castle. Continue 5 miles (8km) west on coast road to *Pendine*, good sands; at *Amroth* enter *Pembrokeshire*. *Pentlepoir*△, near *Saundersfoot*.

Tenby, small port and seaside resort of great charm, unspoilt; historic houses, narrow street; centre for south part of splendid *Pembrokeshire* coast.

EXCURSIONS: (a) via *Lamphey* (ruins of bishop's palace) to *Stackpole* and **St Govan's Head** (from this point to *Elegug Stacks*, 4 miles (6km) westwards is good section of coast). (b) via *Manorbier Castle* and *King's Quoit* (dolmen) to *Lydstep Point* and *Giltar Head*. (c) *Carew* (castle, church and Celtic cross) and delightful scenery of inner creeks of *Milford Haven*, especially the River *Cleddau*.

Pembroke, 3 miles (5km), large castle; continue to *Neyland* and *Milford Haven* rejoining *Pembrokeshire Coastal Path* via *Marloes Sands*△ 24 miles (38km) and *Broad Haven*△ 12 miles (19km). After 20 miles (32km), **St David's**, Britain's smallest city; ancient centre of Christianity, associated with patron saint of Wales. Cathedral, unique site in hollow to escape notice from sea (Viking raiders were active on this coast); superb Norman nave, many interesting details. Ruins of Bishop's Palace of great beauty. Continue on coastal path for 5 miles (8km) to **St David's Head**△: many prehistoric remains; magnificent cliffs typical of whole *North Pembrokeshire coast*, which can only be seen by walkers. Good view from *Carn Llidi* 595ft (181m).

Continue on minor road via *Llanrhian* to *Trevine*△ and on for 17 miles (27km) via *Abercastle* (hamlet on creek), *Abermawr* (storm beach) to *Pwll Deri* △.

EXCURSION: Take path north to *Garn Fawr*, Iron Age fort; then eastwards through *Llandwna* to *Careg Gwastad Point*, scene of last enemy landing on British soil (1797); return along cliffs via *Strumble Head* (lighthouse).

Fishguard, 5 miles (8km), port for *Ireland*; *Newport* (prehistoric camps on *Carn Ingli*, $1^1/_2$ miles, $2^1/_2$km, south); *Nevern*, picturesque village, church and Celtic cross; coast road via *Moylgrove* to *Cemaes Head*, 20 miles (32km) for nearby *Poppit Sands*△.

St Dogmaels and *Cardigan*, both finely placed on River *Teifi;* coracles used for salmon fishing. Turn south for 2 miles (3km), then east to *Cilgerran*, Norman castle above gorge and hidden from view in village. Continue up beautiful *Teifi* valley to *Cenarth*; salmon leap and coracles, *Newcastle Emlyn* via *Henllan* to *Pentre Cwrt*, 21 miles (34km). *Llandyssul*, picturesque market town, $2^1/_2$ miles (4km) east.

From *Pentre Cwrt* return can be made south to *Carmarthen*, 16 miles (26km), or north to central Wales (**R10**) via *Tregaron* with *Blaencaron* Δ and *Tyncornel*Δ nearby.

R10 Central Wales. Shrewsbury — Welshpool — Llanidloes — Devil's Bridge — Aberystwyth — Dolgellau — Llangollen (150 miles, 241km)

From ShrewsburyΔ take *Welshpool* road. At *Middleton,* 14 miles (23km), climb to *Rodney Pillar* on *Breidden Hill* (1,195ft, 364ft), fine viewpoint. *Welshpool,* 5 miles (8km), market town, old houses, Powysland Museum, *Powis Castle* and *Park* with famous gardens.

Cross River *Severn* and turn south. Near *Forden,* 5 miles (8km), *Offa's Dyke,* ancient boundary between England and Wales, runs just east of road. *Montgomery,* 3 miles (5km), picturesque old borough, smallest in country. On to *Newtown,* 9 miles (14km); memorial museum to Robert Owen, social reformer.

Continue up *Severn* valley to *Llanidloes,* 14 miles (23km), small town with old market hall. After 5 miles (8km) enter *Wye* valley at *Llangurig;* take minor road south on west bank for 12 miles (19km) to *Rhayader.*

R10 (i) Elan Valley. Beyond *Elan* village, 4 miles (6½km), road continues past fine series of reservoirs for 8 miles (13km) to *Pont ar Elan;* then 5 miles (8km) on rough road west on north side of river reaching headwaters of River *Ystwyth* and follow down valley 5 miles (8km) west to join road north-west to *Devil's Bridge* 4 miles (6½km). An adventurous route for cyclists.

Main route returns to *Llangurig* and ascends upper *Wye* valley for 8 miles (13km) to *Eisteddfa Gurig,* which is 2 miles (3km) south of *Plynlimon* 2,468ft (752m) source of *Severn, Wye* and *Rheidol.* Road descends 4 miles (6km) to *Ponterwyd.* Turn south for another 4 miles (6km) to **Devil's Bridge;** famous river scenery; bridge across river is superimposed above two earlier bridges. A narrow gauge steam railway runs along *Rheidol* valley between *Devil's Bridge* and *Aberystwyth.*

R10 (ii) *Ystumtuen*Δ to *Borth*Δ. Route for walkers north-west from *Ponterwyd* on mountain road to *Elerch* and *Talybont.* Total distance 19 miles (31km).

Main route follows road above *Rheidol* valley with fine views to *Aberystwyth,* 11 miles (18km), university town and seaside resort. Welsh National Library. *Borth* Δ, 7 miles (11km), bathing. *Machynlleth,* 14 miles (23km), in *Dovey* valley; up *Dulas* valley to *Corris*Δ, slate quarrying village, and down to *Minffordd* in *Dysynni* valley 9 miles (14km), with views of **Cader Idris;** fine route to summit for walkers from *Minffordd* via *Llyn-y-Cau,* descending by *Foxe's Path* to *Kings*Δ. Road continues to *Dolgellau,* 7 miles (11km). Many walks around *Mawddach* estuary, on *Cader Idris* and in wild hills north of estuary.

Railway viaduct across to *Barmouth* has track for cyclists and walkers. Sea bathing at *Barmouth* and *Fairbourne.*

Dolgellau up *Wnion* valley to Lake *Bala,* 20 miles (32km), with *Plas Rhiwaedog*Δ nearby.

EXCURSIONS: (a) *Arenig Fawr* (2,800ft, 853m); (b) *Aràn Benllyn* (2,901ft, 884m); (c) cyclists 42 miles (68km), circuit of rough hill roads crossing *Bwlch Rhiw Hirnant* to *Lake Vyrnwy* and *Llanfyllin*, returning via *Llangynog* and over *Milltir Cerig*.

From *Bala* down beautiful *Dee* valley for 12 miles (19km) to *Cynwyd*Δ, for walks in *Berwyn Hills*. At *Corwen*, 2 miles (3km) join main road and continue 10 miles (16km) to **Llangollen** Δ small town in sheltered valley on *Dee*, famous for scenery and for international Eisteddfod, held annually in July.

EXCURSIONS: (a) *Eglwyseg Valley* and *Valle Crucis Abbey*; (b) *Llantysilio Mountain*; (c) *Dee Valley*; (d) *Ceiriog Valley*.

R11 North Wales. Colwyn Bay — Betws-y-Coed — Snowdon — Caernarvon — Colwyn Bay (74 miles, 119km)

The eastern end of the North Wales coast is spoilt by caravan sites and industry and should be avoided by travelling direct by road or train to *Colwyn Bay*Δ; seaside resort.

EXCURSIONS: (a) *Llandudno, Little Orme's Head, Great Orme's Head*; (b) sea trips *Llandudno* to *Menai Bridge*; (c) steamer up River *Conwy, Deganwy* to *Trefriw*.

Conwy, 6 miles (10km), ancient walled town, thirteenth-century castle; up *Conwy* valley for 5 miles (8km) to *Ro Wen* Δ and on to *Llanrwst*, 7 miles (11km), seventeenth-century bridge; *Betws-y-Coed* is 3 miles (5km) further on.

EXCURSIONS: (a) *Llyn Crafnant, Llyn Geirionydd* and *Llanrhychwyn*, old church; (b) Roman road (*Sarn Helen*) to *Lledr valley* and *Dolwyddelan* (castle); (c) *Swallow Falls* on River *Llugwy*.

*Capel Curig*Δ 7 miles (11km), or *Idwal Cottage*Δ, 13 miles (21km).

EXCURSIONS: walks and climbs on *Tryfan, Glyder mountains, Carnedd Llewelyn* and *Carnedd Dafydd*.

Capel Curig, westwards to *Pen-y-Gwryd* 5 miles (8km) and road continues over *Llanberis Pass*, but take south-west road for 3¹/₂ miles (6km) down beautiful **Nant Gwynant** to *Bryn Gwynant*Δ.

EXCURSIONS: (a) *Watkin Path* route up **Snowdon** (3,500ft, 1,085m, highest summit in Wales); (b) ridge walk, **Snowdon Horseshoe**; (c) *Llyn Dinas, Beddgelert, Aberglaslyn Pass*, returning by *Nanmor valley*; cyclists can extend round to include *Portmadoc* and *Borth-y-Gest* (sea bathing).

On for 4 miles (6km) to *Beddgelert*, turning north-west for 5 miles (8km) to *Snowdon Ranger*Δ beside *Llyn Cwellyn*.

EXCURSIONS: (a) routes up *Snowdon*; (b) *Moel Hebog* and *Pennant valley*; (c) *Nantile valley* and fine ridge walk, *Craig Cwm Silin* to *Rhyd-ddu*.

R11 (i) Beddgelert to Harlech. *Beddgelert, Aberglaslyn.* **Harlech** △, 19 miles (30km); finely situated and well preserved thirteenth-century castle; beach.

EXCURSIONS: (a) *Moel Senigh* (1,019ft, 311m), 1 mile (1¹/₂km) to the east, for view of *Snowdon* and all *Cardigan Bay*; (b) *Llanbedr* and circuit of *Rhinog Fawr* via *Cwm Bychan, Roman Steps* and *Bwlch Drws Ardudwy,* a fine quiet 20 mile (32km) walk (see also **R10**).

R11 (ii) Lleyn. Remote and quiet peninsula; mostly Welsh-speaking. Cyclists can make a circuit from either *Snowdon Ranger*△ or *Harlech* △. Bus service along south coast to *Aberdaron* and up to *Nevin.* Railway to *Pwllheli.* Chief features of interest are *Criccieth* (old town, associations with British Prime Minister Lloyd George); *Abersoch* (small resort, *Penkilan Head,* sea trips to *St Tudwal's Islands*, with cliffs, caves and seabird colonies); *Aberdaron* (picturesque fishing village, cliff walk to *Braich-y-Pwll*, boat to *Bardsey Island*); *Nevin*; the three hills of **Yr Eifl** (1,849ft, 563m) with fine views and Iron Age village, **Tre'r Ceiri**. *Lleyn* has several interesting churches; *Llanengan, Llangwnadl, Llanaelhaiarn* and *Clynnogfawr.*

From *Snowdon Ranger*△ an easy track for walkers crosses hills for 4 miles (6km) to *Llanberis.* Main route follows road for 8 miles (13km) to **Caernarvon**, on *Menai Strait.* Historic walled town with splendid thirteenth- to fourteenth-century castle. *Llanberis*△ is 7 miles (11km) further on.

EXCURSIONS: (a) *Llanberis Pass* and one of the routes up *Snowdon* from *Pen-y-Pass*△; (b) *Cwm Glas*; (c) across *Glyder* mountains from *Nant Peris* to *Idwal Cottage*△ via *Devil's Kitchen.*

Route now returns to coast at *Bangor*△, busy small town with cathedral and university college; elegant Victorian pier. Excellent base from which to explore much of North Wales..

EXCURSIONS: **Anglesey.** (a) by ferry to *Beaumaris*, attractive resort, castle, views of Snowdonia; (b) Telford's suspension bridge (1862) across *Menai Strait*; 4 miles (6km) south-west in parish of *Llandaniel Fab* the great circular barrow at **Bryn-celli-ddu**; then by southern route to *Holyhead* (bus) via *Newborough* (nature reserve), *Aberffraw* and *Rhosneigr.* At *Holyhead* (boat service to *Dublin*) see fine coast scenery of *Holyhead Mountain* (719ft, 219m) with ancient contorted strata.

From *Bangor*, coast road for 6 miles (10km) to *Aber* (glen, waterfall) and a further 6 miles (10km) to *Penmaenmawr*△, thence 10 miles (16km) to *Colwyn Bay*△ via *Conwy.*

Chester△, Roman foundation, their walls encircle city, making interesting two-mile walk; many half-timbered houses and characteristic *Rows* — arcades with shops along house fronts at first floor level. Red sandstone cathedral in several styles from Norman to Jacobean; wide views from central tower.

The Peak District

At their southern end the *Pennine* hills of the north country impinge on the *Midland* plain in a mass of moorland whose dark sandstone (Millstone Grit) edges face inwards upon a landscape of striking contrast — the pastel greens and creams of Carboniferous Limestone country.

The two landscapes make up the *Peak District National Park*, which, though it lacks peaks, has much good hill country containing river valleys of extraordinary interest and beauty.

The following route (which, between *Ilam* and *Matlock*, can form the basis of a walking tour) follows the River *Dove* upwards and strikes north across the limestone to the *Peak* before bearing south again down the *Derwent* to *Matlock*. The quartet of great houses visited is without a rival in any district in England of similar size.

R12 Derby — Edale — Matlock — Southwell (110 miles, 177km)

Derby; industrial city, home of first silk mill (1717), fine porcelain (Crown Derby), Rolls Royce engines. **Kedleston Hall** (1760), lies 5 miles (8km) to northwest, a masterpiece of Robert Adam, work by Chippendale (open April to end of October, Saturday to Wednesday [including Bank Holiday Mondays])

Ashbourne, market town, fine thirteenth-century church. Up *Dove* valley to *Ilam Hall*Δ, centre for walks in *Dove* and *Manifold* valleys (the *Izaak Walton* country). Riverside path for 9 miles (14km) through *Dovedale, Wolfscote Dale* and *Beresford Dale* to *Hartington*Δ.

By footpaths via *Lathkill Dale* and *Over Haddon*, or continue up dale to *Longnor* then east via *Monyash* to *Bakewell*Δ market town, famous for Bakewell pudding; church has important family monuments; Saxon cross. **Haddon Hall**, is 2 miles (3km) to south-east, great house with medieval origins, shows evolution of styles through five centuries (open Easter-September, Tuesday to Sunday and Bank Holidays; closed Sunday in July and August).

Monsal Dale; Cressbrook (early Industrial Revolution mill); *Millersdale*, with *Ravenstor*Δ.

Tideswell, small market centre; finest church in district; *Little Hucklow; Castleton*Δ, overlooked by Norman fortress, many limestone caverns; caving centre, *Blue John Mine, Treak Cliff Cavern, Speedwell Mine* with underground stream explored by boat.

*Edale*Δ under *Kinder Scout* (2,088ft, 636m), south end of *Pennine Way*; village has National Park information centre. Routes up gritstone water-courses (*Crowden, Grinds Brook*, etc) lead to desolate *Kinder Scout* plateau.

Walk over *Win Hill* (view) to *Bamford* and down *Derwent* to *Hathersage*Δ; *Wet Withens* (Bronze Age stone circle); *Eyam* Δ, famous plague village; *Baslow*. **Chatsworth**, superb seventeenth-century Palladian home of Duke of Devonshire; famous for state rooms; huge art collection, pictures, drawings, tapestries, etc; large formal gardens and magnificent deer park (open April-October). *Rowsley* sixteenth-century *Peacock Inn*; *Matlock* Δ, spa town, set in spectacular gorge cut by River *Derwent*. Two miles (3km) to the south is *Cromford*, pleasing early Industrial Revolution village with Arkwright's Mill (1771).

Hardwick Hall, 12 miles (19km) east of *Matlock*, most splendid and least altered of Elizabethan houses; fine furniture, tapestries, pictures, gardens (open April-October, afternoons Wed, Thurs, Sat, Sun and Bank Holiday Mondays).

Southwell, 20 miles (32km) south-east of *Hardwick*, quiet cathedral town in Nottinghamshire almost by-passed by modernity; splendid minster, chiefly Norman, with chapter-house in Decorated style, one of marvels of thirteenth-century craftsmanship.

The Yorkshire Dales

The rivers flowing off from the *Pennines* are famous for their individual beauty. Here, as in the *Lake District*, hill, valley and waterfall become fell, dale and force — the *fjell*, *dal* and *foss* of the Scandanivian settlers, who found this sweeping landscape well suited to their activities as herdsmen. So, at a later date, did the monks, especially the Cistercians, whose large-scale sheep rearing destroyed the woodlands to create the open fellsides seen today. The wealth it brought them accounts for the number and magnificence of Yorkshire abbeys. When the monasteries were dissolved the wool trade survived. Textiles in Yorkshire mean woollen goods, and *Bradford* is still a world centre for wool-clip sales.

The unspoilt dales country, a National Park, is splendid for walking and cycling. The *Craven* district is the principal centre for caving and pot-holing.

R13 Walking Tour: Skipton — Ingleton — Aysgarth — Ripon (130 miles, 209km)
Skipton, once *Sceptone* (sheep town); market centre for dales; castle thirteenth to seventeenth century. Bus to *Linton* Δ from which walking tour begins.

EXCURSION: riverside path down *Wharfedale* by *Burnsall, Barden Bridge*, the *Strid* (where river narrows to little more than 3ft [1m], but extremely dangerous to attempt jumping across). *Bolton Abbey*.

Grassington, picturesque village; path from top end of village through *Grass Wood* to *Conistone; Kilnsey Crag; Kettlewell*Δ.

EXCURSIONS: (a) *Upper Wharfedale* and *Langstrothdale Chase*; (b) *Arncliffe* and *Littondale*.

From *Kettlewell* for 8 miles (13km) via *Kilnsey* and *Mastiles Lane* (old drove road across fells to **Gordale Scar** (chasm in limestone), thence 2 miles (3km) to

Malham △, near precipitous *Malham Cove*, formerly a waterfall.

Continue for 8 miles (13km) via *Kirkby Malham* and *Settle*, small town with pleasant market square, to *Stainforth*△.

EXCURSION: *Penyghent*, 3 hours' climb (2,273ft, 693m).

Thence by footpaths westwards for 10 miles (16km) via *Stainforth Force* (River *Ribble*); *Feizor; Austwick* and *Clapham* to *Ingleton*△. Chief pot-holing and caving centre.

EXCURSIONS: (a) *Ingleborough* (2,373ft, 723m), *Gaping Gill, Trow Gill, Clapham;*
(b) Falls and glens of River *Greta; White Scar Caves* (open to public).
North-eastwards via *Blea Moor*, for 11 miles (18km) to *Dentdale*△.

EXCURSION: *Dent* (picturesque village) and *Deepdale.*

Continue north-east for 8 miles (13km) to *Hawes*△, small market town in *Wensleydale* and north via *Hardrow Force* (highest single fall in England); *Buttertubs Pass* (1,726ft, 526m) and *Thwaite* to *Keld*△ in *Swaledale*, centre for fell-walking and fine river scenery of upper dale.
Muker, Reeth, Grinton (church) and *Grinton Lodge*△, 13 miles (21km).

EXCURSION: *Lower Swaledale* and **Richmond,** historic and finely situated town, castle (1071) with massive keep; circular cobbled market place with church in centre; *Greyfriars Tower*; handsome Georgian houses; steep narrow 'wynd' down to river; riverside path to *Easby Abbey* (1152); *Easby Church* has medieval wall paintings.

R13 (i) Teesdale, *Grinton Lodge*△; *Arkengarthdale Moor, Brignall, Greta Bridge* and *Rokeby* (famous river scenery; *Tees* is boundary between *Yorkshire* and *Durham*): *Barnard Castle*, old gated town and castle (1132). Town has **Bowes Museum** (modelled on the *Tuileries* and containing art collection).

EXCURSIONS: (a) *Middleton-in-Teesdale*, **High Force** (waterfall), **Caldron Snout**;
(b) *Raby Castle*, seat of the Nevilles, a great North Country family, until 1569.

Southwards from *Grinton* for 8 miles (13km) via *Bolton Castle* and *Redmire*, to *Aysgarth*△ in *Wensleydale*, home of famous cheese, many beautiful villages.

EXCURSIONS: (a) *Askrigg, Bainbridge, Semerwater*; (b) *Thoralby, Bishopdale, Buckden Pike* (2,302ft, 702m), *Waldendale*; (c) *Middleham High Moor* to *Middleham* (castle), *East Witton, Jervaulx Abbey, Ellingstring*△.

By road via *Masham* to **Ripon** (cathedral, market square, old houses). **Fountains Abbey**, 4 miles (6km) Cistercian (1132) very extensive remains of abbey church and domestic buildings.

North York Moors and Coast

East of the *Vale of York* are the *North York Moors* (a National Park), the *Vale of Pickering* and the *Wolds*, a continuation via *Lincolnshire* of the chalklands of the south, which reach the coast at *Flamborough Head*.

R14 York — Scarborough — Whitby (65 miles, 105km)
York Δ, Roman *Eboracum*, where Constantine the Great was proclaimed emperor. Medieval wall and gates or 'Bars'; *Bootham, Micklegate, Monk* and *Walmgate*. 'Minster' is the largest ancient cathedral in England; Early English to Perpendicular; famous for stained glass fourteenth to fifteenth century: beautiful chapter house. *St William's College; Treasurer's House; Merchant Adventurers' Hall:* eighteenth-century *Mansion House; Castle Museum (Kirk Collection* notable for reconstructed streets and shops). *Railway Museum.* Walk on town walls and ancient streets, *Shambles, Stonegate*, etc.
    Malton Δ 19 miles (31km). Market centre in *Vale of Pickering*.

EXCURSIONS: (a) *Kirkham Abbey* on River *Derwent; Howardian Hills; Castle Howard*, Vanbrugh's great baroque masterpiece (Easter-September, afternoons; closed Mon and Fri); (b) *Helmsley*Δ (castle); **Rievaulx Abbey**; *Byland Abbey; Coxwold* (where Sterne, author of *Tristram Shandy*, was vicar).

R14 (i) *Pickering*, small market town, castle, church has fifteenth-century wall paintings; *Lastingham*, church has famous early crypt; *Hutton-le-Hole; Farndale* is one of many beautiful dales leading into moors.

Scarborough Δ, 23 miles (37km); large popular seaside resort on two bays with *Castle Hill* between. A fine coast runs south to *Flamborough Head* and north to *Runswick Bay* and *Staithes* (picturesque fishing villages) via *Robin Hood's Bay (Boggle Hole*Δ) and *Whitby*Δ, old seaport town with clustered red-tiled roofs; church steps (199) lead up to abbey, important in early English church history; the home town of Captain Cook.

R14 (ii) Eskdale, the Moors and Cleveland Hills. Good walking country. *Whitby, Little Beck, Goathland, Wheeldale*Δ; *Glaisdale, Castleton, Westerdale*Δ; *Roseberry Topping* (view) 1,057ft (322m) *Guisborough, Saltburn-by-the-Sea*Δ.

The Lake District

Despite its small scale the English *Lake District* has the features of a mountain region. Its fame rests on the infinitely subtle variations on a repeated theme of mountain, dale and lake to be found in a single day's walk. The form of the district, with valleys radiating from a hub, makes it possible to pass from one to another in quick succession and yet have a sense of being in scenery of noble proportions. It is unsurpassed in England as a walking area and the many youth hostels facilitate a great variety of tours. Chief access points by rail are *Windermere, Penrith, Kendal* and *Ravenglass.*

R15 Walking tour: Windermere to Windermere via Patterdale, Keswick and Buttermere (80 miles, 129km)

Bowness-on-Windermere; steamer to *Waterhead, Ambleside*Δ. Footpath east of *Loughrigg Fell* and south side of *Rydal Water; Loughrigg Terrace (High Close*Δ nearby); *Grasmere*Δ; Wordsworth's home, *Dove Cottage*, open to public.

Grisedale Pass to *Patterdale*. From top of pass more strenuous route over *Dollywagon Pike* leads to *Helvellyn* (3,118ft, 950m) and ridge walk over *Striding Edge* and down to *Patterdale*Δ.

EXCURSIONS: (a) steamer on *Ullswater* to *Howtown* and *Pooley Bridge*; (b) *Aira Force* (waterfall), *Dockray, Glenridding.*

Patterdale via *Glenridding, Greenside*Δ and *Sticks Pass* to northern end of *Thirlmere*Δ, or over *Helvellyn*, descending to *Thirlspot Inn.* Bus to **Keswick**Δ.

EXCURSIONS: (a) *Latrigg* (1,203ft, 367m) best general viewpoint of *Derwentwater* and mountains; (b) *Stone Circle, Castlerigg; Wallow Crag, Falcon Crag, Lodore*, boat to *Keswick*; (c) ferry to *Nicol End*, lakeside walk through *Brandelhow Park*, boat to *Keswick* from *High Brandelhow*; boat *High Brandelhow*, walk *Grange-in-Borrow-dale*; over *Grange Fell* to *Watendlath*; *Ashness Bridge*; lakeside road and path by *Stable Hills* and **Friar's Crag** to *Keswick*; (e) *Skiddaw* (3,053ft, 931m); (f) *Saddle-back* (2,847ft, 868m) from *Threlkeld* via *Scales Tarn* (care required over *Sharp Edge*).

Keswick, ferry to *Nicol End*, path south over *Cat Bells, Maiden Moor, Eel Crag* and west over *Dale Head* (2,437ft, 753m), *Hindscarth* and *Robinson* to *Buttermere*Δ.

Buttermere to *Scale Force* (waterfall), *Ling Comb, Red Pike, High Stile, Scarth Gap, Haystacks* and *Fleetwith* to *Longthwaite*Δ.

Brandreth, Green Gable, Great Gable (2,949ft, 898m); *Styhead, Stockley Bridge* and *Seathwaite* (rainiest inhabited place in England) to *Longthwaite*Δ.

Stockley Bridge, Grains Gill, Esk House and south-west to **Scafell Pike** (3,210ft [978m], highest point in England); return to *Esk Hause; Angle Tarn, Rossett Gill* to head of *Langdale;* bus down dale to *Elterwater*Δ.

R15 (i) The South Western valleys. *Elterwater*Δ, *Little Langdale, Tilberthwaite Glen*, **Hawkshead**Δ (picturesque place; Wordsworth was educated at its grammar school). *Coniston* Δ by *Walna Scar* road or *Coniston Old Man* (2,635ft, 803m) to *Seathwaite-in-Dunnerdale*, dale of Wordsworth's *Duddon Sonnets, Duddon* and *Hardknott Pass* (Roman camp) to *Eskdale*Δ. 1¹/₂ miles (2¹/₂km) to *Dalegarth* for narrow-gauge steam railway to *Ravenglass*, 7 miles (11km) on coast.

EXCURSIONS: (a) by *Burnmoor* to *Wasdale Head* and *Wastwater*Δ. For strong walkers a fine return route, requiring local advice or guidance, is via *Lingmell Gill, Mickledore, Lord's Rake*, **Scafell** and *Slight Side*. Alternatively, return via *Wastwater Screes* and *Miterdale*. (b) along *Upper Eskdale* (one of the finest valleys in *Lake District*); climb out east to *Three Tarns*; descend the *Band* to *Langdale*.

The North

Even though disfigured by coal mining *County Durham* is worth exploring. It is the country of Bede, of the most glorious Norman cathedrals, of the Washington family and of the invention of the locomotive steam engine. In the west the *Pennine* moors and dales are as lovely and lonely as those of *Yorkshire*.

Northumberland is one of the most sparsely inhabited of English counties. Memories of the times of Border strife are written into the landscape in its scarcity of villages, many castles and *Hadrian's Wall*. The coast is of outstanding beauty. The fell country from the wall to the *Cheviots* is a National Park.

R16 Durham to Berwick-on-Tweed (120 miles, 193km)
Durham (Δsummer only); on typical medieval town site in sharp bend of River *Wear*. Splendid grouping of cathedral, monastery and castle. Cathedral begun 1093, shrine of St Cuthbert; great Norman nave, stone vaulting, incised pillars; Bede's tomb in twelfth-century Galilee Lady Chapel. Monastic buildings include refectory, now cathedral library. Castle has crypt chapel (1072), dining hall, kitchen and buttery, fine carving of seventeenth-century *Black Staircase*. Riverside walks. Boating.

Washington Old Hall, 12 miles (19km) north, home of Washington family for four centuries to 1613.

*Newcastle-upon-Tyne*Δ, 7 miles (11km), metropolis of the north and not at all unattractive in spite of obvious industry; many bridges, quays, impressive streets and buildings; cathedral; castle with Henry II keep and museum of Roman antiquities.

Hexham, 20 miles (32km), small market town; priory church (Early English with Saxon apse, crypt and bishop's chair). Town has moot hall and other interesting buildings. *Acomb*Δ is 2 miles (3km) north.

From *Acomb* head 2 miles (3km) to reach **Hadrian's Wall** at *Chesters* (*Cilurnum*; military station; excavated forum, gateways). *Housesteads*, 8 miles (13km) (*Borcovicium*; military station; excavations, museum), *Once Brewed*Δ is 3 miles (5km) further.

R16 (i) Once Brewed to Carlisle (26 miles, 42km). *Hadrian's Wall* can be followed westwards past more military stations at *Great Chesters (Aesica), Carvoran (Magnae)* with *Greenhead*Δ nearby, *Birdoswald (Camboglanna)*; those at *Castlesteads* (Fort XIII) and *Stanwix* (Fort XIV) have been destroyed. four miles (6km) south-west of

Birdoswald are *Lanercost Priory* (Augustinian), built of stone taken from Wall and, across fine eighteenth-century bridge is *Naworth Castle*, home of Earl of Carlisle, and *Brampton*, picturesque town with stocks and bullring. *Carlisle*Δ, county town; castle, early Norman keep, dungeons, cathedral, great east window with medieval glass, fine wood carving, nave destroyed in Civil War; *Tullie House*, museum and art gallery; *Redness Hall*, fourteenth century.

Main route continues north for 16 miles (26km) to *Bellingham*Δ in *Tynedale*, *Otterburn* in *Redesdale* and *Rothbury* 23 miles (37km) in *Coquetdale*; good centre for walks; house and gardens of *Cragside* open.

EXCURSIONS: (a) *Upper Coquetdale*, for walks in *Cheviots*; (b) *Simonside Hills*; (c) *Brinkburn Priory*, twelfth century; (d) *Warkworth*, near mouth of *Coquet*, magnificent ruined castle above interesting little town.

Alnwick, 11 miles (18km): castle, home of Duke of Northumberland, finest of the Border fortresses, many art treasures. See also *Hulne Park* with ruins of *Hulne Priory* and *Alnwick Abbey*. *Rock Hall*Δ is 5 miles (8km) north-east.

EXCURSIONS: (a) the coast, with castles of *Dunstanburgh* and *Bamburgh* (open Easter-Sept); (b) **Farne Islands**, spectacular sea-bird colonies, many species; also grey seals; (boat from *Seahouses*); (c) **Holy Island (Lindisfarne)**, by walk at low tide across causeway or sands; monastery founded here by St Aidan (635); present ruins are eleventh century; picturesque small castle by Lutyens; up-to-date museum encompassing seventh to ninth centuries Anglo-Saxon art and monastic life.

Continue for 17 miles (27km) to *Wooler*Δ, pleasant market town, by-passed by main road.

EXCURSIONS: (a) The *Cheviot* (2,676ft, 816m), *Hedgehope* (2,348ft, 716m) and *Harthope* valley; (b) *Yeavering Bell* (Hill Fort) and *College* valley; (c) *Chillingham Park* with herd of wild white cattle.

At *Crookham* 8 miles (13km) north-west take secondary road to *Branxton*, $1^1/_2$ miles ($2^1/_2$km); near church is *Flodden Field Monument* on the site of battle (1513). Nine miles (15km) north by river *Tweed* is *Norham Castle* (of Scott's *Marmion*) fine keep (1160). **Berwick-on-Tweed**, 7 miles (11km), historic Border town, impressive ramparts (1565) and bridges.

FINLAND

Geographical Outline

Land

Finland (Finnish: *Suomi*, 'the land of fens and lakes', is situated between the 60th and 70th degrees of latitude; bordered on the west by Sweden, on the east by Russia, and on the north by Norway. In the south it is a peninsula, between the Gulfs of Bothnia and Finland. Nearly 10 per cent of its area is taken up with lakes and rivers.

The land is largely composed of rocks representing an immensely remote period of earth's history; so ancient that there has been time for parts to be twice uplifted and twice eroded to produce the comparatively level landscape seen today. The solid base is mostly overlaid by sands and gravels left by glaciers of the Ice Age; when these occur as moraines in long parallel lines of narrow rising ground — as in the *Salpausselkä* ridge — they form elevated features running far across the country.

From a coastal plain with hundreds of off-shore islands the land rises to a central plateau of about 300ft (90m) altitude on which most of the lakes (said to number 62,000) are situated. Many, such as *Saimaa* and *Päijänne*, are of great extent. Their smooth surfaces are in strong contrast with the many rivers linking them, one with another, which are often broken by rocks and rapids. In the far north the land rises again, forming an upland region whose highest point is *Halti* (4,356ft, 1,330m).

Climate

The climate is considerably warmer than might be expected; the mildest of all other places of a similar latitude outside Europe. The coldest month is February. In winter the rivers, lakes and sea are frozen but the ports are kept open by icebreakers and the Stockholm/Turku and Travemunde/Helsinki ferry routes are open all year. The warmest month is July, when the temperature in Helsinki is higher than that of London. The summer is warm, bright and exhilarating, the 'midnight sun' is visible at the 70th degree of latitude from the middle of May to the end of July. The winter is cold but dry; it rarely rains for long periods, the annual rainfall is slight, although there are heavy falls of snow.

The main touring season begins in June and continues until the middle of September; July is the most popular month. In the winter there is skiing on gentle slopes in the south from January to March, and in Lapland from March to the end of April.

Plants and Animals

By far the greater part of the country is forest, predominantly spruce and pine, but birch, alder and ash are also evident. Oak occurs only in the south. In Lapland, the forest gives way to a tundra vegetation with lichen and moss.

Reindeer and bear are protected by law; a few wolves and lynx live in the forests. There are many species of birds, especially waterfowl. In Lapland a form of blue capercailzie prized as a game bird is sometimes found. The salmon is common in the Lapland rivers.

The People

Population

Of the population of nearly 5 million, only a quarter live in towns. The largest cities are *Helsinki* (500,000), *Turku* (165,000) and *Tampere* (170,000).

The eastern Finns, who make up the majority of the nation, tend to be fair, broad-headed, and of medium stature. The Swedish Finns of the south and west tend to show the Scandinavian characteristics of long-headedness and greater height. The few thousand Samian Lapps, on the tundra, are sallow complexioned with dark hair and dark eyes, very broad-headed and short in stature.

Language

The country is bilingual — more than 90 per cent of the people speak Finnish, and the rest Swedish. Finnish is a distinctive language. Together with Estonian it is the chief European representative of the Finno-Ugrian group of languages. It is most difficult to learn, as the grammar is particularly complicated. Most educated Finns speak Swedish; and, in the cities, many speak English or German.

Religion

Most of the population belong to the Lutheran Church, but a substantial minority follow the Orthodox faith; an example of influence from East and West.

History

The Finns probably came from the Volga basin (east Russia) and crossed to Finland from Estonia. In 1157 Eric IX of Sweden led a crusade into Finland, introducing Christianity. This union with Sweden, in which Finland had some measure of independence, lasted until 1809. In the seventeenth century a Diet was inaugurated, formed of representatives of the nobles, burghers, clergy and peasants; it lasted until 1906. In 1809 Finland was incorporated in the Russian Empire as a Grand Duchy. She proclaimed her independence on 6 December, 1917, and it was finally achieved by General Mannerheim in 1918.

Finland's decision to remain neutral (1935) in the coming struggle in Europe was unwelcome to Russia who, seeking security for Leningrad, took territory in the south-east at an early stage of World War II. It included the Karelian isthmus and the shores of Lake Ladoga. Later the country was used by Germany as a base for operations against north Russia. The Finns themselves, after temporarily regaining the lost territory, had to cede it again to Russia with certain bases at the armistice of 1944; the bases were later returned but the Finns find it necessary to adopt a cautious policy towards their powerful eastern neighbour, and they do not belong to any western political alliances.

Government

Finland is a democratic republic, the government consisting of the President and the House of Representatives (Diet). The President nominates the Cabinet, which has to have the support of the House of Representatives. There are eight political parties. Finland was the first country in Europe to give women the vote; everyone over 18 has the right to vote. Municipal government is carried out by the burgomaster and aldermen.

Resources

Being the most heavily wooded country in Europe, forests are the main resource. Coal is absent but hydro-electric schemes are well developed. Though less than 10 per cent of the land is suitable for cultivation, agriculture is the foremost occupation; 25 per cent of the working population are thus employed, with 40 per cent in industry. Three-quarters of the agricultural workers are independent farmers. The main exports are timber and paper, but there are rapidly growing textile, clothing and metal industries. Other exports are copper from the *Outokumpu* mine in *Northern Karelia* and glass and pottery of modern design.

Sauna

The sauna steam-bath is a Finnish institution; every house in country districts having its own bath-house. An oven of stones is heated to about 60°C (140°F) and

then sprayed with water; the bathers sit on a high wooden platform in the steam produced and whisk themselves with birch branches to open the pores. This is followed in towns by a cold shower and in the country by a swim.

Costumes and Customs

Local costumes are worn for festivals and sometimes at weekends, especially by the girls. The Lapps have their own distinctive costume, which they wear for the benefit of tourists.

The main holiday of the summer is the Midsummer Festival, which is of pagan origin. Large bonfires are lit on lake shores and the people gather to sing and dance and let off fireworks. Cultural festivals crowd the summer calendar.

Food and Drink

Finnish meals conform to the Scandinavian pattern; coffee and rolls for breakfast, lunch between 11am and 1pm, and the main meal of the day between 5pm and 7pm. Meals ordered outside these times are usually more expensive. Finns eat a great deal of porridge, *puuro*, made not only of oats but of rye, semolina or rice. Potatoes, butter, all kinds of bread from black rye bread, various kinds of brown to pure white, and crispbread are popular foods. A main meal will often begin with a variety of sausage, cheese and salt herring, and continue with a hot dish, probably pork or veal.

Sport

Skiing, which is still a mode of transport in remote country districts, is the favourite winter sport of the entire population. School children are given a week's skiing holiday in February and many people go up to the Lapland fells to ski. In summer, they swim in the sea and lakes. The main sport is athletics, in which they excel; there are many stadiums and gymnasiums. The Finns are a nation of sportsmen, not spectators.

Culture

Architecture

Finnish medieval architecture, simple, in grey stone and almost primitive in form is best seen in such examples as the cathedral at *Turku* and *Olavinlinna* castle at *Savonlinna*. This severe, undecorated style changed little until overtaken in the mid-eighteenth century by a version of Swedish rococo, exampled by the fortress at *Soumenlinna* and wooden houses of this period with their mansard roofs, often seen in rural surroundings. The more modest wooden churches have baroque tendencies, such as those at *Petäjävesi* and *Keuruu* and, with the manor houses, show the Finnish feeling for atmosphere.

Carl Ludvig Engel, a German who died in 1840, is perhaps the outstanding name of the nineteenth century. His neo-classical style is noble and artistic and he designed many of the public buildings of *Helsinki*, notably the Great Square.

The final period of Finnish architecture is likely to be of most interest to the visitor. The essentially functional style of these modern buildings commenced in the 1920s, and was influenced by the work of Le Corbusier and Frank Lloyd Wright. Excellent examples are the *Helsinki* Railway Station (Eliel Saarinen), *Paimio* Sanatorium (Alvar Aalto), *Sampo* Insurance Company building (Erik Bryggman) and the *Helsinki* Stadium (Yrjö Lindgren and T. Jänntti), to mention one by each of the foremost architects. *Helsinki*, and the garden suburb of *Tapiola* contain many recently designed buildings by Aalto and other well-known contemporary architects — the Sirens, Rewell, Ervi and Blomstedt. Their work can be seen in many other towns and some of their most significant examples are in quite remote places.

Literature

Finland's greatest literary work is the national epic — the *Kalevala* — compiled by Elias Lönnrot (1802-84) from the native ballads. It relates the beginnings of the country and its subsequent history, interwoven with love stories and fables; the basis of much of Finland's later art in music, painting and literature.

Translations have been made into many languages and it inspired Longfellow's *Hiawatha*. An English edition *Kalevala, the Land of Heroes* is published by *Dent*. Novels translated into English are Linnankoski's *Song of the Blood-Red Flower*; Sillanpää's *Fallen Asleep When Young*; and Linna's *Unknown Soldier*.

Painting and Sculpture

Great strength and deep feeling characterize the work of Gallen-Kallela (1865-1931) in his portraits, landscapes and, above all, his frescoes as at the Athenaeum, *Helsinki*, illustrating scenes from the *Kalevala*, and those in the Mausoleum at *Pori*. The same can be said of the sculptor Aaltonen (born 1894); his bronze of the runner Nurmi in the Athenaeum, *Helsinki*, and his massive granite figure for the war memorial at *Savonlinna*.

Music

The wonderfully original orchestration of Sibelius (1865-1957) evokes more widely than anything else the beauty and drama of the north — its story, legend and untamed spaciousness. It may be that his great innovation in symphonic form, the breaking out from the mould of conventionally accepted movements, appropriate to a world where man is dominant — was a necessity for one inspired more by nature at work on the grandest scale.

Folk-song and Dance

There has been a revival of Finnish folk-dancing in recent years; it is similar to English, mostly being danced in sets of eight. The *Kantele*, a type of Finnish zither which is mentioned in the *Kalevala* is found only in *Karelia*.

The art of the runo-singer is gradually being lost. Two peasants would sit opposite each other, hands clasped and, swaying to the rhythm, would chant folk stories in turn. From these old folk songs Lönnrot wrote the *Kalevala*.

Design

Finnish designers enjoy world-wide fame for the beauty and simplicity of their glassware, plain or of exquisite colour (Tapio Wirkkala, Timo Sarpaneva, Nanny Still), ceramics both artistic and practical (Kyllikki Salmenhaara, Kaj Franck), textiles and modern versions of the '*ryijy*' rug (Eva Brummer) as well as cutlery, furniture and light fittings.

Touring Information

Access

Finland may be reached by rail via *Hook of Holland, Copenhagen* or *Stockholm* and thence by one of several ferries to *Helsinki* or *Turku*.

Transport

Finnish State Railways have a network of rather more than 3,000 miles (4,800km) covering most of the country except the far north. Locomotives vary from electric to fast diesel engines and long distance fares are cheap. Seat reservation is obligatory in express trains. 8-day, 15-day and 22-day runabout tickets on all trains are on sale.

Buses run by private companies go almost everywhere in the country. Express, long distance, buses run between the cities and directly to Lapland; buses offer an agreeable way of meeting Finnish people and seeing the remotest regions. Fares are cheap and there are ticket offices in all the towns and in many villages.

Steamers ply on many lakes; some routes, as on Lake *Saimaa*, occupy many hours of leisurely cruising. Some steamers with wood-fired engines remain in service, but most have been converted to diesel; hydrofoils are also used.

A comprehensive timetable *Suomen Kulkuneuvot*, includes all rail, bus and steamer services, with useful general map.

Clothing

During the summer season ordinary summer clothing is suitable, but some warmer clothing should be taken, as evenings are sometimes cool. In winter warm clothing, especially underwear, is essential; fur hats are normally worn, and fur-lined or fur coats.

Restaurants

Meals at cafeterias and coffee bars are less expensive than *à la carte* restaurants but, as in all Scandinavian countries, eating out is nowhere cheap. Some youth hostels provide meals and many have cooking facilities.

Public Holidays

1 January, 6 January (Epiphany), Good Friday, Easter Monday, 1 May (Vappu), Ascension Day, Whit Monday, Midsummer (Juhannus; nearest Saturday to 24 June), All Saints' Day, 6 December (Independence), Christmas Day, and 26 December.

Tourist Information

Information and leaflets can be had from the *Finnish Tourist Board, 66 Hay-market, London SW1Y 4RP*, and from the *Matkailutoimisto* tourist information bureaux in most Finnish towns.

Maps

The Geographia map of Finland, 1:500,000 is a good general map showing roads and railways. For cycling or canoeing there is the Suomen Tiekartta, scale 1:200,000, thirteen sheets, or the Autoilijan Tiekartta on a scale of 1:750,000, two sheets. Seven areas of Lapland, including the *Pallas-Ounastunturi National Park* and *Kilpisjarvi* areas are shown on excursion maps at 1:50,000, published by the National Board of Survey.

Accommodation

There are over 100 youth hostels in Finland, mostly small and many of them in school buildings which are open only from mid-June to mid-August; some others are better equipped, provide meals, have family rooms and are open throughout the summer. There are no age restrictions, all are open to motorists and many have bicycles, boats and canoes for hire.

Camping

More than 300 campsites are distributed throughout the country, often on selected sites beside lakes or rivers and some at the seaside; most of them open from early June to late August. 'Wild' camping is discouraged, camp-fires are prohibited and free camping is not allowed without landowner's permission. Offices of Finnish Tourist Board hand out lists of campsites; Finnish Travel Association Camping Office is at Mikonkatu 25, Helsinki 10.

Walking

The scale of the country is not in general suited to walking tours, but there are splendid exceptions such as the *Kainuu* district around *Kajaani* in central Finland and the *Kuusamo* district in the east. There are a number of mapped trails in *Lapland*, and a booklet about them (with maps) is available in Finnish; but details of four trails (the Pallas-Hetta, the Saariselkä, the Five Fells and the Haltia) are also issued in English.

Cycling

Roads are adequately surfaced, except the smaller ones which are likely to be stony and dusty. Cycling is not popular with the Finns, but the Finnish Tourist Information Offices do provide planned cycle routes for visitors.

Canoeing and Boating

Finland, with its myriad winding waterways, large calm lakes and more than 1,250 miles (2,000km) of waymarked routes, is an ideal country for canoeing. Detailed information can be obtained from Suomen Kanoottiliitto Retkeilyo-sasto, Hämeenlinna, Finland.

Motoring

Extra facilities are offered to motorists visiting Finland, who should enquire of their own motoring organisations. Driving licence, international driving permit, registration certificate and certificate of information are essential; international green card is optional but it is expedient to carry it. Main and secondary roads are excellent, except in the far north where surfaces deteriorate. A red warning triangle should be carried, special regulations apply for the use of lights and enforced speed limits are as indicated by road signs.

Helsinki△

The city was founded in 1550 by Gustav Vasa of Sweden to draw some of the trade of the Hanseatic League. In 1812 the Tsar favoured the city as capital to succeed *Turku*, which was regarded as being too close to Sweden and too far away from St Petersburg.

Travel within the city is by tram, bus or by underground train. A tourist ticket can be bought at the City Tourist Office, Pohjoisesplanadi 19 (near South Harbour); it entitles visitors to unlimited journeys for 24 hours on the central network of buses and trams.

On the right of the south harbour is the President's Palace; Market Square, City Hall; west by fine *Esplanadi* to *Mannerheimintie*, bus terminus, Post Office, impressive Parliament Building (Diet), National Museum (Stone Age to modern times). East of Post Office is *Rautatientori* (Railway Square), containing most beautiful railway station in Europe; built 1919, designed by Eliel Saarinen, murals by Järnefelt. In same square, Athenaeum Art Gallery and Finnish National Theatre. Continuing by *Hallituskatu, Senaatintori* (Senate Square) in which are held all parades and celebrations, especially the welcoming of the New Year. Cathedral (*Tuomiotirkko*) dominates the city, built 1830, altar-piece by Russian artist, Neff. On west side of square is University (1832), University Library (fine example of modern style); on east side; Government Offices. Central statue of Alexander II.

Other interesting churches: Johannes Church in *Korkeavuorenkatu*, Gothic style (1893) has three naves and two spires; *Vanha Kirkko*, oldest church in city (1826) in *Lönnrotinkatu; Kallion Kirkko*, on north of city beyond *Töölönlahti*, fine view from tower.

The Opera House and the Museum of European Art are in the *Bulevardi* and there is an open-air Museum of Finnish Buildings at *Seurasaari*, an island north-west of the city.

In Sports Park at end of *Mannerheimintie* is magnificent stadium used for Olympic Games of 1952; here, too, is one of the three youth hostels in the city.

EXCURSIONS: (a) open-air island zoo, *Korkeasaari*, from North Harbour by ferry. (b) *Suomenlinna* from South Harbour; old island fortress. (c) *Porvoo* is about 30 miles (48km) eastwards along the coast, many beautiful eighteenth-century buildings, a picturesque waterfront of old wooden warehouses. Home of poet Runeberg, now a museum. (d) *Gallen-Kallela Museum*, about 2 miles (3km) north of suburb of *Tapiola*; a delightful exhibition of this artist's work displayed in his former studio and home. By tram to end of No 4 route, then 1 mile (2km) walk.

Touring Routes

R1 The Cities of Finland — round trip of 600 miles (965km)
Turku (*Åbo*)Δ, former capital, important all year ice-free port. The Swedish crusaders landed here in 1157. Finland's first monastery and school were founded in *Turku*. Most of the old buildings were burnt down in 1827; the present city is modern with wide boulevards and stone bridges. Cathedral, 1229; thirteenth-century castle. Two universities (Swedish and Finnish), Museums, including Handicrafts Museum in old part of town saved from fire, observatory.

EXCURSION: *Naantali*, 10 miles (16km) north-west by road or by boat in summer; small attractive coastal resort; Presidential summer residence; fifteenth-century convent church.

Tampere (*Tammerfors*)Δ second city of Finland, in a beautiful position between two lakes where the *Tammerkoski* rapids link the waters of one with the other and thus supply industry with hydro-electric power. Founded as an industrial centre by Scottish settlers, many of the Finns still have Scots names. City is cultural centre too; many excellent museums and art galleries; annual theatre season in August; cathedral, with very fine frescoes. View from *Pyynikki*, a ridge 240ft (73m) high overlooking the city, has open-air theatre with revolving auditorium.

Jyväskylä△, cultural centre, with buildings by Aalto, lying at the northen end of Lake *Päijänne*, amid wild and beautiful scenery. Annual Arts Festival in July.

Southwards for 75 miles (120km) by road or steamer on the eastern side of the lake to **Lahti**△, the youngest city in Finland (1905), better known as a winter sports centre. City Hall, designed by Saarinen, is in brick and of unusual style; many other modern buildings, such as Church of the Cross by Aalto and the Concert Hall. Nearby is famous *Vierumäki* athletic academy.

Westwards to **Hämeenlinna**△, birthplace of Jean Sibelius. Fine thirteenth-century castle. Near the town is the tourist centre of *Aulanko*, and the *Aulanko* National Park, a show-piece of tamed wilderness, man-made lakes, exotic trees. Water-bus route, *Tampere — Aulanko*, $5^1/_2$ hours.

> EXCURSION: Northwards for 4 miles (7km) to *Hattula*, to visit one of the oldest churches in Finland (about 1250). A good example of Finnish medieval architecture, with typical pillars, and walls and vault entirely covered by beautifully coloured frescoes.

R2 Lahti — Savonlinna — Kuopio — Lahti (525 miles, 845km)

Via *Kouvola*△ and *Lappeenranta*△, where the *Saimaa* canal connects with the Gulf of Finland via Soviet territory and on to Leningrad. Thence by road along the eastern shore of Lake *Saimaa*, or by steamer, to **Savonlinna**△, attractive spa with steamer services in all directions. Nearby is *Olavinlinna* Castle (1475), built as a fortification against the East. In summer, plays, operas and folk dances are performed here.

> EXCURSION: to *Punkaharju*, winding ridge 4 miles (6km) long. This part of the country is well-provided with youth hostels.

Joensuu△, another lake-side town on steamer route from *Savonlinna*, for access to vast unspoilt and forested lake country of *North Karelia*.

> EXCURSION: to *Koli*△, on Lake *Pielisjärvi*, for *Koli* Peaks (by rail to *Vuonislahti* and thence by motor-boat or by steamer from *Joensuu* in 6 hours), highest land in southern Finland, rising to over 1,000ft (300m), with excellent views of the lakes and forests and multiplicity of way-marked footpaths.

Kuopio△ on Lake *Kallavesi*, is northern terminus of *Saimaa* steamers, has two cathedrals; one Orthodox, another Lutheran. Orthodox Church Museum collection of exhibits is unique in Western Europe. Return to *Lahti* direct via *Mikkeli*△ or by boat via *Savonlinna* and *Lappeenranta*△.

R3 Lapland

A vast wilderness and, in the north, little changed since the last Ice Age, sparsely populated, but with tourist inns and buses to serve the main centres. The Lapps, keep many of their old customs but are no longer nomadic and have settled in permanent houses; they are occupied in breeding reindeer and fishing but many nowadays are employed in industry. Of the total of about 30,000 Lapps only some 2,000 live in Finland, and Finns are in the majority, even in Finnish Lapland.

RovaniemiΔ on confluence of Ounas and Kemi rivers and almost on the Arctic Circle, capital of Finnish Lapland. Eighteen hours by rail from *Helsinki*. Almost entirely rebuilt, after 1944, planned by Alvar Aalto in uncompromising up-to-date style. Starting point for all Lapland routes by road and air. On the borders of wilderness — but many excellent amenities — hotels, shops, theatre, museums, further education.

Pallastunturi (120 miles, 193km, 5 hours by bus from *Rovaniemi*) is in a National Park, in a district of rounded fells. Camping site here and tourist hotel run by Tourist Association. A waymarked trail of 40 miles (64km) to *Enontekio*Δ across the wilderness of the *Pallastunturi* and *Ounastunturi* fells, has unattended huts along the way.

Kilpisjärvi (270 miles, 434km, 10 hours by bus from *Rovaniemi*) is situated among the highest fells of Finland where its frontier meets Sweden and Norway in the north-west. Nature reserve, *Pikku Malla*, can be visited by rowing boat. Bus connections with Norway.

IvaloΔ (209 miles, 336km, 8 hours by bus from *Rovaniemi* or 1 hour by plane) is a good departure point for journeys farther north: eg to *Inari*Δ (24 miles, 38km, $1^1/_4$ hours by bus) on lake; a pretty village, open-air Lapp museum; excellent centre for walking expeditions in vicinity. *Utsjoki* (78 miles, 125km, 3 hours by bus), another hiking centre, almost northernmost point of Finland, on northern frontier with Norway with which there are bus connections.

FRANCE

Geographical Outline

Land

France is more than three times as large as England and Wales, and shows probably the greatest landscape variety of any country in Europe.

Its basic structure consists of the ancient, uplifted blocks of the *Central Massif, Brittany, Ardennes* and *Vosges*, the more recent fold mountains of the *Pyrenees, Alps* and *Jura*, and the two great lowlands of the *Paris basin* and *Aquitaine*.

Aquitaine is watered by the *Garonne* and its tributaries, some flowing from the *Pyrenees*, others from the *Central Massif*. The *Paris basin* contains the *Seine* and its many tributaries. Largely composed of chalk and limestone, it is bounded north by the Channel and the hills of *Artois*, east and south-east by the characteristic chalk and clay scarplands of *Champagne*, by the *Langres* plateau and the heights of the *Côte d'Or*. The valleys of the other chief rivers complete the broad pattern of the landscape. The *Loire*, rising deep in the *Massif*, links several regions, following a lone course through the *Paris basin*, from *Nevers* to *Tours*, and finally across the plain of *Anjou* to *Nantes*. The *Saône* flows in a corridor, between the *Côte d'Or* and the *Jura*, which is continued below *Lyons*, where the *Saône* joins the *Rhône*, coming from the *Lake Geneva*. After a narrow passage between the *Massif* and the *Alps of Dauphiné*, the hills recede south-west and the *Rhône* flows through *Provence* to its delta, the *Camargue*. France has a frontier on the *Rhine*, in its rift valley section between the *Vosges* and the Black Forest, and contains also the headwaters of the *Moselle* and the *Meuse*.

Aquitaine is connected with the *Paris basin* by the 'gate of *Poitou*' and with the plain of *Languedoc* and the *Rhône* valley by the vital gap of *Carcassonne*. Otherwise, the great upland area running south-west to north-east is readily crossed only through the *Belfort* gap south of the *Vosges* and the *Saverne* gap to the north.

Within this structure, fringed by its mountain frontiers and its Mediterranean,

131

Biscayan and Channel coasts, France has an almost infinite variety of regional and local characteristics, partly the result of history but strongly influenced by natural diversity. Regionally, the key to them is to be found in the old provincial divisions, such as *Brittany, Burgundy, Auvergne, Guyenne* rather than in the artifical boundaries of the modern *départements*. Locally the many *pays* — the traditional name applied by its inhabitants to a locality — offer a fascinating study of distinctions often based on land use and types of soil. This is especially true of the *Paris basin*: eg *Pays de Beauce*, with rich arable farms working the fertile covering of loam (*limon*) over limestone; *Pays de Bray*, a clay region of meadows, woods and streams. *Pays* names occur also in the *Alps*: eg the distinction between the upper valley of the *Isère*, known as *Maurienne* and the middle valley, *Grésivaudan*.

Climate

The climate of the north is rather warmer and drier than that of the southern England. But there is a change from oceanic conditions in the west to those of central Europe in the east, felt in the greater range of temperature in *Lorraine* and the change in rainfall from a winter to a summer maximum. In the south, Atlantic conditions prevail over *Aquitaine* in contrast to the warm wet winters and hot dry summers of Mediterranean *Provence*. The main touring season for most regions is summer, though many people prefer to visit the south in late spring or early autumn to avoid the great heat of July and August. The skiing season is from the end of December to the end of March or April in the *Alps, Jura* and *Vosges*, slightly earlier in the *Pyrenees*.

Plants and Animals

More than 20 per cent of the surface is covered by forest. Deciduous woodland is the natural cover of much of the north and west, and the remaining forests of this type include those of *Fontainebleau* and *Compiègne*. Dense conifers clothe the *Ardennes* and the *Low Vosges* and have been extensively planted on the sands of the *Landes*.

Provence is distinct from the rest of the country in its Mediterranean flora. Here the natural forest is of evergreen oak and maritime pine. But reckless felling and over-grazing have brought about large areas of tangled scrub (*maquis*), with wild olive, myrtle, laurel and holm-oak, or *garrigue*, with stunted evergreens and aromatic plants such as lavender and thyme. Along the Provençal coast and the Riviera orange, lemon, almond, Barbary fig and even a few bananas flourish. In the *Cévennes*, chestnuts have replaced beech because of their importance for food.

Animals native to France include the bear, occasionally found in the *Pyrenees*; the wolf still found in the *Cévennes* and the *Vosges*; the fox, marten, badger and weasel in most regions; the marmot in the *Alps*; the chamois and wild goat in the *Alps* and *Pyrenees*. In many of the forests, the red deer and roe deer are preserved while the wild boar is hunted. Hares, rabbits, and squirrels are common.

Insects include the praying mantis and the cigale, or cicada, whose whirring song is so typical of the south.

The People

Population

France has a population of 53 million, of whom more than 9 million live in *Greater Paris*. The ascendancy of the capital is emphasized by the fact that only four other cities exceed 300,000: *Marseille* 1,100,000, *Lyon* 800,000, *Toulouse* 383,000 and *Nice* 350,000. Settlement is dense in the mining and industrial areas of the *Nord* and the *Pas de Calais* but, taken overall, the country is thinly populated, 97 persons per square kilometre against Britain's 220. There are more than 4 million foreigners, with a generous share of coloured people from former French colonies in the towns.

Racially, the people chiefly stem from the three main types of early settlers, Alpine, Mediterranean and Nordic. There has been considerable inter-mixing, but the stocky, broad-headed Alpine type predominates, particularly in a wide zone from *Lorraine*, through the *Savoy Alps* and the *Central Massif* to the *Pyrenees*. In contrast, in *Provence*, the predominant type is slender, with a long head and narrow features and a tendency to be darker than the Alpines. Waves of Nordic immigrants have reached the north at various periods, the most significant being the Salian Franks (fifth century) who gave their name to the country, and the Norsemen (ninth century) who created the duchy of *Normandy*.

The Basques of *Béarn* are probably a survival of much earlier stock, as may also be some of the people of the *Dordogne*. The *Bretons* were emigrants from Britain in the fifth and sixth centuries.

Language

The language derives from the Latin introduced into Gaul by the Romans. With the decline of the Empire, unity of speech was lost. The change into Romance forms produced the Provençal tongue of the intensely Romanized south, still spoken there, and possessing its own distinctive literature. Change went further in the north, to produce various forms of French, of which that spoken in the *Ile de France* became the standard, and the basis of the modern language.

Minority groups speaking other languages occur at the extremes of the country and have been incorporated, chiefly by extension of the frontier, at various times. These languages are Breton, Basque, the Catalan of *Roussillon*, the Italian of *Nice*, the Alsacien of *Alsace*, and the Corse of *Corsica*.

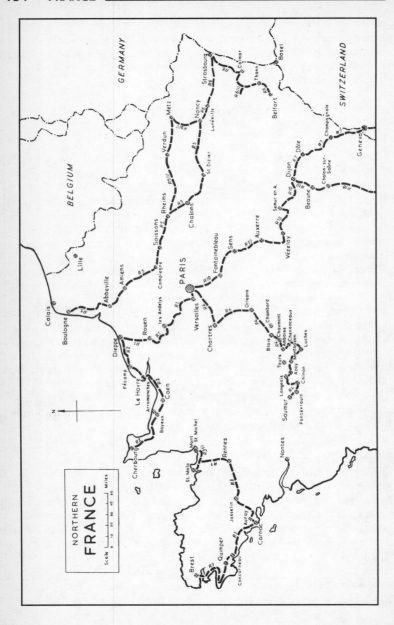

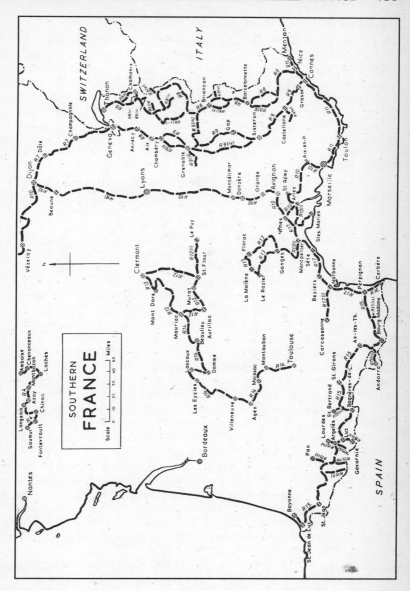

SOUTHERN
FRANCE
Scale
0 10 20 30 40 50 Miles

Religion

The majority of the church-going population is Roman Catholic, but there are a million Protestants (mostly Calvinists) and more than half a million Jews. There is also a very strong anti-clerical (*laïque*) element and the question of religious influence in state schools is still a burning issue in French life.

The dates of the many Roman Catholic ceremonies of interest to visitors can be found in the calendars of events issued by the French National Tourist Office. Amongst the better known are the *pardons* in *Brittany*, the Blessing of the Sea at *Stes-Maries-de-la-Mer* in *Provence* and pilgrimages to *Lourdes* and *Lisieux*.

History

After the fall of the Roman Empire, some continuity of civilized life was maintained in the towns of the south. This made it possible for the distinction between north and south to survive the unification of the country under the Frankish king, Clovis (481), and his Merovingian successors.

Needing the help of Christian *Provence* to rid *Aquitaine* of the Visigoths, Clovis was himself converted to Christianity — the beginning of a process by which the barbarians adopted the superior culture, including the language, of the people they had conquered. Later, under Charlemagne (771-814), they were to become its active champions, a movement culminating in Charles' coronation (800) as Emperor, with dominion over the whole of western Christendom.

At Charles' death the great Frankish Empire fell apart. Not even its partition (843) among his three grandsons could prevent further disintegration. France, now part of *Carolingia* (named after its king, Charles the Bald), was suffering Viking invasions up its estuaries, even including the *Garonne*; *Paris* was sacked four times; *Aquitaine* and *Brittany* were in revolt. People looked to local lords for such protection as they could give; effective authority extended no further than duchies, as in *Gascony*, or was even limited to counties, as in those of the counts of *Blois* and *Anjou*. The norsemen were granted lands on the lower *Seine*, but, in creating *Normandy* (which became a duchy), they discovered a skill in government and administration which did not stop at the Channel.

The recovery of central authority, and with it the rise of *Paris* and of the idea of French nationhood, stems from the election (987) of Hugh Capet, duke of *Francia*, as king of France. At the outset only first among equals, the Capet dynasty gradually increased its power and wealth. Under Philip Augustus (1180-1223), *Paris* was established as the capital. The *Louvre* was built, the university of the *Sorbonne* founded. *Notre Dame* was one of sixteen cathedrals started in his reign in the new Gothic style of the north.

The kings gained prestige through the superior justice of their courts. Their nominal feudal authority was gradually turned into direct sovereignty throughout the land. In the south this followed the horror of the Albigensian war (1209-29), which ended the virtually independent rule of the counts of *Toulouse* and brought the royal power to the Mediterranean. *Dauphiné* was acquired in 1349 and *Provence* (except for *Avignon* and *Orange*) in 1481.

In the north and west, the result of the Hundred Years' War was that the English Crown surrendered its long overlordship of the Angevin dominions. It also discredited the feudal system whose nobility was killing itself off in senseless and greedy warfare. The true heroes of these times are found outside the orders of chivalry in the simple figure of Joan of Arc and in the meek dignity of the burghers of *Calais*.

The fortunate accession of Henry IV of *Navarre* (1589), himself a Calvinist, moderated the terrible civil strife between Catholics and Huguenots. His Edict of Nantes (1598) gave the Huguenots liberty of conscience and full civil rights. His encouragement of agriculture, trade and industry laid the foundations for the Golden Age of Louis XIV. The statesmen-cardinals, Richelieu and Mazarin, further improved the efficiency of the government and the stage was set for Louis himself 'to rule as well as reign'.

During his long reign (1643-1715), the brilliance of the court and French intellectual achievements dazzled the rest of Europe, but Louis' aggressions in his attempts to dominate the continent led to a succession of wars which nearly exhausted the country, and his ill-judged revocation of the Edict of Nantes led large numbers of Huguenots to emigrate with their skills to more tolerant lands.

A further eighty years of wars and colonial rivalries, while the luxury of the court and of the nobility went unreformed, led to the Revolution of 1789-93, the 'Declaration of the Rights of Man' and the violent sweeping away of the *ancien régime*.

Yet the heir of the Revolution turned out to be not democracy but a dictatorship. It seemed that only a strong man could save the new Republic from itself and from its enemies abroad, and in Napoleon was displayed perhaps the most brilliant combination of political and military genius that the world has seen. As First Consul (1799) and later as Emperor (1804), his campaigns made him master of Europe, maker and unmaker of kings and states. The balance of power having gone, Britain was alarmed and alert. She became the ultimate enemy whose defeat was necessary if Napoleon's 'continental system' was to survive. Great schemes — the campaign in Egypt, the attempt to close the Baltic, the assembly of invasion transports at *Boulogne*, even the march to Moscow when Russia went over to the enemy — were designed to that end. But the Channel, Britain's mastery of the seas, and the navy's tenacious years-long vigil off the French ports, proved that, in that age, sea power could be decisive. The march of Allied armies on *Paris* (1814) forced the Emperor's abdication. His return, after a year on Elba, lasted only a hundred days and ended at Waterloo.

Napoleon, in exile, professed that his aims had been liberal and that this would have become more apparent had he been allowed peace. His true glory, he said, lay not in having won forty battles but in his code of civil law. And this Code Napoléon, selecting the best out of the ancient laws and, for the first time, making all men equal before them, has (with the criminal and commercial codes of the same period) been almost universally admired and become a pattern for the codes of many other states.

Napoleon was also modern in his attitude to science and technology — ahead of his time in a country whose industrial revolution came only in the 1850s.

There is space only to list the numerous, and possibly confusing, régimes successively established during France's search for stability after the Revolutionary upheavals.

1789-1804	1st Republic	(Including the Consulate from 1798).
1804-1814	1st Empire	Napoleon I
1814-1830	Bourbon Restoration	Louis XVIII (1814-24). Charles X (1824-30), his attempted return to *ancien régime* led to revolution (1830).
1830-1848	Monarchy 'by will of the people'.	Louis Philippe I, his similar attempt also led to revolution (1848).
1848-1852	2nd Republic	Louis Napoleon (nephew of Napoleon I) elected President.
1852-1870	2nd Empire	Louis Napoleon declared Emperor, after a *coup d'état*, ruling as Napoleon III, with absolute power. An era of progress for France, and of brilliance for *Paris* (in which Haussmann's town planning created the present pattern of boulevards). Ended by France's speedy defeat at Sedan in the Franco-Prussian war.
1870-1940	3rd Republic	Two-chamber legislature. The Republic began with the Germans in occupation of *Paris* (1870) survived the aggressions of World War I, and ended with the German occupation of most of France in 1940.
1940-1944	Vichy Government	Unoccupied France (about one-third Government of the country) under Pétain as Head of State, with supreme power, but increasingly under German instructions. In London de Gaulle formed a provisional government of the 4th Republic.
1944-1958	4th Republic	On the liberation of *Paris* (1944) de Gaulle's government recognized by Allies as government of France, and new constitution drawn up (1946).

		Instability of system shown by fall of twenty-six cabinets, 1946-58.
1958-	5th Republic	De Gaulle recalled. Present constitution drawn up and de Gaulle elected first President of 5th Republic. Pompidou as President 1969-73, Giscard d'Estaing in 1973, François Mitterand in 1981, and re-elected in 1988.

Government

Under the Constitution of the 5th Republic the position of the President (who is elected for seven years) has been greatly strengthened, both as executive head of the Republic and as President of the French Community, ie metropolitan France with the territories overseas. The Executive Council consists of the Prime Minister, the heads of government of each member state and of the ministers responsible to the Community for common affairs. On joining the Council ministers relinquish their parliamentary seats. Parliament consists of two chambers, the National Assembly, elected by universal adult suffrage, with proportional representation, and the Senate consisting of delegates of the Assembly and of those of other member states. Of its 284 members, 186 represent the French Republic.

For the purpose of administration, France is divided into ninety-five *départements* usually named after natural features, such as rivers. They are sub-divided into *arrondissements*, each of which is an electoral unit returning one representative to the Assemblée Nationale.

The *arrondissement* is divided into *cantons* and *communes*. A *canton* is a judicial unit and sends one representative to the Conseil Général of the *département*. The *commune* corresponds to a parish and is presided over by a *maire*. In large towns the *Maire* is a dignity of some importance, but in villages he often follows a humble calling. *Paris* is divided into twenty *arrondissements*, each with its *maire*.

Resources

France is famous for its quality products — fine wines, perfumes and clothing; but in the last fifty years or so large-scale industry has developed rapidly and France is now an important producer of coal, steel, textiles, chemicals and aluminium. Oil and natural gas are worked in the *Garonne basin*, making a major contribution to the country's power supply and although coal imports are necessary, there is a large export of iron ore.

Careful and intensive use of land is encouraged by the predominance of family holdings, and the country is largely self-sufficient in food. Agriculture employs about ten per cent of the working population. Arable farming preponderates north from *Bordeaux* and from the *Central Massif*, wheat being the chief cereal, especially where loam covers the chalk and limestone. Wheat is also grown in the south, as in *Languedoc* and the valleys of the middle *Rhône* and *Garonne*. Barley and oats are grown in the north, rye in the *Central Massif*, rice in the *Camargue*. Other main crops are potatoes (especially in *Brittany*) and beet.

Many varieties of fruit are grown; cider apples in the west and north-west; plums, currants and raspberries in the east; cherries in the *Rhône* valley and *Lorraine*; peaches in the neighbourhood of *Lyon*, and apricots, almonds, figs, oranges and olives in the south.

Cattle are raised to supply the increasing urban population with meat and milk, and to serve the milk product industries, especially for the cheeses, which are world famous. In the mountainous areas the cattle, together with the cowherds and the cheesemakers, spend the summer months on the high pastures (alps) at 6,000ft (1,800m) or more. The Provençal shepherds migrate to the *Dauphiné alps* with their sheep from June to October each year, contributing to beautiful pastoral scenes of chalet villages with cattle grazing, and the mellow sound of cow and goat bells.

Forestry is important, concentrated chiefly in the *Ardennes* and the forests of *Compiègne, Fontainebleau* and *Orléans*.

Sea fishing is practised on all the three great coasts of France, chiefly from the North Sea, Channel and Atlantic ports. The main fishing industry is centred in Brittany. Oysters are cultivated in the Bay of *Cancale*. Sardines are caught in the warmer southern waters and tunny is fished in the Atlantic.

Wines and Vineyards

France is the world's leading producer of fine wines and her vineyards are the most important section of her agriculture. It is interesting in touring France to notice the names of famous vineyards such as *Châteauneuf-du-Pape*, near *Avignon*, and to notice the effect of climate on the vintage; a wet season increases the juice but reduces the sugar content, so that often the quality is in inverse proportion to the quantity.

The principal wine growing areas are *Burgundy, Bordeaux, Champagne*, the *Loire* valley, *Alsace, Lorraine*, the *Rhône* valley and *Languedoc*.

Customs

The customs of hand shaking and cheek kissing are practised much more in France than in English-speaking countries. It is usual to shake hands always on greeting and parting from friends or acquaintances and kiss both cheeks of close friends; in the same way guests in a French home shake hands with their host and hostess when retiring at night and at breakfast next morning. Visiting cards are used for informal invitations and acceptances and for exchanging wishes on New

Year's day, in preference to sending cards at Christmas time. A pleasant custom is that of taking a gift or flowers or a gâteau to one's hostess when invited to dinner.

It is considered discourteous to address a person without using his or her title. In asking the way or shopping, people should always be addressed as Madame, Mademoiselle or Monsieur as the case may be.

Food and Meals

The French give a proper consideration to the art of eating and drinking; in this all classes and all income groups are connoisseurs. There is no hurried eating of snacks; the midday lunch break is from 12 noon to 2pm.

In the south, the cooking is very different from the north as olive oil is used in place of butter and margarine. The finest *cuisine* is said to be in *Touraine*, but every region has its special local dishes which are well worth trying and give an added interest to touring.

Sport

The younger generation is keen on sport and the open air. Association and Rugby football enjoy a considerable popularity. In addition, skiing has a large following, as has hunting (usually of hares or rabbits, on foot) in country districts, whilst the most popular sport of all is bicycle racing, culminating in the great *Tour de France* race in July, in which international competitors race all round France, through streets lined with cheering crowds.

Culture

France has a long tradition of excellence in the arts stretching from Roman times to the present day, and French influence has made itself felt in music, painting, literature and drama, architecture and the cinema.

Architecture

Some of the finest examples of Roman architecture are to be found in Provence. The magnificent theatre at *Orange*, whose façade is still almost complete, gives some idea of what the other theatres in *Paris, Lyon, Vienne* and *Arles* were like. The *Maison Carrée* at *Nîmes* and the similar temple at *Vienne*, the arenas at *Nîmes* and *Arles* and the beautiful *Pont du Gard* aqueduct all influenced the development locally of the Romanesque style of church architecture. This style came late in France (eleventh and twelfth centuries) but produced important regional variations as in *Auvergne* (the *chevet*), *Burgundy* (the pointed arch) and *Normandy* (ribbed vaulting).

From such elements sprang the supreme building achievement of the Middle

Ages — the Gothic style, originating in the *Ile de France* and becoming in the thirteenth century the model for church architecture throughout Christendom. The cathedrals of *Chartres, Amiens* and *Rheims* are among its finest examples.

The Renaissance movement, spreading from Italy, was taken up with enthusiasm and there emerged the French style of classical architecture so familiar today in public buildings all over France. An early example is the François I wing (1515-25) of the château at *Blois*, a later example the Mansart wing (1635-8) of the same château, and still later the *Louvre* front in *Paris*.

France again became the arbiter of taste with the secularized baroque of Louis XIV's *Versailles* (architects Le Vau and Mansart) and with the succeeding style of Louis XV, the rococo, which appealed so greatly to the princely courts of Germany. In the nineteenth century, the classical tradition continued in the great town planning schemes, such as Haussmann's for *Paris*.

Modern French architecture may be seen in all the larger towns. In *Paris*, examples are the *Palais de Chaillot*, the *Beaujon Hospital* and the *Maison Suisse* of the *Cité Universitaire* by Le Corbusier. Just outside *Marseille*, is Le Corbusier's *Cité Radieuse*, a city-within-a-city, with 2,000 inhabitants.

Dams, such as that at *Génissiat*, and beautiful, reinforced concrete bridges, show how successful contemporary French architects have been in combining function and appearance. Perhaps the most distinguished was André Coyne (1891-1960), designer of over a hundred remarkable dams including the great Kariba on the Zambesi.

Painting and Sculpture

Decorative sculpture was greatly developed in the Romanesque period. Its finest examples are included in the routes: *Moissac, Souillac, Beaulieu-sur-Dordogne, Vézelay, Issoire, Clermont-Ferrand (Notre Dame du Port)* and *Toulouse (St Sernin)*. Sculpture was again the characteristic art form of the Gothic period, when a new naturalism finds expression, seen in the west fronts of the cathedrals of *Chartres, Amiens,* and *Rheims. Chartres* is also the richest treasury of stained glass of the twelfth and thirteenth centuries .

With the coming of Renaissance, religious themes (and patrons) were no longer the sole inspiration, and painting becomes the chief means of artistic expression. The two great French artists of the seventeenth century are Poussin and Claude — the one classic, the other romantic; two contrasted modes of feeling which have since constantly recurred in French art. Claude's naturalism and atmospheric effects were developed further in the eighteenth century by Watteau, whose brilliant technique and careful observation prepared the way for the achievements of the nineteenth century.

Nowhere has the search for a satisfying idea of art been pursued with such relentless and uncompromising vigour as in France during the last 150 years. All the great movements have originated there, either through French artists or those attracted to the country to take part in this intellectual ferment.

Beginning with the classic Ingres and romantic colourist Delacroix, the line continues through the out-of-doors realism of Courbet, the painters of the Barbizon school and the Impressionists, with their revolutionary vision, to culminate in Cézanne, Gauguin, and van Gogh. Inspiration, even then, did not flag. Seurat allied classic forms to a *pointilliste* technique, and the twentieth century opened with Bonnard and Vuillard as self-styled prophets. But the shock troops of a new and disturbing artistic vision soon appeared: first, in the group called the Fauves, led by Matisse and Rouault and, a little later, in the first Cubist works of Picasso and Braque. Throughout the subsequent movements in twentieth-century art these men, especially Picasso and Matisse, retained their leadership.

Rodin (1840-1917) stands first among French sculptors in achievement and influence.

Music

Despite the importance of Couperin, Berlioz, Bizet and César Franck, the essentially French contribution to music was made by those who broke with the tradition of the great German composers. In particular, Debussy (1862-1918) opened up a new impressionistic world of sound and feeling; Ravel (1875-1937) was equally in revolt against romantic over-statement.

Literature

French literature, remarkable in range of thought and in versatility of expression, has faithfully reflected all aspects and periods of French civilization. Its writers have had a powerful influence on Western culture in general, particularly during times of transition. Its prestige throughout Europe in the 'Age of Enlightenment' in the eighteenth century was due to its long humanist tradition of confidence in man's powers of reasoning and observing, stemming respectively from Descartes and Montaigne. The tradition was inherited by Voltaire, Montesquieu, Condorcet and other providers of the philosophy of revolution and progress.

In contrast, but serving at first the same end, was the revolt against these intellectual concepts, seen in Rousseau's impassioned emphasis on feeling and the importance of individual freedom. Such ideas, taken up by Madame de Stael, led to the production of many works of romantic imagination by poets and novelists of the early nineteenth century, such as Hugo, Dumas and Stendhal.

A return to close observation of character and of the world around them is seen in the works of Balzac, Zola and de Maupassant. In the same period Baudelaire and the 'Symbolist' poets worked a revolution in the use of words comparable in influence to the work of the Impressionists in painting. They are the originators of modern poetry.

Among the many remarkable French writers of the twentieth century, perhaps the most influential have been Proust, on account of the depth and range of his fifteen-volume novel *Remembrance of Things Past*, and Sartre as the chief exponent of 'Existentialism'.

Theatres

The best known theatre in France is the *Comédie-Française* which has two buildings in Paris, the *Salle Richelieu* and the *Salle Luxembourg*. In the provinces most of the large cities have a theatre or opera house, usually with a weekly change of programme. Perhaps the most interesting are the Roman theatres, such as those at *Vienne* and *Orange*, where performances of plays and music are given during the summer.

Science

French scientists include some with a special claim to fame: Buffon (1707-88) the naturalist; Lamarck (1744-1829) the biologist and first person to state a theory of evolution; Lavoisier (1743-94) the founder of modern chemistry; Pasteur (1822-95) founder of bacteriology and of the techniques of immunization which make him rank as one of the greatest benefactors of mankind; A.H. Becquerel (1852-1908) discoverer of radio-activity; Pierre Curie, who followed up Becquerel's discovery and, with his wife Marie, discovered radium.

The work of Comte (1798-1857), the founder of positivism (which aims to bring all knowledge within the sphere of scientific investigation) has been particularly significant for the social sciences. It was Comte who coined the word 'sociology'.

Touring Information

Touring Areas

The following are the areas described in this chapter (**Route Nos 1-18**). Where, as in most cases, the best approach by train from Britain is via *Paris* (usually involving a change of stations) the station of departure is given in brackets.

Area	*Means of Access*
Normandy (R1 and 2)	Newhaven to Dieppe or Portsmouth to Le Havre.
Brittany (R3)	Southampton to Cherbourg/St Malo, Plymouth to Roscoff or Portsmouth to St Malo.
Châteaux of the Loire (R4)	Paris (Austerlitz) to Orléans or Tours.
Picardy and Champagne (R5)	Folkestone to Boulogne or Folkestone/Dover to Calais.
Ile de France and Burgundy (R10)	Paris (Lyon) to Dijon.

Alsace and Lorraine (R6)	Dover to Dunkerque to Nancy or Folkestone/ Dover to Calais to Strasbourg.
The Jura (R7)	Paris (Lyon) to Dijon.
The Alps (R8 and 9): Savoy	Paris (Lyon) to Chamonix, Annecy or Chambéry.
Dauphiné	Paris (Lyon) to Grenoble or Briançon.
Maritime	Paris (Lyon) to Nice.
Provence (R10)	Paris (Lyon) to Avignon.
Côte d'Azur (R11)	Paris (Lyon) to Marseille.
Auvergne (R12)	Paris (Lyon) or (Austerlitz) to Clermont-Ferrand.
Tarn Gorges and Cévennes (R13)	Clermont-Ferrand to Florac or Alès.
The Dordogne and other valleys of the south-west (R14)	Paris (Austerlitz) to Brive, Cahors or Toulouse.
The Pyrenees (R15):	
Western	Paris (Austerlitz) to Bayonne or Lourdes.
Central	Paris (Austerlitz) to Bagnères-de-Bigorre or Paris (Austerlitz) to Toulouse to Luchon.
Eastern	Paris (Austerlitz) to Perpignan.
Languedoc (R16 and 17)	Paris (Austerlitz) to Perpignan or Paris (Lyon) to Avignon.
Corsica (R18)	Marseille to Bastia or Ajaccio. Nice to Bastia, Calvi or Ajaccio.

Railways

The French Railways (SNCF) are very efficient and the system covers most of the country; their *TGV* trains, the fastest in Europe, operate to *Lyon*, *Valence*, *Aix-les Bains*, *Chambéry*, *Avignon*, *Nîmes*, *Montpellier* and *Marseille* and, except at peak times, ordinary fares apply. 'Tourist' tickets, giving a reduction of 25 per cent for 1,000km return or circular journey, are available. France Vacances tickets offer unlimited rail travel on all SNCF lines for 4, 9 or 16 days. An excess charge, in addition to the fare, is imposed on passengers boarding trains without having first bought a ticket. Although tickets can be bought at any time, they *must* be stamped, or 'composted' before use; orange coloured 'composter' machines stand outside every platform.

Bus Services

Most of these are run by SNCF and they often terminate at a railway station; only a few long distance routes but local bus services exist everywhere. Bicycles are usually carried on the roof. Bus fares are similar to those on the railways but alpine bus fares may be higher and a charge made for luggage.

Clothing

Visitors from countries which enjoy a more subdued climate should note that extremes of temperature can be experienced in the same season and that in the south, or in the mountains, it can be very hot by day and yet cold by night. Particularly when cycling in the mountains, sufficient woollen and windproof clothing should be carried to be donned at the top of the pass before descending. Failure to do this all too often results in a severe chill. Always take extra clothing when walking in the mountains.

Restaurants

Every town in France is amply provided with restaurants almost always providing a good, freshly cooked meal at any hour of the day. Menus are displayed outside, and it usually pays to have the set meal (*menu à prix fixe*) or the *menu touristique*. However, with *à la carte* service you can have as many or as few courses as you wish, and the *plat du jour* (today's special dish) will often make a meal on its own. Particularly economical are cafés advertising *casse-croûte à toute heure* (the nearest equivalent to a snack) and, in the cities, any establishment calling itself a *brasserie*.

It is always very much cheaper to buy fruit outside rather than to have it as a dessert in a restaurant.

Look at the bill after the meal to see if the service charge has been included; if not, the tip should be 12 to 15 per cent of the price shown. There is no service charge for coffee, etc, taken at a buffet counter, but you should add about 10 per cent for lemonade or beer served at a table.

Wine is relatively cheap. Mineral waters such as Perrier, Evian and Vichy are rather expensive, but pleasant. Beer is also obtainable and there are many other alcoholic drinks; the *apéritif* drunk before a meal, and the *liqueur* taken as a *digestif* afterwards.

Drinking Water and Milk

Many people remain doubtful to the safety of tap water in France although, in general, water supplies are regularly supervised and tap water is safe to drink.

Pasteurised milk in bottles is generally available in every town, but unpasteurised milk should always be boiled.

Holidays and Closing Days

There is no early closing day for shops in France and no formal closing on Sundays, still less on Saturdays. Some shops in some areas close on Mondays (either for the morning only or the whole day) while others close on Sundays. Banks are always closed on Sundays and either on Saturdays or on Mondays; on other days they close at 5pm. Most shops and banks are closed daily between 12 noon and 2pm but shops remain open until 6pm. Museums and art galleries are closed on Tuesdays.

Particular attention should be paid to public holidays (*jours de fête*) on which everything closes, almost without exception. In addition to New Year's day, Easter Monday, Whit Monday, and Christmas day the following public holidays are observed: Labour Day (1 May), Ascension (variable date in May), Bastille Day (14 July), Assumption (15 August), All Saints' Day (1 November) and Armistice Day (11 November).

Local Information

Information about local places of interest, train and bus times, pamphlets and maps, can be obtained, usually free of charge, from the office of the Syndicat d'Initiative to be found in all tourist resorts and most towns.

Maps

Michelin map No 989, a road map on scale 1:1,000,000 is recommended. For cycling the best maps are Michelin series, scale 1:200,000, whilst walkers should obtain the French Official Survey maps on a scale of 1:50,000.

Accommodation

In addition to listing youth hostels, the handbook of the French Youth Hostels Association (Fédération Unie des Auberges de Jeunesse), gives details of *maisons amies* and other hostel-type accommodation.

Camping

Possession of a *carte de campeur*, or international camping carnet, is not compulsory for camping in France but such a document is needed when using official campsites. International camping carnets are issued by the Camping and Caravanning Club to its members at 11 Lower Grosvenor Place, London SW1W 0EY and the Cyclists' Touring Club, Cotterell House, 69 Meadrow, Godalming, Surrey GU7 3HS, issues a similar document. Others may join the Camping Club de France, 218 Boulevard Saint-Germain, Paris 7; or the Touring Club de France, whose London agency is at 178 Piccadilly, London W1V 0BA. Camping on what may appear to be common land is always unwise, and discourteous, without first making enquiry and obtaining permission from the office of the local *maire*. Camping in state forests is permitted only on official sites.

Walking

The *Vosges* and the *Jura* provide splendid hill walking, as also do many parts of the *Pyrenees* and the *Alps*, for example the country between *Chamonix* and *Lake*

Geneva. The *Maritime Alps*, which are of little interest to climbers, await discovery by the walker.

In the *Central Massif: Auvergne*, the *Monts du Forez,* and the *Cévennes* offer many possibilities.

River valleys, from the *Meuse* in the north-east to the *Dordogne* and its tributaries, the *Corrèze* and the *Vezère*, in the south-west will repay leisurely and detailed exploration.

Waymarked routes cover more than 4,000 miles (6,500km); details may be had from Fédération Française de la Randonnée Pédestre, 92 Rue de Clignancourt, Paris 18; Fédération des Parcs Naturels de France, 45Rrue de Lisbonne, Paris 8, or from the local Syndicat d'Initiative.

Climbing

The best mountaineering is found in three regions: the *Savoy Alps* (centre *Chamonix*), chiefly comprising the *Mont Blanc* range; the *Dauphiné Alps* — *Meije, Ecrins, Bans* and *Pelvoux group* — centred round the small village of *La Bérarde*; and the *Pyrenees* (the *Vignemale, Mont Perdu, Balaïtous*, etc). *Cauterets* is a good centre.

The *Pyrenees* are a good starting place for guideless climbers who have some experience of gentler mountains. Although the scale is alpine there are only a few small glaciers and the ice-work as practised in *Dauphiné* or *Savoy* is seldom necessary here. While severe climbing may be found, the principal summits may be reached by reasonably easy routes. The Ledormeur Guide is excellent for the normal routes.

It cannot be too strongly emphasized that successful mountaineering in the higher ranges of the *Dauphiné* and *Savoy* is a serious undertaking, demanding considerable technical skill and physical fitness.

The Club Alpin Français, 7 Rue la Boétie, Paris 8, has huts in all the mountain areas, open to members and non-members; overnight fees are reasonable; reduced fees and advance booking facilities are available to members.

Skiing

There is good skiing in all the mountain regions of France. Class instruction is available at the main centres and there are often cable-railways or ski-hoists. The season in the *Alps* and *Pyrenees* is approximately end of December to April and in the *Vosges* and *Auvergne*, January to March. The best centres for skiing are usually those which are less popular in summer and beginners should avoid resorts which are also mountaineering centres, since the slopes are usually steep and difficult, eg *Chamonix*.

The UPCA (Union des Centres de Plein Air), 62 Rue de la Glacière, Paris 13, organises skiing courses in chalet accommodation; also climbing courses in the summer. The French Youth Hostels Association (FUAJ), 27 Rue Pajol, 75018 Paris also arrange winter sports holidays at many skiing centres.

Motoring

France has an excellent road network with many more miles of motorway than most other European countries — but these *autoroutes* are expensive with tolls on most of them. 'N' and 'D' roads are adequately surfaced, usually free from transcontinental freight lorries and, as they have lower speed limits and are often scenically beautiful, make for more agreeable motoring. Minor roads can be even more appealing to discriminating motorists, hence the routes described here shun the motorways.

Motorists belonging to the motoring organisations can obtain information and documentation on request. Speed limits are enforced, priority is given to traffic from the right — unless otherwise signalled by an international road sign, seat belts are mandatory, so too are flashing warning lights and a red warning triangle. Official booklet *Code de la Route* is on sale at all garages.

Cycling

Roads shown in red or yellow on Michelin maps are adequately surfaced and well kept but those shown in white often have a surface of loose stone or earth; cobbled stone surfaces, making cycling uncomfortable, may still be found in some towns.

If a cycle tour in the mountains is planned, it is well to remember that many passes are closed by snow between the end of September and the end of May or June. For cycling in mountainous districts a double chainwheel, giving ten speeds (2 x 5 'double-plateau' deraileur gear) is essential. Hub type 3-speeds are unknown in France and 27 x $1^1/_4$ in tyres nearly impossible to find.

SNCF provide an efficient bicycle hire service at more than 200 railway stations throughout the country.

The French equivalent of the CTC is Fédération Française de Cyclotourisme, 8 Rue Jean-Marie Jégo, 75013 Paris.

Canoeing

Canoeing and boating may be practised in most parts of France, and it is possible to cross the country from the Channel to the Mediterranean by river and canal. There is good sailing on the lakes of *Savoy* and around the coasts. Maps showing the possibilities of the rivers and streams are given in some of the folders on various districts issued by the Ministère de la Jeunesse, des Sports et des Loisirs, 8 Avenue de l'Opéra, Paris 12, and by the French Government Tourist Office, 178 Piccadilly, London W1V 0BA.

Paris

Practical Hints. Boat-trains from the French channel ports arrive at either the *St Lazare* or *Nord* stations; by road from *Dieppe* by D915 from *Calais* by the E15 motorway, from *Boulogne* by N1, or from *Le Havre* by the E05 motorway; by air at the *Aérogare des Invalides*. There are five youth hostels in Paris but only one is near the centre of the city, in *Boulevard Jules Ferry*, near *Place de la République*; others are in *Rue Vitruve*, near *Porte de Bagnolet,* Paris X, at *Choisy-le-Roi, Chatenay-Malabry* and *Cité Universitaire,* 27 Boulevard Jourdan, Paris XIV. Public transport: Métro (Underground) fares are on a flat-rate for single journey, any distance. For a stay of more than one day, or for a party, it is cheaper to buy a *carnet* of ten tickets valid on Métro and buses. Even more economical is the Sesame ticket, valid for 2, 4 or 7 consecutive days on the Metro, RER (suburban trains) and buses. Bus stops are marked by yellow discs on posts which bear route numbers and lists of principal stopping places. Where traffic is heavy, there is a box containing numbered tickets (take one, no charge) to indicate position in queue.

The most 'Parisian' shopping centres are the *Rue de Rivoli* and the area around the *Opéra* — shops such as *Printemps, Galeries Lafayette, Bon Marché*. Central Paris shops are open all day Saturday, closed Sunday and Monday, except for food shops, which open either on Sunday morning or on Monday and department stores, which open on Monday afternoons. Some suburban shops open on Mondays, notably *Boulevard de Clichy* near *Montmartre*.

The City — Quarter by Quarter

Ile de la Cité

The cradle of Paris, inhabited in pre-Roman times. *Pont Neuf*, the oldest bridge has statue of Henri IV. *Quai-des-Orfèvres*, France's Scotland Yard; *Palais de Justice* (Law Courts) old clock on corner, 1370, (closed Sundays). *Saint-Chapelle*, 1248, late Gothic, magnificent windows, carved door to upper chapel. Flower and cage-bird market near *Cité* Métro station. *Conciergerie*, Marie Antoinette imprisoned here. Cathedral of *Notre Dame*, mostly thirteenth century;

Key to plan of Paris
1 Arc de Triomphe. 2 Palais de Chaillot. 3 Eiffel Tower. 4 La Madeleine. 5 Opéra. 6 Place de la Concorde. 7 Louvre. 8 Invalides. 9 Palais de Justice. 10 Hôtel de Ville. 11 Notre Dame. 12 Palais du Luxembourg. 13 Panthéon. 14 The Sorbonne. 15 Tuileries Gardens. 16 Bastille. 17 Chamber of Deputies. 18 Pont Neuf. 19 Air Terminal (Aérogare des Invalides).

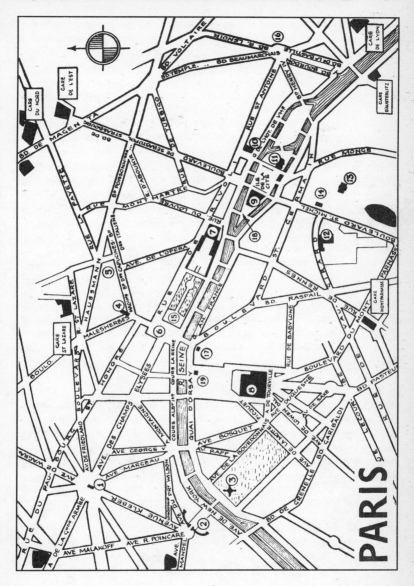

sculptured west door, fine nave, rose windows; scene of national celebrations —
Napoleon crowned here. Outside — flying buttresses, gargoyles. Fine view from
north tower.

Latin Quarter

Student quarter; *Boulevard St Michel* main thoroughfare. *Sorbonne*, University
of Paris, on left going up, between *Rue des Ecoles* and *Rue St Jacques*. *Panthéon*,
at end of *Rue Soufflot*, formerly a church, built 1754-1780; closed Tuesdays.
Contains tombs of great men, eg Rousseau, Voltaire; wall paintings depict history
of France and include Ste Geneviève, patron saint of Paris. Church of *St Etienne-
du-Mont*, north-east of *Panthéon*, sixteenth century; wonderful carved screen,
shrine of *Ste Geneviève*. *Arènes de Lutèce*, remains of Roman amphitheatre, near
Jardin des Plantes (zoo). *Luxembourg Gardens*, across *Boulevard St Michel*. *St
Germain-des-Prés* (1163) oldest church in Paris. Romanesque tower (1014).
Cheap accommodation can be found in this district.

Louvre and Tuileries

The *Louvre* was originally a royal palace, now an art gallery (closed Tuesdays).
Treasures include the *Victory of Samothrace*, *Venus de Milo*, *Mona Lisa*. Outside
are gardens with *Arc de Triomphe du Carrousel*. View under arch through
Tuileries Gardens, across *Place de la Concorde*, up *Champs Elysées* to *Arc de
Triomphe* — nearly 2 miles (3km). *Tuileries* — formal gardens. *Salle-du-Jeu-de-
Paume*, Impressionists paintings (closed Tuesdays). *Rue de Rivoli,* alongside
Tuileries — fashionable shops under arches. *Comédie-Française* — French
National Theatre.

Hôtel de Ville (City Hall) and District

Where Paris receives official guests. Built and furnished on the grand scale. *Ile-
St-Louis*, quiet provincial atmosphere. Old houses. *Place de la Bastille*, site of
prison destroyed in French Revolution (1789); part of site is marked by stones in
pavement between *Boulevard Henri IV* and *Rue St Antione*. Column commemorates revolutions of 1830 and 1848. To the north-west, *Place des Vosges,*
attractive secluded square. *Victor Hugo* museum. *Musée Carnavalet, Rue des
Francs-Bourgeois,* north-west of *Place des Vosges*; house of *Mme de Sévigné,*
museum of old Paris (closed Tuesdays).

Opéra and Madeleine

Opéra (1875), prices moderate, interior splendid. *Place de l' Opéra*, one of busiest
squares in Paris, centre of luxury shopping area. *Madeleine*, nineteenth-century
neo-classic church; *Rue Royale*, expensive shops; *Place Vendôme*, designed by
Mansart, fine architectural unity; Napoleon's victory column.

Place de la Concorde, Champs Elysées

Place de la Concorde, site of the guillotine during French Revolution, obelisk sent from Egypt to King Louis-Philippe. Across the bridge, *Palais Bourbon* (Chamber of Deputies). *Champs-Elysées*, wide avenue leading to *Arc de Triomphe* in *Place Charles de Gaulle*, from which twelve avenues radiate. Arch planned by Napoleon completed 1836. Sculpture by Rude, *Le Départ*, on right pillar. Tomb of Unknown Warrior beneath archway. View from top of arch (closed Tuesdays). *Avenue Foch* leads through smart residential district to *Bois de Boulogne*, large park, trees, ornamental gardens.

Eiffel Tower and Invalides

Eiffel Tower erected 1887-9 for Paris World Fair, 984ft (300m) high. Extensive views. *Palais de Chaillot*, built 1937, for Paris Exhibition, containing *Musée de l'Homme* (fine anthropological collection) and *Musée des Monuments Français et de la Fresque* (copies of frescoes from churches all over France). *Champ-de-Mars*, scene of Roman victory; military pageants under Napoleon. Nearby, in Rue de Lille, is *Musée d'Orsay* (largest collection of Impressionist paintings in France). *Ecole Militaire*, *Hôtel des Invalides*, built by Henri IV for his old soldiers (*invalides*); enlarged by Louis XIV. Tombs of Napoleon and other great military leaders, eg Marshal Foch, General Leclerc (closed Tuesdays).

Montmartre

Artists' quarter on right bank of river; old streets, cheap shops, very expensive restaurants and night clubs. *Sacré Coeur*, twentieth-century neo-Byzantine church; a superb view over Paris. *Place du Tertre* is nearby; almost entire square occupied by restaurant tables. Church of *St Pierre*, twelfth century.

Other Sights

Time should be found to walk along the *quais* by the river, with their second-hand bookstalls; or along the old tow-path, haunt of amateur fishermen.

The modern *Cité Universitaire* is near the *Porte d'Orléans*. Separate buildings house students of each nationality.

The Flea Market (*Marché aux Puces*) near *Porte de Clignancourt* and *Porte de Saint-Ouen* (18th *Arrondissement*) has over 1,000 stalls selling all kinds of antiques, curios and junk (open Saturdays, Sundays and Mondays).

Excursions from Paris

St Denis 6 miles (10km) north; bus from Métro station *Porte-de-la-Chapelle*. Abbey where many French kings are buried.

Versailles, 12¹/₂ miles (20km) south-west. Leave from *Gare Montparnasse*. Palace begun by Louis XIII, but mostly built by Louis XIV, statue is in courtyard. Vast rooms, tapestries, paintings. *Galerie-des-Glaces* (Hall of Mirrors) court ballroom; Treaty of Versailles signed here (1919). Gardens laid out by Le Nôtre under Louis XIV, superb example of formal garden. *Grand Trianon* (Louis XIV) and *Petit Trianon* (Louis XV) built to provide means of escape from court ceremonial. *Hameau* (hamlet) of Marie Antoinette, where she and ladies of her court played at leading a simple country life. *Musée-de-Voitures*, museum of state coaches, open weekday afternoons. Palace closed on Tuesdays.

Fontainebleau, 37 miles (59km); magnificent forest. Former Royal Palace, second only to *Versailles* — various periods, but mainly sixteenth and seventeenth century.

Rueil-Malmaison, 9 miles (14km); by train from *St Lazare* station or by bus from *Pont de Neuilly*. Empress Josephine's palace of *Malmaison* (closed Tuesdays). Rose gardens.

Touring Routes
Normandy

The Normans are partly descended from the Northmen (Scandinavians) who invaded the area in the eighth and ninth centuries. From 1066, when Duke William became King of England, until 1204 Normandy was ruled by English kings.

A pastoral countryside of lush meadows, rolling hills, farms and orchards, some woodland, and cliffs along sections of the coast. The first D-Day landings of the Allied invasion took place between *Arromanches* and *Courseulles* and many towns and villages suffered extensive war damage, now entirely repaired and rebuilt.

Local specialities include cider, perry (a similar drink made from pears), and calvados, a potent spirit distilled from cider; many varieties of cheese (Brie, Camembert, Pont l'Evêque, Petit Suisse); meat dishes based on pork; apple dishes and *pain chocolat*.

R1 Dieppe to Paris via Rouen and Seine Valley (130 miles, 210km)
Dieppe△ (Newhaven ferries tie-up alongside maritime station), fishing port; old castle; church of *St Jacques* thirteenth and fourteenth centuries.

Route from *Dieppe* to *Rouen* not particularly interesting, can well be covered by train in about an hour. If proceeding by road, leave main road N27 at *Sauqueville*, 5 miles (8km), and follow minor road along the valley of the *Scie* to *Longueville* (ruined castle), via *Auffay* and *Clères* (zoological garden in grounds of château); thence along the valley of the *Clérette* to *Malaunay*, rejoining main road N27 for *Rouen*.

Rouen industrial town, but a cultural centre too, important river-port, on the *Seine*, old capital of Normandy. In the Old Market Place Joan of Arc was burned

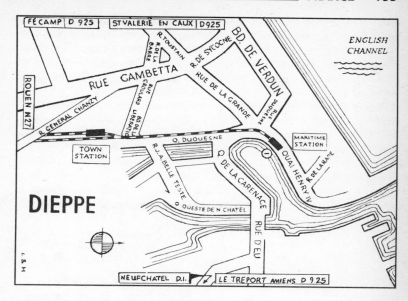

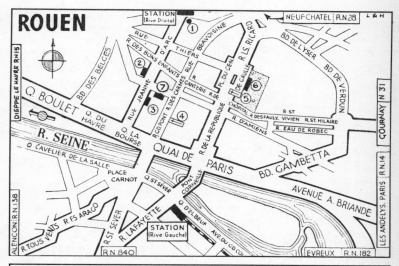

1 Tour Jeanne d' Arc. 2 Post Office. 3 Grosse Horloge. 4 Cathedral.
5 St Ouen Church. 6 Hôtel de Ville. 7 Law Courts (Palais de Justice).

at the stake. Cathedral (thirteenth to sixteenth century), *St Ouen* Church (four-teenth-fifteenth century), Law Courts (old Parliament, sixteenth century), *Grosse Horloge* (clock made in 1447 over an archway), *rue Eau-de-Robec* (old houses lining bridged stream) and several stylish examples of recent architecture. *Musée Flaubert* in *Rue de Lecat*. *Bonsecours* hill on N14 to south-east affords excellent view over city.

From *Rouen* to *Paris* by the *Seine* is a pleasant journey through undulating country, often wooded, with chalk bluffs above the river and a succession of attractive small towns and villages. Follow N840 through the forest of *Rouvray* to *Elbeuf* (cloth industry 600 years old), then by side roads on the north and east side of the river through *Les Andelys* (ruins of *Château Gaillard*; fine view of the *Seine*), forests of *Andelys* and *Vernon* Δ to *Giverny*; follow the River *Epte* to *Gasny*, returning to the *Seine* at *La Roche-Guyon* (old castle); *Haute Isle*, on N313, has a church cut in the rock and some cave-dwellings; on to *Meulan* (old town with *Oinville*Δ nearby) via *Mantes-la-Jolie* to *Saint Germain-en-Laye* (Renaissance palace, with museum of national antiquities). From here to *Paris* either via N13, visiting Napoleon's country house at *Malmaison* or by N184 to *Versailles*. The two trunk roads by-passing *St Germain* and *Versailles* are closed to cyclists.

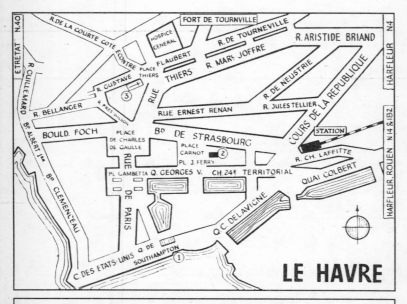

1 Portsmouth ferries dock here. 2 Post Office. 3 Cathedral.

R2 Dieppe to Cherbourg via Le Harve and Bayeux (175 miles, 282km)

Dieppe (see **R1**). Direct by N925, or by picturesque but rough, hilly, coast road D75, to *Saint-Valéry-en-Caux*, small port. Over *Caux* plateau to *Cany-Barville*, Renaissance church; seventeenth-century castle 1¹/₂ miles (2¹/₂km) south. *Fécamp*Δ cod-fishing port and home of Benedictine liqueur; twelfth-century Trinity Church; Benedictine Museum.

Yport (5 miles, 8km) *Etretat*, fine cliffs with the *Aiguille* rock rising 220ft (66m) out of the sea, twelfth-century church of Notre Dame.

On for 61 miles (98km) to **Le Havre**, third most important French port. Frequent ferry service from Portsmouth.

Cross River *Seine* by *Ponte de Tancarville* to *Honfleur*, picturesque port and old town; fifteenth-century church of *Ste Catherine* built of wood, with separate bell-tower; Eugène Boudin museum. *Trouville, Deauville*, seaside resorts which retain much of their turn-of-the-century appeal.

Caen, almost entirely rebuilt; was home of William the Conqueror before he became King of England. He built the castle and the *Abbaye-aux-Hommes* (St Stephen's Church) while his wife, Matilda, built the *Abbaye-aux-Dames* (Trinity Church). Church of *St Pierre* (thirteenth-sixteenth century). Daily ferry services Portsmouth/*Caen*.

EXCURSION: 18 miles (29km) south-west of *Caen* lies the *Bocage*, a region of miniature hills and gorges traversed by the River *Orne*; orchards and meadows alternate with woodlands.

Bayeux, thirteenth-century cathedral; Museum of Queen Matilda, containing the famous *Bayeux Tapestry*, seventy-two scenes of the Norman Conquest sewn on linen 23ft (70m) long, shortly after Conquest.

EXCURSION: to *Arromanches* (7 miles, 11km) one of main British landing points in 1944 invasion; remains of 'Mulberry' artificial harbour. Invasion museum on sea-front.

Through important dairy-farming area via *Isigny-sur-Mer*Δ to *Carentan*, old houses, old church; *Cherbourg*Δ, Atlantic port; ferry services to Channel Islands, Portsmouth and Rosslare. Musée de la Libération in citadel on *Montagne du Route* — and panoramic view — is 1 mile (1¹/₂km) north-west.

EXCURSION: West of *Cherbourg* lies peninsula of *La Hague*; wild rocky coast; fine high-level road from *Cap de la Hague* to *Nez de Jobourg* — cliffs more than 400ft (120m) high.

Brittany

Brittany, the last French province to come under the Crown (1492), did so only on condition that it should keep its customs and liberties, and the Bretons still retain some feeling of isolation and independence. They are descended from Celtic migrants from the west of Britain in the fifth and sixth centuries AD, and many speak Breton (as well as French), a language similar to Welsh and the old Cornish tongue. Women frequently wear the traditional lace cap (*coiffe*) which varies in style from region to region. The local costume, which appears at festivals, usually consists of a black dress, trimmed with velvet, and a beautiful apron richly embroidered and lace-trimmed.

The festivals of Brittany are called *pardons*, with religious processions in traditional costumes, followed by a village fair. *Calvaires*, heavily ornamented crosses with platforms carrying scenes from the New Testament and figures of saints are numerous, so too are churches dedicated to local saints.

Amongst the local specialities are fish and shell-fish (especially lobsters), pancakes and cider.

The most attractive coastal scenery is on the Atlantic seaboard, where magnificent sandy beaches alternate with granite rocks and cliffs, but there are many places of interest inland, and the suggested route includes both types of country.

R3 St Malo to Brest, via Rennes and South Brittany Coast (331 miles, 533km)

St Malo△, formerly a pirates' stronghold; walk around ramparts, almost intact, though medieval town carefully rebuilt after wartime destruction. Daily ferry services from Portsmouth.

R3 (i) to Mont St Michel. By coast road for 33 miles (53km). A rocky island, linked to the mainland (except at very high tide) by a causeway. A picturesque old village, flanks the south-east of the island and on the summit is a thirteenth-century abbey, with a church whose gallery is 400ft (122m) above sea level. From the ramparts superb views over the bay. One of the most interesting sights in France, but very crowded in summer. *Genets*△, on opposite side of bay.

By train or bus to *Rennes*△, capital of the old province of Brittany; *Museum of Breton History*; *Fine Arts Museum* with paintings by French school and Jordaens, Rubens; *Botanical Garden*. West by N24 for 38 miles (61km) to *Ploermel* and *Josselin* — very fine château on bank of River *Oust*. Cross the *Landes* (moors) to **Ste-Anne-d'Auray**, most famous place of pilgrimage in Brittany; Carthusian monastery open to visitors daily; *pardons* 25 and 26 July.

On for 12 miles (19km), south-westerly to **Carnac**, seaside village surrounded by world's greatest concentration of Neolithic and Early Bronze Age monuments. Tumulus of *Saint Michel* (to north-east) has underground tombs, and at *Ménec* (to north-west) are over 1,000 menhirs (standing stones) in long lines. Many isolated standing stones and dolmens (old tombs), including two on *Auray-Plouharnel* road, partly excavated. *Carnac* church is dedicated to *St Cornély*, patron saint of horned animals; blessing of local cattle on second Sunday in September.

Carnac-Plage — sea-bathing; view of *Quiberon* peninsula. At *Quiberon* Δ; *pardon* last Sunday in September.

EXCURSION: by boat from *Quiberon* 35 mins trip to *Belle-Ile*Δ; crumpled coastline, caves and grottoes, many bathing beaches.

From *Belz* across bridge to *Port Louis* and *Hennebont*. Remains of old fortifications at *Lorient*Δ, busy port, rebuilt after wartime bombing and shelling.

EXCURSION: by boat from *Lorient*, 45 mins trip to *Ile-de-Groix*Δ, composed entirely of schist; wild, sharply indented coast, but south shore has sheltered sandy beaches.

Pont-Scorff — picturesque village with pretty river valley to north. *Quimperlé* has upper town dominated by thirteenth-fifteenth-century church, *Notre Dame de l'Assumption*; lower town has church, *Ste Croix*, built on plan copies from that of Holy Sepulchre in Jerusalem. *Forêt de Carnoët* lies 2½ miles (4km) south. *Pont-Aven*; Gauguin lived here; Gauguin museum of Impressionist paintings. 'Gorse Bloom Festival' 1st Sunday in August. *Concarneau*Δ a sheltered beach on western side, tunny-fishing port. *Ville Close* (old walled town) on island; festival on penultimate Sunday in August. On for 4½ miles (7km) by hilly, winding road with pretty views to *La Forêt-Fouesnont*.

*Quimper*Δ In valley at confluence of *Steir* and *Odet*. Gothic cathedral with nineteenth-century twin spires, magnificent stained glass; chancel out of line with nave. Breton museum, rich art gallery in town hall. Festival on 4th Sunday in July. *Mont Frugy* (230ft, 70m) overlooks town; belvedere for view.

Audierne — lobster fishing. *Pardon* last Sunday in August. Beyond *Audierne* the country becomes wilder and the cliffs culminate in the *Pointe du Raz*, most westerly headland of France. Along the north coast the cliffs are continuous as far as *Douarnenez*, fishing port. 'Blessing of the Sea' 3rd Sunday in July. *Morgat* — small seaside resort. Visit caves: *Grandes Grottes* by boat, *Petites Grottes* accessible from shore at low tide. Excursions to magnificent rocky coast all round peninsula of *Crozon*. From *Le Fret*, ferry to *Brest*. Alternative by road: *Douarnenez-Brest* (50 miles (80km), via *Locronan* (fifteenth-century church of *Pénity*), *Châteaulin* (salmon fishing), *Plougastel-Daoulas* (excursions can be made to fruit-growing peninsula of *Plougastel* — old traditional way of life). *Brest*Δ important port and naval station, expertly reconstructed, after wartime devastion, retaining its traditional character. Small beaches westwards towards *St Mathieu*, headland facing Atlantic; *Ushant* in view from lighthouse.

The Loire Valley

This is pastoral country, soft and pleasant, with views of fields, woods and vineyards in every direction. The châteaux, for which this part of France is so well known, are mainly situated about the broad, slow-flowing *Loire* or its tributaries; there are more than a hundred of them between *Gien* and *Angers*.

In summer there are coach tours from *Blois, Tours* and *Saumur*, which enable several châteaux to be visited during one day; at other times of the year the local buses and trains are so infrequent as to make 'one day — one château' the rule, except for motorists or cyclists. Possibly the three finest châteaux are *Blois, Chambord*, and *Chenonceaux*, although the selection is largely a matter of taste. School parties and youth groups can obtain reduced admission charges to the State-owned châteaux *(Chambord, Chaumont, Azay)* and *Fontévrault* abbey by previous application to Service du Droit d'Entrée, Monuments Historiques, 3 Rue de Valois, Paris 1.

From June to October the castles of *Azay, Chambord, Chenonceaux, Loches*, and *Villandry* are floodlit after sundown. But apart from this the *Loire* is best visited out of season when coaches and crowds are absent.

R4 Paris to Saumur (210 miles, 338km)

The most direct route from *Paris* to the *Loire* is via *Etampes*, but the extra 30 miles (48km) spent on the detour via *Chartres* are well worth while.

Chartres △, 55 miles (88km) south-west, or one hour's journey by train, from *Gare Montparnasse*, has the most beautiful Gothic cathedral in Europe. Dissimilar spires — north twelfth century, south sixteenth century. Three magnificent entrances; the west is called a 'Bible in Stone'. Beautiful stained glass, mostly thirteenth century, was carefully dismantled and preserved throughout two World Wars. Carved choir screen, scenes from the life of Virgin Mary. The statues on the exterior of the building are the most important.

On for 45 miles (72km) to **Orléans** △, where cathedral re-built, seventeenth-nineteenth centuries in Gothic style. Famous as the town from which Joan of Arc drove the English in 1429. Important centre for road traffic.

Blois △ pleasant town, mostly rebuilt. Important château with wings in different styles. Church of *St Nicholas*, most beautiful; cathedral of *St Louis*, seventeenth century. Eleventh-century crypt. *Montlivault*△ is 1 mile (2km) further on.

Chambord 9 miles (14km) eastwards, is the largest of the châteaux, built in 1523, the royal palace of *François I*, standing in a vast park. *Beaugency*△ is nearby. *Beauregard,* about 5 miles (8km) south of *Blois,* near *Cellettes*, is a later building with a fine portrait-gallery. *Cheverny*, to the south-east, dates from 1634, but is still lived in; fine interior furnishings of seventeenth century.

Chaumont, standing above the river, and 12 miles (19km) south-west of *Blois* dates from 1475 and is more grimly medieval. *Amboise* castle dominates the small town and gives fine views up and down the river.

Leave the *Loire* by D31 via *Bléré* to *Chenonceaux*, a château whose beauty is greatly enhanced by its unusual situation — it is built like a bridge across the

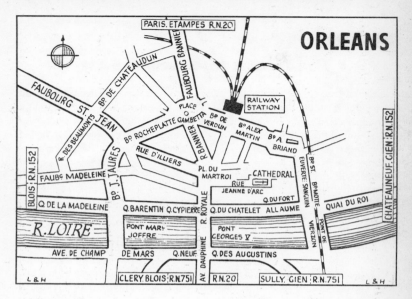

River *Cher*. On for 15 miles (24km) in south-easterly direction for the château of *Montrésor* (eleventh century, restored nineteenth century) with a fine collection of jewellery. Turn westwards for 11 miles (18km) to *Loches,* a charming little fortified town on the *Indre*, within which stands a château, once the home of Anne of Brittany, who married two French kings in succession; one ticket gives entry to the *Donjon, Logis Royaux, Tour Ronde* and *Martelet*.

Follow the River *Indre* westwards to nearby *Tours*Δ (a town less interesting than most others of the *Loire*) to *Montbazon* (ruined fortress); D17 to *Azay-le-Rideau*, a sixteenth-century château of great beauty built partly over River *Indre*.

Turn north to *Villandry*, on the *Loire*, a *château* remarkable for its magnificent ornamental gardens where vegetables are mixed with flowers and herbs. On to *Langeais*, a fortified fifteenth-century château, exterior preserved unchanged and original decoration within. Near the junction of *Indre* and *Loire* is the château of *Ussé*, a turreted building of fairy-tale quality (sixteenth century).

Chinon, on the River *Vienne*, is a picturesque little town whose château is famous for the first meeting between Joan of Arc and the Dauphin (Charles VII).

Near the junction of *Vienne* and *Loire* is the Abbey of *Fontévrault*, which provides a change of scene from the château and is well worth a visit. The abbey, which formerly housed a community of thousands, is a masterpiece of Romanesque architecture, and the church contains the death-masks of several English sovereigns, once buried there.

*Saumur*Δ marks almost the end of the château country and from the summit of its own château there is a fine view over the town and river.

The North and North-East

Flanders, Artois and Picardy will usually be visited en route from one of the Channel ports to the *Vosges* or central Europe. The low hills of *Artois* form the outer northern rim of the *Paris basin* dividing it from the intensely settled and industrialised *Plain of Flanders*, a small but important part of which is French territory. To the south-west of *Artois* lies the chalk upland of *Picardy* cut into separate blocks by the Rivers *Somme, Authie* and *Canche*, and to a large extent covered with the fine loam which permits intense cultivation. Absence of this loam in the chalklands of *Champagne* explains the contrast found here in the vast bare landscape. But the wealth of *Champagne* comes chiefly from its valley slopes with their famous vineyards.

R5 Picardy and Champagne to Lorraine (200 miles, 322km)

*Boulogne*Δ for 23 miles (37km) to *Montreuil*Δ. Continue on N1 until $2^1/_2$ miles (4km) south of *Vron*; take N338 through *Forest of Crécy*: panorama table north-east of village of *Crécy* (22 miles, 35km) on site of battle (1346); D12 to *St Riquier* (9 miles, 14km) abbey church, flamboyant Gothic; *Abbéville* (6 miles, 9km). D3 west side of *Somme* valley for 28 miles (40km) to **Amiens**Δ; cathedral late Gothic, largest in France famed for its perfect form and for statuary on door-arches; *Musée de Picardie*, archaeology, etc, and excellent collection of pictures from fifteenth century to Matisse; water-market on boats sells produce from reclaimed meanders of *Somme*.

D935 for 20 miles (32km) *Montdidier*; cemeteries and memorials of 1918 battles; on to *Compiègne*Δ (23 miles, 37km), Louis XV château, sixteenth-century town hall. D973 through *Forest of Compiègne*; *Pierrefonds* castle (restored); thence by N31 to *Soissons* (19 miles, 30km) market centre of *Soissannais*; cathedral Gothic with beautiful twelfth-century transept. Continue to *Fismes* (18 miles, 29km) and *Rheims* (17 miles, 27km).

RheimsΔ principal city of *Champagne*; has substantial remains of Roman architecture and magnificent cathedral (thirteenth to fifteenth centuries, restored; west front particularly fine); room in technical college where armistice signed at end of World War II; visits to *Pommery's* and other wine cellars can be arranged.

EXCURSION: to **Laon**, 30 miles (48km). Finely situated town with wide views over Picardy; cathedral (1160-1220) one of earliest Gothic buildings; walk on city walls (thirteenth century).

Soon after leaving *Rheims* the *Champagne* vineyards are reached; at *Epernay* the wine cellars of *Moët et Chandon* company can be visited. *Verzy*Δ and

*Châlons-sur-Marne*Δ are nearby; cathedral has interesting exterior and sixteenth-century stained glass. *St Dizier*Δ. *Bar-le-Duc*, old quarter of town has many houses of fifteenth to seventeenth century. *Ligny-en-Barrois*, fascinating small town of eighteenth-century buildings.

R5 (i) Alternative route (25 miles, 40km extra) from *Rheims* to *Nancy* via *Verdun*, scene of the worst battles of the 1914-18 war — a bleak part of France. *Metz*Δ, cathedral, exterior more interesting than interior, good stained glass; eighteenth-century *Hôtel de Ville* and several churches of interest.

Nancy, spacious and beautiful old capital of *Lorraine*; magnificently uniform *Place Stanislas* must be seen for its ensemble and the beautiful wrought-iron work; *Hôtel de Ville* and other buildings in the *Place* are worthy of attention; *Lorraine* museum in Duke's Palace; *Cordeliers'* church. Birthplace of Joan of Arc at *Domrémy*, just south-west of town.

Alsace and Lorraine

The provinces of *Alsace* and *Lorraine* record a chequered history, having been fought over and occupied by French and German troops in many wars. The local dialect (principally in *Alsace*) is basically German, but with a strong admixture of French.

The main attraction of this region for the tourist lies in the **Vosges** mountains, a fine range running from north to south for some 60 miles (about 100km), from *Strasbourg* to *Belfort*. The highest peaks, between 3,500ft and 4,500ft (1,070m and 1,370m), lie in the granite portion of the *Vosges*, south of *Strasbourg* and the River *Bruche*; to the north are the lower mountains of red sandstone. The mountains are well wooded, principally with conifers and beech trees, and the whole region is similar to the Black Forest of south-west Germany. The word *Ballon*, which appears in a number of place names, derives from the rounded shape of the hill tops. There is a good network of youth hostels and it is one of the finest pieces of country for walkers in the whole of France.

R6 Nancy to Belfort via Strasbourg (262 miles, 422km)

Nancy to *Lunéville*, eighteenth-century château; N59 to *Raon-l'Etape* and D392 through attractive forest-covered hills of northern *Vosges* to *Col du Donon*, old frontier between *Lorraine* and *Alsace*; climb to top of *Le Donon* 3,300ft (1,006m), good view of *Vosges*, plain of *Alsace* and Black Forest. *Grandfontaine*Δ, *Schirmeck*, small resort; down valley of River *Bruche* via *Molsheim*; Renaissance town hall.

StrasbourgΔ seat of European Parliament and capital of *Alsace*; one of the most attractive cities in France; cathedral fine Gothic style, built 1015-1439; very fine west front; spire 469ft (143m) high; astronomical clock — mechanical

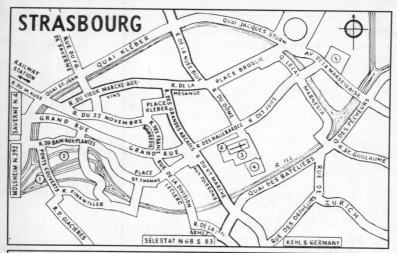

STRASBOURG

1 Ponts Couverts. 2 La Petite France. 3 Cathedral. 4 Château de Rohan.
5 Post Office. 6 Maison Kammerzell.

figures with procession of apostles at noon. Old part of town called *La Petite France* — well-preserved old houses bordering canal; *Rue du Bain-aux-Plantes* — narrow street with fine timbered houses; *Ponts Couverts* — bridges guarded by fourteenth-century towers; *Château de Rohan* — eighteenth-century palace, famous for connection with story of queen's necklace *(Marie* Antoinette*)*, containing fine museum of archaeology, ceramics and paintings; *Maison Kammerzell*, handsome fifteenth-century house.

Between *Strasbourg* and *Colmar* road follows circuitous route through interesting villages. *Obernai*, picturesque market place, sixteenth-century buildings, ramparts. Vineyards, then forest, *Mont Ste Odile*, crowned by convent from whose terrace is the wonderful view of plain of *Alsace*. Pilgrimages at Easter, Whitsun, 15 August. Nearby is *Mur Paien*, ancient wall 6 miles (nearly 10km) long, perhaps Celtic fortifications. *Le Hohwald*△, small resort in high valley surrounded by forests, *Sélestat*, picturesque old town; two interesting churches; ramparts and gateways. A few miles north of *Sélestat* the storks of *Alsace* usually assemble in second half of August for homeward flight to Africa. *Haut Koenigsbourg* — castle reconstructed in its original form; gives a superb panorama over surrounding country.

On to *Ribeauvillé* and then through important wine-growing region (Riesling, Traminer and other wines) to *Riquewihr*, charming little town with many quaint houses and corners.

*Colmar*Δ purely Alsatian in character, storks' nests perched on every height. Fine Museum *de Unterlinden*, cloister (thirteenth century), paintings of religious subjects by great masters, German Primitives. In medieval quarter are beautiful houses — *Ancienne Douane, Maison Pfister, Maison des Têtes.*

Continue up valley of River *Weiss* to *Col du Bonhomme*, along road giving splendid views; thence by mountain road named *Route des Crêtes* to *Col du Luschpach* (3,200ft, 975m) and *Col de la Schlucht* (3,700ft, 1,130m). *Lautenbach*Δ is nearby.

EXCURSIONS: 3 miles (5km) north of *La Schlucht*, footpath leads in 10 minutes to *Lac Vert*; green colour due to lichens suspended in water. Two-and-a-half miles (4km) south of *La Schlucht*, cart track in 1 mile (1½km) to the *Hohneck* (4,500ft, 1,270m) magnificent view; direction indicator.

R6 (i) Via upper valley of River *Vologne* (picturesque lakes), to **Gérardmer**, an all-year-round resort, good centre for excursions in the forests and hills. Fine lake over a mile long. *Xonrupt*Δ is nearby.

Continue on *Route des Crêtes* to *Grand Ballon* (4,700ft, 1,430m) highest point of the *Vosges*. View of three countries; the Alps can be seen on a clear day.

From *Cernay*Δ proceed via *Thann* (fine church of *St Thiébaut* sixteenth-century flamboyant style), via the picturesque *Route Joffre* to **Belfort**, fortified town in the *Belfort Gap* between *Vosges* and *Jura*; most of the houses are seventeenth century; château, and circuit of town ramparts for viewpoints; *Porte de Brisach,* fortified gateway; immense sculptured Lion of Belfort, commemorating defence of town in 1870.

EXCURSION: Via *Giromagny* to *Col du Ballon* Δ 17 miles (27km), fine view, ½ hour to summit of *Ballon d'Alsace*, 4,000ft (1,220m).

The Jura

South of *Belfort* the long ridges of the *Jura* mountains run north-east to south-west along the Swiss frontier. There are comparatively few tourists, and no grand hotels, but narrow river valleys, gorges, forests, waterfalls, and no less than seventy small lakes make an attractive and unspoiled region. The main industry of the mountain farms is the manufacture of Gruyère-type cheese in small co-operatives known as *fruitières*, and during the long rather severe winter a home-craft industry of wooden toy making.

R7 Dijon to Geneva (120 miles, 193km)
From *Dijon* (see **R10**) main road N5 rising on to the foothills at *Dôle*. From *Les Rousses*Δ, passing through an interesting area of forests, caves and subterranean streams to *Champagnole* and crossing main ridge of the *Jura* at *Col de la Faucille*

(4,070ft, 1,230m) with fine views on descent to *Lake Geneva*. From the col, the *Dôle* (5,653ft, 1,723m) can be climbed in 2 hours for possibly the finest view of the lake and the distant *Alps*; it can also be reached direct from *Les Rousses*.

The Alps

The zone of mountainous country, often 60 to 80 miles (100 to 130km) wide, which extends for some 250 miles (400km) from the Mediterranean to Lake Geneva is mostly in French territory, and the French Alps reaching 15,782ft (4,810m) in *Mont Blanc*, contain some of the finest mountain scenery in Europe. The outer ranges are of limestone, often exposed in sheer cliffs, usually with 'back-stairs' of grassy slopes, woods and fertile valleys. The central mass, including the highest peaks, is of granite or other hard rock, forming a landscape on the grandest scale, with extensive snowfields and glaciers, sharp pinnacles, and deep river valleys, forest clad on their lower slopes. South of *Briançon* owing to lower rainfall and brilliant sunshine, the country grows more arid, glaciers fewer, and alpine vegetation is replaced at lower levels by tough plants such as thyme, lavender, Aaron's rod. The chalet houses of Savoy (stone ground-floor, wooden upper storey) give way to square stone farmhouses. Further south are the parched, scrub-covered Maritime Alps, with small villages clinging to their slopes.

Several routes pass through the Alps to the Mediterranean the *Route des Grandes Alpes*, through *Briançon*; the *Route Napoléon*, through *Grenoble* and *Gap*; the railway from *Grenoble* via *Sisteron* or *Digne*. Motor coach services connect most of the main areas, and in summer there are many coach excursions. Buses serve many of the villages, though there may be only one bus each day.

R8 Thonon (Lake Geneva) to Nice, via the Route des Grandes Alpes (450 miles, 724km)

One of the finest mountain road routes in Europe. Many very steep passes 6,000ft (1,800m) or more, but practicable for experienced motorists and cyclists. Highest passes open only July-September, being snowed-up during rest of year, but detours, via valleys, can be taken.

Tourist motor coaches in three stages, each daily in high summer as follows: *Evian* (via *Thonon*) to *Chamonix*, 3 hours. *Chamonix* to *Briançon*, via *Galibier* and *Lauteret* passes, 12 hours. *Briançon* to *Nice* via *Izoard* and *Cayolle* passes, 11 hours.

Thonon-les-Bains, on *Lake Geneva*, a small resort, old town; bathing, sailing, lake steamers to *Geneva, Lausanne* and *Montreux*. Excursions into Alps. Take D902 up the valley of the *Dranse* (gorges), peaks rising to 6,000ft (1,800m), *Pont-des-Plagnettes* (2 miles, 3km to *Lake Montriond*), *Morzine*△ small mountain and ski resort, *Col des Gets*△ (3,845ft, 1,172m, view) through pine forests, *Gorge de Foron, Taninges*. *Praz-de-Lys*△ is nearby.

EXCURSION: by valley of the *Giffre* to *Cirque du Fer à Cheval* (15 miles, 24km, by road to *Sixt*; thence 4 miles, 6km). Here more than twenty waterfalls cascade down a half-circle of cliffs (best seen in June).

R8 (i) by bus to *Sixt* (10 miles, 16km) then on foot for fine two-day trip via *Col d'Anterne* (7,425ft, 2,263km), night at *Chalet de Moëde*, continue via *Col du Brévent* (6,975ft, 2,126m, fine view of *Mont Blanc*) and descend by cable railway or on foot to *Chamonix*. Passes on this route should not be attempted in bad weather or when the snow is still lying.

Continue via *Col du Châtillon*, descent into *Arve* valley, *Cluses* (watchmaking school, museum); road, rail and river continue between crags, valley widens, view of *Mont Blanc*, *Aiguilles de Varens* (8,163ft, 2,488m), *Saint-Gervais-les-Bains*, resort and spa.

R8 (ii) Up *Montjoie* valley to *Les Contamines* (5 miles, 8km south). From slopes of *Mont Joly* fine endways view of *Mont Blanc* range (*Aiguilles de Trélatête*, *Dômes de Miage*, *Aiguilles de Bionnassay*, glaciers).

R8 (iii) To *Chamonix* (13 miles, 21km east) by valley of the *Arve*. Gorges of the *Arve*, *Servoz* (Gorges of the *Diosaz* — entrance fee); narrow rocky defile; *Les Houches* — to the right *Dôme du Goûter*, *Mont Blanc*, *Aiguille du Midi*; *Les Bossons*, just below magnificent *Bossons* glacier. On left of road, practice-rocks of *Les Gaillands*. **Chamonix**, popular but expensive centre; many walks and graded climbs. Cable railways to *Brévent* (8,284ft, 2,525m), for extensive views of *Mont Blanc* range, also to *Aiguille du Midi* (12,608ft, 3,843m) in two stages, 16 minutes' journey. East of *Chamonix* many sharp rocky peaks, *Charmoz*, *Grépon*, *Dru*, etc. Excellent and often very difficult climbs. *Mer-de-Glace*, lower portion of immense *Géant Glacier*, *Argentières* centre for climbing peaks near Swiss frontier and the easier *Aiguilles Rousses* to west. Into *Switzerland* — on foot, *Col de Balme*; by road, *Col des Montets*, both good view points. Owing to the steep valley sides, skiing near *Chamonix* is not recommended for beginners. *Les Pélerins* △.

Chamonix is a suitable starting point for the classic **Tour du Mont Blanc**, a five to six days walking circuit of the range by low passes; *Col de Balme*, *Trient*, *Bovine*, *Champex*, *Ferret*, *Entrèves*, *Col de la Seigne*, *Col du Bonhomme*, *Les Contamines*, *Col de Tricot* and *Les Houches*. A road tunnel connects *Chamonix* with *Courmayeur* on the Italian side.

Mégève, well-known but expensive ski-resort, two cable-cars. Along river *Arly* to *Albertville*; old town of *Conflans*, on hillside, picturesquely medieval.

R8 (iv) To the north-east is the pleasant, unspoilt region of the **Beaufortin**, local costume frequently worn on Sundays, eg, at *Hauteluce*.

The road now enters the valley of the *Isère*, which becomes a long narrow trough, known as the *Tarentaise*. *Moûtiers*, chief town of region, is good centre for excursions.

EXCURSION: Mont Jovet (8,400ft, 2,560m); north-east of *Moûtiers*, 6-7 hours' easy climb; chalet hotel; magnificent view.

R8 (v) To *Pralognan* (18 miles, 29km; 4,600ft, 1,400m) best centre for *Vanoise* group of mountains; pine forests; fine scenery; good skiing.

Continue along *Isère*; valley widens; 19 miles (30km) to *Bourg-St Maurice; Séez*Δ nearby.

R8 (vi) To the **Little St Bernard Pass** (18 miles, 29km; 7,200ft, 2,195m). Excellent approach to the Italian valley of *Aosta* (largely French-speaking). Through bus to Aosta connects with train arriving at *Bourg* in early morning. *Little St Bernard* said to be pass crossed by Hannibal with his elephants.

Take D902 into the upper valley of the *Isère* (average gradient 1 in 17). Village of *Sainte-Foy*, perched 500ft (150m) above river. On the right *Mont Pourri* (12,428ft, 3,788m) and its glaciers, *Tignes*Δ, nearby barrage lake. Country becomes wilder and *Col de l'Iséran* (9,085ft, 2,769m, and seldom open before mid-June) is finally reached by many hairpin bends; fine views. *Tarentaise* group to north, *Maurienne* to south, and peaks along Italian frontier. Down the valley of the *Lenta* (average gradient 1 in 13) and into the *Maurienne* (valley of the River *Arc*); upper valley (above *Modane*) is pleasant; lower part industrialised and oppressively hot in summer. *Lanslebourg*Δ — junction for road via *Mont Cenis* into Italy; *Modane* — start of *Mont Cenis* railway tunnel.

At *Saint-Michel-de-Maurienne* leave N6 for D902 (this road number re-appears at intervals on *Route des Grandes Alpes*) ascending steeply through woods, fine views, to *Valloire*, small ski mountain resort, seventeenth-century church, local costume still worn on Sundays. The valley becomes wilder, gradient up to 1 in 12, *Col du Galibier*, 8,386ft (2,555m) (road through tunnel open only from July to September). Path to top of pass, 8,721ft (2,658m). View north includes three *Aiguilles d'Arves*, southward fine view of *Oisans* group, *La Meije* (13,065ft, 3,982m) surrounded by glaciers. Descend to *Col du Lauteret* (6,752ft, 2,058m) views, *Le Monêtier*, small spa; *Chantemerle* (cable railway to *Serre Chevalier*, 8,150ft, 2,484m with *Le Bez* Δ nearby).

Briançon, fortified old town on hill where four roads meet, picturesque streets, excellent walks in mountains all round town, which is 4,000ft (1,200m) above sea level. Road into Italy via *Montgenèvre* Pass.

Gorges of the *Cerveyrette*, forest, *Col d'Izoard* (7,835ft, 2,388m) fine view. *Casse Déserte*, extraordinary wilderness of sand and red rocks, into the valley of the *Guil*.

R8 (vii) To the east is *Château Queyras*, picturesque fortress, still garrisoned; high isolated *Queyras Valley*, refuge of the *Waldensian* Protestants, *St Véran* (6,693ft, 2,040m).

Gorges de la Guil, aproximately 7 miles (11km) long, road and river pass between marble cliffs then into open country at *Guillestre*. View of *Oisans* mountains to north, forests. *Sainte-Marie-de-Vars*, scree and pastures, *Col de Vars* (6,939ft, 2,115m), the boundary between *Dauphiné* and *Provence*. Descent through pastures and farms, *Saint-Paul-sur-Ubaye*, valley often wild and rugged; *Barcelonnette*, mountain and skiing resort.

Chestnuts and acacias give way to pines and larches, *Bachelard* gorges, waterfalls, *Col de la Cayolle* (7,717ft, 2,352m) fine view of *Var* valley and *Maritime Alps*. From here there is an almost unbroken downhill run of over 80 miles (about 130km) to *Nice*, following the valley of the River *Var*. *Gorges de Daluis* cut by the *Var* through wild reddish rocks, across limestone country to *Pont de Gueydan*.

At *Entrevaux*, an eighteenth-century fortress town, road joins light railway which runs down to *Nice* and follows it to *Pont-de-Cians* (for *Gorges du Cians* about 14 miles (22km) long, lower gorges in limestone, upper through red rocks, wild and picturesque), *Touët-sur-Var*, vineyards and olive groves, *Gorges du Ciaudan*, cliffs rising to 2,000ft (600m). Road continues down the valley of the *Var*, several perched villages. *Nice* (see **R11**). There are several unguarded level-crossings between *Entrevaux* and *Nice*.

R8 (viii) To bypass the *Col d'Iséran*. From *Albertville* follow N90 to *Saint-Pierre-d'Albigny*, then N6 up valley of River *Arc*, narrow and wild, forming the district of *Maurienne*. *Saint-Jean-de-Maurienne*, ancient capital of district, cathedral (twelfth to fifteenth century). *La Toussuire*Δ nearby. Saturday market at *Saint-Michel-de-Maurienne*.

R8 (ix) To bypass the *Col d'Izoard*. From *Briançon* by N94 follows the valley of the *Durance* to *L'Argentière* (for *Vallouise*, *Ailefroide*, excursions and climbs in Oisans group), *Mont-Dauphin*, fortress, *Guillestre*.

R8 (x) To bypass the *Col de la Cayolle*. At *Uvernet* (south of *Barcelonnette*) take D908 via gorges of the *Malune* to *Col d'Allos* (7,382ft, 2,250m, fine view during ascent), *La Foux* Δ, 4 miles (6km) south of col; then 6 miles (9km) to *Allos* village, small summer and winter resort (about 3 hours on foot to charming lake of *Allos*). *Colmars*, old walled town; *La Colle St Michel* (4,940ft, 1,506m); unbroken downhill run from here to *Nice*; beyond *Annot* (picturesque little town) rejoin main route, N202. Alternatively, 12 miles (19km) south of *La Colle St Michel*, join **R9** at *Castellane*.

R9 Geneva to Cannes by the Route Napoléon (290 miles, 467km)

This route, sometimes called the *Route des Alps* has not quite the impressive altitude of the *Routes des Grandes Alpes* (**R8**); it touches little more than 5,000ft (1,500m), and the passes are free of snow for a much longer period. South of *Grenoble* is the *Route Napoléon* proper, the route taken by the Emperor on his return from *Elba* in 1815. Note the milestones topped with the imperial eagle. Tourist motor coaches from *Geneva* to *Grenoble* in 4 hours, from *Grenoble* to *Cannes* in 9$^1/_2$ hours.

From *Geneva* to *Annecy* direct route is via *St Julien*, and N201 (15 miles, 24km) but alternative route via *Mont Salève*, 38 miles (about 60km), is recommended. Motorists and cyclists enter France at *Annemasse*, then follow winding N203 along crest of *Salève*, at 4,000ft (1,200m), with magnificent views over Alps and Lake *Geneva*. Walkers take tram from *Geneva (Rive)* to *Veyrier*, then cable railway to *Salève* and follow footpath and road along crest and down to *Cruseilles* (4-5 hours).

Annecy△ picturesque old town with arcaded streets, canals, medieval castle, in beautiful setting on lakeside; bathing, sailing, lake steamers in summer.

EXCURSION: to *Génissiat* dam, 25 miles (40km) north-west. Bus to *Frangy* (1 hour) thence about 8 miles (13km). Dam, 328ft (100m) high, across upper *Rhône*, with artificial lake 12 miles (19km) long.

Aix-les-Bains△, fashionable spa, about a mile from *Lac du Bourget*, France's largest lake, bathing, sailing. **Chambéry**, former capital of *Savoy*, tourist centre, but too far from mountains for excursions on foot; château, former home of Dukes of Savoy, and *Les Charmettes* (1$\frac{1}{4}$ miles, 2km, south), home of Rousseau and Mme de Warens. From *Chambéry* follow *Grésivaudan* valley (River *Isère*), richly cultivated with maize, vines and fruit.

Grenoble△ capital city of *Dauphiné; Palais de Justice* (sixteeenth century), Museum (good art collection), *Bastille* fort on north side of river (cable railway for view from summit 900ft (270m) above river).

EXCURSIONS: (a) to *St Nizier* from which the **Moucherotte** (6,253ft, 1,905m) can be climbed in 2$\frac{1}{2}$ hours; fine view of *Grenoble, Dauphiné Alps* and *Mont Blanc*. (b) to *Chamrousse*△ centre for climbing and skiing in *Belledonne* range.

R9 (i) alternative route from *Chambéry* to *Grenoble* via the **Grande Chartreuse** range; wooded slopes and sheer rock. D912 from *Chambéry*. *St Pierre-de-Chartreuse*, excellent centre for excursions, finely situated.

EXCURSIONS: (a) to the famous monastery of the *Grande Chartreuse* (3 miles, 5km, north-west) founded 1084, now mostly ruined, but partly inhabited by monks. Remains of big distillery, where *Chartreuse* liqueur made until 1935, are at *Fourvoirie*, 5 miles (8km) further west. (b) easy climbs to *Grand Som, Chamechaude, Charmant Som*, all about 6,000ft (1,800m), or to *Dent de Crolles*, with number of deep potholes.

Continue on D512 via *Col de Porte* (4,440ft, 1,353m) to *Grenoble*.

R9 (ii) South-west of *Grenoble* is the **Vercors** range, famous for the 'Resistance' particularly during 1944. Many forests, rock faces and gorges. Best circuit from *Grenoble* via *Villard-de-Lans*, gorges of the *Bourne, Pont-en-Royans, Petits Goulets, Grands Goulets* (gorges). *Corrençon*; climbing, caving and skiing.

R9 (iii) To join the *Route des Grandes Alpes* (**R8**) at **Col du Lauteret**: tourist bus from *Grenoble* in 3$\frac{1}{4}$ hours. Stiff cycling, but most rewarding scenery. From *Vizille* follow

N91 up valley of *Romanche* (lower part somewhat industrialised), dominated to the north by the *Belledonne* and *Sept Laux* ranges. Good rock-climbing. *Bourg d'Oisans*, small centre for *Oisans* region; excursions to *La Bérarde*, wild valley surrounded by highest peaks of the district. *Alpe d'Huez*△ skiing centre, Gorges of the *Infernet, Chambon Dam* (artificial lake), *La Grave*, large village, climbing and walking centre, fine view of *Meije* and other 13,000ft (4,000m) peaks. Fifty-five miles (88km) to the *Lauteret* pass, 6,752ft (2,058m) (see **R8**).

R9 (iv) From *Grenoble* to *Sisteron* the most direct route is by N75-E712 (89 miles, 143km) or by the railway, both crossing the *Col de la Croix Haute* (3,860ft, 1,177m) and giving a view (on right, between *Monestier* and *Clelles*) of the *Mont Aiguille*, a striking isolated rocky peak, 6,800ft (2,072m) high, first climbed in 1492 by soldiers of Charles VIII (said to be the first recorded mountaineering exploit in history).

The *Route Napoléon* proper, follows N85 from *Vizille*, passing *Laffrey* (four lakes, fine views, statue of Napoleon, commemorating Royalist troops who went over to his support) and *La Mure*, centre for *Valjouffrey* and other attractive valleys leading up to *Massif du Pelvoux* (mountaineering area, nature reserve) which can also be approached by the delightful *Valgaudemar* valley from *St Firmin*. Upper valley of River *Drac* can be explored from *Orcières*△, reached by turning off N85 at *St Bonnet* and taking D14 and D944 up valley beyond *Chabottes*. *Col Bayard* (4,088ft, 1,246m) descent through increasingly Mediterranean vegetation to *Gap* (large town) and valley of *Durance*, 39 miles (63km) further south, *Sisteron*, old town in narrow defile, with fine view from Citadel. Beyond *Digne* are the *Alpes de Provence*, bare sunbaked mountains where torrents have cut gorges known as *cluses*. *Col des Lèques* (3,765ft, 1,147m), hairpin-bend descent to *Castellane*, small town at foot of 600ft (180m) limestone cliff.

R9 (v) To magnificent canyons of the River *Verdon*, 13 miles (20km) long and in places nearly 2,300ft (700m) deep in limestone rock. Excellent views from road south of gorge (*Corniche Sublime*), particularly at *Balcons de la Mescla*. Walkers can follow the *Martel* footpath (occasionally threading through unlit tunnels) from *La Palud* via *La Mescla* to *Point Sublime* (about 8 hours; recommended, but stiff). Bus service *Castellane-Moustiers* passes *La Palud*△ .

Castellane to *Grasse*, fine road, crossing four passes including the *Col de Valferrière* (3,830ft, 1,167m, but open all year) with magnificent views to Mediterranean coast.

Grasse, a picturesque town built on the hillside above a flower-growing plain, is the centre of the French perfume industry. It has a twelfth-century church and museum devoted to the painter Fragonard. From *Grasse* the road winds steeply down to *Cannes* (see **R11**).

Ile de France, Burgundy, Saône and Rhône Valleys

R10 Paris to Marseille (500 miles, 800km)

This is the 'classic' tourist route from *Paris* to the *Riviera* by road N6 to *Lyon* then by N7. From the river valleys of the *Ile de France*, the route enters the wine-producing regions of *Bourgogne* (Burgundy) and *Côte d'Or*, continues between the *Mâconnais* hills and the poultry-farming region of *Bresse*, with distant views of the *Jura*, to *Lyon*, and down the *Rhône* valley into the sun-baked countryside of *Provence*. Depart from *Paris* for *Fontainebleau* and onto *Villiers-sous-Grez* 5 miles (8km) to south. *Sens*, cathedral (1130-60) earliest transitional building in France; treasury has vestments of Thomas à Becket. *Auxerre*, fine Gothic cathedral; church of *St Germain*, fifth and tenth century, ninth-century frescoes in crypt. Continue 25 miles (40km) southwards and at *Sermizelles* take D951 for 9 miles (14km) to *Vézelay*Δ, finely situated little town, magnificent Romanesque basilica, associations with Becket and Crusades. D957 to *Avallon*, thence by N6 to *Rouvray* , D70 to *Précy* and D980 to *Semur*, (39 miles or 63km in all from *Vézelay*), a delightful little town off the tourist routes; fortress, walks on ramparts and on low road from *Pont Joly*; eleventh-century church of *Notre Dame*; fine view of town and River *Armançon* from *Tour de l'Orle d'Or* which contains museum of *Auxois* history. On for 50 miles (80km) by road or railway to *Dijon*.

Dijon Δ old capital of Burgundy. Palace of Dukes of Burgundy — Louis XIV style (museum and art gallery, one of the finest in France); Archaeological Museum, *Magnin* Museum (paintings), *Musée Perrin de Puycousin* (folklore); cathedral of *St Bénigne*, Burgundian Gothic, thirteenth century; also churches of *Notre Dame* and *St Michel*. Many fine seventeenth-century houses. *Dijon* is famous for its good food, for such specialities as gingerbread, mustard, cassis and for Burgundy wines.

N74 for 24 miles (38km) to *Beaune*, famous wine centre; *Hôtel-Dieu* (Hospital), built 1450; nurses wear ancient costume; annual wine sale in November. *Châlon-sur-Saône*Δ (21 miles, 34km). N6 to *Tournus* (17 miles, 27km), *Abbey of l'An Mille; Burgundian Museum. Mâcon* (19 miles, 30km) famous boating centre.

> EXCURSION: Solutré, open-air encampment, late Old Stone Age, remarkable for fine workmanship of flints (small museum).

Lyon (42 miles, 67km); third city of France, on confluence of Saône and Rhône; famous for its *haute cuisine*, silks and many museums, especially *Musée de Tissus*, a new *Roman Museum*, built to mark the 2,000th birthday of the city, and *Fine Arts Museum (Place St Pierre)*. Cathedral of *St Jean-Baptise* (twelfth-century astronomical clock. Good view from tower of basilica of *Notre Dame de*

Fourvière. Picturesque streets; quays of *Rhône* and *Saône*. *Vénissieux* △ is 4 miles (6km) to south of city.

Vienne△, 17 miles (27km) Roman remains; Temple of Augustus and Livia; Roman theatre; twelfth- to fifteenth-century church of *St Maurice*. Route follows *Rhône*, between *Vivarais* mountains to the west and *Vercors* mountains to the east. On through *Valence* (45 miles, 72km) and *Mirmande*△ (18 miles, 29km) to *Montélimar* (9 miles, 14km), hometown of nougat. Canal connects Donzère and *Mondragon* and here is most powerful electricity plant in Europe. *Pont-St-Esprit*, famous bridge over the *Rhône,* largely thirteenth century, twenty-five arches. At *Orange*, 34 miles (55km), route enters *Provence* — Roman triumphal arch, nicely preserved Roman theatre; seats 7,000; plays performed in early August. Birthplace of Dutch royal house of Orange.

EXCURSION: to *Vaison-la-Romaine* (17 miles, 27km, north-east of *Orange*); fine excavated remains of Roman city; medieval upper town with Castle of the Counts. *Séguret*△ nearby.

Avignon 17 miles (27km), famous as the home of the Popes (exiled from Rome) from 1309 to 1403 and, as the residence of the Italian poet Petrarch. Fine city walls and gates. *Palace of the Popes*; open to visitors; guided tours; twelfth-century cathedral; *Promenade du Rocher des Doms*, good view; *Pont-Saint-Bénézet*, the bridge of the song, said to have been built by the shepherd boy *St Bénézet* and his disciples in the twelfth century; only four arches remain.

Across the river is *Villeneuve-lès-Avignon*, former town of the Cardinals. Fine view from *Tour Philip le Bel* and *Fort St André*. *Chartreuse du Val de Bénédiction* (fourteenth-century monastery).

EXCURSION: from *Avignon* by road, 18 miles (29km) eastwards via *L'Isle-sur-la-Sorgue* to *Fontaine de Vaucluse*△, beautiful still pool at foot of cliff, immortalised by Petrarch.

From *Avignon*, N100 west across hills to *Remoulins* (14 miles, 22km), thence 2 miles (3km) north-west to *Pont-du-Gard*, magnificent Roman aqueduct, in three tiers, nearly 900ft (270m) long, constructed 19BC, to carry water from *Uzès* to *Nîmes*. Through wine growing country to **Nîmes**△, 12 miles (19km), many important Roman buildings, *Maison Carrée,* well-preserved temple, finest piece of Roman architecture in France; arenas; Roman amphitheatre, still used for bull-fighting; *Temple of Diana* (ruins); *Tour Magne*, near *Jardin-de-la-Fontaine*, gives wide views.

Arles △, ancient and charming city; immense elliptical *Arènes Romaines*, seated 20,000 in Augustan times, now bull-fights in summer; view of *Camargue* and *Rhône* from top. Théâtre Antique, partly restored and still used. Romanesque *St* Trophîme, formerly cathedral; porch and cloisters are masterpieces. Fourth-century Roman baths, many museums.

R10 (i) The *Camargue*. South of *Arles* stretches the vast wild plain of the **Camargue**, partly cultivated, partly marsh. Nature reserve of the *Etang de Vaccarès*, with ibis, flamingoes and other birds. Cattle-breeding, wine and rice-growing. Herds of bulls and small white horses. Beware mosquitoes by night. *Aigues-Mortes*, city of the Middle Ages, entirely enclosed by walls and towers. At one time on the coast, it is now high and dry on account of the silt brought down by the *Rhône*. Tower of Constance is open to visitors. *Les-Saintes-Maries-de-la-Mer*△, according to tradition the place where Mary Magdalene and her companions landed when fleeing from persecution. Pilgrimage by the gipsies on 24 and 25 May and by local inhabitants on 21 October or first succeeding weekend in honour of their patron, Sarah, maid-servant to the refugees. Processions, local costumes, bull-fights. Picturesque village with fortified church.

Tarascon△ fifteenth-century castle, immortalised in *Tartarin de Tarascon*. Strike eastwards to *St Rémy* and 1 mile ($1^1/_2$km) south (on D5) to site of Greek and Roman city of *Glanum*; Roman mausoleum and triumphal arch still standing. Across the limestone hills of the *Alpilles* to *Les Baux*, curious ruined city built on a rock, with good views over the surrounding country; has given its name to bauxite (aluminium ore). Provençal custom of the shepherds bringing their lambs to Midnight Mass on Christmas Eve survives here.

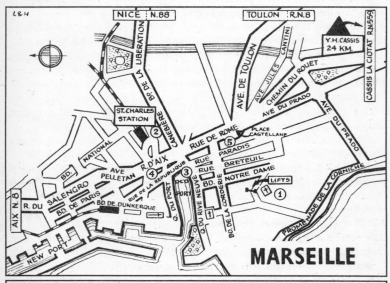

1 Notre Dame-de-la-Garde (church). 2 coaches for Cassis (youth hostel) start here — north side of Canebière. 3 Quai des Belges — boats for Château d'If. 4 Post Office (Rue Colbert). 5 Préfecture.

Continue eastward, up the *Touloubre* valley (gorges) across the plateau and down to *Aix-en-Provence*△, claimed to be the most beautiful town in France. Music festival in July; fifteenth- to sixteenth-century cathedral and cloister; many fine seventeenth- and eighteenth-century houses; many fountains.

Marseilles △, second city and chief port of France. Basilica of *Notre-Dame-de-la-Garde* (nineteenth century) superb viewpoint. *La Canebière* is the main street, centre of life and activity. The Old Port, a picturesque but vicious area to north of the old harbour, was blown up by the Germans in 1943. *Cité Radieuse*, an ultra-modern block of flats designed by Le Corbusier stands south-eastwards of the city.

EXCURSION: boat from *Quai des Belges* (at head of Old Port) to *Château d'If*, a fortress and former prison made famous by Dumas's *Count of Monte Cristo* (about 2 hours' round voyage).

The Côte d'Azur

Between *Marseille* and *Menton,* on the Italian frontier, lies the *Côte d' Azure*, the legendary Mediterranean coast which is frequently, but incorrectly, called the *French Riviera*; the *Riviera* proper is the easternmost of the five natural regions into which the coast is geographically divided.

The *Côte d'Azur* owes its fame largely to its climate, which is unique in Europe; the temperature of the sea, which remains constant at about 55°F (13°C), summer and winter alike, has a strong influence on the climate, giving an extraordinarily mild winter and a relatively fresh summer. This temperature refers to the open area, not to the shallower coastal waters which are much warmer in the summer. The tide rises only a few inches, and the sea, under the almost incessant sunshine, is brilliantly blue. In consequence of its international popularity the *Côte d'Azur* suffers from an excess of tourists and motor cars.

Daily coach service along coast road from *Marseille* to *Toulon* (2¼ hours), *Cannes* (9 hours), and *Nice* (10 hours).

The most famous local speciality is *bouillabaisse*, a kind of fish stew. Others are fish soup, shellfish, and dishes prepared from tomatoes and aubergines, many of them flavoured with garlic.

R11 Marseille — Menton (190 miles, 307km)
Côte des Calanques. The *calanques* are minature fjords between steep limestone cliffs; small sheltered harbours. From *Marseille* over *Col de Carpiagne* (1,070ft, 326m) and fine view to *Cassis*△, picturesque *calanques* to south-west. Good coast walk from here to *La Coitat* (6 miles, 9km). Road continues via *Bandol* and *Sanary*, quiet and attractive little resorts with fishing ports, to *Toulon* — large naval port; charming old town.

Côtes des Maures, wide bays between granite headlands; a few miles inland the wild, wooded hills of the *Maures* rising to 2,000ft (600m) (pine, cork-oak and chestnut forests). The railway leaves the coast at *Toulon* and bypasses the *Maures* region, making this part of the coast less crowded than other parts. Taking the coast road from *Toulon*, proceed to *Hyères*, picturesque old Provençal town. On for 5 miles (8km) to *Giens* for boat to island of *Porquerolles*, ideal for camping, or from *Salins d'Hyères* for boat to island of *Port Cros*. From *Le Lavandou* the road follows the coast for 15 miles (24km) of splendid views, then turns inland through plantations of cork trees to *La Foux;* 3 miles (5km) along coast to fashionable *St Tropez*, then 5 miles (8km) inland to *Grimaud*, good example of *village perchè*, old Provençal village built high on hillside for safety; 8 miles (13km) north is *La Garde-Freinet*. Quiet sandy coast, with pine plantations, ideal for camping (where not forbidden) to *Fréjus*△, town founded by Julius Caesar, Roman ruins, amphitheatre and theatre; fifth-century baptistry, thirteenth-century cloister and cathedral. At *Fréjus* the railway rejoins the coast road.

The Esterel. Splendid coast road, often cut out of the rock; small bays between red cliffs (porphyry) with red rocks and islets. The hills are not high but are wild, with many ravines and gorges; very few villages and inns in the interior; heather and other flowering shrubs grow beneath the pines and cork-oaks. *Le Trayas*△, on coast. **Cannes**, discovered in 1834 by Lord Brougham, a British Lord Chancellor, on his way to Nice. Aristocratic winter resort, now all-year-round haunt of film stars and millionaires. Annual film festival in April. *Boulevard de la Croisette*, fashionable promenade where battles of flowers take place.

EXCURSION: to the beautiful pine-covered *Lérins* (islands) by boat from the harbour near the Municipal Casino. On *Ile Ste Marguerite* is fort which housed the prisoner in Dumas's *Man in the Iron Mask* from 1687-98.

Côte d'Antibes. A flatter coastline, with large bays. From *Cannes* to *Antibes* the coast is almost completely urbanised and unattractive. *Antibes* is the centre of the flower-growing industry. *Cagnes*, old town, picturesque walls, gates, castle.

Nice△ popular, relatively inexpensive resort with Italian atmosphere (it was ceded to France, by the House of Savoy, in 1860). *Promenade des Anglais*, pretty old town and flower market. Port and departure point for *Corsica;* see **R18**. Carnival (early February) for twelve days — processions, fireworks, battle of flowers and confetti.

EXCURSIONS: Numerous excursions into Maritime Alps, such as to *Gorges du Loup* (picturesque winding road, 30 miles (48km), via *Gattières* and *Vence*) 6 mile (10km) long gorge with many waterfalls.

Riviera. Here the *Maritime Alps* rise from the Mediterranean, reaching 4,000ft (approx 1,200m) a few miles inland, and the three *Corniche* roads, with splendid views, lead to *Menton*.

The *Corniche Inférieure* follows the coast to *Villefranche*, for *Cap Ferrat* and the Principality of *Monaco* — no customs barrier, but own postage stamps. *Monaco*, Prince's Palace in Italian Renaissance style. Aquarium is one of best in Europe. **Monte Carlo**, Casino and Opera House, good view from terrace. Art Gallery.

The *Moyenne Corniche* is a road some 1,200ft (350m) above the sea. *Eze*, one of the 'perched villages', built on a rocky height for protection, now almost uninhabited, has picturesque steps and narrow streets, with fine views of coast. The *Grande Corniche* was constructed by Napoleon on an old Roman road, rising to nearly 1,700ft (500m). At *La Turbie* is *Trophée d'Auguste*, ruined but impressive Roman monument. Best view of coast from *Roquebrune*, tenth-century fortified village and castle.

Menton △ favoured climate all the year round. Harbour, interesting old quarter built on the hillside. Lemon-gathering *fêtes*, second half of February. Carnivals begin in August and continue into September.

The Central Massif

The *Central Massif*, occupying one sixth of the country, has great diversity of scenery reflecting its complex geological structure. Uplifted crystalline rocks form the *Limousin* plateau on the west and north-west and again predominate in the forest and meadow-covered *Monts du Forez* between *Vichy* and *Le Puy*; later sediments occur as coal measures and as the bare limestone plateaux of the *Causses* in the south. The heart of the region is characterized by past volcanic activity, seen in the lava plateau of *Aubrac* and the spectacular volcanic cones (*puys*) of *Auvergne*. In the south-east, the *Massif* ends abruptly in the torrent-riven granite and slate scarps of the *Cévennes*, a region of chestnut woods and oak scrub, whose isolated villages were strongholds of the Huguenots and where Protestantism remains stronger than elsewhere in France.

Architecturally the main interest is in the Romanesque churches of *Auvergne*, often built as the place of rest of a treasured statue of the Virgin and the object of pilgrimages from afar. Particularly renowned for their beauty are the exteriors of the eastern ends of these churches; the *chevets* (radiating chapels) were a local feature which later influenced the rise of Gothic in the *Ile de France*.

R12 Circuit of Auvergne from Clermont (260 miles, 420km)
Clermont-Ferrand △ main communications centre for southern central France, lying at the foot of the *Puy de Dôme* and on the edge of a rich plain. Cathedral, thirteenth-century Gothic, some good glass. More interesting is the fine church of *Notre Dame du Port* (eleventh- and twelfth-century Romanesque), fine east end, capitals of pillars of ambulatory carved with figures. Old part of town merits interest — see courtyard of No 3 *Rue des Chausettiers*, thirteenth century. Petrifying springs at *La Fontaine du Pont Naturel* and *Les Grottes du Peron*.

Several museums. Excursions to *Royat*, spa, fortified church of *St Léger*.

Leave *Clermont* by D941A to **Puy de Dôme** (4,800ft, 1,463m), or by footpath from *Col de Ceyssat*. Fine panorama of the *Dôme* group, nearly sixty extinct volcanoes at heights between 3,000 and 4,000ft (900-1,200m), some with rounded summits, others containing craters. Summits easily accessible; two of the most interesting are the *Puy de Pariou* (crater 300ft, 90m deep) and the *Puy de la Vache*, near *Randanne*, where lava stream nearly 4 miles (6km) long has blocked valley to form lake of *Aydat*.

Continue by secondary road via *St Bonnet* to *Orcival*, fine Romanesque church; behind the high altar, twelfth-century statue of Virgin. Return to main road near *Col de Guéry* (4,147ft, 1,264m) fine views of *Roche Tuilière* and *Roche Tanadoire*; Lake *Guéry*. The road enters the *Mont Dore* mountain group. *Banne d'Ordanche* (4,900ft, 1,493m) good view.

Le Mont-Dore△ resort and spa; winter sports. *Puy de Sancy* (6,188ft, 1,886m) highest point of Central France. Ascent by cable railway then 20 minutes walk. Superb view as far as *Dauphiné Alps* on a clear day. Five miles (8km) to *La Bourboule*, pleasant resort; excursion to gorges of the *Avèze*.

By N496 over *Col de la Croix Morland* to *Chambon* — attractive lake, boating, swimming, *Murol*, picturesque (2,500ft, 760m), medieval castle.

At *Grandeyrolles* take D978 to south. Near *Le Cheix* are the *Grottes de Jonas* — caves inhabited in prehistoric times (entrance fee). From *Le Cheix* a detour may be made via *Saurier* and the fine gorges of the *Courgoul*. *Besse-en-Chandesse*, old fortified town, picturesque houses built of lava. Lake *Pavin* — beautiful lake containing large trout. Easy walk to summit of *Puy de Montchal* (4,600ft, 1,402m). To the west the plateau of *Artense*, several lakes and marshes, to the east are the pasturelands of the *Cézallier* mountains. *Condat*, barrage-lake of *Essarts*; fine wooded gorges of the *Rhue*.

Take D679 to *Bort-les-Orgues*, on River *Dordogne*, pleasant little town named after the basalt 'organ pipes' which rise above it; good view from summit. Large hydro-electric scheme has transformed the upper valley of the *Dordogne* into a series of lakes. Dams at *Barrage de Marèges* and *La Triouzoune*. For lower *Dordogne* see **R14**.

Mauriac, agreeable town in pleasant situation; basilica of *Notre Dame des Miracles* is possibly the finest Romanesque church in the *Auvergne*. Continue either via the beautiful valley of *Falgoux* and the gorge of *St Vincent* or via D122 and D22 through *Salers*, picturesque fortified town with fine old mansions; *Grande Place* should be seen; sixteenth-century church. *Col de Néronne* to the *Cirque de Falgoux* below the *Puy Mary* (5,860ft, 1,786m) for a fine view of the *Cantal Mountains*.

Continue by the *Pas de Peyrol* (5,210ft, 1,588m) and the valley of *Mandailles* to *Aurillac*, new town built around picturesque old quarter; fourteenth- and fifteenth-century churches, old mansions; view of old quarter from *Pont Rouge*.

Follow N122 along fine wide valley of the *Cère* at an altitude of 2,000ft (600m), *Vic-sur-Cère* — small spa; House of the Princes of Monaco (fifteenth century); Romanesque church. The road climbs up by the *Pas de la Cère*, a rocky ravine, and the waterfall of *La Roucole*, to *St-Jacques-des-Blats* on the heights of the *Cantal*. Several peaks can be climbed from the head of the valley, such as *Puy Griou* (5,600ft, 1,706m), *Puy de la Poche* (4,900ft, 1,493m) and the *Plomb du Cantal* (6,090ft, 1,856m) highest peak of the *Cantal* group. Through the tunnel of *Lioran* into the narrow valley of the *Alagnon*.

Murat, town dominated by statue of the Virgin on a rocky height. Eastwards on D926 to *St Flour* (3,000ft, 915m) picturesque and fortified; has hottest spa waters in France; cathedral, severe fifteenth-century Gothic, seventeenth-century Town Hall.

> **R12 (i)** From *St Flour*, long but worthwhile detour to town of *Le Puy*. D990 and D590 over the forest plateau of *Margeride*, crossing the *Allier* at *Langeac*. **Le-Puy-en-Velay** — fantastic sight from the distance; town built round three volcanic cones. Fine Romanesque cathedral on steep rock shows Moslem influence and contains famous 'Black Virgin': notice vaults of the nave, west front, cloisters; interesting relics, Bible of the time of Charlemagne; many other churches. Return from *Le Puy* to *Clermont* (80 miles, 130km) via *Brioude*, joining N9 at *Lempdes* (excursion to gorges of the *Alagnon*).

The direct route from *St Flour* to *Clermont* follows N9 over *Col de la Fagéole* 3,373ft (1,028m) on to the plateau of the *Margeride*; valley of the *Allier*, particularly attractive between *Issoire* (which has famous Auvergne-Romanesque church) and *Coudes*. Pass beautiful hilly plateau of *Gergovie*, scene of victory of Vercingetorix over Julius Caesar (monument), and enter *Clermont*.

R13 The Tarn Gorges and the Cévennes — Circuit from Florac (185 miles, 240km)

To the west is the region of the *Causses*, originally covered with forest, but now stony upland plateau with just enough vegetation for sheep grazing, cut by fantastic gorges and narrow river valleys. Eastwards, between the river valleys of the *Ardèche* and *Hérault*, lie the *Cévennes*, wild and beautiful upland country of pine and chestnut forests, barren moors and grassland; little known outside France.

Start at *Florac*, a pleasant little town on the N106, 27 miles (46km) from *Ste-Cécile-d'Andorge* on the *Clermont-Ferrand* to *Nîmes* railway. Original footpath through the Gorges has become D907B, convenient for motorists and cyclists but regrettable for walkers.

After *Florac* go northwards for 5 miles (8km) to *Ispagnac*, small town at entrance to canyon, with twelfth-century Romanesque church. *Quézac* has seventeenth-century bridge and earlier church. *Castelbouc*, curious village worth small detour off route. *Ste-Enimie*, picturesque village below cliffs of gorge. *St Chély* and *Cirque de St Chély*, pretty village and natural amphitheatre of cliffs.

Château de la Caze, fifteenth-century castle in fine setting at river's edge. *La Malêne* is starting point for boat trip through the narrowest part of the gorge where cliffs rise to 1,200ft (360m) to the *Cirque des Baumes*. On to *Pas de Seuci* where river disappears beneath heaps of rocks, then to little village of *Les Vignes* where excursion to *Point Sublime* is recommended; impressive viewpoint at 1,300ft (400m) above riverbed.

Continue to *Le Rozier* at junction of Rivers *Tarn* and *Jonte* and 33 miles (54km) from *Ispagnac*; make excursion to *Montpellier-le-Vieux* where bizarre and lofty assemblage of natural rocks affords fine views. A circular trip can be made down the *Tarn* to *Millau△*, famous for its glove-making industry, among almond and peach trees, returning to *Le Rozier* by the valley of the *Dourbie*, including excursion to *Montpellier-le-Vieux*.

Follow D996 for 13 miles (21km) through the gorges of the *Jonte*; less grandiose than the *Tarn* but equally impressive because of their narrowness. *Belvédère des Terrasses* for fine view over the gorge and on to *Meyrueis*, standing at 2,200ft (670m) at entrance to the gorges.

EXCURSIONS: (a) *Aven Armand* — large underground grotto filled with stalactites and stalagmites of remarkable forms. (b) grotto of *Dargilan* — the most remarkable of the caverns in the district; several impressive chambers containing a variety of stalactite formations. (c) *La Couvertoirade*, fortified centre of Templars of fifteenth century. Twenty miles (32km) south of *Le Rozier*, via *Montpellier-le-Vieux* and *Gorges de la Dourbie*.

Southwards, then eastwards for 15 miles (25km) via *Col de Montjardin* and *Bramabiou* where underground stream reappears as waterfall, and on to *Col de la Séreyède* for excursion to *Mont Aigoual* (5,139ft, 1,567m) highest point of *Cévennes*. Follow river valley of *Hérault* to *Vallerauge* and *Ganges* (30 miles, 48km), then work north-eastwards for 18 miles (30km) to *St Jean du Gard*, typical old town of the *Cévennes*, and by D9 ridge road, *Corniche des Cévennes*, for 33 miles (53km) to *Florac*.

R13 (i) Alternatively, continue south to *St Bauzille de Putois* and make excursion to *Grottes des Demoiselles*, several large caverns with stalactite formations. *Causse de la Selle*, Gorges of the *Hérault*. *St Guilhem le Désert*, eleventh-century abbey church. *Pont au Diable*, thence to *Montpellier* and the Mediterranean (*Ganges — Montpellier* 45 miles, 72km).

Périgord, Quercy and Toulouse

The middle reaches of the rivers of the *Garonne* system, rising either in the *Central Massif* or the *Pyrenees*, provide some of the most beautiful valley scenery in France. The *Dordogne* and *Lot* and their tributaries have cut deeply into high limestone country, making a striking contrast between their fertile banks and the arid *causses* above. The region was much fought over during the Hundred Years' War with England and the *bastides*, towns constructed as fortresses, are reminders of the time when *Aquitaine* was under the English Crown.

R14 Mauriac, Lascaux, Toulouse (290 miles, 470km)

The route is planned to link with **R12** but can be joined direct from *Brive*△, 4 hours by train from *Paris* on main *Toulouse* line. *Brive* can be used as base for walks in the *Corrèze* valley before following the *Vézère* via *Terrasson* to *Lascaux*.

From *Mauriac* (**R12**) on D678 for 11 miles (17km) to *Spontour*△, thence following D18 for 30 miles (49km) to *Argentat*, picturesque town on *Dordogne*; thence on D12 for 15 miles (25km) following river to *Beaulieu*△, Romanesque church of Benedictine abbey, and twelfth-century penitents' church. Take the D940 due south for 5 miles (8km) to *Castelnau*.

EXCURSION: *Gouffre de Padirac*, deep underground river and lakes; *Rocamadour*, village built on cliff below sanctuary of Black Virgin, object of medieval pilgrimages; over-run in summer.

Souillac, 25 miles (40km) fine Romanesque church. At *Montfort*, 16 miles (26km) cross river to *Domme, bastide* town, thirteenth century; *Belvédère de la Barre* for panorama of *Dordogne* valley. Re-cross river on D46 northwards for 6 miles (10km) to *Sarlat*△, lovely little town, once capital of *Périgord Nord*, winding streets, medieval and Renaissance buildings. Near *Montignac* on the *Vézère*, 15 miles (25km) northwards on D704, is **Grotte de Lascaux** where world-famous decorated caves lie $1^1/_4$ miles (2km) south-eastwards at 700ft (216m). Discovered by chance by boys with dog in 1940. Stylised paintings and engravings of the wild animals hunted by prehistoric man crowd the walls. Deterioration by exposure to carbon dioxide and outside air has closed the site to visitors. River follows beautiful course between cliffs for 15 miles (24km) to **Les Eyzies**, *Museum of Pre-historic Art* in castle; engravings and paintings in cave of *La Mouthe* above village, and in those of *Font-de-Gaume* and *Les Combarelles* up side valley of *Beaune*. *Trémolat* 10 miles (16km), southwards where *Vézère* joins *Dordogne*, fine river scenery. Southwards to *Beaumont-du-Périgord* and *Monpazier*, 25 miles (40km), both *bastide* towns, and on for 5 miles (8km) to *Biron*, splendid château. *Villeneuve-sur-Lot*, 20 miles (32km), another *bastide* town, two gateways and bridge.

EXCURSION: Up valley of the *Lot* by D911 to *Fumel* for 18 miles (29km) thence 5 miles (8km) northwards to *Bonaguil*, interesting late medieval castle, built when artillery was coming into use.

N21 to *Agen* △, 17 miles (29km), centre of *Agenais*, rich agricultural and fruit growing district, especially plums; Roman remains, eleventh-century cathedral, old bridges over *Garonne*. Up valley for 26 miles (43km) to *Moissac*, Romanesque abbey-church with fine carvings on porch and in cloisters; south for $3^1/_2$ miles (6km) to *Castelsarrasin*. Eastwards for 13 miles (23km) to *Montauban*, attractive town of pink brick monuments; fruit trade centre; birthplace of Ingres; collection of his paintings and drawings in former bishop's palace.

EXCURSION: Northwards on N20 or rail to *Cahors* 25 miles (59km), medieval town, capital of *Quercy* Romanesque cathedral, superb *Pont Valentré*, finest medieval fortified bridge in Europe.

Road or rail, for 32 miles (51km) to **Toulouse**△, old capital of *Languedoc*, cultural, market and route centre of south-east *Aquitaine*. Substantial remains of Roman architecture, many well-preserved Renaissance mansions. Church of *St Sernin*, supreme among Romanesque basilicas of France; octagonal belfry, treasury rich in relics, among them a thorn reputed to be from crown of crucifixion. University founded 1230. Fine mansions, sixteenth to eighteenth century. *Musée des Augustins* (many notable old master paintings); *Musée St Raymond* opposite *St Sernin* (applied arts and antique sculpture); *Musée Paul Dupuy* (ceramics; history of *Languedoc*).

The Pyrenees

The *Pyrenees*, an impressive mountain chain, 250 miles (400km) in its length from Atlantic to Mediterranean, dividing France from Spain. The western and central districts have a fairly high rainfall; maize, wheat, and fruit are grown at lower levels, and the summer heat in the mountains is tempered by cool air from the west. In the east (*Roussillon*) climate and vegetation become more and more Mediterranean — olives, vines, and figs are cultivated. In the central section the peaks often exceed 10,000ft (3,000m) and reach 11,168ft (3,404m) in the *Pic de Néthou*.

In the western *Pyrenees*, on both sides of the frontier, is the country of the *Basques*, a people racially and culturally distinct and whose language is related to no other European tongue (but French is also spoken). They number about 600,000, of whom a fifth live in France. The local sport is *pelota*, in which a ball is played against a wall with the hand or a special bat; a fast and strenuous game. Local songs, and dances such as the *fandango*, still form part of the life of the country.

R15 Biarritz to Perpignan by the Route des Pyrénées (540 miles, 870km)

This is a fine high-level route, including a number of passes over 5,000ft (1,500m). Although there are many branch lines running up towards the heights there is no public transport over the passes, except for a regular coach tour in summer in four stages, *Biarritz-Lourdes, Lourdes-Luchon, Luchon-Font Romeu,*

Font Romeu-Carcassonne, which can be booked separately. Cyclists will find themselves having to tackle some of the most strenuous ascents of the *Tour de France* route.

*Anglet*Δ near *Biarritz. Route des Pyrénées,* here numbered D918, begins at *St Jean de Luz,* fishing port and resort, vast beach; less expensive than *Biarritz.* Up river valley of *Nivelle* for 4 miles (6km) then on to *Ascain* and continue to *St Ignace* (2¹/₂ miles, 4km) for excursion to summit of *La Rhune,* 2,950ft (900m), by rack railway in 30 minutes, summer only, or on foot in 3 hours.

Continue by D4 and D20 through Basque villages of *Aïnhoa* and *Itxassou* to rejoin D918 for *St Jean-Pied-de-Port;* picturesque, two lines of ramparts, beautiful sixteenth- and seventeenth-century houses in *Rue de la Citadelle.* It stands at foot of pass of *Roncesvalles* (site of epic story of Roland), but the pass itself is 11 miles (18km) from the Spanish frontier.

Follow D933 north-eastwards for 10 miles (16km) to *Chahara,* then rejoin D918 for 6 miles (10km) to *Col d'Osquich* (1,280ft, 390m) and continue for 33 miles (54km) to *Asasp,* where *Route des Pyrénées* crosses N134.

R15 (i) *Asasp* to *Col de Somport* (30 miles, 48km), following the *Gave* (stream) *d'Aspe* up pleasant narrow valley; beyond *Accous* scenery becomes wilder. Just beyond *L'Estanguet* is branch road to *Lescun* for ascent of *Pic d'Anie* (8,200ft, 2,498m, 4 to 5 hours) and several other summits about 7,000ft (2,100m). *Col de Somport* (5,380ft, 1,639m, Spanish frontier, is one of few passes through Pyrenees).

Resume easterly direction on D918 for 13 miles (22km) to *Louvie-Juzon.*

R15 (ii) *Louvie* to *Pau* (15 miles, 26km) northwards. **Pau,** resort once frequented by English visitors in winter: castle (various periods) with fine tapestries; *Boulevard des Pyrénées,* almost 1¹/₄ miles (2km) long, laid out by Napoleon; magnificent views of mountains.

Due south on D934 for 7 miles (11km) to *Laruns,* small town almost encircled by mountains; local costumes worn at festivals, especially on 15 August.

R15 (iii) *Laruns* to *Col du Pourtalet* (18 miles, 29km) by wild, forested valley; near *Gabas* bears are still seen. *Gabas* is a good mountaineering centre (*Pic du Midi d'Ossau,* 9,460ft, 2,884m, not an easy climb); cable railway to *Pic de la Sagette* 6,740ft (2,055m) whence narrow gauge railway for 6 miles (10km) to beautiful *Lac d'Artouste.* Spanish frontier at *Col du Pourtalet,* 5,880ft (1,794m) fine view.

Route des Pyrénées continues via *Eaux-Bonnes,* fashionable spa, and *Gourette,* winter-sports resort, over *Col d'Aubisque* (5,594ft, 1,705), descending to *Argelès-Gazost.*

R15 (iv) *Argelès* to *Lourdes* (8 miles, 13km). Beyond *Agos* stands *Pic de Pibeste* 4,538ft (1,349m). **Lourdes** is of absorbing interest to Catholic visitors; very crowded in summer; spring with reputedly miraculous powers in grotto where it is said that Saint Bernadette had vision of Virgin Mary.

R15 (v) *Argelès* to **Cauterets** (11 miles, 17km), spa (since Roman times) and winter sports resort. Many climbs of varying difficulty; *Pic de Vignemale* is highest point of district (10,821ft, 3,298m, two-day ascent, guide essential). Experienced walkers can reach *Gavarnie* (see **R15**) **(vi)** via *Hourquette d'Ossoue* in about 10 hours.

Southwards for 11 miles (18km) up impressive gorges to *Luz-St Sauveur*△; spa, fashionable in nineteenth century when frequented by Imperial court; notable fortified church of twelfth and fourteenth centuries.

R15 (vi) *Luz* to *Gavarnie* (12½ miles, 20km; bus, 1 hour). *Cirque de Gavarnie* is magnificent natural rocky amphitheatre with cliffs rising nearly a mile high (summit 9,000ft, 2,743m, above sea level). Popular excursion in summer. Tremendous waterfalls (at their best before high summer). Climb *Pimené* (9,197ft, 2,801m, 4 hours) for best view.

Eastwards from *Luz* is the highest and probably the finest section of the route. At *Barèges* (bus from *Luz* in 35 mins) is a mountain railway climbing to 6,500ft (1,950m) on slope of *Pic d'Ayré*. From *Barèges* ascent on foot to *Pic du Midi de Bigorre* in 4-5 hours; 9,400ft (2,865m) peak with superb view; can also be approached by toll road from *Col du Tourmalet* to within few minutes of summit. Cable railway is only for use of observatory, situated just below summit. West of peak (2 hours) is beautiful *Lac Bleu* (6,400ft, 1,944m) on route down to *Bagnères*.
Col du Tourmalet (6,933ft, 2,115m, open July-September) is highest point on the route; splendid view. *Ste-Marie-de-Campan*, junction with D935 for *Bagnères*.

EXCURSION: to caves of *Médous*, 5 miles (8km) down road to *Bagnères*; very fine stalacite caverns, discovered 1948, traversed by boat on underground river. Open in summer.

Col d'Aspin (4,912ft, 1,497m) offers fine view.

EXCURSION: on foot from the *Col* via the *Horquette d'Arreau* to *Arreau* village; about 3 hours.

Continue via *Port de Peyresourde* (5,424ft, 1,653m) and the delightfully named village of *Oô* (rivalled only by *Bun*, 4 miles (6km) south-west of *Argelès*) to *Bagnères de Luchon*. Fashionable health resort (2,070ft, 630m) with *Superbagnères*, still more fashionable (5,906ft, 1,804m).

EXCURSIONS: *Luchon* is a good base for climbs, eg *Pic de Céciré* 7,875ft (2,403m), 2 hours from *Superbagnères*. The *Aneto* (or *Pic de Néthou*), 11,168ft (3,404m), highest peak of the Pyrenees is over the Spanish frontier and demands a two-day ascent, with guides; it lies in the barren *Maladetta* ('Accursed') mountain group. Road over *Col du Portillon* to *Bossost* (2,300ft, 710m) in *Valle d'Aran*.

Follow *Luchon* valley on D125 down to *Cierp*.

R15 (vii) From *Cierp* bridge to *St Bertrand-de-Comminges* (10 miles, 16km), decayed old town but with great past; finest cathedral in Pyrenees (Romanesque-Gothic) *Montrejeau*△ (5 miles, 8km, north).

Turn eastwards for 2$^1/_2$ miles (4km) to *St Béat* and strike northwards for 4 miles (5km) to meet D618, then eastwards again for 38 miles (62km), crossing *Col du Portet d'Aspet* (3,509ft, 1,069m) to *St Girons*, thence via *Gorges de Ribaouto, Massat* and *Col de Port* (4,100ft, 1,249m) to *Tarascon-sur-Ariège*. South-eastwards for 16 miles (26km) on N20 to *Ax-les-Thermes*, a spa since Roman times; excellent centre for mountain walking; *Signal de Chioula* (4,900ft, 1,493m) for view. Road and railway continue up wild and interesting valley, via *Mérens-les-Vals* to *L'Hospitalet*, road junction for *Andorra*.

R15 (viii) To *Pas de la Casa* (frontier) and over highest pass in Pyrenees, the *Port d'Envalira* (7,900ft, 2,407m) into the small independent state of **Andorra**. The country consists of two main valleys and comprises several villages and the capital *Andorra la Vella*. Visit the Parliament House (*Casa de la Vall*) sixteenth century, and church. There is only one main road and the country is entirely mountainous. The *Pic de Casamanya* (9,100ft, 2,773m) gives a view of all the country. French and Spanish are equally understood, but the native tongue is a form of Catalan.

Continue for 19 miles (30km) on N20 from *L'Hospitalet* via *Col de Puymorens* (6,200ft, 1,889m) into the *Cerdagne*, territory south of the watershed and divided between France and Spain. *Llivia*, a Spanish village, remains isolated in French territory. *Bourg-Madame*, on Spanish frontier.

Retrace northwards for 2$^1/_2$ miles (4km) to join D618 to proceed eastwards through the granite wilderness of *Targassonne* to *Font-Romeu*, fashionable resort at 5,900ft (1,800m), has spring with reputed miraculous power and solar power station. *Saillagouse*△ 2$^1/_2$ miles (4km) south on N116. *Mont-Louis*, another high altitude resort; fortified town (*Axat*△ nearby); junction with D118 leading northwards for 74 miles (120km) to *Carcassonne*△ to join **R17 (i).**

Follow N116 for 18 miles (30km), down the valley of the *Têt. Thuès-entre-Valls*, at entrance to *Gorges de la Caranca* and on to fortified village of *Villefranche-de-Conflent*.

R15 (ix) *Villefranche* to *Vernet* and the *Canigou*. *Vernet-les-Bains*, pleasant spa and old village, at foot of **Canigou**, most conspicuous peak of Eastern Pyrenees, delightful shady, winding track (*Escala de l'Ours*) through forest of *Balatg* to *Chalet Hôtel-des Cortalets* (12$^1/_2$ miles, 20km from *Vernet* — overnight); thence in 2 hours, by boulder-strewn slope to summit of *Canigou* (9,137ft, 2,785m); magnificent view over whole of Eastern Pyrenees: direction indicator.

Prades, little town with Gothic church of Moorish influence — in maze of narrow streets; region of orchards and vineyards, olives and cypresses, typical of *Roussillon*, the old name for the country between *Cerdagne* and the Mediterranean, which was Spanish until 1659. Population is Catalan, and a French-Catalan dialect is spoken.

At *Bouleternère* the *Route des Pyrénées* (D618) climbs southwards to reach valley of *Tech* but trip may well be shortened by 30 miles (48km) by continuing down N116 to **Perpignan**Δ, a delightful town with Spanish atmosphere; fourteenth-century brick fortress called the *Castillet; Loge de Mer*, former Exchange, fourteenth and sixteenth century; cathedral of *St Jean*, Gothic, begun in fourteenth century; palace of the Kings of Majorca, Gothic style.

Coast of Languedoc

Comprises two contrasted regions, the 20 miles (30km) stretch of the *Côte Vermeille* where the *Pyrenees* fall abruptly to form a rocky coastline of alternating cliffs and bays; and the long dune belt, with lagoons behind it, lying northwards for about 90 miles (145km), from *Collioure* to the *Rhône* delta.

R16 Perpignan to Cerbère (32 miles, 51km)
The *Côte Vermeille*, unlike the *Côte d'Azur*, is unspoilt and unsophisticated. *Collioure*, picturesque little harbour, favourite subject of Matisse, Dufy and other artists. *Banyuls*, the most southerly seaside resort in France; produces wine similar to sherry. *Cerbère*, fishing port on the Spanish frontier.

R17 Perpignan to Avignon (160 miles, 257km)
A little known part of the Mediterranean coast. Flat, sandy beaches, good bathing. N9, or E15 motorway, *Perpignan* to **Narbonne**, pleasant town, cathedral of *St Just*, Gothic, only choir completed. Town was important Roman settlement. In the distance inland are the *Cévennes* mountains.

R17 (i) *Narbonne* to *Carcassone*Δ, 56 miles (90km) **Carcassonne** is the showplace of the Middle Ages, although much of it is nineteenth-century restoration. The old town or *cité* is completely walled, built on a hill-top and crowned with many conical roofs.

Béziers, old part of town interesting; cathedral of *St Nazaire* (twelfth to fourteenth century) local Gothic. Eastwards 22 miles (36km) to *Mèze*Δ, thence 11 miles (18km) to *Sète*Δ second largest Mediterranean port of France, small shadeless beach; passages on cargo vessels to *Oran* and *Mostaganem* in North Africa at low rate. **Montpellier**Δ, capital of *Hérault*; one of most interesting towns of *Languedoc*; university founded 1289; cathedral; *Musée Fabre,* excellent art collection. (For route to *Gorges du Tarn* see **R13 [i]**.) Continue via *Nîmes* to *Avignon*, on main route *Paris — Riviera* (see **R10**).

R18 The Island of Corsica

For a combination of rich Mediterranean vegetation, sunshine, blue seas, wild mountains and freedom from congestion, Corsica is ideal. Those in search of important works of architecture, museums, and art galleries should look elsewhere. The best time for a visit is May and June; earlier the mountain passes are likely to be snowbound, whilst the summer heat may be found excessive, at least on the east coast.

The language resembles Italian (Corsica having been Italian until the eighteenth century) but most people are bilingual, speaking French also. The only towns of any size on the island are *Bastia* and *Ajaccio*, the usual arrival ports from *Nice* or *Marseille*. Night crossing about 11 hours from *Nice*, 15 hours from *Marseille*.

Cyclists should note that although the road surfaces are generally good the likelihood of obtaining spare parts is remote. Gears and brakes should be suitable for the twisting hills of all the most interesting routes. However, a bycicle is a good way of seeing the island. There is a youth hostel at *Calvi*, and much of the island is ideal for camping; although it should be noted that fires may not be lit in forests.

The topography of Corsica does not lend itself to a description in terms of a continuous road circuit, and in preparing one's own itinerary due consideration must be given to the slow rate of progress on tortuous roads. Bus routes radiate from *Ajaccio* and *Bastia*, but elsewhere services are infrequent and erratic.

Except for a dull stretch southward from *Bastia*, the coast is entirely rocky and much indented, the only beaches being at the heads of some of the bays. Roads cannot generally hug the shore, but offer splendid plunging or distant views of the sea. Foremost of the island's coastal scenery: *Cap Corse*, the northern promontory, which makes a beautiful circuit of 77 miles (124km) from *Bastia*; *Les Calanches* near *Piana*, a wilderness of red granite; the savage *Iles Sanguinaires*, visited by boat from *Ajaccio* (birthplace of Napoleon) and the sea-caves in the white limestone cliffs of the extreme south, visited by boat from *Bonifacio*.

A tour of the interior will leave an impression of continuously exciting views from mountain passes and in narrow valleys, with no one site obviously more memorable than the rest. *Corte*, once the island's capital, is a convenient base for the long *Gorges de la Restonica*, the *Gorges du Tavignano* (on foot only), the *Scala* (defile) *di Santa Regina* and the *Forest of Vizzavona*. The *Col de Bavella* farther south should also not be missed.

The high mountains are best climbed in two days, taking sleeping-bags and provisions, and spending the night close to the summit in the huts of shepherds who are traditionally willing to oblige in this way. The vast views, best appreciated at sunrise, from *Monte Cinto* (8,891ft, 2,710m), *Monte Rotondo* (8,612ft, 2,625m), and *Incudine* (7,008ft, 2,136m), will amply compensate for the rigours of the ascent.

Germany

Geographical Outline

Germany is a big, compact country, some four times as large as England and set squarely in Central Europe. Since 1945 it has been divided into two parts, under Russian and Western influence respectively, with different political and social systems. The eastern part calls itself the *German Democratic Republic (DDR)*; for touring this chapter describes the western part, known as the *German Federal Republic* and the city of Berlin.

Land

Owing to its central position in Europe, Germany is made up physically of parts of three major belts of country running across the continent from west to east: the Northern Lowland, the Central Uplands and the Alps. None of them lies entirely within Germany. The Lowland, for example, which is called the *North German Plain*, is continued westwards in the *Plain of Flanders*, and eastwards through Poland into Russia. This lack of a natural frontier on its eastern and western sides goes far to explain the historic tendency of Germany to fluctuate in size.

The plain is farming country but with many marshes and heaths, including the famous *Lüneburg Heath* between the Rivers *Weser* and *Elbe*, a huge area of rolling moorland. In the extreme south-west of the plain lies the *Ruhr* district where the close mingling of vast industry and farming is typical of the area.

South of the plain lies the Central Uplands, a richly varied region of hills and low mountains, forests and farmland, intersected by numerous rivers. Each range of hills has its own name, from the *Eifel, Taunus* and *Black Forest* in the west to the *Harz* and *Rhön* in the east, and each has its own attraction. They contain every type of rock, from limestone to granite, and the geological picture often changes every few yards, the soil varying from red to violet, black, yellow and ruddy brown. Here is the geologist's happy hunting ground. The soil is much less fertile than that in the North Plain, but there is considerable mineral wealth and a wide variety of industry. It is also the region which best conforms to the picture of the

German countryside of story and legend.

Only a narrow strip of the third belt, the *Alps*, lies within Germany. But between them and the Central Uplands is the interesting region known as the Alpine Foreland. It is a high plain, sloping gently from the *Alps* to the *Danube* and bounded on the west by *Lake Constance*, the largest lake in Germany.

Flowing into and out of *Lake Constance*, and linking all these regions, is the River *Rhine*, the principal waterway of Western and Central Europe. From the lake to *Basel* it forms the German-Swiss border, and from *Basel* to beyond *Strasbourg* the German-French border. In this section it flows through a broad sheltered valley, rich in crops including wine and tobacco, but lacking the spectacular appeal of the gorge which the river enters after flowing westwards from *Mainz* to *Bingen*. The *Rhine* Gorge is probably the most celebrated stretch of river scenery in the world. The mountain-slopes, terraced for vines, fall steeply to the river, scarcely leaving room for a road and a railway on either side. Charming medieval towns and ancient villages line its banks and grim castles crown the towering crags. From *Bonn* the valley broadens again, and, churned by many tugs and no longer beautiful, the river flows past *Cologne* and the great inland port of *Duisburg*, through Holland to the sea.

Climate

Although the climate is temperate, frequent changes of weather occur; cold in winter and hot in summer. The northern *Rhine* valley has a more moderate climate but, with local exceptions, the extremes of heat and cold increase eastwards.

Spring is the season to visit the fruit growing areas of the *Rhine, Pfalz* and *Neckar*, where the blossom provides a wonderful sight.

Summer is popular for touring, but motoring or cycling is best accomplished before noon or in the evening; the afternoon heat can be oppressive, except in the mountains.

The *Rhine* or *Mosel* valleys in September or October can be recommended for the grape harvest, while winter of course is the time for winter sports in the *Harz, Black Forest* or *Bavarian Alps*.

Plants and Animals

More of the natural forest cover has survived than in other densely settled parts of Europe. Forests cover about a quarter of the country, but the oak and beech forest of the north-west has been largely replaced by heath. Conifers, especially Scots pine, are the chief tree further east. Beech predominates in the Central Uplands, except where conditions favour the spruce, as in the *Fichtelgebirge* and the *Bavarian Alps*.

Plants of the Alpine pastures, northern heathlands, coastal dunes and salt marshes are, similar to those found in such areas in neighbouring countries.

Many woodland areas abound with animal life, stag and roe, fox, badger and even wild boar, and the huntsman has been a traditional figure in German life.

The People

Population

The population of the *German Federal Republic* is more than 60 million. A further 1,950,000 people live in *West Berlin*. (The *German Democratic Republic* has about 18 million including the people of *East Berlin*.)

The largest cities of West Germany are *Hamburg* (1,700,000), and *Munich* (1,400,000). Eight others exceed the half million: *Cologne, Essen, Düsseldorf, Frankfurt, Dortmund, Stuttgart, Hanover* and *Bremen*. Two belts of dense settlement, along the northern edge of the Central Uplands and along the *Rhine* valley, converge in the industrial area of the *Ruhr* which has a population of more than 5 million. Distribution of population in the rest of the country is very uneven and many parts are sparsely settled.

Racially, Nordic physical characteristics tend to predominate in the north-west; elsewhere German people are predominantly of the dark, thick set, broad headed Alpine type.

Language

Dialects are widely varied; *Hochdeutsch*, the standard German as taught in schools, is spoken throughout northern and central Germany. Many peasants speak the *Plattdeutsch* dialect but you are unlikely to meet people who do not at least understand *Hochdeutsch*, even if they cannot speak it. Southern speech is soft, and consonants are less strongly articulated, so that Bavarian, Austrian and Swiss dialects are almost different languages. Even northern Germans find them difficult to understand.

English is taught in town schools and is widely spoken and understood by the younger generation, but a knowledge of German will increase the enjoyment of your visit.

Religion

As the home of the Lutheran Reformation northern Germany became and has remained strongly Protestant. Areas of Protestantism extend also through *Hesse* to *Württemburg* in the south-west. On the other hand, *Bavaria* and much of the *Rhineland* are Catholic.

History

Germany's tendency to resist unification makes the history of this great Central

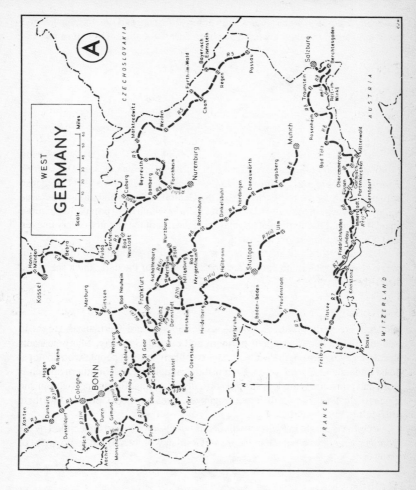

European territory almost impossible to summarise. But certain facts are worth bearing in mind.

It was never fully Romanized. The Roman Empire at its most powerful was only able to hold the *Rhineland* and the areas south of the *Danube*, together with *Rhaetia*, the territory south of an artificial frontier running from *Regensburg* on the *Danube* to *Koblenz* on the *Rhine*. The destruction of three Roman legions by the Germanic tribes under Arminius (AD9) settled the issue in one of the world's decisive battles: the lands around the *Elbe* and the *Vistula* were never to become

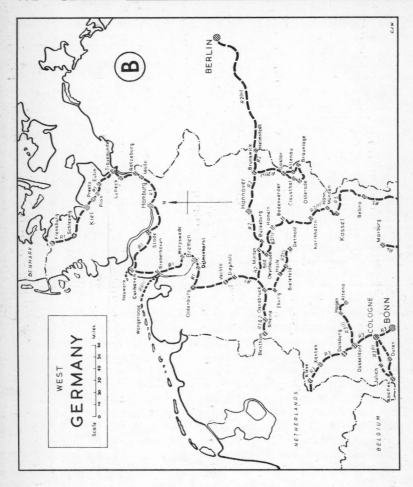

Roman. For the future of the Empire this was a fatal circumstance. From the *North German Plain* came first the tribal penetrations of the Alemanni and the Franks and later the onslaughts of the Goths and Vandals which broke up the civilization of the Empire in the West in 476.

Among the new groupings of restless migrating tribes which had destroyed this pattern of European life were peoples who were to create other patterns of civilization. Some, such as the Bavarians, Swabians and Thuringians, were to develop some of the distinctive regions of modern Germany. Others, such as the

Saxons and Franks, were to play a large part in the building of the English and French nations.

The Franks, in fact, pacified and Christianized the other German tribes. In this work the greatest missionary was the Englishman St Boniface, the 'Apostle of Germany', who died in 754. For a time, under Charlemagne, the Frankish kingdom succeeded where Rome had failed. His great Christian empire, reaching from the *Pyrenees* to the *Elbe*, included a Germany now for the first time united. Its eastern frontier separated Christians from heathens, and Germans from Slavs.

It was in Germany also that, after the period of confusion following the partition of Charlemagne's dominions, the idea of the Empire was revived under Otto I (king 936-73, crowned emperor by the Pope in 962). This new Germanic version of the Holy Roman Empire survived, at least in name, until swept away by Napoleon in 1806, long after it had become an anachronism. But what should have been a partnership of Empire and Papacy became a struggle between them for supremacy, and German resources were wasted in Italian campaigns.

Internally, two systems of succession gave Germany the worst of both worlds. The emperor was elected by seven princes, in whose interest it was generally to elect a weak man. On the other hand, the feudal princedoms were sub-divided by inheritance until Germany became a patchwork of hundreds of tiny states, picturesque but ramshackle and parasitic upon the peasantry. In this way the German states failed to achieve early nationhood at a time when, elsewhere in western Europe and especially in France and England, the opposite tendency was at work creating powerful states.

While the princes fought each other the achievements of the people were local rather than national. The eastern frontier was advanced from the *Elbe* to beyond the *Oder* by penetration of German peasants into the Slav lands, partly by conquest under the Margraves and the Teutonic Knights, partly by invitation. It was their descendants, mostly forming islands of German-speaking people within Slav territory, who made up the tragic streams of refugees from the east after World War II. The remarkable growth of towns was chiefly due to the enterprise of merchants, bankers and industrialists. In the north, the famous Hanseatic League, headed by *Lübeck*, operated as a trading empire independent of prince or emperor. In the south, towns such as *Augsburg* and *Ulm*, commanding routes across the *Alps* or bridges over the *Danube*, grew wealthy because of their central position on the trade routes between northern countries and those of the Mediterranean and the East.

The end of medieval times was marked by two movements; first, the strengthening of some of the princes such as the Habsburgs and Hohenzollerns. Secondly, Luther's call (1517) for Papal reform, made widely known by the recent German invention of the printing press, produced the Reformation and the division of Western Christendom into Catholic and Protestant. After the Peace of Augsburg (1555) the German states, newly independent of both the pope and emperor, enjoyed half a century of prosperity and a cultural activity which produced a northern renaissance.

The Thirty Years' War (1618-48) in which Germany suffered both civil war and the invasion of foreign armies, was a struggle partly religious, partly against Habsburg control. It ended with French power advanced to the *Rhine* and with other losses of German territory. The religious division of the country was confirmed: in broad terms, a Catholic south, a Protestant north and east, and a mixed pattern in the *Rhineland*.

The hundreds of sovereign states remained, making Germany a paradise for princes in the succeeding age of absolutism. Each was concerned primarily with his own magnificence, imitating as far as possible Versailles and the court of Louis XIV. The baroque style mirrored these ambitions. To the prince the glory; to the peasant and townsman the cost. On the other hand, it was in such courts that the genius of Bach was able to flourish; and, after about 1760, there was a brief 'Age of Enlightenment' in some of the smaller states, producing such men as Beethoven, Goethe, Kant and Schiller — the greatest cultural period in German history.

Meanwhile, one state, *Brandenburg,* on the eastern frontier and far from the centre of gravity of the old Germany, was following a policy of war and expansion. This was to make Hohenzollern rulers kings of *Prussia*; its capital, *Berlin*, the capital of Germany; and to produce a philosophy of unscrupulousness and ruthlessness among German leaders for which Germany and the world have paid bitterly. Prussia was faithless even to other German states. She failed them against Napoleon, whose policies reduced the numbers of states from over 400 to under 40, and whose armies brought the liberal revolutionary ideas which the country so greatly needed. But the delayed revolution (1848) was abortive. Later in the century Bismarck, while granting the franchise, ensured that the *Reichstag* then created should have no real power.

By 1871 the whole country had become a federation of states led by *Prussia* under the paternalistic rule of Bismarck, the 'Iron Chancellor'. As a result of his diplomacy Germany was at last united in a Hohenzollern empire and was transformed, within a generation, into one of the greatest industrial powers.

The lack of real democracy and of training in political experience among the people inevitably produced tragic results when control of a nation so powerful passed to leaders less wise than Bismarck. It led, through the actions of Kaiser Wilhelm II, to World War I. It was an important factor (together with the ill-judged reparations policy of the victorious Allies) in the failure of the liberal Weimar Republic (1918-33), Germany's first experience of responsible representative government. Finally, it let in the regime (1933-45) of National Socialism (Nazism) under Hitler. From this new 'dark age' which descended on Europe the continent only escaped by the perilous way of World War II.

Today Germany is again divided. The territory beyond the *Oder*, including

East Prussia and *Pomerania*, has been incorporated into Poland. Between the *Oder* and the *Elbe* is the *German Democratic Republic* under Russian influence. The frontier of West Germany, the *German Federal Republic*, comprising the old west and south German lands, stands again on the *Elbe*.

Government

The *German Federal Republic* sprang from the three western zones of Allied occupation. It acquired a constitution in 1949 and regained full sovereignty in 1955. The President is elected for five years and the Government is headed by the Chancellor. Parliament consists of two Houses, both elected for four years: the lower by direct suffrage, the upper by delegates of the eleven *Länder* (regions) which comprise the Federation.

Resources

Mining and manufacture employ more than half of the working population. Coal and lignite are the most important natural resources and form the basis of Germany's great manufacturing industry. Coal is mined chiefly in the *Ruhr*, with *Saarland* a poor second. Lignite, which occurs more widely, is a much inferior fuel but is economical as a source of electric power. There is great concentration of heavy industry in the *Ruhr* but other industrial activity is widespread. German precision engineering, as in the making of cameras, lenses and scientific instruments is world famous.

About a quarter of the working population are engaged in agriculture or forestry, and farming remains the largest single industry. Most of the farms are small, worked by their owners. Rye and oats are the main cereal crops, wheat and barley being confined to the limited regions of good soils. Potatoes and sugar beet are widely grown, whilst dairying and stock rearing are based on permanent pasture in the north-west and in the Alpine zone. Elsewhere, particularly on the northern plain, arable crops are grown for feeding to animals, as in Denmark.

The valleys of the *Rhine* and the *Mosel* are famous for their vineyards which occur wherever the slope and situation are favourable.

There is a long tradition of good forest management and more than half the forests are publicly owned. Conifer plantations of spruce and pine have ousted much of the natural deciduous woodland, the basis of important pulp, paper and synthetic fibre industries. Wood carving and toy making are old-established crafts in *Bavaria* and the *Black Forest*. An interesting transition in the *Black Forest* has produced the modern clock and watch making industry, based on skills earlier acquired in making the famous wooden cuckoo clocks.

Food and Drink

Based on widespread agriculture, home-produced food is both plentiful and distinctive. It covers a wide range from the plain cheap meal, say, noodle soup, bread and sausage, to the most sumptuous dishes of the more expensive price ranges.

Bread is excellent; Westphalian *Pumpernickel* and *Schwarzbrot* are rye breads, delicious but rather expensive, *Volkornbrot* is made of whole unground grains of wheat.

Sausage is inevitable with the bread and the variety is astounding. *Leberwurst* (liver sausage), *Rinderwurst* (beef sausage), *Bratwurst* (grilled type of pork sausage), *Blutwurst* (black pudding) are common throughout Germany and there are many local varieties, all on display. Bread and sliced sausage with a glass of beer can be had in any restaurant or *Wurstlerei* at a moment's notice.

The variety of cakes, pastry and real fruit tarts and ice-cream is surprising; coffee is served strong with a little cream and is always well made; tea is weak and seldom to English taste.

Beer is everywhere popular, often named after its city of origin, and usually pale coloured, cheap and agreeable. *Dortmund* and *Munich* beers have a reputation for high quality.

Wine, if bought in shops by the bottle, is comparatively cheap and tremendously varied. There are countless named wines, but those from the *Mainz-Bingen* area are said to be the best, especially the famous *Johannisberger*.

Apfelsaft, unfermented apple juice, is a refreshing drink sold at grocer's shops and restaurants.

Culture

Architecture

Germany has not until recent times been an originator of architectural styles. But the Romanesque, Gothic, baroque and rococo were taken up eagerly from abroad and adapted to express German ideas. Romanesque is seen in the cathedrals at *Aachen, Bamberg, Mainz, Osnabruck, Speyer and Worms* and in *Maria Laach* abbey. The finest examples of Gothic are the cathedrals of *Cologne, Marburg* and *Ulm*. The baroque, imported from Italy and France during the Counter-Reformation, became even more exuberant than in its homelands and many wonderful examples occur in the churches of the south.

The Gothic spirit was not limited to church architecture but is expressed also in the houses, streets and market places of the medieval walled towns. Similarly, the baroque imbues many palaces and princely towns of the period as at *Karlsruhe* and *Würzburg*; even more lavish, the rococo flourished in Bavarian churches.

Castles particularly abound along the *Rhine* and its tributaries; the majority are now in ruins but some have been adapted to make magnificent youth hostels as at *Freusburg* and *Altena*.

The modern movement in architecture owes a great deal to German architects, particularly in the design of factories, and in the use of glass and concrete as main materials. The pioneer was Peter Behrens (1868-1940). His pupil Walter Gropius (1883-1969) founded the famous Bauhaus, the ideas and methods of which have had much influence on building and industrial design.

The rebuilding of bombed cities since World War II gave great scope to architects, and imaginative new buildings can be found in most of the towns.

Painting

The greatest German artists worked during the brief period between the spread of Renaissance ideas north of the Alps and the onset of the Reformation. Dürer (1471-1528), the master of drawing, engraving and woodcut, was eagerly receptive to the New Learning while remaining Gothic and German in spirit. His great contemporary, Grünewald, of whom almost nothing is known, preferred to work entirely in the medieval tradition but brought its expression to the highest pitch of intensity. Cranach (1472-1553) is famous for a portrait of Luther but his most significant work, done as a young man, leads the way to a romantic interest in scenery which was developed further by Altdorfer (1480-1538).

The Reformation brought artistic activity to a low ebb in almost every Protestant country. Holbein (1497-1543) was already a master artist when he was forced to leave the continent to seek a living in England, hence English portraiture was enriched by the work of one of the greatest of German artists.

In the field of modern art 'expressionism' found favour early this century with Kendinsky, Barlach and George Grosz. This same movement in the German cinema in the 1920s developed the film as a genre in its own right and was the most significant artistic influence in motion picture set design.

Music

Music is indisputably the art through which Germany has had the greatest cultural influence on the Western World. Bach, Beethoven, Brahms, Wagner, Richard Strauss, to name a few, are all of great importance in the development of music. Almost every German city has its own symphony orchestra and concert hall, while many have municipall- aided opera houses; but more important is the care devoted to musical training in German homes and schools. An ability to play a musical instrument is commonplace, while singing is popular everywhere.

German folk-songs are unique in their variety and tunefulness. In addition to the geniune anonymous folk-songs are hundreds of well-known songs in folk-song style by authors and composers ranging from Goethe and Schubert to the twentieth-century poet Löns.

Literature

In literature, the name of Goethe overtops those of all other German writers, his many-sided genius has enriched Germany and the world, particularly in the fields of drama and poetry. Other famous names are Schiller (eighteenth-century dramatist), Heine and Mörke (nineteenth-century poets), Gerhart Hauptmann (late nineteenth-century dramatist) and Thomas Mann (twentieth-century novelist).

Since the time of Leibniz in the seventeenth century Germany has produced many thinkers of world renown, notably the philosophers of the idealist school — Kant, Fichte, Schelling and Hegel — and others belonging to no group, such as Schopenhauer and Nietzsche.

It is probable that the fairy tales of the brothers Grimm are more widely read outside Germany than the works of any other German author.

Science

Germany has an impressive record of major contributions in every field of science and technology, as the following brief list will show. Gutenberg (1400-68), movable type and book production; Kepler (1571-1630), laws of planetary motion; Leibniz (1646-1716), infinitesimal calculus; Humboldt (1769-1859), naturalist, geographer and explorer; Gauss (1777-1855), mathematics and magnetism; Bunsen (1811-99), spectrum analysis and the 'Bunsen' burner; Kekulé (1829-96), founder of organic chemistry; Koch (1843-1910), bacteriology; Röntgen (1845-1923), X-rays; Ehrlich (1854-1914), medical science; Diesel (1858-1913), internal combustion engine; Planck (1858-1947), quantum theory; Einstein (1879-1955), relativity; Koffka (1886-1941), Gestalt psychology.

Touring Information

Access

The shortest route from Britain is *Dover/Ostend* to *Aachen* by rail/ferry in $9\frac{1}{2}$ hours, rail/jetfoil in $7\frac{1}{2}$ hours. The distance by road from *Ostend* to *Aachen* is 170 miles (274km), and from *Aachen* to *Cologne* is a further 45 miles (72km).

Best route for northern Germany is through Holland crossing the frontier at *Bentheim*. The *Harwich/Hook of Holland* night crossing is recommended, but early reservation is necessary. Other frequent crossings are *Harwich/Hamburg, Hull/Rotterdam* and *Sheerness/Flushing*.

Other approaches are via *Calais* and *Strasbourg* or via *Ostend* and *Luxembourg* to *Trier* — a picturesque route to the *Mosel* and *Rhine*.

Transport

Rail travel is efficient, the express trains being rapid and punctual, and tickets are valid for unlimited breaks of journey. Bus services are run by the Federal Railways (*Bahnbus*) to connect with the trains, and by the Post Office (*Postkraftwagen*) on routes not provided with rail services. The latter are yellow vehicles which penetrate to the remotest mountain villages; they also provide long-distance services in certain tourist areas. Fares are similar to second class rail.

Tourist cards are available for unlimited rail travel throughout West Germany for 4, 9 or 16 days. Holiday runabout tickets (*Tourenkarten*)(10 days within a 21-day period) offer unlimited rail travel within any one of seventy-three regions together with half fare on *Bahnbus* and *Postkraftwagen* and are inexpensive, but their sale is restricted to those with through rail tickets to a point at least 125 miles (200km) inside the German frontier.

On the *Rhine, Mosel* and *Bodensee* there are regular steamer services in summer; rail tickets for the parallel rail route may be used on payment of a supplement of a few Pfennigs per kilometre. On the *Rhine* the fast steamer *Schnelldampfer*, is much more expensive than the ordinary service.

Ferries across the *Rhine* and *Mosel*, *Fähren* — marked 'F' on maps, convey passengers and bicycles.

Money

The *Deutsche Mark* (abbreviated *DM*) is divided into 100 *Pfennigs* (abbreviated *Pf*). Coins are issued for 1, 2, 5, 10 and 50 *Pf*, and for 1, 2 and 5 *DM*, with notes for higher values. Beware of confusing the 1 and 2 *DM* pieces, which are similar in size but not in design.

Clothing

For the mountains (particularly the *Bavarian Alps)* carry a sweater, windproof jacket, scarf and thick stockings or woollen trousers or slacks, with boots or heavy shoes; even in summer there can be sudden cold spells. Women are advised to wear skirts (not shorts) in Catholic areas (*Rhineland* and *Bavaria*).

Restaurants and Meals

There are restaurants in all but the smallest villages and a simple but good meal can almost always be had at quite reasonable cost. The principal types of meat found on the menu are: *Rind* (beef), *Schwein* (pork), *Kalb* (veal), *Wurst* (sausage), *Schinken* (ham), *Speck* (bacon). Other useful words are *Eier* (eggs), *Käse* (cheese), *Gemüse* (vegetables), and *Kartoffeln* (potatoes).

Public Holidays

Whit Monday; 17 June; 16 November (Repentance Day); Christmas Day; 26 December; 1 January; Good Friday; Easter Monday; 1 May; Ascension Day.

Maps

Large-scale walkers' maps of particular tourist areas are published by private firms (eg Stollfuss and Reise-und-Verkehrsverlag); tourist paths and youth hostels are generally marked.

The best choice of road maps on one sheet is Michelin No 984 on a scale of 1:750,000 depicting Germany and Benelux. Kümmerley & Frey publish a general map on a scale of 1:500,000, but sufficientlt detailed for motoring. There are many more detailed motorists' or cyclists' maps including Michelin, 1:200,000, and DGK, same scale but with hostels and footpaths marked.

Accommodation

Germany is the home of the youth hostel movement, founded in 1909 by Richard Schirrmann, and a close network of about 600 hostels covers most of the country. Those in the popular touring areas are often crowded during the holidays, and rather strictly organised. Smaller hostels, off the beaten track, are often more homely and informal. *Bavarian* yourh hostels (routes **R8** and parts of **R5** and **R6**) impose an age limit of 27 years, but smaller country inns (*Gasthaus* or *Gasthof*) will often provide cheap accommodation. Mountain huts of the Deutscher Alpenverein (5 Praterinsel, Munich 22), most of them in *Bavarian Alps*, are open to non-members and provide simple accommodation at low cost.

Camping

There are well-equipped camping sites in many parts of the country; a list can be obtained from the German Tourist Information Bureau, 65 Curzon Street, London W1Y 7PE. A more detailed official handbook is published by the German Camping Club, Mandlstrasse 28, D8, Munich 40. Before camping at places other than the recognised sites the permission of the owner must be sought and, in your own interest, the permission of the local police.

Walking

Although the country lacks the mountain splendours of Austria and Switzerland, the glaciers and fjords of Norway, the limitless sunshine of the Mediterranean, it has many hill regions where forest alternates with meadows and moor, peaks provide unexpectedly wide views and every valley has its stream and neat villages. Waymarked footpaths follow the finest slopes and ridges, often leading away from every trace of civilization except for an occasional wayside inn.

The most famous of these districts is the *Black Forest;* less well known, and visited by foreign tourists are the *Eifel*, the *Odenwald*, the *Spessart* and the *Sauerland*. Footpaths and minor roads on the heights above the *Rhine*, the *Mosel* and other rivers, are preferable to the crowded, noisy roads in the valley below.

Cycling

An excellent way to see the country; a touring model is preferable and a multi-speed gear is almost essential except on the Northern Plain. Cycles can be hired at more than 250 railway stations; rented at one station and returned to another, if preferred. Cycling on the *Autobahnen* is forbidden and cyclists are not officially allowed to cycle two abreast on any road; a wise precaution, as German roads have the highest death rate in Europe.

Motoring

Motorists should carry with them their car registration certificate, international driving licence, international green card — or some other proof of third party insurance; nationality sticker should be displayed and red warning triangle carried. Note that seat belts are compulsory, headlights or dipped headlights must be used at dusk or in poor visibility, that speed limits are 100km/h (62mph) on main road, 130km/h (80mph) on motorways (*Autobahnen*).

Continental highway code applies, driving on the right with traffic coming from the right having priority — except on a few major roads which are indicated accordingly. On-the-spot fines apply for traffic offences.

Touring Routes

R1 Dutch to Danish Frontier via Hamburg (470 miles, 756km)

Leading through flat agricultural country, but recommended to those wishing to get off the beaten track. The direct journey by rail on the route of the Holland-Scandinavia Express is only 300 miles (480km) and can be accomplished in 7 hours, but this route for motorists and cyclists follows a more winding course.

From *Bad Bentheim* Δ (Dutch/German frontier) follow B65, cross the *Ems* at *Rheine*Δ and enter **Osnabruck**Δ, important rail and road junction set between parallel hill ridges — the *Teutoburg Forest* and the *Wiehengebirge*. (See **R2[i]**). Imposing 1,000-year-old cathedral and Gothic town hall with the Hall of Peace of Westphalia, where end of the Thirty Years' War was negotiated in 1648.

Turn north-east by B51. After 15 miles (24km) the *Dümmer* appears on the left, a lake about 4 miles (6¹/₂km) wide with facilities for swimming and sailing, *Damme*Δ is nearby. Smoked eel is a delicacy of this area. Across the marshes fork left at *Diepholz*Δ on B69 to *Vechta*, in the midst of woods, meadows and marshes. Just before the junction with B213 on the right is the *Ahlhorner Heide*, an area of Stone Age funeral monuments called *Hünengräber*. On to *Oldenburg*Δ — castle with gardens, several museums. Halfway to *Bremen* is *Delmenhorst*, magnificent town hall, in middle of wooded *Delmenhorster* marshes.

BremenΔ, the second port of Germany, with interesting dockyards, has all its tourist attractions on the north bank. *St Peter's* cathedral has lead crypt; famous

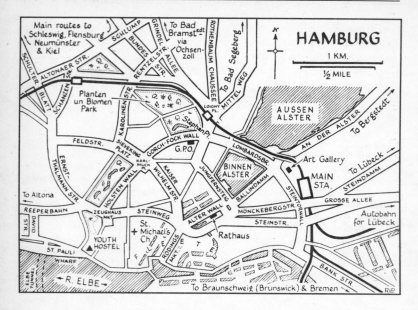

colourful town hall with beautiful Renaissance façade; *Liebfrauenkirche* is one of the finest churches; historical market place with *Roland Monument*; the *Schütting* guildhouse is one of the finest buildings; botanical gardens; several museums. Follow secondary road north-eastwards through *Horn*, turning left to *Worpswede*Δ, artist colony in heart of flat marshy country where typical black-sailed boats can be seen. Cut across country to *Bremerhaven*Δ; largest fisherman's harbour in the world; North Sea Aquarium.

R1 (i) Bremerhaven to Wangerooge (Frisian Islands). Boat service, takes 4 hours, July to mid-September (can also be reached from *Wilhelmshaven*Δ); *Wangerooge*Δ is most easterly of the *Frisian* Islands, pleasant, sandy, good bathing; youth hostel on each island. Other islands can only be reached from the small ports of *Friesland* (*Harle*, *Norddeich*Δ). Most attractive is *Spiekeroog*Δ (Green Island), a nature reserve.

From *Bremerhaven* take coast road northwards to *Cuxhaven*Δ, important fishing town whose symbol is a huge ball-buoy mounted on the end of a jetty. A sail by smack to the island of *Neuwerk* is recommended. Turn east on B73 through *Otterndorf*Δ, *Wingst*Δ and *Stade*Δ with medieval buildings, countryside with farmhouses and steep thatched roofs, and on to **Hamburg**Δ, largest port and second largest city after *Berlin*; at confluence of Rivers *Alster* and *Elbe*. Was principal port of Hanseatic League (thirteenth to seventeenth centuries), later a Free City. Built on marshy soil, frequently on piles. Boat trips to harbour from *St*

Pauli wharf; *Reeperbahn*, famous street of night-life and sailors' entertainments; Renaissance *Rathaus* has half-hourly conducted tours; '*Planten un Blomen*' park — magnificent flower gardens adjoining *Tiergartenstrasse*; boat trip on the *Alster*, leaving from *Alster* Pavilion; Art Gallery (*Kunsthalle*), near main station, many old masters; area of old canals between *Elbe* and *Alster* with interesting old streets around *St Michael's* church.

The Lüneburg Heath

R1 (ii) Hamburg to the Lüneburg Heath. Due south of *Hamburg* — and south-west of *Lüneburg* town stretches the *Lüneburg* Heath (*Lüneburger Heide*). Formerly a vast tract of heather and moorland, much has now been reclaimed for cultivation, and parts disfigured by army manoeuvres, but round the *Wilseder Berg* (550ft, 167m) there is a nature reserve, with fine walking country; *Bispingen*Δ and *Undeloh*Δ give best access. Birch, juniper and pine trees among heather. Romantic associations for many Germans, due largely to writings of Hermann Löns (killed in action 1914), including much-loved song: *Auf der Lüneburger Heide*. Other good parts of the Heath are the *Arloh* (north of *Celle*) and the lonely area east of *Müden* Δ, said to be most beautiful town of Heath, with typical farm settlements protected by huge oaks. At *Walsrode* (on B209) is a Heath Museum in 350-year-old group of farm buildings. *Lüneburg*Δ itself is picturesque old town with Gothic brickwork and half-timbered buildings; old town hall has magnificent carvings and wall-paintings. See brick-built Gothic Michaelis-kirche, fifteenth century, massive pillars warped by unsafe foundations. At *Falling-bostel*Δ, south-west of *Soltau* Δ on B209, are prehistoric stone chambers known as the Seven Stone Houses; many archaeological finds have been made on the Heath.

Niedersächsenweg, long-distance footpath of about 90 miles (145km), way-marked by *Lüneburg Heath Tourist Association*, follows north/south route from *Hamburg* to *Celle*, via *Jesleburg*, *Undeloh*, *Wilseder Berg*, *Soltau* and *Müden*. Niedersächsisches Landesvermessungamt map of *Zentralheide* on scale 1:100,000 depicts this path; Grieben's guide *Lüneburger Heide* describes it.

From *Hamburg* to the Danish frontier follow the North Sea coast, a wind-swept solitude of dunes and dykes; or the Baltic coast, peaceful and wooded with many lakes. Numerous youth hostels on both routes. Rail route crosses the centre of the province, via *Neumünster*Δ.

Schleswig-Holstein, most northerly province, starting point of Anglo-Saxon invasion; now a thickly populated agricultural area.

From *Hamburg* take B435 eastwards, then B207 to *Mölln* Δ, the delightful medieval town of the legendary jester, *Till Eulenspiegel*, in whose memory a festival of plays is held each year. *Ratzeburg*Δ, is an island city on Lake *Ratze-burger*, and only 2 miles (3¹/₄km) from East Germany. It is dominated by its massive cathedral, the oldest brick church in Germany. This whole area is delightful for walking, swimming and yachting.

LübeckΔ, the first large town, is famous for its brickwork; the striking *Rathaus* is the best example, retaining the black glazed tiles characteristic of the area. See *St Marien* cathedral, fortified *Holstein* gate with two massive towers and conical black roofs, the city walls, museum and the *Buddenbrooks* house, background for Thomas Mann's famous novel.

B75 leads to *Travemünde*Δ, a sophisticated seaside resort; ferry services to many Scandinavian ports. Further north along the Baltic coast, particularly north of *Kiel*, are many quieter seaside places, all with excellent bathing on wide sandy beaches backed by pine trees.

Follow the coast road to join B76 leading to *Eutin*Δ gateway to so-called *Holstein Switzerland*, an attractive region of lakes set among woodland; several youth hostels hereabouts. *Bungsburg*, 450ft (137m), highest point, with fine view. *Plön*Δ in the heart of this area, surrounded by five lakes, has magnificent castle. Through the beautiful countryside around *Preetz* where there is an ancient convent, to the university town of *Kiel*Δ where canal affords an exit to the North Sea; *Kiel* Regatta (end of June) is internationally famous.

Continue via *Eckernförde*Δ to *Schleswig*Δ, an ancient Viking city. *Bordesholm* altar, in *St Peter's* cathedral, is famous work of Gothic art, a remarkable wood carving of hundreds of figures. *Gottorf* castle on an island in *Schlei* estuary is largest in *Schleswig-Holstein*; houses *Prehistoric Museum* and *Nydam boat*, fourth-century Viking craft found in marsh country.

On for 20 miles (32km) to *Flensburg*Δ, Germany's northernmost city; charming streets, arcaded market squares. Thirteenth-century *Marienkirche*, *Nordertor* town gate. Music flourishes here with symphony orchestra and opera house; famed too for rum and smoked eels. Visit *Glücksburg*, seaside resort at mouth of fjord, and castle on beech-covered heights.

R2 Dutch Frontier to East German Border via Hanover (190 miles, 306km)
Following the northern edge of the central German uplands and giving access to some pleasant holiday areas. By rail, via the *Hook*, to *Minden* on the *Weser*, in 16 hours from *London*. *Hanover* in a further hour, and *Goslar*, for the *Harz* (see **R2** [iv]) in 20 hours. Follow **R1** as far as *Osnabrück*.

The Teutoburg Forest

R2 (i) Osnabrück to Detmold. Fifty miles (80km). The *Teutoburger Wald*, a long narrow range of wooded hills rising to about 1,000ft (300m), is good walking country with many youth hostels, and footpaths waymarked with white X 6in (15cm) square. The best road for motorists and cyclists (B68) skirts the southern foot of the hills through *Bad Iburg*Δ, a picturesque little town with 900-year-old castle and a Benedictine Abbey from the eleventh century. On to *Halle* with its steep-roofed half-timbered houses, to *Bielefeld* Δ, a beautifully situated manufacturing town symbolised by the pipe-smoking figures of the linen-weavers' monument. Thence by B66 and 239 to *Detmold*Δ, formerly chief town of *Lippe-Detmold*, one of the innumerable small principalities of Germany; fine castle and museum of relics from prehistoric times found in the area. Three miles (5km) south on *Grotenburg* 1,250ft (381m) is colossal statue known as *Hermannsdenkmal*, commemorating victory of Germanic leader Hermann (Arminius) over the Romans in AD9.

From *Osnabrück* follow B65 and keep north of *Wiehengebirge*, a spur of the *Weser* hills via *Bad Essen*Δ to *Lübbecke*, some fine buildings. *Minden*, a former *Hansa* city, has a noble cathedral and remarkable aqueduct carrying *Mittelland* canal over the *Weser*.

The Weser Hill Country

R2 (ii) The River Weser from Minden to Hannoversch-Münden. The *Weser*, a slow-flowing winding river, runs for over 100 miles (160km) through the charming *Weserbergland*, an unspoiled region of beech and oak forests interspersed with fertile farmland. The hills rise to an average of 1,000ft (300m) and a maximum of 1,716ft (523m). Good walking country with many footpaths waymarked with white X: first class for canoeing too, with youth hostels at riverside points every 15 miles (24km) or so. Leisurely steamer service *Hann-Minden-Hameln* in 11 hours, reverse direction in 2 days; May-September only.

From *Minden* by B61 south through the Westphalian Gap (*Porta Westfalica*) a geological curiosity, where the *Weser* in prehistoric times cut through the ridge of hills; *Hausberg*Δ above gap. Fine view from terrace of Kaiser Wilhelm Monument. *Bad Oeynhausen*, small spa. By-roads to *Rinteln*Δ for steamer. *Hameln*Δ (of 'Pied Piper' fame) has a picturesque 'Rat-catcher's house', and sugar rats can be bought in shops. Many fine old timbered houses, with inscriptions and carvings.

EXCURSION: 12 miles (19km) south-west is *Bad Pyrmont*, one of most attractive small spas in Europe; fine gardens, lawns and shady walks.

Next town *Bodenwerder*Δ, was home of legendary Baron *Münchhausen*, teller of travellers' tales; on via *Polle*Δ and to *Holzminden*Δ to *Höxter*Δ near *Corvey* Abbey, parts of which have been untouched since AD850. To east of river is *Solling* forest, densely wooded, rich in game; with highest peak *Grosse Blösse* (1,716ft, 523m) near *Silberborn*Δ. Beyond *Bad Karlshafen*Δ comes the *Reinhardswald*, densely wooded hills where Grimm brothers collected many of their fairy tales (*Reinhardshagen* Δ); nature reserve round *Sababurg*; *Hannoversch-Münden*Δ attractive town at confluence of *Fulda* and *Werra*, which form River *Weser*; **R5** continues south-east.

Six miles (10km) beyond *Minden* is *Bückeburg*, picturesque old town; in surrounding districts women often wear traditional dress. *Stadhagen* has many well-preserved buildings. Hill country to south is worth visiting.

HanoverΔ is former seat of Hanoverian kings; now an important industrial city, mostly rebuilt, with famous trade fair. *Herrenhausen* gardens (west side of city), seventeenth-century baroque style.

R2 (iii) Hanover to Berlin. Hanover is convenient point of departure for *Berlin*; transit visa required to cross East German territory by rail or road, issued on train or at Frontier by stamping passport. Road recommended as frontier formalities usually cleared more quickly. Berlin△, former capital of Germany; is an 'island' in East Germany. Free movement in western part of city, but rapid political changes in Eastern Europe have relaxed many of the former travel restrictions to East Berlin, so visitors should check the latest situation. New luxury buildings in western sectors, show-piece workers' flats in eastern sector. *Charlottenberg* Castle. Famous zoo, aquarium and botanical gardens. Congress hall (interesting modern design) in Tiergarten. *Autobahn* cloverleaf pattern on Potsdamer Chaussee, Dahlem Museum (fine collection of paintings), Egyptian Museum (bust of Nerfertiti). Pergamon Museum in East Berlin. *Waldbühne* (Forest Arena) huge open-air cinema, concerts and sports shows. Pleasant woods (*Grünewald*) and lakes (*Havel*, good bathing) to south-west of city.

Dull route from *Hanover* to **Brunswick**, bustling city dating from ninth century, was former capital of Lower Saxony, has many places of interest. Bronze lion in *Burgplatz* (1166) recalls Henry the Lion, who built the Romanesque cathedral.

The Harz

R2 (iv) Brunswick to the Harz Mountains. Thirty miles (48km) south of *Brunswick*, the *Harz* are conifer-covered hills, rising to about 3,000ft (900m). Better known to German tourists than any others, and linked with many legends, above all the witches' Walpurgis-night in Goethe's *Faust*. There is good skiing on the higher slopes, excellent walking, a number of caves and several well-known spas. The eastern half of the range, including the famous *Brocken* 2,700ft (823m) lies in East German territory, but the frontier is clearly marked and there is no danger of straying.

Goslar△, at northern end of *Harz*, is rare and rewarding old town, containing street after street of domestic architecture of every period from fifteenth century; magnificent guildhouses, solid fortifications, narrow streets. From *Goslar* road B241 rises at times steeply into the *Oberharz* with lakes, and hills of which *Bocksberg* (2,350ft, 716m) rising above *Hahnenklee* is highest and gives fine view as far as distant *Brocken*. Strike north-west by side-road through wonderfully wooded area of *Lautental* to *Bockswiese*△ and *Wildemann*. Westwards to *Iberg*, (1,800ft, 550m), with big stalactite caves. South of *Clausthal-Zellerfeld*△, road B241 leads through idyllic long *Lerbach* valley with heavy black forest on one side and open meadow on the other, to *Osterode*△ a town with fine sixteenth- and seventeenth-century buildings. Follow B243 to *Herzberg*, with lofty 900-year-old castle, caves and some fine views. Beyond *Scharzfeld*△ take winding hilly road over the *Grosse Knollen* (1,970ft, 600m) to *Sieber* and up the *Sieber* valley to *St Andreasberg*. This is the highest of seven well-known *Harz* towns, in strange, barren but fascinating countryside. Strike down to B27 for ski centre at *Braunlage*△ close to border of Russian Zone. Thence by B4 over bleak and boggy country above 3,000ft (900m) to *Torfhaus*△ which faces the *Brocken*. Follow by-road to *Altenau*△ past a large reservoir and wild and romantic *Oker* valley; at *Romkerhall* the narrow defile lays bare many layers of the earth's crust. Return from *Oker* to *Goslar*.

The above circuit is about 140 miles (225km) from *Brunswick* to *Brunswick* or 80 miles (129km) from *Goslar* to *Goslar*.

Eastward from *Brunswick* road B 1 skirts wooded hills known as the *Elm* and joins *Autobahn* at *Helmstedt*, frontier town.

R3 The Rhine from the Dutch Frontier to Mainz (228 miles, 367km)

The *Rhine* is not merely the largest river in Western Europe, it is also a main artery of transport; huge barges ply from the industrial Ruhr to Holland and the North Sea. Passenger steamers do not run on this section, and because of the flatness of the country the Lower *Rhine* is not often visited by tourists. But motorists and cyclists entering Germany from Holland should cross the frontier near *Nijmegen* to the picturesque little town of *Kleve*Δ on the edge of the *Reichswald* forest. *Kalkar* and *Xanten* are also historical small towns.

*Duisburg*Δ, on the east bank, is the second-largest inland port in the world, handling the coal, steel and other products of the *Ruhr*. Further south is **Düsseldorf**Δ, a spacious city lying outside the industrial region, has parks, tree-lined street, elegant shops and the *Königsallee*, a magnificent avenue.

The Sauerland

R3 (i) Düsseldorf to the Sauerland Hills. An excursion for visitors wishing to get away from fellow tourists, to walk the *Sauerland* hills where the youth hostel movement first began.

By busy road for 50 miles (80km) or by rail in 2 hours, via *Hagen*Δ to *Altena*Δ, in valley of *Lenne*. World's first permanent youth hostel opened here in 1909 by Richard Schirrmann, young school-teacher, in castle above town. South of *Altena* stretches wooded hill country of *Sauerland* some 60 miles (96km) from east to west, which, with the contiguous *Bergisch Land* hills to the west forms popular place of recreation from nearby *Ruhr*. Many footpaths waymarked with white X by *Sauer-ländischer Gebirgsverein* of *Iserlohn*; their maps on scale 1:50,000 depict these paths, their guide *Führer durch das Hauptwegenetz* describes them. Close network of youth hostels, some of them purpose-built; several are converted castles. Thinly populated, hills rise to maximum of 2,733ft (833m) (*Kahler Asten* south-east of *Meschede*Δ), but cut by deep river valleys giving impression of greater height; many reservoirs including that formed by the *Möhne* dam of wartime fame. *Möhnsee-Körbecke*Δ nearby.

Twenty-five miles (40km) south of *Düsseldorf* and 87 miles (140km) from the Dutch frontier: **Cologne**Δ (**Köln**), founded by Romans in 38BC; many Roman remains, especially *Dionysus* mosaic. Cultural and commercial capital of *Rhineland*; magnificent Gothic cathedral (begun 1248, finished in nineteenth century) is one of most beautiful in world. Golden reliquary on high altar, fine view from tower — note semi-circular arrangement of streets, following former fortifications, and roads converging on city from all directions. The fifteenth-century *Gürzenich*, built for dancing and celebration, is still so used, especially during the carnival on Shrove Tuesday and days immediately preceeding it.

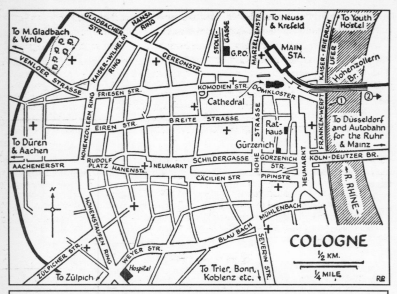

1 Rhine steamers land here. 2 To youth hostel at Deutz.

R3 (ii) Cologne to Aachen, 45 miles (72km). Not an interesting journey, but important as most direct rail access via *Ostend*. By fast train in 1 hour. Choice of roads via *Jülich* or *Düren*. For *Aachen* itself see **R3 (iii)**.

The Rhine Valley

South of *Cologne* the *Rhine* valley is about 25 miles (40km) wide and not at all spectacular. River steamers ply from *Cologne*, and travellers with time can go to *Mainz* by fast steamer in fourteen hours. Travellers with less time to spare should take cheaper slow steamer from *Koblenz* to *Rüdesheim* in six hours. Road and railway on each side of the river, with numerous ferries. Road B9 follows the west (left) bank of the river, and B42 the east; both packed with motor traffic in summer. Use steamer or make for quiet hill country on either side.

Rheinhöhenwege following course of river, often at distance from it; right-bank footpath from *Beuel*, opposite *Bonn*, to *Wiesbaden* Δ, left-bank from *Bonn* to *Andernach* and from *Koblenz*Δ to *Mainz*Δ; both waymarked with white R. Stollfuss map of *Hunsrück* on scale 1:100,000 depicts these footpaths.

Leaving *Cologne*, take road B9 to **Bonn** Δ. Beethoven's birthplace; ancient university town; celebrated *Rheinisches Landesmuseum*; *Poppeldorfer* castle; seat of government; *Bundehaus* is attractive modern building, by riverside.

*Bad Godesberg*Δ, first of many tourist resorts on the route; small and elegant redoubt palace, and eighteenth-century castle.

EXCURSION: Ferry to *Königswinter*, then on foot into the **Siebengebirge** (Seven Mountains), former volcanoes; highest peak is *Olberg* 1,498ft (456m) but wider view from *Drachenfels* (Dragon's Rock — named after Siegfried legend, based on this area) which rises immediately above river and has ruined castle. Rack railway up from *Königwinter* in 10 minutes. *Siebengebirge* have well-marked paths, good walking.

South of *Godesberg* the valley narrows and wine growing area begins; make for *Bad Honnef*Δ; on to *Linz*, charming old walled town, many half-timbered houses.

R3 (iii) Sinzig to Aachen via Ahr Valley and Eifel, 156 miles (250km). A pleasant journey for motorists and cyclists by relatively quiet by-roads. Follow graceful *Ahr Valley* (Germany's largest red wine area) past sophisticated spa of *Bad Neuenahr*Δ to small towns of *Ahrweiler* and *Altenahr*Δ, entering *Eifel* mountains.

The Eifel

An unspoiled region with numerous extinct volcanic craters, many now filled by small lakes (*Maare*) particularly near *Daun*, in sombre forest surroundings; frequent hot springs. Average height of region about 1,800ft (550m).

Six north/south footpaths waymarked with solid black triangle on white ground, six east/west footpaths waymarked with arrow on white ground. Crater path from *Andernach* to *Gerolstein*, waymarked with black V. Waymarking by Eifelsverein of *Düren*, depicted on their *Wanderkarte* on six sheets at a scale of 1:50,000

South from *Altenahr* on B257 to famous motor-racing circuit of *Nürburg Ring* (17 miles, 27km, 170 curves) crowded when racing in progress. Track dominated by *Höhe Acht* (2,430ft, 740m), highest peak in *Eifel*. Continue by B257 to *Daun*Δ centre of crater lakes. North and west by *Gerolstein*Δ (small spa) to *Prüm*Δ with 1,200-year-old Benedictine abbey, one of many abbeys which helped to open up *Eifel* for settlement in Middle Ages. West of *Prüm* is *Schnee-Eifel*, high and desolate range. North-east by B51 via *Kronenburg*Δ to *Blankenheim*Δ near source of River *Ahr*. Proceed north-westwards to *Gemünd* Δ for vast reservoir of *Urfttal*, supplying water and electric power to Rhineland towns. West by B258 to *Monschau* Δ, frontier town, many half-timbered houses, tourist centre. Road 258 now crosses tongue of Belgian territory (*Hautes Fagnes*), traverses *Rötgen* forest, and enters *Aachen*.

Aachen Δ (Aix-la-Chapelle) is historic town, capital of Charlemagne's empire; cathedral partly built by him; Holy Roman emperors were crowned here for seven centuries. Warm springs (hottest in Europe). Main rail approach to Germany via *Ostend*.

From *Sinzig*, 7 miles (11km) upstream to *Brohl*.

EXCURSION: 6 miles (10km) by road to *Laacher See*, largest lake in *Eifel*, with ninth-century *Maria Laach* abbey and fine abbey church.

Continue on left bank via *Andernach*, town established in pre-Roman times, to **Koblenz**△, confluence of *Mosel* and *Rhine*, important wine trade; *Deutsches Eck*, point at which the *Mosel* enters the *Rhine* and their different-coloured waters mingle. Cross to *Ehrenbreitstein* fortress (climb, or take chair lift, for magnificent view). See **R4** for *Mosel* and *Lahn* valley routes from *Koblenz*.

The Rhine Gorge

Between *Koblenz* and *Bingen* (40 miles, 64km) the *Rhine* winds its way between steep hillsides, often covered with vineyards and dotted with ruined castles. Follow road B42 to *Lahnstein*, ancient town; picturesque houses and streets; Castle *Lahneck* worth visiting. Fine views of *Stolzenfels* Castle on opposite bank (thirteenth century). *Braubach*, ancient battlements; *Marksburg*, 700ft (215m) above river, a medieval castle. Continue up road B42 and ferry to *Boppard*, charming old town, excellent starting point for excursions.

Ferry back to east bank, and continue through *Kamp* to *Bornhofen*. At *Wellmich*, 5 miles (8km) farther on is *Burg Maus* (Mouse Castle), a name given in contempt by the owners of *Burg Katz* (Cat Castle) a short distance upstream.

Next comes the narrowest part of the *Rhine* gorge where the river is barely 200yd (180m) wide, but more than 70ft (20m) deep, fast-flowing, and with whirlpools. On the west bank is *St Goar*△, a pleasant town with *Rheinfels* castle on heights above. On opposite bank is *St Goarhausen* △, with steeply rising cliff, the **Loreli**, where a beautiful maiden is supposed to have sat, combing her golden hair, and luring boatmen to their deaths on the rocks below.

Beyond *Urbar* comes *Oberwesel*△, a picturesque old town, surrounded by a thirteenth-century wall with fourteen watchtowers. To the south of town is the ruined castle of *Schönburg*, on a lofty cliff.

On a small island near *Kaub* stands the many-turreted *Pfalz*, built as a toll house in the fourteenth century; above *Kaub* is the magnificent castle of *Gutenfels*. *Bacharach* △, another walled town of great charm, is dominated by the castle of *Stahleck* (Hall of Knights, and a superb view from battlements).

Beyond *Lorch* △ comes a series of castles, *Heimburg, Sooneck* and *Rheinstein*, on the west bank. The river then bends eastwards, entering the *Binger Loch*, formerly rapids which could not be navigated. *Bingen*△, river port on confluence of *Rhine* and *Nahe*; tenth-century *Mäuseturm* (Mouse Tower) on small island nearby. Opposite *Bingen* stands the *Niederwaldenkmal*, a monumentally ugly statue of Germania, 120ft (36m) high, erected in 1877 to commemorate the creation of German unity by Bismarck; a fine view from here.

Rüdesheim△, famous for wines but crowded with tourists. *Rüdesheim* to *Mainz* landscape is quite flat and richly agricultural; *Rheingau* vineyards for finest Rhenish wines. *Geisenheim* for *Schönborn* castle; *Eltville*; celebrated wine town; *Schlangenbad*, thermal open-air swimming pool; *Wiesbaden* Δ, celebrated spa since Roman times, attractively planned town in sheltered position.

MainzΔ was an illustrious city in Roman times; retains traces of former glory and now capital of *Rhine Palatinate*. Romanesque cathedral houses remarkable collection of church art. Gutenberg museum in fine Renaissance building, hand-presses and Gutenberg Bible; see too Chagall windows in St Stephen's church.

R4 Trier to Marburg via Mosel and Lahn (186 miles, 299km)

An unusual, but rewarding route; less over-run than the *Rhine* valley, and considered to be preferable. *Trier* can be reached via *Ostend* and *Luxembourg* and this *Mosel* valley journey can well be combined with a tour in *Luxembourg*.

TrierΔ, oldest city in the country, and focal point of church for many centuries. Now resembles gigantic open-air museum. *Porta Nigra*, massive gateway, northern entry to Roman Empire; Roman baths, basilica and amphitheatre.

The Mosel

At *Trier* enter *Mosel* valley where the river meanders in huge leisurely curves, between the *Eifel* and the *Hunsrück*. From *Trier* to *Koblenz*, in a straight line is 60 miles (96km), but the river doubles this distance. River banks are terraced with vineyards; wine taverns in the sleepy red-roofed villages and towns. Some castles but few of the grim ruins characterising the *Rhine*. Ideal river for canoeists; several riverside youth hostels. By road, take B53 to *Bullay*, then B49 to *Koblenz*.

Moselhöhenwege follows course of river, waymarked with white M from *Brodenbach*Δ to *Bernkastel*Δ on right bank, similarly waymarked from *Koblenz*Δ to *Karden* and from *Cochem* Δ to *Mehring* on left bank, by *Hunsrückverein* of *Bernkastel*. Stollfuss map *Das Moseltal* on scale of 1:100,000 depicts these footpaths.

First place of note is *Neumagen*; Roman stone model of wine ship with tippling crew discovered here. *Bernkastel-Kues*Δ, one of many wine towns; market square of timbered buildings from sixteenth century. Town dominated by ruined *Landshut* castle. Notable wine festival on first Saturday and Sunday in September.

The Hunsrück

R4 (i) Bernkastel to Idar Oberstein 25 miles (40km). South of the *Mosel* lies heavily wooded hill country, the *Hunsrück*. Southwards to *Morbach* Δ and follow B269 to foot of *Erbeskopf* (2,600ft, 792m) highest peak in *Rhineland* area, then take byroad eastwards to *Idar Oberstein* Δwell known for precious stone cutting industry; workshops can be visited. *Hunsrück* range continues westwards, past *Hermeskeil*Δ into *Saarland*.

Long-distance footpath, waymarked with white X, by Hunsrückverein of *Bernkastel*, follows highest ridges in north-easterly direction from *Merzig* in *Saarland* to *Bacharach* on the *Rhine*. Stollfuss map of *Hunsrück* on scale 1:100,000 depicts this footpath.

Continue along *Mosel* valley past *Urzig*, which has fine old timbered buildings. *Traben-Trarbach*△, modern town dominated by ruined castle of *Grevenburg*. Between *Reil* and *Alf* on left bank is particularly fine section of *Mosel* path; picturesque *Marienburg* ruin, south of *Alf* where ridge separating two loops of river is barely 1,480ft (450m) wide; one of the finest views in *Mosel* area.

At *Eller* railway enters (2^1/$_2$ mile, 4km) tunnel; road follows river valley to *Beilstein* with picturesque market square partly cut out of rock.

Cochem △, originally pre-Roman, has remains of walls and gateways; castle above town rebuilt in nineteenth century to original plans. *Eifel* footpath to *Prüm* begins here.

Series of attractive small towns and villages both sides of river. *Moselkern*, confluence of River *Eltz*, beautiful valley with several castles.

EXCURSION: on foot in 1 hour by *Eifel* path (motorists and cyclists can approach by by-road) to **Burg Eltz**, best preserved of all *Mosel* castles. Vast building with many towers; parts date from twelfth century. Castle can be visited (guide available). To north lies ruin of castle *Trutz-Eltz*, built by Bishop Balduin of *Trier* in fourteenth century to control insubordinate knights of *Eltz*.

Brodenbach △ on right bank, small tourist centre, marks end of most attractive part of *Mosel*; to north is fruit-growing area of *Maifeld*, to south is spur of *Hunsrück*.

R4 (ii) Brodenbach to the Rhine. Motorists and cyclists can follow by-road over heights via *Gondershausen* to *St Goar*△ (25 miles, 40km) on *Rhine*. For walkers, choice of several fine footpaths in 4-5 hours to *Boppard*.

Koblenz (see **R3**) for *Rhine* valley. Follow east bank of *Rhine* southwards to *Niederlahnstein*, for confluence of River *Lahn*.

The Lahn

A graceful river, flowing in smaller loops than the *Mosel*, between *Taunus* and *Westerwald*. Narrow valley near mouth, meadow and hill country nearer source. Many interesting small towns. Some wine-growing. Railway follows river from *Koblenz* to *Marburg*; fast train via *Giessen* in about 2 hours; main roads leave valley, but side roads recommended, following river most of way.

B260 to *Bad Ems*△ celebrated spa, known in Roman times and more recently by Bismarck's 'Ems Telegram' of 1870; continue to *Nassau*, whence comes

Dutch royal family name of *Orange-Nassau*; sixteenth-century castles and half-timbered houses. Take winding secondary road via *Diez*△ to *Limburg*△, medieval town, thirteenth-century cathedral with seven towers; expeditions into *Westerwald* and *Taunus* from here.

Runkel, 5 miles (8km) beyond *Limburg*, has fine castle and old bridge over *Lahn*; *Wetzlar*△ has associations with Goethe, a very fine cathedral, an unusual number steep streets and steps, and the Leitz factory where the famous Leica camera is produced. *Giessen*△ is rail junction and centre of scientific reseach. On to **Marburg**△, a town from the Middle Ages, set on the hills; *St Elisabeth* church, first Gothic cathedral built in Germany; Gothic town hall with noteworthy old clock; first Protestant university founded here in 1527.

The Taunus

One of the many ranges forming the central uplands. To the north, bordering River *Lahn*, its woodlands are interspersed with pleasant farming country. To the south the land rises to an average of 1,500ft (450m), thickly wooded. Four principal footpaths, waymarked by *Taunusbund* and *Rhein-Taunus Club*, who publish maps *Maintaunus* and *Rheintaunus* on scale 1:50,000 depicting them; *Stollfuss* map *Taunus* on scale 1:100,000 shows these footpaths too. Highest point is *Feldberg* (2,860ft, 871m — not to be confused with *Feldberg* in *Black Forest*). A western spur of *Taunus* forms *Rheingau* hills, sheltering famous wine-growing region of that name (see **R3**). *Königstein* is railhead for ascent of *Feldberg*.

R4 (iii) Giessen to Mainz via Homburg, 45 miles (72km). An alternative return to *Rhine*, skirting east and south of *Taunus* hills to *Bad Nauheim* (fashionable spa) then B455 to *Bad Homburg*△, another spa, which gave name to Homburg hat; castle with fine garden. Follow choice of footpaths via *Wiesbaden* △ to *Mainz*△.

R5 Kassel to Passau by the Eastern Mountains (350 miles, 563km)

Leading into remote and unspoilt country. A long route for any but most leisured motorist or cyclist, and hilly all the way. Closely follows border of East Germany and of Czechoslovakia.

Kassel △, a garden city on the *Fulda* may be reached by extending **R2 (ii)** from *Hannoversch-Münden* (14 miles, 22km) or **R4** from *Marburg* (43 miles, 69km) or by rail from England via *Hook of Holland* has fine art gallery, with many old masters; museum of tapestry and wallpapers in *Wilhelmshöhe* castle.

Twenty-five miles (40km) eastwards lies *Höher Meissner*, hill plateau (2,437ft, 743m) overlooking East German border. *Ludwigstein*△; south via *Rotenburg*△ to *Bebra*, a rail junction with many old half-timbered houses; along River *Fulda*, via *Bad Hersfeld*△ and *Schlitz*△ to *Fulda*△, important religious centre (tomb of St Boniface, English monk of eighth century); many fine baroque buildings. Continue south-east to the *Rhön*.

The Rhön

A thinly wooded hill region of volcanic origin, with interesting flora; *Wasser-kuppe* is highest peak (3,037ft, 925m); gliding and skiing popular here.

Footpaths north/south from *Tann* to *Gemunden* Δ and north-east/south-west from East German frontier near *Fladungen* to *Gemunden*; also seven footpaths west/east. All waymarked with red triangles by *Rhönklub* of *Fulda*. *Rhönklub* map of *Rhön* on scale 1:100,000 depicts them.

Franconia

Franconia is a historical rather than geographical entity; one of the duchies of medieval Germany, it comprises northern and eastern *Bavaria*, centred on *Nuremberg*. Has many medieval cities and some pleasant hill country in *Fränkische Alb* and *Frankenwald*. It is the land of the Meistersinger.

B279 leads through *Bischofsheim*Δ into *Bad Neustadt*, pleasantly situated spa on River *Saale*. Over the steep-wooded ridges of the *Hassberge*, via *Königshofen*, fine market-place, many timbered buildings, to **Bamberg**Δ. Beautiful cathedral city, famous equestrian statue of *Knight of Bamberg*; many fine old houses in area between cathedral and town hall; former Bishop's residences, now museums.

R5 (i) Bamberg to CoburgΔ, 28 miles (45km). *Coburg*, home of Albert of Saxe-Coburg-Gotha, Queen Victoria's consort, to whom there is a statue in market place. City with many buildings in Gothic and Renaissance styles, dominated by massive *Veste*, one of largest and finest fortresses in Germany, which has many connections with Luther and the Reformation, now museum with huge collection of engravings.

R5 (ii) Bamberg to Nuremberg, 38 miles (61km). South by narrow valley of River *Regnitz* via *Forchheim* and *Erlangen*Δ, part of which was built to a plan in baroque style, to house Huguenot refugees in seventeenth century. **Nuremberg**Δ, at crossroads of medieval trade routes, hence prosperity and rich heritage in architecture, either original or carefully rebuilt in original style; house of sixteenth-century artist Albrecht Dürer (in *Bergstrasse*); city wall and castle; many lovely Gothic churches including the *Frauenkirche* (on the market square) which has clock with famous set of mechanical figures showing seven electors paying homage to Emperor Charles IV; clock constructed 1509, plays at 12 noon daily; many associations with troubadours and Meistersinger, large Germanic National Museum, including interesting collection of toys and dolls. *Nuremberg* is centre of German toy industry and *Lebkuchen* (gingerbreads) are a special *Nuremberg* delicacy.

From *Bamberg* follow **R5 (ii)** to *Forchheim* and eastwards along valley of River *Wiesent* into *Fränkische Schweiz*, characterised by steep-walled valleys, jagged rock formations, summits rising to about 2,000ft (600m), caves, picturesque villages such as *Gössweinstein*Δ, *Pottenstein*Δ and *Streitberg*Δ.

The Fichtelgebirge

A horseshoe shaped range, covered with spruce forests; mountainous, with granite peaks up to watershed of tributaries of the *Elbe, Danube* and *Rhine*. Excellent walking and skiing country; many footpaths waymarked by Fichtelgebirgeverien of *Wunsiedel* and depicted on their map on scale 1:50,000.

Main highway is the *Ostmarkstrasse*, but secondary roads preferable for cyclists and leisurely motorists. Ascend *Steinach* valley to *Oberwarmensteinach*Δ at foot of *Ochsenkopf* (3,360ft, 1,024m) winter-sports centre. Beyond *Fichtelgeberg* join B303 for *Wunsiedel*, pleasant small resort; on *Luisenburg*, southwards, is extraordinary maze of rock. From *Marktredwitz*Δ follow *Ostmarkstrasse* through the *Oberpfälzerwald*, with many youth hostels, to *Cham* — for *Bavarian Forest*.

The Bavarian Forest

The frontier here is formed by a mountain barrier, heavily forested, unspoilt and little visited. The *Bavarian Forest* extends unbroken along the *Danube* from *Regensburg* to *Passau*, with the *Oberpfälzerwald* as its northern spur. On the Czech side lies the *Bohemian* Forest.

Motorists and cyclists can follow B85 for whole length of forest to *Passau*. *Furth-im-Wald*Δ has *Drachen-Stich* celebration on second Sunday in August. Highest peak *Grosser Arber* (4,780ft, 1,457m) with beautiful *Arbersee* below, can be climbed from *Bayer — Eisenstein*Δ or *Bodenmais*Δ. Southwards is *Grosser Rachel* (4,765ft, 1,452m) accessible from *Waldhäuser*Δ; so, too, is the bare rock-strewn summit of the *Lusen* (4,452ft, 1,357m).

Passau, small town of character at confluence of *Inn* and *Danube*; see fifteenth-century St Stephen's cathedral, in exuberant baroque. *Danube* steamers to *Linz* in 4 hours, to *Vienna* in 13 hours.

> *Ostlicher Haupwanderweg*, long-distance footpath of about 105 miles (170km), waymarked with green triangle by Bayerischer-Wald-Verein of *Straubing*, follows highest ridges of mountains from *Furth-im-Wald* to *Obernzell* on *Danube*, east of *Passau*, with many youth hostels on route. Fritsch map of *Bayerischer Wald* on scale 1:100,000 depicts this footpath.

R6 Mainz to Munich by the 'Romantic Road' (225 miles, 362km)
Highway from *Würzburg* on River *Main* to *Füssen* in Alps is named *Romantische Strasse* and goes through series of picturesque places and areas in *Franconia* (see **R5**) and *Upper Bavaria*. Side roads, although circuitous, are numerous and preferable for motorists with time to spare, and for cyclists.

From *Mainz* follow River *Main* to **Frankfurt** Δ, formerly prosperous merchant city, home of German liberalism and of wealthy Jewish families; associations with poet Goethe; museums, art galleries and *Palmengarten*, one of finest botanical gardens in Europe.

On through *Offenbach* and *Aschaffenburg*Δ, where river valley narrows and acquires great charm, winding its way in huge bends past delightful old market towns like *Miltenberg*Δ and *Wertheim* Δ.

The Spessart

R6 (i) Aschaffenburg to Wertheim by the Spessart 32 miles (51km). An alternative to the *Main* valley route. Trunk road B8 is attractive though busy, crossing highest part of *Spessart*, but many footpaths and minor roads also follow this route.

This is a triangle of forested hill country, some 1,000ft (300m) high, enclosed by huge bend on River *Main*. Oak and beech trees, including some of oldest trees in Germany around *Rohrbrunn*, alternate with pines. Southern portion, centred on village of *Rohrbrunn* (on B8) is most attractive. Highest point is *Geiersberg* (1,900ft, 579m) above *Rohrbrunn*. Nature reserves round *Rohrberg*. Most visited place is fifteenth-century castle of *Mespelbrunn* on by-road from B8, 10 miles (16km) south-east of *Aschaffenburg*Δ; castle stands on island in lake among woods; magnificent Hall of Knights.

Spessart has four *Höhenwege*, footpaths based on disused medieval trade routes, waymarked with initial letters in black on white ground by Spessartbund of *Aschaffenburg*. Ravenstein map of *Spessart* on scale 1:100,000 depicts these paths.

R6 (ii) Wertheim to Würzburg, 25 miles (40km). WurzburgΔ, old university town, seat of bishop, many masterpieces of baroque architecture; see the *Residenz*, reputed grandest baroque palace in the country, built in horseshoe shape; royal apartments and grand staircase are superb.

At *Wertheim* route leaves River *Main* to follow its tributary, the *Tauber*, via *Tauberbischofsheim*Δ, *Ingersheim*Δ and, after seeing the castle at *Weikersheim*Δ, on to *Creglingen*Δ. On to *Rothenburg*Δ, much visited showplace of the Middle Ages; see treasures in *St James'* church. *Rathaus* tower for view over town; walk around encircling walls.

Southwards to *Feuchtwangen*Δ, and on to *Dinkelsbühl*Δ, another medieval town, as is *Nördlingen* Δ. At *Donauwörth* Δ, on the River *Danube (Donau)*, route enters **Swabia**, another imprecisely defined region, like *Franconia*. The *Swabians* have a reputation, even among Germans, for their hard work.

AugsburgΔ, a medieval city, famous in its day for wealthy merchant families; Dürer, Holbein and Titian worked here. Cathedral has oldest stained glass in world, famous eleventh-century bronze doors and altarpiece by Holbein. *Maximilianstrasse*, one of finest streets, part of Roman road leading to Venice; *Schaezlerpalais* art gallery has magnificent collection. Alps visible on clear days from top of *Perlach* tower of *Rathaus*.

MunichΔ, capital of *Bavaria*, third largest city, intellectual, artistic and industrial centre. *Frauenkirche* with famous twin dome-capped towers. *Rathaus*,

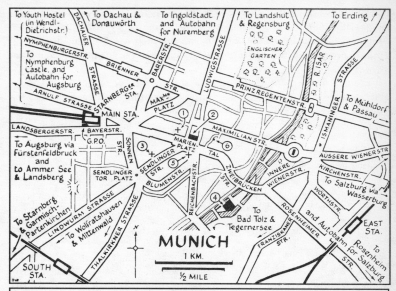

1 Frauenkirche. 2 Town Hall. 3 St Nepomuk Church. 4 Deutsches Museum. 5 St Peter's Church. 6 Hofbräuhaus.

overlooking *Marienplatz* has remarkable mechanical clock with enamelled copper figures which daily perform knights' tournament and shepherds' dance; *St Nepomuk* church, in exuberant rococo. *Theatinerkirche* on the *Ludwigstrasse*, baroque, façade and interior crowded with cherubs. *St Peter's* church, on *Marienplatz*, oldest in city but many times restored, baroque interior. *Deutsches Museum*, one of finest science museums in world. Fine art collection in *Pinakothek* galleries. Imposing broad streets; *Prinzregentenstrasse, Maximilianstrasse, Ludwigstrasse*. On outskirts of city is *Nymphenburg Palace*, fine baroque building in lovely park with pavilions and lakes; *Amalienburg*, hunting lodge in the park, decorated in sumptuous rococo.

South-West Germany

The state of *Baden-Württemberg* occupies the south-west of Germany in the angle of the *Rhine* and Lake *Constance*. It is an area of great variety and charm — orchards, wooded uplands, winding rivers, old towns, villages and castles and, above all, the *Black Forest*. The eastern portion of *Württemberg* is called *Swabia*, an area which overlaps into *Bavaria* (see **R6**).

R7 Mainz to Lake Constance (240 miles, 386km)

Across hill and mountain country above the *Rhine* valley. Rail from *Mainz* to *Freiburg* in 3 hours; from *London* to *Freiburg* via *Ostend/Cologne* in 18 hours. Post bus in summer from *Freiburg* to *Schaffhausen*, rail connections to *Constance*.

From *Mainz* to *Darmstadt*△, across flat *Rhine* valley, journey by rail advisable, thence by B3, the *Bergstrasse*, skirting *Odenwald*; succession of charming villages and many youth hostels.

The Odenwald

R7 (i) Bensheim to Miltenberg via the Odenwald, 46 miles (74km). Road B47, the *Nibenlungenstrasse*, is supposed to mark route to Wagner's *Nibelungen*. It crosses the *Odenwald* forest, a compact woodland area between the *Main* and *Neckar*. Western portion, above *Bergstrasse*, has deciduous trees, fruit and vineyards, and is substantially populated. Eastern portion is coniferous forest, wilder and less frequented.

To the north is peak of *Melibocus* (1,690ft, 515m) good view, much visited; *Lindenfels*, health resort. Southwards to pleasant area around *Wald Michelbach* △ and the 1,900ft (579m) *Tromm*. *Michelstadt*, *Erbach* △ and *Amorbach* △ are all very picturesque towns. At *Miltenberg* reach River *Main* (see **R6**).

Heidelberg△, famous university city, charmingly situated on River *Neckar*; see the *Hauptstrasse* at foot of ruined castle; and take funicular railway to *Königstühl* (1,846ft, 562m) for superb view of *Neckar* valley.

R7 (ii) Heidelberg to Ulm via Neckar and Schwäbische Alb, 136 miles (219km). By rail (via *Heilbronn* and *Stuttgart*) in about 4¹/₂ hours.

River *Neckar*, flowing through gorge between *Odenwald* and hill country to south is most attractive; vineyards, old castles, picturesque towns and villages: *Neckargemund-Dilsberg*△ for *Neckarsteinach* where four castles dominate the river. *Eberbach* △ probably most beautiful point on river; rail and road into *Odenwald* via *Mosbach* △ to *Bad Wimpfen*△ where River *Neckar* joined by two tributaries: *Jagst* and *Kocher*, flowing through rolling wooded limestone plateau of *Höhenlohe*. *Heilbronn*△ former free city.

South and east of *Heilbronn* stretches **Swabian Forest**, little known country similar to *Black Forest* but less lofty (rising to less than 2,000ft, 600m); small streams, sleepy villages; central points, *Backnang* and *Murrhardt*△.

Stuttgart △, capital of *Baden-Württemberg*, economic and cultural centre of south-west Germany. Noted for lovely setting between hills and vineyards. Spa with many mineral water springs, full of architectural interest, lavishly endowed with parks and gardens, museums and castles. Famous engineering works: *Mercedes-Benz*, *Bosch* and *Porsche*.

The Schwäbische Alb

Road B10 from *Stuttgart* to Ulm crosses the *Schwäbische Alb*, a plateau over 100 miles (160km) long, with white rocks, deep valleys, heights rising to over 3,000ft (900m). Forms continuation of Swiss Jura, hence sometimes called Swabian Jura, with similar rock formations — much limestone, many gorges and caves. Northern slope falls steeply to River *Neckar*, with fortresses on rocky summits; southern slope falls gently to River *Danube*. Many beech forests. As fine a walking country as *Black Forest*, but less well known; many youth hostels and huts of *Schwäbischer Albverein* and *Naturfreunde*.

Footpaths follow northern and southern edges of *Alb*, from *Donauwörth*Δ to *Tuttlingen*Δ, both waymarked by *Schwäbischer Albverein* with red triangles pointing towards *Tuttlingen*. Reise und Verkehrsverlag maps of *Schwäbische Alb* on two sheets on scale 1:100,000 depict these footpaths.

Highest levels at south-western end, known as *Heuberg*; above *Lochen*Δ are many heights above 3,000ft (900m), good skiing. Castle of *Hohenzollern* family, rebuilt nineteenth century, 5 miles (8km) north-west of *Balingen*. *Tübingen*Δ, *Wildenstein* and *Sigmaringen* Δ for southern approaches to *Alb*. Central portion known as *Rauhe Alb* between *Reutlingen* and *Geislingen* has several youth hostels.

Ulm Δ, ancient imperial and modern industrial city, commercial and route centre on *Danube*, fine Gothic cathedral, with highest spire in world (528ft, 161m). Many medieval buildings, a leaning tower named *Metzgerturm* and an excellent museum; riverside promenade. *New Ulm*, across *Danube* in Bavaria, has interesting modern buildings including Catholic church of striking design.

South from *Heidelberg* through unexciting country to *Karlsruhe*Δ, former princely city now busy with lawyers and technologists; eighteenth-century fan-shaped town plan; on to *Pforzheim*.

The Black Forest

Pforzheim Δ on northern border of dense spruce forest, deeply cut valleys, mountain lakes, vineyards and orchards; delightful area for walkers, but popular in summer. Grassy summits at about 4,000ft (1,200m) afford wide views; *Hornisgrinde* (3,820ft, 1,164m) in north, *Belchen* (4,637ft, 1,414m) and *Feldberg*, the highest (4,900ft, 1,493m) in the south.

Many villages with shingled cottages, steeply-pitched thatched farmhouses, centuries old. Sundays and holidays bring out authentic, if local, costumes. Many youth hostels and *Naturfreunde* huts.

Three north/south footpaths, excellently waymarked; transverse and subsidiary footpaths waymarked with blue or yellow in horizontal diamond by Schwarzwaldverein of *Freiburg*. Reise und Verkehrsverlag maps of *Schwarzwald* on scale 1:75,000 on three sheets depict all of them.

Main tourist centres from north to south are *Baden-Baden*Δ, fashionable spa, elegant early nineteenth-century casino and *Kurhaus*; climb nearby *Merkur* (2,278ft, 693m) for wide views across forest. *Sohlberghaus*, in magnificent situation high above *Ottenhöfen* near *Hornisgrinde* peak, and *Freudenstadt* Δ a hill-top town with arcaded square. *Alpirsbach*Δ and on to *Triberg*Δ, at junction of three valleys, noted for cuckoo-clocks; nearby *Gutach* waterfall has cascade of 500ft (152m).

FreiburgΔ, favourite town of the Habsburgs; many fine old buildings, carefully restored Gothic cathedral with open lace-work spire; the *Kaufhaus*, sixteenth-century merchant's hall; the *Schwabentor*, an old city gate.

EXCURSIONS: (a) by bus and cable railway onto the *Schauinsland* (4,173ft, 1,272m) in 45 minutes, or on foot in 4$^1/_2$ hours. Very fine view. (b) by rail in 35-50 minutes. Eighteen miles (29km) up the *Höllental* (Hell Valley) to *Titisee*Δ, beautiful but very crowded lakeside resort, thence on foot in 3-4 hours to summit of *Feldberg* (4,900ft, 1,493m); superb views but over-run owing to easy access by many paths and roads. *Altglashütten*Δ nearby, south-east of summit. Nature reserve round *Feldberg*, with many sub-alpine flowers.

From *Freiburg*, either south through lovely country to *Basel*, or south-east through *Titisee*, by equally lovely parts of the forest with many youth hostels on both routes, emerging into *Hegau*, an area of former volcanic peaks, immediately north of Swiss frontier, to reach Lake *Constance*.

Lake Constance

Lake *Constance (Bodensee)*, 40 miles (64km) long and 1,300ft (396m) above sea-level; in places 8 miles (13km) wide; mild climate; orchards and vineyards; bathing from May to October. Picturesque towns and villages, including *Konstanz*Δ itself and *Uberlingen*Δ. Island of *Mainau*, north-east of *Konstanz,* has castle of former Teutonic knights, surrounded by lemon and banana trees. *Friedrichshafen* Δ, was home of the Zeppelins and the Dornier aircraft. *Lindau*Δ, medieval walled town, almost entirely surrounded by lake. Excellent lake-steamer service.

The Bavarian Alps

R8 Lake Constance to Salzburg via the Bavarian Alps (240 miles, 386km)
Separated from the mountain massif of Austria by the *Inn* valley, the *Bavarian Alps* have north/south valleys but few through routes, no east/west valleys and no peaks as high as those beyond the frontier. Our route follows the west/east extent of the mountains, with rail connections to all parts from *Munich*. Motorists and cyclists can take the entire route without difficulty; walkers can take advantage

of *Postkraftwagen* bus service between *Lindau* and *Berchtesgaden* for easy stages on the route.

From *Lindau* by roads B18 and B308 and the *Deutsche Alpenstrasse*, rising with many curves to about 3,000ft (900m) into the *Allgäu Alps*, lying in *Württemberg* and *Schwaben*, beautiful mountain region forming the western section of the range, from Lake *Constance* to the River *Lech*. Many ski resorts, mountain peaks top 8,000ft (2,400m) and rich alpine meadows yield well-known soft cheeses.

R8 (i) Immenstadt to OberstdorfΔ, 13 miles (21km). Road B19 from *Sonthofen* via *Fischen* to *Oberstdorf*, a mountain centre at 2,700ft (823m) gives access to seven valleys, including *Klein-Walser-Tal* across Austrian frontier. German money is used as no road communications with rest of Austria exist through *Bregenzer* Forest.

EXCURSION: *Nebelhorn*, 6,279ft (1,914m) cable railway followed by chairlift, and to *Kanzelwand* (6,800ft, 2,072m, 16 minutes' journey from valley station at *Rielzlern*). *Nebelhorn* can be climbed on foot in 4 hours. Circular trip on foot round slopes of *Hofat*, via *Oylat* and *Dietersbach*, 8 hours.

From *Immenstadt* by B310 to *Füssen*Δ, charmingly situated old-fashioned town on River *Lech*; fine castle, parts of town wall preserved. To north lies network of small lakes; eastwards into *Ammergebirge*, foothills of *Wetterstein* mountains, for *Neuschwanstein* and *Hohenschwangau*, former residences of Bavarian royal house. **Neuschwanstein**, built in 1870s by extravagant King Ludwig II, one of the most romantic sights in Europe, fairy-tale castle of turrets and towers, perched on rock.

Hohenschwangau, grim neo-Gothic restoration of medieval castle. Bridle path from here goes just inside Austrian frontier, thence on narrow by-road through nature reserve of *Ammer* valley, to *Linderhof*, another of Ludwig II's castles in French eighteenth-century style. On to **Oberammergau**Δ, famous for play first performed 1634 in thanksgiving for end of plague, then every ten years; 1,200 performers, all village people, and sincerity of religious presentation maintained.

Garmisch-PartenkirchenΔ, twin villages at head of *Loisach* valley, famous winter-sports centre; huge ski and skating stadiums. *Garmisch*, on western side of valley, is fashionable and expensive; *Partenkirchen* quieter and cheaper. Brightly painted timber houses, peasant costumes.

EXCURSIONS: (a) by *Zugspitze* rack railway to *Scheefernerhaus*, $1^1/_4$ hours, then by cable railway in 4 minutes to summit of **Zugspitze** (9,720ft, 2,962m), Germany's highest mountain. (b) by cable railway in 10 minutes to summit of *Wank* (5,677ft, 1,730m). (c) by cable railway in 8 minutes to the *Kreuzeck* (5,630ft, 1,716m). Both *Wank* and *Kreuzeck* can be ascended on foot, each in about $3^1/_2$ hours. Ascent of *Zugspitze* (via *Raintal*) for experienced climbers only, 10–11 hours.

From *Garmisch* to *Mittenwald* Δ by B2, 11 miles (18km), or by footpath via *Ferchen* valley and *Elmau*, 5$^1/_2$ hours. *Mittenwald* lies in *Isar* valley, dividing *Wetterstein* from *Karwendel* mountains; in Middle Ages a key transit point for goods from Venice and Orient to the cities of south Germany; in seventeenth century Italian-trained violin maker founded now famous violin industry; violin-makers' school and museum. Many gaily frescoed houses.

EXCURSIONS: (a) by chair-lift and cable railway to the *Höher-Kranzberg* (4,565ft, 1,390m); on foot in 2-2$^1/_2$ hours. (b) by rail to *Scharnitz*, then on foot up lovely *Karwendel* valley (4-day trip).

B11 to *Walchensee*, broad lake with steep, forest-clothed banks, dark-green waters, background of alpine peaks. *Urfeld*Δ on northern shore.

EXCURSIONS: (a) Hydro-electric works (water tunnel from lake to *Kochel See*). (b) tour of lake on foot — 6 to 7 hours. (c) on foot in 3 hours, or by chairlift in 11 minutes, on to *Herzogstand* (5,680ft, 1,730m) with magnificent views; thence by narrow, precipitous ridge path in 1$^1/_2$ hours to neighbouring peak of *Heimgarten* (5,875ft, 1,790m) with footpath link to *Ohlstadt* in *Loisach* valley (3 hours).

From *Urfeld*, pleasant by-road for 11 miles (17km), or by footpaths in 6 hours, through *Jachenau* valley where farmhouses often in possession of same families for centuries to *Lenggries*Δ, small resort on River *Isar*; where timber rafts are floated downstream.

From *Lenggries* to *Scharling*Δ at the southern end of the *Tegernsee* lake is 25 miles (40km) by road via *Bad Tölz*, picturesque old town and spa, but by choice of pleasant footpaths journey can be made in about 6 hours. *Tegernsee* is sophisticated, with many small villas, but not so attractive as smaller neighbour *Schliersee*. Again, choice of footpaths to *Josefstal*Δ in about 4 hours.

Mountain road via *Bayrischzell*Δ mountain resort, to B15, or footpath in 3 hours via *Birkenstein*, on to summit of *Wendelstein* (6,028ft, 1,837m) down to and thence by rack railway (55 minutes) or on foot (3 hours) down to *Brannenburg* in upper *Inn* valley; same river which forms Swiss Engadine, but now a powerful stream. On through *Rosenheim* to *Sims See*, good bathing, and *Chiemsee*, largest of Bavarian lakes; low-lying, marshy area, lacks grandeur of mountain-girt lakes, but notable for magnificent castle of *Herrenchiemsee*, built by King Ludwig II and modelled on Versailles, open to public; steamers from *Stock*, near *Prien*Δ.

Skirt northern shore of lake, via *Hemhof*Δ, on to *Traunstein*Δ spa and rail junction and southwards, by *Bergen*Δ, to small resort of *Ruhpolding*.

R8 (ii) Ruhpolding to Reit im Winkl 15 miles (24km). On the German *Alpenstrasse*, leading into little known part of Bavarian Alps. *Reit im Winkl* has good skiing (very heavy snowfalls, excellent learners' slopes). *Nattersberg-Alm* (3,300ft, 1,006m) is approached from *Seegatterl*, on *Alpenstrasse* by steep path.

EXCURSION: from *Nattersberg-Alm*: ascent of *Fellhorn* (5,800ft, 1,767m, 3 hours) with fine view over Alps.

On B305 from *Ruhpolding* into grandiose mountain scenery of the *Berchtesgadener Land*, projecting into Austria. *Berchtesgaden* Δ, picturesque town, famous for woodcarving, winter sports and Hitler's mountain eyrie on the *Obersalzberg*. Dominated by the *Watzmann* (8,704ft, 2,653m, can be climbed from *Ramsau-Wimbachbrücke* via *Münchener* hut in 6-7 hours). **Königssee** lies 3 miles (5km) southwards from *Berchtesgaden*, one of the most beautiful alpine lakes, with clear green water 580ft (180m) deep, surrounded by almost vertical cliffs rising to nearly 6,000ft (1,800m).

EXCURSIONS: (a) circular tour on lake by motor-boat, 1 hour 50 minutes. (b) by cable railway from northern end of *Königssee* on to the *Jenner* (6,149ft, 1,875m) 22 minutes. (c) by cable railway on to the *Obersalzberg* (3,345ft, 1,020m), 10 minutes; or on foot from *Berchtesgaden* in 1 hour. (d) by lake boat to *St Bartholomä* on *Königssee* thence on foot (2-3 days) via *Funtensee* hut, *Steinernes Meer* (an extraordinary wilderness of boulders) and *Reimann* hut to *Saalfelden* in Austria.

From *Berchtesgaden* to *Bad Reichenhall*, spa; concentrated saline springs gave rise to important salt trade in Middle Ages. Interesting old monastery of *St Zeno*.

GREECE

Geographical Outline

Land

The mainland of Greece is the southern extension of the *Balkan* peninsula into the Mediterranean, together with the coastlands of *Thrace* separating Bulgaria from the *Aegean Sea*.

The *Aegean* lies between the Greek mainland and Turkey, and all its many islands, except two nearest the mouth of the *Dardanelles*, are part of Greece. South-east of the mainland lies the wide curve of islands comprising *Crete* and the *Dodecanese* and close to the west coast lie the *Ionian* islands.

Greece is a mountainous country and even the islands are, with a few volcanic exceptions, drowned extensions of the mainland ranges. The central spine is the *Pindus* range running north-north-west to south-south-east from the Albanian frontier towards the *Gulf of Corinth*. From this spine a series of ranges run south-eastwards which form the promontories of the east coast and which can be traced, partly drowned, in lines of islands in the *Aegean*. In the *Peloponnesus* the ranges follow the same general direction, but curve eastwards and then north-eastwards in their extension in *Crete* and *Rhodes*. With some important exceptions limestone is the dominant rock.

Many peaks exceed 7,000ft (2,130m) in *Central Greece*, the *Peloponnesus*, and in *Crete*, and several exceed 8,000ft (2,440m). Mount *Olympus* in *Thessaly* is 9,550ft (2,910m).

Much of the scenery is moulded by the close juxtaposition of white limestone mountain ranges, tiny plains and valleys — sometimes dusty with sparse vegetation, sometimes green with olives and other trees — and deep inlets of the blue sea. It is a scenery with remarkable variety over small distances.

There are few important rivers and many are dry, or nearly so, in the summer months. In the north the lower reaches of the *Vardar* and *Struma* rivers are in Greek territory, but these rise deep in the *Balkan* peninsula.

Climate

Greece has the typical Mediterranean climate of hot dry summers with little rain and mild winters. Only the higher mountains of the north have any appreciable rainfall in summer.

Average winter rainfall is heavy on the west coast and in the mountains in central and northern Greece, but on the east coast it is quite light. Rain in Greece tends to come in downpours interspersed with long periods of clear sunny weather. Winters are mild, particularly in the coastal regions, although the coastlands around *Salonica*, in the north, are subject to cold spells coming down from the interior of the *Balkans*. Many visitors who do not take kindly to the summer heat, even though this is tempered with afternoon sea breezes in the coastal areas, find the climate more acceptable from mid-March to the end of May, when temperatures are more like those of mid-summer in England, except that the sunshine is more reliable.

Plants and Animals

Only a quarter of the land is suitable for cultivation, a tenth is forest or woodland — mainly in the mountains — and two-thirds of the country is barren or rocky.

The vegetation is very much determined by the dryness of the climate and the porous nature of the limestone soils.

Whole areas have been denuded of forest by human action, as for example in *Attica*, and goats in particular have prevented it from returning. Forests have tended to persist in the mountains formed of crystalline rocks. Oak, beech, chestnut, plane, pine and fir are found here, the latter mainly on the higher ground.

Sparse scrubland, mainly of the Mediterranean type, such as the *maquis* of the *Peloponnesus*, covers much of the uncultivated country. The Mediterranean vegetation on lower ground is of trees, evergreen shrubs and herbaceous plants. In *Attica* a more thorny scrubland is common. A feature of the stony ground in the south and in the islands, in spring, are the brilliant flowers: crocus, tulip, iris, narcissus, anemone, poppy and others.

Among the fauna are porcupines, wolves, wild goats and jackals. Rarities in the remoter mountain areas include the European brown bear and the chamois. There is a great variety of birds, including eagles and vultures. Reptiles are common, especially in the *Peloponnesus* and the *Cyclades*, but only two kinds of snake are poisonous.

The People

Population

Of the 9 million nearly half live in rural areas. *Athens*, the capital, with its port, *Piraeus*, has more than 2 million. *Salonica (Thessaloniki)*, with 750,000, is the

second city. All other towns are much smaller; the next largest is *Patras* (120,000).

It is generally supposed that the Greeks of classical times were a tall people, fair in colouring, of the Nordic racial type. Sculptures suggest as much, but how far these were a true likeness and how far they represented an ideal will probably never be known.

In the intervening centuries many non-Greek peoples have mixed with the indigenous population, eg Syrians, Slavs, Franks, Turks, Albanians. The Greeks of today are generally short of stature and dark in colouring.

Language

Greek is spoken by all but a tiny fraction. In *Thrace* there are small pockets of Turkish speaking people and in *Macedonia* there are Slavonic speaking minorities.

Modern Greek is a direct descendant of the language of classical times, more closely related to it than, for example, is modern Italian to Latin. Its divergence is greater in pronunciation than in its written form.

To speak of 'Modern Greek' is in fact to speak of two languages — Demotic (common) and Katharevoussa (pure). Demotic is the living spoken language and the language of songs and ballads. Katharevoussa is a conscious and artificial return to Ancient Greek. It is the official language and is taught in schools and generally used in newspapers. What particularly distinguishes it from Demotic is its refusal to use the many foreign words which have crept into the spoken tongue. The common language is, however, gaining on the purist form.

The written language uses, of course, the Greek alphabet. The visitor should at least acquaint himself with the symbols corresponding to the Roman alphabet so as to be able to read place names, menus, etc, which might otherwise be unintelligible.

English is fairly widely understood, particularly in places frequented by tourists.

Religion

The vast majority of Greeks are of the Greek Orthodox faith, which is the established religion under the Constitution. There are small Moslem minorities in the north of the country.

History

By 2,500BC, possibly earlier, a civilization flourished in Greece (centred on *Crete*) known to us as *Minoan*. Clear evidence of its existence was first revealed by the excavations of Sir Arthur Evans at the *Palace of Knossos*. It is still not known where the people who developed it came from or who they were.

Some time after 2,000BC the centre of civilization began to shift to the mainland, particularly the *Peloponnesus*. This had developed by about 1,600BC into what has come to be called the 'Mycenean culture' after one of its principal cities — *Mycenae*.

In its later stages this civilization was probably Greek speaking, but it differed in many important respects from the later classical Greek civilization, and the transition from the destruction of *Mycenae* and its culture to the classical Greek period is obscure. Homer's story of the Trojan War, once regarded as myth, almost certainly relates to this *Mycenaen* age, although he lived many centuries after the events related.

Classical Greece, through colonization, began to emerge in the eighth century

BC and by 600BC its culture had spread, as far afield as Marseille and the Crimea.

Although the Greeks were conscious and proud of their common 'Hellenic' history and culture and regarded themselves as set apart from the rest of mankind — a view which their achievements do much to support — they were never a single nation. They were a large number of fiercely independent city states sharing a common culture, but seldom sharing much else. By the fifth century BC most of these city states had developed the first form of democratic government by various paths from early monarchies through aristocratic oligarchies. Supreme among these was *Athens*, and the prime exception to this was *Sparta*.

The golden age of Greece was the fifth century BC, when a unique civilization flourished. This age was ushered in by two wars with the Persian Empire in which Greece fought for survival. The first, in 490BC, was fought alone by *Athens* and was decided and won at *Marathon*. The second, ten years later, was the grand test and, for once, the Greek world united against the common enemy, with the exception of *Thebes*. The Persians were defeated at sea in the battle of *Salamis*, and on land at *Plataea*. The victory left *Athens* supreme as a maritime power and on this she built what was virtually an empire of city-states, known as the *Delian League*. In the next half-century *Athens* was at the height of her power, and it was during this period that Greece's greatest achievements in architecture, literature, philosophy and many other fields were witnessed. The power of *Athens*, however, was rivalled by that of *Sparta* and inevitably the two states clashed. The Peloponnesian war began in 437BC and dragged on until 404BC. *Athens* was defeated and Greek civilisation did not recover from the devastating effect.

The hegemony of *Sparta* lasted until 371BC when *Thebes* triumphed at the battle of *Leuctra*, but the Golden Age had ended. A weakened Greece fell prey to a new semi-Greek power in the north — *Macedonia* — under King Philip. When Philip was assassinated (336BC) his son, Alexander, succeeded him and began a new chapter in the history of Greece. In the remaining thirteen years of his life he led Greek armies to conquer the Persian Empire and penetrated as far as Afghanistan and India. His empire collapsed shortly after his death but the spread of Greek ideas into Asia had an incalculable influence on history.

Macedonia eventually came into conflict with the growing power of Rome. The issue was finally decided in 168BC. Greece passed to the Romans and for five hundred years the country was in their hands; but the influence of Greece on the Roman Empire in the field of thought was profound.

When the Roman Empire split into east and west, at the beginning of the fourth century AD, Greece came under the Eastern Empire based on *Constantinople*.

The Eastern (later, Byzantine) Empire was, however, often unable to defend its Greek territories and between the fourth and eighth centuries Greece was over-run by Goths, Visigoths and Vandals, Huns and Slavs in turn, all of whom caused much devastation. In 1204 a Crusade intended for the Holy Land was diverted to attack *Constantinople* and, as a result, Greece fell into the hands of the Franks.

There followed an age of strife, and, although the Byzantines returned for a short time, the country fell an easy victim to the Ottoman Turks in the fifteenth century. Ottoman rule lasted until the nineteenth century, although Greece was often a battleground between Turks and the Venetians, and the latter held many footholds on Greek territory, particularly the islands.

The modern state of Greece had its beginnings in 1832 after the people had risen against the Turks in the War of Independence — a long drawn out and bitter struggle. The new state consisted initially of little more than the *Peloponnesus*. Its growth was far from easy, hindered both by internal dissensions and by rivalries of the Great Powers over their interests in the *Balkans*. Little by little Greece added more to her territories — the *Ionian Islands* (from Britain) in 1864, *Thessaly* in 1881, and most of the north of the country and the *Aegean* islands in the Balkan War of 1912 (against Turkey). After World War I the Greeks endeavoured to occupy the Turkish side of the *Aegean* but were driven out by Kemal Atatürk with disastrous results. There, but for the acquisition of the *Dodecanese* from Italy in 1947, the expansion of Greece has ended — although her interest in Cyprus is still considerable.

When Greece was freed from German occupation in 1944, civil war broke out, and dragged on until 1949, seriously hindering the country's recovery.

Government

Since 1832 Greece has been a kingdom most of the time. The fortunes and popularity of the monarchy have however fluctuated, and of her six kings since independence four have been deposed and one assassinated. Since the Constitution of 1844, and more particularly since that of 1864 Greece has been a democracy but, like the monarchy, the strength and popularity of the democratic institutions have fluctuated and on a number of occasions near-dictators have held power. Since 1974, however, the country has been a democratic republic, and in 1981 it became a full member of the European Economic Community.

Resources

Greece is a poor country by West European standards. It lacks the raw materials to create the industries that have brought wealth to Western Europe and its agricultural land is under severe pressure from over-population. It is essentially an agricultural country, more than half the population being directly engaged on the land, although only a quarter of the land is suitable for cultivation. Despite the compulsory break-up of large estates there is serious overcrowding and the average peasant farmer's holding is very small.

Tobacco, wheat, olives, maize, barley, citrus fruit and grapes are the principal agricultural products. Grapes are grown for wine, for dessert fruit, and for drying as currants and sultanas.

Tobacco, grown mainly in the north, is by far the most important export. Currants and sultanas are also important, *Patras* being the centre of this industry. The cultivation of the vine is mainly concentrated in the *Peloponnesus*. Much of the wine produced is for local consumption although some, like the sweet Mavrodaphni and Samos wines, are exported. Wheat is grown mainly in *Thessaly* and the north but much has to be imported.

A wide variety of minerals are mined, notably non-ferrous metals at *Lauion* and on *Euboea* and bauxite, used in the aluminium smelting plant near *Mount Parnassus*. Lignite fuels the electric power stations and factories. Such industries as there are, mainly textiles and petrochemicals, are concentrated around *Athens*. Fishing is an important occupation and Greece also has a large Merchant Navy although many of the ships are registered under foreign flags.

Customs

The Greeks are a kindly, hospitable, emotional people with an uninhibited curiosity about strangers.

Like their classical forebears they take a passionate interest in politics, and feelings can run high on controversial issues.

A great deal of their time is spent in social life and in the *tavernas* talking politics, listening to national music and watching dancing. The dances are a mixture of Turkish influence and the traditions of classical Greece. The music will often sound strange to Western ears, having a distinctly Eastern character.

There are many festivals, ranging from picturesque local ones connected with saints' days to the performance of classical plays in the ancient open-air theatres of *Epidaurus, Delphi* and *Athens*. Easter is the time of great religious ritual and festivity, but its date is often different from Easter in western countries.

Food and Drink

Greek wines include *Demestica* (red or white), *Castel Danielis, Naoussa* (red), *Mavrodaphni, Kampa* and *Samos* (very sweet). Wine impregnated with resin, most often white wine from *Attica*, called *retsina*, is very popular but is an acquired taste.

Greek brandy comes in two best-known varieties, *Outrys,* pale and light in flavour and harmless in moderation; *Metaxa* is sweet, rough and rather potent. Both are cheap.

Ouzo — a spirit rather like *Pernod* — is widely drunk. Another spirit is *Mastica*, which is made from the gum-plant of that name.

Much of the traditional food is of Turkish origin and the specialities mentioned here are worth trying. *Dolmas*, a richly seasoned rice wrapped in vine leaves and cooked in oil (as are many other foods); *pilaff*, stuffed tomatoes, paprikas, and aubergines; *moussaka*, minced meat mixed with rice, covered with aubergines, tomatoes and cheese sauce. *Kopanisti*, roe with sharp cheese. *Feta* is cheese made from goat's milk, often the main ingredient of Greek salad.

Kataife — noodles with nut fillings are exceedingly sweet, so, too, is *baklava*, a rich pastry of chopped nuts, raisins and honey. *Loukoumi* (Turkish Delight) is eaten all over Greece, and other sweet delicacies like crystallized fruits are common. Many fish dishes such as red mullet, shellfish and octopus are excellent.

Turkish coffee, usually served in tiny cups, is practically a national drink. Varieties are: *sketo* (without sugar), *gleeko* (very sweet and strong) and *metrio* (medium sweet and strong).

A visitor having difficulty with the menu may well be invited to the kitchen to select his food there.

Dress

National costume is largely of Turkish or Albanian origin — although in the *Ionian Islands* there is Venetian influence. Western dress is widespread, particularly in the cities, although it is often mixed with the traditional. National costume has not entirely disappeared for Turkish costume is still to be seen — notably in *Crete*, the islands and in the north of the country. Perhaps the most traditional Greek costume is that worn by the Evzone — the ceremonial Greek soldier — with the short pleated skirt, white wool leg bindings and leather slippers. This is of Albanian origin.

Sport

Swimming, fishing, sailing and underwater swimming are the favourite sports during the summer. In winter there is skiing on *Mount Parnes*.

Culture

Architecture

Greece is a country rich in architecture, particularly from the classical and Hellenistic periods, and from the Byzantine age.

The earliest remains are those of the Minoan civilization in *Crete*, the most famous being the ruins of the palace of *Knossos* (near *Candia*) excavated by Sir Arthur Evans at the turn of the century. There had been continuous occupation here since before 2,500BC but most of the remains date from the centuries just before 1,400BC. The throne room and the royal apartments give a breath-taking glimpse of the architecture of this time. *Knossos* is by no means the only Minoan site to be seen; others include the palaces at *Phaestos* and *Hagia Triada* near the south coast of *Crete*.

With the Mycenean age the centre of power shifted to the mainland — particularly to the *Peloponnesus* — where many remains of this period are to be found. Foremost is *Mycenae* (south of *Corinth*) the great deserted citadel of Agamemnon dominating the plain of *Argos*. The town reached the height of its power some time after 1,400BC but was later abandoned. Notable here are the *Lion Gate*, the Cyclopean walls, the shaft graves, and the beehive tombs by the road to the palace. Other Mycenean sites of interest are the palace of *Pylos* near *Navarino* on the west coast.

Most of the surviving architecture of the classical Greek period consists of temples, monuments and secular public buildings — notably theatres. Temples and other buildings are generally classified into three styles: Doric, Ionic and Corinthian. All three developed and existed alongside each other, although the Corinthian is a later style more popular among the Romans than the Greeks. In mainland Greece the older buildings tend to be Doric, eg the sixth-century *Temple of Apollo* at *Corinth*. The greatest achievement of the Doric style is the *Parthenon*, on the *Acropolis* at *Athens* (started in 447BC). Another, almost complete, example is the *Theseum*, below the Acropolis. Other notable Doric buildings are the *Treasury of the Athenians* at *Delphi*, the remains of the *Temple of Zeus* at *Olympia*, the *Temple of Aphaea* on *Aegina*, and the *Propylaea* at *Athens*. Foremost among Ionic buildings are the *Erechtheum* and the *Temple of Athene Nike*, both on the *Acropolis* at *Athens*, built a little after the *Parthenon*. Greek Corinthian buildings are rare; the earliest known example is that of the *Monument of Lysicrates* in *Athens* (334BC).

Among the finest examples of classical secular architecture are the theatres at *Epidaurus*, and of *Dionysus* in *Athens*, and the *stadium* for the Pythian games at *Delphi*.

Apart from the beauty of the buildings themselves the outstanding feature of the classical period is the marrying of the architecture with its physical surroundings. The great classical centres like *Athens, Delphi, Epidaurus, Delos* and *Olympia* all bear witness to this, even if today often only ruins remain.

Much of the architecture of the period when Greece was part of the Roman Empire carries on the classical styles and traditions. Examples are the Corinthian *Temple of Olympian Zeus* (finished by Hadrian), the *Theatre of Herodes Atticus* in *Athens*, and the *'House of Cleopatra'* at *Delos*. Town building, however, was more characteristically Roman in style, as can be seen in the ruins of Roman *Corinth*.

Byzantine architecture is in marked contrast to that of classical Greece, and Greece has many splendid examples — ranging from the fifth-century church of *St George* at *Salonica*, through the monasteries on the peninsula of *Mount Athos* (tenth to sixteenth century) to the church at *Daphni* (near *Athens*) and the town of *Mistra* in the *Peloponnesus*. *Mistra* is a deserted Byzantine town, surmounted by a Frankish fortress, dating from just before the Turkish conquest in the fifteenth century.

The island of *Rhodes* has a very rare feature in the architecture of the Knights of St John (fourteenth to sixteenth century) with the distinctive fortresses, streets, villas, and palaces of the city.

The Turks and their rivals, the Venetians, have left many examples of their architecture in Greece, although little that can be described as great. Venetian fortresses occur in many places in the *Aegean islands*, the *Ionian islands*, and in the *Peloponnesus*, and here and there are houses and churches of Venetian influence. Turkish town architecture, particularly the overhanging houses of slightly Tudor appearance, occurs in many areas, especially in the north of the country, in *Epirus*, *Macedonia*, and *Thrace* and in the *Aegean islands*. A number of mosques also survive, eg the *Aslan Aga Mosque* in *Jannina*.

Art

Most of the surviving art of classical and pre-classical Greece is to be found in Greek museums, notably those in *Athens* and *Delphi*. Some can be found in other European museums.

At *Knossos*, frescoes of the Minoan period are still to be seen *in situ* and give the impression of a carefree civilization. Pottery and jewellery and other art of the period can be seen in the museum at *Candia*.

Many of the artistic finds from *Mycenae* are in the *National Archaeological Museum* at *Athens*; the metal-work in particular, is of a very high standard.

Archaic Greek statues (seventh and sixth century BC) are very stiff and wooden, although often beautiful in execution. Statues of the fifth century BC onwards show vivid movement and remarkable observation of the human form. Many great artists, eg Phidias, Praxiteles, and Polycleitus, are known to us from later Greek and Roman copies of their works, but one statue is certainly an original, the Hermes of Praxiteles at *Olympia*. The museums of *Delphi, Athens*, and *Olympia* contain fascinating examples of the sculpture of the period.

Sculpture was the most perfect form of artistic expression in classical Greece. In addition to free-standing statues, sculpture work was applied in great variety to adorning temples with friezes, pediments, etc, often depicting scenes from mythology. Perhaps the most famous of all friezes is that from the *Parthenon* (the *Elgin Marbles*) depicting the procession of the Panathenaic Festival — much of this is in the British Museum in London.

Burial steles are another form of sculpture, interesting for depicting scenes in the lives of ordinary people of the classical cities. The *Ceramicus* in *Athens* has yielded many examples, a number of which have been removed to the museums.

Of classical Greek painting little or nothing survives, but in painted pottery there are rich remains. These are of three basic forms: black figures on a red background, red figures on a black background, and coloured figures on a white background (used mainly for burial purposes). This art reached its highest expression in *Athens* in the fifth century BC. The subjects are usually scenes either from mythology or from everyday life.

The art of Greece, in the Hellenistic and Roman periods derives from the classical period but lacks its restraint and simplicity. The *Winged Victory of Samothrace* (now in the Louvre) is a splendid example.

Byzantine art contrasts sharply with that of classical Greece. It is the expression of the beliefs of the Orthodox Christian church, reaching its greatest achievements in the interior decoration of religious buildings. Classical Greek art gave beauty to the exterior: in Byzantine art the interior is all important and wall mosaics and paintings are its dominant medium. The *Pantocrator* at *Daphni* (AD1100) is one of the finest examples of this art. In *Salonica* important mosaics of the fifth century survive (churches of *St George* and *Hosios David*) and also of the fourteenth century in the church of the *Holy Apostles*. Splendid examples of New Testament scenes dating from the early eleventh century are to be found in the *Monastery of Hosios Lukas*, near *Delphi*. The monasteries on *Mount Athos* have many examples of later wall paintings and mosaic work. The deserted town of *Mistra* in the *Peloponnesus* is particularly rich in Byzantine wall paintings of the fourteenth century.

Literature

With the shadowy figure of Homer the literature of Greece, and of the whole Western world, begins. He lived in *Ionia* (the modern coastland of Western Turkey), probably about 950BC. He produced two epics — the *Iliad* and the *Odyssey* — of unsurpassed genius, and they formed the backbone of Greek education throughout the classical period.

Only a few works survive from the five centuries between Homer and the great period of *Athens*; notably the love poems of Sappho, a few fragments of the satirist Archilochus, the shrewd and factual works of instruction on farming and sailing (in verse) of Hesiod, and some lyric poems of Pindar.

Fifth-century Greece, and especially *Athens*, produced a wealth of literature, breath-taking in its scope and genius. From this period dates the birth of drama (tragedy and comedy), of history, philosophy, and scientific thought. Herodotus was the first historian, with a fascinating blend of absorbing stories and scientific fact. Thucydides, the Athenian, wrote a dramatic but objective account of the Peloponnesian War, through which he lived, which marks him as a great historian. Xenophon followed on from Thucydides but is less masterful, although his *Anabasis* (the retreat of the 10,000 from Persia) is a fascinating and human account of Greek discipline and heroism.

From the golden age of Athens three tragic dramatists stand above all others: Aeschylus, Sophocles, and Euripides. Nineteen of the latter's plays survive, seven by Aeschylus, and eight by Sophocles. Fragments of many others are known. Even after 2,500 years the works of these three are among the greatest. Living in the later years of Sophocles and Euripides was the great writer of comedy, Aristophanes. He did not hesitate to take a dig at the writings of his tragic contemporaries and although much of his humour is based on contemporary events his plays are still enjoyed.

Plato's contribution to philosophy is enormous and the dialogue form in which he generally wrote has literary merit.

In the fourth century BC, although the power of Greece had declined, literature still flourished. Among the great names are Aristotle the philosopher, Menander the father of modern comedy, and Demosthenes the orator. After this, classical Greek literature died and the writers of the centuries that follow, although they often owe much to classical literature and wrote in Greek, drew their roots from other civilizations, notably the Roman and the Hebrew. Among these are Plutarch the historian, and Lucian, and the authors of the New Testament.

The long Byzantine age produced works mainly of theology and history. It is not strictly speaking the literature of Greece. Its authors were drawn from all over the Byzantine world and relatively few came from what is now modern Greece. The language used was a fossilized form of classical Greek and faced an ever widening gulf from the living changing Greek language of the day.

Modern Greek literature has to some extent been a struggle between this classical language of the Byzantine period and the living language (*demotic*) of the people, from which the latter has emerged victorious. Notable writings in the living language date from the Cretan literature of the sixteenth and seventeenth centuries and the so-called *Klephtic Ballads* of the period of Turkish occupation. The War of Independence brought in its train a revival of Greek literature, particularly in the form of poetry and the novel of which the novelist Kazantzakis is best known by his *Zorba, the Greek*.

Science

The Greeks, from the sixth century BC onwards, were the first people to make a systematic attempt to understand the natural world. Their achievements in most branches of science during the next 350 years make them the 'most remarkable people who ever yet existed'.

Abstract reasoning was their greatest strength: mathematics and astronomy best demonstrate their genius. Even today our geometry is largely theirs — developed by Greeks from Thales to Euclid, Archimedes and Apollonius. Heracleides discovered the rotation of the earth; Eratosthenes calculated its circumference; and Aristarchus anticipated Copernicus in suggesting that the sun was the centre of the solar system. Hipparchus, their greatest astronomer, calculated the lunar month to within half a second and greatly developed trigonometry.

Aristotle was not only a philosopher but took the whole field of knowledge for his subject. He was the first to make biology a science, his achievements in marine biology and in the study of bees and other insects being especially remarkable. His pupil Theophrastus excelled in botany.

Hippocrates, the father of medicine, also belongs to the classical period. His ideal of conduct, embodied in the Hippocratic oath, still serves as a model for medical men, and much of the practice of his school is still accepted as sound. Much later, near the beginning of the Christian era, the work of Celsus shows a further advance in medical knowledge.

Early in the Christian era two names are outstanding: Galen, the physician, and Dioscorides, the botanist and pharmacologist. The works of these two, with those of Aristotle, became the basis of scientific knowledge in the Arab world and in Christendom up to the Renaissance.

Concerts and Festivals

The *State Symphony Orchestra* has a high reputation. Festivals include *Athens Music Festival*, August/September, *Epidaurus Drama Festival*, June/July. Various places stage national dances, eg *Megara*, 25 miles (40km) from *Athens*, Easter Tuesday.

Touring Information

Access

London to *Athens*; (i) by air; APEX return; must be booked one month in advance, valid one month. (ii) by rail daily via *Ostend* and through Yugoslavia, 3 days. (iii) by rail daily via *Calais/Milan — Brindisi*, 36 hours, thence by sea. Service from *Brindisi* is to *Corfu, Igoumenitsa* and *Patras* nightly in summer, less frequent in winter; from *Patras* a motor coach connection continues the journey to *Athens*. Other less frequent services to *Piraeus* are (iv) from *Marseille, Genoa, Naples* or *Venice* (v) by motor coach; *London* to *Athens* 3-days' journey. Cheaper fares for students are offered by most Greek shipping companies.

Transport

Long distance motor coaches are cheaper, faster and more comfortable than rail which is mostly slow, infrequent and apt to be crowded on long distance trains, although local diesel electric trains are more comfortable. The Peloponnesus Railway connects *Athens* with *Corinth, Patras* and *Kalamata* — branching at *Corinth* for *Tripolis* — while the *Northern Railway* runs to *Salonica*. Student concession fares are offered, so too are 10, 20 or 30-day tickets for use on the entire railway network. Trolleybuses and buses in Athens are very cheap, so, too, is the Elektriko (electric railway) which runs from *Piraeus* into central *Athens* and out to the suburbs. Main line railway tickets should be bought in advance, as quite often the ticket office opens only an hour before departure when immediately a long queue forms. Bus or steamer tickets should be booked the day before.

Clothing

For a summer visit go prepared for very hot and dry weather from early July to early September, when shade temperatures are often in the nineties, and insects troublesome.

Restaurants

There are numerous small cafés and restaurants which, however dilapidated they look, are likely to prove good and reasonable. The *tavernas*, or restaurants with local character, are among the cheapest eating places, although you may occasionally come across one which is on the smarter side and therefore more expensive.

Public Holidays

National holidays on 1 January, 6 January, 25 March, Ash Wednesday, Good Friday, Easter Monday, Whit Monday (note that Greek Easter is fixed in accord with Julian calendar which may be later than in the West), 1 May, 15 August, 28 October, 25 and 26 December.

Maps

A useful general map is published by Hallwag on a scale of 1:1,000,000, complete with index and showing the mainland and all the islands on one sheet.

Accommodation

The Greek Youth Hostels Association has about thirty hostels; seven of them on *Crete*, one on *Corfu*.

There are many village guest houses, where visitors stay quite cheaply with families. Visitors are accommodated in many of the monasteries either for a small charge or free.

Tavernas often have rooms to let, but they can be noisy. Many cheap boarding houses offer limited facilities and small inexpensive hotels are usually clean and unprententious.

In the countryside if you ask at a café or inquire of the '*proedros*' or village headman you can usually be accommodated very cheaply. Most hotels and *pensions* give a reduction for students.

Camping

Camping is officially prohibited except on government approved sites; there are more than 200 of these as indicated on the Hallwag map of Greece.

Walking

Good areas for a walking holiday are to be found within a radius of *Athens* or in the *Peloponnesus*, an area of fertile plains, rich coastal strips and mountains, with many small towns and villages. *Mount Parnes* 20 miles (32km), from *Athens* is popular with both climbers and walkers. There are mountain huts, used as youth hostels, on *Olympus* and *Parnassus*.

Motoring

Motorists are required to carry their own national documents — vehicle registration certificate, certificate of insurance, international driving licence together with a red warning triangle and national identity sticker and an adequate first-aid outfit. It would be prudent, too, to have an International Green Insurance card.

Motoring in Greece should conform to International Traffic Regulations, plus speed limits beginning at 50km/h (32mph) in built-up areas and parking is forbidden in front of public buildings, churches and banks.

Motorists should heed additional advice from their own motoring organisations and note that the Greek Automobile Association offer reciprocal membership; their headquarters is in Athens at 2/4 Rue Messogion, and there are branch offices in other towns.

Road surfaces, their standards of engineering and maintenance, are not equal to those in many other European countries. Toll motorways connect *Athens* and *Salonica* and *Athens* and *Patras*; metalled surfaces on main tourist routes, but many dirt-roads in country districts.

Cycling

Minor roads are poor and the summer heat is great, but apart from this cycling is an excellent way of touring.

Weights and Measures

While the metric system is in common use, there is also the *Oka*, a unit of weight equivalent to 2.83lb, and subdivided into smaller units. Among other measures is the *Peke*, equivalent to 25 inches.

Athens△

The modern city dates from the nineteenth century, after the War of Independence. It is not very spectacular, but is pleasant and spacious, dominated by the *Acropolis* and *Mount Lycabettus* and surrounded at a distance by the mountains of *Attica*.

The **Acropolis** and immediate surroundings are the great centre of attraction.

The buildings on it date mainly from the age of Pericles, and, even in their ruined state, are some of the most famous and beautiful in the world. They are the *Parthenon, Erechtheum,* and the *Temple of Athene Nike*, with the great entrance way, the *Propylaea*. The *Acropolis* is open until midnight when there is a full moon, and a visit then is particularly recommended.

To the south of the *Acropolis* lie the *Theatres of Dionysus* (fourth century BC) and of *Herodes Atticus* (built second century AD by a rich noble). In the original *Theatre of Dionysus* many plays of the great Athenian dramatists were first performed.

South-west of the *Acropolis* is the hill of the *Pnyx* where assemblies of Athenian citizens once met, and nearby is the hill of the *Areopagus*. To the west is the site of the ancient *Agora*, which has two buildings of great interest: the extremely well-preserved temple called the *Theseum* (fifth century BC), and the recent reconstruction of the *Stoa of Attalus* built to house the vast quantity of antiquities found in the *Agora*.

Other interesting remains are the *Tower of the Winds* (first century BC), the *Arch of Hadrian* and the *Temple of Olympian Zeus*, in the Roman quarter, and the *Ceramicus* and other cemeteries situated near the *Dipylon* and the *Sacred Gate*.

A visit to the *National Archaeological Museum* is highly recommended; it has some of the most splendid examples of Greek work uncovered by excavation.

Three Byzantine churches of note — all close to *Constitution Square* — are those of *Kapnikarea*, the *Small Metropolis* and *Sts Theodores*.

EXCURSIONS: (a) *Piraeus* 2 miles (3km) south, the port of *Athens*; little remains of the famous ancient port, but the modern one is busy, thriving and colourful; *Phaleron*, near *Piraeus*, bathing resort for the Athenians. (b) **Cape Sunion**, southernmost tip of *Attica*, 36 miles (58km) south, bus from *Aigypta Square*; has impressive remains of **Temple of Poseidon** on lofty cliffs and magnificent views out to sea. (c) **Marathon**, 18 miles (29km) east, beyond *Mount Hymettus*, on bay of same name; site of victory of Athenians over Persians, 490BC. Burial mound of Athenians killed in the battle can still be seen, 5 miles (8km) south of village. Approach either on foot (9 miles, 14km) from *Pendelis monastery* (reached by bus from *Kaningos Square*) via summit of **Mount Pentelikon** (3,635ft, 1,108m, fine view) returning by bus, or on foot (8 miles, 13km) by road and path from *Ekali* (bus from *Kaningos Square*), or all way by bus from *Aigypta Square*. (d) **Daphni**, 4 miles (6km); on *Corinth* road, eleventh-century Byzantine church, one of finest examples extant. Particularly fine mosaic head of Christ in the dome. (e) **Aegina**, island in *Saronic Gulf*; early morning steamer, $1^1/_2$ hours, from *Piraeus*. Quiet beaches; picturesque villages; Ruins of **Temple of Aphaia**, with commanding view (bus, 7 miles, 11km, from harbour).

Touring Routes

R1 Athens to Delphi and Hosios Lukas (138 miles, 222km)

Leave *Athens* by *Corinth* road north-west, just beyond *Eleusis*; slight remains of *Hall of Eleusinian Mysteries*. At *Mandra*, road climbs into wooded *Cithaeron* hills; at entrance of *Kaza* gorge by-road branches left to *Villa*. Main road enters plain of *Boeotia* descending to *Thebes*, city of Oedipus. Road continues past mountain of classic *Sphinx* to *Levadia*, 73 miles (117km). Take left fork by direct mountain road to *Delphi*, 28 miles (45km).

Delphi Δ, high on the slopes of **Mount Parnassus**, looking over northern shore of *Gulf of Corinth*, was main religious centre of ancient Greece, famous for its Oracle which issued advice and predictions — often shrewd though cryptic — to those who consulted it.

The classical ruins are imposing, set in beautiful spectacular surroundings. The *Temple of Apollo* was the focal point; foundations and several columns remain. Nearby, on *Sacred Way*, is *Treasury of the Athenians*, almost completely restored. Other remains, contributions of other city states, line the *Way*. Above the *Temple* is a well preserved *Theatre*, and higher still the *Stadium of the Pythian Games*. Further towards the valley is another group of ruins, including the *Gymnasium*, the *Sanctuary* and *Temple of Athena Pronaea*, and the *Tholos*. The museum nearby, contains many interesting and beautiful works of art found on the site.

Twenty miles (32km) east, along road back to *Levadia*, take the *Stiris* road on right to reach 17 miles (27km), *Monastery of Hosios Lukas (St Luke)*. Its church contains very find examples of Byzantine mosaic work, particularly the *Pantocrator* in the dome, and scenes from the New Testament.

The Peloponnesus

R2 Athens — Corinth — Mycenae — Nauplion — Epidaurus (106 miles, 170km)

From *Eleusis* (**R1**) road follows splendid mountainous coast with view, to island of *Salamis*; ferry from *Megalo Pefko*. Continue through *Megara* and cross the isthmus and canal to *Corinth*, 53 miles (85km); modern town, rebuilt since earthquake in 1928, not very interesting. On for 5 miles (8km) south-west to *Acrocorinthos*, which has impressive remains and famous view. Most of the classical Greek city was destroyed by Romans in 146BC, but a few Doric columns of *Temple of Apollo* (sixth century BC) still stand. Nearby are the numerous remains of the Roman city, notably *Fountains of Peirene, Senate House, Agora, Odeon* and *Amphitheatre*.

Road through *Dervenakia Gorge* to plain of *Argos*, dominated by lonely rocky hill bearing remains of **Mycenae**△, 24 miles (39km) centre of civilization to which it gives its name. Approach is along by-road 2 miles (3km) from main road through *Charvati*. Entrance to the citadel with its gigantic walls is by the famous Lion Gate. Inside are shaft graves of *Royal Cemetery* (splendid finds from here are in *National Archaeological Museum* in *Athens*), remains of *Royal Palace*, and fascinating subterranean staircase leading to a water supply outside the walls. On road up to citadel are the curious Beehive Tombs, of which the two best known are the so-called *Tombs of Agamemnon (Treasury of Atreus)* and of *Clytemnestra*.

Continue south through *Charvati* on by-road past *Heraion*, site of *Temple of Hera*, to *Chonika* and *Tiryns* 9 miles (14km): Mycenaean fortified palace, considerable remains.

Nauplion△ 2 miles (3km), picturesque port of *Gulf of Argolis*, dominated by *Acronauplia* (ancient *Acropolis*) and the *Palamedes* fortress, with their Venetian and Turkish fortifications. For a short time *Nauplion* was capital of modern Greece until *Athens* was captured from the Turks.

Epidaurus, 18 miles (29km) east, has what is probably the most perfect example of a classical theatre in Greece, lying almost complete in natural armchair in the hills; extraordinarily good acoustics. Drama festival June/July. Nearby are ruins of *Sanctuary of Asclepius*, a sort of religious health resort in classical times. *Ligourio,* 4 miles (6km).

R3 Nauplion — Sparta — Monemvasia (160 miles, 257km)

From *Nauplion* (**R2**) through *Argos* and the magnificent mountain scenery descending to valley of *Arcadia* in which town of *Tripolis*, 48 miles (77km), is route centre for much of *Peloponnesus*.

Sparta, 40 miles (64km). Remains of ancient city, some 2 miles (3km) from modern town at foot of *Taegetus* mountains. Remains are not very extensive: mainly walls on the *Acropolis*, small *theatre*, and foundations of *Temple of Artemis*.

Mistra, 4 miles (6km) west, clinging to slopes of *Taegetus* mountains, is deserted Byzantine town, mainly fourteenth century, crowned by earlier Frankish fortress constructed by William de Villehardouin. It was for a time capital of the *Peloponnesus* and an important cultural and religious centre. Below the fortress is the upper town with impressive ruins of *Palace of the Palaeologi* and then the lower town. Many Byzantine churches and monasteries in various states of preservation — notably *Peribleptos* monastery (well preserved), church of *St Sophia* (well preserved) and convent of *Pantanassa* (still occupied). This town with its curious haunted air is one of most remarkable historic remains in Greece.

Monemvasia, 63 miles (101km) south-east of *Sparta*, picturesque and historic port on high rocky promontory; occupied in turn by Franks, Byzantines, Turks and Venetians, it contains examples of architecture of each.

R4 Tripolis — Bassae — Patras — Athens (307 miles, 494km)
From *Tripolis* (**R3**) road through mountains to *Megalopolis*, 22 miles (35km);
Karitaina, 11 miles (18km), attractive village below thirteenth-century Frankish
castle; *Andritsaina*, 18 miles (29km), attractive small town.

> EXCURSION: New road up to **Temple of Bassae (Apollo Epicureius)** remote in hills
> at 3,776ft (1,151m). Doric temple in fine state of preservation; built by Ikintos, one of
> architects of *Parthenon*, fifth century BC. Often considered most beautiful in Greece
> after *Parthenon*; splendid setting, with great views.

> From *Andritsaina* bus to *Pygros*, 31 miles (50km) from which bus or train to
> **Olympia** Δ 15 miles (24km) in pleasant wooded valley of River *Alpheus*, where
> Olympic Games were held throughout classical Greek and Roman times. It was
> never a town, but a religious and athletic centre. Remains extensive, but not
> particularly well preserved: destruction by man and nature (earthquakes and
> changing courses of rivers) have taken their toll. Notable are the stadium, with
> entrance way and starting and finishing lines preserved. *Temple of Zeus* (the
> centre of the sanctuary) and ancient *Temple of Hera* (seventh century BC). The
> museum contains a great quantity of the finds from excavation on the site, in
> particular the statue of Hermes by Praxiteles.

> From *Olympia* by road or rail through *Patras*Δ, largest town of *Peloponnesus*
> to *Athens* 215 miles (346km).

The Northern Provinces

Places of outstanding interest are: in *Thessaly*, the *Tempe Valley*, *Mount Olympus*,
Mount Pelion and *Meteora*; in *Epirus*, *Jannina*, its chief town; in *Greek Macedonia*,
Salonica, *Kastoria* and the peninsula of *Chalcidice* with its monasteries of *Mount
Athos*.

R5 Volos — (Mount Pelion) — Meteora — Jannina (172 miles, 277km)
Volos, 241 miles (428km) from *Athens* by rail-car via *Stavros*, or by steamer in
12 hours.

> EXCURSIONS: (a) **Mount Pelion** Δ (5,252ft, 1,601m) 4 hours' walk to summit from
> *Portaria*, very fine view; (b) to charming villages along *Pelion Range*, such as
> *Makrinitsa*, 11 miles (18km), *Zagora*, 31 miles (50km), *Tsangarada*, 36 miles (58km)
> and *Ayios Jannis (Ionannis)*, which contain many splendid Turkish houses.

Larissa, 38 miles (61km) home of Hippocrates. Storks nest here.

> EXCURSIONS: (a) **Tempe Valley.** *Tembi*, 22 miles (35km) by rail whence 4 hour
> walk through valley between *Olympus* and *Ossa* to *Stomion*, small coastal resort. (b)
> **Mount Ossa** (2 days), guide necessary. *Ayia* 20 miles (32km) by bus, *Anatoli* 3 hours
> and a further $3^1/_2$ hours to summit (6,490ft, 1,978m).

Trikkala, 38 miles (61km), on classical River *Lethe*. *Kalabaka*, 14 miles (23km), rail terminus at foot of *Meteora*, famous monasteries built on great and almost inaccessible rocks in fourteenth century; originally twenty-four each on its own pinnacle; four still occupied.

Continue by road for 82 miles (132km) through *Pindus Mountains* over *Metsovon Pass* (5,594ft, 1,705m) into *Epirus*, to **Jannina**; important in Turkish times and retains much architecture of the period, particularly in the old town within the walls, with its narrow streets and Turkish houses. The *Kastro* is a well preserved Turkish fortress; *Aslan Aga Mosque* is a landmark built on a cliff above the lake. On an island in Lake *Jannina* are several interesting monasteries (eleventh to thirteenth century).

Daily coach service between *Jannina* and *Athens* (343 miles, 552km).

R6 Salonica — (Mount Athos) — Kastoria (139 miles, 224km)

Salonica △ (*Thessaloniki*), chief port of north, 321 miles (517km) by rail from *Athens*. Modern city is on seafront; picturesque old Turkish quarters lie on hills behind. Much of old city walls remain. The architectural riches are the Byzantine churches covering 1,000 years of Byzantine art. Outstanding are fifth-century church of *St George, St Sophia* (with splendid mosaics), *St Demetrius*, seventh century or earlier, almost destroyed by fire in 1917, but some old work survives), the lovely fourteenth-century *Church of the Twelve Apostles*, and the little church of *Hosios David* in the old town with superb mosaic of the *Pantocrator*.

R6 (i) Mount Athos Peninsula. Easternmost extension of *Chalcidice*, 31 miles (50km) long rising to 6,670ft (2,033m). Cut at isthmus by Xerxes' canal (482BC). Here lives a unique community of monks, either in monasteries or as anchorites or hermits — an autonomous republic. *Ayion Oros*, under Greek sovereignty. No women allowed to enter peninsula; men must obtain permission from Ministry of Foreign Affairs in Athens, through own Embassy.

Approach by sea from *Salonica* (Friday evening) arrive *Dhafni* next morning. (Return service leaves *Dhafni* Monday evening.) Visits to monasteries (there are twenty) either on foot or by mule or boat.

Pella 24 miles (39km), site of capital of Alexander the Great; *Mount Paikon*△ is 20 miles (32km) to north-east. *Edessa*, 31 miles (50km), finely situated town. Lake *Vegorritis*, 11 miles (18km). *Florina* 30 miles (48km), market town (2,230ft, 679m). *Pisodherion Pass* 5,183ft, (1,580m), 18 miles (29km).

Kastoria, 25 miles (40km), town like *Jannina*, built beside a lake, near Albanian frontier. Its history goes back to classical times, but little remains of this period. Chief attractions, apart from its lovely setting, are interesting Byzantine churches of *Taxiarch, St George* and *St Alipois* and old Turkish quarters and bazaar.

The Islands

From *Piraeus* boats can be taken to almost all the islands of Greece. Sailings are regular and cheap, and the choice of which to visit is a difficult one. None will be disappointing and most are enchanting. The brief descriptions below cover only some of the highlights.

Crete

By far the largest of the islands; 140 miles (225km) long and mountainous along its entire length. Cradle of European civilization. In addition to its important archaeological sites *Crete* offers splendid scenery, quiet and colourful villages, many customs and links with the past and almost all-year-round swimming. Eight youth hostels on the island.

Heraklion△, the chief town. Fortified by the Venetians. Much Turkish architecture. *Archaeological Museum* particularly interesting, containing many of the finds of *Knossos*.

Knossos, 3 miles (5km), Minoan palace earlier than 1,400BC. Highly complicated site, excavated and restored with much imagination, not all of it fortunate. Layout and artistic work quite different from classical Greek buildings. Courtyards, throne rooms, store rooms, stairways, frescoes, and even bathrooms are of great interest.

Phaestos, 40 miles (64km) from *Heraklion* (bus; accommodation at Tourist Pavilion). Another Minoan palace near south coast, reached by splendid journey over central mountains. Remarkable physical setting overlooked by *Mount Ida (Psiloriti)* (8,193ft, 2,497m). Palace similar in many ways to *Knossos*.

Rhodes

Largest of the twelve islands of the *Dodecanese*. Claims most favoured climate in Greece. A beautiful island, noted for its flowers and gardens, medieval towns and villages.

The city of **Rhodes** has palaces and houses built by Knights of St John in varying forms of the Gothic style. Much medieval architecture, Turkish mosques and houses and several interesting Byzantine churches, all within the old town completely enclosed by medieval walls. Unusual feature of harbour is *Quay of the Windmills*. Behind city is the *Acropolis*, with ruins of *Temples of Apollo* and *Zeus* and well restored theatre.

As interesting and picturesque as city of *Rhodes* is town of **Lindos** 35 miles (56km) on south-east coast, dominated by fortress built by Knights of Rhodes, and containing fascinating mixture of classical ruins, Byzantine churches (particularly *St Demetrius*) and medieval houses.

The Cyclades

Mykonos. The attraction of this island is centred in the little port of *Mykonos* itself, with its brilliant white houses, narrow street, numerous churches, and the canvas-sailed windmills which dominate the town. It is the archetype of picture postcard scenes of the *Aegean*, and is much visited by tourists.

Delos. Small and uninhabited island approached by motor-boat from *Mykonos*. Once great religious and commercial centre; virtually open-air museum of whole period from classical Greeks to Romans, in a spectacular setting. Remains are extensive and complex.

Remaining islands of *Aegean* are visited, not so much for their historic monuments, although there are many to be found and admired, but for their character and atmosphere springing from a harmony of architecture and natural surroundings, enhanced by the sunshine of a favoured climate. Three such islands, in the *Cyclades*, outstanding in their charm are **Naxos**, **Paros** and **Santorin**.

The Ionian Islands

Of this group, lying off the west coast of Greece, the most popular is **Corfu**Δ (*Kerkyra*) much more verdant than the others, covered with forests of pine, and orchards, cypresses and olives. Fine sandy beaches and pleasant towns where influence of Venetians is strong.

ICELAND

Geographical Outline

Land

Iceland lies in the North Atlantic about 500 miles (800km) north-west of Scotland and, as the crow flies, midway between New York and Moscow. Measuring 300 miles (480km) from west to east and 190 miles (300km) from north to south, it is just under 40,000 sq miles (103,000 sq km) in area — about one-fifth larger than Ireland. Its coastline, except on the south, is heavily indented with fjords and extends to some 3,700 miles (6,000km) with numerous islands around the coasts, some of them inhabited, the largest of which are the *Vestmannaeyjar* (Westman Islands).

The name is deceptive; the mainland barely touches the Arctic Circle and only about one-eighth is covered with ice. It is much more a land of fire: signs of volcanic activity, past and present, are to be seen everywhere; numerous gaping fissures running in a north/south direction in the north and in a north-east/south-west direction in the south make striking features in the landscape. Its rocks are all of igneous origin and are added to periodically by eruptions of lava and volcanic ash, occurring two or three times in a decade. Several volcanoes have been active in the past, some of them many times, notably *Hekla*, the last time in 1947 when the eruption lasted more than a year and the lava flow covered 25 sq miles (65 sq km) and *Helgafell*, on the *Westman Islands*, which erupted in 1973. They occur along a crescent from *Eldeyjar* in the south-west through *Hekla* and *Laki* to *Leirhafnarskördh* in the north-east. Acid hot springs follow the same line, but alkaline hot springs occur in all parts. Some are spouting springs or geysers, the most famous at *Haukadalur*, about 50 miles (80km) north-east of *Reykjavík*. Earthquakes are frequent, but seldom harmful.

Vatnajökull 3,240sq miles (8,400 sq km) reaches a thickness of 3,000ft (900m) and is as large as all the glaciers on the European mainland put together. *Hvannadalshnukur,* 6,954ft (2,120m) in *Öræfajökull* is the highest summit. Other extensive glaciers are *Langjökull, Hofsjökull* and *Myrdalsjökull*. Lakes are

246

innumerable, and powerful rivers with many waterfalls stem from the glaciers. Apart from the ice caps the interior largely consists of a wilderness of rock, boulders and lava fields forming a tableland 2,300 to 3,300ft (700 to 1,000m) above sea level.

Climate

Iceland's climate may be described as cool temperate oceanic; it is variable and capricious. Winters are relatively mild, summers cool, with generally high humidity due to the prevailing south-west winds. Regional differences are caused by the set of ocean currents (Polar or Gulf Stream) and by the barrier effect of the high mountains of the south. Rainfall is heaviest along the south and south-west coasts. In the interior snow can fall at all seasons. Brilliant sunshine is frequent; air is generally marvellously clear but fog does occur in coastal districts.

For two or three months in summer there is continuous daylight; long twilights are enjoyed in early spring and summer. The Northern Lights are often seen in autumn and early winter. Best season for touring is mid-June to early September.

Plants and Animals

Plant cover is continuous in only a small part. Species are about one-sixth as numerous as in the British Isles, but are of great interest in illustrating early post-glacial conditions. The lowlands have Arctic and southern plants, with grasses and dwarf willow dominant; in summer the higher exposed places are covered with yellowish mosses, while sheltered patches show up a vivid green. Woodlands of birch and mountain ash were once extensive, but now occur only in a few places.

With the exception of reindeer, Arctic fox and mink, wildlife in Iceland is winged and the abundant bird life, especially sea birds and water fowl, is a great attraction to naturalists. More than 200 species of migrant birds visit the country. Waterfowl abound on *Lake Myvatn* in the north-east; sea birds teem on cliff faces.

The People

Population

The most sparsely populated country in Europe; average of two inhabitants per square kilometre. Most of the 232,000 people live on the coast in small towns or villages, but there are a few thousand farmsteads in pastoral valleys or on the better parts of the lowlands of the south-west. *Reykjavík*, the capital, has almost 90,000 inhabitants; *Kopavogur*, only 4 miles (6km) away, is the next largest town, population 13,000. *Akureyri*, capital of the northern part of the island, has 12,000.

The people are descended from the original Norse and Celtic colonists.

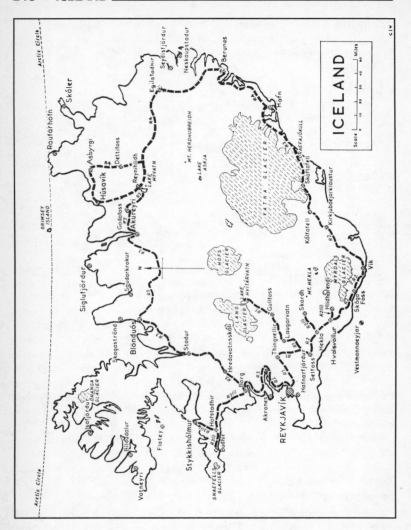

Language

Icelandic is the purest of the Germanic languages, having changed little from the Scandinavian of western Norway spoken by the first settlers. It includes also a few Gaelic names introduced by those Vikings who came from settlements in western Britain.

Religion

The national religion is Lutheran, but there is complete freedom of worship. *Reykjavík* has a Roman Catholic cathedral.

History

Iceland was the last European country to be inhabited. Irish monks and hermits reached it late in the eighth century. Then came Scandinavian explorers, one of whom, Floki Vilgerdharson, after a hard winter, called it *Island* (Iceland). In 874 came the first Norse settlers: Ingólfur Arnarson, founder of *Reykjavík*, and his foster-brother, who was soon murdered by his Irish slaves. The Irish fled to some islands, but were pursued and killed by Ingólfur, the islands ever since being known as the *Vestmannaeyjar* ('islands of the men from the west').

By 930 the settlement was complete, there being about 400 chief settlers, some, with their dependants, seeking freedom from the overlordship of King Harold Fairhair in Norway, others, including some who had become Christians, coming from the Hebrides and other Viking settlements in western Britain. But Christianity soon died out.

In 930, also, Iceland became a nation, forming a General Assembly, the Althing, and adopting a code of law recited annually to the Althing from the Rock of Law at *Thingvellir* where it met annually until 1798.

During the existence of the independent Republic (then unique in the world) Greenland was colonised (985), some Icelanders including Leif Ericsson reached North America (1000) and Christianity was accepted following a mission sent by the king of Norway. But dissension brought the Republic to an end in 1262 when the sovereignty of the Norwegian king was acknowledged.

After the Union of Kalmar Danish influence gradually became dominant. The Reformation was forced on Iceland. Danish monopoly of trade brought economic decline, hastened in the eighteenth century by natural disasters — eruptions, plague and famine.

Recovery began in the 1830s. A cultural and political movement, parallel to those in Norway and elsewhere, awakened a new national consciousness, fostered by scholars and leaders, above all by Jón Sigurdsson (1811-79), the founder of modern Iceland. The Althing was revived (1843), the right of free trade won (1854) and a constitution within the Danish kingdom obtained (1874).

In 1918 Iceland became a sovereign independent state united with Denmark under a common king. In 1944 it returned to being an independent republic.

Government

The President and Parliament (Althing) are elected for four years. The modern Althing has sixty members, one-third in an Upper House, the remainder in the Lower House. There is proportional representation and adult suffrage.

Resources

The grasslands are the basis of Iceland's agriculture; hydro-electic power and geothermal energy support industry, but by far the most important natural resource are the rich fishing banks. The yield is much greater than that of the land; a fifth of the working population is employed in fishing and its associated industries. Cod-fishing is centred particularly on *Reykjavík, Isafjördur* in the north-west peninsula, and the *Westman Islands*. Herring fishing is concentrated on the north and east coasts, notably on *Siglufjördur*, which has large processing plants, and *Raufarhöfn*.

Agriculture occupies almost a quarter of the working population, though very little of the land is cultivated. Farming is based on grass cultivation and animal husbandry; hay is harvested twice every summer and turnips, oats and barley are grown. Cattle breeding, sheep rearing and dairy farming are important. Hot-house cultivation, using hot springs, yields tomatoes, green vegetables and even grapes and bananas.

Collecting of sea birds' eggs for food is specially important in the *Westman Islands* and the north-west peninsula and eider-down from the nests of breeding birds is collected at many places on the north and east coasts, particularly *Flatey* in *Breidhifjördur*.

Food and Drink

Typical dishes are *skyr*, a creamy substance, not unlike curdled milk, served as dessert with sugar and cream; *hangikjot*, well smoked mutton, usually eaten with boiled potatoes or peas; *hardfiskur* or *ryklingur*, smoked dried fish, generally served with butter. Wafers or small pancakes with whipped cream are often served with tea or coffee. Local beer is bland and expensive; coffee, often generously served, is a better buy.

Sport

Glima is a form of wrestling peculiar to Iceland. Swimming is the most popular participation sport; naturally heated pools abound and swimming in geothermal water is a year-round event. Skating, skiing, football and athletics are popular, so too are chess (there are two Icelandic grand masters) and bridge.

Culture

Literature

The twelfth and thirteenth centuries were periods of intense literary activity, producing the *Eddaic* poems, dealing with the gods and heroes of Europe, especially of Scandinavia; the *Landnámabók*, a unique prose record of the settlement; and the *Sagas*, also in prose, a northern equivalent of the Homeric poems. The sagas include the *Heimskringla*, a history of the kings of Norway, and many others such as the *Saga of Burnt Njál*, giving a vivid picture of Icelandic life or of historic events. There are many English translations.

The nineteenth-century cultural revival brought renewed interest in the sagas and a new phase of literary activity which still continues. The realist novels of Icelandic life by Halldór Kiljan Laxness (Nobel Prizewinner, 1955) are available in translation.

Icelanders are avid readers; the annual number of books published per capita in Iceland is greater than anywhere else in the world.

Music and Drama

Drama, opera and ballet are staged at the *National Theatre* in *Reykjavík*. There is a biennial arts festival of international status, and professional theatres in *Reykjavík* and *Akureyri*. The native folk songs have been recovered by collectors but Icelanders have also been much influenced by the musical traditions of the Continent. There is a Conservatory of Music and a National Symphony Orchestra; music ensembles flourish and choral singing is popular.

Sculpture

The *Einar Jónsson Museum* in *Reykjavik* houses the works of Iceland's first and greatest sculptor.

Applied Art

Wood carving and tapestry working were practised from early times. Examples can be seen in the *National Museum, Reykjavík*.

Touring Information

Touring Areas

In the south-west, the neighbourhood of *Reykjavík* and *Thingvellir*, combining scenic, natural history and historic interest; routes east or north-east from *Selfoss* towards ice caps or to the central uninhabited areas; in the north, *Akureyri* and *Myvatn*.

Access

By sea, summer only, by Smyril Line car and passenger ferry from *Scrabster*, via *Thorshavn*, to *Seydisfjördur* (one night on board). London/Glasgow-*Reykjavík*, by air. Excursion return fares (valid 30 days, minimum stay of 6 days); one week package-trips by air in winter are inexpensive.

Transport

There are no railways, but regular coastal services, starting from *Reykjavík* and *Akureyri* call at all the main ports around the coast.

Car ferries ply between *Reykjavík* and *Akranes* from *Thorlákshöfn* to the *Westman Islands* and, in the west, from *Stykkishólmur* to *Brájanlækur* via the *Breidafjördur Islands*.

An extensive system of scheduled bus services reaches most outlying towns and villages and in the holiday season extends into the uninhabited highlands.

Domestic air services reach every inhabited part of the country; connecting bus services link outlying districts to the nearest air-strip.

Money

The Icelandic monetary unit is the *krona*, which is equal to 100 *aurar*. Coins are 10*kr*, 5*kr*, 1*kr*, 50 *aurar* and 5 *aurar*. Banknotes are 10*kr*, 50*kr*, 100*kr*, 500*kr* and 1,000*kr*.

Clothing

Ordinary clothing is usually sufficient for normal excursions. If a longer inland trip is planned, heavy sweaters, boots and an anorak are essential. Take a bathing costume as there are opportunities for swimming in water from hot springs.

Restaurants and Meals

Cafeterias, snack bars, fast-food bars and small restaurants of the less expensive kind can be found in many places, but eating out is seldom cheap.

Maps and Guide Books

Danish Geodetic Institute publish a general map, 1:750,000 and 1:1,000,000, on one sheet; also nine sheets depicting the country on a scale of 1:250,000 and eighty-seven sheets on the 1:100,000 scale. Shell Road Map, 1:600,000, showing useful detail, can be bought at garages in Iceland. Iceland Tourist Board, 172 Tottenham Court Road, London W1P 9LG also stock maps.

Place Names

Many natural and other features can be recognised on the map with the aid of a slight knowledge of the meaning of Icelandic words, such as the following:

Akvegur	road	*Foss*	waterfall
Bær	farm	*Gigur*	crater
Brú	bridge	*Hraun*	lava field
Eldjia	volcanic fissure	*Hver*	hot spring
Eydibær	deserted farm	*Kaupstadhur*	town

Kauptun med kirkju	market town with church	*Sjóporp*	fishing village
Kauptun an kirkju	market town without church	*Skogur*	wood
		Sogustadhur	historical place
		Syslumot	county bound-
Kirkja	church		ary
Kjarr	copse	*Vatn*	water, lake
Laug	hot spring	*Vegur, gata*	bridle path
Reykja	steam, smoke	*Verzlunarstadhur*	trading station
Sandur	sand	*Viti*	lighthouse

Accommodation

Youth hostels are open only in the summer months, except *Reykjavík* and *Akureyri* which are open all year. A canteen set should be brought. Tourist huts, owned by the Touring Club of Iceland (*Ferdhafélag Islands*) and from whom permission to use them has to be obtained, are usually of a good standard, with heating equipment, fuel and cooking utensils, but sleeping bags and food must be brought. Other accommodation in primitive huts or shelters, primarily for farmers when gathering sheep. Some country hotels and private houses provide accommodation for those having their own sleeping bags.

Walking

Best undertaken from centres rather than as a place to place tour, unless a fully planned trek into the interior, with ponies in support to carry food and equipment, is arranged.

Camping

Camping sites in *Reykjavík, Laugarvatn, Thingvellir, Húsafell, Isafjördur, Varmahlid, Akureyri, Myvatn, Egilsstadir, Jökulsárgljúfur* and *Skaftafell*. In some places, camping is restricted to specially marked areas; elsewhere, although camping is generally free, it is not permitted in the National Parks. Campers must, however, request permission from local farmers to camp on any fenced land.

Mountaineering

Only for experienced parties, and requires expedition technique. Movement on the larger ice caps, in particular, requires more than alpine methods. On *Vatnajökull* polar equipment is essential; frequent five-day blizzards must be prepared for.

Motoring

Motorists must carry their car registration certificates, driving licence and international driving permit, international green card of insurance and national identity sticker.

Driving is on the right, giving way to traffic from the right; speed limit in built-up areas is 40km/h (25mph), elsewhere it is 70km/h (43mph).

Although Iceland has nearly 6,000 miles (9,600km) of road much of it is ungraded gravel, dusty and hardly suitable for touring by car or bicycle. A main highway encircles the country, but some stretches are poorly surfaced.

Health

First aid kit should include burn ointment, as springs and geysers can burn even through climbing boots. Be cautious where you walk in areas of thermal activity. An insect repellent should also be taken as midges abound.

Touring Information

Reykjavík Δ, most northerly metropolis in the world, beautifully situated on north shore of *Seltjarnarnes*, a city of neat streets, brightly coloured roofs, bordered by pastures, lava fields and the sea — a panorama best seen from top of *Hallgrim's* church tower on south-east side of harbour; here, too, is statue of *Leif Ericsson*, discoverer of America, and nearby is *Einar Jónsson Museum*.

At old city centre is *Tjörnin*, lake with ducks and seabirds; hub of commerce, Government and culture; here are *Parliament House* (1881), *Old Government Buildings* (mid-eighteenth century) and *National Theatre*. Beyond *Tjörnin* comes *National Museum and Art Gallery*, *Nordic House* (designed by Aalto) *Magnusson Manuscript Museum* (housing precious saga manuscripts) and the *University*.

River *Ellidaár*, one of Iceland's best salmon rivers, runs through eastern side of capital; here, too, is Árbaer *Folk Museum* — old Reykjavík houses reconstructed in original style, traditional country church and farmhouse, complete with furniture of the period.

Reykjavík is best centre for organised tours in south-west, or further afield, for which Tourist Information Centre, Ingólfsstræti 5, Reykjavík, YHA Office in Laufásvegur 41, 101 Reykjavík or *Ferdhafélag Islands* should be consulted.

EXCURSIONS: (a) *Hafnarfjördur*, 7 miles (11km), cod-fishing port, built on lava, then across lava fields to *Krisuvik*, 18 miles (29km), boiling mud pools and sulphur pools. (b) **Heimaey, Westman Islands** Δ ($^{1}/_{2}$ hour by air), town partly buried in volcanic dust, fishing centre, famous breeding place of sea birds, including large gannet colony.

R1 Reykjavík — Thingvellir — Selfoss — Hvítárvatn (135 miles, 217km)
North-east for 35 miles (56km) to *Thingvellir*, meeting place of Althing for over 850 years; lava plain between mountains and *Thingvallavatn*, largest lake and 360ft (109m) deep; birds include whooper swan, whimbrel, ptarmigan and redwing. Continue for 30 miles (48km) on east side of lake and down valley of

River *Sog* through farming country to *Sogsbrú* and *Selfoss*.

EXCURSION: *Hveragerdi*, 7 miles (11km), village with hot springs used for hot-house cultivation.

Laugarvatn, 23 miles (37km), beautifully situated on warm water lake; **Great Geysir**, 14 miles (22km) to north-east, most famous geyser in world, all others named from it, many others in locality; on for 3 miles (5km) to **Gullfoss**, magnificent fall of 105ft (32m) on River *Hívtá*.

Hvítárvatn is 30 miles (48km) to the north, in central stone desert under *Langjökull*, from which glaciers descend to lake.

R2 Selfoss — Skóga Foss — Vík — Kirkjubæjarklaustur — Höfn (140 miles, 225km)

Selfoss (**R1**) to *Thjórsárbrú*, 10 miles (16km), bridge over River *Thjórsá*.

R2 (i) Hella, 6 miles (10km) beyond bridge, road north-east to *Skardh*, 18 miles (29km), for ascent of **Hekla** (4,748ft, 1,447m) and treks to *Landmannahellir* and *Landmannalaugar* with fine scenery in desert area north of mountain. Alternatively, ascent can be made from *Leirubakki*Δ, 6 miles (10km) west of *Hekla*.

Ægisidha, 12 miles (19km), ancient artificial underground caves. From *Hvolsvöllur*, the road follows the beautiful and historic *Fljótshtid* for 17 miles (27km) to *Fljótsdalur*Δ, beside the *Tindfjallajökull* glacier.

R2 (ii) Hvolsvöllur to Hlidharendi, 11 miles (18km), farm mentioned in *Njál's Saga*.

Road skirts *Eyjafjöll* (5,470ft, 1,667m) affording views of *Surtsey Island*. outcome of sub-marine volcanic eruption in 1963, and *Westman Islands*Δ. On for 15 miles (24km), past ice mass of *Myrdalsjökull* to **Skóga Foss** , 200ft (60m) fall. *Vík*, a small fishing settlement is 24 miles (39km) further on, followed by *Kirkjubæjarklaustur* after 43 miles (69km). On for 23 miles (37km) to *Skaftafell National Park*, a strikingly beautiful area on southern fringe of *Vatnajökull* glacier streaming with melt-water to the sea across desert of black volcanic sand. Road skirts *Öræfajökull* follows southern edge of *Vatnajökull* close to the sea, giving on to beautiful scenery towards ice cap. *Höfn*Δ one of the larger fishing ports and base for expeditions on to the glacier and trips to the eastern fjords.

R3 Reykjavík — Hredavatnsskáli — Akureyri — Lake Myvatn (350 miles, 563km)

Road follows coast, skirting *Hvalfjördur* to head of *Borgarfjördur*, 70 miles (112km).

R3(i) Snæfellsnes Peninsula. From *Borg* on *Borgarfjördur* follow road for 55 miles (88km) across plain of Myrar with many lakes via Búdir to *Arnarstapi*.

EXCURSIONS: (a) spectacular basalt sea cliffs below Snæfellsjökull with caves and stacks. (b) lava fields and glacier of *Snæfellsjökull* (4,745ft, 1,446m, extinct volcano).

From *Búdir* return 20 miles (32km) east to near *Hofstadir* where road crosses peninsula, for a further 20 miles (32km) to *Stykkishólmur* where ferries ply to *Flatey* and other islands in **Breidafjördur**.

Hredavatnsskáli is 15 miles (24km) north-eastwards; beautiful volcanic scenery. Road reaches north coast at *Stadhúr* on *Hrútafjördur* after 45 miles (72km). *Blönduós*Δ is 60 miles (96km) further on.

On for 95 miles (153km) to **Akureyri**Δ (bus and air connections with *Reykjavík*), principal town of the north, in sheltered situation at head of *Eyjafjördur* about 37 miles (60km) from the open sea. Excellent botanical gardens and several museums.

Turn eastwards for 30 miles (48km) to the *Godafoss* waterfall, thence southeast for another 30 miles (48km) to **Lake Myvatn,** famous for variety of its volcanic landscape of craters, fissures, ashes and lavas; and, for ornithologists, equally famous as breeding place of many species of duck and other wildfowl. Northwards to *Húsavik*, fishing village, along foot of *Tjórnes* to *Asbyrgi*, horseshoe-shaped rock formation and then south for 20 miles (32km) to *Dettifoss*, Europe's most powerful waterfall, and back to *Myvatn*.

EXCURSION: an expedition, requiring planning, can be made into desert area to south notably to *Askja*, a vast eruption depression chosen as training area by NASA for US astronauts preparing for their first trip to the moon, and *Herdhubreidh*, a climbers' mountain.

R4 Circular Tour of Iceland (890 miles, 1,430km)

From *Reykjavík*, over *Hellisheidi* and through farming country via *Hveragerdi*Δ to *Selfoss* to follow route **R2** to *Höfn* Δ; thence by coast road alongside fjords via *Stafafell*Δ and *Berunes*Δ and on to *Egilsstadir*, having passed Iceland's largest wood. From *Egilsstadir* it is only 17 miles (27km) over the mountain road to *Seydisfjördur*Δ, or directly across uplands and desert to *Lake Myvatn*. **R3**, in reverse, completes the tour.

IRELAND

Geographical and Historical Outline

Land

Ireland, the second largest of the British Isles, has an area of about 32,000 sq miles (83,000 sq km); rather more than three-fifths of this consists of the independent *Republic of Ireland*, the remainder, ie six of the nine counties of the old province of *Ulster*, forms *Northern Ireland*, which remains a part of the United Kingdom.

Structurally Ireland is a western continuation of Britain. The main mountain districts lie around the coasts whilst the centre is a limestone plateau. A striking feature is the large number of rivers and lakes, including the two largest lakes in the *British Isles — Lough Neagh* in *Northern Ireland* and *Lough Corrib* in the *Republic*. The basalt of the north-east gives rise to spectacular coastal features including the famous *Giant's Causeway*. The western seaboard is characterized by many islands, drowned valleys and deep bays.

Climate

The climate is like that of England, with very variable weather, though rather wetter, especially in the west, and with less snow and ice in winter. The prevailing wind is south-west. May and June are usually dry and pleasantly warm; July and August rather more changeable.

Plants and Animals

Though in many parts of the country the underlying rock is limestone, most of the mountain areas have a peaty soil, with great stretches of heathery moorland, similar to the Highlands of Scotland. The peat of the central bogland is of great interest to ecologists and botanists. Ireland became a separate land mass early in the Ice Age, and many species which have since spread across Britain are unknown there. In compensation there are special rarities known also only in Portugal and north-west Spain, or even in North America. The *Burren* of *County*

257

Clare supports an astonishing mixture of Arctic-alpine and Mediterranean species, which makes it most worth visiting in early summer.

The country has suffered greatly from deforestation during the past three centuries, but efforts are now being made to re-afforest numerous mountain areas, largely with foreign conifers.

The fauna also show the effects of isolation; the Irish hare and Irish stoat are examples. Snakes are noted for their absence. There is a wealth of bird life.

History

Ireland was never part of the Roman Empire — a circumstance which brought it two great if temporary advantages: the Celts, who had overrun the island about the beginning of the Christian era, were able to develop a native culture comparatively free of outside influences until the Christianizing mission of St Patrick in the fifth century; and the country avoided the general ruin which engulfed most of Europe when the Empire collapsed in the face of the barbarian invasions. Ireland in fact became in the Dark Ages a beacon of culture and peaceful progress which gave it a name in Europe as 'the island of saints and scholars'.

For centuries it remained divided into a number of separate kingdoms represented by the provinces of *Leinster, Munster, Connaught* and *Ulster*, the title of 'high king', to whom the others owed allegiance, being held most of the time by the O'Neills of *Ulster* but subsequently, in the eleventh and twelfth centuries, by the O'Briens of *Munster* and the O'Connors of *Connaught*.

Viking invasions in the ninth and tenth centuries led to the founding of Norse settlements at *Dublin, Wexford, Waterford, Cork* and *Limerick*.

Two centuries of Anglo-Norman overlordship began in 1167 with the intervention of Henry II in Irish affairs. The country became divided into the Anglo-Irish territories within a boundary called the 'Pale' and independent Celtic Ireland 'beyond the Pale'.

The subsequent history of relations between England and Ireland is not a happy one. The English land proprietors became for a time free of allegiance to the English Crown. When the Tudors and Stuarts regained authority England became Protestant and old Catholic proprietors were expelled to be replaced by Protestants. Catholicism itself was repressed, the process being carried furthest by Oliver Cromwell.

Much of *Ulster* had been settled by Protestant immigrants from England and Scotland. Their support of William of Orange against James II in the famous siege of *Londonderry* (1689) was important in establishing the success of the English Revolution and the effective end of Jacobite hopes.

The English Parliament now virtually controlled Irish affairs, but it was not until the Act of Union (1800) that Irish representatives became entitled to seats at Westminster. The chief benefit was the gaining of Catholic emancipation (1829) largely due to the tenacious and valiant campaigns of Daniel O'Connell. But Parliament's belief in free trade operated to the disadvantage of Ireland. Except for linen and shipbuilding in the north-east the poorer country was unable to establish industries. The potato famine of 1845-9 was a disaster for its dense population (over 8 million in 1841) and led to decline by death and emigration.

Home rule for Ireland became an issue associated on the Irish side particularly with Parnell and on the English side with Gladstone, and by 1913 many were demanding a republic. Both contentions were opposed by Protestant *Ulster* and by a majority in England. Eventually, in 1921 an Irish Free State with dominion status was established, except for the six counties of *Northern Ireland* which elected to remain within the Union as a federal province. In 1937 the Free State became the sovereign independent democratic state of *Eire (Ireland)*, and in 1949 it became a Republic formally separated from the Commonwealth.

The Republic of Ireland

The People

Population

Of the population of about almost 3,000,000, about 1,000,000 live in *Dublin*. *Cork* (150,000) is the second city, and about 270,000 more live in towns of over 10,000 inhabitants. Settlement is therefore predominantly rural. In many counties (such as *Donegal, Kerry, Clare* and *Meath*) and in the whole province of *Connaught* population is remarkably sparse.

There is probably some survival of pre-Celtic stock. The Celtic type known to antiquity, tall and blond or often red-haired, is to be found most often in *Co Donegal*, while the black-haired blue-eyed types of the south and west are also regarded as typically Celtic. Many Normans, Flemings, Welsh and English settled in the country following the Norman invasion and there has been a gradual influx of English and Scottish blood over the centuries, especially in the towns. Germans from the *Rhine-Mosel* region who settled mainly in *Co Limerick*, and French Huguenot refugees, have also left their mark.

Language

Irish, the ancient language of the country, is closely related to Scots' Gaelic. It is spoken as a mother tongue in certain remote areas of the south and the west and in *Co Donegal*, but English remains the language of common use in the country as a whole.

Religion

The population is overwhelmingly Roman Catholic.

Government

The head of the state is the Uachtaran (President) and the executive head of government is the Taoiseach (Prime Minister) acting with an Executive Council or Cabinet. Parliament consists of the Dail, with 147 members, elected by citizens of 18 years and over, and a Senate or upper house, chosen partly by indirect election on a mainly vocational basis and partly by the Taoiseach's nomination.

Resources and Occupations

The main source of income is agriculture, particularly the raising of beef cattle, which are exported mainly to England. The soil, except in the mountain areas, is well suited to dairying and horticulture, though high summer rainfall makes cereal crops other than oats somewhat hazardous. The excellent bone-forming properties of the limestone soil make the rearing of thoroughbred horses an important national enterprise.

The want of minerals has in the past restricted industrial development, but an intensive programme of electrical development, using both waterpower and peat fuel from the bogs, has done much to fill the gap, so that now more than half the employed population is engaged in industry. Manufactured foodstuffs, beer, stout and whisky are exported, together with handwoven tweeds and carpets.

Culture

Architecture

The Romanesque style of the pre-Norman period may best be seen in *Cormac's Chapel* on the *Rock of Cashel*, the doorway of *Clonfert* cathedral in south-east *Co Galway*, and various ruined churches, especially *Clonmacnoise*. For the Gothic period the most important buildings still in use are the two cathedrals in *Dublin, St Patrick's* and *Christ Church*, and *St Canice's* cathedral in *Kilkenny*. Of the many imposing monastic buildings of the Middle Ages, most are now in ruins; especially noteworthy are those of *Mellifont Abbey* and *Jerpoint Abbey* in *Co Kilkenny*. *Dublin* has many examples of Regency and Georgian architecture. Contemporary architecture is not much in evidence, though *Dublin's* fine airport is a notable exception, and many recently built churches show a pleasing blend of traditional and modern styles. Much good modern stained glass is produced in Ireland: fine examples are to be found in *Donegal* town and *Loughrea*, *Co Galway*.

Music and Dances

There is an astonishingly rich background of folk music, modal in type, with many melodies of intense and haunting beauty. Singing in the traditional style may often be heard at local *'feiseanna'* — festivals in Irish music, dancing and story-telling somewhat on the lines of the Welsh *eisteddfod*. Irish traditional dancing is very like the Scottish; many tunes and dances are in fact identical, though differently named.

Drama

The Irish excel in the art of the theatre, having a talent for acting which makes for a high standard both professional and amateur. The *Abbey Theatre* in *Dublin*, the centre of the Irish dramatic movement of the beginning of the twentieth century, is world famous. It specializes in plays with an Irish setting, while the *Gate Theatre* productions usually have a more cosmopolitan flavour. The *Damer Hall* in *St Stephen's Green* is often used by Irish-speaking amateur companies both from Dublin and the provinces. Dramatic societies are numerous in provincial towns and even in some of the remote country districts, particularly in Irish-speaking areas.

Literature

Among the Gaelic languages Irish was for a long time the only literary form. Its classic stories, probably first written down in the ninth century, include heroic tales built around the lives of Cuchulain and Deirdre (the Gaelic equivalents of Achilles and Helen of Troy) or around the doings of Fingal and Ossian. The creation of Irish-Gaelic literature has been stimulated in the twentieth century by the revival of interest in the spoken language.

Of wider significance has been the famous revival of Irish literature in the English language which developed as an expression of national consciousness at the same time as the growth of republican sentiments. Its chief glory was the dramatic movement based principally on the works of W. B. Yeats and J. M. Synge and whose later playwrights have included Lord Dunsany, St John Ervine and Sean O'Casey. Yeats was also chief among the poets of the revival, while in prose there appeared the figure of James Joyce besides many excellent storytellers of more local achievement.

Apart from such writers in the Irish tradition, authors of Irish origin have made major contributions to the general body of English literature. They include Congreve, Swift, Goldsmith, Sheridan and Burke, and, more recently, Wilde and Shaw.

Touring Information

Touring Areas

The scenic areas which attract the most visitors are the *Wicklow Mountains*, south of *Dublin*; the mountains of *Cork* and *Kerry* in the south-west, with Ireland's highest mountain *Carrantuohill*, (3,414ft, 1,040m); the mountain and moorland region of *Connaught*, lying between *Galway Bay* and *Sligo Bay* in the west; the hills of *Donegal* in the extreme north-west. Less known mountain areas of great beauty are the *Galtee* and *Comeragh Mountains* of *Counties Tipperary* and *Waterford* in the south, and the *Carlingford Peninsula*, on the east coast, north of *Dundalk*.

Access

By sea from Great Britain. *Liverpool-Dun Laoghaire* (Sealink), day and night services, both directions, 8 hours. *Holyhead-Dun Laoghaire* (Sealink), day and night services, both directions, $3^1/_4$ hours. *Fishguard-Rosslare* (Sealink), daily service, except Sundays, and night services in mid-summer, $3^1/_4$ hours. *Swansea-Cork* (Cork Car Ferries), daily services, 10 hours. *Pembroke-Rosslare* (Sealink), daily services, 4 hours. Sailing tickets required at peak periods on all these services.

By Air. Aer Lingus, in conjunction with British Airways, Dan Air and Brymon Airways, operate services between *Dublin, Shannon* or *Cork* and many UK airports. Reduced fares on 3 months Apex and 1 month excursion tickets.

Transport

The railway network links the towns, but does not extend into all the scenic areas.

The bus service covers most of the country; services infrequent except in the neighbourhood of *Dublin* where weekday and Sunday buses serve points within walking distance of several *Co Wicklow* youth hostels.

Coras Iompair Eireann issue 8- or 15-day Rail Rambler tickets and composite rail and bus tickets.

Money

British money is acceptable in Ireland, but visitors are advised to buy their Irish money at banks. Banking hours in small towns vary widely where banks may be open only a few days a week.

Public Holidays

St Patrick's Day (17 March), Good Friday, Easter Monday, Whit Monday, First Monday in June, First Monday in August, Last Monday in October, Christmas Day, Boxing Day and New Year's Day.

Restaurants

Restaurants serving cheap and simple meals are rare, except in towns. Meat courses are generally good and generously served.

Maps

The Ordnance Survey publishes maps, scale 1in to 1 mile, for the *Dublin, Wicklow, Cork* and *Killarney* tourist areas; also a series at $^1/_2$in to 1 mile in 25 sheets covering all the country. Bartholomew maps, scale $^1/_4$in to 1 mile cover the country in five sheets.

Accommodation

The Irish YHA, *An Oige*, has about 40 hostels; most of them are small. Booking in advance is essential at weekends, particularly for hostels within reach of *Dublin*, and at all times for parties of any size. Cooked meals are not provided, but self-catering facilities are available. The *Wicklow Mountains*, the south-west and *Co Donegal* are the areas best covered, but the other main scenic areas are also accessible and a circular cycling tour of Ireland can be made from hostel to hostel without runs over 100 miles (160km).

Walking

Admirable walking country in most of the mountain areas served by hostels; in *Co Wicklow* it is possible to plan a complete cross-country walking tour from hostel to hostel.

Motoring

Motoring conditions are similar to those in England and Wales.

Cycling

Main roads are good; rough conditions may be met on minor roads and routes should be planned accordingly. The frequency of strong south-west winds should also be allowed for.

Dublin

Dublin △. Centre of city is formed by *O'Connell Street* and its intersection with River *Liffey*. Main shopping streets (a) south of river: *Grafton Street*, where most fashionable shops are situated, and *Great George's Street*, parallel with it, nearer the river; (b) north of river: *Henry Street, Mary Street* and *Talbot Street*, parallel to the river and crossing *O'Connell Street*.

Eighteenth-century classicism is predominant architectural influence, seen in many streets and squares, especially in neighbourhood of *Merrion Square*. See also the *Custom House* (1791), on north quayside east of *O'Connell Bridge*, the *Law Courts* (1796) known as the Four Courts, on north quays west of *O'Connell Bridge*, the *Bank of Ireland* (formerly Parliament House) (1729), *Trinity College*, of which the west front buildings were completed in 1759, the house of the Provost of *Trinity, King's Inns* in *Henrietta Street, King's Hospital School*, and the former *Newcomen's Bank* now corporation buildings, beyond top of *Dame Street*. *Dublin Castle*, off *Dame Street*, consists of a series of quadrangles (now government offices) of varying date, from medieval *Record Tower* to early nineteenth-century *Chapel Royal; State Rooms* are open for conducted tours.

The squares and playing fields of *Trinity College* form a green and peaceful oasis in middle of city; its library has some of greatest treasures of Celtic art, especially the **Book of Kells**, an early ninth-century copy of the Gospels with illuminations of extraordinary complexity and beauty.

National Museum, Kildare Street, has superb examples of Celtic art; celebrated *Tara brooch* and *Ardagh chalice*. *National Gallery, Merrion Square*, has a particularly fine El Greco, a Tiepolo and a Correggio Nativity. *Municipal Gallery, Parnell Square*, mainly nineteenth- and twentieth-century artists.

There are two medieval cathedrals, *Christ Church* and *St Patrick's*, the latter containing burial place of Jonathan Swift. *St Michan's* church on north side of river has fine eighteenth-century interior and vaults with a gruesome collection of naturally mummified bodies. The *University Church*, on *St Stephen's Green*, is a fine example of modern building in the Byzantine style.

Touring Routes

R1 Dublin to Aghavannagh through the Wicklow Mountains (122 miles, 196km)

Dublin△ — Glencree△ — Knockree△ — Glendaloch△ — Aghavannagh△ — Glenmalure△ — Ballinclea△ — Baltyboys△ — Dublin.

The area is of great scenic beauty, with heather-clad mountains rising to 3,039ft (926m) at their highest point, *Lugnaquilla*, easily climbed either from *Glenmalure, Ballinclea* or *Aghavannagh*. The valley of *Glendaloch* is a celebrated beauty spot; ruins of pre-Norman monastic settlement (*St Kevin's*) with round tower and other buildings, sixth to twelfth century. *Avoca* valley and *Glenmalure*△ are also particularly beautiful. *Wicklow* is a county to linger in rather than pass through; several hostels are excellent centres for hill walking. Rock climbing in *Glendaloch* and at some points on flanks of *Lugnaquilla*.

R2 Tir Chonaill (County Donegal) (301 miles, 484km)

Sligo — Ball Hill△ — Carrick — Crohy Head△ — Aranmore Island△ — Errigal△ — Tra-na-Rossann △ and back by Ball Hill to Sligo.

Donegal is wild and rocky, and contains some of Ireland's most spectacular scenery, especially *Slieve League*, near *Carrick*, where a mountain of 1,972ft (601m) falls in a sheer cliff to the Atlantic, impressive cliffs of *Bloody Foreland*, near *Derrybeg*, and *Horn Head*, near *Tra-na-Rosann*. Highest mountains are *Errigal* (2,466ft, 752m, accessible from *Tra-na-Rosann* by bicycle) and *Muckish* (2,197ft, 669m, 8 miles, 13km, from *Tra-na-Rosann*). *Errigal* is in heart of Irish speaking area. County has little industry, but *Donegal* tweeds, hand-spun and hand-woven, are world famous; *Carrigart* is main local centre for their sale.

R3 Dublin to Cork, via County Kilkenny and the Galtee Mountains (176 miles, 283km)

Dublin Δ — *Foulksrath*Δ — *Mountain Lodge*Δ — *Ballydavid Wood* Δ — *Cork*Δ.

This route makes accessible the *Barrow* valley and *County Kilkenny* and the mountain area of *County Tipperary*. *Foulksrath*Δ can be the base for a visit to *Kilkenny*: important in Irish history, fine thirteenth-century cathedral and other medieval churches. The *Galtee Mountains*, between *Mountain Lodge* and *Ballydavid Wood* are worth exploring; magnificent panorama from highest point, *Galteemore* (3,018ft, 920m). The *Rock of Cashel*, with cathedral ruins, chapel of *Cormac*, and an Irish high cross, is within reach for cyclists, and should not be missed. Near *Mountain Lodge* are *Mitchelstown* caves, a chain of limestone caverns.

R4 Cork and the South-West (301 miles, 484km)

Cork Δ, second city of Republic; partly built on island in River *Lee*, many bridges, fine quays. Protestant and Roman Catholic cathedrals; *St Anne Shandon's* church, unusual sandstone and limestone spire. University has sixteenth-century cloisters, charmingly laid out grounds, and *Honan* chapel — a tiny but exquisite gem of mosaic and stained glass. *Turner's Cross* church, one of few uncompromisingly modern churches in the country. Riverside walks and wooded heights give city a picturesque and tranquil charm, in contrast to the well known energy of its inhabitants.

Within easy reach by bus is *Blarney Castle*, in park-like grounds, where those who wish to acquire the gift of eloquence the easy way can do it — or so they say — by kissing the *Blarney Stone*. Numerous seaside resorts around shores of *Cork Harbour*; swimming, boating, and sea fishing. *Cobh*, on island in harbour, is port of call for transatlantic liners. *Cork's* most important cultural event is annual film festival, which has an international reputation.

The mountain area of *Counties Cork* and *Kerry* contains Ireland's highest mountain, *Carrantuohill* (3,414ft, 1,040m) and most famous beauty spot, *Killarney*. Like *Wicklow*, it is a region to be lingered in; splendid opportunities for hill walking and scrambling, with *Black Valley*Δ and *Killarney*Δ well situated for the purpose. On west coast is *Ballinskelligs*Δ, sea-fishing, swimming, boating, and within easy reach of *Valentia Island*Δ, while *Skellig Rocks* (on largest, *Skellig Michael*, are buildings of an early hermit settlement) stand 9 miles (14km) offshore. *Cape Clear Island*Δ reached from *Baltimore* harbour by ferry.

Cork to *Kinsale*Δ, 18 miles (29km); small fishing port, place of James II's landing (1689) in attempt to recover English Crown. *Cape Clear*Δ is 40 miles (64km) further west. Then via *Bantry* and *Bantry Bay*, one of many fine examples of drowned valleys of this coast, and through beautiful *Glengariff* valley noted for mild climate and Mediterranean vegetation to *Kenmare* and on for 80 miles (129km) to *Black Valley*Δ, mountainous going, and hardly practicable in one day except for the tough. *Ballinskelligs*Δ is 56 miles (90km) westwards, then east for 48 miles (77km) to *Killarney*Δ. The famous lakes are sheltered by two sandstone ranges: *MacGillicuddy's Reeks*, which include *Carrantuohill*, with *Beaufort*Δ nearby, and that which runs from *Cahirbarragh* (2,239ft, 682m) to *Mangerton* (2,756ft, 840m). *Lough Leane* has many wooded islands; *Muckross*, on Lake *Muckross*, is site of ancient abbey; semi-tropical plants abound; many fine walks. Return, easterly for 59 miles (95km) to *Cork*, via *Loo Bridge*Δ and *Macroom*.

Other districts of great beauty are (i) the *Beare Peninsula*, with Lake *Glanmore* Δ and *Allihies*Δ, running west from *Glengariff*; (ii) the *Dingle Peninsula*, chief Irish-speaking district of the south-west; youth hostel at *Dun Chaoin*. (iii); *Gouganebarra*, in the heart of the mountains between *Bantry* and *Macroom*.

R5 Galway, Connemara and the Joyce Country

Galway, cross-country by road or by train in 3 hours; capital of the west; picturesquely situated on estuary of River *Corrib*; was formerly second city of Ireland, though of its medieval grandeur not much remains save imposing church of *St Nicholas* and sixteenth-century house in main street known as *Lynch's Castle*. Now flourishing seaside resort, and has many factories. Fine university buildings. Boating on River *Corrib*, and on lake from which it flows, is a favourite local pursuit. *Galway* races, last week of July, are sporting event of national importance.

Galway's western hinterland is a lonely but beautiful district of bare mountains and desolate boglands; countless lakes, from the great *Lough Corrib* to tiny moorland pools barely large enough to hold a trout, make it an angler's paradise. *Connemara*, properly so called, is the southern coastal region which remains largely Irish-speaking. The more mountainous northern section, the *Joyce Country*, is accessible from *Killary Harbour*.

The *Connemara* coast is ideal for a holiday of boating, fishing and swimming; many good beaches, mostly empty, except at weekends.

Aran Islands: at head of *Galway Bay*; fishing boats make frequent crossings from *Lettermullen*. Those interested in antiquities should certainly make this trip and see *Dun Aengus*, prehistoric circular stone fortress on *Inishmore*, the largest island; also early Christian chapels, shrines and beehive huts. The islands are formed of limestone; their sparse soil is mixed with seaweed for the growing of barley and potatoes.

*Killary Harbour*Δ; among some of finest scenery in the west; on southern shore of long sea inlet, opposite *Mweelrea* (2,688ft, 820m) highest mountain in county. Rock climbing on it and on mountain groups of *Beanna Beola (The Twelve Bens)* and *Maumturk* range.

Circular tour from *Galway*, along coast road for 36 miles (56km) via *Indreabhan*Δ, to *Lettermullen*, thence north to *Maam Cross* and west via *Ben Lettery*Δ to *Clifden*, capital of *Connemara*, near which first transatlantic fliers,

Alcock and Brown, made their landing in 1919; then north and east circling mountains via *Letterfrack* and *Kylemore*, to *Killary Harbour*△, making a route of 53 miles (85km) from *Lettermullen*. Continue for 45 miles (72km) by *Leenane*, through *Joyce Country* to *Maam Cross* and *Oughterard* (fishing centre on *Lough Corrib*) and back to *Galway*.

If time can be spared, coast road can be followed all the way from *Lettermullen* to *Clifden*, via charming small fishing town of *Roundstone* and, a little beyond it, *Dog's Bay*, finest bathing beach in *Connemara*.

R5 (i) From *Leenane* turn north via *Westport* and round north shore of *Clew Bay* to *Currane* on *Achill Sound*, 45 miles (72km) for a visit to *Achill Island* (linked to the mainland by bridge); spectacular scenery, especially cliffs of *Croaghan* (2,192ft, 668m) plunging to Atlantic, and beautiful cone of *Slievemore* (2,204ft, 672m); fine bathing beaches.

NORTHERN IRELAND

The People

Population

Of the population of about 1,550,000 more than 50 per cent are town dwellers, including some 400,000 in *Belfast*, the capital.

The people are of varied ancestry: Irish, Scots, English and a few French. This diversity arises from the history of the province — the 'plantations' of the seventeenth century, for example, when Scots and English settlers were brought in. This explains the terms 'Scots-Irish' and 'Ulster-Scot' by which the Ulsterman not obviously of Irish origin is often known abroad. It also explains the political abyss between 'Orange' (Protestant, in favour of continued union with Great Britain) and 'Green' (Roman Catholic, in favour of union with the Republic).

Language

English is spoken everywhere, and in a variety of local accents, in some places closer to Elizabethan than to modern English, and sometimes influenced by the idioms of Gaelic. Almost all place names are of Gaelic origin.

Religion

The various Protestant denominations (Church of Ireland, Presbyterian, Methodist, etc) account for 65 per cent of the population, the remainder being Roman Catholic. The term 'Church of Ireland' does not signify a state church. In spite of the strong religious affiliations of almost all its people, Northern Ireland is legally a secular state, no denomination receiving state support.

Government

Northern Ireland has, since 1880, been part of the United Kingdom and sends twelve members to the United Kingdom Parliament at Westminster.

Resources

Farming is the chief occupation in a land of small farms which, under a system of Government loans, are becoming the property of those who farm them. The standard is constantly being raised by application of scientific methods and mechanisation.

The other main occupations are in the world-renowned Irish linen industry; ship-building in *Belfast*; and the manufacture of aircraft.

Mineral resources are few. Only a little coal occurs and even this cannot be mined easily. This and the lack of raw materials has led to a policy of manufacturing goods of high specific value: for example, electronic computers and radio and electrical goods. Many of these industries are in the smaller towns, but *Belfast* itself has a great diversity.

As in the rest of Ireland there is a marked lack of woodlands. Fishing is carried on from a number of small ports, particularly in *Co Down*. There is a considerable tourist trade.

National Characteristics

The characteristic of the Ulsterman most likely to be noticed by the visitor is his interest in the stranger and his desire to help him — in particular in seeing those parts of the country which should not be missed, and to which he will be directed with obvious pride. A 'bit of a crack' (a chat) is always appreciated and often worth the time spent on it.

In country districts a greeting may be expected from all passers-by — usually a comment on the weather.

Food and Drink

The pattern is very like that in Scotland, particularly in the variety of bread and scones, including 'soda' bread and 'potato' bread, both usually in the form of *farls* baked on a griddle.

Sport

Most town dwellers are keenly interested in sport, principally Association, Gaelic, or Rugby football, golf, cricket and hockey (or its Gaelic counterparts, hurley and camogie). In Gaelic football (a cross between the other two codes) a player can take three steps with the ball in his hands. Water sports, including sailing, canoeing and fishing, are popular and facilities are excellent.

Culture

Folklore

Ireland as a whole has been described as a 'treasure house of old ways unrivalled in Western Europe' and *Ulster* is its most representative region.

While Northern Ireland is rich in folklore, systematic attempts at recording it have only been made in recent times. In some country districts vestiges remain of the old '*ceilidhe*' system of entertainment, by which people gathered in the home of a neighbour for conversation, song and dance, story telling, or even card playing, according to age. Superstitions abound, largely based on legends of the 'wee people' (fairies) and even a hard-headed farmer will leave a 'fairy thorn' tree standing in a ploughed field. In some parts, wishing wells are common, often with a nearby tree bearing pins or strips of cloth taken from the clothing to transfer ailments from the person to the tree. Charms against the evil eye, and for the treatment of human ailments are still sometimes used. St Brigid's Crosses are made of rushes cut on the eve of St Brigid's Day. Such charms are really of pagan origin and design; samples of the many ancient practices still to be found in the *Ulster* countryside.

Music

Music is more for the participator than the listener, though there are worthwhile orchestral and choral concerts mainly during the winter. Bands abound: brass, bagpipe, flute and accordion. Choirs are numerous. There are well-supported musical festivals in *Belfast* and other places.

Touring Information

Touring Areas

The *Antrim* coast and basalt plateau of the north-east; the *Mourne Mountains*; the *Sperrin Mountains*; the lake district of *Co Fermanagh*.

Access

By sea from Great Britain. *Stranraer (Scotland)—Larne* (Sealink), day and night services, 2^1/$_2$ hours. *Cairnryan—Larne* (P & O European Ferries), daily services, 2^1/$_2$ hours. *Minnigaff*△ 20 miles (32km) from *Stranraer*. *Ballygally*△ 4 miles (6km) north of *Larne* at start of *Antrim* coast chain. *Liverpool-Belfast* (Belfast

Ferries), nightly, 10 hours. Sailing tickets required at peak periods on all these services.

By air. Services between *Belfast* and most UK airports.

From the Republic. *Dublin-Belfast*, by train, serving *Portadown, Lurgan* and *Lisburn* en route. Elsewhere, access is mainly by local bus. Travelling to and from the Republic and Northern Ireland involves a customs examination.

Transport

The railway system consists of the main lines *Belfast, Portadown* (on to *Dublin*) and *Belfast-Londonderry* with branches *Belfast-Bangor* and *Larne* and *Coleraine-Portrush*. There is an intricate network of bus services, all under the control of the Ulster Transport Authority.

Public Holidays

The chief general holiday is 12 July, the day of the parades of Orangemen; in *Belfast* 20,000 men with bands and banners take part. The week in which this day falls is the traditional holiday week. Bank holidays are the same as in England, with the addition of 17 March (St Patrick's Day) and 12 July.

Restaurants

Outside *Belfast*, not abundant; but in all towns it is possible to get a meal either in a restaurant or a hotel at prices similar to those in England.

Maps

For the walker, the Ordnance Survey maps, scale 1in to 1 mile, covering the country in nine sheets, are excellent. Bartholomew maps, scale $1/_2$in to 1 mile, on two sheets, are adequate for cyclists and motorists.

Accommodation

There are now only three youth hostels along the *Antrim* coast. Others are in *Belfast*, in *Newcastle* (for *Mourne Mountains*) and *Castle Archdale* (on *Lower Loch Erne*). All the hostels are small and meals are not provided, but members' kitchens are everywhere well equipped, though without cutlery.

Walking

The best walking can be in open country, especially in the upland areas mentioned above; often there are no roads or tracks. Hostels are within walking distance of each other.

Rock climbing is practised in some parts of the *Mourne Mountains*, but for ordinary hill walking no special skill is needed beyond the common sense always called for in such country.

Motoring

Conditions and regulations are similar to those in England and Wales.

Touring Routes

R1 Belfast to Londonderry via Antrim Coast Road (120 miles, 193km)

Belfast Δ, lively industrial city and seaport. Around City Hall is excellent shopping centre and busy commercial area. Much of city given over to factories and terraces of workers' houses, product of rapid expansion in nineteenth century, but there are pleasant suburbs and public parks, and surrounding hills provide a beautiful setting. *Bellevue* and *Hazelwood Parks* for panoramic views of city, port area (massive cranes and gantries of shipyards) and surrounding countryside. Buses for tour of city from City Hall (*Donegal Square East*). *Ulster Museum* near the Botanic Gardens is worth a visit.

Parliament House at *Stormont* is pleasantly situated on low hill; extensive views.

Leave *Belfast* by *York Street*, *York Road* and *Shore Road*, passing shopping centre and factory area (linen and tobacco). *Carrickfergus*; massive Norman castle (1200) and ancient church of *St Nicholas*. Along shore of *Larne Lough*, noted for sea birds and wild fowl, to *Larne*, or train to Larne from *York Road Station*. Those who have crossed on the *Stranraer-Larne* Ferry could make this their starting point.

At *Larne* the famous **Antrim Coast Road**, one of most attractive roads in Europe, begins. Below lies the sea; behind lie extensive moors and beautiful **Antrim Glens** — all worth exploring by taking an extra day or two at one or other *County Antrim* hostel.

*Ballygally*Δ, attractive village 4 miles (6km) north of *Larne*. Continue by road, either to *Carncastle*, across moors, or to *Glenarm* and *Carnlough*, each with small harbour. Route continues north between cliff and sea round *Garron Point* (walkers can cross moors above *Carnlough* to *Parkmore* at head of *Glenariff*, and so avoid the dangerous *Glenariff* cliffs) and to *Red Bay* (good and quiet beach) and *Cushendall*Δ from which three of *Glens of Antrim* radiate. Here main road swings inland, but by-roads lead to *Cushendun*, quiet village, popular among artists.

To *Ballyvoy* and *Ballycastle*, choice of routes: main road; or *Torr Head* road by coast, with steep hills and very sharp bends; or, for walkers, by open moors east or west of main road. *Murlough Bay* and wild, open country around *Fair Head* are worth a detour, or separate day's walking.

Ballycastle quiet seaside resort, except on last Tuesday in August when famous Lammas Fair is held. *Rathlin Island* can be reached by motor boat.

Continue on road nearest coast, passing *Carrick-a-Rede Island* (linked to mainland by rope bridge), to beautiful strand of *Whitepark Bay*Δ, chalk cliffs, sandhills, views over Atlantic to islands of Scotland.

Giant's Causeway, is 4 mile (6km) west; largest and most perfect example of columnar formation of basaltic lavas. Regular hexagonal columns, formed by rapid cooling of molten lava. From the Causeway, either by footpath to *Portballintrae* and road to *Dunluce Castle* (ruin), *Portrush* and *Coleraine*; or by road via *Bushmills* to *Coleraine*; then by *Murder Hole Road* to *Stradreagh*, or if motoring or cycling, by either main (mountain) or coast road, via *Downhill* to *Limavady* and *Londonderry*.

Londonderry. 'Derry' means an oak grove; the prefix 'London' commemorates colonization of city by the Companies of the City of London during the reign of James I. On the site of modern Derry (the term always used in Ireland) St Columba established a religious community before he went to Iona (sixth century).

In 1689 Derry endured a siege of 105 days. It is the only city in the British Isles which preserves its city walls complete; they have a circuit of about a mile and are pierced by seven gates. Many of the old guns are still in position, and relics of siege can be seen in *St Columba's Cathedral*.

R2 Londonderry to Newry via Sperrin Mountains (93 miles, 150km)
Leave *Londonderry* by main *Belfast* road. Where huge *Altnagelvin* Hospital dominates landscape is a striking example of modern art — the bronze figure of Princess Macha. At village of *Claudy,* take road on right towards *Park* where the ridges of *Sperrin Mountains* are now visible.

Walkers can take an interesting route on rough roads crossing the *Sperrin* ridges, by *Park*, the *Dart Pass*, *Cranagh* (a tiny village notable in local story for having wearied of politicians and attempted to set up its own republic) and the *Barnes Gap to Gortin*. Motorists and cyclists can reach *Gortin* via *Plumbridge*.

Continue via *Omagh*, small market town, beautifully situated on River *Strule*, *Aughnacloy, Caledon* and *Killylea* to orchard country of *Co Armagh*. *Armagh* is small ancient city with two cathedrals, observatory and some fine Georgian architecture; was site of St Patrick's metropolitan church in fifth century, and is seat of two Archbishops, the Roman Catholic and Protestant Primates of all Ireland.

R2 (i) *Omagh* via *Portadown* to *Belfast*Δ 70 miles (112 km).

R2 (ii) *Omagh* to *Enniskillen* (lake district) via *Castle Archdale*Δ, near *Irvinestown*, and routes to *Sligo* and west coast of *Republic of Ireland*.

R3 Newry to Belfast via Mourne Mountains (100 miles, 161km)
Newry, at head of *Carlingford Lough*, between *Mourne Mountains* and *Slieve Gullion*, contains pleasant Georgian buildings and is surrounded by very attractive country.

To *Warrenpoint* and *Rostrevor*. Then by hill routes to either *Kinnahalla* or

Newcastle△, within a short distance of each other and with easy access to the
Mourne Mountains.

A suggested route for walkers is from *Knockbarragh* by road and rough hill
tracks and lanes to *Kinnahalla* then by *Spelga Pass* or by open mountain track to
Silent Valley and by road to *Dunnywater Bridge*; then by track round flank of
Spence's Mountain to *Bloody Bridge*. On by mountain track (the *Brandy Pad*) via
Slievenaman and by pleasant route through *Tollymore Forest Park* to *New-
castle*△, a popular seaside resort at the foot of the mountains.

For motorists and cyclists: from *Restrevor*; by *Kilbroney* river valley to
Hilltown and *Kinnahalla* or by River *Glen* to *Kinnahalla* (follow signposts
marked '*Spelga Dam*' until hostel is reached). Then by *Spelga Pass* to *Silent
Valley* and via *Kilkeel* and *Annalong*, two attractive small fishing ports, to
Newcastle△.

Route continues with fine views of mountains via *Dundrum* (impressive ruins
of Norman castle) to *Minerstown* near *St John's Point*, with lighthouse and old
church.

From *Minerstown* take road to *Strangford* and cross strait by ferry to
Portaferry. Route now runs north alongside *Strangford Lough* to *Newtownards*
and *Belfast*.

R3 (i) *Minerstown* to *Downpatrick* (ancient town, with reputed grave of St Patrick,
who began his ministry at *Saul*, 2 miles, 3km, distant), thence from *Saintfield*, to
Belfast (28 miles, 45km).

ITALY

Geographical Outline

Land

Italy has four main physical divisions: the peninsula, centrally situated in the *Mediterranean* and whose core is the mountain range of the *Apennines*; the northern plain, watered by the River *Po* and its tributaries, and by the *Adige* and other Alpine rivers reaching the *Adriatic* direct; the *Alps*, continues with the *Apennines* in the west, and forming a crescent-shaped barrier on Italy's frontier with France, Switzerland, Austria and Yugoslavia; the large islands of *Sicily* and *Sardinia*, and a number of small islands of which the best known are *Elba, Ischia* and *Capri*. Within these divisions there is great regional diversity.

Italy shares with France the highest mountain in the *Alps, Mont Blanc* (15,782ft, 4,810m); with Switzerland *Monte Rosa* (15,217ft, 4,638m) and the *Matterhorn* (14,782ft, 4,505m). The *Gran Paradiso* (13,324ft, 4,061m) in the *Graian Alps*, is the highest peak entirely within the country. The *Apennines* reach 9,560ft (2,914m) in the *Gran Sasso*.

Grouped around the southern end of the *Tyrrhenian* sea are several areas of continuing volcanic activity: *Vesuvius* (3,880ft, 1,182m) and the *Phlegraean Fields* near *Naples*; *Etna* (10,742ft, 3,274m) in *Sicily*; the *Lipari* islands, including *Stromboli* and *Vulcano*.

Climate

Italy is a land of sunshine and, for the most part, of low humidity, with clear crisp air. Summer temperatures are high and particularly trying from *Rome* southwards in July and August. The hottest parts are *Sicily* and the *Gulf of Taranto*.

Winter shows greater ranges of climate over comparatively short distances, seen in the contrast between the mildness of the *Riviera* and the severe cold of the lowlands of *Piedmont*, and again in the warmth of the lake region (*Como, Garda* and *Maggiore*) below the *High Alps* where the coldest winters occur.

Rainfall is only typically Mediterranean, occurring in winter with summer

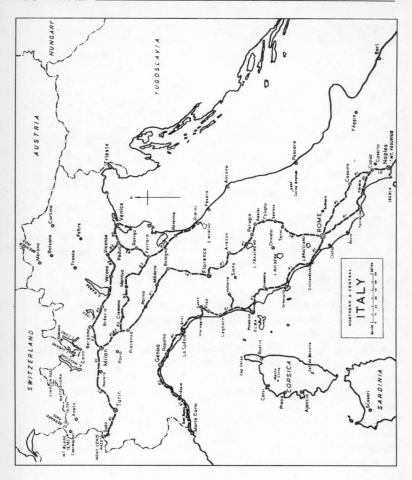

drought, south of *Naples*. Elsewhere in the peninsula and on the northern plain it is greatest in spring and autumn, whilst in the *High Alps* precipitation occurs chiefly in summer and winter.

Plants and Animals

The vegetation of the Alps and of the northern plain is Central European in type; that of the peninsula is Mediterranean.

Both types include coniferous forests. The broad-leaved trees and brush-

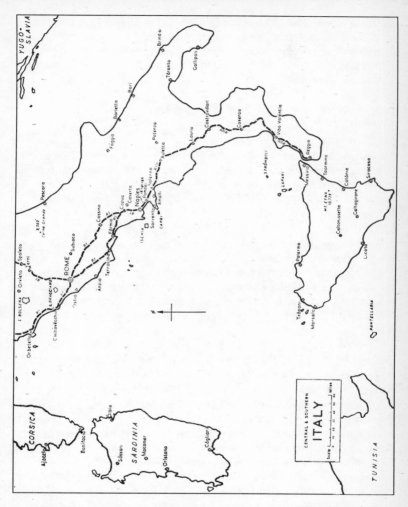

woods of the north yield in the peninsula to evergreen trees and to a *maquis*-type of brushwood. But in the mountains beech forests extend as far as *Sicily*. A further contrast is between the meadows and pastures of the north, which remain green in summer, and those in the south which have to survive in parched conditions.

The natural vegetation has been replaced over large areas: the vine and groves of olive, lemon and orange are important features in the landscape.

Among wild animals lizards abound, somewhat making up in interest for the comparative lack of birds. The wild pig, wolf, bear, deer, chamois and moufflon occur. Also the ibex, in the *Gran Paradiso National Park*. Dangerous smaller animals include scorpions, certain centipedes and spiders, and vipers. In some country districts precautions may need to be taken against mosquitoes, but there is no danger of malaria.

The People

Population

The population of about 57 million is highly urbanised; the majority living in the considerable number of small towns of fewer than 20,000 people. The six cities of over half-a-million inhabitants are: *Rome* (2,800,000), *Milan* (1,800,000), *Naples* (1,235,000), *Turin* (1,180,000), *Genoa* (848,000), and *Palermo* (650,000).

Language

Italian developed in the thirteenth century out of the Florentine dialect, one of the many local vernaculars based on Latin which gradually replaced the classical language after the break-up of the Empire. With the growth of trade there was again a need for a national language and Dante's writings provided a model to which others were glad to conform in writing and, to a lesser extent, in speech.

Italian is a finely resonant, smoothly flowing tongue, lending itself naturally to song.

French is the language of some of the alpine districts such as the *Val d'Aosta* and *Val Pelline*. Parts of the *Trentino* are German-speaking.

Religion

Italy is almost entirely Roman Catholic. Church influence, exercised through large numbers of clergy, is strong.

The position of the *Vatican City* as a sovereign state independent of Italy emphasises its world-wide responsibilities in spiritual matters. But the Pope is also Bishop of Rome and Primate of Italy.

Saints' days are numerous and widely observed. Visits to shrines are popular and common. A great shrine such as that of St Anthony of *Padua* draws people from great distances.

Protestants are the most numerous non-Catholic community. They include the Waldensians of the alpine valleys west of *Turin* whose history of persecution endured is as heroic and tragic as that of the Huguenots.

History

It was in Italy that Greek and Christian ideas found a powerful advocate in the practical genius of Rome and so acquired their profound influence on the whole of Western culture. The story of Italy abounds in local episodes glorious and sordid, but its great themes — the Empire, the Church, the Renaissance — occupy the world stage and command recognition in any assessment of man's limitations and possibilities. Italy has, too, its own noble if more local theme of the search, during 1,400 years, for unity after collapse of the Empire in the West.

From the eighth century BC there were Greek colonies in *Sicily* and southern Italy (*Magna Graecia*), whilst north of the *Tiber*, another people, the Etruscans, were extending their power widely in the peninsula.

Rome itself emerged in about 600BC from a union of communities of Latin and Sabine stock. Ruled first by kings, including the Etruscan Tarquins, it later became a republic (509BC) and grew rapidly in organisation and power. First *Latium* was conquered, then the whole of Italy. By war and diplomacy in the East, in Africa and Spain all the countries of the Mediterranean became Roman provinces.

After 400 years of republican rule, civil strife brought dictatorship. Julius Caesar conquered Gaul but his attempt to seize power for life was a misjudgement which brought his assassination (44BC). Yet when Octavian, his adopted son, acquired full power he did so as Augustus Caesar and his long reign as emperor (30BC to AD14), bringing peace and prosperity, confirmed the transition from Republic to Empire.

The Empire, surviving until AD476, became synonymous with civilisation in the West. Wherever the Roman peace was accepted cities were founded, communications were improved and men had before them the example of Roman power and love of order which found particular expression in architecture, town life and Roman law.

Christianity, at first persecuted, forced underground to the catacombs and its adherents spectacularly martyred by Nero, was later recognised by Constantine and adopted as the offical religion of the Empire. In a sense it succeeded the Empire in the West. With the founding of Constantinople (AD30), and with the barbarian invasions, the civil power of Rome declined, but the city found a new role as centre of the Christian church. The barbarians overran it, but the Papacy survived.

Italy was conquered by the Visigoths under Alaric, who sacked Rome (410); then, more happily, by the Ostrogoths under the wise rule (493-526) of Theodoric the Great. Imperial power was again secured under Justinian (famous for his code of law and his splendid Byzantine churches at *Ravenna*), only to be lost to the unruly Lombard invaders (568).

Henceforward, political unity was lost. Charlemagne took *Lombardy* (775); the Arabs, after a fifty-year struggle, conquered *Sicily* (878) and disputed southern Italy with the Byzantine Empire. Elsewhere, power was in the hands of local lords until Otto I revived the Western Empire and the royal power. His coronation as Holy Roman Emperor (962) united Germany and Italy (except the south). The next major event was the Norman conquest of *Sicily* (1061-91) and the south, both being united in the feudal Kingdom of Sicily.

The famous medieval struggle between popes and emperors on the question of supremacy was partly due to a difference of views on the relationship of spiritual to temporal power, later echoed in other countries. But popes were also temporal rulers in the Papal States and were opposed to imperial attempts to unify Italy. These seemed likely to succeed when the crowns of the Sicilian Kingdom and the Empire came to be held by one man—the Hohenstaufen prince, Frederick II. But the popes proposed instead to unify Italy themselves by a federation of states with the Pope at its head. From this there arose the notorious party factions of Guelphs and Ghibellines, supporters respectively of papal and imperial supremacy.

Neither was successful. When the emperors ceased to interfere in Italy the newly risen and prosperous city states (*Florence, Milan*, etc) refused to submit to papal authority. The Papacy fell; the pope fled to exile in *Avignon* (1303-77). Nor was an attempt by Rienzo to revive the Roman republic more successful. Instead, each city went its own way either as a republic (such as *Venice*) or as an autocracy (such as *Milan* under the Visconti and *Florence* under the Medici).

These cities, with the returned Papacy and a new power in the south — the Kingdom of Naples, under Aragonese rule — were the principal states at the beginning of the Renaissance in the fifteenth century. With many other lesser but still brilliant states they provided unexampled patronage and stimulation to artists and scholars imbued with the new humanism. Yet politically they were a danger to each other, although they had some success in co-operation. Their disunity encouraged outside intervention. First France (1494), then Spain (1503), then the Emperor Charles V (1521) invaded. Except for *Venice* and *Savoy* Italy was dominated by Spain (1559-1700) and by Austria (1713-96 and again 1815-70).

It was Napoleon's conquest of Italy (1796-9), and the liberal ideas then brought in, which opened the way to the *risorgimento*, as the movement of unification was called. But it was not achieved without a further sixty years of struggle. Success was due finally to four leading patriots: Mazzini, its prophet, and the founder of the 'Young Italy' movement; Cavour, its statesman and political genius; Garibaldi, its popular hero and man of action; Victor Emmanuel II of the House of Savoy, its focus of loyalty, as constitutional head, when a united independent Kingdom of Italy was proclaimed (1861).

In the century since unification the salient facts have been the economic expansion of northern Italy; the problem of the impoverished south (eg, Danilo Dolci's work in *Sicily*); colonial expansion in Africa; the Irredentist movement to secure the *Trentino, Trieste*, etc; the loss of political liberty under fascism; the creation of a sovereign *Vatican State* (1929); the Abyssinian War; alliances alternating between western and central Europe (including the fatal Rome-Berlin axis); Allied invasion and occupation; proclamation (1946) of a republic, brought a return to progress under representative government and, with the Treaty of Rome in 1957, Italy became a founder member of the EEC.

Government

Parliament consists of two houses; a Chamber of Deputies whose 596 members are elected for five years by universal adult suffrage; and a Senate of 246 members elected for six years on a regional basis. Executive power rests with the Cabinet presided over by the Prime Minister. The President holds office for seven years.

Italy is divided into nineteen *regioni* most of which are further divided into provinces. Four of the *regioni* are autonomous, having their own parliaments and governments: *Sicily, Sardinia, Aosta* (French speaking) and *Trentino-South Tirol* (whose two parts are respectively Italian and German speaking).

Resources

There are over eight million workers in agriculture, a feature being the large numbers who live in towns but who go to work in the countryside. Holdings are generally small. Wheat, grown chiefly in the northern plain and in *Apulia* and *Sicily*, is by far the most important crop. Other cereals are maize and rice, grown chiefly in parts of the northern plain. Potatoes and sugar beet are widely grown. Olives and the vine are cultivated in every *regioni*; citrus fruits, almonds and walnuts in *Sicily* and the south. Other crops include tobacco, hemp and cotton.

Many coastal villages have markets for fish caught locally, particularly sardines and tunny.

Minerals are generally inadequate for the country's needs. But Italy is a major exporter of sulphur and mercury and has important reserves of bauxite, zinc and lead. The comparative deficiency of coal is partly compensated for by abundant hydro-electricity resources, chiefly in the Alps.

The northern cities are the chief industrial centres. More than a million people are employed in clothing and textiles. Next comes engineering, including well-known motor vehicle, typewriter and electrical concerns. Pasta-making and the processing of other food, wine and tobacco employs more than half a million.

Among luxury products Venetian glass and Tuscan *majolica* represent a centuries-old tradition.

Food and Drink

The main meal is taken in the evening. Animal fats are used in cooking in the north; olive oil takes their place further south. The staple item is pasta (processed wheat) in various forms — *spaghetti, fettuccine, macaroni, etc* — the latter predominating in the south.

The variety of regional and local dishes adds to the pleasures of travel.

Specialities include: fish soups — *brodetto* (Adriatic coast), *cacciucco* (Tuscan coast); other soups — *minestrone al pesto (Liguria), busecca (Milan)*; meat dishes — *abbacchio (Rome)*, sausages *(Emilia* and the *Marche)*; fish dishes — *baccalà alla veneziana* (cod with milk and onions) *(Venice)*, *triglie* (red mullet) *(Leghorn)*; cheese dishes —*fondau* and *bagna cauda (Piedmont)*, *mozzarella in carrozza* and *pizza Napolitana (Naples)*; other savouries: — *fettuccine* and *gnocchi alla romana (Rome)*, *cappelletti* and *tagliatelle alla bolognese (Emilia)*.

Ice cream is an Italian and particularly a Sicilian speciality and is excellent in all its many varieties. Italy is, of course, the home of *caffè espresso*.

Wine is the main drink and is inexpensive, Italy being the world's second greatest producer, mostly for home consumption. It is worth while to ask about the local wines and in this way discover, in *Verona* for example, the sparkling Valpolicella.

Culture

Italy is a treasure house of all the arts, the country of origin of the great movement of ideas of the Renaissance, of major styles in the Romanesque and the baroque, and of a host of other components of Western culture.

Architecture

Among Greek temples in *Sicily* and the south, those of Neptune at *Paestum* and of Concord at *Agrigento* are among the best preserved in Europe. There is a fine Greek theatre at *Syracuse*.

The Romans, looking beyond Greek models, took the arch, the dome and the Etruscan vault and used them with a new grandeur to reach the technical achievements of the *Pantheon*, the *Colosseum* and the *Baths of Caracalla*. Specially interesting for their influence on the form of early Christian churches are the Roman basilicas, or courts of justice, now best seen in the *Basilica Aemilia* in the *Forum* and the *Underground Basilica* near the *Porta Maggiore*.

The least altered Christian basilicas in *Rome are Sant' Clemente* (AD392) and *Santa Sabina* (425). Two fine early churches at *Ravenna* — *Sant' Apollinare Nuovo* (525) and *Sant' Apollinare in Classe* (549) — are also basilican in form.

Byzantine architecture is represented by the other great church of *Ravenna*, *Sant' Vitale* (526), and, above all, by *St Mark's, Venice*. In the twelfth century churches of *Palermo* it is combined with Arab and Norman features.

Romanesque is well seen in the fine group at *Pisa: Baptistry, Cathedral* and *Leaning Tower*; and in *Sant' Ambrogio, Milan; Sant' Zeno Maggiore, Verona; Sant' Miniato, Florence; Santa Maria in Cosmedin, Rome*; and *Monreale Cathedral*.

Gothic came late to Italy and was accepted only partly and in modified form.

Its chief examples are *Milan Cathedral; Florence Cathedral* and *Campanile; Sant' Francesco, Assisi.* In *Venice* the *Doge's Palace* and several other *palazzi* are local variants of the style.

Renaissance architecture, a return to classical forms, began in *Florence* with Brunelleschi (it is significant of humanism that architect's names now appear, in contrast to the earlier impersonal tradition) and reached its height in *Rome* with Bramante, who began the rebuilding of *St Peter's* (1506), and in *Venice* with Sansovino and Sanmichele. Its later freer development by Michelangelo in *Rome* and *Florence* led to the so-called Mannerist style. Its chief architect, Palladio, worked chiefly in his native *Vicenza* where his designs for villas became the models for other countries, especially England. Two well-known churches in *Venice* — *Sant' Giorgio Maggiore* and the *Rendentore* — are also his.

The exuberance of baroque architecture is seen particularly in the work of Borromini and Bernini in *Rome*, and in Longhena's *Santa Maria della Salute* in *Venice*.

Adventurous experiments in contemporary building can be seen in *Milan* and *Rome*.

Painting and Sculpture

Mosaic floors, portrait busts and reliefs on triumphal arches were the chief artistic forms of the Roman period, but some paintings survive in *Pompeii, Herculaneum* and *Rome*.

There are early Christian paintings in the catacombs. Then, for a thousand years, the art of wall mosaic was dominant— at first Roman, later Byzantine in style, as in the great groups at *Ravenna, Cefalù* and *Monreale*.

The transition from mosaic to fresco came in the thirteenth century with Cavallini, Cimabue, Duccio and the great new vision of Giotto. In sculpture Nicola Pisano's famous pulpit (1260) in the Baptistry at *Pisa* began a new tradition of naturalism in modelling the human form which was developed by his son Giovanni. The long dominance of medieval ideas was coming to an end. Simone Martini (about 1284-1344) was the first artist since classical times to paint a non-religious subject. Men were not only looking back to those times but were beginning to look about them with wonder and delight. These two sources of inspiration produced the Renaissance — a re-birth of thought and feeling.

Ghiberti (1378-1455) in bronze, Masaccio (1401-28), Uccello (1397-1475) and Piero della Francesca (1418-92) in painting, progressively solved the problems of light, shade, movement and perspective presented by the new interest in naturalistic representation. Pisanello (1397-1455), Antonio Pollaiuolo (1432-98), and Signorelli (c1440-1523) learnt to model with scientific realism. Botticelli (1444-1510) gave elegant form to pagan myths. But he and most artists of the time could also combine the new freedom with traditional piety.

Donatello (1386-1466) was the supreme sculptor of the early Renaissance and had perhaps the greatest influence on the future. He had great pupils in Pollaiuolo and Verrocchio (1435-88) and a follower in the painter Mantegna.

The masters of the High Renaissance, heirs of all this achievement, built on it each according to his own noble vision: the calm insight of Leonardo da Vinci (1452-1519), the grace and harmony of Raphael (1483-1520), the turbulent restless idealism of Michelangelo (1475-1564).

Mantegna (1431-1506), bringing to paintings a sculptural quality, influenced the schools of *Padua, Ferrara, Milan* and *Venice*. The Venetians, Giorgione (1478-1510) and Titian (1477-1576), now created a new wordly art of gorgeous colour and sensuous form, and Veronese (1528-88) added an imaginary classical background to scenes of Venetian pageantry. But Tintoretto (1518-94), no less grandiose, turned this richness to religious themes in numerous and enormous paintings. Religion also found a sophisticated interpreter in Correggio (1489-1534), working in *Parma*.

In *Rome*, reactions against Mannerism — the ineffectual attempts to imitate Michelangelo — came with Caravaggio's (1573-1610) return to realism and with Annibale Carracci's (1560-1609) refined classicism. In *Rome* also, a little later, the French masters Poussin and Claude were at work and Bernini (1598-1680) was making fluent sculpture an integral part of his baroque architectural schemes. Salvator Rosa's (1615-73) wild landscapes started a fashion which influenced particularly the English cult of the picturesque.

The most attractive works of the eighteenth century are those by a group of artists in *Venice*: Piazzetta, Guardi, Canaletto, Tiepolo and Longhi. Painting then declined but Canova (1757-1822) produced finely carved if frigid sculpture in a further revival which looked back to classical Greece.

The most famous Italian contributors to modern art are Modigliani (1884-1920) and the surrealist painter De Chirico (1888-1978).

Art Galleries

The greatest galleries are the *Uffizi* and the *Pitti* in *Florence*, the *Vatican Museums* in *Rome*, *Accademia di Belle Arti* in *Venice*, *Brera* in *Milan* and *Capodimonte* in *Naples*.

Many of the finest works are in churches and palaces; the churches of *Rome* and *Florence* in particular are rich in outstanding paintings and sculptures.

Museums

Very important are the *Vatican Galleries*, the *Capitoline Museum* in *Rome* and the *National Museum* in *Naples*. There are many more, including museums dealing with weapons and armour, Christian and Roman excavated relics, etc. Public buildings and museums are often closed on Sunday afternoons, Mondays and public holidays. Churches are frequently shut between noon and 3pm and after 5pm.

Music

Italians of the eleventh century invented our system of musical notation and also the tonic sol-fa. Most of the indications of expression — *andante, adagio*, etc — are Italian as also are the names of many musical instruments including the pianoforte. The violin and its relations were first produced in *Brescia*, reaching perfection in *Cremona*, where Antonio Stradivarius (1644-1736) was only the greatest of a succession of famous makers.

Corelli (1653-1713) and Vivaldi (1675-1741) were among early developers of the violin concerto. Domenico Scarlatti (1685-1757) was the first great composer for the harpsichord.

The Renaissance had seen the culmination of Italian religious music in the unaccompanied masses of Palestrina (1525-94) and the beginning of the operatic tradition in the works of Monteverdi (1567-1643) who was also the first to use an orchestra. Classical opera was continued by Alessandro Scarlatti (1659-1725).

The popular fame of Italian opera today rests on the great series of works by nineteenth-century composers writing in a romantic idiom: Rossini (1792-1868), Donizetti (1797-1848), and Verdi (1813-1901). Puccini (1858-1924), continued this tradition into the twentieth century.

The opera house was an Italian creation and is found in many towns. The main centres are *La Scala, Milan; San Carlo, Naples*; the *Teatro dell' Opera* and *Teatro Adriano, Rome*. A visit to an open-air performance in the *Baths of Caracalla, Rome*, or the *Arena, Verona* provides a memorable experience.

Theatres

Summer visitors will probably be most interested in the open-air performance of plays in, for example, the Greek theatre at *Syracuse* and the Roman theatre (not to be confused with the *Arena*) at *Verona*.

Cinema

Italy was one of the first countries to discover the excellent cinematic material provided by scenes of ordinary life if presented in a simple straightforward way and backed by good technique. Italian films maintain their international reputation in this respect.

Customes and Dances

The chief areas for 'local colour' of this kind are *Sardinia, Abruzzi, Umbria, Tuscany*, and the alpine districts of the north. They are particularly to be sought away from the main centres, in out-of-the-way villages and towns.

Literature

Dante (1265-1321) represents the medieval world at a time when the first signs of change were appearing. His immediate successors, Petrarch (1304-74) and Boccaccio (1313-75) are the first humanists.

The poets of the Renaissance have little appeal today, but its vigorous prose writers capture the spirit of the period and are wonderfully readable: eg Cellini's (1500-71) uninhibited account of his life and times; Vasari's (15ll-74) *Lives of Painters, Sculptors and Architects* and Machiavelli's (1469-1527) politically realistic writings inspired by his vision of a united Italy. Among novels available in translation is Manzoni's (1785-1873) great work *The Betrothed*; those of Alberto Moravia are also widely read. Giuseppe Lampedusa's *The Leopard*, translated 1959, has become a classic.

Science

Leonardo da Vinci (1452-1519), the all-round man of the Renaissance, was as much scientist as artist and contributed to nearly every branch of the science of his time. Galileo Galilei (1564-1642), almost as versatile, devoted his life to observation and experiment to become both the founder of modern scientific method and the champion of its results against ideas surviving from the medieval period. His trial by the Inquisition was one of the turning points of history.

Reti (1621-97) and Spallanzani (1729-99), naturalists and micro-biologists, were rigorous experimenters, as unready as Galileo to take anything on trust. They disproved the various theories of spontaneous generation which were popular in their times.

Avogadro (1776-1856) was the first to distinguish between atoms and molecules. Dorati (1826-73) was the founder of spectroscopic astronomy. Another astronomer, Schiaparelli (1835-1910) is particularly associated with the study of Mars.

To Marconi (1874-1937) are due the first effective developments in radio-telegraphy.

Touring Information

Touring Areas

In no other land are there so many cities of major artistic and architectural significance. The countryside, also, ranges in beauty from the grandeur and romantic wildness of the *Alps* and the *Abruzzi* to the classic calm of *Umbria* and *Tuscany*. Each of the following areas would fully occupy a holiday visit.

Piedmont and *Aosta*: *Turin* and the mountains bordering France and Switzerland.
Genoa and the *Western Riviera*.
The lakes of *Como, Garda* and *Maggiore*.
The cities of *Lombardy*.
The *Venice* region and the *Dolomites*.
Emilia and *Romagna*: *Piacenza* to *Ravenna* and *Rimini*.
Florence, Pisa, Siena: a fine-art region in the lovely countryside of *Tuscany*.
Perugia and *Assisi*: Franciscan Italy, old and unchanged towns in the soft,
pleasant countryside of *Umbria*.
Rome: a magnificent city rich in noble buildings and requiring a visit of at least
a week.
The *Abruzzi* and the *Marche*: a wilder, more primitive Italy.
Naples, Pompeii, Vesuvius, Salerno and the south: different in physical condi-
tions, history and culture, and with a climate similar to that of North Africa.
Picturesque and often primitive.
Sicily.
Sardinia.

Access

For *Turin, Genoa* and the *Western Riviera* the best and cheapest rail route is via
Paris and *Modane*, changing stations at *Paris*. For all other areas it is advisable
to use the through boat train from *Calais* or *Boulogne* via Switzerland to *Milan*,
for *Venice* and for *Rome*.

British Airways run excursion flights to *Milan, Venice* and other destinations
at fares competitive with travel by railway.

Transport

Rail, or bus, are the cheapest means of travel. On certain fast diesel or electric
trains (*Rapido*) a supplement is charged. There are cheaper fares for families,
where four or more of the same family travel together; 8, 15, 21 and 30 days travel-
at-will tickets, circular tickets, from frontier to same or different frontier, for an
itinerary of not less than 1,000km and the bargain-priced *Kilometric ticket*, valid
for 3,000km for 30 days.

Motoring

Traffic moves at speed. Main cities are served by *autostrade*, all of which are toll
roads; other main roads are well maintained, but motoring on them is not so fast.
Motorists should carry their car registration papers, driving licence, red warning
triangle (in case of breakdown); an international green insurance card is a
necessity, so too is a country-of-origin sticker. Police can impose restrictions on
traffic noise; look out for '*Zona di Silenzio*' notices.

Money

The unit of currency is the *lira* (plural *lire*). Coins are issued for 5, 10, 50, 100, and 200 *lire*; notes for 500, 1,000, 5,000, 10,000, 20,000, 50,000 and 100,000 *lire*.

Clothing

Lightweight clothing is suitable in summer, but pullovers will be useful for occasional chilly nights, or for expeditions in mountain areas. Shorts are widely worn in the country during the summer. It is well to avoid being conspicuous, and every effort should be made to wear clean and tidy clothing, especially when visiting galleries and churches.

In churches, particularly *St Peter's* and the *Vatican*, everybody (but especially women), is required to be dressed with simple dignity, no shorts, no uncovered shoulders.

Avoid wearing mountain boots or heavy shoes in southern cities; but sandals should have thick soles — pavements become uncomfortably hot.

Restaurants

Trattorie, restaurants with a local character, are among the cheapest and most interesting eating places. Cafés are more specifically for coffee, fruit drinks and ices, but sell also small cakes. In *bottiglierie*, provided wine is ordered, you may eat your own food and make use of plate and cutlery.

One must get used to food cooked in olive oil, particularly as one travels further south. The various forms of *minestra* (*pasta*, rice and vegetables) provide a nourishing and often substantial dish (*primo piatto*).

Buying own Food

It is quite easy to buy bread, cheese and fruit, even in villages. Shops marked *Panetteria, Pane e Pasta* or *Fornaio* sell *pasta*, also bread and dry groceries. Shops marked *Pasticceria* sell sweets and biscuits.

Public Holidays

1 and 6 January, Easter Sunday, Easter Monday, 25 April, 1 May, Ascension Day, 2 June, Whit Sunday, Corpus Christi, 15 August (Assumption), 1 November, 8 December, Christmas Day, 26 December.

Maps and Guide Books

Michelin No 988 is an adequate road map, scale 1:1,000,000. Italian Touring Club maps on a scale of 1:200,000 are published in 30 sheets. For some of the popular alpine areas the Italian Touring Club publishes fine maps on a scale of 1:50,000 suitable for walkers and climbers.

Wonders of Italy series (*Rome, Florence*, etc), published in English by Fattorusso of Florence, are excellent picture guides with accurate text, forming useful handbooks and souvenirs of the chief cities.

The *Guide Books to the Museums and Monuments in Italy* (in English) published by the Ministero dell' Educazione Nazional and obtainable at all the main sites (eg, *Pompeii*), are far cheaper to buy than paying for the services of a guide.

Tourist literature can be obtained from the Italian State Tourist Office, 1 Princes Street, London, W1 and from the Ente Provinciale per i Turismo at each provincial capital; also plans and guide books of every town from the appropriate Azienda Autonoma di Soggiorno or Pro Loco.

Accommodation

The AIG (Italian Youth Hostels Association) has about sixty hostels, spread over nearly all parts of the country. They are too far apart for walkers, however, so that the use of some means of transport is unavoidable.

Mountaineering

In the *Courmayeur, Aosta, Mont Blanc* area conditions are similar to those of Switzerland. Mountaineering of all grades is possible and plans are best made in consultation with climbing clubs.

The *Dolomites*, close to the Austrian border, is a magnificent mountaineering area with many mountain huts. The rock is always good, and there are many routes world-famous for their length and severity.

In the *Apennines* the best climbing areas are in the wild massifs of the *Abruzzi (Gran Sasso and Maiella)* east of Rome.

Winter-sports take place in all three districts and all are equipped with mountain huts. The Club Alpino Italiano (CAI) has 200 local branches in Italy. It publishes guides to the Italian mountains and organises assistance and aid of various kinds. It maintains about 600 huts in the finest mountain areas. Further information from CAI, Via Ugo Foscolo, 3, Milan.

Touring Routes

In the following tours the chief cities have been linked in two circular routes:

(i) From the French frontier along the peninsula to Naples and back, via *Turin — Milan — Bologna — Florence — Perugia — Rome* returning via *Rome — Leghorn — Pisa — La Spezia — Genoa.*

(ii) Across the north Italian plain from *Milan* to *Venice* and back, via *Brescia — Verona — Padua* returning via *Mantua* and *Cremona.*

In addition there are two Alpine areas which can be described as regions rather than routes:

(a) The *Pennine Alps, Aosta Valley, Mont Blanc* (on the French frontier).

(b) *Upper Adige, Trentino, Dolomites* (on the Austrian frontier).

R1 The Peninsula: Turin to Rome and Naples, returning via Genoa (1,430 miles, 2,300km)

The route leaves France by the *Mont Cenis* tunnel and enters *Piedmont*, a region of rugged mountain scenery, the country of the House of Savoy, the kings of which became the builders of modern Italy.

Bardonecchia, small mountain resort, *Susa*, old town, Roman arch, **Turin**△ 69 miles (111km), on River *Po*, well-planned city, with network of fine avenues, arcaded shops, beautiful squares. Capital of Italy for a while in nineteenth century. Fiat, Lancia and Pininfarina factories are here — and the Cinzano and Martini vermouth distilleries. Old Roman gateway; Castle, seventeenth century onwards; Egyptian Museum (second only to Cairo Museum), interesting churches in baroque style, eg, the *Superga* (in outskirts, at 2,200ft[(670m], 6 miles [10km] from city centre). *Palazzo Cavour*, where the statesman lived and died.

> EXCURSIONS: (a) *Colli Torinesi*, hilly area giving good views of city. (b) *Piedmont Plain*, many attractive little towns with cobbled streets and painted churches. (c) *Torre Pellice*, 35 miles (56km), headquarters of the Waldensians (*Valdesi*), the only considerable Protestant community in Italy, who took refuge in the high valleys near the French frontier; attractive and little-known mountain area; highest peak *Monte Viso*, 12,609ft (3,843m).

Route continues to *Vercelli*, through rice-growing district to *Novara*, 63 miles (101km).

> EXCURSIONS: (a) Lake of *Orta*, 25 miles (40km), set amidst trees. (b) the alpine valleys east of *Monte Rosa* mountain group (centre *Varallo*, 35 miles, 56km). (c) Lake *Maggiore* (40 miles, 64km, long) with picturesque *Borromean* Islands. Chief resorts are *Stresa, Verbania* and *Baveno*; many attractive villages, steamer services. North end of lake is in Switzerland (*Locarno*).

Milan△ 30 miles (48km), the most important commercial and industrial city in the country, cosmopolitan and independent; a vast city with great blocks of flats. Once the greatest of the Italian city states, it now has few ancient buildings. Immense Gothic cathedral is third largest in the world; a mass of gleaming white marble; has 200 statues. View from roof includes the Alps. The *Piazza del Duomo* (cathedral square) is the scene of big meetings. *Sforza Castle* (fifteenth century); *Scala* Theatre, famous opera house; *Brera* Picture Gallery, one of the best collections in the world; church of *Santa Maria delle Grazie* contains Leonardo da Vinci's *Last Supper*; *Galleria*, vast arcade of shops and restaurants; immense railway station; several interesting churches.

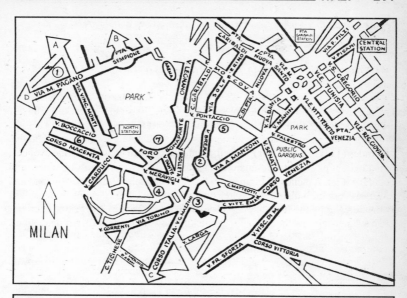

1 Galleria. 2 La Scala Theatre. 3 Duomo. 4 Post Office. 5 Brera Gallery.
6 Santa Maria della Grazie. 7 Sforza Castle.
A to youth hostel. B to Como. C to Pavia. D to Novara.

EXCURSIONS: (a) Lake *Maggiore* (see *Novara* above). (b) *Pavia*, 24 miles (39km), famous university, interesting churches; the *Certosa*, important monastery now secularised and its land used for agricultural experiments; chapel has early Renaissance marble facade. (c) monastery at *Chiaravalle* (on road to *Pavia*). (d) *Como*Δ 29 miles (47km), on beautiful Lake *Como* (31¹/₂ miles, 50km, long). Many steamer excursions on lake; chief resorts: *Cernobbio, Bellagio, Menaggio*Δ; also at *Domaso*Δ and *Lecco*Δ.

Continue through *Piacenza* to *Parma*Δ, 80 miles (129km), home of violets, hams and Parmesan cheese; on for 30 miles (48km) to *Modena*. The railway runs near the *Via Emilia*, ancient road between the *Apennines* and the *Po* Plains, and alongside the *Autostrada del Sole*, motorway from *Milan* to *Reggio Calabria* via *Bologna, Florence, Rome* and *Naples*.

Bologna Δ, 26 miles (42km), important commercial centre, with many old buildings; university founded in twelfth century, fine arcaded streets. Leaning Towers; Civic Museum, collection of Roman antiquities; churches of *San Francesco, San Petonio* (never finished), *San Domenico, San Giacomo*.

EXCURSIONS: (a) *San Michele* in *Bosco* for view of city. (b) the Adriatic coast, via *Faenza* (the home of *majolica* porcelain — French *faïence*) — and *Rimini*∆ to *San Marino* (about 90 miles, 130km); **see R2(i).** (c) Fertile plains north of *Bologna*; rice is grown; you can walk along the dykes built to control the spring rise in river level; a typical little town is *Budrio*, 12 miles (19km) north-east.

South across the mountains for 68 miles (110km), via passes at *Raticosa* and *Futa*, with their elaborately repeated S-bends, characteristic of *Apennine* roads. Approaching *Florence*, note the softness of *Tuscany* compared with harsh plains of the north.

Florence

Florence∆ on the River *Arno* is one of the world's loveliest cities; has art treasures of the highest rank; many interesting churches, Gothic and Renaissance buildings, museums.

Cathedral (Duomo) of St Mary of the Flowers, begun by di Cambio in 1296, dome by Brunelleschi 1434; inside is Michelangelo's *Descent from the Cross*. Giotto's Campanile, 267ft (81m) (good view from top). *Baptistry* has magnificent bronze doors by Ghiberti; thirteenth-century mosaics in ceiling.

Piazza della Signoria (this was the centre of Florentine life); on it stands the *Palazzo Vecchio*, now the city hall, open to the public. Statues include Donatello's *Judith and Holofernes*, Benvenuto Cellini's *Perseus with Head of Medusa*, and copy of Michelangelo's *David* (original in *Accademia di Belle Arti*).

Churches of *Santa Maria Novella*, thirteenth-century Tuscan-Gothic, frescoes by Ghirlandaio, *Strozzi Chapel* — frescoes by Orcagna; *San Lorenzo*, begun 1491 by Brunelleschi, never finished, recently discovered Michelangelo drawings; *Santa Croce*, thirteenth century, fine frescoes by Gaddi and Giotto, tombs of famous Italians, including Michelangelo; *San Marco*, lovely cloisters, frescoes by Fra Angelico, Savonarola's cell.

The *Medici Mausoleum*, splendidly gloomy; very fine statues by Michelangelo in sacristy.

Palazzo Strozzi (fifteenth century), has delightful lanterns, torch-holders, etc. *Palazzo Medici-Riccardi* (fifteenth century) home of Lorenzo the Magnificent and the great Medici family; wall-painting of *Journey of the Three Kings*; *Palazzo Pitti*, begun 1450, first attempt to build artistic building with blocks of unhewn stone. Art gallery on first floor with paintings by Raphael, Titian and Tintoretto; cross *Ponte Vecchio* to *Uffizi Palace* where art gallery has one of finest collections in world — Botticelli's *Primavera* and *Birth of Venus*. Michelangelo's *Holy Family* and many other masterpieces. *Boboli Gardens* lie behind *Uffizi Palace*, a refuge from sightseeing in terraced greenery, ornamented with antique statues, shady tree-lined paths, a grotto, pool and fountain. At highest point the *Citadel Belvedere* affords fine view.

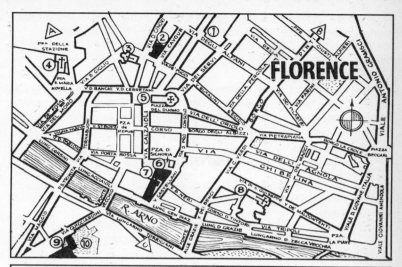

1 Accademia. 2 Palazzo Medici-Riccardi. 3 San Lorenzo. 4 Santa Maria
Novella. 5 Duomo. 6 Palazzo Vecchio. 7 Uffizi Gallery. 8 Santa Croce.
9 Pitti Gallery. 10 Boboli Gardens.
A to railway station. B to youth hostel. C to Son Miniato

Cross *Ponte di Ferro* and climb hill to *Piazzale Michelangelo* and up steps to
San Miniato (eleventh to thirteenth century). This view of Florence, set amidst
hills, should not be missed.

EXCURSIONS: (a) *Fiesole*, 5 miles (8km) medieval villas, Roman theatre. (b)
Pontassieve, at confluence of *Sieve* and *Arno* (13 miles [21km] east) for *Sieve Valley*
and *Vallombrosa* (south) area rich in old monasteries, including *La Verna*, where St
Francis received the Stigmata. Lovely views, suitable walking district. (c) *Siena*, 38
miles (61km) by railway or bus. Carefully planned and well-preserved medieval city,
encircled by ramparts. *Piazza del Campo*, beautifully proportioned fan-shaped square,
faced by *Palazzo Pubblico* with *Torre del Mangia*, 288ft (88m) high, sublime panorama from top. *Corsa del Palio*, daring horse race, around *Piazza del Campo*, held
annually since 1636, takes place on 2 July and 16 August.

Continue south-east through *Arezzo*, 55 miles (88km), town of lovely
squares. Church of *Santa Francesca*, frescoes. Route follows upper *Arno* valley,
past the *Chianti* wine country to the *Tiber* valley. *San Sepolcro* and *Gubbio*, to the
east, fine examples of medieval towns, are worth a visit. *Cortona*, hill city 800ft
(243m) above railway; Lake *Trasimeno*, where great Roman Army was defeated
by Hannibal in 217BC.

Perugia, 48 miles (77km), centre of *Umbria*, 1,000ft (300m) above valley, ancient city with fine Etruscan arch. *Palazzo dei Priori* (fourteenth century); *Cambio* (exchange); Great Fountain; all in main square; many perfect medieval streets, particularly *Maesta della Volte* and *Viale Priori*. From church of *San Pietro*, view to *Assisi*.

Assisi, 18 miles (29km) medieval town, home and work-place of St Francis. *Basilica of San Francesco*, built over his tomb; story of the saint's life in twenty-eight frescoes by Giotto; *Santa Chiara* at other end of town.

EXCURSIONS: (a) Convent of *San Damiano* twelfth century. (b) The *Carcere*, 2 miles (3km) by the lanes past *Santa Chiara*, 1,000ft (300m) above town, amid woods. (c) baroque *Santa Maria degli Angeli* housing *Porziuncola* chapel where St Francis began his life's work.

The pastoral and agricultural countryside of *Umbria* is one of the loveliest parts of Italy and well repays exploration.

Foligno△ 22 miles (35km), railway junction for lines to Adriatic coast. *Spoleto*, 18 miles (29km), medieval town amid hills; Filippo Lippi's frescoes in cathedral.

EXCURSION: *Orvieto*, medieval buildings, cathedral with fine frescoes by Signorelli.

Route enters dry grassy *Campagna*; the ancient Roman road surface may be seen again and again alongside the modern road. *St Peter's* dome can be seen in the distance when 30 miles (50km) north of *Rome*.

Rome

Rome△ on the River *Tiber* is the capital of modern Italy. The finest city in the world cannot be 'done' in a few hours and it is important not to destroy enjoyment by attempting too much. Interest will be heightened by finding out something about the Roman Empire and the Roman Catholic Church before your visit. Georgina Masson's *Companion Guide to Rome* published in paperback by Fontana describes detailed itineraries for sightseeing throughout the city on foot; a practical and enjoyable guide.

Metropolitana underground railway from main station. Line 'A' goes north-west to *Ottaviano* (for *St Peter's*), thence to *Piazza de Spagna* and on beyond city limits; also goes south-east to *St John Lateran*. Line 'B' goes south-west to *Colosseum, Pyramide, St Paulo fuori le Mura* and on to *Ostia*. Many bus services in city, cheap fares.

The ancient city was built on the Seven Hills. The River *Tiber* flows from north to south on western side. Modern buildings, many of indifferent style, extensively surround the ancient city.

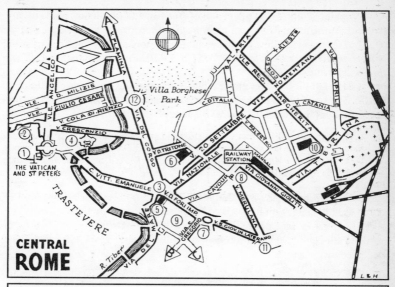

1 St Peter's. 2 Vatican. 3 Piazza Venezia. 4 Castel Sant' Angelo.
5 Capitoline Museum. 6 Quirinal Palace. 7 Colosseum. 8 Santa Maria
Maggiore. 9 Forum. 10 University. 11 St John Lateran. 12 Piazza del
Popolo.
A to youth hostel. B to Porta San Paola. C to Baths of Caracalla

Walk No 1: Ancient Rome

From *Piazza Venezia* (city centre), fifteenth-century *Palazzo Venezia*, huge
Vittorio Emanuele monument (commemorates unity of Italy), Tomb of Unknown
Solider, to north-east Trajan's Column (second century). Along *Via dei Fori
Imperiali* are remains of Imperial Forums, built when Roman Forum became too
small. Take the steps from *Via del Mare* up to *Piazza del Campidoglio*, designed
by Michelangelo (site of Capitol of Ancient Rome), Church of *Santa Maria in
Aracoeli*, *Capitoline Museum*, magnificent Roman sculptures. Descend to *Via dei
Fori* for entrance to **Roman Forum** area. Centre of ancient Roman life, now
bewildering spectacle of neglected ruins; Arch of Septimus Severus (AD203)
temples and public buildings. Arch of Titus (AD70). Leave Forum, cross to
Colosseum, immense amphitheatre built AD72-82, scene of gladiatorial combats
and public spectacles. South of Forum is Palatine Hill, Roman ruins older than
Forum. North-east of *Colosseum* in park, remains of Nero's palace. Along *Via
San Gregorio*, through park of *Porta Capena*, to *Baths* of *Caracalla*, once most
magnificent baths in Rome. Open-air opera in summer.

See also old city walls, particularly east of main station, and near *Lateran Gate*.

Walk No 2: Vatican and St Peter's

Corso Vittorio Emanuele, cross river, *Via della Conciliazione*, to **Vatican City**, headquarters of the Roman Catholic Church, once capital of the old Papal States (most of central Italy) and now an independent city state. The Vatican Palace has been official residence of the Popes (Bishops of Rome) only since 1377, though they have lived in Rome since 498.

St Peter's, the largest cathedral in the world, stands on the site of Nero's Circus, where St Peter was executed in AD66. The present magnificent Renaissance and baroque church (partly designed by Bramante and Michelangelo) was built 1506-1626 over reputed tomb of St Peter.

The *Piazza San Pietro*, over 250yd (230m) across; colonnade by Bernini, 284 columns, 140 statues on balustrade; Egyptian obelisk from Nero's Circus. To right, Vatican Palace; official entrance by 'Bronze Doors', Swiss guards in seventeenth-century uniform; Pope uses only a few of the 1,400 rooms, rest occupied by museums.

Façade of basilica 124yd (113m) wide, height of dome, 435ft (133m). View from roof and cupola. Brass marks in centre of floor indicate size of other cathedrals. Bernini's *Baldacchino* (canopy) over High Altar; mosaics; bronze statue of St Peter, his foot kissed smooth by multitudes of pilgrims.

Gate to left of façade leads into Vatican City for exterior of basilica and palace gardens. The City has its own printing and publishing works, wireless station (transmitting almost every language of the world) and post office, and its own stamps and coins.

For museums, leave *Piazza* on right, take *Via di Porta Angelica* and follow the walls to entrance.

Museum of Antiquities, remarkable collection of sculptures, etc (note Laocoön and Apollo Belvedere); Vatican Library; Borgia Apartments (frescoes by Pintoricchio); *Stanze* (rooms) of Raphael — magnificent wall and ceiling paintings by Raphael; **Sistine Chapel** (where Popes are elected) celebrated paintings by Michelangelo on ceiling and altar wall; Picture Gallery (Pinacoteca), Italian paintings. It is advisable to follow the marked itinerary.

On Tiber, near Vatican, *Castel Sant'Angelo*, originally mausoleum of Hadrian (AD136) later made into fortress, and connected to Vatican Palace by wall-top corridor.

Walk No 3

From *Piazza Venezia* into *Via del Corso*, baroque Palazzo *Doria*, turn left and continue to *Santa Maria sopra Minerva*, Gothic, built on site of Temple of Minerva; *Pantheon*, pagan Roman temple, converted into church; work north-west to *Piazza della Colonna*, column of Marcus Aurelius (second century) elaborate carvings. Continue up *Corso*, then left for Mausoleum of Augustus; north to *Piazza del Popolo*, for gardens of *Pincio* and *Villa Borghese*. Return south by attractive *Piazza di Spagna*, Quirinal Palace, east to *Piazza del' Esedra*, church of *Santa Maria degli Angeli* transformed from part of *Baths of Diocletian*. From station square, take *Via Cavour*, **Santa Maria Maggiore**, original magnificence is preserved; floor and columns of nave, also mosaics on arch and walls, date from fifth century. According to tradition, the Virgin appeared in a vision asking that the church be built where snow fell in morning, anniversary (5 August) commemorated by shower of white flowers during Mass. Nearby, *Santa Pudenziana*, oldest church in Rome, founded AD145, fourth-century work oldest visible.

Walk No 4

From *Piazza Venezia*, take *Via del Mare* — Theatre of Marcellus, along river, near *Ponte Palatino* note small classical temples and church of *Santa Maria in Cosmedin*, cross river to district of *Trastevere*, see churches of *Santa Cecilia* and *Santa Maria*, go up *Gianicolo* (Janiculum Hill), gardens, fine view, monuments to Garibaldi and his wife, and cross river again near Vatican.

Other important churches: **St John Lateran**, a mile (1$^1/_2$km) south of station. The cathedral of Rome — various periods. Statues of the Apostles; canopy over high altar traditionally containing skulls of St Peter and St Paul; mosaic in apse; gold leaf roof decorated with arms of all the Popes; cloisters. The nearby Baptistry is fifth century.

The *Lateran* palace (museum) was once residence of the Pope. Opposite is building containing *Scala Santa*, said to be a staircase from Pilate's house; may only be ascended on the knees.

St Paul Outside the Walls (*San Paolo fuori le Mura*) 1 mile (1$^1/_2$km) south of *Porta San Paolo* (old city gate). Founded 323, badly damaged by fire 1823, rebuilt on original lines 1854; fifth-century mosaics on triumphal arch escaped fire; interesting light from alabaster windows; fine cloisters (twelfth century).

There are over 200 churches in Rome; almost all have some interest; many are closed 12noon-3pm, except the four major basilicas *St Peter Vatican, Santa Maria Maggiore, St John Lateran* and *St Paul Outside the Walls*.

Recommended: *San Lorenzo fuori le Mura* (east of station, beyond Città Universitaria) sixth and thirteenth century. *Sant' Agnese fuori le Mura* (1mile, 1$^1/_2$-2km, north-east on *Via Nomentana*) 625, built over best preserved catacombs in Rome. *Santa Costanza* (nearby) unusual blue and white fourth-century mosaics. *San Clemente*, near Colosseum, archaeologically most interesting. *San Anselmo; Santa Sabina* (both on quiet and leafy *Aventine*). *Santi Cosma and Damiano* (near *Forum*) 527. *San Pietro in Vincoli* (near *Via Cavour*) contains Michelangelo's famous sculpture of Moses.

EXCURSIONS: (a) Appian Way (*Via Appia Antica*) for **Catacombs** of *San Callisto*, originally burial places of early Christians, then their places of refuge during persecutions, Circus of *Maxentius*; ancient Roman tombs line the old road. (b) *Tivoli* (20 miles, 32km, east) *Hadrian's Villa*, extensive ruins of the emperor's favourite residence; *Villa d'Este*, fine Renaissance villa and gardens, superb ornamental fountains. (c) *Ostia* (15 miles, 24km, west) excavated city; good bathing at *Castel Fusano*. (d) volcanic *Alban Hills* (about 15 miles, 24km, south-east), crater lakes of *Albano* and *Nemi*, attractive villages and towns. (e) *Subiaco* (about 50 miles, 80km, east), fine monasteries, founded by St Benedict; beautiful scenery, pine trees. (f) from *Avezzano*, 70 miles (112km) east, both the *Gran Sasso* mountain region (*Carno Grande*, 9,560ft, 2,914m, highest peak of *Apennines*) and the *Abruzzi National Park* (wild mountain scenery, hills rise to 4,700ft, 1,430m) can be reached — cool and refreshing after Rome.

Leave Rome by *Porta Maggiore* and *Via Casilina*, across the *Campagna* and the *Latium* mountains. *Monte Cassino*, monastery founded 529, destroyed for the fourth time in 1944, now rebuilt.

Caserta, with magnificent nineteenth-century Royal Palace; has ornamental water 2 miles (3km) in length fed by aqueduct 30 miles (nearly 50km) long. Road continues through four-fold avenue of plane trees, then through vines (strung high, so that ploughing can continue underneath), reaching Naples, 150 miles (240km) from Rome.

Naples

Naples△ is on a picturesque bay with *Vesuvius* in distance. It was originally a Greek city, then Roman for seven centuries; a long time part of Spanish Empire. It is totally different from Rome and the cities of the north — a mixture of fine buildings, elegant quarters, and the squalid dwellings of the larger number of its people. The great heat will discourage a lengthy stay in summer. *Naples* is a city of noise, motor-cars, buses, lorries and vociferous abandon — but its main quality is gaiety.

Castel Nuovo, thirteenth to fifteenth century: National Museum, paintings and ancient sculptures, particularly interesting for its collection of objects found at *Pompeii* and *Herculaneum*; Cathedral (fourteenth century restored) with chapel of *San Januarius* in rich baroque style, Gothic churches of *San Lorenzo Maggiore* and *San Domenico*; many baroque churches — *San Paolo; Castell dell'Ovo*, on small island, for view; seventeenth-century Royal Palace.

EXCURSIONS: (a) **Vesuvius** (10 miles, 16km), volcano over 3,000ft (900m) high; can be ascended by rail, bus and chair-lift. Several important eruptions, eg AD79 which buried *Herculaneum* under a sea of mud and *Pompeii* under a heap of ash; 1631, when 20,000 people were killed. A famous wine called 'Lacrima Cristi' is grown on its slopes. (b) **Pompeii** (15 miles, 24km). Vast excavated area, advisable to work out route beforehand, book and plan issued by Ministero dell'Educazione. (c) **Herculan-**

eum (6 miles, 10km). A smaller city than *Pompeii*; the excavated portions are compact. See especially the Theatre. (d)cCircuit of *Sorrento* peninsula, and *Salerno*. *Castellamare di Stábia* (20 miles, 32km). *Agerola*Δ (11 miles, 18km), **Sorrento**Δ (12 miles, 19km), towns with fine sea views across Bay of Naples. From *Sorrento* by boat to **Capri,** holiday island of the millionaires, with its town perched 500ft (150m) up. Blue grotto. *Anacapri* is pretty village. Spectacular route along south side of peninsula to *Amalfi*, picturesque resort, *Praiano, Ravello*, magnificent Norman buildings; *Salerno*Δ in beautiful position on bay.

R1 Naples to Sicily

The route proceeds inland from *Salerno*Δ through *Eboli* and *Auletta*, then south to *Lauria* (80 miles, 130km) through the limestone country and chestnut forests of *Basilicata*. On to *Castrovillari* (35 miles, 56km), an agreeable little town on sunlit uplands of *Calabria* — mountainous peninsula forming 'toe' of Italy and one of the poorest regions, but has splendid forests and mountain flora — then due south to *Cosenza* (45 miles, 72km) via *Spezzano Albanese* (medicinal springs) and along wide gravel valley of the River *Crati*. *Tiriolo* (45 miles, 72km) has fine view of both *Tyrrhenian* and *Ionian* seas. Road turns westwards via plateau of *Maida* — scene of British victory against Napoleonic Army in 1806 — hence Maida Vale in London; *Pizzo Calabro* (Δin castle) on coast; *Vibo Valentia* (32 miles 52km) — formerly military outpost of ancient Greece — has Norman castle affording magnificent view from battlements. After 30 miles (48km) to *Palmi* route takes coast road — steep, looped and zigzagged to **Reggio Calabria** (30 miles, 48km) via *Scilla* (Δin castle) of Scylla and Charybdis of the *Odyssey* — through olive groves and luxuriant vegetation.

Sicily

Frequent steamers ply across narrows to *Messina*. Mountainous extension of *Apennines*; highest at *Mount Etna*, 10,800ft (3,292m), largest active volcano in Europe. Cloudless skies, mild winters, but too hot and dry in mid-summer; delightful in spring and autumn. Vines, almonds and lemons are grown, sulphur is mined near *Agrigento*, oil and asphalt exploited in south-east corner of island, sword-fish and tunny are netted. Remains of Greek and Roman buildings, Saracen mosques, Norman castles and baroque churches abound. **Messina** — almost entirely destroyed by earthquake 1908 and aerial bombardment 1943; now rebuilt, broad street parallel with sea; fine views from hills above town. Railway runs all around the island, mostly single track.

EXCURSION: *Lipari*Δ, largest of *Aeolian Islands*. By hydrofoil from *Messina*, or steamers from *Milazzo*. Seven islands, all volcanic; *Stromboli* remains active.

Coast road westwards to *Castroreale*Δ (30 miles, 48km) and on to **Palermo** (125 miles, 200km) via *Cefalu* — backed by formidable cliff, twelfth-century cathedral, splendid mosaics, *Palermo* rich in baroque palaces and churches, luxuriant gardens. Massacre of Sicilian Vespers here Easter Day, 1282.

EXCURSION: *Monte Pellegrino* (8 miles, 13km), 2,000ft (610m), headland affording magnificent panorama.

Road to *Trapani* (60 miles, 97km) goes inland past *Segesta* (fine ruins of Doric temple) through rolling, hilly terrain. Remote, little-known region northeast of *Trapani* to *Cape St Vito*, via *Erice* — a little medieval town of Phoenician origin on isolated calcareous hill; incomparable views.

Marsala (20 miles, 32km) famed for golden wine. On to *Agrigento* (90 miles, 145km) visiting *Selinunte* en route — site of ruined Hellenic temples in romantic desolation. *Ragusa* is 65 miles (105km) further on in south-east corner of island, delightful for lovers of baroque, as is *Noto* (32 miles, 50km, towards *Syracuse*).

Syracuse (24 miles, 39km). Ancient rival of Athens and Carthage; many classical ruins, *Catania* (33 miles, 53km), a thriving commercial city, built among the lava-flows which have repeatedly destroyed it.

EXCURSION: **Etna.** Lower slopes extremely fertile; scattered forest up to 6,000ft (1,800m) barren beyond. Snow-capped most of year; winter sports centre. Bus from *Catania* to *Rifugio Sapienza*. CA1 hut, or Observatory, for overnight accommodation.

Taormina (32 miles, 51km) balcony site above sea, with view of *Etna:* Greek, Roman and medieval monuments. Warm winter resort. *Messina* is 32 miles (51km) further on.

Return R1 Naples to Genoa and San Remo

Take road to west through the 'Phlegraean Fields' (*Campi Flegrei*), region of attractive volcanic hills, used as holiday resort by ancient Romans; main centre *Pozzuoli*, with Roman amphitheatre. Route follows coast to *Minturno*, Roman aqueduct and theatre; resorts of *Formia* and *Gaeta* (peninsula was fortress — huge castle). *Sperlonga* 71 miles (114km). Turn inland across the *Pontine Marshes* — intensively cultivated in ancient times, then became malarial, now reclaimed, with model farms and villages. Near *Rome* imposing remains of Claudian aqueduct.

After 74 miles (120km) enter *Rome* by *Porta San Giovanni,* leave on northwest by *Piazza del Popolo* and make for *Bracciano*, Renaissance castle, large crater lake; return to coast at *Civitavecchia*.

Sardinia. Daily steamer from *Civitavecchia* to *Olbia* (7 hours). Mountainous, thinly populated, greater part uncultivated; much scented brushwood of eucalyptus, myrtle, medlar and wild rose. Prehistoric monuments abound, especially '*Nuraghi*' — conical towers built of large blocks of unmortared stone. *Olbia* to *Sassari* (55 miles, 88km) across granite heights and volcanic hills, through cork woods on to *Fertilia*Δ (65 miles, 90km) south by third class coast road via *Bosa* to *Oristano*. Cross-country to southeast for 65 miles (105km) to *Cagliari* — Pisan fortifications and port for crossing to

Palermo. East coast route to *Olbia* is less frequented, more mountains and spectacular than west-facing coast.

Route now mainly follows ancient *Via Aurelia* to French frontier. *Tarquinia*, medieval buildings, underground Etruscan tombs, Etruscan Museum; *Orbetello*. Etruscan walls; *Grosetto*, agricultural centre, sixteenth-century ramparts; *Piombino*, for steamers to *Elba* where Napoleon was exiled, and escaped to France before Waterloo; inland to *Volterra*, considerable Etruscan remains, many medieval buildings; *Leghorn (Livorno)* modern port, 170 miles (273km); good bathing along the coastline southwards.

Pisa, 12 miles (19km) in eleventh century was maritime republic like *Venice;* birthplace of Galileo. The architecture is mainly Romanesque, *Piazza del Duomo*, around which loveliest buildings are grouped. *Duomo* began 1063, note delicate work in façade; leaning tower, 1173, marble, view from top. *Baptistry*, 1152, first expression of new sculpture in Italy. The pulpit in *Baptistry* by Nicola Pisano, and that in *Duomo* by Giovanni, his son, are very fine. *Civic Museum*, Gothic *Medici* Palace, *Santa Maria della Spina* (fourteenth century), *Camposanto* (cemetery) with Gothic arcading and frescoes. Inland to *Lucca*Δ: sixteenth- and seventeenth-century walls (now with dry moats and charming gardens); fine Pisan Romanesque buildings, *Duomo* housing crucifix reputed to be miraculous, church of *San Michele*; some Gothic buildings.

Viareggio, largest coastal resort; *Marina di Massa*Δ, 30 miles (48km), good beach; *Carrara*, marble quarries; *Lerici* 20 miles (32km), village on bay in which Shelley was drowned. **La Spezia**, big naval port on lovely gulf. Excursion to village of *Portovenere*.

North of *La Spezia* the *Riviera di Levante* stretches as far as *Genoa*. Towns such as *Levanto, Sestri Levante, Rapallo* and *Santa Margherita* are coastal resorts. *Portofino* on attractively hilly peninsula.

Genoa, largest port in Italy and rival to Marseille. Birthplace of Christopher Columbus. Contrasts in streets between old houses and palaces and modern commercial buildings, due to former decay and modern revival of the city. Fine streets: *Balbi, Cairoli, Garibaldi; Piazza de Ferrari*. Modern area, *Via 20 Settembre*, with *Victory Square*; old quarter, south of cathedral of *San Lorenzo* (twelfth-sixteenth century). Several attractive churches. Excursion along the *Circonvallazione a Monte* for wide views of the city.

The coast between *Genoa* and the French frontier is known as *Riviera di Ponente*. Between the cosmopolitan resorts are primitive peasant villages. The poor land encourages the teeming local population to seek a living in fishing, hence innumerable fishing villages.

Albissola Marina, 27 miles (43km), good bathing. *Savona*Δ, iron industry and port; *Finale Marina*Δ, 18 miles (29km), another bathing resort. *Alassio*, less sea-side resort than a residential town, well laid out; *San Remo*, largest and most fashionable of Italian winter resorts; centre of early flower-trade; some pictur-esque old street. Excursions to *Baiardo*, 3,000ft (900m) up in hills, magnificent panorama of *Riviera*.

R2 Milan to Venice and return (410 miles, 660km)
Milan (see **R1**) to *Bergamo*△, 36 miles (58km), modern industrial town with walled Venetian town at higher level. *Torre del Comune*, twelfth-century tower, *Palazzo della Ragione, Colleoni* Chapel, *Santa Maria Maggiore*.

EXCURSION: northwards to alpine valleys and Lake *Iseo* (15 miles, 24km, long).

Brescia, 33 miles (53km), situated between Alps and plains, a town where Lombardic and Venetian artistic ideas mixed. *Broletto*, twelfth-century govern-ment house with tower; *Rotonda*, eleventh- to twelfth-century cathedral; *Loggia*, attractive Renaissance square; Roman museum; many Renaissance churches and palaces. *Desenzano*, on south shore of Lake *Garda* (32 miles, 52km, long).

EXCURSION: by steamer or bus along lake, many attractive resorts and villages, among them is *Riva del Garda*△. Road on west side gives best views.

Verona△, 41 miles (66km), on River *Adige*; fine Roman remains: arena, forum, theatre; cathedral, many churches; *San Zeno*, particularly interesting Romanesque style. Birthplace of Paolo Veronese.

EXCURSIONS: (a) foothills of Alps, *Soave* wine-growing district. (b) *Montagnana* (△in castle) enclosed by splendid walls with 24 towers; Veronese 'Transfiguration' in cathedral.

Vicenza, 32 miles (52km), north of *Berici* hills, renowned for architectural work of Andrea Palladio.

Padua, 20 miles (32km), noted university and one of the old city states; under Venetian rule for 400 years; Basilica of *Sant'Antonio*, astonishing mixture of Lombardic Gothic and Venetian Oriental (cupolas); Donatello's statue of Gattamelata; *Scrovegni* Chapel (1303), fine frescoes by Giotto. *Venice* 20 miles (32km).

Venice

The barbarian invasion of the Dark Age drove refugees to seek safety on islands in shallow lagoon; the city of **Venice**△ was founded in 811 and grew rapidly after 1000; kept independence as city republic until 1797; 'Queen of the Adriatic' from 1400 onwards; eventually lost importance through discovery of America, and working of new routes to east.

Railway and road reach the 118 islands of the city by a 2 mile (3km) causeway, beyond which no motor traffic is allowed. You travel by boat, or by footpath crossing the canals by countless beautiful little bridges. The city is not too large to be explored on foot, and the narrow footways between tall buildings are shady. An excellent book on walks in Venice is *Venice for Pleasure* by J.G. Links, published by Bodley Head; Hugh Honour's *Companion Guide to Venice*, published in paperback by Fontana is recommended, so too is *Venice* by Jan Morris, published in paperback by Faber & Faber.

The gondola is the 'taxi' of *Venice* but fares are expensive. Fares are cheap on the water-buses (*vaporetto*); frequent service along the length of the Grand Canal and there are also numerous motor-boat services (*motoscafi*).

Tour No 1 By Boat

From station by water-bus for 2 miles (3km) along **Grand Canal**, lined by palaces facing the water-front, to *Piazza San Marco. Ca' 'd'Oro*, fine Gothic palace; sixteenth-century **Ponte di Rialto**, bridge carrying shops; *Palazzo Rezzonico* (seventeenth century); churches of *Santa Maria della Salute* on south bank, and *San Giorgio* on island opposite *Piazza San Marco:* land at *San Zaccaria*.

Tour No 2 On foot from San Zaccaria landing stage to Rialto

Left along promenade, *Ponte dei Sospira* (**Bridge of Sighs**) joining prison to *Palazzo Ducale* (**Doge's Palace**) finest non-church Gothic building, fourteenth to fifteenth century, magnificent interior; paintings by great Venetian artists, including Tintoretto's *Paradise* — longest canvas painting in world. On quay, column with Lion of St Mark. Opposite palace is *Libreria Vecchia*, by Sansovino (sixteenth century), the *Loggetta*, and *Campanile*, 300ft (91m), lift, good view.

Piazza San Marco, elegant square surrounded by buildings of many periods. **Church of St Mark**, without parallel in western Europe. Founded ninth century as shrine for body of St Mark; rebuilt eleventh century, its mainly Byzantine style reflects *Venice's* trade with the east. The four bronze horses (third century BC) brought to *Venice* in 1204 after conquest of Constantinople, together with shiploads of other loot, adorn the church. Fine marble facings, and twelfth-seventeenth-century interior and exterior mosaics.

Past clock tower (bronze figures strike the hours) into *Merceria*, attractive shopping street, *San Salvatore* (Renaissance interior). *Merceria* bears right then left to *Rialto* Bridge, centre of busy district.

Interesting Gothic churches of *Santa Maria dei Frari, Santo Stefano, Santi Giovanni e Paolo* (with many tombs of Doges).

Ghetto (north-west of city), *Arsenale* (ancient naval arsenal of Republic, with fine walls), island of *San Pietro* for pretty gardens and quayside views.

EXCURSIONS: (a) *Murano* (water-bus from *Fondamenta Nuove*), museum of ancient glassware and world-famous glass factories (b). *Torcello* (water-bus as [a]), fine cathedral. (c) Lido (water-bus from *Riva degli Schiavoni*), celebrated and sophisticated bathing resort, remarkable contrast to *Venice*.

Route continues across the last stretches of the *Po basin. Po* and its tributaries here are all embanked; in spite of this, flooding often occurs. *Rovigo*, centre of the *Polesine*, tract of land which has been drained by good engineering work, thence through a region of lakes and marshes to **Ferrara**△, 22 miles (35km); cathedral, Renaissance houses; see *Castello Estense*, and walk along medieval *Via delle Volte.*

EXCURSION: to isolated abbey of *Pomposa* for mosaics and view from campanile.

R2 (i) Ferrara to San Marino. Southwards to **Ravenna**△, 46 miles (74km). Former capital of west Roman Empire; Byzantine monuments and mosaics, also Dante's tomb. Thence to *Rimini*△ 33 miles (53km), resort with wide sandy beaches, and **San Marino**, an independent republic, perched on *Monte Titano*; one of the smallest states in world and very old — sixth century.

West to **Mantua**△. The River *Mincio* forms a string of lakes round the city. *Palazzo Ducale*, thirteenth to eighteenth century, third in size only to *Vatican* and *Caserta*, frescoes, picture gallery; several other palaces built for Gonzaga family; church of *Sant' Andrea.*

Cremona, on River *Po*; the *Torrazzo* (thirteenth century) rises to 350ft (107m); Lombardic Gothic cathedral and twelfth-century baptistry; thence 50 miles (80km) north-west to *Milan.*

R3 The Pennine Alps and Aosta Valley

This region is contained roughly between two international railway lines — the *Mont Cenis* route (via *Modane*) and the *Simplon* (via *Domodossola*). Much of the highest ground forms the frontier with France and Switzerland (*Mont Blanc, Matterhorn, Monte Rosa*); the *Gran Paradiso* group is all in Italy. Area offers everything from interesting valley walks to mountaineering of highest order; reached by train and bus from *Turin*; or by road from France and Switzerland.

Main valley, formed by *Dora Baltea*, tributary of the *Po*, is **Val d'Aosta.** French or a Franco-Italian dialect is spoken by many of the people, particularly in the west, and the French form of place names is frequently used.

Aosta (80 miles, 130km, from Turin), founded in 25BC, called *Augusta Praetoria*, after Caesar Augustus; interesting Roman and medieval buildings, surrounded by Roman walls.

EXCURSIONS: (a) **Great St Bernard Pass** (8,170ft, 2,490m), 20 miles (32km), route shows glaciers of *Grand Combin*; hospice, famous pass route to Switzerland (*Martigny*). (b) *Cogne*, centre of *Gran Paradiso National Park*. (c) *Valsavaranche* for ascent of *Gran Paradiso*, 13,324ft (4,061m). (d) from *Pré St Didier* **Little St Bernard Pass** road (7,200ft, 2,195m) leads into France (*Bourg St Maurice*). Good views. Short cuts for walkers. Excellent view of *Mont Blanc* from *Monte di Nono*, 2 hours' walk from main road.

Courmayeur (25 miles, 40km, from *Aosta*), Italian counterpart of *Chamonix*; background is the *Mont Blanc* range in its wildest and most rugged aspect. For serious climbers Italian Alpine Club huts are plentiful; qualified guides in *Courmayeur*.

EXCURSIONS: (a) west; *Col de Chécroui* or *Val Veni*. (b) east: *Val Ferret* or *Mont de la Saxe;* all excellent for views of the high peaks. (c) for strong walkers; whole day, night at hut; rough steep track to *Rifugio Torino*, just below *Géant* glacier. Expensive cable railway goes across French border to *Chamonix* with tremendous views; *Mont Blanc* road tunnel links *Entrèves* near *Courmayeur* with *Les Pélerins*Δ near *Chamonix*.

R4 The Dolomites and Alto Adige

Contained between imaginary lines running north from *Brescia* and *Venice*. The mountains are of dolomitic limestone, coloured grey, yellow and even rose-red according to the light; sheer cliffs and towers frequently rise abruptly from meadows or forests. *Feltre,* grouped around its castle; elegant arcaded square. *Asiago*Δ all-year-round resort. Many Italian Alpine Club huts and simple hotels, as well as expensive resorts, in this district.

In the northern part of the area German is widely spoken and towns and villages resemble Austria rather than Italy.

Approach via *Trento* or from *Innsbruck* over the *Brenner* Pass. Can be conveniently combined with visit to *Venice*. Many motorcoach services.

Trento, on River *Adige,* Italian-style chief town of *Trentino Alto-Adige*, which, like *Val d'Aosta*, has partial independence.

EXCURSIONS: (a) *Lake Molveno*. (b) *Madonna di Campiglio*, centre for *Brenta* group and return via *Malè*. (c) *San Martino di Castrozza*, in heart of mountains, via *Cembra* valley and *Rolle* Pass (6,488ft, 1,978m).

Continue north through typical *Adige* country along *Brenner* route to **Bolzano**, industrial town but good centre for Dolomites.

EXCURSIONS: (a) *Mendola Pass*, 4,462ft (1,360m), 15 miles (24km) (tram part way). (b) by 'Dolomite Road' with magnificent views, including *Catinnacio (Rosengarten)* peaks. *Marmolada* (10,960ft, 3,340m), *Pordoi Pass* (7,356ft, 2,242m) to *Cortina d'Ampezzo* (67 miles, 108km), mountain resort, with road and rail connections to **Lienz**. (c) through the *Val Gardena* and *Ortisei* to *Sella* Pass (7,262ft, 2,214m). (d) through **Merano** (well-known winter and summer resort) and *Venosta* valley for the *Ortler* group and *Stelvio* Pass into the *Engadine* (Switzerland).

Main route to Innsbruck continues up *Isarco* valley to Austrian frontier at *Brenner* Pass.

LUXEMBOURG

Geographical Outline

The Grand Duchy of Luxembourg, with an area of 1,000 sq miles (2,590 sq km)
and no more than 50 miles (80km) from north to south and 35 miles (56km) from
west to east, is one of the smallest states of Europe. But, for several reasons, it has
an importance out of proportion to its size. Situated between Belgium, France and
Germany, it lies on routes between the Rhine and the Paris basin and between the
Belgian ports and central Europe. The basis of its prosperity is the large iron and
steel industry. For touring, especially walking, its smallness and accessibility
offer advantages and it has some very attractive and varied country with historical
associations.

Land

The northern part, called *Oesling* or *E' slek*, is part of the *Ardennes* uplands 1,300
to 1,800ft (400 to 500m), consisting chiefly of ancient slate formations into which
rivers have cut steep-sided narrow valleys and spectacular winding defiles. The
remaining two-thirds of the country, the *Bon Pays* (or *Gutland*), is some 400ft
(120m) lower and is a continuation of the adjoining scarpland of *Lorraine*. Its
resistant limestones and sandstones produce many striking landscape features,
especially in the district known as the *Petite Suisse*. As in the *Oesling*, the *Bon
Pays* is deeply cut by river valleys including the wine-growing *Moselle*. Most of
the streams drain towards the *Sûre* which itself joins the *Moselle* at *Wasserbillig*.

Climate

The prevailing winds are between south and west, producing a mild climate, west
European rather than 'continental'. The lower valleys are humid in summer, but
the hill country is cool and has less rainfall than the Belgian *Ardennes* by which
it is sheltered.

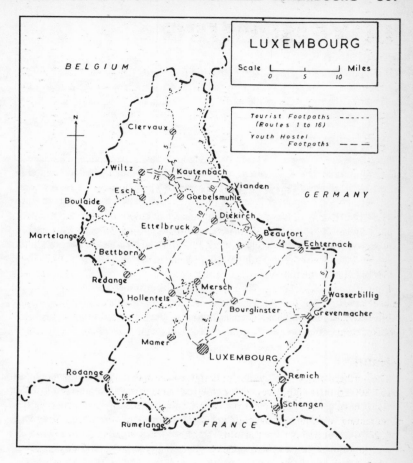

Plants

One-third of the country is wooded. In the *Ardennes* the valley slopes, thickly covered with oak and spruce forest, contrast with the plateau above, which is open and largely cultivated. For a few weeks about Whitsuntide, when the broom is in flower, this part of the country takes on a golden glow. In the *Bon Pays* magnificent beech woods cover the sandstone plateaux of the centre.

The People

Population

Of the population of almost 400,000 about two-thirds live either in the capital, *Luxembourg* (78,000) or in the iron and steel districts. Racially the people are a product of the mingling of the early Celtic inhabitants (Belgae) with the first Roman and later Germanic invaders.

Language

The people are tri-lingual. The mother tongue and everyday spoken language is Luxembourgian (*Letzeburgesch*), a Germanic West Frankish dialect, which is used by all classes of the community. The written languages, used everywhere, are German and French; both are taught to all children at school and there is no language barrier between one area and another. There is, however, a tendency for the languages to serve different purposes, German predominating in everyday life (most newspapers are in German), while French is the language of the law courts and the council chamber. Such facility produces good linguists and English is widely known.

Religion

Practically all the people are Roman Catholics. Since 1867 the country has been a bishopric centred on the cathedral of *Notre-Dame* in *Luxembourg City*.

History

Strategically part of the troubled borderland between France and Germany, the territory now known as Luxembourg has experienced many changes of fortune in accordance with the varying strengths of the great European powers. At the break-up of Charlemagne's empire in 843 it became part of the Middle Kingdom of *Lotharingia* whose name still survives in neighbouring *Lorraine*. But in 925 it became a fief of the kingdom of Germany. In 963 its immediate ruler, Siegfried, Count of Ardenne, built a stronghold on the site of the capital city, and this became known as '*Lucilinburhuc*' ('Little Fortress'), from which the present name derives. His descendants increased their domains by marriages until, by 1354, these were four times the size of the state today. The prestige of the house of Luxembourg was such that, between 1308 and 1410, four of its members were elected emperors of the Holy Roman Empire.

A curious relic of these times survives in the most famous device in English heraldry. John the Blind, ruler of Luxembourg, died fighting for the French at the battle of Crécy (1346). His heroism so moved the Black Prince that he took from John's helmet the motto *Ich Dien* ('I Serve') and the three feathers above it and adopted them as the device of the Prince of Wales.

Luxembourg's brilliant medieval period ended in 1443 with its purchase by Philip the Good of Burgundy. It then formed part of the Netherlands, and came in succession under Burgundy, the Spanish and Austrian Habsburgs and France. It did not achieve independence, as the modern Grand Duchy, until 1815. During these centuries, particularly in the wars of Louis XIV, the fortress was besieged a number of times and frequently changed hands. Its territory also, was reduced in size.

In 1815 William I, King of the Netherlands, of the dynasty of Orange-Nassau-Vianden, became the first Grand-Duke. But Prussia was given the right to garrison the fortress. When, in 1830, Belgium became independent, there was a popular movement for union with it. The question was settled by the powers of the Treaty of London (1831), ratified 1839, when the western (Walloon) part was transferred to become the Belgian Province of Luxembourg. The independence of the remainder (now a linguistic unit) was guaranteed, but the fortress was left under Prussian control. Later Luxembourg was again involved in the rivalries of the great powers. But popular feeling turned against union with any other country and independence was realised in the second Treaty of London (1867), which guaranteed perpetual neutrality, settled the sovereignty as hereditary in the ruling house and required withdrawal of the Prussian garrison and the dismantling of the fortress. The Treaty has remained the basis of Luxembourg's existence as a state and though over run by the Germans in both World Wars its independent political status has each time been restored. More recently Luxembourg has become the home of EEC institutions, such as the European Court of Justice and the Secretariat of the European Parliament.

Government

The Grand Duchy is a parliamentary democracy under a constitutional monarchy. Parliament consists of the chamber of deputies, elected for five years, by men and women aged 18 and over, by proportional representation. The Cabinet, called the Council of Government, is headed by the President who is appointed by the Sovereign. An unusual additional body, which functions as second chamber, is the Council of State of twenty-one members appointed by the Sovereign.

Resources

Agriculture, forestry and wine production give work to about a quarter of the population. The estates are generally small to medium sized and cultivated by their owners, rented farms being exceptional. Vine growing, for the production of both still and sparkling wines, is concentrated along the slopes of the *Moselle* valley bordering Germany. While some of the forest is State owned and some in private hands, most of it is owned by the village communes and used to meet local requirements. There is a tendency for the oak of the *Ardennes* and the beech of the *Bon Pays* to lose ground to softwood plantations.

The chief industry is iron and steel production, formerly based on the ore mines of the south-west, but now increasingly dependent on iron ore imported from France; coal, coke, and petroleum have to be imported too. Ninety-eight per cent of the steel is exported. Currently a member of the Benelux Union, the European Coal and Steel Community (administered from *Luxembourg City*) and the European Common Market, Luxembourg, because of this great industry, has an important place alongside larger nations on the continent.

Other industries include tanning, metal work, ceramics, brewing and cement.

Food and Drink

The specialities include Ardennes ham, cooked cheese, trout and pike. The national drinks are white Moselle wine and beer. Coffee is much more frequently drunk than tea.

Culture

Architecture

Apart from their often fine situations, the many medieval castles are interesting as buildings. The most imposing are *Vianden, Clervaux, Bourscheid, Beaufort, Hollenfels* and *Bourglinster*. The city of *Luxembourg*, once an imposing fortress particularly after being strengthened by Vauban, Louis XIV's famous military engineer, has preserved important works of military architecture.

At *Echternach*, which grew up around the abbey founded in 698 by St Willibrord of Northumbria, are the considerable eighteenth-century baroque buildings of the present Benedictine abbey, with an eighth-century (Merovingian) crypt. The Town Hall, the famous *Dingstuhl*, was originally built in the thirteenth century as a court of justice.

Other churches of interest are *Vianden* (thirteenth-century Gothic), *Luxembourg* cathedral (Renaissance), *Koerich* (baroque), *Rindschleiden* (for its frescoes) and *Junglinster* (for its knights' tombs). Many churches newly built or re-built after World War II have remarkable modern stained glass windows. Carved field crosses, mostly eighteenth century, are found all over the country.

Touring Information

Access

Luxembourg City is within $10^{1}/_{2}$ hours' journey from London by rail and boat via Ostend and Brussels, the most direct route. By air in about 2 hours on daily flights.

Transport

There is a good railway system, largely electrified, but some local journeys are more easily made by bus.

Money

The Luxembourg *franc* is tied to the same exchange value as the Belgian *franc*, divided into 100 *centimes*, but due to inflation these latter have almost disappeared. Belgian money is accepted in Luxembourg, but not vice versa.

Maps

The whole country is covered by the Michelin map No 7, scale 1:200,000; more detailed maps, showing footpaths, on scales of 1:100,000, 1:50,000 and 1:20,000 are sold by Centrale des Auberges de Jeunesse Luxembourgeoises in *Luxembourg City*.

Public Holidays

New Year's Day, Easter Monday, 1 May, Ascension Day, Whit Monday, National Day on 23 June. Assumption Day on 15 August, All Saints Day on 1 November, Christmas Day and Boxing Day.

Walking

Luxembourg has some of Europe's finest hill country for moderate walking tours. The marked long-distance footpaths listed here give access to some idyllic forest and meadow country.

1 **Haute-Sûre Track**: Martelange— Ettelbrück.
2 **Attert Track**: Martelange — Redange — Useldange — Mersch.
3 **Our Track**: Ouren — Vianden — Diekirch.
4 **Seven Castles Track:** Gaichel (Eischen) — Mersch.
5 **North Track**: Wemperhardt — Kautenbach — Diekirch.
6 **Basse-Sûre Track**: Wasserbillig — Echternach.
7 **Moselle Track**: Wasserbillig — Stromberg (Schengen).
8 **Alzette Track**: Dommeldange (Luxembourg) — Mersch.
9 **Pre'tzerdall Track**: Boulaide — Pratze — Ettelbrück.
10 **Victor Hugo Track**: Vianden — Brandenbourg — Ettelbrück.
11 **Charles Mathieu Track**: Esch-sur-Sûre — Wiltz — Vianden.
12 **Moellerdall Track**: Section Mersch — Larochette; Beaufort — Echternach.
13 **Maurice Cosyn Track**: Diekirch — Beaufort.
14 **Mamer Track**: Mamer — Kopstal — Mersch.
15 **Wiltz Track**: Goehelsmühle — Kautenbach — Wiltz.
16 **South Track**: Rodange — Ramelange.

Additional footpaths, marked with white triangles, link the youth hostels.

Motoring

Belgium's motoring regulations apply equally in Luxembourg. Only about 30 miles (50km) of motorway, southwards from *Luxembourg City*; elsewhere satisfactory main roads but many variously surfaced and circuitous minor roads. Automobile Club du Grand Duché de Luxembourg, is at Route de Longwy 13, Luxembourg — Helfenterbrück.

Cycling

Although hilly in all its parts. Luxembourg is an ideal country for cycling as all roads are in good condition. Touring cyclists should avoid the few heavy traffic roads.

Canoeing and Boating

The *Moselle*, broad, calm and slow, with many disembarkation points and camping grounds along its banks, provides easy conditions. The *Lower Sûre*, from *Ettelbrück* to *Wasserbillig*, is swifter than the *Moselle* but presents no serious difficulty; all the dams are provided with water-passes. Above *Ettelbrück* its practicability depends on the water level, and its sand banks and other obstructions require greater experience. The same can be said of the swift flowing *Our* and, with greater emphasis, of the *Wiltz*. *Lultzhausen* △, close to *Haute-Sûre* lake, offers facilities for canoeing, sailing, surfing, swimming and diving.

Touring Route

R1 Arlon — Luxembourg — Moselle Valley and the Ardennes,
143 miles (230km)

Coming from *Arlon* (Belgium) enter Luxembourg by secondary road through *Septfontaines* (medieval church and castle) and *Ansembourg* (medieval and Renaissance castles) to *Hollenfells*△. Picturesque road to *Luxembourg City*, with footpath or bus connection from *Kopstal*.

Luxembourg City△, capital of the Grand Duchy, about equidistant from the borders of Belgium, France and Germany. Once one of the most important fortresses of Europe, the old town is situated on a steep-sided, rocky plateau and many picturesque ruined bastions and towers are still to be seen. The main part of the town is almost surrounded by a belt of parkland at the edge of the rocky slopes. The *Cathedral of Notre Dame* dates from 1618 and has an interesting baroque portico. In the oldest part of the town amongst interesting, narrow streets, stands the Grand Ducal Palace, a building in sixteenth-century Spanish style. Well worth seeing also is the view of the valley from the *Roc du Bouc*.

East from *Luxembourg* by road for 29 miles (47km) or by footpath to

Key to Plan of Luxembourg City

1 Notre Dame Cathedral.
2 Grand Ducal Palace.
3 Post Office.
4 Tourist Office.
5 youth hostel.
A to Bouillon.
B to Brussels/ Clervaux.
C to Echternach/ Clervaux.
D to Trier.
E to Metz.

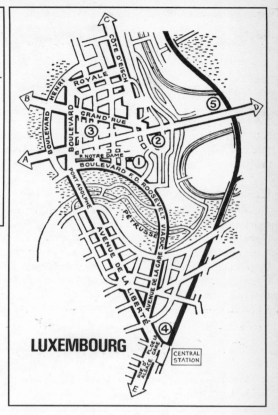

LUXEMBOURG

*Grevenmacher*Δ, ancient and picturesque town on the *Moselle*, famous for sparkling wine, similar to champagne; wine cellars can be visited. Then turn northwards to follow by road or footpath the meanders of the *Moselle* and *Sûre* to *Echternach*Δ, small town, rich in folklore and tradition, with remarkable ancient buildings including town hall, medieval ramparts, lovely fifteenth-century abbey founded by Northumbrian monk, St Willibrord in seventh century; famous dancing procession at Whitsun commemorates his cures of epilepsy and plagues. Fine modern stained glass windows in choir of Basilica.

From *Echternach* through *Petite Suisse*, area of narrow valleys, cliffs, sandstone rocks and beech woods, to *Beaufort*Δ. By minor roads northwards through *Reisdorf* following River *Our* through *Bettel* to *Vianden*Δ, most picturesque little town in the *Ardennes*; Gothic church and cloisters, dominated by impressive ruins of medieval castle, chairlift to belvedere (1,380ft, 420m). Thence for 11 miles (17km) by roads B17 and A7, or waymarked footpath, to *Ettelbrück*△ and on north-westwards by A15 for 11¹/₂ miles (18km), turning sharply westwards on minor road for 5 miles (8km) to *Lultzhausen*△ on River *Sûre*.

NETHERLANDS

Geographical Outline

The Kingdom of the Netherlands covers about 16,000 sq miles (41,000 sq km), but this figure is increasing as more and more land is won from the sea. The name 'Holland', generally used to describe the whole country, should properly be applied only to the provinces of North and South Holland, which form the north-west portion of the country.

Land

More than one-fifth of the land is under sea-level and would be invaded by the sea if the country was not protected by dykes and dunes. The area between the dunes along the sea-shore and the higher land of the south and east was formerly lake and marshy swamp; but through much human effort the swamps, together with a large part of the *Zuider Zee* (now called *Ijsselmeer*), have been converted into pasture and arable land known as polders. The pastures are split up by innumerable little ditches, very necessary in order to regulate the water level.

To safeguard the dunes, which are the natural defence against the North Sea, long-rooted grasses have been planted and dykes and piers have been built.

Climate

The climate is temperate but with seasonal extremes of temperature due to the continental influence. The prevailing winds from the west are noticeable, as they pass unhindered over the flat country, tending to produce damp weather, but without excessive rainfall.

The coldest month is January, and July the hottest. A visit is well worth while at any time of the year, although spring and summer are the best touring seasons. April and the beginning of May are the best times for visiting the bulb fields, when they are a mass of colour.

Plants and Animals

The undulating sand-hills are extremely beautiful; they are like mountain ranges compared with the level polders behind them. There is a large variety of vegetation on the dunes; near the shore are tangled masses of thorn and brambles, and further inland there are fragrant birches and pines, twisted by the storms into fantastic shapes. The ground is carpeted with wild flowers. Rabbits are evident, as well as hares, lizards, pheasants and many sea-birds.

Just behind the dunes, between *Alkmaar* and *Leiden*, is a strip of sandy ground, mixed with clay, where the famous bulbs are grown. Daffodils, tulips, hyacinths and gladioli in their season transform flat fields into wonderfully coloured acres of flowers.

Between the *Hague* and the *Hook* is *Westland*, the most important market-gardening area, where peaches, tomatoes, grapes and strawberries are grown under acres of glass.

In the province of *Drenthe* is a region of heather and moorland, while the provinces of *Friesland* and *Groningen* are predominantly given over to pasture.

The People

Population

With more than 14 million people the country is the most densely populated in Europe, and one of the most densely populated in the world.

Language

The language, Dutch, is a Germanic tongue. In towns you should have no difficulty in being understood, as many people have a working knowledge of English and are eager to help.

Religion

About 36 per cent of the population is Protestant and another 37 per cent Roman Catholic; the remainder are unclassified. Protestants, who are divided into many sects, are more numerous in the north. Roman Catholics are predominant in the provinces of *Limburg* and *North Brabant*.

History

The Dutch are the outstanding example of a nation forced to engage in unremitting struggle against the sea and in efforts to contain the great rivers which would otherwise flood the richest parts of their country. For a thousand years from Roman times the waters were victorious: the sea level tended to rise, the dune belt was pierced and towards the end of the period the Zuider Zee was formed.

These northern Netherlands were therefore much less developed than those of the south (see Belgium) when they came first under Burgundian and later under Habsburg rule in the Middle Ages. A change of fortune came with a new phase in which the sea level tended slightly to fall and with the introduction of windmills for pumping in the fifteenth century. The Dutch, schooled in self-reliance by the battle against nature, needed only this to turn to advantage their otherwise favourable situation for international trading. Wealth increased. The towns, particularly *Amsterdam*, prospered.

The ideas associated with the Reformation were naturally congenial to matter-of-fact merchants whose wealth was independent of the Church and of the feudal system represented by the Spanish overlordship of the Netherlands.

The rebellion, the famous Revolt of the Netherlands, which broke out against Philip II in 1555, reflected the new-felt strength of a people already forging the financial and commercial forms in which the trade of the modern world was to develop, and their impatience at a control which was both alien and rigidly traditional. It was successful only in the northern provinces. Here it found an apt leader in Prince William of Orange, called 'William the Silent' (1533-84), and a new ally in the sea as a spring-board for assault. The east-west course of the Lower Rhine and Maas was also a decisive factor in determining that the two parts of the Netherlands should develop differently. The growth of Amsterdam at the expense of Antwerp, which remained tied to imperial Spain, symbolizes the new force affecting the balance of power. The revolt was only the beginning of an eighty years' war. Not until 1648 was the independence of the young 'Republic of the Seven Provinces' acknowledged by its former master.

Something of the spirit of this heroic age continued for another generation as shown in the development of Dutch sea power, Dutch rivalry with England in trade and empire building, and in scientific and artistic achievement. But, from the death of Rembrandt (1669), the sharp decline in artistic conviction may reflect a similar inadequacy of vision in the factions controlling the nation's policy, seen in the rivalries for the position of head of state (*stadtholder*) and in the intervals when the position was dispensed with. The House of Orange was alternately looked to for leadership and suspected as having dynastic ambitions. These, by a strange turn of fate, were satisfied when William III came to double the part of *stadtholder* with the sovereignty of Great Britain (1688-1702) held jointly with his wife, Mary Stuart — a spectacular example of the swiftly changing relationships between the powers of western Europe which were to continue throughout the eighteenth century.

The end of the Republic came with an unhappy period of French domination during the Napoleonic wars. The modern kingdom dates from 1815 when William I of Orange-Nassau was proclaimed king. His rule was autocratic but his son, William II, was sympathetic to liberal ideas and the Netherlands were therefore more fortunate than other countries in 1848 in achieving a democratic constitution without a revolution. In 1890 the Dutch Crown passed to Wilhelmina, then only 10 years old, who became a great queen, exiled in London during World War II and a focus of national loyalty for her peoples in occupied Europe and Asia. Queen Juliana succeeded her mother in 1948 and, in 1980, abdicated in favour of her daughter, Beatrix.

In recent times the traditional neutrality of the Netherlands has lapsed in favour of partnership with Belgium and Luxembourg (*Benelux*) and membership of the EEC and NATO. Influence has been exerted on the side of moderation in international affairs; the permanent Court of International Justice is situated at the Hague, so too is the International Institute of Social Studies.

Government

The Kingdom of the Netherlands is a parliamentary democracy under a limited monarchy. The 'States General' is the legislature, while the Cabinet, led by the Prime Minister, coordinates policy and functions as the executive. There is too, a Council of State, an advisory body, presided over by the Sovereign. All citizens aged 18 or over have a vote and elections are based on proportional representation.

Resources

Cereals, potatoes and sugar-beet are grown on the higher lands of *Groningen, Friesland* and *Zeeland*, while on the damp lower ground of *Friesland* and the provinces of *North* and *South Holland* large numbers of cattle are reared, both for meat and dairy products. The bulb fields around *Haarlem* are a highly productive specialist industry supplying an international market.

Fishing is another important occupation and there are many fishing ports along the North Sea coast, notably *Ijmuiden*, *Scheveningen* and *Vlaardingen*.

The importance of industry is increasing. There are oilfields and natural gas in *Drenthe*, shipyards in a number of towns, and a variety of industries producing consumer goods. Philips radio and electrical works dominating the town of *Eindhoven*, is the biggest industry, employing more than 40,000 people.

Amsterdam and *Rotterdam* are great commercial cities. *Rotterdam*, one of the main transit centres for goods passing to and from Central Europe via the *Rhine*, is the world's largest port, while *Schiphol*, near *Amsterdam* is one of the biggest airports.

Food and Meals

Breakfast and lunch are similar, consisting of bread, thickly buttered, with cheese, sugar, chocolate, and perhaps slices of sausage and meat. The cheese is served in thin wafers, often with different kinds of bread and biscuits. Dinner, between six and seven, is the most substantial meal; meat, vegetables and gravy is the usual dish. Fruit is abundant and good in season.

Among Dutch specialities are:

Smoked eels, called *paling*.

Fresh salted herrings garnished with raw onions, eaten at stalls in the streets.

Hutspot, which is mashed potatoes, carrots and onions with meat.

Boerenkool met worst, curly cabbage with smoked sausage.

Pancakes, eaten with bacon or treacle.

Rolpens, fried smoked sausage.

Beefsteak and sauté potatoes.

Rijsttafel, consisting of rice and various kinds of Malay curry with a dozen or more different chutneys and garnishes.

Sport

Among the usual sports, in which there is a natural emphasis on those connected with water, special interest attaches to the traditional 'Eleven Towns Race' in the province of *Friesland*, a one-day skating race over 125 miles (200km), in which thousands of enthusiasts take part; it dates from the seventeenth century.

Culture

Architecture

There are many medieval castles (one of them houses the youth hostel at *Heemskerk*) and some notable Gothic and Renaissance churches. Many of these are mentioned at appropriate points in the itineraries. The main glory of the country, however, lies in its domestic architecture — the old houses which line the canals in *Amsterdam* and other cities, with their stepped gables and weathered façades.

Painting

An indication of Dutch influence in this field may be seen in the Dutch origin of such words as *landscape, easel, etch* and *sketch*. In a period of 50 years from 1625 Dutch painters made a contribution to European art which, in several ways, was of the greatest significance. Catering for the tastes of a merchant class, their typical subjects were portraits, landscapes and domestic interiors. Realism was sought through precise observation and a technical competence which achieved complete mastery in recording the play of light. The many great names include Vermeer, Pieter de Hoogh, Frans Hals and Jan Steen. But all are transcended by Rembrandt for whom outward realism was only the starting point of a deeper study of men and nature.

Among the moderns, Van Gogh (1853-90), has the same intense interest in the visible world and a great range of human sympathy expressed not in terms of light and shade but of strong colour in the full glare of the sun.

Museums and Art Galleries

No one should miss the *Rijksmuseum* in *Amsterdam*, with its magnificent collection of paintings by Rembrandt and others, or the *Mauritshuis* in the *Hague*. Other fine galleries are the Frans Hals museum at *Haarlem* and the *Boymans-van Beuningen Museum*, in *Rotterdam*.

Music

There are many good concerts, especially in *Amsterdam*, where the *Concertgebouw* Orchestra is world-famous. All the large towns have a concert hall as well as a theatre.

Science

Erasmus (1467-1536), did more than any other man to further the revival of learning associated with the Renaissance. The University of *Leiden* (founded 1575) quickly achieved eminence and fame abroad in many branches of learning. Among its professors was van Groot (Grotius, 1583-1645), for long the great authority on international law.

Less known, perhaps, is the work of the draper's assistant, Leeuwenhoek (1632-1723) one of the originals in the world of science — inventor of the microscope, and, throughout a long life, a prince of observers and recorder of unprecedented accuracy. His contemporary, Huygens (1629-95), improved the telescope, invented the pendulum clock and studied the properties of light. De Vries (1848-1935), the botanist, put forward the mutation theory of evolution.

Folklore

Folklore remains a part of Dutch life, often associated with the church. There is an Easter Monday dance at *Ootmarsum* during which each house in the village is entered; over the whole of *Twente* bonfires are lit; Island of *Terschelling*: Oppenried procession; *Limburg* and *Brabant:* carnival festivities; *Zwolle*: St Martin's Market; *Hindeloopen*: Whitsun wreaths; *Veluwe* region: folk dances.

National Costumes

National costumes can still be seen at the islands of *Zeeland: Marken* and *Volendam* (near *Amsterdam*); *Spakenburg* and *Bunschoten* (near *Amersfoort*); *Hindeloopen*; *Veluwe*; *Staphorts* (near *Zwolle* and *Meppel*); *Scheveningen* and other resorts.

Touring Information

Access

The most convenient route is by boat from Harwich to the *Hook of Holland*, a 6-hour crossing. The night service, in particular, is very comfortable, with sleeping berths or rest chairs available. There are also ferries from Sheerness to *Vlissingen*, Dover/*Zeebrugge* and Felixstowe/*Zeebrugge*. Motorists and cyclists may prefer to travel via Dover-Ostend, crossing Belgium to the Dutch frontier. Passengers from the north of England will find the steamer services from Hull/*Zeebrugge* and

Hull/*Rotterdam* useful, but summer bookings must be made early.

Touring Areas

For touring purposes the Netherlands can be divided into nine main areas, as follows:

1 *Friesland* and *Groningen*: a land of lakes, big farmhouses and pleasant pastureland.

2 The Provinces of *North* and *South Holland*: flat country, polders, lakes, rivers, windmills, big towns.

3 The North Sea coast: sandy beaches, dunes, fishermen's villages; the seaside resorts of *Scheveningen, Noordwijk* and *Zandvoort*.

4 *Betuwe*: orchards, big rivers.

5 *Veluwe:* woodland, heather.

6 The *Ijsselmeer*: four polders reclaimed from the sea, with picturesque old towns on the original land.

7 *Limburg*: lovely hills, but partially industrialised.

8 The former islands of *Zeeland*.

9 The so-called *Wadden Islands* in the north of the country.

Transport

There is a close network of railways, wholly electrified, and most of the main towns are less than an hour's journey apart by rail.

A season-ticket is available, valid for eight days on all railway lines, also on buses *Amsterdam* to the *Hague* and on ferry *Enkhuizen* to *Staveren*.

There are frequent bus services between neighbouring large towns, but no long-distance services; the bus terminus is nearly always near the railway station.

There is a comprehensive system of boat services; a particularly worthwhile trip is the tour of the waterways of *Amsterdam* by motor-launch.

Money

The currency unit is the guilder (*gulden*), alternatively named *florin*, abbreviated as *Fl* or *F*, and divided into 100 cents. Notes are issued for 5, 10, 25, 50, 100 and 1,000 guilders and in some higher denominations; metal coins are issued for 5, 10, 25 cents, 1 and $2^1/_2$ Guilder. A 5-cent bronze coin is called a *stuiver*, a 10-cent nickel coin a *dubbeltje* and a 25-cent nickel coin a *kwartje*.

Restaurants

Eating out can be expensive, but there are cafeterias in all large towns, where food is moderately priced. A service charge is included in bills in restaurants, so tipping is usually unnecessary.

Information Services

Every town and village of importance has its own information bureau, identifiable by the sign, *VVV*, often in or near railway stations, or central squares; many offer an accommodation service.

Public Holidays

New Year's Day, Good Friday, Easter Monday, Queen's Birthday on 30 April, Ascension Day, Whit Monday, Christmas and Boxing Day.

Maps

The Michelin maps Nos 1, 5 and 6, scale 1:200,000, or No 410, scale 1:400,000, are recommended; other good maps are those of the Royal Netherlands Touring Club (ANWB), obtainable only in the Netherlands.

Youth Hostels

There is an excellent network of over fifty youth hostels, mostly large (more than 100 beds) and all providing substantial meals. They are busy in July and August; prior reservations should be made.

Walking

The Netherlands does not claim to be a country for the walker, being for the most part flat and intensively cultivated. Some of the moorland areas in the east can, however, be covered pleasantly on foot. An international four-day long-distance walk around *Nijmegen* is arranged annually, usually in July, participants from thirty or more countries number at least 20,000.

Cycling

It is ideal country for cycling and most Dutch people, including the Royal Family, are cyclists; whole families with quite young children are often seen out cycling in the country.

There are excellent cycle paths through woods and parks, along many interesting routes denied to the motorist. Bicycle hire is popular; a deposit may be required; enquire at dealers and railway stations. The weight is not so important as the land is flat everywhere except in parts of *Limburg, Gelderland* and *Overijssel.*

Cycling westward is tiring at times, as the winds are unchecked by hills. If you intend to travel by cycle, boat and train, be sure to cycle with the prevailing west and south-west winds behind you as far as possible.

Cycles may not be left unattended in a town at the kerbside; they must be immobilised and placed in one of the many slots provided in the pavement, or leaned against the wall. It is advisable to make use of the many cycle parks (*Rijwielstallingen*) for a small charge.

Cyclists **must** use the cyclepaths indicated by a round blue sign on which a cycle is shown in white, but **have the option of doing** so when the sign is a black oblong with the word '*rijwielpad*' in white.

Motoring

Netherland's road system is excellent; even minor country roads are properly surfaced and maintained. Speed restrictions are 50 km/h (30mph) in towns, 100km/h (60mph) outside built-up areas. A driving licence and registration papers are necessary, so too is a red warning triangle and country-of-origin sticker. An international green insurance card is recommended — for visitors from USA or Canada it is a necessity. Driving is on the right, overtaking on left and traffic coming from the right has priority. Netherlands Automobile Club (KNAC) is in the Hague, at Sophialaan 4; Netherlands Toeristenbond (ANWB), also in the Hague at Wassenaarseweg 220.

Canoeing and Boating

Almost all the country can be traversed by canal, river or lake. The cruising office of the Royal Netherlands Touring Club (ANWB), 5 Museumplein, Amsterdam, has charts for sale. A small scale map, with the regulations of the waterways can be had from the VVV Tourist Offices.

Amsterdam△

The city gets its name from the dam which was laid across the mouth of the River *Amstel* in the thirteenth century, and the name *Dam* still exists in the square which forms the hub of the city, on which stands the Royal Palace and the New Church.

The centre of the city is built on islands formed by the intersection of two series of canals — one series forming concentric semi-circles and the other radiating outwards from the middle. The canals are bordered on either side by quiet quays, tree-lined and crossed by picturesque bridges. The old houses along the quays are full of architectural interest and complete a picture of great charm and character. This central area of canals and quays repays prolonged and leisurely exploration on foot.

The two most attractive waterways are probably the *Oudezijdsvoorburgwal*, running from north to south in the centre of the old city, and the *Reguliersgracht*, also running from north to south, but lying south of the River *Amstel*. Owing to the complicated layout of streets and canals it is almost essential to buy a good street plan, with index.

The **National Museum** (*Rijksmuseum*), *42 Stadhouderskade* — one of the

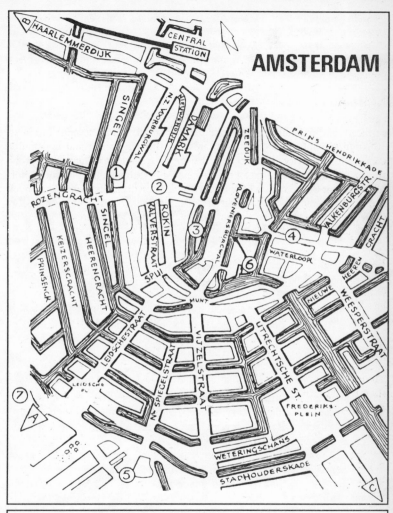

1 Post Office. 2 Royal Palace. 3 Town Hall. 4 Rembrandt's House.
5 Rijksmuseum. 6 Youth hostel on Kloveniersburgwal. 7 Youth hostel in
Vondelpark.
A to Schiphol Airport. B to Haarlem. C to Utrecht.

greatest art galleries in Europe, with a world-famous collection of masterpieces, including Rembrandt's *Night Watch*. The Municipal Museum (*Stedelijk*), *13 Paulus Potterstraat*, has a good collection of modern art. There is, too, the *Van Goghmuseum*; the Nautical Museum, *57 Corn Schuytstraat*; the Historical Museum, *4 Nieuwmarkt; Willet Holthuysen* Museum, *605 Heerengracht*, a seventeenth-century residence with a splendid collection of furniture; the Tropical Museum, *2 Linnaeusstraat*.

Other buildings worth seeing are the Royal Palace (1648); the oldest house, *1 Zeedijk*, an example of fifteenth-century architecture, with a wooden façade and side walls of brick; *Leeuwenberg*, on the *Oudezijdsvoorburgwal*, one of the most magnificent houses, built about 1600. *Oude Kerk* (Old Church) on the *Oudekerksplein*, consecrated in 1306, enlarged several times; the slender octagonal spire dates from 1564. *Nieuwe Kerk* (New Church) next to the Royal Palace; building begun in early fifteenth century; tombs of admirals, including the celebrated de Ruyter. Amsterdam University, *Oudemanhuispoot*. Asscher's diamond-cutting workshops, *127 Tolstraat*. Mint Tower, on the *Muntplein*, built 1620. Rembrandt's House, *4-6 Jodenbreestraat*, where the great Dutch painter lived from 1639 to 1658, is well worth a visit. Anne Frank House is at *Prinsengracht 263*. Modern architecture can be seen at the Exchange in the *Damrak*. The Exchange, built in 1903, is important for its influence on subsequent twentieth-century Dutch architecture. *Kalverstraat*, a busy shopping street, free of traffic.

The most interesting excursion in *Amsterdam* is the *Rondvaart*, a motorboat journey through the docks and canals of the city, lasting about an hour and a quarter.

Touring Routes

R1 Amsterdam to Amsterdam round the Ijsselmeer (518 miles, 834km)
This route encircles the country, except *Limberg*, and has been planned for motorists or cyclists; it can however be accomplished by train and bus and makes a very satisfactory 14-day cycling tour.

Leave *Amsterdam* northwards across the *Schellingwoude* bridge to *Monnickendam* thence 7 miles (11km) to *Broek in Waterland* and a further 2 miles (3km) where a ferry, as well as a dyke-road, connects to the former island of *Marken* in the new *Markerwaard* polder. Also buses (NACO) from *Amsterdam* (leaving north of the *Ijsselmeer*) and from *Monnickendam*. **Marken** is famous for its picturesque wooden houses and the costume of its inhabitants which, although a tourist bait, is quite genuine.

From *Marken* another ferry crosses in 30 minutes to **Volendam**, an interesting fishing village, where national costume is worn as everyday attire. *Marken* is Protestant and *Volendam* Catholic and, as with other isolated communities in the

Netherlands, the inhabitants rarely marry outside their own sect, so that individuality in manner and costume is still retained.

North of *Volendam* lies **Edam**, famous for its cheese. *Grote Kerk*, rebuilt in the seventeenth century, has fine stained glass windows and an interesting collection of hour-glasses. *Speeltoren* is most significant landmark; has ancient carillon.

Bear west across *North Holland* to **Alkmaar**, world-famous for its cheesemarket held every Friday morning. Colourful uniforms are worn (May to October) by the Guild of Cheese Porters. *Alkmaar* is, however, worth some attention on any day; sixteenth-century Weigh House overlooking the market; the church of St Lawrence; the Town Hall; and many other fine buildings. Weigh House contains a carillon of thirty-five bells, and mounted figures appear at the base of the tower and take part in a tournament every time the clock strikes the hour. Youth hostels at *Schoorl* 6 miles (10km), *Bakkum* 8 miles (13km) and *Egmond-a/d Hoef* 8 miles (13km).

East of *Alkmaar* on the *Ijsselmeer*, lie *Hoorn, Enkhuizen* and *Medemblik*, three dreamy old towns which were once flourishing seaports; many handsome seventeenth-century buildings. West Frisian Museum at *Hoorn* and *Zuider Zee* Museum at *Enkhuizen*. *Petten* is small bathing resort 12 miles (19km) north of *Alkmaar*. *Den Helder*, a naval base, 13 miles (21km) further north, has car ferries to the island of *Texel*Δ.

*Den Oever*Δ, at the north-east tip of *North Holland* province, is starting point of **Great Dyke** enclosing the former *Zuider Zee*. The road (with cycle track) along the top of the dam is 18 miles (29km) long. Fine view from tower on dyke near *Den Oever*. At east end of the dyke the road forks; the main route continues right to *Bolsward*, but there is an interesting excursion to *Groningen*.

R1 (i) To *Groningen* and the Frisian Islands. At east end of dyke, bear left, for 6 miles (10km) to *Harlingen*, fair-sized port; boats from here in about 2 hours to *Vlieland* and *Terschelling*, two of the Frisian Islands. *Franeker*, town hall (sixteenth century) and church (fifteenth century); Eise Eisinga Planetarium constructed in eighteenth century by a local wool comber is still a great curiosity. Eighteen miles (29km) farther, *Leeuwarden*, capital of *Friesland*, architecturally interesting, several museums. *Holwerd*, 18 miles (29km) north, has regular ferry service to *Ameland*, third of Frisian Islands. All of these islands are admirable in summer for camping and bathing; miles of beach and sand-dunes. Youth hostels on *Terschelling, Ameland* and *Schiermonnikoog*.

Groningen, university town and capital of province of same name, can be approached direct from *Leeuwarden* or from *Holwerd* via *Dokkum*. It is a pleasant, well laid out town but, although over 900 years old, has only a few historic buildings left, such as the fifteenth century *Martinikerk* and other old buildings near the *Grote Markt*. The market, held on Tuesdays, Fridays and Saturdays is most interesting.

Continuing on main route, *Bolsward*, ancient town. Town Hall and Gothic church, 1446, are architectural jewels. On for 7 miles (11km) to *Sneek* △ among attractive lakes, good sailing and bathing; similarly at *Heeg*△ south-west of *Sneek*. Leave main road at *Heerenveen* and turn north-east to fine woodlands of *Beesterzwaag* and eastwards through *Donkerbroek* and *Appelscha*, turning south-westwards across moorland to *Steenwijk*, pleasant little town with medieval churches. Follow road beside the canal to **Giethoorn**, a remarkable and lovely village with no roads; the houses are connected by numerous wooden bridges spanning the many waterways. *Meppel*△ is 4 miles (6km) east. To *Vollenhove*, for visit to north-east polder, or direct by *Genemuiden*, noted for innumerable haystacks.

Kampen, interesting Hanseatic town on River *Ijssel*, entered by one of town's three fine old gateways. Old Town Hall (1350), the New Tower (*Nieuwe Toren*) seventeenth century; *Bovenkerk*, fourteenth century. *Urk*, a former island, now part of north-east polder is nearby and retains evidence of one-time isolation, including picturesque local costume.

Zwolle, capital of *Overijssel* Province, surrounded by gardens and waterways, previously the ramparts and moats. The *Sassenpoort* (gateway) dating from 1408, is only part of ramparts still standing. *Grote Kerk*, fifteenth century, by *Grote Markt*, has fine organ. Fifteenth century Town Hall; *Onze Lieve Vrouwekerk* (Church of Our Lady) with 250ft (70m) fifteenth-century tower known as the *Peperbus* (pepperbox); houses in *Diezerstraat*: many fine buildings in modern style. *Oldebroek* △ 8 miles (13km) south-westwards.

Elburg, town near *Ijsselmeer* and *East Flevoland* polder; sixteenth-century fortifications, fine gateway and thirteenth-century church, small harbour. Return inland across a pleasant landscape of moorland and woods to *Emst*. Take *Apeldoorn* road to *Cannenburg* castle and on to seventeenth-century royal palace *Het Loo* (now Orange-Nassau museum), in beautiful grounds just before *Apeldoorn*.

Apeldoorn△, popular resort set in wooded countryside. *Berg en Bos* is area of natural woodland famed for its flower gardens and ponds; open-air swimming pool in beautiful setting adjoining this park.

South through wooded country to *Hoenderloo*, to **Hoge Veluwe National Park**, 22sq miles (57sq km) of unspoilt countryside between *Apeldoorn* and *Arnhem* where deer, moufflon and wild boar roam at liberty in their natural habitat. *Kröller-Müller Museum*, modern building in park, housing paintings, including many by Vincent van Gogh, costly furniture, fine sculpture and rare porcelain. *Doorwerth* △, with its thirteenth-century castle is nearby.

Arnhem△, on *Lower Rhine*, scene of desperate fighting after the airborne landing of September 1944. The *Airborne Museum* at *Hartenstein* and the cemetery and monument are at *Oosterbeek* to the west. City Hall, sixteenth-century Renaissance palace, known as *Duivelshuis* because of devilish figures carved on front; sixteenth-century gateway by the *Grote Markt*; *Provinciehuis* near the *Rhine* bridge; Aquarium of the Moorland Reclamation Society, *Zijpen-daalseweg,* a wonderful collection of Dutch fresh water and tropical fish. *Bronbeek* Museum: East Indian specimens, and live exhibition of silk worm cultivation.

EXCURSIONS: (a) north (No 3 bus, 15 minutes) to **Open-Air Museum**, unique collection of Dutch houses and costumes, farmsteads, windmills, and old-time arts and crafts from every province. (b) *Sonsbeek, Zijpendaal* and *Rozendaal* Parks.

Leave *Arnhem* by *Nijmegen* road, south through rolling *Betuwe* countryside, famous for its blossom-laden orchards in spring.

Nijmegen, frontier stronghold since Roman times; see the *Valkhof,* ruined castle with chapel built by Charlemagne; Renaissance Town Hall with Gobelin tapestries; fourteenth-century Gothic *Grote Kerk*; seventeenth-century Weigh House in Market Place. View into Germany from the heights of the town.

Continue by *'s-Hertogenbosch* road, via *OyerasseltΔ* and cross River *Maas* to *Grave*. Fork left through *Uden* and *Veghel* to *St Oedenrode*, scene of a guild festival, and straight on, across the the *Eindhoven-'s-Hertogenbosch* main road to *Oirschot*. Branch left to *Hilvarenbeek*, turning right again for *Tilburg*, industrial town, textile factories, but has palatial town hall.

On through wooded countryside of *Brabant* to **Breda**, from which Charles II returned to England at Restoration, 1660. *Begÿnhof*, founded 1270 by Flemish sisters of mercy; Renaissance castle, now occupied by Royal Netherlands Academy; *Grote Kerk* thirteenth-century Gothic; admirable town planning in factory and residential districts on outskirts; lovely countryside all around. *ChaamΔ* is nearby.

Road continues across flat heath and woodland via *Roosendaal* to *Bergen-op-ZoomΔ*, former flourishing seaport on the *Scheldt* estuary; Town Hall, four-teenth-century Gothic *Grote Kerk*, from tower of which Antwerp can be seen; sixteenth-century *Markiezenhof* and medieval gateways of *Gevangenpoort* and *Wouwpoort*. Religious procession on 15 August.

Southwards from *Bergen-op-Zoom* and into province of *Zeeland*, through sand-dunes for about 4 miles (6km) then westwards to *Goes* where many local costumes can be seen at the Tuesday market; sixteenth-century church and part of fifteenth-century Town Hall. Boat from *Katseveer,* north-west of *Goes*, to *Zierikzee* on *Duiveland* Island; 199ft (60m) tower of *Grote Kerk*, visible from far off, begun in 1454, never completed.

Fourteen miles (22km) west of *Goes* is *MiddelburgΔ*, chief town of *Zeeland* in centre of interesting island of *Walcheren*, with ornate fifteenth-century town hall, twelfth-century abbey and adjoining *Nieuwe Kerk* with 280ft (85m) tower affording wide views. Circuit of island by bus from *Middelburg* goes via *Veere*, where former trade with Scotland is shown by sixteenth-century *Scotse Huizen*; pretty road westwards *via DomburgΔ* to Netherlands' most westerly town of

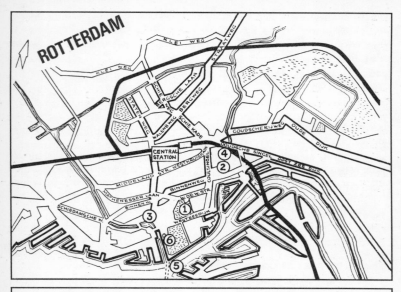

1 Boymans Museum. 2 Post Office. 3 youth hostel on Rochussenstraat.
4 Town Hall. 5 Maas Tunnel. 6 Euromast

Westkapelle and then along north shore of *Scheldt* estuary with views of ocean liners on their way to and from *Antwerp*; road then turns inland back to *Middelburg. Vlissingen*, summer resort and port, but quiet and picturesque.

Return to *Zierikzee* and on north-east to *Willemstad*, thence due north to *Rotterdam.*

Rotterdam△, second city of Netherlands, and largest port in the world. From *Willemsplein* a most interesting cruise of $1^1/_2$ hours round the docks. See the *Boymans Museum*, old masters, modern art and sculpture; the *Maas Tunnel* (3,525ft, 1,000m long) which links the two sections of the city; *Blijdorp Zoo* on northern edge of the city is most modern in world; *Delfshaven*, where the Pilgrim Fathers embarked for Plymouth and America. Zadkine statue commemorates wartime devastation of city, almost completely rebuilt in impressive style of contemporary Dutch architecture. 'Euromast', 600ft (183m) look-out tower, with café-restaurant at 341ft (104m), constructed 1960, made higher in 1979. Nine miles (14km) of underground railway now ease traffic and sightseeing.

Vlaardingen, old fishing port, lies 6 miles (10km) westwards, then 12 miles (19km) north to **Delft**, famed for its china, a delightful little town with tree-lined canals and handsome seventeenth-century houses. *Nieuwe Kerk* (fifteenth-century), where the Dutch kings are buried; *Oude Kerk* (thirteenth-century); *Prinsenhof*, where the nation's founding father, Prince William of Orange, was murdered in 1584 (now a museum); Town Hall and *Oostpoort*.

On for 5 miles (8km) to **The Hague**Δ (*Den Haag* or '*s-Gravenhage*), the seat of government and foreign embassies, a well-planned city with many fine buildings, parks, royal palaces and boulevards. By the *Hofvijver*, an oblong lake in the centre of the city, is the *Mauritshuis* Art Gallery, magnificent collection of paintings by Dutch old masters. Near the *Mauritshuis* is the *Binnenhof* (old palace of Counts of Holland, now the seat of Parliament), surrounding thirteenth-century *Ridderzaal* (Knights' Hall). The *Gevangenpoort*, sixteenth-century prison gate, open daily, is near large square known as *Buitenhof*, where is City Hall, and beyond it the fourteenth- and fifteenth-century Gothic *Grote Kerk* (good view from tower).

In the north of the town is the Peace Palace, with its beautiful gardens, founded by Carnegie and built 1907-13. All nations contributed large sums towards furnishing and equipping it. Municipal Museum, *41 Stadhouderslaan*; Mesdag Panorama, *65b Zeestraat*; Postal Museum, *82 Zeestraat; Bosch* Park, *Madurodam*, a miniature town, scale models, showing development through a thousand years.

Continue north-easterly for 10 miles (16km) to **Leiden**, university town with many lovely old houses, almshouses and public buildings, birthplace of Rembrandt, Jan Steen and other great Dutch painters. In town centre is the *Burcht* (castle); to south-east is sixteenth-century *Hooglandsekerk*; to west across *New Rhine*, are the Fish and Eel markets and seventh-century Weigh House and Butter-market, and the Gothic *Pieterskerk*. Across the *Rapenburger* lies the University, housed in a fifteenth-century convent. *Noordwijk* Δ is 8 miles (13km) to north-west.

Take the road north-west through *Voorhout* to *Lisse* and **Keukenhof**, a former country house, whose grounds are given over to displays of Dutch bulbs, best seen in April or early May. Flower processions between *Sassenheim, Lisse* and *Hillegom* usually take place in second half of April, always on a Saturday.

Continue through *Vogelenzang* to **Haarlem**Δ, in the midst of bulbfields; market square has fine examples of medieval and Renaissance architecture. Many museums, especially Franz Hals which has admirable collection of his portraits. Sixteenth-century *Grote Kerk* has famous organ of 5,000 pipes, with frequent recitals.

A straight road leads back to *Amsterdam*, 12 miles (19km) to the east, but the road via *Bloemendaal* to *Spaarndam* and thence to *Halfweg* is preferable. At *Spaarndam* is small monument inspired by symbolic story of the little boy, Hans Brinker, who held his finger in the dyke and saved the whole district from destruction by flood.

R2 Amsterdam — Aachen via Eindhoven (140 miles, 225km)

This route crosses the central Netherlands from north to south and includes the hill-country of *Limburg* province.

Leave *Amsterdam* by road skirting *Ijsselmeer* in south-east direction. *Muiden*, small port; *Muiderslot* castle, on coast of former *Zuider Zee* near *Weesp*, is ancient stronghold with many historical associations; *Bussum*, town on edge of the *Gooi*; a pleasantly-wooded region. **Hilversum**, an elegant town, with parks and gardens and notable for attractive modern architecture; see Dudok's Town Hall; *Loosdrecht* lakes are nearby. *Hilversum* is the Dutch broadcasting centre.

Continue south-east passing the Royal Palace at *Soestdijk*, residence of the Queen, to *Soest*Δ and to **Amersfoort**. *Koppelpoort* (fourteenth century) across River *Eem* is one of fine gateways; fifteenth-century tower of Our Lady and ancient houses, '*Muurhuizen*', within former town wall. Thence across wooded heathland to **Utrecht**, seat of cardinal-archbishop; an old town with two canals cut deeply below the houses. Cathedral Tower fourteenth century (370ft, 112m, high) and remaining portions of Gothic cathedral (the nave having been destroyed by a hurricane); Central Municipal Museum (history and art), Gold and Silver Museum and Old Dutch Clocks Museum. *Bunnik* Δ is 3 miles, 5km south-east of town.

South of *Utrecht* road crosses flat plain between Rivers *Lek* and *Waal* (twin branches of *Rhine*) and *Maas*, to '*s Hertogenbosch* (*Bois-le-Duc*), pleasant town with magnificent Gothic cathedral and seventeenth-century town hall.

Southwards again for 20 miles (32km) to *Eindhoven*, dominated by huge Philips electrical works and DAF motor-car factory. *Valkenswaard*Δ, 3 miles (5km) due south.

South-east, through attractive woods and heather country via *Beegden* into province of *Limburg* to *Sittard*Δ. Southern *Limburg* is an area for lovers of wilder country, with ruined castles. Explore, in particular, valley of River *Geul*, leading to *Valkenburg*, popular tourist centre (grottoes). *Maastricht*Δ, the provincial capital and old fortress town, has many fine churches including *St Servatius*, the oldest in the Netherlands.

German frontier is reached at *Vaals* and *Aachen* is $2^1/_2$ miles (6km) beyond.

NORWAY

Geographical Outline

The Norwegian saying, 'the sea unites but the land divides', reflects the nature of this country which stretches 1,100 miles (1,770km) from the North Cape, 320 miles (515km) north of the Arctic Circle, to the latitude of northern Scotland. It lies on the north-west edge of Europe and varies in breadth from 270 miles (435km) in the south to 4 miles (6km) near *Narvik*.

Land

Norwegian scenery may be imagined as a gigantic mass of rock, whose whole surface has been worked over by a small sharp tool. At a very early period the area north and west of a line from *Stavanger* to *Veranger* was subjected to tremendous mountain building movements which folded and buckled the Palaeozoic rocks into mountain ranges running north-east and south-west, extending into what eventually became the Scottish highlands. Then followed a long period when the mountains were gradually worn down by weathering and running water to a fraction of their original height. Except for a few peaks of more resistant rock, the land was reduced to a series of high plateaux. Partial subsidence of some ranges produced the line of skerries and islands which protect the coastal waters and fjords from storms.

During the comparatively recent glacial period, a thick ice sheet covered Scandinavia and a new surface was imposed on the basic pattern. Now the ice sheet has melted, revealing the characteristic marks of a glaciated region; steep sided valleys with U-shaped cross-sections, bare rock surfaces often polished and scored with grooves, side valleys entering main valleys high above the main valley floor so that streams descend in waterfalls — a source of cheap electric power. Valleys are often blocked by heaps of detritus which dam up the waters into long narrow lakes; the area of these lakes is greater than that of the cultivable land. The deepest glacial valleys become fjords, making a convenient means of reaching the interior of the country where land travel is often difficult. The depth

of the fjords is approximately equal to the height of the surrounding mountains. The coast-line has the astounding length of 21,000 miles (33,800km).

Climate

In west Norway the climate is quite temperate, but tends to be moist. The country lies on the continental shelf, that part of Europe now submerged under shallow seas; the warm surface waters of the Atlantic increase the temperature throughout the year and harbours as far north as *Hammerfest* are ice-free in winter. The long hours of daylight help to raise the average summer temperature. Norway lies in the track of prevailing south-west winds, bringing moisture at all seasons; rain in summer, snow in winter. Towards the eastern border the climate becomes drier and the annual range of temperature greater.

Plants and Animals

In the south, or at low altitudes, forests of spruce and fir containing some deciduous trees are found. As one moves north, or reaches higher levels, these gradually disappear to be replaced by pine and birch forests, thickets of willow and dwarf birch; then open moors covered with mosses and lichens.

Flowering herbaceous plants belonging to continental Europe are found in the south-east; many berry-bearing plants occur in the forests; Arctic perennials, together with heaths and saxifrages, are found on the highest mountains if there is sufficient soil, as well as in the north.

Similarly, Arctic animals — polar hare, polar fox, wolverine, lemming and reindeer — are found in the north and also above the conifer line among the mountains. There are elk and roe deer in the forests of east Norway, red deer on the west coast. The bear, lynx and wolf, once numerous, are now rare, though the wolf is found from the *Røros* district northwards into *Finnmark*.

Many birds native to Norway are also known in Britain, while many that breed in Norway visit Britain as winter migrants. The moors shelter ptarmigan and capercaillie, and the coasts and islands of the north are the home of ducks and gulls valuable for their feathers or their eggs.

The People

Population

One reason why Norway is an excellent country for the visitor is that it has only about four million inhabitants. *Oslo*, with about 470,000 inhabitants, is the largest city, followed by *Bergen* (212,000), *Trondheim* (135,000) and *Stavanger* (90,000).

Language

Norway has two official languages which, though members of the same language family, differ in pronunciation, grammer and vocabulary.

Bokmål (formerly called *Riksmål*) derives from the Norwegianised Danish used by the educated classes. This is the language of Wergeland, Ibsen, Bjørnson and Sigrid Undset.

Nynorsk (formerly called *Landsmål*) builds directly on the village dialects. It developed rapidly as a medium for depicting country life, but was not so quickly accepted as the legal, artistic and social equal of *Bokmål*. It was used by Vinje, Garborg and Dunn.

Samisk, the language spoken by the Lapps of northern Norway, also has official status.

The long struggle between the supporters of *Bokmål* and *Nynorsk* has ended in a compromise. The local council decides which shall be the local official language, used on road signs, public notices and in schools. About one third of the children are educated in *Nynorsk*. A plan for gradually fusing the two into a single national language has been started but will take generations to complete. The latest spelling is wholly phonetic: 'chauffeur' is *sjafør* and 'all right' is *ålreit*.

However, guidebooks have an English key: in the towns and tourist centres most people speak English and many country people also speak it.

Religion

Almost the entire population belongs to the Evangelical-Lutheran State Church. There are eight dioceses and about a thousand parishes, but many of these have to share a minister so that a clergyman's work in thinly populated areas may be very difficult.

In matters of belief, the Church preserves its independence. In 1942, for example, practically all the ministers resigned simultaneously rather than obey Nazi orders. The Church enters into political life and there is a Christian People's Party in the *Storting*.

History

During the Viking age, Norway developed as a nation and colonial power under vigorous leaders. By 885 the country was united under one king, Harold Fairhair. Settlements were made in the Faroes, Orkneys, Shetlands, the Hebrides, Man, Ireland, northern Scotland, northern England and Iceland. Christianity was firmly established in the reign of Olaf Haroldson (1015-30), the St Olaf of tradition. His brother, Harold Hardrada, aimed to conquer England but was killed at Stamford Bridge in 1066 a few weeks before the Norman invasion.

Norway itself developed a strong central government on the Norman model and, under Magnus VI (1263-80), reached the zenith of its medieval achievements as the first European country to have a national code of law.

Decline came with the increasing influence of Denmark, especially after the Union of Kalmar in 1397 and with loss of trade to the Hansa monopolists. For four centuries control lay with Danish administrators; the Danish language became compulsory in churches and later in schools; links with the colonies were weakened and eventually broken.

Recovery began with the discovery of deposits of iron ore and the development of an export trade in timber. Norwegian merchants benefitted when, in 1560, the Hansa monopoly was abolished. Under the absolutist regime of Christian IV (1588-1648), both countries had nominally equal status as twin kingdoms.

A movement for self-assertion began late in the eighteenth century. Its form and the nature of its demands are of interest as an example of emergent nationalism. It looked with pride to early Norwegian history and across the sea to English views of liberty and to those of revolutionary France. It founded a society of sciences and letters, called for a national university and a national bank, found ways of circumventing the Danish mercantile system, encouraged the growth of a nation-wide economic community and in 1810 founded a society to unite the country's liberal forces.

Matters came to a head in 1814, when on the ceding of Norway to the king of Sweden, he claimed the Crown by right of inheritance. The people's resistance was decisive and a national assembly, meeting at *Eidsvoll*, adopted a free constitution providing for a limited monarchy, a one-chamber parliament, liberty of religion and freedom of the press. On these terms the king was accepted and Norway was independent except for foreign policy and the king's right to appoint a governor. Both caused friction. The latter right was abolished in 1873. Subservience in foreign policy became ever more irksome. Sweden, with greater natural resources, could be comparatively self-contained; Norwegian prosperity depended on international connections for the growth of her great merchant fleet and of distant enterprises such as Antarctic whaling.

The union with Sweden ended in 1905 and Haakon VII was elected king by popular vote. He was succeeded in 1956 by the Crown Prince, now King Olav V. Norway has become an outstanding example of a sparsely populated country, with difficult natural conditions, achieving a remarkably high standard of living.

Government

The system of democratic government is similar to that in Britain. Executive power is nominally vested in the king, who governs through a cabinet (the *Statsråd*) chosen from the leaders of the majority in Parliament (the *Storting*). The *Storting* has, however, only one chamber, though for some purposes it divides into two houses, the *Oldesting* (112 members) and *Lagting* (38 members). Of its 150 members, elected for four years by a system of proportional representation, two-thirds must come from country districts.

Resources

Norway is the world's largest producer of sulphur pyrites and is one of the few countries with molybdenum. Valuable reserves of North Sea oil are drilled offshore, producing 40 million tons annually and employing 32,000 people in the industry, otherwise mineral resources are meagre. Her fisheries are the largest in the world, forestry is important, and she leads Europe in the use of water-power.

Only about 3 per cent of the land is cultivated, mainly in valley-bottoms and around the fjords, and the Norwegian peasant farmer's life is a hard one. In mountain districts the cattle are taken up in summer to the high pastures by the women and children, who live in isolated *saeter* (mountain farms) while the men stay behind to look after the crops in the valleys.

Industry and agriculture each support about 30 per cent of the population. Nearly a tenth is engaged in shipping, about 7 per cent in fishing and whaling, and commerce supports rather more, for Norway has the third largest merchant fleet in the world.

Customs

Easter, Ascension, Whitsun and Christmas are all observed and other public holidays include New Year's Day, Labour Day, and Constitution Day (17 May). The main Christmas celebrations are held on Christmas Eve, though Christmas tree parties go on for some time. The great national holiday, 17 May, is marked in every town by decorations, flags and a children's procession. People celebrate Midsummer with bonfires and dancing. Private parties, family gatherings and especially weddings are always an excuse for great celebrations. A real country wedding lasts three days.

With their long tradition of country hospitality, Norwegians are excellent hosts, overflowing with friendliness and with a sound sense of humour. They enjoy explaining their country to foreigners. They are lovers of the open air and of many kinds of sports.

Travellers a century ago admired the scenery more than the people. Modern Norway, however, has a high standard of living; her authors, musicians, statesmen and explorers have won international fame. In their efforts to improve their country, Norwegians willingly spend public money on social services, new public buildings, theatre subsidies, university research, or temperance propaganda. Profits from the government football pools and the wine monopoly are used for some of these purposes.

Food and Drink

Breakfast consists of coffee and *smørbrød* (an open sandwich). Several kinds of bread and six or more coverings may be available at breakfast. Many Norwegians, particularly in the towns, make no break for lunch but eat *smørbrød* — a national 'packed lunch' — at the office or the factory. Work ends about 4pm and the day's big meal, *middag*, follows at once. The final evening snack will be more smørbrød.

Norwegians get good fish and cook it well. Tinned fish, meat-paste and jam appear on *smørbrød*, as do various kinds of cheese including the special brown goat's-milk *gjetost*.

As a rule, coffee is strong and tea is weak. Milk, fruit juice (*saft*) and a non-alcoholic beer (*vørterøl*) are served everywhere, but the sale of stronger beers can be prohibited by the local council.

Culture

Architecture

The cold winters have always forced Norwegians to build substantial, warm houses. Timber is the traditional material, and the earliest houses were usually simple log cabins, with a fire in the centre. Each district developed a different style. From about 1600, stone flues, and later iron stoves, altered the plan of the rooms. Windows were introduced, and partitions divided the single room. The older houses with low walls and turf roofs often remained in use as barns. Such farms are still common.

Wood-carvings often decorated beams and doorposts in these houses. The best carvings, however, are found on the remaining Viking stave churches, the finest old buildings in Norway.

Older town houses and contemporary suburban houses are also of wood, usually timber frame type of construction. Many pleasing modern designs can be found, but fires have ravaged so many towns that old buildings are rare.

The larger modern buildings are of reinforced concrete or brick. They follow general European trends, but are bold in character and show a care for detail worth further study. Churches are particularly noticeable, for many are rebuilt in post-war design, replacing those destroyed by the Nazis.

Painting and Sculpture

Little but decorative art was produced before the nineteenth century. Wood and stone carving, however, were very highly developed during the Viking and Danish periods, and decorative painting was also widespread.

The twentieth century is dominated by Edvard Munch (1863-1944). Many of his best works are in the *Oslo* National Gallery and the frescoes in the University *Aula* are also his.

Frescoes decorate many of *Oslo's* modern buildings. See especially the City Hall. Many were painted by disciples of Matisse, such as Revold, Per Krogh, Sørensen.

Sculpture did not achieve national importance until *Vigeland* (1869-1943). His work dominates all Norwegian sculpture. Besides the *Frogner Park* plan, he produced many of the memorial statues in *Oslo*. The work of later sculptors can be seen on the restoration of *Trondheim* cathedral and on the *Oslo Rådhus*.

Museums

There are many local historical museums, but, except in *Oslo* and *Bergen*, few general or scientific museums. *Bergen*, however, has a fishery and an industrial art museum, while the university now controls the famous science museums.

Some of *Oslo's* fifteen museums will chiefly attract specialists, though others will interest everyone. There are three general historical museums; the City Museum in *Frogner Park* and *Akerhus* fortress by the harbour cover *Oslo's* history, while there are Viking and medieval exhibits in the university's historical collections.

The theatres have their special museum and there is a ski museum at *Holmenkollen*. Nansen's *Fram*, the Kon-tiki raft *Ra II* at *Bygdøy*, and Amundsen's home at *Svartskøg*, commemorate Norway's great explorers. Three Viking ships and the Norwegian Maritime Museum are also at *Bygdøy*.

In most counties there is an open-air folk-museum, and every visitor ought to see one. The most famous are at *Bygdøy*, near *Oslo*, and '*Old Bergen*', a bus trip away from Bergen city centre. The old Norwegian way of life can be studied not only in furniture, tools and clothes, but in houses and complete farms, reassembled in the museums, where guides wearing *bunad* (national costume) show visitors around.

Music

Of native instruments, the Hardanger fiddle (*Hardingfele*), which has four sympathetic drone strings, as well as the normal strings, had a strong influence on the melody and an even stronger one on the harmony of Norwegian music. The cultural revival of the 1840s was marked in music by the collection and publication of traditional ballads and dance airs.

Greig is the greatest Norwegian composer. His songs, piano pieces and orchestral works are well known everywhere. His contemporary, Svendsen, is Norway's greatest symphonic composer. Of modern composers only two are well known outside Norway — Halvorsen, a theatre composer, much of whose work is incidental music, and Sinding who is known for his symphonies and much excellent chamber music.

There are few orchestras and only two concert halls, the *Grieg Hall* in *Bergen* (1976) and the *Oslo Concert Hall* (1977).

National Dances

There is a living folk-dance tradition though many dances were only revived earlier this century. Two kinds are practised: song-dances (*folkeviseleik*) and music dances. In the song-dances old ballads and newer songs are given dramatic interpretation in ring-dances like those popular in medieval Norway. Such dances still flourish in the *Faroes*, where the steps were rediscovered.

The typical traditional music dances, the solo *Halling*, and couple-dances like the *Springar* and *Gangar* are extremely difficult, and give the man chance to demonstrate his prowess; there are also easier couple-dances, set, and longways dances. They are danced to a fiddle, either the violin or the *Hardingfele*.

National Costumes

Most parts of Norway preserve their special traditional dress or *bunad* and within each district there are many local variations, with costumes for everyday use and special occasions. Local patterns may derive from seventeenth-century or even Renaissance costume, but the different styles, graceful for women, gallant for men, have evolved in the home: the cloth is always hand-woven and home-dyed.

A girl's festival *bunad*, with its white blouse and apron, embroidered skirt and silver brooches, is a precious heirloom. Though everyday *bunad* is now rarely used, many girls, especially those from country homes, always wear the festival *bunad* on formal occasions or public holidays. A national committee ensures that traditional standards are maintained.

Literature

Norway shares with Iceland the pre-Christian *Eddaic* poems (eighth to ninth centuries) on historical and mythological themes, and the scaldic verse which spanned the transition (ninth to tenth centuries) from pagan to Christian themes. In prose, also, the early Icelandic sagas, including the *Heimskringla*, a history of the kings of Norway, are Norwegian in inspiration.

In the nineteenth century, following the attainment of independence, Norway again produced writers of international significance. Wergeland (1808-45) is the poet of freedom, both in political ideas and in his claim for stylistic freedom for the poet. Bjørnson (1832-1910) was a powerful advocate of emancipation of the European peoples through democracy and education, and a great representative Norwegian. His comtemporary, Ibsen, (1828-1906), probes individual personality as well as social problems. He is the dramatist of self-realization. In his psychological analysis, and technically as a master of stagecraft, his influence on the theatre has been profound.

Among more recent writers Sigrid Undset should be mentioned; her novels, which secured for her a Nobel Prize, are available in translation.

Theatres

The theatre is a town institution and even today Norway has only a few, many of them dependent on public funds. All have permanent companies, and often produce, in translation, foreign works.

The *National Theatre* in the centre of *Oslo*, which produces *Bokmål* plays, is Norway's biggest playhouse, and has a reputation for fine, sincere acting. *Det Norske Teatret*, the *Nynorsk* theatre nearby, was established to show that *Nynorsk* could rival *Bokmål* in this field also. Both are now subsidised.

In *Bergen*, the home of the first nationalist theatre, where Ibsen worked in the 1850s, *Den Nationale Scene* sets a high standard and has a wide repertoire. The *Rogaland Theatre* in *Stavanger* and *Tröndelag Theatre* in *Trondheim* also have permanent companies.

Touring Information

Hostellers are Welcome

In Norway the traveller of modest means, with a rucksack or bicycle is always welcome.

Access

Norway Line ply between Newcastle and *Bergen*; summer only. Fred Olsen Lines run a weekly service Newcastle/*Bergen* and Newcastle/*Oslo*, via *Kristiansand* and *Hirtshals* (Denmark).

There is a variety of cheaper air fares London/*Bergen* and Newcastle/*Bergen*, all with various booking restrictions.

Transport

The main land routes start from *Oslo, Bergen* and *Stavanger*. Buses serve most major routes in summer. If not too crowded they will carry bicycles and luggage.

The mountainous nature of the country made railway building extremely expensive and most lines keep to the valleys or coast except the celebrated *Oslo-Bergen* railway (see **R2** and **R6**) which climbs over the mountains between east and west. Rolling stock is modern and comfortable; long distance trains, except a few diesel expresses, make 10-minute halts at certain stations, allowing passengers time to obtain coffee at the buffets.

Boats are the oldest and still best means of transport in coastal districts, and the best way of seeing much of Norway's finest scenery. They are also vital links in the country's economic life, and on a boat journey one learns a great deal about Norwegian life. In many villages the arrival of the boat, with post, cargo and passengers, is an important event. The boats run in sheltered water between the islands and the mainland on almost all routes. Fares are low by comparison with buses and trains.

Timetable

A useful publication for planning a tour is the Norwegian Tourist Board's *Tourist Timetables*, distributed free to members of the public; a selective timetable of trains, boats, aircraft, buses and ferries operating a regular service. Such information is particularly important in a country of big distances where transport services are infrequent and the traveller may run the risk of missing the only bus or ferry connection of the morning or afternoon; hence it is prudent to check, and recheck, information from tourist offices.

Money

The unit of currency is the *krone*, which is divided into 100 *øre*. There are coins of 5, 10, 25 and 50 *øre*, 1 *krone* and 5 *kroner*, and notes of 10, 50, 100, 500, and 1,000 *kroner*.

Prices

Food is rather expensive, but the quality, especially in restaurants, is good. Clothing and other manufactured articles are also expensive and there are no bargain souvenirs to be had.

Clothing

Although ordinary clothing is sufficient in summer, in the mountains it is colder and a sweater, wind-proof jacket, thick socks and a scarf are necessary.

Boots are essential for walking in the mountains; waterproofs and sou'wester are often worn. Towards the end of the season an extra sweater for the evening is advisable.

Women are advised to wear slacks, or shorts for cycling, and nowhere is there any objection to this.

Slacks and long-sleeved shirts should be worn in the evenings as a protection against *mygg* and *knott* (mosquitos and gnats). Both are troublesome on summer evenings all over Norway and are a menace in the north and in *Finnmark*, particularly during July.

Restaurants

There are restaurants in most villages, but some are often for the short summer season only. It can be difficult to find anywhere else to eat, even in the fjord country, because hotel restaurants are seldom open to non-residents. Reasonably priced food is often indicated by *Nynorsk* names like *Kaffi* and *Stova*. *Restaurant* will be more expensive, and *Turist* very expensive. Service is often slow, and a lunch bar or take-away (*gatekjøkken*) is often best for a quick meal in towns. The *kafeteria* found in large stores will close at the same time as the store, ie 4pm.

Fish is cheap and always excellently cooked, but fishcakes (*fiskekaker*) are not to everyone's taste; sausages are plentiful and good. *Varme pølser* (hot sausages) are often sold in the street.

Restaurants always supply tea, coffee, milk, fruit juice and, unless they are *avhold* (temperance) cafés, beer as well.

Maps

The Norwegian Ordnance Survey (Norges Geografiske Oppmåling) publish sheets covering the *Bergen-Hardanger* area on a scale of 1:100,000, the *Jotunheimen* mountains on a scale of 1:50,000 and the *Jostedalsbreen* and *Hardangervidda*. An excellent series of general maps on a scale of 1:325,000/1:400,000 covering all Norway on five sheets is published by Cappelen.

Norwegian maps are confusing because the same place may appear under different names on different maps and an unimportant place (from the point of view of communications) may appear in larger type than a more important place, particularly in the fjord country.

Place Names

Many natural features can be recognised on the map with the aid of a slight knowledge of the meaning of Norwegian place names. Here is a list of some of them with the *Nynorsk* forms in brackets.

botn	bottom (of valley)	*nes*	headland
bre	glacier	*nord*	north
by	town	*saeter (støl, stul)*	mountain farm
bygd	village	*sjø*	sea, lake
dal	valley	*steinbrott*	quarry
elv (Å)	river	*sund*	sound, channel
fjell	mountain	*syd (sør)*	south
fjellstue	mountain hut	*tind*	peak
fotsti	footpath	*tjern (tjørn)*	tarn
foss	waterfall	*ur*	scree, boulders
gate	street	*vatn, vann*	lake (small)
gård (gard)	farm	*vest*	west
hei	moor, heath	*vidd (a)*	mountain plateau
hytte	hut (cottage size)	*vik (våg)*	inlet, creek
jøkul	glacier	*ost (aust)*	east
leirplass	camping site	*øy*	island

Tourist Huts

The mountainous plateau in the centre of Norway offer walkers and mountaineers unrivalled opportunites. The Norwegian YHA caters primarily for tourists using the roads, but there are some hostels in the mountains which serve as starting points. Mountain tourist huts, equipped not unlike hostels, fill the gaps. Some are privately run, and are expensive, but many are owned by the Norwegian Mountain Touring Association (DNT) or by local district touring clubs. Membership can be obtained, in person or by post, from Norske Turistforening, Stortingsgate 28, Oslo 1.

The association has also marked out the routes between the huts with cairns and supplies sketch maps of each district, which give the number of hours needed for each route. These schedules make no allowance for loitering.

The main area served by the district clubs are *Jotunheimen* with *Jostedalsbreen*, the *Hardangervidda*, *Rondane* and *Trollheimen*.

Mountaineering

British mountaineering expeditions, at the turn of the century, discovered that Norway was a mountaineer's paradise; there are still many unclimbed peaks, walls and ridges.

Among the great *Jotunheimen* mountains the best climbing, for novices and experts, is found in the *Horungen* group, capped by the *Store Skagastølstind*. North-west lie the *Sunnmøre Alps*, around the *Hjørundfjord*. *Oye*, on the *Norangsfjord* (an arm of the *Hjørundfjord*) is the best climbing area. In *Romsdal* there cannot be many unclimbed routes but the mountains are fascinating, having taken on fantastic shapes and been given fanciful names. *Andalsnes* is the best centre.

Opportunites for pioneers can still be found in the *Nordmore* mountains, east of *Kristiansund*, and new routes might also be opened-up on the *Trolla* ridge. Among the hundreds of peaks in the *Lofotens*, some remain unclimbed and although climbers here have to take tents, the climate is ideal for camping, and supplies are obtainable everywhere. Some islands can be reached only by rowing boat, but the main ports *Svolvaer*Δ and *Stamsund*Δ are served by the regular coastal steamers.

Skiing

Skis were invented in Norway (in the *Telemark*) and all Norwegians learn to ski at an early age. Foreign visitors are increasingly making their first acquaintance with skis in Norway, where snow conditions are usually excellent from Christmas until late March and tuition and the hire of skis can be inexpensively arranged. Winter daylight is short but Norwegian hostels provide comfortable and pleasant facilities in the evenings.

Motoring and Cycling

Motorists should carry their car registration certificate, insurance certificate, international driving permit, red warning triangle and national identity sticker as well as their own national driving licence; an international green insurance card is recommended, although not compulsory. Motorways are few, toll charges are payable on some of them and on some minor roads in the mountains; river-ferries are free, fjord ferries are not. Speed limits commence at 50km/h (31mph) in built-up areas; on-the-spot fines can be imposed.

Motorists belonging to their own national organisations should enquire of them regarding facilities offered by the NAF and KNA — their Norwegian counterparts.

Roads in the cities and main roads throughout the country are well surfaced; some secondary roads, however, have loose surfaces. Many roads become muddy during the spring thaw, and dusty in summer. Mountain roads are liable to be snowbound from November until late May, but roads at lower levels are open all year round.

The steepness of the hills gave road engineers many problems, but tunnels, spirals and zigzags have lessened the gradients, although a low gear is essential. Norwegian drivers are usually considerate about dipping their headlamps, but less careful about signalling, and give little elbow room. Tunnelled roads are best avoided by cyclists; they are unlit, often pitch-black, and consequently hazardous, even with bicycle lights.

Traffic keeps to the right, and the vehicles approaching from that side have right of way. Cyclists must signal all turns, carry a white front light, white patch and rear reflector. The strict rules about reporting accidents and against driving under the influence of drink apply to cyclists.

Norwegians regret that it is now necessary to carry a cycle-lock.

Canoeing and Sailing

The Norwegian coast, with its thousands of islands and bays, is an ideal place for canoeing and sailing, both of which are popular sports. There are clubs everywhere along the coast from *Trondheim* to the Swedish frontier. There is, however, no large scale hiring of boats.

The coast is well charted and buoyed, but local knowledge, easily obtained on the spot, is helpful and sometimes essential. There are practically no irksome restrictions on camping, bathing, etc, anywhere along the coast.

Inland canoeing is less practicable. There are many beautiful lakes, but at many places the rivers are too rapid for navigation.

Practical Hints

A tour of Norway needs planning. Distances are vast and walkers in particular will need to study the bus, train and ferry timetables. For cyclists it may often mean hard work to average more than 50 miles (80km) a day and the distance between the hostels is often greater than that. The Norwegian YHA discourages hitch-hiking.

Most offices are open until about 4pm and in the summer shops close early. After *middag*, however, it is usual to take a rest, or walk out of doors. Cinemas run non-continuous programmes and the doors are closed when the programme begins, even to ticket holders. Smoking is not allowed in cinemas or theatres.

The Norwegian postal system is efficient. Parcels can be sent in advance to the hostels but they are not delivered. An 'accompanying letter' (*Følgebrev*) is delivered, authorising the addressee to collect the parcel at the post office.

An eiderdown duvet is usually the only covering on a Norwegian bed; it is wise to anchor it with a blanket. All doors in Norway have draught-preventing raised thresholds.

A particular conversational phrase which requires explanation is '*vaer så god*' (literally, 'be so good') often pronounced *vesgoot*. It has innumerable meanings, of which the following are the most important:
'Can I help you?' (used by shop assistants).
'Fares please' (on a bus).
'Here you are, please' (used when handing anything to anyone at a meal or elsewhere).

Touring Routes

These routes are intended to be followed in the summer season of mid-June to early September; outside this period many bus and steamer services cease to operate, or operate only on certain days of the week, and many youth hostels are closed.

Most of the routes are based on *Bergen*, the most popular approach to Norway from the west.

The Western Fjords

For many people, the western fjords, running deep into the heart of the country typify Norwegian scenery, with their towering rock walls, snow capped peaks and magnificent waterfalls.

The great fjords all follow a similar plan. At the mouth the channel winds through a group of islands before entering the fjord itself; the sides at first slope gently but soon become steeper until they tower over a narrow inlet which penetrates the heart of Norway's mountain massif.

Local boats and ferries run within the fjords, while faster boats connect the important villages with the ports at the mouth, or direct with *Bergen*, the capital of the fjord country. Visitors arriving at *Bergen* can thus sail up any fjord and then take the road that climbs into the mountains and over to the valleys beyond. In the reverse direction, the head of any fjord can be reached from *Oslo*, and thence to *Bergen* by boat.

Of the many fjords along the west coast, the most important are *Boknfjord* and *Hardangerfjord* south of *Bergen*, and further north, *Sognefjord, Nordfjord* and *Storfjord,* the last leading to *Geirangerfjord.*

Bergen△

Norway's second city is an important port, industrial and fishing centre. Founded in 1070, it was in the twelfth century the capital of Norway and from the fourteenth to sixteenth a trading port controlled by Hanseatic merchants. All these phases of its history have left their mark and, in spite of fires, *Bergen* has more old buildings than any other town. There are, for example, the twelfth-century Church of St Mary (*Mariakirken*), the thirteenth- century *Håkonshall*, damaged

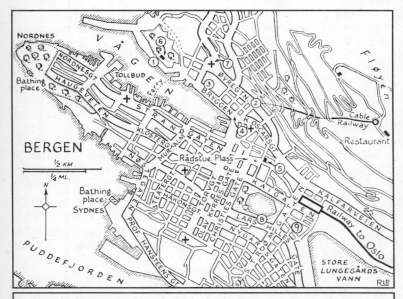

1 Quay for Newcastle ships. 2 Funicular for Fløyen. 3 Hanseatic Museum.
4 Fish Market. 5 Post Office. 6 Hakonshall. 7 Mariakirken. 8 Meyer
Gallery. 9 Bus Station.

during the war, the Hanseatic Museum and the old Quay (*Bryggen*). The thirteenth-century cathedral is less interesting. Adjoining the *Bryggen* is the market place and open-air fish market. Funicular railway station is nearby, and a trip to top of *Fløyen* (1,050ft, 320m) affords magnificent views of city and coast. There is also a cable lift up to Bergen's highest point, *Ulriken* (1,860ft, 567m). The theatre, *Den Nationale Scene*, is centre for annual *Bergen* International Music Festival. The town has its picture gallery (*Billedgalleri*), and there is also the *Rasmus Meyer* collection of paintings (some by Edvard Munch) and furniture.

Due south of the city at *Fjøsanger* stands the *Fantoft* stave church; not far away at *Hop*, is *Trollhaugen*, Grieg's home, and a little hut where he composed, with his furniture and belongings. At *Fana,* further south, is a twelfth-century church, and nearby at *Lyse*, 15 miles (24km) south of *Bergen*, are the ruins of Norway's earliest Cistercian monastery (twelfth century). On the nearby islands, especially at *Askoy* and *Godøysund*, are good bathing beaches which can be reached by motorboat.

The travel section of the Norwegian Youth Hostels Association is to be found at Strandgaten 4.

R1 Bergen to Geilo via the Hardangerfjord (156 miles, 250km)

This route is recommended for the visitor who lacks time to travel farther afield. It gives a glimpse of fjords and of wild semi-mountain country and if completed by a homeward trip on the *Oslo-Bergen* railway from *Geilo* to *Bergen* (see **R2**) glaciers and mountains will be included as well. The through journey by bus and boat requires a minimum of one night's stop en route — but both walker and cyclist can well spend a week on the trip.

By bus from *Bergen* to *Norheimsund* in 2 hours. Winding road, within sight of fjords most of way, through *Samnanger* and up on to the *Kvamskogen* plateau. From *Kvamskogen* easy climb to summit of *Tveitakvitingen* (4,200ft, 1,280m, magnificent view over *Hardanger*); good walking country. Road descends steeply, with many tunnels and fine views, to *Norheimsund* on *Hardangerfjord*.

The *Hardangerfjord* is about 100 miles (160km) long and flanked by mountains rising to 5,000ft (1,500m) at some points, but because of its greater width it lacks the canyon-like appearance of some of the more northerly fjords. It is seen at its best in May, when the fruit trees are in bloom. Local costume is still worn on special occasions, and *Hardanger* embroidery is famous.

At *Norheimsund* a steamer connects with the bus, travelling up the fjord to *Lofthus* in 2 hours, glimpses of *Folgefonn* glacier to south.

R1 (i) Northeimsund to Kvanndal by bus (alternative to main road) via *Oystese*, good beach, *Fyksesund* suspension bridge and hydro-electric station at *Alvik*. From *Kvanndal*, ferry to *Kinsarvik* on main road *Lofthus-Geilo*.

Lofthus is tourist centre for western part of *Hardangervidda* and for impressive

Sørfjord (see **R4**). Buses leave *Lofthus* (change at *Kinsarvik*) for *Geilo*, 5 hour journey. At *Eidfjord* road leaves fjord and begins steep ascent onto *Hardanger-vidda* (rise of more than 4,000ft in about 30 miles, or 1,200m in 50km) by way of wild *Måbø* valley; on left, 26 miles (16km), from *Eidfjord*, the *Vøringfoss* is one of finest waterfalls in Norway, 530ft (162m) high; best view from *Fossli* hotel, but also footpath from road to foot of fall. On to the *Dyranut* pass (4,070ft, 1,241m) and mid-way across the *Hardangervidda,* a high plateau about 60 miles (100km) by 40 miles (65km), admirable walking country, practically uninhabited, intersected by many lakes and tarns; it is a mixture of bare rock with snow lying on the higher points, coarse moorland with bilberry and occasional patches of lush grass with reindeer herds, many tourist huts, linked by paths.

Beyond the *Dyranut* pass the road reaches the small *Skiftesjø* lake, followed by a series of larger lakes. At *Haugastøl*, 43 miles (70km) from the *Har-dangerfjord*, the road meets the *Bergen-Oslo* railway (see **R2**); on Lake *Ustevann* lies *Ustaoset*, much-frequented ski-centre, with the *Hallingskarv* mountain range behind it. This is the head of the *Hallingdal* valley, and from here the barren plateau landscape gives place to trees and meadows.

On for 156 miles (250km) to **Geilo**Δ, pleasant summer and winter-sports resort, junction of roads to *Numedal* and *Hallingdal*. For route from *Oslo* to *Geilo* see **R6**.

R2 Bergen to Geilo by the Bergen — Oslo Railway (148 miles, 238km)

This is the most attractive portion of the famous railway line. The journey to *Geilo* takes 4 hours, but express trains take little more than 3 hours. There is no road on the central section of this route, and for many villages the train provides the only communication with the outside world. The railway, completed in 1909, is an amazing piece of engineering, no less than 45 miles (72km) out of a total of 305 miles (491km) being taken up by tunnels or snow shelters. Although it does not reach altitudes of alpine mountain railways its operation is no less difficult, owing to rigorous winter conditions.

From *Bergen* line crosses the peninsula in tunnels, then skirts *Sørfjord*, not to be confused with a branch of *Hardangerfjord* bearing the same name, and *Bolstadfjord*; fine views of the water, but many tunnels. On for 63 miles (101km) to **Voss**Δ, rail junction; oldest house in Norway (*Finneloftet*, built 1250), thirteenth-century church; summer resort and winter sports centre.

R2 (i) Voss to Granvin (Hardangerfjord), 17 miles (27km), 50 minutes' journey. Electric railway, pleasant but unexciting countryside, mostly forested. From *Granvin* buses connect to *Norheimsund* and other points on *Hardangerfjord*.

R2 (ii) Voss to Gudvangen (for Sognefjord), 30 miles (48km). Bus (six services daily) in 1 hour 50 minutes, shortest and cheapest route from *Bergen* to the inner *Sognefjord*. Following road No 60 past *Skulestadmo* to *Lønehorgi*, a mountain 4,670ft

(1,424m) and worth climbing. Beyond *Upheimsvann* enter upper *Nærøy* valley, on watershed of *Sogn. Stalheim*, tourist centre, finely situated. Descend to *Gudvangen* at head of **Næroyfjord**, narrow and rocky walled, probably second only to *Geirangerfjord* (see **R5** [ii]) for grandeur. Ferry to *Kaupanger* for *Jotunheimen* (see **R3**) or by bus to *Vangsnes*Δ and then ferry to *Balestrand*Δ for *Nordfjord* (see **R5**[i]).

Voss is only 150ft (46m) above sea level, but from this point the railway rises steadily, following attractive *Raundal* valley, which grows increasingly wild, the river becoming a torrent. *Mjølfjell*Δ, 84 miles (135m) from *Bergen*, well-known ski-centre; mountain walks to *Ulvik* (upper *Hardangerfjord* (6 hours). Pass through *Gravehalsen* tunnel, 3 miles (5km) long, to *Myrdal*, at head of *Flåm* valley.

R2 (iii) Myrdal to Flåm by electric railway (12 miles, 19km, 53 minutes' journey). The *Flåmsbane*, said to be the most expensive railway in world to construct, has gradient of 1 in 18, many loops and tunnels, fine views, including numerous waterfalls; train stops at viewpoints for benefit of tourists. *Flåm* lies on beautiful **Aurlandsfjord**, branch of *Sognefjord*: ferries via *Aurland* to *Kaupanger* and other places on *Sognefjord*.

Train continues to ascend, affording fine view of *Flåm* valley on left just beyond *Myrdal* station. Enters barren treeless region where many timber snowsheds screen railway line. Shortly before *Finse*, railway reaches highest point of 4,260ft (1,300m). *Finse*, 118 miles (190km) from *Bergen* and highest railway station in north Europe, has fine view over lake to *Hardanger* glacier; Scott of the Antarctic and his party trained here — monument by lakeside. Good centre for high mountain and glacier tours.

R2 (iv) Finse to Aurland on foot, 5 to 7 days; magnificent wild country with many lakes; overnight stops at tourist huts *Geiteryggen, Steinbergdalen* and *Steine. Osterbø*; bus *Steine-Aurland.*

Railway continues between *Hardanger* glacier and *Hallingskarv* mountain range (peaks 6,230ft, 1,900m), through tundra country, all above tree line. At *Haugastøl* railway joins road from *Hardangerfjord* and follows it to **Geilo** (see **R1**).

R3 Bergen to Otta, via Sognefjord and Jotunheimen Mountains
This route combines some of the finest fjord country with the grandest mountains; a rather expensive journey, but most rewarding. Take cargo steamer for overnight voyage from *Bergen* to *Sogndal*Δ, calling at all small ports en route; thence by bus to *Krossbu*. Quicker route by express boat from *Bergen* to *Leikanger* in 5 hours, connecting bus to *Sogndal,* and continue to *Krossbu* in 4 hours. Quickest route is via *Voss* and *Gudvangen* (see **R2 [ii]**) to *Kaupanger* and *Sogndal* thence by bus to *Krossbu*, as above; a night must be spent at *Sogndal*, but breaks of journeys recommended also at other places en route, eg *Voss, Gudvangen.*

Sognefjord, the country's longest, provides access 125 miles (200km) inland to the foot of the *Jotunheimen* mountains; reaches depths of more than 3,940ft (1,200m) and some surrounding rock faces rise sheer to 2,000ft (600m) above the fjord. The offshoots, *Aurlandsfjord* and *Fjærlandsfjord*, are narrower and grander than the main fjord, but are not entered by the express boats.

From *Bergen*, boat threads maze of islands, reaching entrance to *Sognefjord* after about $2^1/_2$ hours (express boat) or $5^1/_2$ hours (slow boat). Fjord here is up to 3 miles (5km) wide.

R3 (i) Lavik to Stryn (Nordfjord), 120 miles (190km). Bus connects with boat from *Bergen*; a 5 hours' trip on winding roads, but reaching no substantial heights, via *Førde* (centre of area known as *Sunnfjord* — no actual fjord of this name) and Lake *Jølster*; fine views south-eastward to *Jøstedal* glacier. Cross *Utvikfjell* (2,100ft, 640m, fine views) to *Byrkjelo*△ and descend to *Utvik*, on southern arm of *Nordfjord*; continue along fjord by series of tourist resorts — *Olden* and *Loen*, each with attractive narrow lakes, to *Stryn*△ at head of fjord (see **R5 [i]**).

Høyanger (on small *Høyangersfjord*) is modern industrial town, with large hydro-electric works. At *Vik*, on south shore (express boats do not call) is fine twelfth-century stave church. *Balestrand*△, at entrance to *Fjærlandsfjord*, summer resort amid orchards, with many upland footpaths, an English church and a tourist office. *Vangsnes*△ on opposite shore.

R3 (ii) Balestrand to Stryn (Nordfjord), 77 miles (48km) 6 hours' journey, including hour's break at *Vassenden*. This is a longer but more exciting route than **R3 (i)**. After leaving fjord, road rapidly reaches 2,300ft (700m) before descending to series of lakes in *Viksdal*. At *Moskog* this route joins **R3 (i)** for rest of way to *Stryn*.

At *Hermansverk* a short cut can be taken to the *Jotunheimen* by taking a bus journey to *Sogndal*△ and thence to *Krossbu*. Fjord boat continues to *Solsnes*, a stopping place in mid-fjord where passengers transfer to ferries for *Gudvangen* (see **R2 [ii]**) and *Flåm* (see **R2 [iii]**). On to *Lærdal*△ (also called *Lærdalsøyra*), a village surrounded by high mountains and out of reach of sun during more than six months a year; dry climate, like the rest of innermost *Sogn*.

R3 (iii) Lærdal to Gol, 77 miles (124km). A good route for motorists and cyclists wishing to return to *Bergen* by **R1** or **R2**. Also bus service in 3 hours. Road climbs narrow valley of *Lærdal* river (many rapids; famous for salmon fishing) to *Borgund* with one of finest stave churches in Norway, twelfth century; decorated doors and roof-hole lighting. At *Borlaug*△ branch road across *Fillefjell* Mountains to Lake *Tyin* (southern approach to *Jotunheimen*). Route follows road up to Lake *Eldrevatn* (3,790ft, 1,155m) on *Hemsedal* mountain plateau, down into valley of rapid-flowing *Heimsil* river, past *Hemsedal*△ to *Gol* on *Oslo-Bergen* railway (see **R6**). Thence to *Bergen* by **R1** or **R2**.

From *Lærdal*, express steamers turn into *Årdalsfjord*, passing *Fodnes*, remains of enormous landslide to north-east, and on other side of fjord the mountain *Bodlenakkjen* (3,100ft, 945m), to reach *Årdalstangen*, village at head of fjord.

R3 (iv) Årdal to Tyin (Jotunheimen), 32 miles (51km), $1^1/_2$ hours by bus. A fine approach to *Jotunheimen* mountains from the south. Spectacular climb from *Ovre Årdal* (hydro-electric works and aluminium factory) on brilliant green Lake *Årdal*, up valley of *Ardøla (Tya)* river by road with forty-three sharp bends, reaching height of 3,400ft (1,035m) above sea level in 7 miles (11km). Lake *Tyin*, 3,500ft (1,065m) above sea level, is second largest of *Jotunheimen* lakes with fine views of peaks to north-east. Bus, twice daily *Tyin* hotel to *Eidsbugaren* on Lake *Bygdin* and boat connection to *Bygdin*; fine boat trip, $1^3/_4$ hours. *ValdresflyaΔ*, about 6 miles, 9km, north of *Bygdin*).

Express boats terminate at *Årdalstangen*, but there is a bus service to *Skjolden* from *Sogndal* ($2^1/_2$ hours) up the west side of the *Lusterfjord*, gentler than most of *Sogn*, with several bays and small ports. On precipitous east side lies *Urnes*, with oldest stave church in Norway; animal carvings. Northern end of fjord is warm, dry and fertile, even tobacco can be grown.

SkjoldenΔ, extreme inland point of *Sognefjord* complex. Buses leave for *Jotunheimen* and *Otta*. Road blocked by snow October to May or longer. Leaving *Skjolden*, road climbs stiffly near *Opptun*, offering magnificent views over *Fortun* valley below. *Turtagrø*, tourist station (2,900ft, 883m), centre for rock-climbers and starting-point for exploring the *Jotunheimen*.

EXCURSION: to *Fannaråki* (6,780ft, 2,066m) highest inhabited point in Norway, meteorological station; ascent in 4 hours, marked path.

Ten miles (16km) beyond *Turtagrø* is one of highest road passes in Norway (4,690ft, 1,429m) near the old *Sognefjell* pass. *Krossbu* (22 miles, 35km, from *Skjolden* and 60 miles, 96km, by road from *Sogndal*) is good centre for western *Jotunheimen*.

The poet Vinje christened Norway's highest mountains, which are also highest in northern Europe, '**Jotunheimen**' or home of the giants. Many peaks over 6,500ft (2,000m); the highest, *Galdhøpiggen*, is 8,100ft (2,467m). Numerous tourist huts in the mountains with clear connecting paths which can safely be followed. Ascent of most peaks, however, involves crossing of glaciers, and it is foolhardy to attempt this except with a party, owing to many crevasses. *Galdhøpiggen* can be climbed from *Spiterstulen* without crossing a glacier.

Galdesand (between *Elveseter* and *Roisheim*) is probably best northern approach to high *Jotunheimen*.

R3 (v) Jotunheimen Walking Tour. Among many possible tours in this area this one occupies 8 days; moderately strenuous. Nights are spent in tourist huts at places named. 1st Day: *Galdesand*, stay at *BøverdalenΔ*, to *Juvass* hut ($3^1/_2$ hours). 2nd Day:

climb *Galdhøpiggen* and return to *Juvass* Hut. 3rd Day: Walk to *Spiterstulen* (3$^1/_2$ hours). 4th Day: walk to *Glitterheim* Hut via *Skautflya* (5 hours). 5th Day: walk to *Gjendesheim* (7 hours). 6th Day: rest day at *Gjendesheim*, on Lake *Gjende*. 7th Day: make early start to follow Peer Gynt's route along rock ridge of *Besseggen* (5,500ft, 1,676m) to *Memurubu* and catch midday boat to *Gjendebu* (40 minutes' sailing). 8th Day: walk via *Eidsbugaren* to *Tyinholmen* (6 hours). Bus to *Tyin* Hotel whence connecting bus to *Lærdal*Δ (See **R3 [iii]**).

Lom, 50 miles (80km) by road from *Skjolden*; in valley of River *Otta*; junction of road to *Nordfjord*. Continue down valley to **Otta**, in upper *Gudbrandsdal*, on *Oslo-Trondheim* railway (90 miles, 145km, from *Skjolden* and 128 miles, 206km, from *Sogndal*). See **R7 (i)**.

R4 Bergen — Kristiansand, via Setesdal (328 miles, 527km)

A long tour, for the motorist or cyclist wishing to avoid the more crowded central fjord area. Can also be undertaken by bus and ferry in minimum of 3 days. It includes the remarkable *Setesdal* valley, and at *Kristiansand* gives access by sea to Danish ports.

Bergen to *Odda*Δ, may be made by following **R1** to *Lofthus*, thence alongside *Sorfjord*, narrow arm of *Hardangerfjord*. *Folgefonn* glacier, third largest in the country, lies westwards of the fjord.

EXCURSION: from *Tyssedal*, 3$^1/_2$ miles (6km) north of *Odda*, road leads up to huge *Skjeggeda* dam and power station; many waterfalls; boat trips on lake at top (*Ringedalsvatn*).

Continue by series of fine waterfalls to *Seljestad*, then steep climb of 3,000ft (915m) in 6 miles (10km) (fine backwards views towards *Folgefonn* glacier) and descend to *Røldal*. Road now crosses *Haukeliseter*, southern extension of *Hardangervidda*; wild country, traditional meeting point of routes between east and west Norway. *Dyrskar Pass* (3,720ft, 1,135m) has snow all year, but is accessible for vehicles June-October, *Haukeligrend*, 65 miles (104km) from *Odda*.

R4 (i) Haukeligrend to Dalen (for Telemark). 40 miles (64km). Direct approach to *Telemark* (see **R9**) from *Bergen*, and attractive route to *Oslo*. *Dalen* terminus of the *Telemark* waterways (see **R9**).

At *Bjåen* road begins steep descent in **Setesdal** valley, one of most interesting parts of Norway. Upper part of valley was cut off from rest of country until road was built in 1938; many traditions preserved, national costume worn, folk-dancing popular. On west side of valley many extensive plateaux with small lakes providing good fishing.

Bykle is typical village of area, many ancient houses, church decorated with traditional rose-paintings. *Valle*, 19 miles (30km) south, was formerly principal place of upper *Setesdal*. Mountain paths lead east and west; fine eighteenth-century wooden church with carved altar. *Bygland*, on *Byglandsfjord*, has ancient tumuli.

Lower *Setesdal* is less interesting, and cyclists can shorten journey by taking train from *Byglandsfjord* to **Kristiansand**Δ 45 miles (72km), where journey may be continued to *Stavanger* or *Oslo* by **R10**.

R5 Bergen — Kirkenes by the North Cape

Voyage takes 5$^1/_2$ days by *Hurtigrute* steamers, serving forty ports; stopovers may be made. Boats carry two.

Måløy, reached on first morning after leaving *Bergen*, is junction for *Nordfjord*.

R5 (i) Måløy to Loen (Nordfjord) by boat to *Sandane*, thence by bus. Approach to *Nordfjord* would not be by *Hurtigrute* but by smaller fjord steamer leaving *Bergen* daily, although some boats do not go as far as *Sandane*.

Nordfjord is typical Norwegian fjord, long and narrow with several arms; less accessible than *Hardanger* or *Sogn* while not as magnificent as *Geiranger* (see **R5** [ii]), has tourist centres of *Stryn*Δ and *Byrkjelo*Δ. From *Stryn* bus connections to *Lom*, change at *Grotli*, or to *Geiranger*, via *Hellesylt*Δ.

Beyond *Måløy* boat enters complex of islands and inlets known as *Sunnmøre* and *Storfjord*. Boat calls at *Ålesund*, important herring fishery port and commercial centre; good museum of *Sunnmøre* history.

R5 (ii) Ålesund to Geiranger by the Storfjord. No regular boat service whole length of fjord but connecting bus and ferries. Bus *Ålesund-Magerholm*, ferry to *Sykkylven*, bus (by pleasant *Velledal* valley, rising to 1,740ft [530m], fine views) via *Stranda* and *Hellesylt*, then by boat up *Geirangerfjord*.

Geirangerfjord is probably most remarkable of all Norwegian fjords; 9 miles (14km) long, barely $^1/_4$ mile (400m) wide, bounded by cliffs more than 3,280ft (1,000m) high, down which pour such famous waterfalls at *Brundesloret* (The Bridal Veil) and *De Syv Søster* (The Seven Sisters). From *Geiranger* bus climbs to *Grotli* and *Lom* (for *Jotunheimen*, see **R3** [v]).

Further ports of call are *Molde*Δ, facing southwards and abundant in roses; annual international jazz festival (for *Åndalsnes* and *Romsdal*, see **R7** [ii]), *Kristiansund*Δ, a trawler port (not to be confused with *Kristiansand* in south Norway) and *Trondheim*Δ — see **R7**.

On third morning after leaving *Bergen*, boat crosses Arctic Circle and enters the 'Land of the Midnight Sun' (see **R11**). After calling at various ports in the *Lofoten* Islands, at *Hammerfest*, most northerly town in the world, boat rounds *North Cape*, a 984ft (300m) cliff which can be approached by road from *Honningsvåg*Δ, and reaches *Kirkenes*, close to Soviet frontier, mineral port, terminus of route.

The Eastern Valleys

Five great valleys, *Osterdal, Gudbrandsdal, Valdres, Hallingdal* and *Numedal* run north and west from *Oslofjord*. Their rivers are broader and quieter than the fierce streams of the western fjord country. Their sides are steep, but not vertical, and are often thickly wooded, while on the upper slopes are many *saeters*. The valley floors are broad, perhaps contain a lake, and big agricultural villages have developed. Each valley has its individual way of life, its traditional architecture, and its own beauty.

The valley roads climb gradually but steadily until they leave the shelter of the forests and emerge on to high, open moors. From *Gudbrandsdal* roads connect with all the north coast ports, while the road through *Osterdal* provides an alternative route to *Trondheim*. The *Valdres* roads lead to *Jotunheimen* and *Sognefjord*, and the *Hallingdal* and *Numedal* roads to *Hardangerfjord*. Mountain roads link the upper valleys together.

R6 Oslo to Geilo by the Hallingdal (157 miles, 253km by road)
This is the route of the *Oslo-Bergen* railway and of the main road. Rail journey in 4 to 5 hours.

Railway skirts edge of *Nordmarka*, an area of woods and lakes popular with *Oslo* inhabitants for ski tours, and at *Jevnaker* touches *Randsfjord*, in fact an inland lake, not a fjord. Beyond *Orgenvika* is the beautiful Lake *Kørderen*, at foot of *Hallingdal*, a valley bounded by forest-clad mountains. Note typical high chimneys of houses. *Nes* has a *Hallingdal* museum, with many folklore treasures.

R6 (i) From Nes to Vassfaret. Paths lead into vast forest area of *Vassfaret*, where bears are still to be found.

At *Gol* valley bends sharply westward; junction for **R3 (iii)** to *Lærdal* on *Sognefjord*.

R6 (ii) Gol to Fagernes, 33 miles (53km). Attractive road from *Hallingdal* to *Valdres* via *Sanderstølen* plateau (2,790ft, 850m, but open all year). Bus twice daily.

Railway climbs steeply into upper *Hallingdal*, which widens considerably. *Torpo* has fine stave church, twelfth century, with carved doorway. *Geilo*△, just below tree line.

For continuation of route to *Bergen* by rail see **R2**; by road and ferry see **R1**.

R7 Oslo to Trondheim by the Gudbrandsdal (346 miles, 557km)
Of several alternative routes to *Trondheim* this is probably the most attractive. Train in approximately 8 hours. Rail and road follow Lake *Mjøsa*, Norway's largest lake (62 miles, 100km, long). From *Eidsvoll* to *Lillehammer* journey may be made by paddle-steamer (6 hours).

*Hamar*Δ is ancient town, over 900 years old; ruins of twelfth-century cathedral outside town to north. *Lillehammer*Δ is well-known tourist centre, particularly for winter sports, as snow lies later than in west Norway. Nearby is *Maihaugen* open-air folk museum, buildings from past centuries, reconstructed and furnished, also medieval farm from *Gudbrandsdal* and a stave church.

Gudbrandsdal valley begins here; generally narrow, with steep rocky sides; has youth hostel at *Sjoa* and many farms and villages; rough-hewn timber farmhouses often arranged in form of square. Woodcarving and weaving are typical crafts.

Ringebu has stave church dating from 1250. *Kvam*, 175 miles (280km) from *Oslo*, for approach to *Rondane*.

R7 (i) Kvam to Rondane Mountains. The *Rondane* is an attractive mountain area with dry climate well provided with tourist huts and clearly-marked paths. Many peaks exceed 5,900ft (1,800m) and are above snow line. *Rondane* can be also approached from *Otta* or *Sel*.

Otta is junction for routes to *Jotunheimen* (**R3**) and *Nordfjord* (**R5 [i]**). Beyond *Sel* valley rises steeply, grows narrower, and scenery becomes wilder. *Dombås*Δ (2,166ft, 660m) is junction for road and railway to *Åndalsnes*.

R7 (ii) Dombås to Åndalsnes via Romsdal, 67 miles (108km). By train in 2$^1/_2$ hours journey. Rail and road follow upper *Gudbrandsdal*. *Lesjaskog* is good centre for little-known walking country to north centred on *Aursjø* hut. *Romsdal* (valley of River *Rauma*), thickly wooded. *Åndalsnes*, small port, was scene of British landing in 1940. *Setnes*Δ is nearby.

EXCURSIONS: into **Romsdal** mountains by fine *Trollstigs* road between peaks of *Trolltindene* (5,900ft, 1,800m) and fantastically shaped peaks named *Dronningen* ('Queen'), *Bispen* ('Bishop'), etc. Excellent climbing.

From *Dombås* railway climbs steeply onto *Dovrefell*, a high mountain plateau reaching highest station at *Hjerkinn* (3,357ft, 1,023m), then descends, via *Oppdal*Δ to *Trondheim*.

TrondheimΔ chief port of northern Norway and third largest town, was Viking capital when founded in 997; modern city retains many memorials of its past. Gothic cathedral begun in 1090 as the shrine of *St Olav*; archbishops' palace is almost as old. See the *Stifts-gården*, governor's residence built in 1774-6, largest wooden building in the country; *Ringve* museum of music and *Trøndelag* folk museum. Fjord here is very wide, bounded by rolling hills, with fields and woodland.

Sør-Trøndelag county provides excellent walking and skiing.

For continuation northwards from *Trondheim* to north Norway by land see **R11**; by sea — **R5**.

R8 Oslo to Fagernes by Valdres (120 miles, 193km)

Railway, via *Dokka*, in $4^1/_2$ hours. Bus, via Lake *Sperillen*, twice daily, 5 hours.

Valdres valley can be approached by two routes. The eastern route, via Lake Lake *Randsfjord* and *Dokka*, gives varied scenery — farming country, woods, moorland — and, near Lake *Tonsvatn* reaches height of 2,460ft (750m). The western route, via *HønefossΔ*, follows Lake *Sperillen* and the *Begnadal* valley, skirting the edge of *Vassfaret* forest (see **R6 [i]**).

Routes join at *Bjørgo* to enter **Valdres**, one of the most beautiful valleys in Norway; thought to have been inhabited for at least 4,000 years. *Fagernes*, the only town, is picturesquely situated on Lake *Strandefjord*, 1,180ft (360m) above sea level. It has a museum of local history and culture. Bus connections to *Gol* in *Hallingdal* (see **R6 [ii]**), also to *Lærdal* (*Sognefjord*) and to southern *Jotunheimen* massif (*Tyin, Bygdin*).

The Telemark

Telemark is an inland area of unspoilt mountains and lakes, lying south-west of *Oslo*. The people still preserve many of their native crafts; as well as their own costumes and dialects. It is the original home of skiing; ski-jumpers from *Morgedal* were first to introduce the sport into *Oslo* in 1870-80.

R9 Oslo to Dalen by rail and canal

An attractive, and leisurely approach to the *Telemark*, and a possible stage on the route to *Bergen* is the boat service on the *Telemark* waterway; 180 miles (130km) voyage in 10 hours through 18 locks, canals and lakes between *Skien* on the south coast and *Dalen*.

Some of this route can be covered by train from *Oslo* on the *Stavanger* line (**R10**) as far as *Lunde* (3 hours). Thence on the *Telemark* waterway for 6 hours on meandering voyage among mountains and forest, past *KviteseidΔ* (thirteenth-century church) to *Dalen*, small village at head of Lake *Bandak*. For continuation to *Bergen* see **R4 (i)**.

R9 (i) Dalen to Rjukan, 58 miles, 93km. This route crosses wild country at northern edge of *Telemark*, where it adjoins the *Hardanger* plateau. Buses twice daily, 3 hours. *Rauland* (35 miles, 56km, slightly off road) is good example of *Telemark* village architecture and crafts. Cross *Møsvatn* Pass (3,280ft, 1,000m) and pass *Møsvatn* dam, a barrage containing the waters which provide power for the hydro-electric works at *Rjukan*. Road descends, with many bends, from the wild country above into a deep valley which bustles with industrial activity. Here is the *Norsk Hydro* company's hydro-electric plant, built underground, with adjoining chemical factories, etc. *RjukanΔ* has a cable railway which climbs 1,640ft (500m) to *Gvepseborg*. It is also starting point for ascent of *Gausta* (6,000ft, 1,830m), highest peak in *Telemark*. Return to *Oslo* by direct route via *KongsbergΔ*, bus and rail in 5 hours.

The South Coast

The west coast of the *Oslofjord*, and all the south coast from *Tønsberg* to *Stavanger* is a popular holiday area for the people of *Oslo*, and is quite unlike the rest of the country. There are no deep fjords; the tree-clad hills are not so high or steep; there are many bathing beaches and holiday resorts, sheltered by islands and skerries and ideal for picnics.

R10 Stavanger to Oslo (404 miles, 650km)

StavangerΔ, port and fishing centre, and home of the canning industry. North Sea oil has brought rig construction yards and boomtown prosperity, but it remains Norway's best preserved town of wooden houses in narrow streets. The cathedral, begun in Romanesque style by English monks in 1130, has a Gothic choir dating from 1280, some fine stained glass and a baroque carved pulpit. The town has a museum and art gallery. The tourist bureau is the old fireguard's tower — *Valbergstårnet* — from which there are good views. No other roads lead from *Stavanger* except that to the south, but there are regular ferries to *HaugesundΔ* and the *Ryfylke* fjords.

   South of *Stavanger* lies the flat, marshy but fertile plain of *Jæren;* so mild here that sheep can feed out of doors in winter; renowned for bird life, especially in the migration season. *Jæren* is one of the few parts of the coast not protected by islands from the westerly gales.

   On via *Mandal*, a sea-bathing resort, and *Flekkefjord* to **KristiansandΔ**, an important port, built on a peninsula, with street layout planned by Christian IV in 1641; many charming streets. *Vest Agder* open-air museum, biggest in country, at *Grimshaug* to west of town. Junction for *Setesdal* valley (see **R4**). Do not confuse with *Kristiansund*, near *Trondheim*.

   EXCURSION: to *Grovane*, 12 miles, 19km, north on road 405, for *Grovane/Beihölen* steam railway, 3 miles, 5km, run on narrow gauge track.

Lillesand is attractive little town with many timber houses. *GrimstadΔ*, home-town of Ibsen; Ibsen musuem in *Ostergate* is oldest house of town (1750). There follows a series of ports, many connected with whaling industry. *KragerøΔ*. *Larvik* has ferry to *Fredrikshavn* in Denmark and road and rail connections to *Skien,* for *Telemark* waterway (see **R9**). Then entrance to *Oslofjord*, a broad and beautiful approach to capital, with many summer resorts such as *TønsbergΔ*, *Horten*, which has interesting naval museum and *DrammenΔ* with an open-air museum. *Oslo* is 20 miles (32km) farther on.

Oslo△

Norway's only large city, capital and chief home of Norwegian learning and culture. Though central built-up area is small, and retains much of the atmosphere of a small town, it is probably the most spacious city in Europe.

Oslo was founded in 1050, but after a disastrous fire (1642), Christian IV had it rebuilt on its present site behind *Akershus* fortress. He re-christened it *Christiania*, the old name being restored in 1925. The only old buildings besides *Akershus*, now a museum, are the eleventh-century *Gamle Akers* Church and *Gamlebyen* Church (1298), both now restored. *Oslo's* cathedral, *Vår Frelsers Kirke* (Church of Our Saviour), built in 1699, has been restored twice.

Oslo's modern buildings are more striking. Visitors arriving by boat see first the new *Rådhus* (**Town Hall**) with its two broad towers and its big clock. The main sight of the town hall, and one of the most interesting in the whole city, is the series of mural paintings and sculptures, by Norway's leading modern artists, showing scenes from her history.

Modern *Oslo* is a spacious city, with wide streets, and many parks. In **Frogner Park** there is a unique sculpture exhibition, devoted entirely to the work of the twentieth-century sculptor Vigeland: some 150 statues depicting every type of human figure, from babyhood to old age, bursting with life and emotions.

Karl Johans Gate is the heart of *Oslo*, and on or near it lie the *Storting*, the University, the theatres and art galleries, the *Rådhus*, the Royal Palace and many of the best shops and hotels. Shops named *Heimen* and *Den Norske Husflids Forening*, exhibit and sell traditional handmade pottery, cloth and pewter work.

Bygdøy, by ferry (summer only) from the quays in front of the *Rådhus*; buses connect throughout the year. See the *Kontiki* raft *Ra II* and Nansen's ship *Fram*, open-air folk-museum of houses and other buildings, some from Middle Ages, assembled from different parts of Norway, and three Viking ships, more than 1,000 years old, painstakingly re-assembled from fragments dug out of coastal mud.

The Far North

Northern Norway proper begins about 190 miles, 300km, north of *Trondheim*. The climate is unexpectedly mild and, in the summer, with almost 24 hours of sunshine each day, there it little suggestion of the 'Arctic Circle'. The '**midnight sun**' is visible at *Bodø* from 1 June to 13 June, at *Troms* from 18 May to 25 July *North Cape* from 12 May to 1 August. *Hammerfest*, the most northerly town in the world, is nearer the North Pole than it is to London yet the country is neither desolate nor barren. Bare rocks, glaciers and snow-covered mountains are indeed there but every patch of soil is cultivated and has its small farm, while the little

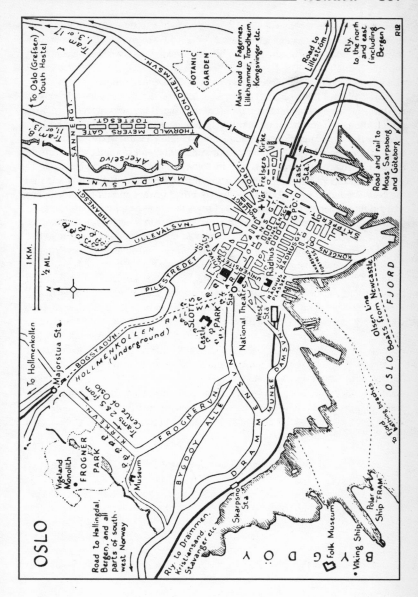

OSLO

To Oslo (Grefsen) Youth Hostel

Tram 13 or 17

Tram 13 or 17

TRONDHJEIMSVN.

BOTANIC GARDEN

Main road to Fagernes, Lillehammer, Trondheim, Kongsvinger etc.

Road to Lillestrøm

Rly. to the north and east (including Bergen)

SANNERGT.

THORVALD MEYERS GATE

TOFTESGT.

AKERSELV

Road and rail to Moss, Sarpsborg and Göteborg

MARIDALSVN.

THRANESGT.

ULLEVALSVN.

1 KM.

½ ML.

N

PILESTREDET

POLICE

TORG

Vår Frelsers Kirke

G.P.O.

East Sta.

SKIPPERGT.

KONGENS

PARK

UNIVERSITY

Rådhus

RÅDHUSGT.

Castle

SLOTTS

National Theatre

West Sta.

To Hollmenkollen

Majorstua Sta.

BOGSTADVN.

HOLLMENKOLLEN RAILY. (underground)

Trams 2&5 from Centre of Oslo

KIRKEVN.

FROGNER PARK

Vigeland Monolith

FROGNERVN.

BYGDØY ALLE

Museum

DRAMMEN

MUNKE DAMSVN.

Skarpsno Sta.

Rly. to Drammen, Kristiansand, Stavanger etc.

Road to Hallingdal, Bergen, and all parts of south-west Norway

OSLO FJORD

Olsen Line Boats from Newcastle

to Bygdøy beach

Boats to Bygdøy

BYGDØY

Folk Museum

Viking Ship

Polar Ship 'FRAM'

Lofoten ports shelter the world's largest cod-fishing fleet and have many fish-curing factories. Summer temperature inland in **Finnmark** may reach 30°C (85°F). Swarms of mosquitoes make life unpleasant for a short time in early July.

R11 Trondheim to Kirkenes by road (1,200 miles, 1,930km)

The 450 miles (720km) from *Trondheim* to *Bodø* by rail, the remainder by bus and ferry, is a 5-day journey, more expensive than the 4-day coastal ferry trip. Road is open May to September approximately; sometimes rough, always with a loose surface, but is well-engineered and makes use of six ferries. Many youth hostels, several hotels and tourist stations. Good centres for walking and cycling, are *Mo i Rana*Δ, *Bodø*Δ and *Tromsø*Δ. The *Finnmarksvidda* provides the best walking country in Norway and hostellers can use travellers' huts at hostel prices. The *vidda* is inhabited only by Lapps — the last nomadic race of Europe — following their reindeer herds. They differ from Norwegians in appearance, dress, language and way of life. *Kautokeino* and *Karasjok*Δ their centres, can be reached by road; or by 2-day river trip from *Tana* to *Karasjok*; interesting, though expensive.

PORTUGAL

Geographical Outline

Land

Portugal occupies less than one-sixth of the *Iberian Peninsula*, but includes most of its western seaboard. Its length from north to south is about 358 miles (576km), and it varies in breadth from about 140 miles (225km) in the north to about 75 miles (120km) in the south.

Physically the country can be roughly divided into the region north of the *Tagus* which is mainly hilly or mountainous, with a narrow coastal plain; and that south of the river, which is much flatter, although with some hilly districts.

Across the mountainous country the principal rivers cut deep valleys from east to west; the *Minho* on the northern frontier, the *Douro*, the *Mondego* and the *Tagus*. All but the *Mondego* rise in Spain. They are difficult to navigate and are, therefore, not important for communication. The mountains are not high by alpine standards; the highest are in the *Serra da Estrêla* at 6,500ft (1,980m), over against the Spanish frontier, but most are not much above 4,600ft (1,400m). They are, however, often bare and rugged in character and form wild and impressive scenery.

A remarkable and pleasing feature of Portugal is that, although a small country, the scenery is diverse due both to its physical features and to the uses to which the land has been put, and the appearance of the country often varies considerably within small distances.

South of the *Tagus*, especially, this diversity owes much to human influence, and wide stretches of bleak heathland are interspersed with areas of cork oak and olive, and of extensive wheat growing. In the extreme south are the coastlands of the *Algarve* which have much of the character of Andalusia and of the neighbouring coasts of Africa.

Climate

Portugal has an equable climate, influenced by the Atlantic. It does not experience extremes of heat or cold — particularly near the coast — and this makes it suitable for touring at any time of the year.

Rainfall is heaviest in the northern coastal areas and in the mountains. It is least in the extreme south.

In summer *Oporto* (in the north) is generally cooler than *Lisbon*, but in coastal areas the heat is tempered by on-shore breezes. In the extreme south (the *Algarve*) and towards the interior of the country, and also in valleys sheltered by the mountains from cooling breezes, the heat of summer is greater.

Winters in the coastal regions are mild, but coastal fogs, caused by cold Atlantic currents, are common.

Plants and Animals

The vegetation is a mixture of the temperate and the sub-tropical. Pines and deciduous trees familiar in Northern Europe frequently exist side by side with cacti, tree-ferns, palms and aloes from Africa and elsewhere — a characteristic well demonstrated in the *Sintra* hills near *Lisbon*.

North of *Lisbon* pinewoods are common along the coastal plain, and forests of oak and chestnut cover the lower slopes of the mountains above the cultivated valleys. Lime, elm and poplar are also common.

Cork oaks are widely distributed, but particularly important in the *Alentejo* (south of the *Tagus*). They will be seen with the bark stripped from the trunks, to provide the cork which is of great importance in Portugal. The olive is also common and so too is the locust tree with its curious edible seed pods. The *Algarve* is rich in fruit trees, especially almond and fig.

Three crops in particular produce a countryside unfamiliar in Northern Europe: maize is important in the north, grape-vines as far south as the *Tagus*, and rice is grown in the valleys of several rivers.

In the north oxen are still used for ploughing and as draught animals. Donkeys and mules are the usual beasts of burden. Wolves are found in the wilder areas, notably the *Serra da Estrêla*, and wild boars are preserved in certain districts.

The People

Population

Of the population of almost 10 million people, a very high proportion live in the rural areas. The visitor will find that there is often a surprisingly large number of people to be seen in the countryside. This density of settlement often belies the nature of the soils which are not on the whole particularly fertile.

The only large cities are *Lisbon* (population 850,000), *Oporto* (350,000) and *Setubal* (59,000). Otherwise no town exceeds 50,000.

Ethnically the Portuguese are predominantly of Mediterranean type, but in the

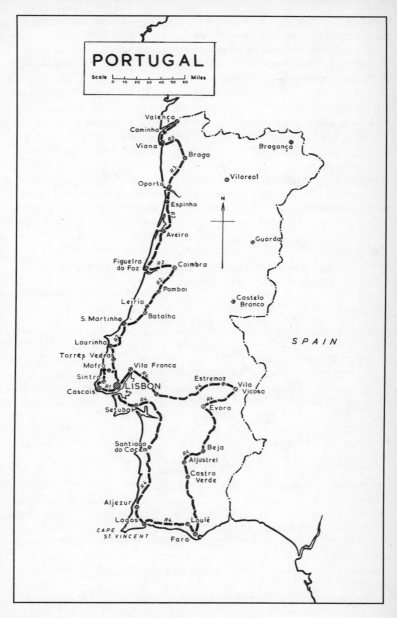

course of the country's long and complex history of invasion and exploration there has been intermingling with stocks from outside Iberia — Romans, Visigoths, Moors, Jews and Negroes. The present-day characteristics are generally of a short dark sturdy people, but in the north there are some traces of the fairer Germanic peoples.

Language

Portuguese is one of the three surviving Latin-derived languages of the Iberian Peninsula, the others being Castilian (Spanish) and Catalan. Resulting from this common origin it has some likeness to Castilian, particularly in written form, but it is a distinct language. Galician, the dialect of north-west Spain, is directly linked to Portuguese, but has declined under the influence of Castilian.

A visitor with a knowledge of Spanish, or even French, might find it comparatively easy to get a grasp of written Portuguese, but the spoken language presents more difficulties.

Religion

The overwhelming majority of the people are Roman Catholic. The Church plays a considerable part in the life of the country.

History

Portugal has no separate history until the twelfth century; before that time its history was that of the whole Peninsula. Phoenicians and Greeks traded with the Iberian peoples and later the Carthaginians established an Empire here. This fell to the Romans at the end of the third century BC, although for more than a century the tribes of the Atlantic seaboard held out against them. In 27BC, the emperor Augustus created the province of *Lusitania*, which included most of the area of modern Portugal, and this lasted until the series of invasions which brought about the collapse of the Roman Empire. Of these invaders the most important were the Visigoths. They incorporated *Lusitania* in an unstable kingdom which survived until it fell an easy prey to the Moslems in the early eighth century AD.

The name Portugal was first applied to the district around modern *Oporto* and was derived from the Roman name for the city — *Portus Cale*. The birth of Portugal dates from 1125 when this district established its independence of the Christian kingdom of *Léon*. In the next 125 years the remainder of her frontiers were carved from land under Moorish (Moslem) control, but more than a century passed before Portugal decisively defeated the territorial designs of the neighbouring kingdom of Castile. This was achieved by John of Aviz at the battle of Aljubarrota (1385) which ushered in Portugal's great age of exploration and expansion.

By the end of the fifteenth century Portuguese explorer-traders such as

Bartholomew Diaz and Vasco da Gama, inspired by the work of Prince Henry the Navigator, had discovered the Azores and Madeira, explored the coasts of Africa, and established themselves in India, the East Indies and China. In 1500 they landed in Brazil.

In the first half of the sixteenth century Portugal was at the height of her power, but the efforts of so great an expansion had overtaxed the small country's strength and in 1581 she was conquered by Spain. Independence was regained sixty years later, but, although she was still to exploit the wealth of Brazil, she never fully recovered her strength and went slowly into decline. Her ascendancy in the East passed first to the Dutch, later to the British.

The country was occupied by the French during the Napoleonic Wars (until they were expelled by Wellington) and the royal family fled to Brazil. A few years later Brazil seceded from her union with Portugal.

The constitutional struggle of the nineteenth century culminated in the assassination of King Carlos in 1908 and the establishment of a republic two years later. The new democracy was at first extremely unstable, but the appointment of Dr Salazar as finance minister in 1928, and prime minister in 1932, brought a more lasting political peace, disrupted by a popular uprising in 1974 and the setting-up of a democratic regime, now with membership of NATO and EEC.

Government

The President and the Government have very wide powers even though the country has many of the characteristics of a parliamentary democracy.

Resources

Although Portugal is a predominantly agricultural country it has become much more industrial in the last few years; in the past ten years or so exports of manufactured goods have trebled, with particular emphasis on machinery. Grapes, olive oil, wheat, maize and potatoes are among the principal products of the soil.

Portugal is the world's largest producer of cork. The famous port wine is very much a wine for export; other wines, more to the taste of the Portuguese, are produced for home consumption. The pine forests give rise to a considerable industry in timber, resins and turpentine. Another industry is the canning and export of sardines, caught by the coastal fishing communities.

Customs and Dress

There are considerable regional variations in customs and dress, as yet largely unaffected by the modern tendency throughout Europe for standardisation in dress and the preservation of local costume mainly for the tourist trade. Picturesque costumes may be seen at their best at the *romarias* or pilgrimages which combine religion with secular festivities. Dancing and singing play a prominent part of the life of the people. The traditional songs are of a slower rhythm than those of Spain. In *Lisbon* this is typified by the *fado*, popular in many cafés and restaurants. The climax of the harvesting (eg treading the grapes, stripping the maize cobs) is often made an occasion for lighthearted festivals.

Food and Drink

The staple diet is of fish, particularly cod, vegetables and fruit. Meat is rarely eaten by the ordinary people, in whose diet rice, maize bread and beans play an important part. Cooking is usually done in olive oil.

Sport

Bullfighting, usually conducted without the bulls being killed, is a popular sport; so, too, is football.

Culture

Architecture

With one or two exceptions — such as the Roman Temple of Diana at *Évora* and the Byzantine style church of *São Frutuoso* at *Braga* — the existing notable buildings date from times later than the creation of the kingdom of Portugal.

The familiar labels of the successive architectural styles, from Romanesque through to baroque and later, can be attached to the great buildings, but in the Portuguese setting they often contain distinctive elements which set them a little apart.

Thus the Romanesque, found mainly in the north (which was conquered earlier from the Moors) is often a rather forbidding style, as for instance in the fortress-like cathedrals of *Braga* and *Coimbra*.

The Gothic comes, therefore, as a rather greater contrast to the Romanesque than do the same two styles in, for example, England. Its two finest achievements are both monastery churches — at *Batalha* and *Alcobaça*.

The Gothic passed into the Manueline, a style exclusively Portuguese, containing much Moorish influence and coinciding with the country's great age of discovery and conquest. Two famous examples exist close to each other in the *Belém* district of *Lisbon* — the monastery of *Jerónimos* and the tower of *Bélem*.

Renaissance architecture was established in the sixteenth century, eg the cathedral of *Leiria*; and later the baroque style — of which the monastery at *Mafra* is probably the most extravagant example — became predominant. In connection with these and later styles mention must be made of the unique Portuguese *azulejos*, glazed tiles used for interior and exterior decoration. Introduced by the Moors, *azulejos* were developed by the Portuguese and for centuries they have been used to add colourful decoration to buildings, both religious and secular. Although still produced, and in evidence everywhere, modern trends in building are curtailing their use.

Literature

Portugal has a long and imposing literary history but its works are not generally accessible to those lacking knowledge of the language.

An outstanding exception, however, are the poems of Camões (Camõens) (1524-80) who has a universal appeal as one of the greatest figures of the Renaissance. Both in the circumstances of his life and in his great epic *Os Lusiadas* (*The Portuguese*), which has been translated into English several times, he epitomises one of the supreme European achievements, the voyages of discovery and the linking up of the West with the Orient.

Touring Information

Access

London to *Lisbon*; by rail, via Dieppe and Paris, in 2 days: by coach London to *Lisbon* frequent service by Europabus, 46 hours en route; by air, direct flight in about $2^1/_2$ hours; by sea, ships going to the Caribbean and South America accept passengers to *Lisbon*, but the voyage is expensive.

Transport

Portuguese trains have two classes, and run on broad-gauge track as in Spain. A supplementary charge is payable on some expresses, marked Rapide in time-tables. Tourist tickets for the entire railway system are issued for 7, 14 or 21 days. An excellent network of buses is run by Rodoviaria Nacional; fast and direct services between main towns, less frequent and more leisurely between smaller towns and villages.

Money

The *escudo* is divided into 100 *centavos*. Nickel coins are used for 50 *centavos* and 1 *escudo*; silver coins for $2^1/_2$, 5, 10 and 25 *escudos*.; notes are issued for 50, 100, 500, 1,000 and 5,000 *escudos*.

Clothing

Although the climate is one of the best in Europe, and it is warm and sunny most of the year, there can often be a cool breeze in the evenings, and a waterproof is essential as rain can be heavy, particularly in the mountains.

Restaurants and Meals

Food is plentiful and wholesome; cooking is appreciated as an art and is often excellent. Sea foods, such as *caldeirada* (fisherman's stew), *porco a Alentejana* (pork stewed with clams) and *bacalhau*, the national dish of codfish, served in various forms are popular, as well as sweets and delicacies rich in eggs and sugar, such as *ovos moles de Aveiro* or *trouxas d'ovos das Caldas*.

Public Holidays

1 January, Shrove Tuesday, Good Friday, 25 April, 1 May, 10 June, Corpus Christi, 24 June, 15 August, 5 October, 1 November, 1 December, 8 December and Christmas Day. In addition each town celebrates the feast of its own patron saint (St Anthony in *Lisbon*, 13 June).

Maps

Michelin No 37, scale 1:500,000, depicts all the country on one sheet.

Accommodation

The idea of youth hostelling has not yet become popular in Portugal; there are fewer than twenty youth hostels.

Other simple, clean and cheap accommodation is readily available in all parts of the country. The government regulates the prices charged and grades the standard. This information is obtainable in a free booklet from the Portuguese Tourist Offices and visitors are recommended to obtain a copy. It will provide accurate, reliable and invaluable information for finding accommodation.

Motoring

Motorists should carry with them their driving licence, car registration certificate — together with a 'Green Card' of insurance and a 'bail bond', both issued by the insurance company. A nationality sticker and a red warning triangle are also necessary. The Portuguese motoring association is Autómovel Clube de Portugal, Rue Rosa Araujo 49A, Lisbon.

Upper speed limits of 60km/h (37mph) apply in built-up areas, 120km/h (75mph) on the motorway *Setubal/Lisbon/Oporto* and 90km/h (56mph) elsewhere. Portuguese motorists favour high speeds, they are notoriously rash; cautious motoring is seldom seen.

Cycling

Portugal is a comparatively small country, and cycling is a convenient way of seeing it. Secondary roads are best used; although surfaces may be indifferent, motor traffic is not likely to intrude. Cycles are carried cheaply on buses and trains and less rewarding areas should be crossed quickly this way.

Lisbon△

Built along the north bank of the *Tagus* where the *Mar de Palha*, the wide part of the estuary, becomes a narrow channel before entering the sea, its history dates from Roman times, possibly before. For 500 years a Moorish city, it later became capital of the newly formed kingdom of Portugal, reaching its greatest prosperity with the age of Portuguese exploration and conquest overseas.

Much of it is built on hills, where streets are often narrow, steep and tortuous. Between the hills and along the *Tagus* run spacious avenues, the main link between different parts of the city.

Lisbon was almost entirely destroyed by earthquake in 1755. Much of the present plan of the city dates from the reconstruction, by the Marquis of Pombal, following the catastrophe. There are very few complete buildings older than this and therefore relatively little dating from the period of Portugal's greatest prosperity — the fifteenth and sixteenth centuries. Nevertheless, *Lisbon* is a beautiful and historical city, as well as being one of the busiest ports of Europe.

Its four districts are, from east to west:

(a) The *Alfama* (old town), site of Roman and Moorish Lisbon; a hilly quarter of narrow streets, retaining much of their medieval appearance, dominated by Moorish castle of *São Jorge* (many later additions). Other interesting buildings; the old cathedral (*Sé Patriarcal*), with Gothic façade and choir, but rest of later date; church of *São Vincente de Fora* (Renaissance); church of *Madre de Deus*, containing museum of *azulejos* in cloisters.

(b) *The Cicade Baixa* (lower town), centre of modern *Lisbon* planned after 1755 by Marquis of Pombal. The **Rossio** (the fine spacious *Dom Pedro IV Square*) is the hub of city life. National Theatre is on north side. The Rossio railway station at the north-west corner is a nineteenth-century copy of the Manueline style. Northward runs fine spacious *Avenida da Liberdade*. To the south parallel streets of good proportions lead to *Praça do Commercio*, sometimes known as *Black Horse Square*, flanked on three sides by arcaded buildings, on fourth by *Tagus*. Ferry to *Cacilhas* from near south-east corner.

(c) The *Bairro Alto* and (d) *Alcantara* districts contain buildings of great interest, in particular the ruins of the *Carmo* church, destroyed in the earthquake, the *Estrella* church with white marble dome and twin towers visible for miles around, finely decorated church of *São Roque*, and *Aqueduct of Aguas Livres* (eighteenth century), still in use.

At **Belém**, the western suburb, are the two most important Manueline buildings; the **monastery of Jerónimos**, full of beautiful detail, and the lovely **tower of Belém** standing out into the river.

The visitor should not fail to see two of Lisbon's finest aspects; the many parks and gardens of exotic plants and trees, and the splendid view of the city from the top of the gigantic stele of Christ at *Cacilhas* on the south bank of the *Tagus*.

Touring Routes

As described, these routes are intended for motoring or cycling, but travellers by train and bus can use them with only minor modifications.

R1 Lisbon to Lisbon via Mafra, Sintra and Cascais (86 miles, 138km)

Leave *Lisbon* by N8 (due north) and follow the road through *Loures*. After 20 miles (32km) turn left along N116 for *Mafra*; small town dominated by vast baroque monastery and palace started in 1713 by King John V; church with famous carillons.

Seven miles (11km) west is fishing village, *Ericeira*, famous for lobsters; King Manuel II fled from here in 1910 on board a British destroyer. To north are wild deserted beaches.

South along N247 across plain towards *Sintra Hills*. *Sintra* is charming little town, favourite summer residence of Portuguese royal family. Royal palace of Moorish, Gothic and Manueline appearance, dominated by two tall conical chimneys; remarkable interior decoration and secluded walled garden. Moorish castle on crags above town; walk length of battlemented perimeter wall and ascend staircase of royal tower for view. Nineteenth-century Pena palace on nearby hill top, motley of several architectural styles; staterooms open to visitors.

The rugged volcanic *Sintra Hills*, with lush, sub-tropical vegetation, continue westward to the sea.

Continue west to *Cabo da Roca*, westernmost point of Europe, fine cliff scenery. Then, still on N237, round coast to *Cascais*, fishing village and seaside resort for *Lisbon*. Nearby is *Estoril*, fashionable winter resort; famous casino.

On coast road N6 from *Estoril* back to *Lisbon* is *Catalazete*△, near *Oeiras* on shore of *Tagus* estuary.

R2 Lisbon to Oporto (283 miles, 456km)

This route takes in many places of interest and beauty along the narrow coastal plain from *Lisbon* to *Oporto*. It combines many sites of historic and artistic interest with fine beaches and coastal scenery, and pleasant and varied countryside.

Leave *Lisbon* by N8 (due north) and follow road for 40 miles (64km) through *Loures* to *Torres Vedras*, centre of wine producing region and a town with strong associations with Wellington in the Peninsular War; he was made Marquis of Torres Vedras by the Portuguese.

North-westwards, via *Lourinha* and *Areia Branca*△ to *Peniche*; interesting fishing town; seventeenth-century ramparts on edge of headland of impressive cliffs. Opposite lies island of *Berlenga*, worth an hour's boat trip from *Peniche*.

Six miles (10km) inland, on N114 stands *Obidos*, fortified town, protected by medieval walls and dominated by castle; scene of Wellington's first confrontation with French army. Follow N8 north through *Caldas da Rainha*, a spa with sulphur springs, patronised in 1484 by Queen Leonor, hence town's name; fine Manueline church. After 7 miles (11km) turn off to *São Martinho do Porto* (nearby is *Alfeizerão*△, a hamlet, well-known for its pastry); peaceful fishing village in wide bay, with sandy beaches, connected with sea by narrow exit through cliffs. *Nazaré*, 7 miles (11km) north, a fishing village in two parts, one on the cliffs, one on the shore, connected by funicular. Much frequented by tourists; best seen out of season, no harbour, the boats are launched from the beach into the Atlantic breakers. Fisherman wear traditional costume at folk festivals, shirts and trousers of rough wool tartan; the women wear dresses underlaid with many layers of petticoats.

Eight miles (13km) inland is small town of *Alcobaça*, famous for the Cistercian monastery of *Santa Maria* founded by Afonso Henriques, the first king of Portugal, to commemorate the capture of *Santarém* from the Moors. The Gothic church with later additions is the largest in the country and contains the tombs of King Pedro I and his mistress, Inez de Castro.

Thirteen miles (21km) north-east along N1 is the equally famous church of the monastery of *Our Lady of Victory at Batalha*, celebrating the victory of *Aljubarrota* (1385) over the Castilians. The victor, King João I, lies buried here in the Founder's Chapel with his Queen, Philippa of Lancaster (daughter of John of Gaunt) and their sons, of whom the most celebrated was Prince Henry the Navigator. A beautiful and impressive church, with some English influence in its design, and later pure Portuguese influence in the Manueline additions.

The next town along N1 is *Leiria*△, dominated by a medieval castle; ruins of Romanesque church of *São Pedro* below castle; sixteenth-century Renaissance cathedral. Westwards for 14 miles (22km) through forest of *Leiria* is *São Pedro de Moel*△, on the coast.

From *Leiria* continue on N1 via *Pombal*, overlooked by medieval castle of the Templars, to *Condeixa*, where nearby Roman excavations at *Conimbriga* are finest in Iberian Peninsula. On for 9 miles (15km) to *Coimbra*.

Coimbra△, third city of Portugal, overlooked by university, one of Europe's oldest, high above the *Mondego*, with architecture from Romanesque to modern. The old cathedral is Romanesque; the new cathedral is eighteenth century. The *Machado de Castro Museum*, in former episcopal palace, has Roman galleries in basement. In the lower town is the *Monastery of Santa Cruz*, founded by Afonso Henriques but rebuilt in the sixteenth century. In the *Praca do Comercio* is the church of *São Tiago*, rebuilt in eighteenth century but retaining its Romanesque doorways.

Leave *Coimbra* by N111, following north banks of the *Mondego* through several historically interesting villages to *Figueira da Foz*, a modern and popular resort with fine sandy beaches.

North on N109 through pinewoods and farmlands of *Beira Litoral* with its distinctive windmills and water-wheels. *Aveiro*, a fishing town on edge of landlocked lagoon; canals lined with houses with sixteenth- and seventeenth-century façades. Several interesting churches of same period. The lagoon can be seen by a trip along the road to the coast at *Barra*, or better still by boat from the town. Salt drying in shallow beds around lagoon.

From *Aveiro* N109 north to *Ovar* and along coast to *Espinho*, a seaside resort; 10 miles (16km) farther is *Vila Nova de Gaia* on the south bank of the *Douro*, facing *Oporto* where wine from up-river vineyards is blended, matured in vats, decanted into wooden barrels and stored in port wine 'lodges', where free tasting is offered to visitors and many thousand litres exported.

Oporto△, on steep northern bank of *Douro*, crossed by three noteworthy bridges, one designed by Eiffel, the French engineer, another iron bridge carrying two roads, one above the other, and a daring single-span structure in reinforced concrete, built in the 1960s. Second city of Portugal; a busy commercial centre with long connections with England; many historic buildings; modern university. *São Martinho da Cedofeita*, Romanesque with seventeenth-century restorations. Church and convent of *Santa Clara*, Gothic and Renaissance with splendid gilding in interior. Cathedral, Romanesque with considerable eighteenth-century restorations.

R3 Oporto to Valença (Spanish Frontier) (98 miles, 157km)
This route covers the far north of Portugal to the *Minho* province on the Spanish frontier.

Leave *Oporto* by N14 via *Vila Nova de Famalicao* to **Braga** △, important as *Bracara Augusta* in Roman times; occupied by Moors from late eighth century to mid-eleventh century. Became ecclesiastically important after Reconquest and has remained so; archbishop is primate of all Portugal. Richly endowed with Renaissance and baroque architecture, and Romanesque cathedral with Gothic and later additions.

EXCURSIONS: a few kilometres east and south-east are two hill-top pilgrimage churches — *Bom Jesus do Monte* (eighteenth century) and *Sameiro*; fine views towards mountains on Spanish frontier. Further east from *Bom Jesus* is ancient Iberian hill fort at *Briteiros*. The wild granitic *Serra do Gerês* is within the *Parque Nacional da Peneda-Gerês* and is best explored from *Lindoso*△ and *Vilharinho das Furnas*△, both lying close to the Spanish frontier, 56 miles (90km) to the north-east. North-westwards by N201 for 2 miles (3km) trip to Byzantine church of *São Frutuoso*, a unique pre-Moorish relic.

Nineteen miles (30km) from *Braga* is *Ponte de Lima*; pleasant little town where road crosses River Lima by bridge built in 1360 on Roman foundations. From here follow N202 on north bank of *Lima* down its lovely valley to *Viana do*

Castelo; attractive seaport with Manueline and Renaissance architecture, interesting churches. Funicular to *Monte de Santa Luzia*, gives splendid views of the coast, the town and the *Lima* valley.

Leave *Viana* by N13 which hugs coast as far as mouth of *Minho*. *Caminha*, attractive small town; main square with fifteenth-century battlemented buildings, sixteenth-century church and fountain.

Continue along delightful *Minho* valley, the frontier between Spain and Portugal, to *Vila Nova de Cerveira*△ and *Valença do Minho*, old border citadels each within encircling ramparts. *Vigo* in Spain is 20 miles (32km) further.

R4 Lisbon — Evora — Faro — Lagos — Lisbon (509 miles, 819km)

This route covers southern Portugal, first the *Alentejo*, a province occupying almost a third of the country, then the *Algarve*, southernmost province and most westerly region of Iberian peninsula conquered by Moors; so named from Arabic *El-gharb*, meaning 'west'. Moorish influence lasted longer, and population is sparser, than in the north. The *Algarve* can be very hot in summer.

Leave *Lisbon* by N10, or by motorway, to *Vila Franca de Xira*; bull breeding centre; arena with frequent bullfights during summer season. Cross River *Tagus* by modern toll bridge and across flat monotonous sparsely inhabited country for 28 miles (45km); then turn left at crossroads on to N4 to *Vendas Novas*. Soon the *Alentejo* is entered and the scenery changes, with rolling country and many cork-oak trees. *Montemor-o-Novo*, small town dominated by castle. Fifteen miles (24km) further is *Arraiolos*, noted since Middle Ages for woollen carpets; more castle ruins. Continue on N4 to **Estremoz**, hill town in marble quarrying locality; overlooked by medieval castle, surrounded by seventeenth-century ramparts and famous for *Alentejo* pottery. Top platform of thirteenth-century keep of castle affords distant views in all directions.

Continue on N4 to *Borba*, a town notable for extensive use of marble in its construction, then take N255 to *Vila Viçosa*, favoured by monarchy, has become museum town; sixteenth-century marble palace of Dukes of Bragança overlooks a great square, together with church and convent.

South-westwards on N254 to **Évora**△, a walled town since Roman times, retains almost intact *Temple of Diana* with granite Corinthian columns, marble bases and capitals. Medieval ramparts to north and west of town; much Gothic, Renaissance and Manueline architecture. See the cathedral (and view from roof), battlement chapel of *São Bras*, church of *São Francisco*, the buildings of *Praça do Giraldo* and numerous fine houses and squares.

5Fifty-one miles (82km) south, across hilly country along N18 lies *Beja*, another hill town of Roman origin, convent of *Conceição*, now a museum (Gothic-Moorish façade); thirteenth-century keep of castle which dominates the town.

Continue for 13 miles (21km) on N18 to *Ervidel* and join N2 to *Aljustrel*, a mining town. From here to *Castro Verde* road runs across flat wheat-growing plain. From *Almodovar* ascent of *Serra do Malhão* begins, and after *Ameixial* the descent into the *Algarve*, the most popular province of Portugal for the visitor. Olive, almond, fig, mulberry and other fruit trees are to be seen mile after mile on the road to *Faro*, an ancient town, but most of its historic buildings destroyed by earthquakes; now an international resort.

EXCURSION: *Olhão*, 6 miles (10km) east, fishing port with canning industry, separated from sea by long sandbar; town of Moorish appearance with white cubic houses.

Leave *Faro* by N125 to *São João da Venda*, fork right to *Loulé* in centre of some of loveliest *Algarve* countryside. Thirteenth-century church; town famous for number and variety of Moorish-style chimneys that adorn the houses. West along N270 to rejoin N125. *Alcantarilha*, picturesque village. Twelve miles (19km) west is fishing port of *Portimão*Δ. Nearby is *Praia de Rocha*, excellent bathing, fine beaches and cliffs. Continue to *Lagos*. Seaside resort and fishing port with many old houses; in the *Praça da Republica* is the Customs House where, at one time, slave markets were held. Remarkable cliff formation at *Ponta da Peidade*, 1 mile (2km) south.

EXCURSIONS: (a) to **Cape St Vincent**, 20 miles (32km) west along N125. Wild barren plateau, ending in lofty cliffs around the cape, most south-westerly point of continental Europe. At *Ponta de Sagres*Δ are the remains of Prince Henry the Navigator's fortress now restored, where he established his maritime school and planned the explorations which established Portugal's empire. See particularly the stone compass dial in the courtyard. (b) to the *Serra de Monchique*, 26 miles (42km) via *Portimão* by N125, N124 and N266 to *Monchique*. The *Serra* form a range of beautiful hills, covered in lush vegetation and commanding fine views, particularly from the peak of *Foia* (2,960ft, 902m) above village of *Monchique*.

Leave *Lagos* by N120, which crosses *Serra de Espinhaço de Cão* to *Aljezur* and on to *Santiago do Cacém* at southern end of range of low hills notable for their windmills. 10 miles (16km) west lies fishing village of *Sines*: harbour protected by rocky headland; birthplace of Vasco da Gama.

Continue on N120 from *Santiago do Cacém*, first over hills, then across rice growing plain of River *Sado* (bridge for motor vehicles only) to *Alcácer do Sal*. Here take N5 for 20 miles (32km) and at village of *Marateca* take N10 for *Setubal*, port and industrial town, but many interesting monuments; famous for export of seed oysters and muscatel wine; church of *Jesus* in daring Manueline style. Top ramparts of *St Philip's* castle, sixteenth-century, for breathtaking panorama. On for 25 miles (40km) to *Tagus* estuary to *Cacilhas* where ferry can be taken across to *Lisbon*.

EXCURSION: a pleasant diversion from *Setubal* is to *Sesimbra*, interesting fishing port set in a coast of splendid cliffs, haven for underwater swimmers and swordfish, 16 miles (25km) west along *Serra da Arrabida* (leave Lisbon road at *Vila Nogueira de Azeitão* and take N379 to *Sesimbra*).

SCOTLAND

Geographical Outline

Scotland is a country in its own right, differing from England and Wales in history, tradition, institutions and culture.

Land

Scotland has an area of about 30,000 sq miles (77,000 sq km). Its mainland extends 274 miles (441km) from the *Mull of Galloway* in the south-west to *Cape Wrath* in the north. To the north lie the *Orkney* and *Shetland* island groups, the latter on the same latitude as Labrador and the southern tip of Greenland. Off the west coast lie the *Hebrides* and other islands; more than 100 are inhabited.

The mainland has four regions: *the Southern Uplands*, *Central Lowlands*, *Highlands*, and *North-East Coastal Plain* — a layout mainly determined by the nature of the rocks out of which erosion has fashioned the scenery of today. The rocks of the *Central Lowlands* (Old Red Sandstone and Carboniferous) have proved less resistant than the older formations of the *Southern Uplands* and *Highlands* on either side and from which they are marked off by geological faults.

Another major fault, dividing the *Highlands* in two, has smashed the hard rocks along its course so completely that erosion of their debris has been easy and has produced the *Great Glen (Glen More)* from *Inverness* to *Fort William*. The scale of faulting has been such that the rocks on one side of the glen have travelled horizontally 65 miles (104km) past their opposite numbers on the other.

The *Highlands* have more than 500 summits over 3,000ft (900m) in height. They are the worn stumps of a range many millions of years older than the Alps and were originally of comparable altitude. The glorious landscape of the *North-West Highlands* is the front of this ancient range.

Contemporary with the upheaval of the Alps, volcanoes were active, notably along the line of the present islands of *Arran, Mull, Rum* and *Skye*. The basaltic island of *Staffa*, including the famous *Fingal's Cave*, cut by the sea in columnar basalt, is part of a lava flow from *Mull*. A fine example of an extinct volcano is

378

Arthur's Seat in *Edinburgh*.

Drowning of the western coast is seen not only in the numerous islands but also in the deep indentations of the sea lochs.

More recently the Ice Age contributed to the detailed shaping of the landscape, as in the corries and lake basins of the *Highlands* and, more particularly, the crag and tail sculpturing of the site of *Edinburgh* and the 'parallel roads' of *Glen Roy*. In *Edinburgh* it is easy to see how the bottom currents of an eastward flowing glacier or ice-sheet were deflected by the resistant basalt of the *Castle Rock*, so that they gouged out the hollows of *Princes Street Gardens* and the *Grass Market*. In between they left a sheltered 'tail' destined after time to carry the *Royal Mile*. In *Glen Roy* the so-called 'parallel roads' represent three terraces of former lakes which were temporarily dammed by glaciers at different levels.

Climate

The weather varies almost from hour to hour. Atlantic depressions particularly affect the north and bring high winds to the *Orkney* and *Shetland* islands. There is considerable difference in climate between east and west. Winters in the *Outer Hebrides* are mild, while in the north-east there may be heavy snow. Annual rainfall ranges from about 150in (380cm) in the north-west to less than 26in (66cm) in the *Lothians* and around the *Moray Firth*. Spring is generally the driest season. June is the finest month, especially along the western seaboard. July and August are warmer but wetter. September and October often provide good weather for the late holidaymaker. Long daylight is a feature of the northern summer.

Plants and Animals

The original extensive forests of Scots pine which were the natural vegetation of most land below about 1,250ft (400m) were gradually destroyed through the expansion of cultivation, the need to drive out wolves and the use of timber for smelting, charcoal and shipbuilding. Remnants of the primeval forest remain in the *Highland*s, the best example being the *Black Wood* of *Rannoch* in *Perthshire*, *Rothiemurchus Forest* in *Speyside* and the *Glen Affic* area.

On higher ground heather moorland is dominant on the poorer soils, but there are extensive areas of grass where conditions are more favourable.

A large number of Arctic-alpine plants are widespread in the Highlands above the moorland. During June and July the rock ledges are festooned with flowers. Several species found at these high altitudes are relics of the Arctic flora which existed in Britain during the Ice Age. Many of the same species of flora are still found in Northern Canada, Greenland, Spitzbergen and Novaya Zemlya.

Red deer range over the *Highlands* and the Royal stags with their twelve-pointed antlers make a splendid sight. Roe deer are found in the lower woodland.

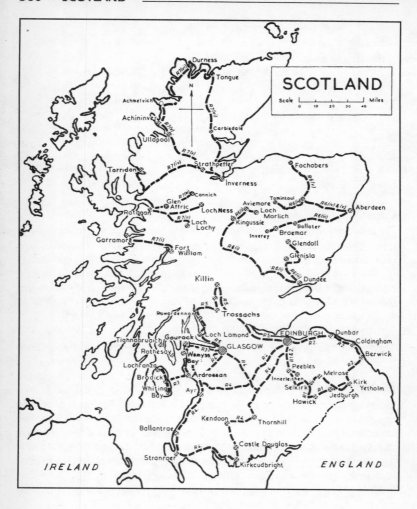

A herd of reindeer was introduced some years ago to a reserve in *Speyside*. The wild cat, the most savage of British animals, is still common in the north. The pine marten, once almost extinct, has found shelter in the increasing State forests.

The golden eagle with a wing span of up to 8ft (2½m) is sometimes seen. The osprey, or white-tailed sea eagle, is again nesting in *Speyside*.

The People

Population

Scotland has rather more than five million inhabitants; three-quarters live in the industrial belt of the *Central Lowlands*. The shifting of population to the towns, common to so many countries, has been experienced in acute form and only about half-a-million now remain in rural areas. There has been great emigration, principally to Canada, the USA and New Zealand. Depopulation has been most serious in the *Highlands* and *Islands*; north of *Perth* there are now vast areas with only scattered houses.

There are four cities: *Glasgow* (900,000), *Edinburgh*, the capital (456,000), *Aberdeen* (215,000) and *Dundee* (191,000).

The Scot is an amalgam of many races. Scots, Picts, Britons, Angles, Norsemen and Danes have all contributed something to the character of the people. Small groups of Flemish traders settled on the east coast and in more recent times the Irish have found in the industrial belt opportunities denied them in their native land.

The Highlanders, isolated by geography and language from the rest of the country, have retained longest their individual temperament, mode of life and culture.

Language

The Scots tongue is more than a dialect of English. It has its own dialects, differing in pronunciation and vocabulary. In the common speech of the country people some words can be traced to the 'Auld Alliance' over many centuries between Scotland and France or to the earlier Viking influence. In the Old Norse colonies of *Orkney* and *Shetland*, especially, many Norse words survive. Many Scots who speak good English still seek out old Scots words or phrases to describe something graphically or to emphasise a point.

Gaelic is still spoken by some 90,000 people in the north and west, but all but a few are bilingual. The careful speech of many Highlanders is due to their thinking in an idiom completely different from English. Place names, including many in the southern counties, show the one time wide distribution of Gaelic.

Religion

The Church of Scotland is Presbyterian in organisation, ie its ministers are all of equal rank and are chosen by the congregation. Each parish is administered by a kirk session of elders. Among other Presbyterian churches the most influential is the Free Church, which is strongest in the west and north-west *Highlands*, where strict Sabbatarian principles are maintained.

The Roman Catholic Church with some 780,000 members is strong in the industrial west where there are many people of Irish extraction. In the *Highlands* and *Islands* there are Catholic communities, eg *Morar*, which remained unaffected by the Reformation.

The Scottish Episcopal Church is part of the Anglican communion.

History

The Picts of the north baulked Rome in its aim to conquer the whole island of Britannia. Even the hold on the *Lowlands* was abandoned. The legions drew back from the *Antonine Wall* at the narrow neck between the *Firths of Forth* and *Clyde*. *Hadrian's Wall*, from the *Tyne* to the *Solway* became (AD211) the northern frontier of the Empire.

Other invaders were perhaps better fitted to penetrate. By the fifth century the Scots, a Celtic people from Ireland, had established themselves in *Argyll*; the British (Welsh) held *Strathclyde* in the south-west; and Anglian people occupied *Lothian* in the south-east. The introduction of Christianity from Ireland by St Columba in AD563 (following St Ninian and St Kentigern) ensured the dominance of Irish influences for 500 years. A united kingdom of *Alban* (of Picts and Scots, and later to be known as Scotland) was formed in 843 under Kenneth Macalpine of *Dunstaffnage*. Meanwhile Norsemen had settled in the *Western Isles, Orkney* and *Shetland* and by 875 they began to occupy the northern mainland. The kingdom annexed *Lothian* in 1016; *Strathclyde* was united with it by dynastic succession in 1034.

English cultural influences became strong when Malcolm III married an English princess — the St Margaret of Scottish history. Under David I (1124-53) a modified Norman feudal system was established. The Norsemen were pushed out of *Sutherland* and *Caithness* (1196), but English claims to overlordship of Scotland were the most pressing problems and led to the beginning (1200) of the 'Auld Alliance' of Scotland and France. The defeat of Haakon of Norway by Alexander III at *Largs* (1263) ended the Norse supremacy in the *Western Isles*. (*Orkney* and *Shetland*, however, remained Norse until 1469 when they were acquired as a pledge for a marriage dowry). But on Alexander's death (1286) the whole kingdom passed to Margaret, the Maid of Norway. Her death on the voyage to Scotland left the throne open to many rival claimants. The English king, Edward I, acting as arbitrator, awarded it to John Balliol but insisted on his own supreme overlordship. The subsequent rebellion led by William Wallace, the seizing of the throne by Robert Bruce and his victory against the English army at *Bannockburn* (1314) are among the most stirring chapters of Scottish history.

The crowning of Bruce's grandson, Robert, the High Steward, as Robert II (1371) marks the beginning of the House of Stewart (Stuart), so fateful in the later story of England and Scotland. An important link with the Tudors, ruling in England, was the marriage (1503) of James IV to Margaret, daughter of Henry

VII. But the alliance with France continued and provoked disastrous war with England.

Around the powerful figure of John Knox the Reformation gathered strength from 1559. Along with the Protestantism of Elizabethan England it was fatal to the spirited but tragic Mary, Queen of Scots. Her French connections, Catholic upbringing and capacity for intrigue were so dangerous to the new Protestant state that they led to her execution in 1587. It was her son, James VI, who became James I of England at the Union of the Crowns (1603).

Most of the country had by this time become Presbyterian and was resentful of Charles I's attempts at reaction. It therefore took the side of Cromwell in the English Civil War. For a time, during Cromwell's Protectorate, the two Parliaments were united at Westminster. After the Restoration of the Stewarts (1660) religious issues again clouded the relations between the kings and the Scottish people. Yet the loyalty of the *Highlands* to the Stewart House was seen in the revolt which was crushed at *Killiecrankie* (1689). It persisted after the Union of the Parliaments (1707). The rebellion (1715) in support of James Stewart, the Old Pretender, was followed by the more stirring and romantic rising (1745) around his son Charles Edward (Bonnie Prince Charlie), the Young Pretender, who met final defeat at *Culloden*.

The long-term result was the pacification of the *Highlands*, where the clans gave up their habit of raiding the industrious *Lowlands* and turned instead to arable cultivation wherever possible. But much of this work was undone by the Highland Clearances (1840) when thousands of inland crofters were either moved to the coast or forced to emigrate to make way first for sheep farms, later deer reserves.

In other parts of the country the Industrial and Agrarian Revolutions took place at the same time as in England and with similar results.

Government

Details of new legislation concerned solely with Scotland are considered at Westminster by the Scottish Grand Committee to which all Scottish members belong. Administration of many departments of government is carried out from *Edinburgh* under the Secretary of State for Scotland. The many and ancient differences between Scots and English law also necessitate separate Law Officers.

Resources

Heavy industry has been the mainstay for more than a hundred years. There are shipyards on the *Clyde* and the iron and steel industry which grew up on the *Lowland* coalfields. As the coal measures of the west become worked out new seams have been opened in *Fife* and the *Lothians*. Other industries include jute (*Dundee*), granite (*Aberdeen*), chemicals (*Grangemouth*), thread (*Paisley*) and woollens (for which the *Border* towns have an international reputation). *Edinburgh* is primarily an administrative centre but has printing and associated industries and brewing.

Vast reserves of North Sea oil are drilled on the continental shelf off Scotland and numerous oil fields are 'on flow' to Scottish terminals.

Much of the abundant water of the *Highlands* has been harnessed for power. More than fifty hydro-electric stations have been built.

More than two-thirds of the land is mountain, moorland or treeless deer forest and more than half the area of the country is rough grazing. Grass is the most important crop and the main produce is livestock: in the south-west, the world-famous Ayrshire dairy cattle and the hardy black Galloway; in the north-east, the Aberdeen Angus and the Shorthorn. Sheep — the Blackface, Cheviot and Border Leicester — are plentiful. Intensive use is made of arable: along the east coast and around the *Moray Firth* is some of the best farmed land in the world. Most of the wheat is grown in the counties of *Fife, Angus, Perth* and the *Lothians*. Seed potatoes are an important export. Poultry-keeping is on the increase. Eggs are the main produce of *Orkney*.

The type of agriculture carried on in the *Highlands* is known as crofting. There are some 20,000 crofts consisting usually of small areas of arable combined with common (ie shared) hill grazing. Crofts are to an increasing extent worked in combination with some other occupation such as fishing or catering for tourists.

Forestry is a major industry; trees have been planted in peaty soil formerly regarded as useless and plantations set up in many remote areas. The *Forestry Commission* has over 4 million hectares under woodland, the private sector has a further 300,000 hectares.

Sea fisheries are of greater relative importance than in England and numerous towns and villages have for generations been dependent on fishing, but there is now a trend towards centralisation. Most of the white fish catch is landed by trawlers based at *Aberdeen* and *Granton*. Scottish trawlers do not usually go so far as English trawlers and they cater more for the 'quality' market.

Customs

The Scots calendar retains survivals of Celtic and Norse festivals. Yule, the New Year, is still celebrated with Scandinavian fire rites such as the Burning of the Clavie at *Burghead* in *Moray*, the Fireballs ceremony at *Stonehaven*, Burning the Old Year Out at *Biggar* and the spectacular Up-Helly-a' at *Lerwick* in which a Viking galley is sacrificed to the flames.

Other customs include 'first footing' in the 'wee sma oors' of New Year; handball games at *Jedburgh* and other Border towns at Candlemas (St Bride's Day: 1 February); face washing in dew on *Arthur's Seat, Edinburgh* and crowning of a Beltane Queen at *Peebles* on Beltane (1 May) (many of the Border

Common Ridings, although now spread over a period, are believed to have their origins in Beltane ceremonies); fairs at *Kirkwall, St Andrews* and some other towns and the procession of the Burry Man (the spirit of vegetation) at *South Queensferry* at Lammas (1 August), traditionally a herd's festival. Hallowe'en (31 October), the season of the earth's decay, when our forefathers remembered their dead, is still a time when children (the *guizers*) dress up, blacken their faces and carry lanterns made of hollowed turnips. Bonfires lit at dusk show the Celtic origin of the night's festivities; the highlight of the children's parties — 'dookin' for apples in a tub of water — is believed to have a Druidic origin.

Food and Drink

Scots cookery is not sophisticated but prime Scotch beef, salmon, grouse, venison and Scotch broth are worthy of any menu. The treatment of fish has received most attention. These include *Finnan* haddock, the coffee-coloured *Arbroath* smokie, the copper and gold *Loch Fyne* kipper and that delicate luxury, smoked salmon. Oatmeal porridge with cream still compares with packaged breakfast cereals. There is of course the haggis, 'chieftain o' the pudding race', which has a brief moment of glory at Burns' suppers on 25 January.

Scots bakers are outstanding and there is a great variety of sweetcakes. Shortbread is world famous. Oatcakes with jam or cheese are excellent. In Scotland pancakes are English drop scones; crumpets are pancakes; cookies are buns. Buttery baps are well known in *Aberdeen* where the best are made. Among many other local pastries are *Forfar* bridies.

Skirlie, oatmeal fried with onions, is a tasty addition to a grill or fry. Athol brose, sometimes served as a sweet, is a potent mixture of whisky, cream and oatmeal, the proportions a well-guarded secret. Marmalade had its origin in *Dundee*.

Scotland's most famous product is whisky, produced in numerous distilleries throughout the country. The best quality whisky is made in the *Highlands* and is called 'malt whisky'; its principal raw material is malted barley.

Dress

The wearing of the kilt has increased in popularity in post-war years. In the *Highlands*, however, its wearing is regarded as the mark of the landlords. Despite bemedalled girl dancers at Highland Games it is a masculine garment. Traditional women's dress is worn by dancers at some Highland Games. On festive occasions another form is worn by East Coast fisherwomen.

Sport

The Highland Games — sports meetings which draw great numbers of visitors — originated in the gatherings of clansmen around their chiefs. The contests include tossing the caber (a tree trunk), putting the shot, throwing the hammer, wrestling, hill races, piping and Highland dancing. The principal gatherings are at *Braemar* and *Aboyne* in *Deeside, Lonach* in *Donside*, the Northern meeting in *Inverness* and the *Oban* and *Cowal* Games.

Golf had its origin in Scotland and there are few places without a course. Curling is another game which has spread from Scotland to many countries; indoor ice rinks have increased its popularity. There is a considerable winter sports industry, particularly in the *Cairngorms* area. Shinty — a vigorous form of hockey, with a dash of lacrosse — is a distinctly Scottish game which still has many enthusiasts in the *Highlands*. Bowling differs from the crown game played in much of England; the bias is built into the bowls and the greens are flat.

Association football is popular and rugby also has a large following. Seven-a-side tournaments — a variant introduced by rugby clubs in the *Borders* — provide fast-moving exciting games.

Culture

Architecture

The broch, a circular defence tower with walls up to 16ft (5m) thick, is found only in Scotland and is probably attributable to the Picts. The best example is at *Mousa* in *Shetland*. There are others in *Skye* and in *Glenelg*.

The oldest church is *St Margaret's* chapel in *Edinburgh Castle*. The Roman-esque is represented by *St Regulus* in *St Andrews*, *St Magnus Cathedral* in *Kirkwall, Dunfermline Abbey*, the ruined abbeys of *Jedburgh* and *Kelso* and restored churches at *Iona, Dalmeny* and *Leuchars*. Gothic examples are *Glasgow Cathedral* and the ruins of *Arbroath, Dryburgh* and *Holyrood Abbeys* and *Elgin Cathedral*. Decorated Gothic: *Sweetheart Abbey* near *Dumfries*, *Melrose Abbey* and *Dunblane Cathedral*. Notable examples of late Gothic are *St Michael's, Linlithgow* and *St Machar's Cathedral, Aberdeen*. This late period produced work of distinctively national character such as the open crown spires of *St Giles', Edinburgh* and *King's College, Aberdeen*.

Castles show less outside influence than churches. Examples of domestic burgh architecture are preserved in most towns, but *Culross* near *North Queensferry* has the greatest number.

The era of the great architects and large mansions of the late seventeenth and eighteenth centuries is well represented. *Edinburgh University* was designed by Robert Adam, the architect of the classic revival. *Edinburgh's New Town* was built in the late eighteenth and early nineteenth centuries. *Glasgow School of Art* (1894) by Charles Rennie Mackintosh had a wide influence on the growth of the modern idiom on the Continent.

Music

The *Lowlands* have songs associated with Burns and the Jacobites and more modern songs inspired by Gaelic airs; *Hebridean* and *Highland* working songs, rowing songs and lullabies have great beauty. There has recently been a revival of country dance tunes, *reels*, *strathspeys* and other traditional forms. Bagpipe music — a developed form of folk music — reaches its most advanced level in the intricate *pibroch*.

Literature

The poems of Robert Burns — catching the very lilt and tone of Lowland Scots — have a unique place; he is popularly cherished and annually remembered in Burns' Night celebrations.

Scots writers have made notably spirited contributions to writing in standard English. They include James Thomson, the poet of *The Seasons,* Boswell, the biographer of Dr Johnson, Thomas Carlyle and, among novelists, Smollett, Scott, R.L. Stevenson and John Buchan.

Science

Adam Smith's *Wealth of Nations* makes him the founder of political economy. Hugh Miller's *Old Red Sandstone* is a charming classic of writing on geology. The Scottish genius for practical application of knowledge is particularly well illustrated in the fields of transport and medicine. Telford, the engineer of canals and roads; Symington, the pioneer of steam navigation; and the inventors of the steam engine (James Watt), the bicycle (Kirkpatrick MacMillan), hard road surfaces (Macadam) and the pneumatic tyre (J.B. Dunlop) — all were Scots, as also were Simpson, the first user of chloroform as an anaesthetic; Lister, the pioneer of antiseptic surgery; and Fleming, the discoverer of penicillin.

Museums

In addition to the large collections in *Edinburgh* and *Glasgow* (see Touring Routes), others of special interest include the *Albert Institute, Dundee* (whaling), *Dunhope Museum, Dundee* (archaeological and technological), *Aberdeen Art Gallery Museum* (wildlife, natural resources and history of the north-east), *Marischal College Museum, Aberdeen* (prehistoric), *Inverness Museum* (Highland relics), *West Highland Museum, Fort William* (tartans, Jacobite treasures and weapons), folk museums at *Glamis* and *Kingussie*, Hugh Miller's cottage at *Cromarty*, Burns' cottage, *Ayr* and David Livingstone's birthplace at *Blantyre*. There are many local museums in the *Borders*.

Touring Information

Transport

Trains provide the fastest means of long distance travel; bus services in the more populous areas are good. In remote districts services are maintained by small operators often on a one-bus-a-day basis. Steamer services on the *Clyde* and in the *Western Isles* are operated by Caledonian MacBrayne.

Details of all transport services, including Postbuses, are set out in the booklet *Getting Around in the Highlands and Islands* published annually in April by Highlands and Islands Development Board, Bridge House, Bank Street, Inverness.

There are no trains in the *Western Highlands* on Sundays and bus and ferry services are extremely limited.

Money

Scottish banks issue their own pound notes and although these are legal tender in England it may save argument if they are exchanged for Bank of England coins before returning south.

Clothing

Ordinary outdoor clothing with the addition of a heavy sweater (or better two thin ones), or windproof jacket is all that is required by the ordinary traveller. Midge cream is recommended for summer use. Clegs (horse-flies) are persistent attackers in bracken and heather.

Restaurants

Cheap if you find the right place, and so it is worth seeking local guidance. High tea is the great Scottish meal and usually consists of fish or an egg dish, tea, scones and cakes. Good value almost everywhere. Mutton pies are traditional fare.

Fish and chips are now a national institution. A northern variety is chips and oatmeal pudding which sometimes appears on the bill of fare as a 'mealie jimmy'.

Maps

For walkers, the Ordnance Survey maps, scale 1:50,000 in eighty-five sheets. Particularly useful for cyclists are the Bartholomew National series scale 1:100,000, twenty-four sheets. The Ordnance Survey 1:250,000 *Routemaster* series are excellent maps for motorists. SYHA map of Scotland, 9 miles to 1in, shows hostels and places to visit. Regional guides include those published by Her Majesty's Stationery Office for the Forestry Commission: *National Forest Park Guides to Argyll, Forests of North-East Scotland, Glen More (Cairngorms),*

Queen Elizabeth, Ben Lomond, Loch Ard and the Trossachs.

Climber's guides, detailing rock climbing routes in the main areas are published by the Scottish Mountaineering Club.

Accommodation

There are about eighty youth hostels, providing good coverage for every touring area. Meals are provided at only a few hostels. Periods during which advance booking is advised are stated separately for each hostel in the SYHA handbook.

Camping

Permission to camp should always be asked of farmers and landowners. Membership of Camping and Caravan Club of Great Britain, 11 Lower Grosvenor Place, London SW1 is an advantage.

Walking

The country provides an inexhaustible variety of experience for the walker, particularly for the tough and strenuous; but tours of all grades are possible.

Mountaineering

Most of the mountains rise either directly from the sea or the low-lying glens and so gain the full advantage of their height. This fact, and the possibility of experiencing very severe, even sub-Arctic, conditions on the heights, makes proper preparation essential.

Of the vast tracts of uninhabited mountain country the finest is the *Cairngorms* area. The *Cuillin Hills* and *Glencoe* provide innumerable rock climbs of all grades of difficulty. In the north a number of fascinating peaks — among them *Liathach, Beinn Eighe, An Teallach* and *Stac Polly* — give good climbing and ridge walking. *Ben Nevis*, Scotland's highest mountain (4,406ft, 1,343m) can be easily reached by the path from *Glen Nevis* but its northern precipices offer superb rock climbing. In the *Loch Lomond* area the *Arrochar* peaks, near *Ardgartan*, offer enjoyable excursions and a training ground in rock climbing for the longer climbs further north. There is excellent ridge walking on the *Isle of Arran*.

Skiing

In good conditions skiing can be as good as at the best resorts in Norway and Central Europe. But weather conditions change quickly. The most stable snow conditions are in the *Cairngorms* where the best time is in March and April. There is snow in January and February, and even in December, but bad weather then often makes skiing difficult.

In January and February, the *Southern Grampians* are most frequented as their weather is less severe than in the *Cairngorms* and the hostels at *Glen Clova (Glendoll)* and *Killin* are nearer for weekend skiers. In the west, there is a reliable snow field on *Meall a' Bhuiridh* in *Glencoe* (with ski and chair lift).

Motoring

Motoring conditions and requirements are very similar to those in England and Wales, except that in many areas of the Highlands most roads are single track with passing places.

Cycling

Even on small by-roads surfaces are generally good, and such roads should particularly be taken in the south, where there is much traffic on main roads. They are, in any case, much more picturesque. In the north, main roads are crowded only in July and August. Distances between hostels in the north-west are just right for easy cycling.

A low gear is an advantage for some of the steep hills, particularly in the north, and also to counter strong winds on exposed moorland routes.

Canoeing

The finest canoeing is among the many fjords, inlets and islands of the west coast, but experience is required because of tides and currents. The best area is round the *Firth of Clyde*. The whole of the coast has been canoed. The extreme north, however, is very stormy and should be visited only after long apprenticeship in calmer waters.

The principal rivers are the *Spey, Tay* and *Tweed*, but care neede to be exercised not to interfere with fishing interests. The fastest is the *Spey*. The *Tay*, near *Stanley* (just north of *Perth*) affords a magnificent stretch of white water which is used for the Scottish Slalom Championships. The *Tweed* is suitable, usually, only in spring and autumn as it is generally too low in summer. The finest resort for the average canoeist is the *Loch Lomond* with its many bays and islands.

Sailing

As with canoeing, the west coast and the *Clyde Estuary* are the finest areas although there is a great deal of sailing on the *Firth of Forth* and *Firth of Tay*. Dinghy sailing is popular; at most seaside resorts there are weekly races in which visitors can generally take part.

Fishing

Brown trout, sea trout and salmon abound in the lochs, rivers and streams. Much of the fishing is privately owned and strictly preserved, but a large part is controlled by local angling associations who, for a modest charge, will issue permits to individual anglers to fish by the day, week, or month. They are non-profit-making concerns; fees received go towards re-stocking and to improvement of the fishing generally.

Many private owners of trout waters will give permission for a day's fishing now and again to any angler who asks for it. Some never refuse, believing that the presence of anglers on the water acts as a deterrent to poachers who take fish other than by means of rod and line. Most of the salmon fishing is strictly preserved, but some good sport can be obtained on payment of very reasonable fees.

Pony Trekking

This is popular in summer. The *Borders*, the *Angus Glens*, *Deeside* and *Speyside* are the main centres but in many other areas ponies — usually Icelandic, Exmoor or the sturdy Highland 'garron' — are available for those who want to get away from the beaten tracks.

Edinburgh△

Edinburgh occupies one of the finest sites of any city in the world. Its *New Town* (1767) is a famous example of eighteenth-century town planning. Best starting point is the **Castle**; view of city from ramparts; regalia of Scotland; from half-moon battery is fired city's time signal, the one o'clock gun. **Scottish National War Memorial** crowns highest part of rock. Oldest part of *Castle* is eleventh-century *St Margaret's Chapel*.

Between *Castle* and **Palace of Holyroodhouse** (chief royal residence in Scotland) stretches the '*Royal Mile*' which, with the closes and wynds on either side, was *Old Edinburgh*. *Outlook Tower* and *Camera Obscura* (view of *Princes Street*, *Forth* and hills). **Greyfriars Churchyard** where the National Covenant was signed in 1638, and **National Library of Scotland** (see exhibition rooms) are both in *George IV Bridge*. **Royal Scottish Museum** in *Chambers Street*.

Separated from *Old Edinburgh* by *Princes Street Gardens* is the **New Town** with spacious streets and handsome squares. In *West Princes Street Gardens* is famous *Floral Clock* and *Scots-American War Memorial*. **Scott Monument** in *East Princes Street Gardens* may be climbed. Between the two gardens is the *Mound*; at foot is **Royal Scottish Academy**, behind which is **National Gallery**.

At eastern end of **Princes Street** (one of most beautiful streets in the world) is **Calton Hill**, more remarkable for view from it than for its monuments.

National Portrait Gallery and (in the same building) **Museum of Antiquities** are in *Queen Street*. **Royal Botanical Gardens**, north of *New Town*, finely laid out.

International Festival of Music and Drama, three weeks annually, late August and early September.

EXCURSIONS: (a) **Linlithgow Palace**, birthplace of Mary, Queen of Scots. (b) **Forth Bridge** and new road bridge at *Queensferry*; **Dunfermline Abbey**, burial place of King Robert Bruce. (c) **Culross**, a whole seventeenth-century village of great architectural interest.

Touring Routes

The Borders

A close-knit region, in the valleys of which are many towns rich in history. Excellent touring country for motorists and cyclists. The intervening hills provide fine walking.

R1 Walking Tour: Peebles — Kirk Yetholm — Peebles (110 miles, 177km)
Peebles, on River *Tweed*. Bus for 6 miles (10km) to *Innerleithen* where tour begins. Cross river to *Traquair* and by hill path over *Minchmuir* (1,856ft, 566m) to *Broadmeadows*Δ, 8 miles (13km), above *Yarrow Water*.

Selkirk, 5 miles (8km), town on hill above *Ettrick Water*; statues of Sir Walter Scott and Mungo Park; *Abbotsford*, 5 miles (8km), Scott's home, containing many relics; *Melrose*Δ, 4 miles (6km), small town with famous abbey repeatedly destroyed in border warfare (Cistercian, 1136).

EXCURSION: *Eildon Hills* (1,385ft, 422m) and ruins of **Dryburgh Abbey**, finely situated by *Tweed*: return by *Old Melrose* and *Newstead* (Roman fort, *Trimontium*).

Bus to *Jedfoot*. Walk to *Jedfoot Station*, then by Roman road south-east over *Shibden Hill* to *Hounam*, 10 miles (16km); path to *Bowmont Water* and *Kirk Yetholm* Δ, 6 miles (10km), northern terminus of *Pennine Way* and centre for walking in *Cheviot Hills*.

Morebattle, *Oxnam* and *Mossburnfoot* to *Ferniehirst Castle*, 15 miles (24km).

Main road for 2 miles (3km) to **Jedburgh**; ruins of **Abbey** (twelfth century); *Queen Mary's House* in *Queen Street*, relics of Mary, Queen of Scots. Bus up *Teviotdale* to *Hawick*, chief town of Roxburghshire, then on foot for 6 miles (10km) to *Snoot*Δ.

Continue for 14 miles (22km) via *Ale Water* and *Wollrig* to *Ettrick Water*, and by *Bowhill* to *Broadmeadows*Δ.

Bus up *Yarrow Water* to *Douglas Farm* (near *Gordon Arms Hotel*). Walk by *Stake Law* (1,784ft, 544m) and *Glen Sax* to *Peebles*, 11 miles (18km).

R2 Motoring or Cycling Tour: Edinburgh — Melrose — Berwick — Dunbar — Edinburgh (190 miles, 306km) (see also **R1**)
*Edinburgh*Δ to *Peebles* (visit *Neidpath Castle*) and on via *Barns*, *Traquair*, *Gordon Arms* and down *Yarrow Water* to *Broadmeadows*Δ, 56 miles (90km).

Selkirk, Abbotsford, Melrose Abbey, 12 miles (19km).

Newstead (Roman fort, *Trimontium*), *St Boswells, Dryburgh Abbey* and *Wallace Monument*, **Jedburgh**, *Ferniehirst Castle*, 19 miles (27km).

Cornhill, Flodden Field (site of battle, 1513); *Norham Castle*; **Berwick**; *Eyemouth*, fishing village; *Coldingham* Δ, 36 miles (58km). (Sea bathing and popular centre for skin-divers; coastal scenery: *St Abb's Head; Coldingham Priory*).

Dunbar, 17 miles (27km) and through fertile *East Lothian* countryside to *Haddington* (county town, many interesting buildings, statue of John Knox) and thence returning to *Edinburgh* after 31 miles (50km).

The Clyde Coast and Isle of Arran

There are several holiday resorts along the southern shores. The islands of *Arran* and *Bute* are within easy reach, the former with a compact group of peaks for the hill walker. The sea lochs of the northern shores are well worth exploring.

R3 Glasgow — Arran — Glasgow (135 miles, 217km)
GlasgowΔ, largest city; many industries. Gothic *Cathedral of St Mungo* with fine twelfth-century crypt. *Art Gallery and Museum* in *Kelvingrove Park*, Chief European schools of painting well represented; *Pollok House*, 3 miles (5km) south, also has good art collections.

Train from *Glasgow* Central station to *Ardrossan*, whence ferry to *Brodick*, **Isle of Arran**; bus to *Whiting Bay*Δ.

EXCURSIONS: (a) *Kildonan Castle*, 4 miles (6km), and fine coast from *Bennan Head* to *Dippin Head*. (b) *Holy Island* and *Cave of St Molios* (Runic inscriptions). (c) *Glenashdale* and hills behind hostel.

Bus all, or part, way to *Lochranza*Δ, 24 miles (39km).

EXCURSIONS: (a) **Goatfell** (2,866ft, 873m). (b) **ridge walk**, *Ben Nuis, Ben Tarsuinn, Beinn a Chliabhain*. (c) **ridge walk**, *Goatfell, Cir Mhor, Beinn a Chliabhain*. (d) walk by *Catacol Bay, Lennymore Church* and *Lochain*.

Return to *Brodick*; steamer to *Ardrossan*; bus to *Weymss Bay* for ferry to *Rothesay*; or bus to *Gourock* for ferry to *Dunoon*, or train to *Glasgow*.

EXCURSION: *Benmore Forest* and *Puck's Glen* (arboretum) in *Strath Eachaig*.

The South-West

The magic of Robert Burns draws people towards *Ayrshire*, but *Galloway*, the *Stewartry (Kirkcudbrightshire)* and *Dumfriesshire* are being discovered by tourists. The coastal scenery varies from magnificent rocky headlands to great stretches of sand. Inland lies some of the finest scenery of the south.

R4 Glasgow (or Edinburgh) to Kirkcudbright, Stranraer and Ayr (280 miles, 450km)

At *Abington* (43 miles, 69km, from *Glasgow*, 40 miles, 64km, from *Edinburgh*), in upper *Clydesdale*, B797 south-west up *Glengonnar Burn* to *Leadhills* and *Wanlockhead*△, 8¹/₂ miles (14km) (1,380ft, 420m), highest village in Scotland; centre for walks.

EXCURSIONS: (a) *Lowther Hills* and *Enterkin Pass*. (b) *Wanlock Water*. (c) by *Willowgrain Hill* to *Sanquhar*, 10 miles (16km), town famous in Presbyterian history.

B797 to *Mennock*, 8 miles (13km). Up *Nithsdale* to *Thornhill*, 10 miles (16km), across *Nith* to *Penpoint*, 2 miles (3km). *Keir*, 1¹/₂ miles (2km) to south-east, birthplace of Kirkpatrick MacMillan, inventor of bicycle (1839); tablet in *Courthill Smithy*. *Maxwelton*, 3 miles (5km), birthplace of 'Annie Laurie'. *Moniaive; High Bridge of Ken; Kendoon* △ 17 miles (27km).

EXCURSIONS: (a) *Lochinvar*, home of Scott's *Young Lochinvar*. (b) ridge walks on *Rhinns of Kells* (2,668ft, 813m). (c) *Cairnsmore of Carsphairn* (2,612ft, 796m).

Castle Douglas, 20 miles (32km); *Carlingwark Loch* and *Threave Castle*, *Kirkcudbright*, 10 miles (16km), handsome small town on *Dee* estuary.

Cardoness Castle, 1 mile (1¹/₂km) from *Gatehouse of Fleet*. Along beautiful coast road to *Dirk Hatteraick's Cave*; ruins of *Barholm Castle* and *Carsluith Castle*. *Creetown*, 11 miles (18km). *Newton Stewart*, 6 miles (10km), finely situated market town of cattle raising district of *Galloway*. *Minnigaff*△ nearby. *Glenluce Abbey*, 15 miles (24km). *Stranraer*, 10 miles (16km), for ferry to Larne, Northern Ireland.

EXCURSIONS:(a) *Mull of Galloway*, via *Kirkmadrine* church, sub-tropical garden of *Logan House* and sea-fish pond at *Port Logan*. (b) **Loch Trool** and *Glen Trool National Forest Park* (camping site at *Caldons*). (c) *Whithorn*, site of first Christian church in Scotland, built by St Ninian, 397; museum has well-known early lettered stones and crosses.

North by *Loch Ryan, Glen App, Ballantrae*, valley of River *Stinchar* to *Pinwherry*, returning to coast at **Girvan**, 35 miles (56km), fishing port and resort. Motor boat to **Ailsa Craig**, 10 miles (16km), precipitous granite rock islet (1,114ft, 339m), bird sanctuary, breeding place of gannets.

Kirkoswald: the country of 'Tam o' Shanter'; *Culzean Castle*, eighteenth-century building in Gothic style by Robert Adam; fine interior; gardens; *Auld Brig o' Doon, Alloway Kirk, Burns Monument, Burns' Cottage* and Museum. Ayr△, 22 miles (35km).

EXCURSIONS: (a) *Brown Carrick* (912ft, 278m), 6 miles (10km) south-west, very extensive view. (b) *Crossrague Abbey* (Cluniac, thirteenth century, fine ruins), 12 miles (19km) south.

Tarbolton, 8 miles (13km), *Burns' Batchelors' Club; Mossgiel*, where *Burns* farmed; *Burns Memorial and Museum: Mauchline*, 5 miles (8km), *Tavern of 'Poosie Nansie'*.

From *Mauchline* either north-west by *Symington* and *Dundonald* (castle) and north by ancient burgh of *Kilmaurs* to *Glasgow*△, 36 miles (58km); or by *Sorn, Muirkirk, Carstairs* and *Carnwath* to *Edinburgh*△, 62 miles (100km).

Loch Lomond, Trossachs and Central Highlands

This, the best known and most readily accessible part of the *Highlands*, has much beautiful scenery, hills for climbers and walkers, and many lochs.

R5 Balloch to Killin and either Edinburgh (130 miles, 209km) or Fort William (165 miles, 265km)

Balloch (bus from *Anderstown Cross Bus Station*, or train from *Glasgow*). *Loch Lomond*△. Walk 2 miles (3km) to steamer (June to mid-September) or bus to *Balmaha*. Walk 7 miles (11km) to *Rowardennan* △, (or steamer all way).

EXCURSIONS: (a) **Ben Lomond** (3,192ft, 973m) by track in 3 hours. (b) path along banks of *Loch Lomond* through *Craig Royston* to *Inversnaid*.

Steamer *Inversnaid*; walk 4 miles (6km) to *Stronachlachar* on *Loch Katrine*: steamer to *Trossachs Pier*; walk 4 miles (6km) through woods and along shore of *Loch Achray* to *Brig o' Turk* and *Trossachs* on *Loch Vennachar*.

EXCURSIONS: the many walks and climbs include (a) **Ben A'an** (1,750ft, 533m), best viewpoint, 1$^1/_2$ hours from *Trossachs Hotel*. (b) **Ben Venue** (2,393ft, 730m).

Continue by road north from *Brig o' Turk* to *Achnahard* and by track up to *Gleann nam Meann* to top of pass; descend to ford (boggy ground) and cross to cart track to *Bailemore*; road to *Balquhidder*, 12 miles (19km).

EXCURSIONS: (a) several walks along shores of **Loch Voil** (associations with Rob Roy, who is buried in churchyard). (b) hill walks on *Braes of Balquhidder*. (c) ascents: **Stobinian** (3,921ft, 1,195m); **Ben More** (3,845ft 1,172m), very extensive view and *Crianlarich*△, 4 miles (6$^1/_2$km) westwards.

Path over *Kirkton Pass* through forestry plantation and down to *Ledchary*, 6 miles (10km), in *Glen Dochart*; road to *Killin Junction*, 2 miles (3km); bus to *Killin*△, at head of *Loch Tay*.

EXCURSIONS: (a) *Stronachlachar* (1,708ft, 520m), 1 hour, view of *Loch* and *Ben Lawers*. (b) *Finlarig Castle* and *Falls of Lochay*, 4 miles (6km). (c) **Ben Lawers**, (3,984ft, 1,214m) of particular interest to botanists. (d) walks on southern side of *Loch Tay*. (e) *Glen Ogle*.

Bus to **Stirling**△, 40 miles (64km), historic burgh; *Castle; Argyll's Lodging* (seventeenth century) and other old houses; *Wallace monument*. *Dunblane*, 6 miles (10km), beautiful Gothic cathedral. Site of *Battle of Bannockburn* (1314) is 2 miles (3km) south of *Stirling*. *Edinburgh* 36 miles (58km).
Alternatively continue to **Western Highlands**.
Crianlarich△, 14 miles (23km), many splendid hill walks. *Tyndrum*, 5 miles (8km); *Dalmally*, 12 miles (19km). By foot of *Loch Awe* and *Falls of Cruachan*, 7 miles (11km). *Pass of Brander*, under *Ben Cruachan* (3,689ft, 1,124m). *Taynuilt*, 6 miles (10km); road follows *Loch Etive* to *Oban*△, 12 miles (19km), route centre for *Western Highlands* and *Islands*, finely situated on *Sound of Kerrera*.

EXCURSIONS: by steamer (a) *Staffa*, uninhabited island, famous basaltic formations, **Fingal's Cave** and other caves; and **Iona**, St Columba's island: *St Oran's Chapel* (Romanesque) and historic *Cemetery*, ancient crosses; **Cathedral** (sixteenth century); **Abbey**, rebuilt by Iona community; (b) *Tobermory*△, **Island of Mull**. Many other excursions by land and sea.

Ballachulish, 37 miles (59km) via *Appin*. **Glencoe**△, 2¹/₂ miles (4km). Centre for experienced walkers and climbers.

EXCURSIONS: (a) Site of Massacre (1692), *Bridge of Coe, Clachaig*. (b) **Five Valleys walk**: morning bus 5¹/₂ miles (9km) up Glen; footpath southwards along *Allt Lairig Eilde* to *Dalness*; down *Glen Etive* to school ³/₄ mile (1km) south of *Inver-charnan*; follow *Allt nan Gaoirean* and cross to *Caol Creran*; from *Corbhainn* west below *Meall an Aodainn* to bridle road from *Glen Creran* and along it to *East Laroch* and *Glencoe*, 19 miles (30km). (c) **Bidean nam Bian** (3,766ft, 1,147m). (d) **Aonach Eagach**, formidable ridge route, needing a head for heights; take local advice.

Ballachulish Bridge; Onich, and by shores of *Loch Linnhe* to **Fort William**, 15 miles (24km). *Glen Nevis*△, 3 miles (5km) (see **R7**). For walkers, fine route in good weather by *Gleann Seileach, Beinn na Gucaig* (2,017ft, 614m), splendid view, and north-east to old military road to *Fort William*, 10 miles (16km).

EXCURSIONS: Ben Nevis (4,406ft, 1,343m), highest mountain in British Isles; many other walks and climbs.

The Eastern Grampians

North-east of *Glen Garry* is the most extensive continuous upland region dominated in the north by the *Cairngorms* and in the east by the *Braes of Angus*.

Among its famous rivers are the *Dee*, the *Don*, and the *Spey*. Its hills, though closely preserved for deer forest and grouse, have become a great mountain playground for walking, skiing and pony trekking. Separated from the *Cairngorms* by *Strath Spey* are the little-known *Monadhliath Mountains*, a haunt of the eagle, drained by the *Findhorn*, one of the most beautiful of Scottish rivers.

The route is divided into five sections, each penetrating the hills by different valleys.

R6 (i) Perth to Dunkeld, Kingussie, Aviemore and Loch Morlich (100 miles, 161km)

Perth△ to *Dunkeld* 14 (22km), old town and ruined cathedral, finely situated on River *Tay*.

Leave *Strath Tay* at *Ballinluig*, 9 miles (14km), and by River *Tummel* to **Pitlochry**△, 5 miles (8km) (see fish ladder for passage of salmon).

EXCURSIONS: (a) *Queen's View* and road south of *Loch Tummel*. (b) *Ben Vrackie* (2,757ft, 840m), easy route by path from *Moulin*.

Pass of *Killiecrankie* to *Blair Atholl* 8 miles (13km). Road and rail follow lonely *Glen Garry* to cross *Pass of Drumochter* (1,484ft, 452m) to *Dalwhinnie*, 24 miles (39km). **Kingussie**△, 14 miles (22km), on River *Spey; Highland Museum*; many walks. **Aviemore**△, 12 miles (19km), principal ski resort of the Highlands.

EXCURSIONS: (a) *Loch an Eilean* and *Wolf of Badenoch's Castle*. (b) *Loch Einich (Eunach)*; **Braeriach** (4,428ft, 1,350m) from *Glen Einich* (not in stalking season). (c) *Dulnain Valley* in **Monadhliath Mountains**. (d) *Strathspey* steam railway from *Aviemore* to *Boat of Garten*; ospreys nest here.

Loch Morlich △, 7 miles (11km).

EXCURSIONS: ascents include **Cairn Gorm** (4,084ft, 1,244m), chairlift to top in summer and winter, and **Ben Macdhui** (4,296ft, 1,309m).

R6 (ii) Dundee to Glenisla and Glendoll (38 miles, 61km)

Dundee to *Alyth*, 17 miles (27km), and on to *Glenisla*, 9 miles (14km).

EXCURSIONS: (a) *Mount Blair*. (b) *Glen Canlochan* and *Glas Maol* (3,502ft, 1,067m), source of River *Isla*.

Glendoll△, 12 miles (19km) by hill route or 19 miles (30km) from *Kirriemuir,* by *Glen Clova*; walking and climbing centre.

R6 (iii) The Dee. Aberdeen to Ballater, Braemar and Inverey (64 miles, 103km)

Aberdeen△, port and third city; 'the granite city'. *Old Aberdeen, King's College,*

Cathedral of St Machar; Bridge of Balgownie (fourteenth century); *Harbour* and *Fish Market; Art Gallery and Museum; Brig o' Dee.*

A943 on south bank of River *Dee* to *Brig o' Feugh* and *Feughside*, 20 miles (32km).

EXCURSIONS: (a) *Kerloch* (1,747ft, 532m) and *Glen Dye.* (b) *Forest of Birse.* (c) *Crathes Castle.*

Continue up *Dee* valley; *Banchory; Aboyne* (Highland Games, 1st Saturday in August). **Ballater**Δ, 11 miles (18km).

EXCURSIONS: (a) *Craigendarroch, Pass of Ballater, Bridge of Gairn* and riverside track to *Ballater.* (b) *Pananich, Cambus o' May, Vat Burn, Loch Kinord.* (c) *Glen Gairn* and *Morven* (2,862ft, 872m). (d) *Glen Muick* and *Mount Keen* (3,077ft, 938m).

Crathie Church 7 miles (11km), closely associated with the Royal Family. **Balmoral Castle**, 1 mile (1¹/₂km), residence of the Queen; castle grounds open to public May, June, July — daily, except Sunday. *Invercauld Bridge*, 6 miles (4km). On for 3 miles (5km) to **Braemar**Δ (Braemar Games, early September).

EXCURSIONS: (a) *Creag Choinnich* (1,769ft, 538m). (b) **Morrone** (2,819ft, 859m) view. (c) **Lochnager** (3,786ft, 1,154m). (d) *Ben Avon* (3,843ft, 1,171m). (e) *Ben a Bhuird* (3,924ft, 1,196m).

*Inverey*Δ, 4¹/₂ miles (7km), at southern end of **Larig Ghru** route.

EXCURSIONS: (a) *Glen Ey* and *Colonel's Bed.* (b) *Glen Lui* and **Ben Macdhui** (4,296ft, 1,309m). (c) *Loch Etchachan* and **Loch Avon.** (d) **Pools of Dee** (source) and **Braeriach** (4,248ft, 1,295m) or **Cairn Toul** (4,241ft, 1,293m).

R6 (iv) The Don. Aberdeen to Corgarff and Tomintoul (63 miles, 101km)

AberdeenΔ. By valley of River *Don* to *Alford*, 26 miles (42km); ruins of *Kildrummy Castle*, 10 miles (16km); *Glenbuchat Castle*, 5 miles (8km); *Strathdon* 7 miles (11km); *Corgarff*, 9 miles (14km).

EXCURSION: Sources of *Don, Inchrory* and *Ben Avon* (3,843ft, 1,171m).

Continue by old military road (the *Lecht*) to *Tomintoul*Δ, 11 miles (18km), highest village in the *Highlands* and centre for walks in *Strathavon.*

R6 (v) Lower Spey and Lower Findhorn. Alford to Fochabers (33 miles, 53km)

One mile (1¹/₂km) north of *Kildrummy* turn north from *Don* valley. *Huntly*, 14 miles (22km), town and castle; *Keith*, 11 miles (18km); *Fochabers*, 8 miles (13km), on River *Spey.*

EXCURSIONS: (a) **Elgin**, ancient royal burgh, ruined cathedral. (b) *Forres*, 20 miles (32km), for beautiful lower **Findhorn Valley**, *Findhorn Estuary* and *Culbin Sands*.

Hill routes between hostels, linking the above sections are: *Inverey* (**R6 [iii]**) to (a) *Kingussie* (**R6 [i]**) by *Glen Feshie*. (b) *Aviemore* (**R6 (i)**) by *Larig Ghru*. (c) *Loch Morlich* (**R6 [i]**) by *Larig Ghru* or by *Shelter Stone* and *Glen Derry*.

The Northern Highlands

North and west of the *Great Glen* lies the finest scenery in Scotland. The mountains of *Ross-shire* and *Sutherland* are of great interest to the geologist as well as the climber. The *Cullin Hills* of *Skye* are the most difficult and savage range in the British Isles — a challenge and an attraction to the climber. Associations with the Young Pretender, Bonnie Prince Charlie, abound in the country between *Inverness* and *Skye*.

Communication, except by water, is difficult. The route is divided into six sections, each based on a different approach from the *Great Glen* to various parts of the region.

R7 (i) Fort William to Mallaig (43 miles, 69km)
Fort William, *Glen Nevis△*. Ferry to *Camusnagaul* for road on south bank of *Loch Eil*. *Glenfinnan*, 18 miles (29km) on *Loch Shiel*: Prince Charlie's Monument. *Lochailort*, 7 miles (11km); *Arisaig* 10 miles (16km); *Garramore△*, 3 miles (5km); fine coast scenery, views to islands; bathing.

EXCURSIONS: (a) coastal walks. (b) **Loch Morar** (deepest loch, 1,080ft, 330m). Boat from *Mallaig* to (c) **Loch Nevis**. (d) **Loch Hourn**.

Mallaig, 5 miles (8km); rail terminus; steamers to **Western Isles** and points on coast; ferry to *Armadale△* on *Isle of Skye*. *Broadford△*, 8 miles (13km) from *Kyleakin* (ferry from *Kyle of Lochalsh*), or 15 miles (24km) from *Armadale* (ferry from *Mallaig*). Centre of a crofting area.

EXCURSIONS: (a) *Elgol* (bus) via *Torin* for motor-boat across **Loch Scavaig** to **Loch Coruisk**. (b) **path** (experienced walkers only) to *Loch Coruisk* by the *bad step* from *Strathaird House*.

Road follows north-east coast to *Sligachan*, 18 miles (29km), climbing centre. By bus via *Drynoch*, or walk 9 miles (14km) over *Bealach-a-Mhain* to **Glenbrittle△** climbing centre; coastal and forest walks with spectacular views of *Cuillins*.

EXCURSIONS: (a) *Rudh 'an Dunain*. (b) **Cuillin Hills** (only for experienced climbers).

From *Sligachan* thence 24 miles (39km) to *Dunvegan; Castle Skeabost*, 17 miles (27km) and on for 11 miles (18km) to *Uig*Δ for steamer to **Outer Hebrides** for *Stockinish*Δ and *Lochmaddy*Δ — and Gatliff Hebridean Hostels Trust Δs at *Rhenigidale, Bernerey, Claddach Baleshare* and *Howmore*.

EXCURSIONS: *Kilbride* (Prince Charlie's landing place), *Kilmuir* (grave of Flora MacDonald) and *Duntulm Castle*.

Road over the *Quiraing*, fantastic rock scenery; *Staffin*, 9 miles (14km).

EXCURSIONS: (a) boat, *Kilt Rock* and outlet of *Loch Mealt*. (b) **The Storr** (2,360ft, 719m) and **Old Man of Storr** (pinnacle).

Portree, chief settlement.

R7 (ii) Loch Lochy to Kyle of Lochalsh (57 miles, 92km)
Loch LochyΔ; fishing and windsurfing, as well as interesting walking on north side of loch.

EXCURSIONS: (a) *Glen Roy* and its '*parallel roads*'. (b) **Loch Arkaig**. (c) *Spean Bridge* and *Commando War Memorial*.

Invergarry, 3 miles (5km) to the north-east, then west for 9 miles (14km) by *Glen Garry* (large hydro-electric scheme) and new road to *Glen Loyne* and *Glen Moriston* (or from *Loch Ness*Δ, by *Invermoriston* to junction with this road, 18 miles (29km). West by *Glen Clunie* and *Glen Shiel* to *Shiel Bridge* and *Ratagan*Δ, 21 miles (34km), on *Loch Duich*.

EXCURSIONS: (a) **Falls of Glomach** (370ft, 112m) highest in British Isles. (b) *Loch Duich* and *Eilean Donan Castle*. (c) *Glen Lichd* and *Sgurr Fhuaran (Ouran)* (3,505ft, 1,068m), one of '*Five Sisters of Kintail*'.

Mam Ratagan Pass (1,116ft, 340m) to *Glenelg*, 9 miles (14km).

EXCURSIONS: (a) two Iron Age *brochs* at *Corrary* in *Gleann Beag*. (b) *Arnisdale* on **Loch Hourn**.

From *Glenelg*, ferry to *Skye* or continue on mainland. *Kyle*, terminus of railway from *Inverness*; ferry to *Kyleakin* Δ, *Skye*. From *Ratagan* 23 miles (37km) by *Shiel Bridge* and *Dornie*, or 17 miles (27km) by *Totaig* and *Dornie Ferry*.

R7 (iii) Inverness to Kyle of Lochalsh via Glen Affric (89 miles, 143km)
(walking route only)
InvernessΔ; capital of the *Highlands*; view from terrace by *Castle; Highland Museum*; Islands in River *Ness; Culloden Moor* nearby.
    Beauly, 13 miles (21km); bus along *Strath Glass* to *Cannich*Δ, 17 miles (27km), walking centre. *Glen Affric*Δ, 21 miles (34km), at head of *Glen Affric*.

EXCURSIONS: ascents include (a) *Ben Attow* (3,383ft, 1,031m). (b) *Mam Soul* (3,862ft, 1,177m).

Path by *Glen Fionn* and *Glen Lichd* to *Ratagan*Δ 14 miles (22km) to join **R7(ii).**

R7 (iv) Inverness, Strathpeffer, Strome, Torridon (92 miles, 148km)

Inverness to *Beauly*, 13 miles (21km); *Strathpeffer*Δ, 10 miles (16km), walking centre; *Garve*, 9 miles (14km). *Achnasheen*, 16 miles (26km) (view) fork left for *Glen Carron; Achnashellach*, 9 miles (14km), walking and climbing centre. *Lochcarron*, 12 miles (19km), fishing village. *Strome*, 4 miles (6km). *Kyle of Lochalsh*, 7 miles (11km).

EXCURSION: *Bealach-nam-Bo* road and the mountains of *Applecross*.

Shieldaig, 10 miles (16km), fishing village; 7 miles (11km) eastwards to *Torridon* Δ, centre of vast wilderness area cared for by Scottish National Trust.

EXCURSIONS: (a) *Diabaig*, fishing village, and coast; *Craig*Δ nearby. (b) *Beinn Alligin* (3,232ft, 985m). (c) climbs (not in stalking season) of splendid peaks. **Liathach** (3,456ft, 1,051m), **Beinn Eighe** (3,309ft, 1,008m) and Nature Reserve at *Kinlochewe.*

R7 (v) Inverness, Ullapool, Achininver, Achmelvich (128 miles, 206km)

Garve, 32 miles (50km). Road up *Strath Garve*, 15 miles (24km) and down *Dirrie More* to *Falls of Measach* 6 miles (10km). Road forking left, A832, leads to *Dundonnell*, 13 miles (21km) on *Little Loch Broom* under impressive ridge of precipices of *An Teallach* (3,483ft, 1,062m).

*Ullapool*Δ, 12 miles (19km), fishing town on *Loch Broom.*

*Achininver*Δ, 27 miles (43km) (14 miles, 22km for walkers), centre for climbing **An Stac (Stac Polly)** (2,009ft, 612m) and fantastic sandstone peaks of *Coigach* district.

From *Ullapool* north by *Drumrunie Lodge*, 10 miles (16km), turn north-west by *Loch Lurgain* through wild scenery to *Lochinver*, 21 miles (34km); *Achmelvich*Δ, 4 miles (6km). Excellent coast walks, fine scenery, white sands and bathing beaches.

EXCURSIONS: (a) along coast to *Cnoc Poll* (352ft, 107m); ascents of (b) **Suilven** (2,399ft, 731m), (c) **Canisp** (2,779ft, 846km) and **Ben More Assynt** (3,273ft, 997m).

R7 (vi) Inverness, Carbisdale, Tongue, Durness, Achmelvich (204 miles, 328km)

Ardgay (bus from *Inverness*, 60 miles, 96km); *Carbisdale Castle*Δ, 4 miles (6km). *Invershin Ferry; Lairg*, 7 miles (11km), on *Loch Shin*. Fork right up *Strath Tirry; Altnaharra*, 21 miles (34km). Continue north by *Loch Loyal. Tongue*Δ, 16 miles (26km); fishing.

Continue round head of *Kyle of Tongue* for 9 miles (14km), then take road west to foot of *Loch Hope*, 6 miles (10km). Round head of *Loch Eriboll* and north coast to *Durness*△, 21 miles (34km), splendid beaches.

EXCURSIONS: (a) Smoo Cave. (b) **Cape Wrath** by ferry and minibus.

Road south-west to *Rhiconich*, 15 miles (24km), at head of *Loch Inchard* and across primeval landscape to *Laxford Bridge*, 4¹/₂ miles (7km); *Scourie*, 7 miles (11km). By coast with many small islands to *Kylesku Ferry*, 12 miles (19km). Road south over pass (818ft, 250m) between *Quinag* (2,653ft, 808m) and *Glasven* (2,541ft, 774m) to *Skiag Bridge*, 7 miles (11km), on *Loch Assynt*. *Lochinver*, 11 miles (18km); *Achmelvich*△, 4 miles (6km).

SPAIN

Geographical Outline

Land

Spain, occupying most of the *Iberian Peninsula*, has been called a 'kaleidoscope of landscapes', its regions being as distinct as if they were different countries.

Its central feature is the *Meseta*, the plateau of *Castile*, *León* and *Extremadura*, crossed by mountain ranges including the *Sierra de Guadarrama* and the *Sierra de Gredos* which roughly divide it into a higher northern and a lower southern section.

South of *Madrid*, the Rivers *Tagus* and *Guadiana* thread westwards across the plateau, their valleys separated by the *Montes de Toledo*. In its upper part the *Guadiana* crosses the desolate tableland of *La Mancha*.

The plateau stands isolated and distinct. The *Ebro*, the longest river, occupies the depression between it and the *Pyrenees*. The *Douro* and its tributaries separate it from the *Cantabrian* mountains of the north, which back the narrow coastal plain running from *Finisterre* in *Galicia* through *Asturias* and *Old Castile* to the *Basque* provinces.

In the south the plateau ends abruptly in the *Sierra Morena* above the broad basin of the river *Guadalquivir*, the heart of *Andalusia*, beyond which rise the highlands of *Granada*. Here, behind the Mediterranean coast, rises the beautiful snow-capped *Sierra Nevada*, culminating in the *Pico de Mulhacen* (11,410ft, 3,480m), the highest point in Spain.

In *Murcia* and *Valencia* the important coastal lowlands are isolated from the rest of the country by complex groups of *sierras*. In *Catalonia* the coast, cutting across the grain of the country, has stretches of spectacular scenery, as in the granite cliffs of the *Costa Brava*.

From *Catalonia* the *Pyrenees* and their foothills run through *Aragon* and *Navarre* to the *Basque* country, forming a continuous mountain barrier between the peninsula and the rest of Europe.

The *Balearic* and *Canary Islands* are politically part of Spain; the former are

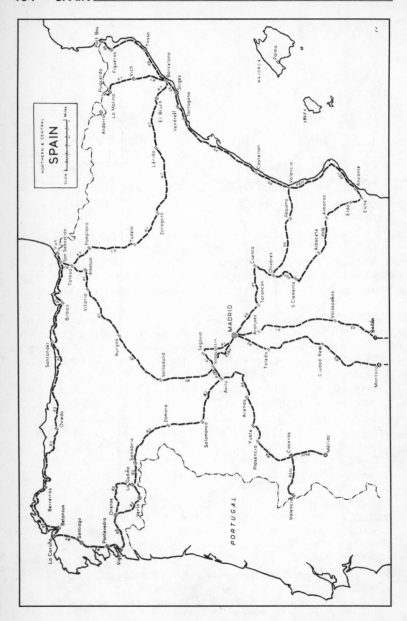

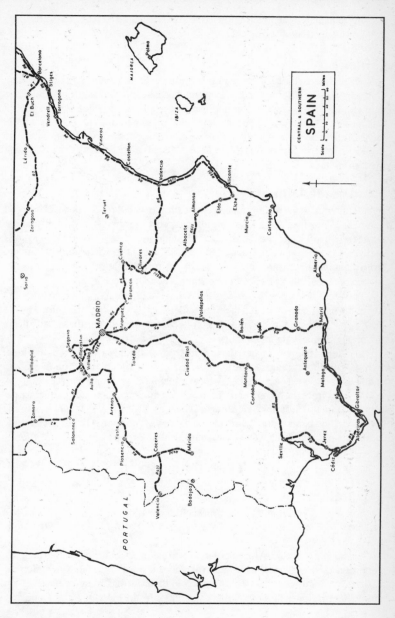

Mediterranean, but the latter, lying in the Atlantic nearer to Africa than Europe, are volcanic and almost tropical.

Climate

The northern coast has frequent rain and mist even in summer. On the central plateau, the wettest season is in March and April, but rainfall is low generally; its temperature extremes of winter and summer can be very wide, -12°C to 35°C (10°F to 95°F). In the Mediterranean provinces temperatures are usually a little lower in summer, but humidity makes the climate more trying, especially in *Valencia*; frost seldom occurs. In *Andalusia* there is no real winter except on very high ground.

Plants and Animals

In the wetter parts the plants of meadow, heath and woodland are those of western and central Europe. The arid parts either support evergreens such as ilex and a shrub (*mattoral*) similar to the *garrigue* of southern France, or are lacking in soils and vegetation. But Spain is rich in species, because of its wide range of climate, from plants similar to those of highland Britain, found in the hill areas of the north, to the cacti and sub-tropical flowers of the Andalusian coast.

The olive flourishes on lower ground in the southern half of the country and along the north-east coast and the *Ebro* valley. In *Extremadura* it is joined by the cork oak. On the other hand the beech is confined to the northern half of the country, especially the mountains.

In contrast to many other parts of Europe small birds are not common in great numbers. Vultures, eagles, and hawks frequent the mountains. The dunes and marshes south-west of *Seville* now form a magnificent nature reserve.

Wolves from the *Pyrenees* and *Cantabrian* mountains spread south in winter to the mountains just north of *Madrid*. There are still a few Spanish ibex in the *Pyrenees*, and bears in the *Pyrenees* and *Asturias*. The animal life of the extreme south has obvious links with Africa, such as the 'Barbary apes' of *Gibraltar*.

The People

Population

Total is about 37 million. The six largest cities are *Madrid* (3 million), *Barcelona* (1,750,000), *Valencia* (745,000), *Seville* (645,000), *Malaga* (502,000), *Saragossa* (571,000).

Physically the basis of the population is a fusion of Celtic and Iberian peoples, conditioned by 600 years of Roman rule, after a short period during which the eastern seaboard was under first Greek and then Carthaginian influence. Visigothic penetration in the sixth century was ended by the Mohammedan Conquest.

The 700 years of Moorish rule in *Andalusia* have left a considerable legacy of racial and cultural influences.

Language

Castilian, a form of Spanish native to the capital, is the official language of the whole country. It is derived from Latin but includes many words of Arabic origin. Catalan, spoken in the north-east and *Balearic Islands*, is distinct and is more like Provençal; the Galician dialect has a closer affinity to Portuguese. The Basques, who live near the Bay of Biscay, have a completely different language of unknown origin.

History

The cave paintings at *Altamira* and other sites are a vivid link with a hunting culture of perhaps 12,000 years ago. Celtic cromlechs and Iberian remains, including the bust of the Lady of Elche (*Prado Museum*), relate to peoples native to the peninsula at the time of the Phoenician traders and the early historic settlements by Greeks and Carthaginians. Such settlements were at first confined to the coast, but later extended inland for the sake of the silver mining and to secure recruits for the Carthaginian army of Hannibal.

As a result of the Punic wars between Carthage and Rome, Spain fell under Roman rule (206BC), control being gradually extended to the whole peninsula. Only the extreme north-west, where Celtic traditions (though not the language) still linger, felt little of this influence.

At the collapse of the Western Empire, Spain was over-run by the Visigoths, a Germanic people, who made their capital at *Toledo*. But the conquerors soon adopted both the language and the religion of the inhabitants. The Arab invasion in 711, under Tarak, overthrew their kingdom, although a remnant of the nobles continued resistance in the *Cantabrian* mountains for 300 years.

Until 756 the Arab Emirs were dependent on the Caliphate at Damascus, but in that year an independent Emirate was established. In 912 it was constituted a Caliphate. During this period Moslem Spain, with its capital at *Cordova*, earned a reputation for science, arts and luxury without equal in the Western world.

In the tenth century the Christians of the north-west began a revival that in the course of the next three centuries gradually reduced the area of Moslem rule. Corruption and schisms contributed to the decline of Moorish Spain. In 1212 Alfonso VIII defeated the Moors at *Navas de Tolosa*, and soon their dominion was restricted to the kingdom of Granada, where their philosophy continued to flourish. It finally fell, however, in 1492.

During the period of the re-conquest Christian Spain consisted of a number of independent kingdoms and only with the marriage of Isabella of Castile and Ferdinand of Aragon in 1479 did the basis of the modern state rise. In their zeal to maintain a strong central power the rulers persecuted and drove out the Jews and later the Moors and tolerated the Inquisition in a drive for unity of state and faith.

Shortly after the unification the Spanish king Charles I (who had already inherited the Netherlands) became Emperor (as Charles V) of the Holy Roman Empire (1520). Together with the discoveries in America this converted Spain almost overnight into the major world power. Brilliant leadership under Charles, who abdicated in 1556 to the monastery of *Yuste*, was followed by the less flexible rule of Phillip II whose solemn palace at *El Escorial* contains the tombs of all subsequent kings. His policy of war against Protestantism, continued overseas expansion and a naval attack on England, overstretched the economy and resources of the country. From his death in 1598 Spain sank gradually into powerless decadence.

The eighteenth century saw a brief attempt under the Bourbon Charles III to revitalise and centralise Spain, but his ideas found little favour and in a few years the Napoleonic Wars, here as elsewhere, were interrupting the course of history. Ties with the colonies were severed and Spanish life was split into a liberal and a clerical party whose vendetta for power dominated the unstable parliaments and frequent dictatorships of the nineteenth century.

In more recent times the dictatorship of 1923-9 led to the abdication of the king, the brief rule of a left-wing republic and the bitter civil war during 1936-9. General Franco, the nationalist leader, became dictator; upon his death in 1975 Prince Juan Carlos, grandson of the late King Alfonso XIII acceded to the throne. Democracy was restored and a new constitution promulgated in 1978.

Government

Spain is a constitutional monarchy, now belonging to both NATO and the EEC. The *Cortes* (parliament) consists of 350 members who form the Congress of Deputies, elected every four years by universal adult suffrage, together with a 248-strong Senate consisting of directly elected representatives of the provinces, islands, autonomous regions and *Ceuta* and *Melilla*.

Resources

Spain is a predominantly agricultural country and over 5 million people are employed on the land. Wheat is the chief grain crop; the vine is cultivated in all districts; the olive in the south and east and notably in the huge plantations around *Jaén*; figs and cork in *Extremadura*; dates in *Murcia*, especially around *Elche*; oranges (the main export) around *Seville* and in *Valencia* and *Castellón*; lemons in *Murcia*; onions in *Valencia*. The sherry of *Jerez* is perhaps the most distinctive export.

A special feature, providing some of the richest crops, is the *huerta* (irrigated) cultivation, highly developed in the south-east, notably the rice fields of *Valencia*. The best cattle land is in the wet north and north-west. Sheep and goats are important in more arid areas and transhumance is practised over great distances.

Forest products include eucalyptus and resin in addition to cork and an extensive afforestation programme run by the state has created many new plantations.

Coastal fishing is chiefly for sardines, tunny and cod, mostly for the home market; the balance is mainly sardines, canned for export.

Mineral resources are rich and varied. They include iron (*Bilbao*), coal (*Asturias*), copper (*Riotinto*), mercury (*Almadén*) and lead (*Sierra Morena*). Some 300,000 workers are employed. A uranium plant was established in 1960.

Heavy industry is largely concentrated in *Catalonia* which is also noted for its textiles. The *Basque* provinces, with much dispersed industry, are the other chief manufacturing areas. In both regions, and generally throughout Spain, industry relies on hydro-electric power; drought can therefore seriously restrict production. There is little coal; charcoal remains an important domestic fuel.

Customs and Dress

Each region has its own. As holidays are still holy days pilgrimages and saints' days are the centre of most festivities; Holy Week is celebrated with great ceremony.

It is unusual, and hazardous, for women to walk alone at night; even in daylight, expect comments from passing men.

In *Galicia* women wear the *monteo*, a bell-shaped skirt, and a shoulder cape. Men frequently wear a brown cloth hat with high crown and a rush cape. Handicrafts include lace making, basketry and jet ornaments. The local dance is the *muneira*, danced to the bagpipes. Pilgrimages centre on *Santiago de Compostela*, the chief shrine of Spain.

In the *Basque* country men wear a traditional red beret on festive occasions. Basque bands consist of pipes and drums. There is a tradition of impromptu singing in a style reminiscent of the Middle Ages.

In *Catalonia* the traditional headgear is the *barretina*, a long fisherman's cap, coloured to match the sash. Footgear is the rope-soled boot. The local dance, the *sardana*, is danced by a whole village in concentric rings to the music of a *cobla*. *Montserrat* with its black Virgin is the chief object of pilgrimage; this monastery up in the hills has a world famous boys' choir.

In *Valencia* and the *Levant* silks and linen are common for women's dresses. Men working in the fields wear white trousers and, instead of a jacket, the blanket which serves as a basket and rug combined. The great festival of the year is *Las Fallas* on St Joseph's Eve when each district constructs a satirical tableau of *papier maché* which is burnt amid a deluge of fireworks.

Andalusia shows the greatest Moorish influence in style of dress, as in much else; in *Granada* a traditional type of weaving with cubic designs, and boxes decorated with inlaid mosaics derive from the Muslim past. All the towns celebrate Holy Week with magnificent processions, each district competing for the most splendid figure of the Virgin. The original penitents' clothes, with pointed hooded head-dresses, have become very ornate and represent the various guilds of the town. At various dates in spring and summer the *ferias* (fairs) are held. *Seville's* being the most famous. The *flamenco* dances are better seen at country festivals than at the commercialised *Sacromonte* at *Granada*.

In *Madrid* at Christmas the old *Plaza Mayor* is filled with Christmas trees, clay models for the cribs, and tambourines of all sizes. On New Year's Eve thousands crowd into the *Puerta del Sol* to eat a grape for each of the strokes of midnight.

Food and Drink

Regional specialities include; in *Galicia*, a maize cake, *borona*, baked in cabbage leaves, fish dishes, dairy products and Ribeiro wine; in *Asturias*, cider and Rioja wines; in *Andalusia*, cold soups, called *gazpacho*, salads, fish dishes and sweets such as *yemas de San Leandro*, sherry, manzanilla. In *Catalonia, pasta* is the main element in the food of the people, with a fair proportion of meat; in *Valencia, paella*, a rice dish, and a very unusual drink, *horchata*, made from crushed sweetened nuts; on the central plateau, stews, bread dipped in garlic, breadcrumbs and milk. *Madrid* is famous for its bars, with every type of fish and marine product.

Sport

The national sports are bullfighting and football, in which Spain has won many honours in recent years. In the *Basque* country the chief sports are the annual log cutting competitions and sailing regattas. *Pelota*, the national game of the Basques, has spread all over Spain. *Seville* shares the honours with *Madrid* as a centre of the art of bullfighting.

Culture

Architecture

Extensive Roman remains can be seen at *Mérida* (theatre and amphitheatre), *Itálica, Ampurias* and *Tarragona* as well as the great aqueduct at *Segovia*.

Certain Visigothic churches have the horseshoe arches which later became a characteristic feature of Moorish architecture. The great mosque at *Cordova* was built during the early centuries of Moorish occupation; later examples of their architecture are the *Giralda Tower* and *Alcázar* at *Seville* and the splendid

Alhambra of *Granada*. Christian refugees to the north founded many churches during the ninth century in a hybrid style, Mozarabic. Mudejar architecture is in the Muslim tradition, occurring between the eleventh and fifteenth centuries in regions of Christian re-conquest. Romanesque is often a foreign import in Spain, as with the pilgrims' churches along the route to *Santiago de Compostela*.

Of Gothic, introduced by the Cistercians, there are many examples of several periods; early, including the cathedrals of *Burgos, Toledo* and *León*; middle, including the cathedrals of *Barcelona, Gerona* and *Pamplona*; late, including the cathedrals of *Segovia, Seville* and the new cathedral of *Salamanca*.

Castles in Spain are so numerous that they have given their name to an entire region, *Castile*; most are fifteenth century, but many in the south are Moorish, impressive though often in ruins.

Renaissance motifs entered Spain as decorative features in a style called Plateresque, especially well displayed at *Salamanca*.

The baroque style reached its most extreme in the fantastic excesses of ornamentation practised by the Churriguera family in the early eighteenth century. The best examples of this elaborate manner are in the cathedrals of *Santiago, Salamanca* and *Valladolid*.

The nineteenth and twentieth centuries have brought few innovations to Spanish architecture, but the work of the Catalan Gaudé must be mentioned; his church of the *Sagrada Familia* in *Barcelona* attracts much attention.

Painting

The world famous museum of the *Prado* in *Madrid* houses the greatest collection of Spain's masterpieces, though many outstanding individual items are found in the numerous palaces and churches with royal associations.

El Greco, the Cretan, using elongated features and striking colours, is almost modern in his effects. Velasquez, the Court painter of the seventeenth century, is strictly objective. Murillo captures in his laughing boys the carefree moments of ordinary people. Goya's searing realism brought home for the first time the horrors of war and delusions of terror and the madhouse. Spain is also the birthplace of Picasso, though his life's work was done beyond the Pyrenees.

Music

The popularity of folk music and dancing since the Middle Ages, is probably even stronger and truer in Spain than in any other European country. Pilar Lopez and Antonia have made folk music famous all over the world; in classical music its motifs have been woven into the work of Albeniz, Granados and Manuel de Falla.

Literature

The golden age of Spanish literature coincided with England's Elizabethan age.

Lope de Vega, Calderon and Alarcon produced between them some thousands of full length plays. Cervantes' masterpiece, *Don Quixote*, gave birth to the European novel. A long history of lyrical poetry stands behind the passionate verse of Garcia Lorca, and a succession of historians, from Bartolme de las Casas to Pindal have chronicled Spain's unique contribution to the heritage of the West.

Touring Information

Access

By *rail:* there is a break of gauge between France and Spain and in each direction it is usually necessary to change trains after crossing the frontier. London to *Barcelona* via Dieppe-Paris, 27 hours; London to *Madrid* via Dieppe-Paris, 35 hours. By air London to *Barcelona* direct, London to *Madrid* direct. Also direct flights in summer to *Málaga, Valencia* and *Bilbao.* By *sea:* car ferry from Plymouth to *Santander*, twice weekly, 24 hour voyage.

Transport

Supplements are payable for travel on many of the fastest trains, such as the 'Talgo' with specially articulated rolling stock. Reduced price 'mileage tickets' (*carnets kilometricos*), for a minimum total distance of 3,000km (approximately 1,900 miles) offer a significant saving to those intending to travel extensively by train; obtainable only in Spain.

Spanish railways (RENFE) run a widespread network of buses, numerous lines, low-priced; details from railway stations. Many private bus companies too.

Money

The *peseta* is divided into 100 *centimos.* There are coins of 1, 5, 10, 25, 50, 100, 200 and 500 *pesetas*, and notes of 100, 200, 500, 1,000, 2,000 and 5,000 *pesetas.*

Seasons for Touring

The central plateau is often arid and desolate and always dusty and hot in summer. This, and the long distances between towns and villages, makes it advisable to cross these stretches by rail.

The south is best visited in spring or early autumn. In the east, the *Costa Brava* has become so popular that in mid-season it is difficult to get accommodation even on campsites.

Clothing

As the climate ranges from delightfully mild in the north to sub-tropical in the south one should dress accordingly.

In towns, or when travelling by public transport, and in the evenings everywhere, women should wear a skirt or dress; and men slacks and long-sleeved shirt. In religious buildings women should cover the head; both sexes should cover the arms. Shorts, jeans, etc, are acceptable on beaches, for mountain walking, or for cycling in the country or through towns. The most popular tourist beaches of Spain are now as international as any others, but elsewhere bikinis are likely to attract unfavourable comment.

Restaurants and Meals

Lunch is served in restaurants from 1pm, dinner is eaten late, not before 9pm — but Spaniards prefer any time after 2pm and 10pm.

Food is excellent and abundant; the tastiness and delicacy of the different regional dishes is remarkable. *Cocido*, a stew made of boiled chickpeas, with meat, vegetables and dumplings, is a national dish, so too is *paella*, made of rice with small pieces of meat, or fish, with vegetables; both dishes have many local variants with their own names.

Public Holidays

1 and 6 January, 19 March, Maundy Thursday, Good Friday and Easter Monday, 1 May, Corpus Christi (second Thursday after Whitsun), 24 June, 18 and 25 July, 15 August, 12 October, 1 November, 8 December and Christmas Day. In addition to these national *fiestas* each town celebrates the feast day of its patron saint.

Maps

Michelin No 990, scale 1:1,000,000, is an adequate road map of Spain and Portugal. Large scale maps can be obtained only in the major cities; they are not of good quality. Climbing guide books, in Spanish, complete with simple maps, describe the mountain areas of the north-east.

Accommodation

Although there are more than 100 youth hostels, many of them are open only from mid-July to mid-September. Except in popular resorts, hotels are much cheaper in Spain than in the rest of Europe. Prices are fixed by the Government, and clearly displayed in each room.

Camping

Although a camping carnet is not indispensable, it assists in gaining entry to officially approved campsites; there are more than 500. Camping elsewhere is discouraged. More information can be had from Spanish National Camping Association, Duque de Medinaceli 2, Madrid-14.

Skiing

Season usually December to March. Resorts at *La Molina, Nuria* and *Salardú* in the *Pyrenees*, and at *Pajares* and *Reinosa* in the *Cantabrian* mountains. Skiing can also be enjoyed in the *Sierra Guadarrama* within 40 miles (65km) of *Madrid*, and in the *Sierra Nevada* near *Granada*.

Cycling

Cyclists will find the terrain agreeable in the northern provinces and on the east coast as far south as *Barcelona*. Further south, and on the central plateau, the un-relieved heat and hard, dusty going on unsurfaced roads are likely to deter. On many minor roads gradients and poor road surfaces make low gearing essential. Cycling means racing in Spain; touring gear, in particular is seldom seen and most spares are in metric dimensions. Start with new tyres and tubes, together with spares.

Practical Hints

Permission should be obtained for photographing interiors of museums, churches, etc, and close-ups of bullfights. It is forbidden to photograph airfields, military zones and certain areas in the *Pyrenees*.

Milk should be boiled. Tap water is safe enough in the higher mountain areas and in the cities but elsewhere there is an occasional danger of typhoid, especially in summer.

Shops and offices are open from 9am to 1.30pm and from 5.30pm to 8pm banks 9am to 2pm; monuments and museums 10am to 1pm (where they are open in the afternoon it is not usually before 3 or 4pm). All are closed on *fiesta* days, which are numerous.

Motoring

Motorists should carry with them their driving licence, car registration certificate, certificate of insurance together with a 'bail bond' — and an international driving permit; a nationality sticker and red warning triangle are also necessary.

'A' roads are toll motorways with a speed limit of 120km/h (75mph); those designated 'N' are main roads with speed restricted to 90km/h (56mph) per hour, while 'C' roads may be described as secondary, used by local traffic and by visitors with time to spare.

The 'rule of the road' is to drive on the right, overtake on the left and, in built-up areas and crossings to give preference to traffic coming in from the right.

Touring Routes

R1 Irún to Madrid (348 miles, 560km)

Irún, frontier town on River *Bidasoa*, scene of one of Wellington's coups against Napoleon. *Hondarribia* Δ. Take road N1 for 13 miles (20km) to **San Sebastian**Δ, capital of *Basque* province of *Guipúzcoa* and centre for *Basque* games and folklore festivals; favourite summer-resort for Spaniards; *La Concha* beach has strict rules on bathing dress. Many agreeable excursions to coast and hill country are possible.

Continue on same road for 13 miles (20km) to *Tolosa* where road climbs for 25 miles (40km) to pass of *Echegárate* (2,100ft, 640m) and enters countryside less watered by Atlantic rains. *Alsasua*Δ, is 4 miles (6km) beyond the pass.

On for 28 miles (45km) to *Vitoria*, capital of *Alava* province; has two cathedrals and equestrian statue of Wellington to commemorate famous battle of Napoleonic War. Thence 21 miles (34km) to crossing of River *Ebro* at *Miranda de Ebro*Δ.

Burgos Δ, 50 miles (80km), magnificent thirteenth-century Gothic cathedral with fine western façade and twin spires; other interesting churches; *Castillo* where Edward I of England was married, fine view of city; in *Casa del Cordón* Columbus was received by Ferdinand and Isabella on his return from America. Two great monasteries on outskirts; one, *Las Huelgas*, contains many fine royal tombs and a good museum. During Civil War (1936-9) *Burgos* was administrative capital of Nationalist Spain. N1 continues due south to *Madrid*, 152 miles (245km), but has little of interest either in towns or change of scenery.

*Palencia*Δ, 52 miles (83km) south-west, just off through road N620; cathedral. **Valladolid** Δ, 30 miles (48km); one-time capital of *Castile*, Holy Week ceremonies here are particularly splendid. Cervantes museum and many sixteenth-century sculptured façades.

N403 to *Villacastin*, 65 miles (104km); N110 to **Segovia** Δ, 23 miles (37km); altitude 3,300ft (1,006m), almost completely enclosed by Roman wall. Has best preserved Roman aqueduct in existence, sixteenth-century Gothic cathedral, castle, many fine old houses. Minor road to *San Ildefonso de la Granja*, 8 miles (13km), summer palace of kings of Spain with wonderful tapestries, some in designs by Goya; huge formal gardens where on special occasions magnificent fountains play.

Continue through wooded hill country up long pass to *Puerto de Navacerrada*Δ (6,100ft, 1,860m) 11 miles (18km); winter sports area with teleski and rack railway from valley. Excellent area for hill walking and rock climbing. Most Spanish mountaineering clubs have huts in the pass; *Cercedilla*Δ and San *Rafael*Δ are nearby.

Road descends, through similar country to village of *Villalba*, 13 miles (21km) NVI to *Madrid*, 25 miles (40km), passing *La Voz de Madrid* radio station and *Casa del Campo*, permanent exhibition site for agriculture and regional crafts, entering *Madrid* near the University city.

Madrid△

At geographical centre of the country, 2,300ft (700m) above sea-level, the highest capital in Europe. A lovely city of wide avenues and spacious parks. *Puerta del Sol*, busy square at city centre from which all main roads in Spain radiate and distances are measured; focal point, too, of *Metropolitano*, the underground railway. *Plaza Mayor*, a vast square in old city, was scene of bullfights, jousting and burning at the stake by Inquisition, now quiet, surrounded by narrow streets, steps and vaulted alleys. Former royal palace on western edge of town has sumptuous state apartments, art treasures, carriage museum and *Armeria Real*, world's finest collection of arms and armour.

Plaza de España with its skyscraper, *Avenida José Antonio* and *Calle de Alcalá* are fashionable. *Calle de Alcalá* bisects broad north/south avenue at *Square of Cibeles*, central post office here, and continues as *Paseo del Prado* to **Prado Art Gallery**: one of finest collections in Europe, unequalled for Velasquez, Goya and El Greco. Behind Gallery is main park, the *Retiro*, with boating lake.

The two big bull rings stage fights every Sunday and on special *fiestas*. A worthwhile visit on Sunday mornings is to the *Rasto*, secondhand market, south from *Plaza Mayor*.

R2 Madrid to Vigo (408 miles, 656km)

Leave *Madrid* by NVI, forking left after 10 miles (16km), on to new road through *Galapagar* to **El Escorial**△ 18 miles (29km); huge fortress-like monastery and royal palace in commanding position, built by Philip II; fine period rooms, full of art treasures; pantheon has tombs of kings.

At *Guadarrama* village, 7 miles (11km), turn left to visit *Valley of the Fallen* where huge cross and church hewn out of rock commemorate the dead of the Civil War. Return to *Guadarrama* and climb very steep and long pass on road NVI, which motorists can avoid by using tunnel, and descend to *San Rafael*△. At *Villacastin*, 23 miles (37km), turn south-west on N501 to **Avila**△, 18 miles (29km) at altitude of 3,600ft (1,097m); fine example of medieval walled city, built of red granite; cathedral; Romanesque churches; birthplace of St Theresa, joint patron saint of Spain. *Peñaranda de Bracamonte*△, 35 miles (56km), a rather decrepit little town.

Salamanca, 27 miles (43km), one of oldest university towns in Europe; spacious arcaded *Plaza Mayor*; fine university buildings; especially famous Plateresque gateways; two cathedrals; many fifteenth- and sixteenth-century houses.

N630 to *Zamora*Δ, 55 miles (40km), and for a further 13 miles (21km), turning left on N525 to cross hilly, remote area of *León* province to *Puebla de Sanabria*, 55 miles (88km), *Lago de Sanabria*Δ, beautiful lake 10 miles (16km) north of village.

N525 continues through mountains to *La Gudiña*, 37 miles (59km). Here either go north on C533 to join main road at *Freijido*, 33 arduous miles (53km) or west and north via *Verin* to *Orense*Δ, 68 miles (110km) (62 miles, 99km, from *Freijido*), with famous bridge. Thence to *Vigo*, 66 miles (106km), some of them close to the Portuguese border in the inaccessible gorge of *Miño*.

*Vigo*Δ, most important fishing port in Spain, set amid pinewoods and gardens; close to beautiful coastal scenery, fine sandy beaches just south of the town.

R3 Vigo to Irún (635 miles, 1,021km)

Vigo (see **R2**). N550 past airport to *Pontevedra* Δ, 20 miles (32km) picturesque town with many churches and palaces.

Santiago de Compostela, 35 miles (56km): the object of massive pilgrimages to the tomb of St James the Apostle, was second only to Jerusalem and Rome in Middle Ages; cathedral with twelfth-century interior and sculpture, Churrigueresque front.

CorrunaΔ (*La Coruña*), 40 miles (64km), naval base on Atlantic coast; countryside akin to Scotland; likelihood of frequent rain. *Betanzos*, 15 miles (24km), fork left and at *Xubia*, 23 miles (37km), right on C641 for 4 miles (6km), where fork left on C642, following north coast to *Vivero*Δ, 50 miles (80km) *Luarca* Δ, 80 miles (128km).

*Oviedo*Δ, 60 miles (96km), mining and industrial centre; cathedral, fine museum, *Arriondas*, 41 miles (66km); best approach to *Picos de Europa*, wild and beautiful mountain range, with *Covadonga National Park*. *Ribadesella* Δ 15 miles (24km) on coast, and on to *Llanes*Δ, 20 miles (32km).

SantanderΔ, 70 miles (112km), sophisticated resort, but busy port too. *El Sardinero* on narrow *Magdalena* headland, fashionable since nineteenth century when Spanish royal family took to sea bathing; excellent beaches. On for 13 miles (20km), to *Solórzano*Δ

EXCURSION: Caves of **Altamira** (*Polanco*Δ, nearby) with famous prehistoric drawings.

Bilbao, 55 miles (89km), industrial and mining port. Good minor roads to *Bermeo* and *Guernica*, 30 miles (48km), scene of infamous bombing raid by Germans in Civil War, subject of one of Picasso's most famous paintings. *Amorebieta*, 8 miles (13km). *San Sebastian* (**R1**), 56 miles (90km).

R4 Madrid to Badajoz (327 miles, 526km)

Madrid to *Avila* (see **R2**). In *Avila* take C502 to *Venta del Obispo*, 30 miles

(48km), on eastern part of the wild *Sierra de Gredos*. Road over *Puerto del Pico* (4,480ft, 1,367m) to *Arenas de San Pedro*, 21 miles (34km), and by C501 to monastery of *Yuste*, 48 miles (77km), where Emperor Charles V retired after abdication. *Plasencia*, 27 miles (43km), encircled by twelfth-century walls; fourteenth-century cathedral is remarkably beautiful. N630 to *Cáceres*Δ, 53 miles (85km), picturesque provincial capital, rich in Moorish architecture.

R4 (i) Cáceres to Valencia de AlcántaraΔ. N521 through sparsely populated olive and charcoal producing country to Portuguese frontier beyond *Valencia de Alcántara*, 55 miles (88km) Lisbon via Santarem 164 miles (264km) along *Tagus* valley, to *Alburquerque*Δ 20 miles (32km) south-east of *Valencia de Alcántara* on C530 to *Badajoz*.

Mérida, 45 miles (72km), some of richest Roman remains outside Italy; aqueducts, theatre, amphitheatre, numerous arches.

*Badajoz*Δ, 38 miles (61km), provincial capital in key position on Portuguese frontier; besieged, attacked and pillaged in Wars of Succession, Peninsular War and Civil War.

R5 Madrid — Granada — Malaga — Seville — Cordova — Madrid (850 miles, 1,370km)

The main road to the south, NIV, which crosses the flat tableland of *La Mancha*, has little of interest except the splendid royal palace and gardens at *Aranjuez*, 33 miles (53km). The wine growing district is reached at *Valdepeñas*, 95 miles (152km), road then crosses *Sierra Morena* through a rocky defile to *Bailén*, 60 miles (96km).

N323 to *Jaén* Δ, 25 miles (40km) centre of ranch country and area of large estates, olive plantations and orchards. Renaissance cathedral has holy relic, claimed to be St Veronica's veil, showing the imprinted image of Christ's face. Road crosses *Sierra de Lucena* to *Granada*, 62 miles (99km).

*Granada*Δ was last outpost of Moorish rule in Spain, and in the *Alhambra* palace a great variety of splendid Arabesque detail is preserved; delightful gardens where nightingales sing adjoin the *Generalife*, summer palace of Moorish kings. Fine Renaissance tombs in *Capilla Real* of cathedral. Gypsy caves on *Sacromonte*, now commercialised.

EXCURSION: *Sierra Nevada*, light railway to 4,600ft (1,402m), road to 10,720ft (3,268m). Many fine walks but little accommodation.

Road continues south to *Motril*, 46 miles (74km), on Mediterranean coast. An area of great contrast of climate; cane and palm plantations only a few kilometres from mountain snows.

N340 is winding road, westwards through fine coastal scenery to *Málaga*Δ, 65 miles (105km), founded by Phoenicians; much to see in cathedral (view from tower), *Bishop's Palace* and eleventh-century Moorish *Alcazaba*.

Coast road west from *Málaga is Costa del Sol*, spoilt by unsightly tourist development, *Torremolinos*△, *Mijas Costa*△ and *Marbella*△, 37 miles (59km). Inland is *Sierra de Ronda*, attractive mountain area.

Algeciras, 50 miles (80km), overlooks bay of *Gibraltar*. Ferries to Tangiers and Ceuta in Morocco which can be seen clearly from headland of *Tarifa*, 15 miles (24km).

Cadiz, 63 miles (101km), major port of Spanish Empire in earlier times, now a naval base; Spain's biggest prison here. *Jerez de la Frontera* △, 32 miles (51km), gave its name to sherry from former English spelling of town's name *Xeres*; white walls, patios and many bodegas for trying the local product. *Alcázar*, charming Mudéjar palace, fourteenth century but much restored. In this district, which for 200 years was border with last Moorish kingdom, many towns are known as *de la Frontera*.

Seville△, 160 miles (96km), was a centre of Moorish culture. Gothic cathedral is biggest in Spain, massive exterior, richly decorated interior; retains in its structure minaret of former mosque (fine view from top); tomb of Columbus; many art treasures. *Seville's* celebrations during Holy Week and its *Feria* during first week of April are unique and world-famous.

EXCURSION: *Itálica*, 5 miles (8km) north-west, Roman amphitheatre.

NIV to *Carmona*, 20 miles (32km); Roman cemetery. **Cordova** (Cordoba), 65 miles (104km) was Moorish capital; *Mosque*, although partly rebuilt as a cathedral, remains the finest example of Muslim art in western Europe. Old town is a maze of alleys with many picturesque patios.

Shortest route onward is by NIV rejoining outward route at *Bailén*, 65 miles (104km). Tougher but more interesting is to turn north at *Montoro*, 28 miles (45km) by N420 to *Ciudad Real*, 90 miles (144km) and N401 to *Toledo*, 74 miles (119km); desolate highland areas with poor roads, seldom visited.

Toledo△, on eminence overlooking, and encircled by, ravine of River *Tagus*; once capital of *Castile*. Splendid Gothic cathedral is best visited in afternoon when chapels are open, especially *Capilla Mayor* containing huge *Transparente*, remarkable example of Spanish baroque. Many narrow streets with medieval and Renaissance buildings, including El Greco's house and museum of his works.

Continue 45 miles (72km) north-north-east via *Seseña* to return to *Madrid*.

R6 Madrid — Valencia — Barcelona — Costa Brava (617 miles, 992km)
N111 from *Atocha* railway station for 53 miles (85km) to *Tarancón*, then another 53 miles (85km) on N400 to **Cuenca**△, medieval walled town with houses overhanging cliffs above River *Júcar*.

EXCURSION: *Ciudad Encantada*, 26 miles (42km) north, extraordinary rock formations.

From *Cuenca* turn south on N420 to *La Almarcha*, 39 miles (62km) so rejoining NIII. *Cuestas de Contreras*, 60 miles (96km), impressive scenery where River *Cabriel* breaches central plateau. Descend to coastal plain through orange grove district to *Valencia*, 63 miles (101km).

R6 (i) Alternative route La Almarcha to Valencia. NIII to *Honrubia*, 8 miles (13km) south-west to *San Clemente* to join N301 for *Albacete*, 70 miles (112km) provincial capital with steel, especially cutlery, industries. N430 to *Almansa*, 45 miles (72km) N330 via *Villena* to *Elda* 36 miles (58km). Fork right 6 miles (9km) beyond, through *Novelda* to **Elche**, 12 miles (19km), town of white cube-shaped houses in largest date palm grove in Europe (reputedly 300,000 trees). Outside town are many Iberian, Phoenician and Visigothic remains, and here was found the famous *Dama de Elche*, a very early sculpture now in the *Prado*.

N340 to *Alicante*△, 15 miles (24km), busy port (steamers for *Mallorca* and North Africa); modern town on bay; old town on hill. Coastal road. N332; much fine scenery, but locally spoiled by overgrown resorts such as *Benidorm* and *Denia*. *Valencia*, 115 miles (185km) via *Piles*△.

Valencia △, provincial capital and port and centre of rich agricultural area, irrigated since thirteenth century, producing citrus fruits, rice and wheat. Many churches, museums and towers; cathedral has many treasures and *Fine Arts Museum* has paintings by El Greco, Goya and Velazquez. Spectacular *fiestas* in mid-March (San José), Holy Week, May and late July. Regular ferries ply to *Palma* and *Ibiza*.

Northwards along coast road for 31 miles (49km) to *Nules*, 11 miles (17km) to *Castellon*△, thence 6 miles (10km) to *Benicasim*△ and a further 32 miles (51km) to *Benicarló*△. *Tortosa*, 33 miles (53km) a granite built, walled town on River *Ebro* lies some way from main road. Much damaged in Civil War, but Gothic cathedral still worth seeing for its fine carvings.

Tarragona△, 53 miles (85km) splendidly grouped, ancient city with extensive Roman remains surrounded by cyclopean walls, probably pre-Roman. Romanesque-Gothic cathedral. On for 8 miles, 12km, to *Altafulla*△ and at *El Vendrell*△, 16 miles (25km) take coast road, C246, via *Sitges* to *Barcelona,* 40 miles (64km).

Barcelona△, second city, chief port and industrial centre of Spain; capital of Catalonia; bustling, noisy and colourful; many fine buildings, Romanesque, Gothic, Renaissance and baroque; Gothic cathedral in old town and other lovely buildings nearby, including sixteenth-century palace *Archivo de la Corona de Aragon* and fourteenth-century chapel of *Santa Agueda*. Unfinished church of the Holy Family (*Sagrada Familia*), begun 1882, by Gaudé (blocks of whose flats can also be seen), is a unique example of eccentric art. Permanent exhibition of regional crafts (examples can be purchased) at *Pueblo Español* on outskirts. *Mount Tibidabo* (funicular), fine panorama of city and coast.

North-east by NII along coast for 9 miles (15km) to *El Masnou*△ and a further

13 miles (20km) to *Cabrera del Mar*Δ. Where NII turns inland, keep to coast, through *Lloret* and *Tossa*, popular seaside resorts.

*La Escala*Δ, 27 miles (43km), small fishing port near which is *Ampurias* with remains of early Greek settlement, *Emporion*, and Roman town (excavated); museum. Road leaves coast to rejoin NII at *Figueras*Δ, 15 miles (24km), with Salvador Dali museum. Between *Palamós* and *Figueras* a number of attractive villages and bays can be reached on roads at right angles to through route.

> EXCURSION: **Gerona**, 25 miles (40km), finely situated medieval town, dominated by Gothic cathedral with widest nave in world and beautiful Romanesque cloisters. Churches of *San Feliú* and *San Pedro de Galligans*.

Figueras to frontier by NII to *Col de Perthus*, 15 miles (24km), or by C252, a more eventful route, to *Port Bou*, 23 miles (37km).

R7 Puigcerdá — Barcelona — Saragossa — Irún (493 miles, 794km)

From frontier, *Puigcerdá*, mountainous road N152 and, after 8 miles (13km), turn off to *La Molina*Δ, fine winter sports resort. Cross pass to *Ribes de Freser* 23 miles (37km).

> EXCURSION: *Nuria*Δ (6,000ft, 1,829m), rack railway.

On for 9 miles (14km) to *Ripoll* where monastery of architectural merit has particularly fine twelfth-century cloisters. *Vich*, 23 miles (37km) has vast cathedral adorned with remarkable frescoes; episcopal museum. Continue southwards for 35 miles (56km) to Barcelona (see **R6**). North-west by local road over hill to *San Cugat*, 11 miles (18km), village with Benedictine abbey and church with twelfth-century cloisters. *Tarrasa*, 11 miles (18km), town with three very fine Romanesque churches. West to *Esparreguera*, 10 miles (16km).

Montserrat, 14 miles (22km), famous monastery and place of pilgrimage, grandly situated on terrace of curiously serrated mountain; funicular to summit 4,260ft (1,300m). Continue west for 7 miles (11km) to rejoin NII; *Lérida*Δ, 67 miles (107km), provincial capital, has two cathedrals.

> **R7 (i) Lérida to Andorra**. C1313 up *Segre* valley to *Seo de Urgel* (2,273ft, 693m), 85 miles (136km). Enter **Andorra**, 6 miles (10km) beyond.

> **R7 (ii) Lerida to France over Pyrenees**. *Lérida*, C47 to *Pobla de Segur*, 70 miles (112km), *Esterri*, 36 miles (58km). Over *Bonaigua* pass (6,800ft, 2,072m) to *Salardú*Δ, 23 miles (37km); less inaccessible than most parts of Spanish Pyrenees. On down valley to *Viella* 6 miles (10km); and N230 to border and *Cierp*, 26 miles (42km).

Saragossa Δ 89 miles (143km), former capital of *Aragon*; industrial and commercial city, rebuilt after heroic siege against French in Peninsular War; two cathedrals remain: *La Seo*, twelfth-seventeenth century; *Nuestra Señora del Pilar*, seventeenth century, huge building with many domes; Gothic alabaster altar.

R7 (iii) Huesca and Pyrenees. *Huesca*, 45 miles (72km), provincial capital. *Sabiñánigo*, 33 miles (53km), turning for **Ordesa National Park**, 28 miles (45km), magnificent scenery. *Jaca*△, 10 miles (16km), *Canfranc*△, 14 miles (22km), *Somport*, 6 miles (10km), historic frontier pass at 5,380ft (1,640m).

N232 along *Ebro* valley to *Tudela*, 50 miles (80km), notable church and bridge. Four miles (6km) north near N121 are remains of very considerable Roman town.

Pamplona, 60 miles (96km), capital of former kingdom of *Navarre*; citadel built by Philip II; Gothic cathedral. Bullfighting *fiesta*, 6 to 20 July annually, evening bullfights and early morning bull-running through streets. Many byroads lead up interesting Pyrenean valleys.

Tolosa, 41 miles (66km) and on to *Irún*, 23 miles (37km) (see **R1**).

The Balearic Islands

These islands lie well out into the Mediterranean, and cannot conveniently be described in any of the touring routes in Spain, but their interest to visitors to that country merits a mention here.

Majorca (*Mallorca*) is the largest island of the group. **Palma**△, its capital is served by overnight steamers from *Barcelona, Valencia* and *Alicante*. The city is dominated by its Gothic cathedral, and many other old buildings merit attention. Tourist purchases have helped to keep local craft industries alive. There are good beaches nearby.

Tour of Majorca (187 miles, 301km). West to *Paguera*, then inland to *Andratx*, 19 miles (30km). From here a splendid road threads its way through the mountains high above the island's long north-west coast. *Valldemosa*, 27miles (43km), fourteenth-century monastery, associations with Chopin. *Sóller*, 13 miles (21km). Constantly winding road comes down to *Pollensa*, 33 miles (53km), *Puerto de Pollensa*, 4 miles (6km). *Cape Formento*, 4 miles (6km) north-east marks end of this ragged coast. South-east to *Alcudia*△, 5 miles (8km) and *Artá*, 24 miles (38km) splendid seashore caves, 6 miles (10km) to the south-east. Then south to *Cuevas del Drach*, 14 miles (22km) for more impressive stalactite caves. The circuit is completed by continuing south-west to *Santany*, 19 miles (30km) and north-west to *Palma*, 33 miles (53km), but as this southern corner of the island is uninteresting visitors may prefer to return directly to *Palma* via *Manacor*, 39 miles (62km) from *Cuevas del Drach*.

The other islands are much smaller. **Minorca**, the most easterly, is rocky without being mountainous, and has many prehistoric remains. There are three steamers a week from *Barcelona* to *Mahon*, and weekly services from *Palma*. **Ibiza**, the most westerly, also has unusual antiquities. Steamers ply from *Barcelona, Alicante* and *Valencia*.

SWEDEN

Geographical Outline

Land

From the southern tip of *Skåne* to the borders of Norway and Finland in the north, Sweden extends for nearly 1,000 miles (1,600km) whilst from the Skagerrak to the Baltic its greatest width is about 300 miles (480km). Sweden's northernmost point, 200 miles (320km) beyond the Arctic Circle, is the same latitude as the northern coastline of Canada, while the city of *Malmö* is almost as far south as Newcastle-upon-Tyne. The country's total area is about twice that of Great Britain.

The geographical isolation of Sweden has played no small part in her history; water surrounds her on three sides, and the northern Baltic is icebound in winter. In the north-east, the River *Torne* forms the border with Finland, and the frontier with Norway is a formidable mountain barrier.

From these mountains the land slopes steeply to the west to give Norway her rugged grandeur, but more gently to the east. Sweden's northern landscape is typified by undulating forests cut by large rivers running in a north-west to south-east direction. The southern part is a plain, relieved only in the centre by hilly country.

The Swedes divide their country into three parts: *Norrland*, the north; *Svealand*, the district around the great lakes, centre of the ancient kingdom of *Svea Rike* (hence *Sverige*, the modern Swedish name for the country) and *Götaland*, the southern plain, once the home of the Goths.

Climate

Sheltered from the west by the mountain frontier with Norway, Sweden, except in the south, is less affected by Atlantic than by continental conditions to which it is open on the east. It has, therefore, a comparatively dry climate.

Spring is the driest and probably the most exhilarating season. In the short space of a month or so the sunshine gains in intensity and soon brings about the thaw of river and lake ice and the budding of trees and wild flowers. In the north, the change is so sudden that full summer follows in a matter of weeks. March and April are the best months for winter sports.

Summer is short; June, July and August in the south; even shorter in the north. The sunlight, however, is intense and the hours of sunshine exceed those of Italy and Spain, though temperatures are lower. The midnight sun can be seen beyond the Arctic Circle for many weeks, and even in the south summer nights resemble a twilight. Most summer rain — what there is of it — falls quickly, and sometimes heavily, usually following thunder, out of blue skies decked with billowy clouds.

Autumn, the wettest season, has superb colourings both in sky and landscapes, especially in the north. The south-west has a tendency to damper weather, with coastal mists.

Winter days are short; so short in fact in the north that artificial light must be used almost continuously in the home. Nevertheless the weather is often crisp, with brilliant sunshine and clear nights, giving fine opportunities for skiing and sleighriding. Again, the south-west has a tendency to damper, mistier weather.

Plants and Animals

Forests cover more than half of the total area. Many are of the graceful silver birch, interspersed with rowan, alder and aspen, but the greater part is of sombre conifer, spruce and pine, and also juniper. In the far north-west, however, stunted birch and willow are best able to withstand the hard conditions. In the south, the deciduous trees which we know so well give a softer face to the landscape, and beech thrives particularly well in the chalk soils. This region therefore more nearly resembles Britain's woodlands, and the bird-life there is much the same. In central and south Sweden there are marshes where waders abound, and some islands around the south and east coasts are kept as bird sanctuaries. The far north is the most interesting area for a study of plant and animal life. The wild flowers and shrubs are magnificent in spring; since all follow one another in quick succession, there is a range of colours hardly to be rivalled elsewhere; Arctic flowers such as those found in the Alps, flowers of the woods and meadows, ling and alpine rhododendron. Then, in great profusion, come the edible cloudberry (*hjortron*) and whortleberry (*lingon*). The latter is found in the woods all over Sweden and forms a distinctive item in the cuisine.

The north, however, is not alone in having a show of colour; the island of *Gotland* has a magnificent display of roses in the capital, *Visby*, during the summer, and orchids and lilies in many varieties appear in the meadows in early June.

Members of the eagle and allied families nest among the crags of the north-west, and blackcock is the most common gamebird. Even the cuckoo can be heard over the Arctic Circle. The reindeer is now only to be seen in the semi-tame herds kept by the Lapps, but deer and also elk are now relatively common since laws and heavy fees were introduced to limit hunting to a few days of the year. The lynx is found sometimes even in the central forests, but the wolf and bear have now been pushed well up into the mountain regions. Game-fish abound in the rivers and lakes; on the open parts of the big lakes, fishing is free; elsewhere licences can usually be obtained very cheaply. Crayfish are a delicacy much sought after in the autumn.

The People

Population

Sweden has a large area, but owing to the barren nature of most of *Norrland* her population is only 8,300,000, and the majority of these live in the southern tip and the cities of central Sweden. *Stockholm*, the capital, has a population of about 1,400,000 but only two others, *Göteborg* and *Malmö*, have over 250,000.

In the far north there are some 8,500 nomadic Lapps. Other groups include 50,000 Finnish-speaking farmers, fishermen and lumberjacks settled along the Finnish border, and 100,000 refugees, mostly from Baltic countries.

Language

The three Scandinavian languages are very similar to each other and bear a general resemblance to the other languages of the Germanic family (English, German and Dutch). Swedish is a pleasant sounding language, many of the hard sounds of English and German being softened; this however makes it a difficult language to understand until the ear has grown accustomed to its rising and falling lilt. It is said that Swedish intonation comes easier to the Welsh than to other people.

Very many Swedes speak at least some English, but it is helpful to have some idea of the pronunciation of place-names, as even a Swede who speaks good English may find it difficult to understand the foreigner who cannot pronounce the name of the place he wants to get to. It is difficult for English-speaking people to acquire a really good Swedish pronunciation, but easy to get near enough for understanding.

The vowel sounds are similar to English, and can be long or short. The *o* in words like *god* (good), *bror* (brother) is long, like the English 'oo' in 'school'. The modified vowels *ä* and *ö* are pronounced like the 'e' in 'bet' and the 'u' in 'fur' respectively. The vowel *å* is similar to the Scottish 'o'; a Scotsman saying 'boat' and a Swede saying *båt* will sound just the same. Consonants are as in English with three exceptions; *j* and *g* are softened before certain vowels to a 'y' sound; *k*, while retaining the hard sounds in words like *kaka* (biscuit) is softened to 'sch' in words like *skina* (shine), *kyrka* (church). 'W' is not used in Swedish except in

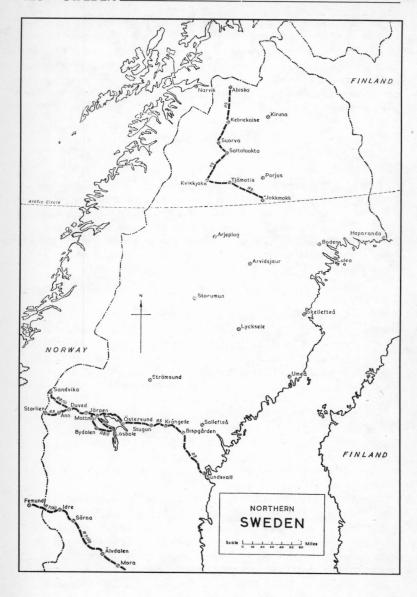

NORTHERN
SWEDEN

Scale |___|___|___|___|___|___| Miles
0 10 20 30 40 50 60

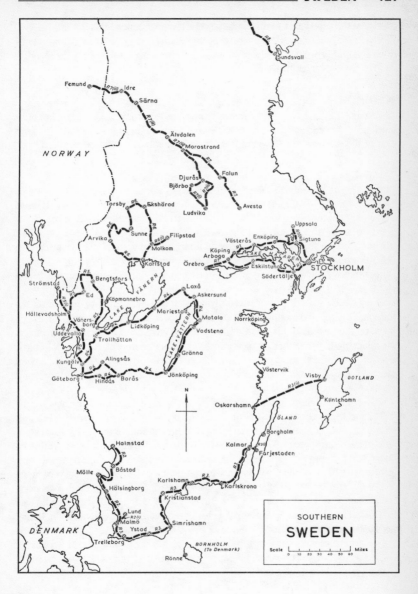

SOUTHERN
SWEDEN

Scale |___|___|___|___|___|___| Miles
0 10 20 30 40 50 60

foreign words and some family names, when it is pronounced like the English 'v'.

A few place-names, indicating prononunciation, may help in pronouncing others; *Göteborg*, 'Yuh-t-boy'; *Gällivare*, 'Yell-i-var-e', *Västerås*, 'Vesterohs'; *Norrköping*, 'Nor-chuh-ping.'

Religion

The State Church, to which the majority nominally belong, is Lutheran, but only a fraction of the population can be reckoned regular churchgoers. *Uppsala* is the seat of the Archbishop. There is freedom of worship for other denominations.

History

In the ninth/tenth centuries the Swedish Vikings raided eastwards for the slaves and furs which they traded to the Arabs via the Russian waterways. This ceased in the next century with the adoption of Christianity and the Swedes turned their energies more to colonizing their own territory. The early kings were often challenged by a strong aristocracy, even after a feudal system was established in the thirteenth century. But the Union of *Kalmar* (1397), by which Eric of Pomerania was crowned king of the three Scandinavian countries, strengthened royal power. Denmark was for long the dominant partner, but by the fifteenth century the balance of power was shifting. The peasants, already represented in the *Riksdag*, reacted against Denmark and, in 1523, placed the forceful Gustavus Vasa on the throne. In his reign of thirty-seven years the Lutheran Reformation was accepted, the power of the church curtailed by confiscation of its lands, central government was further strengthened, and the monarchy, which had been elective, was declared hereditary; agriculture and mining were developed and commerce encouraged by freeing it from the Hanseatic league.

Swedish influence as a European power was at its height in the century following the accession (1611) of Gustavus II Aldophus, the warrior king and strategist who, until his death in 1632 was the outstanding figure on the Protestant side in the Thirty Years' War (1618-48). By systematically seizing the southern and eastern shores of the Baltic he secured Swedish domination of the sea, reinforced (1658) under Charles X by the taking from Denmark of the provinces of *Skåne, Halland, Blekinge* and *Bohuslän*. Sweden's hold on them was confirmed by the victory at *Lund* in 1676. But her fortunes changed in the Nordic war (1700-21) when many of the powers were ranged against her. Unwisely challenging Russia she was defeated at Poltava (1709), her invasion of Norway (1718) failed, and thereafter she was forced to give up her Baltic empire.

A period of party strife between groups called the 'Caps' and 'Hats' (somewhat akin to Whigs and Tories in England) was ended by the strong rule of a reforming king, Gustavus III (1772-92), a patron of learning under whom the arts and sciences flourished. But his home and foreign policy made the nobles his enemies and led to his assassination.

A constitutional monarchy with ultimate power in the hands of the *Riksdag* was set up in 1809, with French Marshal Bernadotte as crown prince. As king (1818-44) he demonstrated the advantages of neutrality, a policy consistently followed by subsequent governments. The 1850s were a period of industrial revolution (notably in the iron, timber and woodpulp industries), social reform and a new feeling of kinship with Denmark. Modern Sweden has enjoyed progressive governments and a firm attachment to the arts of peace.

Government

The Crown has executive authority, but in practice this devolves on the Cabinet, led by the Prime Minister, which must have constant parliamentary support. The *Riksdag* (Parliament) consists of one House elected every three years by proportional representation.

Resources

Research and mechanisation in agriculture ensure a high yield and Sweden is self-supporting in the principal foodstuffs. About ten per cent of the country is arable land; two-thirds of this is in the south, mainly in the form of large farms in *Skåne*, *Västergötland* and *Östergötland* and smaller ones in *Svealand*. In the north, farms occur in small areas along the river banks, and the farmers have to depend on fishing and logging to make ends meet.

Things to notice on the farms are; in the south, the tethered cattle, and in the north, the drying racks for hay; and in *Dalarna* the raised larders (*härbre*) in the farmyards. The red colouring, Falun-red, used everywhere for preserving the wooden buildings, is an iron oxide by-product first produced in the copper mine at *Falun*, hence the name.

Both salt and fresh water fishing are of importance. On the northern rivers, the *karsinapata*, a type of salmon-trap is often set up across the rapids, and off the *Bohuslän* coast, the *sjöbodar*, the long-eaved fishing huts are built out on piles into the sea.

Forest products, mainly in the form of pulps, paper, wallboard, matches, prefabricated buildings, chemicals and wood alcohol constitute about 40 per cent of Sweden's export trade. Most of the large sawmills and factories are on the north-west shores of the Baltic, on *Lake Vänern* and at the mouths of the rivers down which the logs are floated in the spring.

Mining is very important, but an almost entire lack of coal restricts smelting to high-grade ores; low-grade iron ore from the *Norrland* fields is exported through Narvik in Norway. Copper, lead and aluminium are processed in the *Boliden* district in the north-east.

Many Swedish inventions or developments, such as dynamite, turbines, separators, ball-bearings and refrigerators, are in use throughout the world and engineering products are a major export. Craft industries of glassware and woodwork centred in *Småland* and a varied domestic industry in *Dalarna*, are important in the industrial scheme.

Customs

Along with her conventions, Sweden has preserved a charming folklore. Most of the festivals are connected with the seasons, and are celebrated in song and dance, sometimes with feasting.

Valborgsmässsoafton, the eve of the first of May, is the occasion when students make a special greeting to spring with bonfires and singing. *Midsommarafton* is celebrated in town and country all over Sweden. In the country districts, and especially in *Dalarna*, the national costumes and dances are seen at their best during this celebration. St Lucia Day, 13 December, originally a pagan exorcising of the dark spirits of winter, is now a festival day marking the opening of the Christmas season.

Foresters and fishermen in various communities have their own special festivals, but a nation-wide custom is the holding of crayfish suppers by lantern light, often outdoors towards the end of summer.

Food and Drink

A Scandinavian speciality is *smörgås*, which may be described as an open sandwich. The famous *smörgåsbord* is an elaborate assortment of cold dishes, such as pickled herring, sliced sausage, shrimps, salad, cheese, smoked salmon and other fish — with a choice of crispbread called *knäckebröd* of various degrees of hardness, white bread (*franksbröd*) and a dark sweet-tasting bread. The sweet course, not usually served with midday lunch, is generally a light fruit mixture. Various kinds of junket are also popular.

Milk is commonly drunk with meals, or beer (confusingly called *öl*) usually *Pilsner* or similar. There is a variety of soft drinks of superior quality. Anything ending in *-saft* is some kind of fruit juice. *Pommac* is somewhat like the German or Swiss *Apfelsöft*. *Solo* and *Loranga* are orange juice.

Culture

Architecture

A visitor will not go far before noting the preponderance of modern buildings even in the smallest of country towns. This applies as much to the far north as to the south, though for different reasons. The development of the northern towns came about so recently that due regard could be paid to modern conditions. Farther south, however, replacement has often been necessary following the effects of fire on the older buildings, the majority of which were of timber.

The isolation of Sweden meant that Christianity arrived late, and consequently she is not so rich in religious architectural relics as countries closer to Rome. There is, however, much to see, reflecting the culural development of the country from Stone Age burial grounds to medieval churches, Renaissance palaces and modern social architecture.

Under the Vasa dynasty (1520-1654) castles were built on royal initiative at strategic points such as *Kalmar, Mariefred (Gripsholm), Uppsala* and *Vadstena*; and, notably in Skåne, others were built by the nobility. Many remain as monuments of a period when Swedish architecture was much subject to influences from abroad.

The first decades of the twentieth century were characterized by a romantic national movement which attained its highest expression in the Town Hall of *Stockholm* (1923). New incentives were given by the Stockholm Exhibition (1930), where Functionalism was the dominant theme. Buildings of this character had, however, appeared earlier than this, the first being the Art Gallery in *Stockholm* (1916).

A new shopping area, claimed to be the largest in Europe, has been built in the city-centre. Space has been gained by building at different levels, including a new street, *Sergelgatan*, solely for pedestrians, and a system of roof gardens linked by bridges forms an elevated park.

Art

Artists working in Sweden in the seventeenth and eighteenth centuries were mostly foreigners; among native painters, Roslin (in Paris) and Martin (in London) had an international reputation. Zorn (1860-1920), recorder of peasant life, was sought after as a portraitist; Prince Eugen (1865-1947) represents the school of sentimental painting prevailing in Sweden at the turn of the century. Sculpture is dominated by Milles (1875-1955), considered one of the great sculptors of the twentieth century.

Sweden makes a notable contribution to the arts in industrial design: furniture, glass, china and many other everyday objects are almost always superbly designed.

Museums and Art Galleries

Most large towns have at least one museum, which houses also sculpture and paintings, and the smaller towns often have a museum of some kind. In the country there are often parks called *gammalgård*, in which typical buildings of the district have been carefully preserved, completely equipped with furniture. *Skansen* Open Air Museum in *Stockholm* is an example on the national scale, since almost every province is represented.

Literature

Swedenborg (1688-1772) is known to the world for the many mystical and theological works of his later life. Strindberg (1849-1912), poet and dramatist, innovator, and master of many styles, has been specially influential through his naturalistic novels and plays. In a different vein, the historical novels of Selma Lagerlöf (1858-1940), the first woman to receive a Nobel Prize for Literature, include the classic *Gösta Berlings Saga*, a story of Varmland, and should be read for their vivid pictures of Swedish life and character.

Theatres

There are theatres and concert halls in *Stockholm, Göteborg, Malmö, Norrköping, Helsingborg* and *Gävle* but, like the cinemas these have few, if any, performances in summer. Concerts are, however, held on summer evenings in *Stockholm* in the National Museum (Art Gallery), in *Skansen* Open Air Museum, in *Kungsträdgården*, and on the piazza of the City Hall. *Stockholm* Festival of Music, Drama and Ballet is held annually in early June. Operas, performed at other times in the Royal Opera House, are given in summer at the *Drottningholm Court Theatre*.

Science

Sweden's best known eighteenth-century scientists are Celsius, in physics, and von Linné (Linnaeus) in botany. Swedenborg too, wrote widely in mathematics, mineralogy and physiology before he became a mystic. Natural scientists in the nineteenth century include Retzius, and Berzelius and Alfred Nobel, inventor of dynamite and founder of the Nobel prizes, most highly regarded of international awards; in the twentieth century, de Geer, the geologist, and Svedberg, the physicist.

Touring Information

Touring Areas

Sweden is such a large country and contains so many different types of landscape that you cannot hope to see it all on foot, by bicycle or even by motor car. Distances are so great that the most you can do is to explore one of the many areas.

First in importance comes the lake and canal district of central Sweden. This is undulating country, alternating between open farmland and woods, with frequent glimpses between clearings across the lakes. Many of its modern industrial towns have historical associations from the days when they were trading centres.

Bohuslän and *Dalsland* lie to the west of the central lakes. The rocky coast of

Bohuslän with its many fishing villages and bathing resorts contrasts with the wooded hilly district of *Dalsland* dotted with small farms and lakes.

Värmland is a province of lakes, fertile valleys and wooded ridges. The atmosphere of the old *bruk* and manor houses of this district gave Selma Lagerlöf the inspiration for the novels she wrote portraying the life of the people. Modern cellulose factories in forest settings now dot the landscape.

Bergslagen is the name of the central (mining) district included in the provinces of *Värmland, Västmanland* and *Dalarna*. The latter is one of the most popular provinces for touring since here, especially around *Lake Siljan*, can be seen many of the customs and colourful local costumes in idyllic surroundings: woods, lakes and meadows, small white stone churches, and mellowed wooden farmhouses, some containing unique wall hangings (*dalmålningar*).

Skåne, district of fertile plains, Sweden's richest agricultural country, has castles and manor houses surrounded by parks and gardens, and, along the coasts, sandy bathing beaches; *Blekinge* is an area of cultivated valleys between beech-wooded hills; then there are the unique islands of *Öland* and *Gotland*. *Jämtland* is an area for mountain walking and winter sports. *Ångermanland* and *Medelpad* are provinces of forests, lakes, mountains, large rivers and forest industries.

In the far north lies a vast area of pine forests, giving way to treeless lake-dotted mountains, the land of the Lapps. This is splendid country for mountain walking, climbing, fishing and skiing, and is best reached by train from *Stockholm* to *Kiruna* by the main route, returning by the inland route through *Östersund*.

Access

The most direct route is by DFDS steamers to *Gottenburg* (*Göteborg*), sailing from Harwich thrice weekly, or from Newcastle twice a week. Another route, for those wishing to combine Sweden and Denmark, is by DFDS steamers from Harwich or Newcastle to Esbjerg. Many services between Denmark and Sweden include Copenhagen to *Malmö*, Dragör to *Limhamn* and Elsinore to *Halsingborg*, the shortest route.

Transport

Swedish State Railways are run efficiently and, together with their own bus services, make almost all the country readily accessible. Special holiday tickets (*Semesterbiljett*) for long distances, cheap circular tour tickets and the low-priced card *Lågpriskort*, which qualifies for remarkable reductions on rail fares throughout the country, are on offer.

The Post Office run the bus services (*Post diligensen*) in *Norrland*, connecting north-south railway lines with remote inland districts and the coast. Regular steamers ply, in summer, on the *Gota* and *Dalsland* canals and on Lakes *Vättern* and *Siljan*; river ferries are free and run according to demand, and many small ferries run out to the islands off the coasts and on some lakes in *Lapland*.

The national timetable, *Sveriges Kommunikationer*, with international sign language, includes rail, some lake-boat and most bus services. *Trafikleder i Lappland* is a special bus and boat timetable for the *Kebnekaise, Sjöfall* and *Sitasjaure* areas, issued free by *Svenska Turisföreningen*.

Public Holidays

1 January, 6 January, Good Friday, Easter Monday, 1 May, Ascension Day, Whit Monday, Midsummer Day (nearest Saturday to 24 June), All Saints' Day, Christmas Day and 26 December.

Clothing

Fairly light clothing can be worn in summer, but spring nights can be sharp with frost, especially farther north. Be prepared for sudden bursts of thundery rain and take anti-midge protection in summer.

Restaurants

Most towns have inexpensive restaurants in the department stores which serve good quality food and even the smallest communities can be relied upon to have a *kafé* which serves coffee and pastries. Restaurants do not escape Sweden's high cost of living; *à la carte* eating is expensive, but set bills of fare — offered between fixed hours — are often reasonably priced and fish dishes in suprising variety, are less expensive.

Maps

The largest series is Topografiska karten över Sverige; the far north is at a scale of 1:100,000 and the rest of the country at 1:50,000. Motorists and cyclists should use the new Turist kartan, ten very large sheets at 1:300,000. General-purpose road maps can be bought cheaply, or free of charge, at most filling stations.

Walking Tours

Swedish youth hostels are often too far apart for hostel-to-hostel walking tours. The best walking country served by youth hostels is to be found in *Värmland*, to the north of Lake *Vänern* (see **R6**), and round Lake *Siljan* in *Dalarna* (see **R7**). Undoubtedly, however, the finest walking is to be had in the mountain areas of the north.

Mountaineering and Fell Walking

The Swedish highlands span more than 500 miles (800km) through *Lapland* (see **R9**), *Jämtland* (see **R8**) and *Härjedalen* to *Dalarna* (see **R7**). The highest (nearly

7,000ft, 2,140m) and most rugged mountains, with glaciers in some parts, occur in north-west *Lapland* and will attract mountaineers. But they and the other mountain areas are particularly suitable for long fell-walking tours.

Almost uninhabited, the highlands have a wild spaciousness hardly to be found elsewhere in Europe. Careful planning and some experience is essential before attempting a long tour, which should not in any case be undertaken alone. Conditions are quite different from those found in the Alps, notably the remoteness from habitation, and so it may be necessary to carry provisions for several days.

The Swedish Touring Club (STF) has marked tracks, provided bridges, rowing boats, motor boats on lakes and accommodation in their mountain stations and huts; concession fees are available for YHA members.

(a) STF mountain stations; beds, meals, and usually a store and self-cooking facilities; make reservations: in *Lapland* at *Abisko, Kebnekaise, Saltoluokta, Ritsem*, and *Kvikkjokk*; in *Jämtland* at *Blåhammaren, Sylarna* and *Storulvån* and in *Dalarna* at *Grövelsjön*.

(b) STF mountain huts; no staff, no meals and no advance booking: about fifty huts on the cairned trails between tourist stations, equipped with bedding, cooking utensils and, in most cases, firewood.

(c) STF shelters (unlocked); Lapp style conical huts, unfloored with turf-covered sides.

Leave huts and shelters as you would wish to find them: wood supply inside; windows, doors and outbuildings secured. Carelessness could be fatal as an open window could mean a snow-filled hut. Similarly at unmanned boat crossings leave a boat at each side. This means rowing three times.

Skiing

All the above mountain regions are excellent for skiing. In *Lapland* the best months are March and April, but in the far north it may still be possible to ski as late as the end of May.

Motoring

Motorists should enquire of their own motoring organisations for advice of additional facilities for motorists in Sweden. Driving licence, international driving permit, registration certificate and certificate of insurance must be carried; international green card is not compulsory but it is prudent to carry it. Motorways (no toll charges) are well-engineered and excellently surfaced, secondary roads are occasionally loosely finished, in the north frequently so. A red warning triangle should be carried, and a national identity sticker displayed. Enforced speed limits are indicated by road signs.

Cycling

Principal roads have permanent surfaces suitable for cycling; other roads may be roughly surfaced. Apart from the north-west, Sweden is not difficult terrain for cyclists and winds are comparatively light. Most towns have cycle shops where running repairs can be carried out but most spares are in metric dimensions.

Canoeing and Boating

Canoeing is possible for long stretches on many canals, rivers and lakes, along the shores of which convenient camping sites can easily be found. At some tourist hotels, canoes are loaned out by the STF (*Grövelsjön* in *Dalarna* and *Tärnaby* in *Lapland*). Suggested routes are through the *Göteborg — Hindås — Alingsås* lake district, the *Dalsland Canal, Mälaren* and surrounding lakes and rivers, *Grövelsjön* and surrounding lakes and down River *Torne* from *Torneträsk* to *Jukkasjärvi*.

Sailing is popular around the coast, especially from *Stockholm* and *Göteborg*. Most boats are privately owned, so that hiring out is not so usual. There are, however, sight-seeing trips on the waterways of these ports.

Stockholm△

The city, beautifully situated on its islands, comprises the Old City, the 'Stone City' and the suburbs and satellite towns of recent growth.

A useful plan of the city and its communications is SL Stockholmskarta which can be bought on buses, but an adequate street-plan is supplied free to visitors by the Tourist Association Bureau, on the *Hamngatan*.

Its centre is the island known as the 'city between the bridges', or the old city (*gamla staden*). In direct contrast to the historical buildings found here are modern flats lining the waterfront and concrete and steel bridges which span the waterways.

Boats arriving from the west, ie from Lake *Mälaren*, tie up close by the railway station at *Norr-Mälarstrand* and *Klara Strand*, while sea-going steamers arrive at *Skeppsbron* on the east side.

The focal point of roads from the north is *Norra Bantorget*, just north of the station, and from the south, the clover-leaf crossing known as *Slussen*.

Most public service vehicles are electric; a standard fare is charged, valid for buses and underground (*Tunnelbanan*), and the ticket can be used for a further journey in the same zone within an hour of issue. Excess is charged for journeys into other zones and double fare after midnight. During summer tourist tickets are on sale, valid for 24 hours on the city's entire transport system.

The main shopping-centre lies to the north of the old city, the main streets being *Drottninggatan, Hamngatan* and *Kungsgatan*; NK, Åhléns and PUB are the most popular stores.

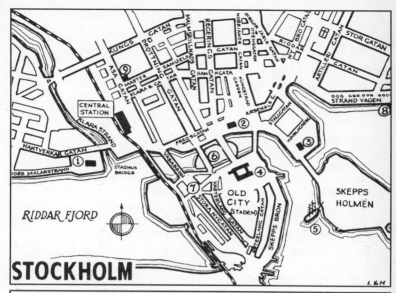

STOCKHOLM

1 Town Hall. 2 Opera. 3 National Museum. 4 Royal Palace. 5 youth hostel ship *Af Chapman*. 6 Riksdag (Parliament House). 7 Riddarhuset. 8 Road to Skansen. 9 Post Office.

The Old City

The Bank of Sweden and Parliament House (*Riksdagshuset*). Visitors can be shown round Parliament House unless a session is in progress, when the visitors' gallery can be used. The Great Church (*Storkyrkan*) oldest church in Stockholm. Great Square (*Stortorget*). Royal Palace (*Kungliga Slottet*); eighteenth century. Watch for the smelt fishers on the waterways here in summer.

Riddarholmskyrkan: thirteenth-century abbey, Swedish Pantheon, burial place of kings and notables; on *Riddarholm* island, south-west of *Riddarhuset*; free admission on Sunday afternoons.

Riddarhuset: Assembly Hall of Swedish nobility, seventeenth century; often used for concerts.

Immediately North of the Old City

City Hall (*Stadshuset*) 1911-23, synthesis of romantic and modern styles; free admission on Sunday afternoons.

Law Courts (*Rådhuset*), 1915; Concert Hall (*Konserthuset*), 1926, neo-classical; faces the lively flower and produce market (*Hötorget*), with *Orpheus* fountain by Milles. *Kungliga Teatern* (opera and ballet) season August-May. *Royal Dramatic Theatre*, season September to mid-June. *National Museum*; painting and sculpture, and concerts on summer evenings.

To the North, but farther from City Centre

Stadium built for Olympic Games in 1912; football and athletic events on Sunday afternoons. College of Technology (*Tekniska Högskolan*) with fountain *Monument of Industry*, by Milles, at front. Gustavus III Pavilion 1790 in Haga Park with exquisite period furnishings. Natural History Museum (*Naturhistoriska Riksmuseum*) botanical garden; train from *Ostra* Station to *Frescati*, or by underground to '*Universitetet*' *Millesgarden*, with Milles's works on terraces overlooking city.

East of Old City (Skeppsholmen and beyond)

Nordic Museum (*Nordiska Museet*) and Royal Armoury (*Kgl Livrustkammaren*) historical collections. *Skansen*, open-air cultural museum, theatre, zoological gardens, music and dancing. *Waldemarsudde*, art collection. National Historical Museum (*Stat Historiska Museum*); fine collection of religious art and archaeology. *Wasavarvet*, royal man-of-war *Wasa*, foundered in Stockholm harbour in 1628, raised 1961, restored and carefully preserved. Other museums farther east are the Maritime Museum (*Stat Sjöhistoriska*), the Ethnographic Museum, the Technical Museum (with unique Atomarium) and the Museum of Modern Art on *Skeppsholmen*.

Outside the City to the East

Stockholm Archipelago for superb bathing and boating. Popular resort of *Saltsjöbaden*, 25 minutes by suburban railway from *Saltsjöbaden* station at *Slussen*, or by steamer from *Nybroplan* in $1^1/_2$ hours.

South of Old City

Katarina lift for fine view; Civic Centre (*Medborgar huset*); Handicraft Institute (*Stat Handverksinstitut*); fine view from building over city. Southern Hospital (*Södersjukhuset*), one of Sweden's finest modern hospitals. Ericsson's telephone factory; an example of industrial architecture.

Outside City to the West

Drottningholm Castle by steamer from *Klara Strand* in 40 minutes, or by bus from *Brommaplan* underground station. Seventeenth century, French baroque, museums; theatre is eighteenth century and preserved in original form. Open in summer when performances of operas are staged.

Gripsholm Castle, Mariefred. Sailings from *Klara Strand* in summer in $3^1/_2$ hours or by railway in $1^1/_2$ hours. Mainly sixteenth century; portrait collection one of the finest in Europe.

There are many indoor and outdoor swimming baths and it also possible to bathe during the summer in the maze of creeks to be found at some distance from the city.

Vällingby and *Farsta* are modern suburbs of interest to architects and can be reached by underground from the centre of Stockholm in about 30 minutes. Modern apartment buildings of different kind, surround an attractive shopping centre and underground station.

Touring Routes

R1 Stockholm — Örebro — Stockholm, round Lake Mälaren (250 miles, 403km)

This district is the cradle of the Swedish nation and abounds in historical monuments and associations. It contains a large number of fine castles and country houses. Lake *Mälaren* is dotted with innumerable islands, many of them extremely beautiful. Steamer service in summer from *Stockholm (Klara Strand)* to some places mentioned in this route; a pleasant means of exploring the lake, although route is based on road travel.

From *Stockholm* take road E4 through north-western suburb of *Ulriksdal* with palace built by Charles X (seventeenth century) for 23 miles (37km) to **Sigtuna**△, one of oldest and most picturesque towns in Sweden. Nearest railway station *Märsta* is 3 miles (5km) eastwards. Town founded eleventh century; ruins of four large churches testify to its former importance. *Sigtunastiftelsen* is well-known college for ecclesiastical studies and adult education.

EXCURSION: *Skokloster* Castle, with collection of trophies from Thirty Years' War, is one of finest in Sweden. Boat trips in season.

R1 (i) Sigtuna to Uppsala△, 20 miles (32km). Do not omit this detour unless very short of time. From *Sigtuna* continue north to join main road from *Stockholm* at *Alsike*. **Uppsala** is older of the two ancient universities and seat of Archbishop of Sweden. Many associations with great botanist Linnaeus. Cathedral is beautiful Gothic building. Castle (sixteenth century) mainly occupied by County Council, but great hall open to visitors — here Queen Christina abdicated in 1654. University library ('*Carolina Rediviva*') contains valuable collection of books and manuscripts, greatest treasure being Codex Argentius, translation of Bible into ancient Gothic by Arian Bishop Ulfilas (fifth century) so-called from silver colour of its lettering.

EXCURSION: *Gamla Uppsala*, (2$^1/_2$ miles, 4km) by bus or train, is site of capital of pre-Christian kingdom of *Svea Rike* (hence *Sverige*, the modern Swedish name for the country). Little church said to stand on site of Temple of Odin. Great mounds are burial places of ancient chieftains. On one of these the royal council was held and assembled tribes were addressed by their kings.

From *Sigtuna* take secondary road via *Erikssund* to join E18 at *Overgan*, then through *Enköping*Δ, old market town with monastery ruins, crossing county boundary from *Uppland* into *Västmanland*.

VästeråsΔ, 26 miles (42km) from *Sigtuna* is a manufacturing town, and county capital, pleasantly situated on bay of lake. ASEA factory in Romanesque style in weathered red brick is said by local people to be frequently mistaken for cathedral. *Djäkneberg* is pleasant open space affording good view over town and lake; names and dates cut on rocks and stones are work of local eccentric.

EXCURSION: 10 miles (16km) south-west to *Tidö* castle (1620): stands in fine park on peninsula in lake.

Continue on E18 via *Kolbäck* and *Munktorp* to *Köping*Δ (22 miles, 35km) with small open-air museum.

On for 10 miles (16km) to *Arboga*Δ, a small town with many interesting fifteenth-century buildings. Here Sweden's first parliament was held in 1435 under Engelbrekt, whose statue, 1935, commemorates 500th anniversary. Beyond *Arboga* main road crosses county boundary into small province of *Närke* and continues along Lake *Hjälmar* to mouth of River *Svartån* to *Örebro*Δ, 45 miles (72km), important in Swedish history from its foundation in fourteenth century to 1810 when Bernadotte was here elected crown prince.

Returning, take roads on south of Lake *Hjälmar* for 25 miles (40km) to **Eskilstuna**, home of Swedish steel industry. Before the days of safety razors and electric shavers *Eskilstuna* razors were world famous. Town takes its name from English missionary St Eskil (eleventh century) martyred by pagans and buried here. Fine public park and country open-air museum where two ancient smithies are preserved. Continue eastwards for 20 miles (32km) on road E3 to *Strängnäs*, delightful cathedral town on lakeside.

Mariefred, for *Gripsholm Castle*, is 12 miles (19km) farther on.

Boat services to bathing beaches on islands of *Segerön* and *Granliden*. Through picturesque wooded country to *Södertälje*Δ for another open-air museum and on for 15 miles (24km) by motorway to suburbs of *Stockholm*.

R2 Skåne and Halland. Malmö to Halmstad (104 miles, 167km)

This part of Sweden was for a long time under Danish rule, and it is said that inhabitants are still more happy-go-lucky than their fellow Swedes. Certainly the traveller crossing from Denmark will be struck by the Danish look of the towns and countryside of fertile plains.

MalmöΔ is third largest town in Sweden and ancient capital of Skåne. Many fine old buildings; St Peter's Church, 1319, *Malmöhus* castle. Sixteenth-century and modern architecture; City Theatre, 1944, *Friluftstaden* Garden Suburb. Ferry service to Copenhagen.

R2 (i) Malmö to LundΔ (11 miles, 18km). *Lund* is ancient town, well worth a visit. Founded by *Knut* (Canute) the Great, King of Denmark, Norway and England. University founded 1666. Romanesque cathedral is one of oldest and most interesting churches in Sweden; astronomical clock plays on weekdays at 12 noon and 3pm when moving figures of knights on horseback clash, trumpeters blow, organ plays and three kings pay homage to infant Christ. Restaurant in University club house is open to public.

*Landskrona*Δ 25 miles (40km) along coast road from *Malmö* has well-preserved seventeenth-century fortifications surrounding moated castle.

EXCURSION: by steamer, 35 minutes to Island of *Ven*, to see observatory built by Danish astronomer Tycho Brahe (sixteenth century).

HelsingborgΔ, fine modern town built round older nucleus. Wide view from castle tower (*Kärnan*), 186 steps. Maritime museum at *Råd* to south of town, bathing beach at *Pålsjöbaden* nearby. Ferries to Helsingör in Denmark and Travemünde in Germany.

Northwards for 4 miles (6km) to *Kulla-Gunnarstorp* for *Sofiero Castle*, summer residence of royal family; park open each morning in summer. *Viken*, popular seaside resort is 2 miles (3km) farther on; *Höganäs,* 4 miles (6km), has Sweden's only coal mine.

Mölle is pleasant resort on *Kullen* peninsula, below *Högkull* hill (615ft, 187m) with high cliffs and some interesting caves; area is nature reserve, and there is an entrance fee. Powerful light-house on point of peninsula.

Continue along coast via *Ängelholm*Δ and *Margretetorp*Δ through *Hallandsås* hills by attractive *Sinarp* valley to *Båstad*Δ, fashionable resort with international tennis and golf tournaments, fine gardens.

Turn east on road No 115 via *Ö Karup* and, at *Hasslöfs* church, take road south to *Lugnarohögen* for fine ship-form burial mound dating from Bronze Age. North to *Laholm*Δ, on River *Lagan*, picturesque little town; ruins of medieval fortress, moat now salmon nursery. Excellent bathing on coast at *Melbystrand*.

Take coast road again, 14 miles (22km), to *Halmstad*Δ, port with remains of old fortifications; sculpture by Milles, *Europa and the Bull* on fountain in *Stora Torg*. Coast road continues for 90 miles (145km) to *Göteborg*, but less interesting than *Malmö* to *Halmstad* route.

R3 The extreme South. Malmö to Kalmar (255 miles, 410km), Öland and Gotland

Route follows coast of provinces of *Skåne, Blekinge* and *Småland*. Take road E6 for 20 miles (32km) to *Trelleborg*Δ, port for ferry to Travemünde; continue on road No 10 past several fishing villages and small resorts to *Ystad*Δ which has preserved its medieval character; many half-timbered houses, Franciscan monastery and museum. *Ystads Saltsjöbaden*, modern seaside resort, lies eastwards.

District contains many castles and manor-houses. Steamer service to Rönne on Danish island of Bornholm.

Continue from *Ystad* on road No 10 for 8 miles (12km), then turn northwards on to road No 103 for magnificent sixteenth-century castle of *Glimmingehus*, well-preserved, four-storey keep. Coast reached again after 17 miles (25km) at *Simrishamn*, old seaport with medieval atmosphere; favoured by artists. *Kivik*, fishing village and bathing resort is 10 miles (16km) farther on. *Havång△*, near *Ravlundabro* — take track near shore from *Vitemölla* for 2 miles (3km).

Beyond *Degeberga* is well-preserved castle of *Vittskövle* (sixteenth century). *Kristianstad* is garrison town; two ancient city gates are preserved on new sites. Trinity (*Trefaldighets*) church is good example of seventeenth-century architecture. At *Sölvesborg*, 18 miles (29km), road No 15 enters province of **Blekinge**, former Danish possession often called 'Garden of Sweden' owing to its well-tilled valleys. Road circles *Pukaviks* bay for 19 miles (30km) to *Karlshamn△*, port and industrial town; boat excursions to *Blekinge* archipelago.

Kullåkra, 10 miles (16km) by rail from *Karlshamn*, is station for *Tjärö△* reached by road to *Järnavik*, 2 miles (3km), then motor boat. *Ronneby△*, 11 miles (18km), has picturesque wooden houses and mineral wells.

Karlskrona, 16 miles (26km), principal naval base, built on islands; founded by Charles XI in 1679; planned in baroque style, with fine streets and buildings. *Blekinge* Museum in *Våstra Prinsgatan*. *Kristianopel△* is 15 miles (24km) along coast.

After 5 miles (8km), at *Brömsebro*, leave *Blekinge* for *Småland*; name means small lands, derived from former division into many small estates; soil is poor but the province has won fame for its glass and furniture industries.

Kalmar△ is historic town. Fine example of seventeenth-century planning. Baroque cathedral; town hall; merchant houses; city wall and gates. Massive castle, partly twelfth century, partly Renaissance. Fine interior. Swedish American Day celebrated in courtyard on second Sunday in August.

EXCURSION: west-north-west for 26 miles (42km) to *Orrefors△*, known throughout world for its artistic glassware.

R3 (i) Kalmar to Island of Öland. Linked to mainland by Europe's longest bridge (4 miles, 6km) or by boat from *Oskarshamn△* to *Byxelkrok*, north *Öland*.

Apart from narrow coastal strip, island consists of long chalk ridge, infertile but with interesting flora and bird life. Archaeological remains and windmills abound. Bus service on circular route links *Borgholm△* (capital and only town) with *Ölands Skogsby△*, *Böda* and *Ottenby*.

R3 (ii) To Island of Gotland. Steamers daily from *Oskarshamn* to **Visby**. Also from *Öland* to *Klintehamn△* on *Gotland*. Can also be reached from *Stockholm*. *Gotland* 'Isle of the Goths' lies 50 miles (80km) from Swedish coast; sunny climate, with southerly type of flora in lowlands and pine and heather on uplands. *Visby△*, capital and only town is former Hansa city which in twelfth and thirteenth century was fabulously wealthy. Most of churches now roofless, but merchants' houses still stand along narrow streets, giving vivid impression of Middle Ages; city wall, still almost complete, is over 2 miles, 3km, in length (recommended walk). Nine youth hostels on island; bus services connect most places.

Whole island is rich in prehistoric remains, interesting churches, old manor houses; many bathing beaches. Island of *Stora Karlsö*, off west coast and by motor boat from *Klintehamn*, is bird sanctuary.

R4 Göteborg and The Great Lakes. Göteborg — Jönköping — Göteborg (361 miles, 581km)

GöteborgΔ was founded 1619 when south of Sweden and all Norway were under Danish rule; it was well placed for trade with the New World and the Far East. Dutch merchants and town-planners helped in its development and the signs of their influence remain in the buildings and canals in parts of the city. *Göteborg* has always tended to look west; connections with English and Scots families remain in surnames.

The principal sights are *Götaplatsen* (*Gota* Square), with Milles sculpture *Poseidon*, Art Museum, Concert Hall (one of finest in Europe), and Municipal Theatre. Botanical Gardens and *Trädgardsföreningen*, a terrace restaurant with music and dancing in beautiful garden surroundings. *Gustav Adolfs Torg*, main square at centre of busy street *Östra Hamngatan*. *Liseberg* amusement park is a smaller edition of the famous Tivoli in Copenhagen with gardens, music, restaurants and entertainments.

From *Göteborg* follow course of canalised River *Göta* for 12 miles (19km) to charming ancient little town of *Kungälv*Δ. On opposite side of river is fourteenth-century fortress of *Bohus*. Take road on east side of river for 12 miles (19km) to *Alvängen* and continue for 25 miles (40km) to *Trollhättan* Δ, industrial town and tourist centre. Here are locks which raise canal to level of Lake *Vänern*. Hydro-electric station at *Trollhätten Falls*, one of largest in Europe, can be visited by arrangement. Many walks and viewpoints in neighbourhood.

EXCURSION: 9 miles (14km) to *Vänersborg*Δ, lake and canal port at entry into Lake *Vänern* (Sweden's largest lake). Journey from *Göteborg* to *Vänersborg* can be made by *Göta* Canal steamer (about 8 hours).

Take side-road north-eastwards for 50 miles (80km) to *Lidköping*Δ, small industrial town on bay, and then follow lakeside road to *Kinnekulle*Δ, peculiarly terraced rocky hill, 1,000ft (305m) with wide views. Look-out tower on *Högkulle* (ascend from either *Råbäck* or *Gassäter*). Several ancient castles in neighbourhood. On to *Mariestad*Δ (34 miles [55km] from *Lipköping*), pleasant lakeside town, seventeenth-century cathedral. Continue for 28 miles (45km) on E3 via *Hassle* to *Laxå*, a small industrial town with interesting wooden church and museum, on main railway line *Stockholm-Göteborg*, and most northerly point on this route. *Örebro* on route **R1** is 40 miles (64km) north-east. Turn south on road

No 205 for 26 miles (42km) via *Röfors* and past two small lakes to *Askersund*Δ at northen end of Lake *Vättern*; follow road No 50, one of most beautiful lakeside roads in Sweden, for 20 miles (32km) to *Medevi*Δ and continue for 18 miles (29km) to *Motala* Δ, industrial town and port for *Göta* Canal; thirteenth-century cathedral; tomb of von Platen, engineer of canal, in lakeside park.

Bathing beach at *Varamobaden*. *Vadstena* Δ 10 miles (16km) south, is port of call for canal steamers; Renaissance castle (1545); abbey established by St Birgitta, founder of Birgittine religious order. *Borhamn* Δ is nearby, and then at *Väversunda*, 10 miles (16km), is Lake *Tåkern*, haunt of many birds. On for 2 miles (3km) to *Omberg*Δ (760ft, 231m) a wooded hill rising sheer from lake, famous for its bird-life and plants; a broad view from summit. Nearby are abbey ruins and prehistoric lake- dwelling site. After 1 mile (2km) is *Rök* with ninth-century runic stone, biggest in the country. *Hästholmen* is nearby, lake port with steamer to *Hjo*Δ on opposite bank. *Ödeshog*Δ is 5 miles (8km) south of *Hästholmen*. *Gränna* Δ is 20 miles (32km) farther on; charming village in district famous for its orchards; a 300-year-old pear tree is preserved as ancient monument; *André Museum* contains relics of ill-fated attempt to reach North Pole by balloon (1897).

EXCURSION: to island of *Visingsö* by steamer or motor boat in about half an hour; many ancient barrows and earthworks; medieval churches; rich vegetation.

Jönköping is 25 miles (40km) farther along E4 at south end of lake; new museum at *Fiskartorget*; seventeenth-century Town Hall; open-air museum in park; modern match industry (with museum). Turn west on road No 40 for 35 miles (56km) to *Ulricehamn*Δ, health resort with sanatoria on Lake *Åsunden*. Continue for 20 miles (32km) to *Borås*Δ, textile manufacturing town. From here two routes to *Göteborg*: 52 miles (84km) via *Alingsås*Δ and *Näs*, on Lake *Sävelången*, famous school of arts and crafts, or 45 miles (72km) via *Hindås*, noted winter sports centre.

R5 Bohuslän and Dalsland. Göteborg — Hällevadsholm — Vänersborg — Göteborg (248 miles, 399km)

From *Göteborg* take road No 160 on west bank of River *Göta* for 12 miles (19km) to *Kungälv*Δ. Fork north-west on E6 for further 12 miles (19km) to *Jorlanda*Δ and 5 miles (8km) on to *Spekeröd*; to north is magnificent coastal scenery: *Stenungsund* (3 miles, 5km) has good bathing beach. After another 3 miles (5km), is *Ödsmål*Δ. On for 22 miles (36km) to *Uddevalla*Δ in valley between tall cliffs. Nearby are gravel-beds with biggest mass of fossil shells in world. Motor-boat services and tours to nearby islands including *Bassholmen*Δ. *Hällevadsholm* lies 25 miles (40km) to north.

R5 (i) **Hällevadsholm to Strömstad** (28 miles, 45km). *Tanumshede* (15 miles, 24km) is centre of district abounding in tumuli, rock carvings, rune-stones and many other prehistoric remains. Leaving main road at *Skee*, descend to *Strömstad*Δ.

EXCURSION: to *Koster* Islands, by motor boat (*Sydkoster* is of interest to botanists), and by road to *Blomsholm*, with remarkable standing stones in ship form dating from Iron Age.

Main route continues past beautiful *Bullaren* Lakes via *Mon* to *Ed*Δ, charming tourist centre at end of Lake *Stora Le*. Take lakeside road for 20 miles (32km) to *Nössemark*, then ferry across lake to *Sund* and continue for another 20 miles (32km) to *Bengtsfors*Δ. Good views from hills where marked footpaths are shown on local maps. *Köpmannebro*, 30 miles (48km) away on Lake *Vänern*, may be reached either by road or by **Dalsland Canal**, pleasant and little used route, composed of lakes and canals, 168 miles (270km) of waterway with twenty-nine locks; steamer services from *Bengtsfors* in 6 hours.

From *Köpmannebro* turn south on lakeside road to *Vänersborg*Δ. Bathing and motor-boat excursions. Return to *Göteborg* on route **R4** via *Trollhättan*Δ.

R6 Värmland. Karlstad — Arvika — Torsby — Karlstad (330 miles, 530km)

By railway from *Göteborg*, changing at *Kil*, to *Karlstad*Δ, ancient county capital on north shore of Lake *Vånern* and at mouth of River *Klarålven*, in springtime thick with floating logs; open-air museums; early eighteenth-century cathedral; excellent centre for excursions into varied countryside.

Take road westwards for 28 miles (45km) to *Vårmskog*Δ. Turn north for 25 miles (40km) to *Arvika* and, via *Åmotsfors*Δ and series of delightful small lakes — *Racken, Gunnern*, and *Rottnen* — eastwards for 55 miles (88km) to *Sunne*Δ, attractive small resort on isthmus between middle and upper *Fryken* Lakes. These lakes and surrounding countryside (*Fryksdalen*) form background to Selma Lagerlöf's novel *Gösta Berlings Saga*.

EXCURSIONS: (a) *Mårbacka* farmhouse, home of Selma Lagerlöf (8 miles, 13km). (b) boat excursions on Lake *Fryken*. Youth hostel at *Fryksta*.

Turn north along magnificent upper lake for 32 miles (51km) by road or by lake steamer to *Torsby*. Here and at *Gräsmark* farther south, on Lake *Rottnen*, are hills, such as *Tossebergsklätten* (1,120ft, 340m), worth climbing for views. Northwards on road No 234 for 22 miles (35km), then turn southwards on road No 62 for 21 miles (33km) to *Ekshärad*; fine views from *Ekesberget*. Continue south along River *Klarälven* into an old mining district, via *Ransäter*Δ, to *Molkom*, 45 miles (72km).

R6 (i) Molkom to Filipstad (28 miles, 45km). Pleasant little town, centre of Bergslagen, an area in which mining has been carried out for six hundred years or more. Mausoleum of John Ericsson, the inventor.

Main route returns to *Karlstad* (45 miles, 72km).

R7 Dalarna. Ludvika — Falun — Avesta (173 miles, 278km)

Dalarna is one of the most picturesque districts in Sweden. In some places old costumes are still worn for festivals, and traditional songs and dances still performed. *Dalarna* (name means the dales) derived from two great valleys. The eastern *Dalälv* flows into Lake *Siljan*, one of most beautiful lakes in Sweden. This route is practicable for walkers, with some assistance from lake steamers; twice weekly from *Leksand*Δ to *Tällberg, Rättvik*Δ and *Mora*Δ.

From *Filipstad* (see **R6(i)**; or by railway from *Stockholm*) to **Ludvika**, industrial town on Lake *Väsman* from where there is choice of two routes to *Djurås*.

R7 (i) Ludvika to Djurås, via Björbo (53 miles, 85km). Skirting pleasant Lake *Väsman*, then through good hill country to *Björbo* (fine bridge over western *Dalälv*) and *Floda*, typical *Dalarna* village. Walkers can take hill path from *Skalberget*, 10 miles (16km) south of *Björbo*. *Djurås* lies at junction of eastern and western *Dalälv* valleys. *Tjärnboberg* (1,240ft, 377m) can be climbed from *Sifferbo*. Look-out point on *Djurmoklack* (1,196ft, 365m).

R7 (ii) Ludvika to Djurås via Borlänge (38 miles, 61km). Main road via *Rämshyttan* on Lake *Rämen* and forested hill country to **Borlänge**Δ, main town of *Dalarna*, with largest steel plant in the country. Interesting open-air museum. Thence by *Dalälv* valley to *Djurås*.

From *Djurås* through district famed for rural handicrafts via delightful village of *Gagnef* and on to *Leksand*Δ on Lake **Siljan**; midsummer festival here, open-air play, maypole dance, longboats rowed across lake. Views over lake from several nearby hills, from top of church tower on *Sollerön* island and from *Gesundaberget* (1,500ft, 457m). *Mora*Δ is goal of annual ski-contest '*Vasaloppet*' run by as many as 10,000 competitors from *Sälen*Δ, 53 miles (85km) away, to commemorate message sent by ski-runners to Gustav Vasa in 1521 to tell him that *Dalarna* supported him. Statue of Vasa by Zorn, famous Swedish artist; museum of his works on display here.

R7 (iii) Mora to Femund (Norway) via Österdalälven (76 miles, 122km). An approach to Eastern Norway, through wild and little-frequented country. Rail to *Älvdalen* (26 miles, 42km), then by buses, changing at *Särna*Δ and *Idre*Δ. From Femund connections by boat and bus to *Røros*.

By road No 70 for 18 miles (29km) on north side of lake to *Vikarbyn*, or same distance by footpath over *Fåsås* hill.

EXCURSION: (3 miles, 5km) north to attractive mountain village of *Röjeråsen*, famous view over lake, etc. Look-out tower.

On for 4 miles (6km) to *Rättvik*Δ, tourist centre; notable white church with unique mural painting, open-air museum.

South-east on road No 80 for 30 miles (48km), via *Bjursås* to *Falun* △, famous for its copper-mine worked since thirteenth century under same company; museum at mine buildings and the old mine town.

Skirt Lake *Runn* to *Vika* on road No 266 and enter picturesque **Säterdal**, deep and fertile, with many old villages. *Säter*△, once a provincial capital, has fine old houses. Good views from *Bipsberg* (1,020ft, 311m). *Hedemora*△ has fine church and houses of eighteenth century and earlier and an old theatre. Tour ends at *Avesta* (steel works) whence train to *Stockholm* in 1¹/₂ hours.

R8 Jämtland. Sundsvall to Storlien (235 miles, 378km)

This region rivals *Dalarna* for varied charm and surpasses it in the height of its mountains, which rise to 5,000ft (1,500m) near the Norwegian frontier. Excellent walking country. Walkers should make *Östersund* starting point for their tours, but cyclists or motorists should start from *Sundsvall*.

Sundsvall△ is busy timber export centre; factory on offshore island of *Alnö* which is largest wood-pulp plant in Sweden. From tower on rocky height of *Norra Stadsberget* is extensive view over Gulf of *Bothnia*.

Route follows road and River *Indal*, used for logging; numerous power-stations. *Bispgården* 58 miles (93km), fine view of valley, 5 miles (8km) farther are the *Döda Fallet*, waterfalls formed by a sudden change in course of river in eighteenth century. *Ragunda* has thirteenth-century church. At point where river leaves Lake *Gesunden* rapids have been harnessed to feed one of largest underground hydro-electric stations in Sweden. Follow pleasant north shore of lake to *Stugun*, at foot of *Stugunberget* (1,234ft, 376m); rare orchids in nearby forests, protected by law. At *Näverede* leave river valley and cut across plateau to **Östersund**△, beautifully situated on arm of Lake *Storsjön*, county capital, tourist centre and only sizeable town in *Jämtland*; founded in 1786; second highest town in Sweden (1,200ft, 366m); new church on hill above station is fine example of modern architecture. *Jamtli* open-air museum (one of best in Sweden) has many old buildings re-assembled from various parts of province.

EXCURSIONS: (a) round *Frösö* by steamer. (b) over bridge to island of *Frösö* and climb *Östberget* (1,536ft, 468m), magnificent view over lake and surrounding mountains; *Frösö* church, and near it open-air theatre where Petersen-Berger's opera *Arnljot* is performed every year in July.

Lake *Storsjön*, not to be confused with another and smaller Lake *Storsjön* lying to south-west in province of *Härjedalen*, lies nearly 1,000ft (300m) above sea level, amongst fertile country, with fine mountain background; road round lake is one of most beautiful in Sweden. Take this road, or railway, along east and north side of lake via *Mattmar* to *Järpen*.

R8 (i) Östersund to Järpen on foot. Walkers should start their tour at *Östersund*, (thence by railway to *Mattmar*, on by bus to *Hallen* (tourist hotel), then footpath inland to tourist hotel at *Bydalen* in beautiful *Storån* valley; excellent centre for mountain tours (eg ascent of *Drommen* (3,740ft, 1,140m, fine view, $2^1/_2$ hours climb). From *Bydalen* strike north over summit of *Västerfjället* (3,800ft, 1,157m, 2 hours) and continue in $3^1/_2$ hours to *Sällsjö* (tourist hotel) for visit to fine waterfall *Storbofallet*; thence by footpath or road for 5 miles (8km) to *Morsil* and rail or bus to *Järpen*.

Slagsån is 3 miles (5km) west of *Järpen* on road E75 and marks the beginning of series of tourist resorts such as *Hålland* and *Undersåker* in valley of same name; many excursions into mountains. *Åre*△ on lake of same name, is one of finest tourist centres in *Jämtland*, both summer and winter.

EXCURSION: ascent of *Åreskutan* (4,658ft, 1,420m), one of highest peaks in *Jämtland*, via *Östra Plantån* and *Mörvikshummeln* by funicular and ski-lift. Entirely on foot takes 6 hours, return.

Duved, where road and railway separate, is 5 miles (8km) on, and from here *Mulffjället* can be climbed in 4 hours.

R8 (ii) Duved to Sandvika (29 miles, 47km). This was once road to Norway (for Trondheim); wild but beautiful country. Bus as far as Tännforsen (magnificent waterfalls, 85ft, 25m, drop). Tourist station at Sandvika, on Norwegian side of frontier.

Railway and road E75 bears south-west to *Ann*△, where lake of same name lies at 1,700ft (518m) and continues for 8 miles (12km) to *Enafors* for the approach to one of finest mountain regions in Scandinavia, comparable to Norwegian *Jotunheimen*, well equipped with tourist huts, tourist hotels and marked footpaths. Northern group is called *Snasahögarna* (highest peak *Storsnasen*, 4,799ft, 1,463m, one day's ascent); farther south are *Sylarna, Helagsfjället* and other groups.

Railway continues from *Enafors*, climbing to highest rail point in Sweden (1,970ft, 600m) and passes *Storlien*△, popular winter sports centre, to cross Norwegian frontier.

R9 The Far North — Lapland and the 'King's Way'

This is one of the most fascinating but inaccessible parts of Sweden. Formerly inhabited only by Lapps, now a popular tourist area for Swedes but distance puts it beyond reach of most other tourists. It is a region of vast mountain masses, solitary lakes, with sparse vegetation surprisingly beautiful in the season of summer flowers. Best months for touring are late May, August and early September.

Best approach point is *Jokkmokk*, or *Porjus*, reached either by train from *Östersund* in 14 hours, or from *Stockholm* by rail to *Boden* in 17 hours, thence by bus in 4 hours. Travellers coming via Norway can approach by rail from Narvik to *Abisko* in about 2 hours, taking this route in reverse direction.

Jokkmokk △, just north of Arctic Circle, is important Lapp church and market centre, with a Lapp high school for adult education.

From *Jokkmokk* via *Tjåmotis* in about $1^1/_2$ hours to *Kvikkjokk* — magnificent approach up beautiful Lake *Saggat*, ringed with mountains rising to 4,000ft (1,200m).

Kvikkjokk △, oldest tourist resort in *Lapland*, lies on the **Kungsleden**, a through footpath of about 220 miles (350km) from *Jäkkvik* to *Abisko*, waymarked by STF and provided with tourist huts, tourist stations or farmhouse accommodation at day's walking distances. Numerous lake crossings are necessary, and boat booking should be made by telephoning from previous tourist hut. Routes between mountain stations refer to actual days of travel and one day in every three must be set aside for resting or bad weather.

From *Kvikkjokk*, 52 miles (84km), 5 days' walking through forest, across watershed and moorland to *Saltoluokta* △, finely situated on Lake *Langas*. Boat and bus to *Vakkotavare*, then on foot for 32 miles (51km) in 3 to 4 days, skirting eastern edge of *Stora Sjöfallets National Park*, to *Kebnekaise* △, for *Kebnekaise* mountain group (highest peak 6,966ft 2,123m, highest mountain in Sweden); popular mountaineering centre. Final section of journey, *Kebnekaise* to *Abisko*, 54 miles (87km) 4 days' walking largely above level of vegetation; huts on route are locked, and keys must be taken from *Kebnekaise*.

Abisko △, at northern end of *Abisko National Park* (flowers and wildlife preserved in 11sq miles, 29sq km, area of upland valley), is very popular tourist centre on Lake *Torneträsk*; motor boats on lake; midnight sun visible 12 June to 4 July. Rail across frontier to Narvik in 2 hours.

SWITZERLAND

Geographical Outline

Land

Switzerland, a mountainous country set in the heart of Europe and totally cut off from the sea, occupies an area of about 16,000sq miles (41,000sq km), at least half of which is accounted for by the *Alps*. A further sixth is covered by the *Jura* mountains. The *Foreland* between the two ranges is a broad region of low hills and lakes and is the most important economically.

The *Swiss Alps* are the highest and grandest portion of the alpine chain. From the neighbourhood of the *St Gotthard* pass two main ranges extend to the west, the *Bernese Alps* (sometimes loosely described as the *Bernese Oberland*, which correctly describes only their northern slopes) and the *Pennine Alps*, highest peak *Monte Rosa*, 15,217ft (4,638m). A further two ranges extend to the east, the *Glarus* and the *Grisons Alps*, whose main peaks are somewhat lower.

The *Jura* range stretches along the Swiss-French frontier for some 200 miles (320km), rising abruptly from the central plateau. Its highest ridges, about 6,000ft (1,800m), are to the west of *Lake Geneva*.

Climate

The range of climate for such a small country is immense, being influenced by height, the western rain-bearing winds and the shelter of the mountains. The *Valais* and the *Engadine* are amongst the driest regions, while the *Lugano* region enjoys a mild winter and abundant sunshine. The *Föhn*, a warm south wind from Italy, influences the central mountain area, while the *Bise*, a bitter north wind from Central Europe often blows across the *Foreland* in winter. The permanent snowline occurs at about 10,000ft (3,000m).

Plants and Animals

Mixed forests occur up to about 4,500ft (1,370m), followed by coniferous forests

450

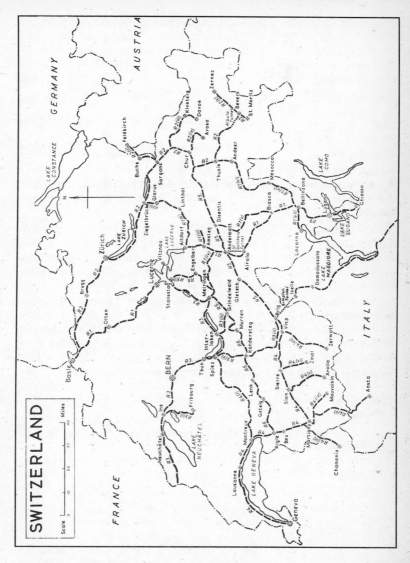

and meadows (the true 'alps' used for summer grazing) up to about 7,000ft (2,130m). Juniper and rhododendron then give place to the alpine flora, including gentians, saxifrages and edelweiss, and to bare rock before the snowline is reached. On south-facing slopes cereals can be grown as high as 6,000ft (1,800m). The warm trench of the *Valais* is famous for its wines, apricots and peaches, and around the lakes of *Canton Ticino* the vegetation has Mediterranean features.

Among the wild animals are the alpine partridge, mountain hare, chamois and marmot, whose shrill whistle is often heard near the snowline. Laws exist for protecting wildlife and there are many preserved areas and parks.

The People

Population

Most of the 6 million people live in the *Foreland* — chief cities *Zürich* (410,000), *Basel* (212,000), *Geneva* (175,000), *Bern* (150,000). The foot of the *Jura* and the shores of the larger lakes are closely settled, but the alpine districts are sparsely inhabited.

Language

German is the language of over 70 per cent of the people; when writing (or speaking to foreigners) there is little to distinguish their German from that of Bavaria, but in conversation amongst themselves, they use a dialect ('*Schwyzerdütsch*'), virtually a separate language, varying considerably from canton to canton.

French is the language west of a line drawn from *Delle*, on the French border, to the *Matterhorn*, and is spoken by about 20 per cent of the population. Italian is spoken in the southernmost canton, *Ticino*. In the *Engadine* and *Upper Rhine Valley* they speak *Romansch*, an ancient language of Roman origin.

Religion

More than 60 per cent of the population are Protestant. Others are Roman Catholic, mostly in *Fribourg, Lucerne, Ticino* and *Valais*; the church is subject to federal control.

History

From the four language groups, history has forged a Swiss nation united and independent, proud of its traditional liberty and democracy.

On 1 August 1291, the leaders of *Uri, Schwyz* and *Unterwalden* met together in the *Rütli* Meadow, taking a solemn oath of Perpetual Alliance. 'One for All and All for One'; they demanded, and obtained, certain concessions from their Habsburg overlords, eventually becoming independent. This event is regarded as the foundation of the Swiss Confederation and is commemorated on the National Day each year. Other cantons gradually joined the Alliance and some areas, such as *Ticino*, were added by conquest. Swiss pikemen on many occasions repelled larger armies, forcing other countries to recognise the nation's internal unity. But the nature of the Confederation, each canton retaining self-government, prevented Switzerland from becoming a European power, and the country was further divided by the Reformation led by Zwingli in *Zürich* (1521-31) and Calvin in the then independent republic of *Geneva*. Napoleon and his allies overran Switzerland but in 1815 the country was freed and assumed its present form. Since 1815, the Swiss have maintained a strict neutrality in all wars, and this has contributed to their prosperity and high standard of living.

Government

The Confederation consists of twenty-three cantons, each with its own government and administration. The Federal Government is responsible for defence, foreign affairs and the transport and postal systems. The canton constitutions are similar to each other and to the Federal constitution, except that in the three small cantons of *Glarus, Appenzell* and *Unterwalden* the ancient custom of the *Landsgemeinde* is still in existence; inhabitants meet together once a year in an open-air 'parliament' to discuss policy and administration for the ensuing year, and to elect their Council.

Resources

The tourist trade based upon the unrivalled scenic beauties of the Alps is important, but the machine and chemical industries are principal sources of wealth; agriculture is significant too. Small-scale farming is carried out with meticulous care, and every square foot of cultivable land is put to good use. Cattle are kept in all regions and the higher altitudes are grazed whenever the season permits, while hay is harvested from mountain slopes from late spring until late summer.

The mountain grazing period is from June to October. The flocks and herds are taken up the mountain as soon as the receding snow permits, allowing only a few days for the preparation of the summer huts. The life is arduous, and in many cases only the men accompany the animals; they descend gradually as the high grasslands, or 'alps' (from which the mountains derive their name) are grazed. The milk during this period is made into cheese.

But the *Foreland* is the most important region both for agriculture and industry. The latter is not confined to the towns but is dispersed widely to take advantage of the abundant hydro-electric power. This has enabled Switzerland to become a highly industrialized country, despite the necessity of importing most of its raw materials. The main enterprises are precision engineering, watch and clock making and textile manufacture. Banking and insurance also add considerably to the wealth of the country. Vines are grown on the warm slopes overlooking the western lakes and the dairy industry is renowned for cheeses and chocolate.

Customs

The people are of great integrity and extremely industrious; their hard work and business sense have created a prosperous state out of a small mountainous country. They are also very thrifty; almost everybody is privately insured against sickness or accident, and there is no national health service, although there is an unemployment, disability and old-age pension scheme. The Swiss cherish their old traditions and national costumes and processions. Most of the festivals take place in the mountain regions in the spring, and are concerned with the departure of the snow and preparation for the summer on the alps.

The *Basel* carnival, on the first Monday in Lent, is an occasion for processions of grotesque figures, masked dances and abandoned jollity. At *Zürich*, about the middle of April, a procession takes place wherein an effigy of winter is burned to the accompaniment of the church bells. In *Lugano*, in the vine district, a vintage procession with dancing and singing is held on the last Sunday of September and, in *Neuchâtel*, the first weekend of October. Lesser vintage festivals are held in the regions of *Locarno, Lake Geneva* and the lower *Valais*. The most interesting religious festival is that of Corpus Christi in the *Lötschental*, see **R3(ii)**.

1 August (National Day) is celebrated in the country districts with processions in local costume, dancing, fireworks and bonfires lit on the surrounding heights. In the large towns more sophisticated amusements are added and processions usually include carnival floats.

Food

Breakfast is continental, with excellent coffee, rolls and butter. The main meal is at midday when practically everything closes down for two hours; a light supper is taken in the evening, often a meat or fish dish; but cheese, eggs or sausages are popular.

Various cantons and regions have their own culinary specialities. In the alpine regions there is 'hard food' such as cheese, dried meat, fruitbread, etc, while in the lakeside regions there are various fish specialities. From the farmhouses of the plateau comes the *Berner platte* — smoked sausage, bacon, ham, sometimes boiled beef, pickled cabbage and potatoes or green beans; but the national dish of German-speaking districts is *rösti*—potatoes boiled, diced, fried and then baked. French-speaking districts favour the *fondue* — pieces of bread dipped into a communal pot of melted cheese; and in the south Italian dishes such as *risotto*, *spaghetti* and *minestra* are found.

Culture

Architecture

Gothic and Renaissance architecture are to be found in the main towns, particularly in *Bern*, which has retained its charming old-world character. In *Zürich*, *Geneva* and other places a remarkable harmony has been achieved between old and new.

Perhaps the most typically Swiss popular art is to be seen in the domestic buildings of the countryside. In the *Emmental* district the large timber-built farmhouses are particularly fine, with their wide-spread roofs, balconies and verandas. The traditional chalet is chiefly found in the *Oberland*. The chalet of the *Valais* is more roughly built, usually quite black, and the houses are crowded together on the hillsides, separated only by narrow cobbled lanes or alleyways. In the south-east, the houses are solidly constructed of stone, while in the Italian-speaking regions they resemble those of north Italy, with shallow-pitched roofs and tiled floors.

Painting

Konrad Witz (early fifteenth century) has a place among European painters as perhaps the first to include realistic representations of landscapes in his pictures. Hodler (1853-1918) treated landscapes in a forcefully simple yet naturalistic style. The strange art of Klee (1879-1940) owes nothing to either of these compatriots but stems from his theory that each work should grow according to its own laws.

Local Costumes

There is a great variety of local costume worn mostly for festivals and processions, but likely to be seen on Sundays in the *Valais, Appenzell* and in villages off the beaten track in central Switzerland.

Literature

The attraction of its lakes and, later, its mountains; its political liberty, and convenience as a refuge for exiles, have led writers from many countries to visit or settle in Switzerland; they include Voltaire, Mme de Staël, Rousseau, Gibbon, Byron, Shelley and Samuel Butler. But its native contributions to civilization have been distinctive in several fields.

Pestalozzi (1746-1827) by his writings and practice was the founder of modern ideas of primary education. Gottfried Keller (1819-90) was famous as a lyric poet. Burckhardt (1818-97) is well-known for his history of Renaissance art. Karl Barth (1886-1966) was one of the leading contemporary Protestant theologians.

Science

H.B. de Saussure (1740-99), inspirer of the first ascent (1786) of Mont Blanc, was the chief pioneer in the study of alpine botany, geology, meteorology and mineralogy. The professors Auguste Piccard (1884-1962) and his twin brother J.F. Piccard (1884-1963) pioneered the exploration of the upper atmosphere by daring balloon flights. Auguste also began investigation of the ocean depths by descents in a steel sphere, and this work has been continued by his son Jacques (born 1922). Jung (1875-1961) ranks second only to Freud in the study of the processes of the pysche.

Touring Information

General

For generations past, Switzerland has been the holidaymaker's paradise. The scenery is superb, the hotel industry is highly developed, communications are good, and everything is clean, punctual and well ordered.

There are so many foreign tourists in the main holiday regions, however, that real contact with the local people becomes difficult. In these regions, even on the mountain peaks, there are signposts, restaurants, and other attributes of civilization, restricting opportunity for adventure or solitude. The answer, as in many other countries, is to avoid the main holiday centres and make for the lesser known areas, such as the upper *Rhône* valley and the *Jura*.

Touring Areas

The most popular mountain areas are the *Bernese Oberland*, approached via *Interlaken*, the *Engadine (St Moritz)* and the Alps of southern *Valais (Zermatt)*. Lower-lying but no less popular are *Lucerne* and the sunny vine-clad valleys of the *Ticino*. Less well-known areas are the *Jura* mountains, approached via *Basel* or *Geneva*, and the *Grisons* south of *Chur*, both well provided with youth hostels.

Seasons

The winter sports season starts before Christmas in the alpine regions, slackens off in January owing to short days and intense cold, and reaches its climax in mid-February when hours of sunshine are longer and weather conditions more stable. Spring, the season of alpine flowers, comes to the mountain areas in late May. Mid-July to mid-August is the most popular holiday time in the Alps. Accommodation is easier to find in June, early July and September, all suitable months for walkers and cyclists. The season in southern *Ticino* is Easter to June, or autumn; in July and August it is likely to be uncomfortably hot.

Access

Through trains from French channel ports, Boulogne and Calais; quickest connection leaves London mid-afternoon in summer; arriving Basel early next day. Via Dieppe and Paris is a little cheaper, but this route involves a longer journey and an inconvenient change of stations in Paris. You can purchase through tickets from London entitling you to enter Switzerland at one frontier station (eg *Basel*) and leave at another (eg *Delle* — see **R3**) on the homeward journey, with options of travelling via Paris.

Transport

A network of excellent roads and railways climbs or penetrates the mountains in breathtaking feats of engineering. Among the principal passes are the *Simplon, St Gotthard, Great St Bernard, Susten* and *Furka*; open to traffic from mid-June to end of October, although the *Simplon* is open all year (with chains). Railway tunnels under the *Simplon* and *Lötschberg* carry cars in a shuttle service, and toll roads go under the *Great St Bernard* and *St Gotthard* passes.

Almost all Swiss railways are electrified, and three-quarters of the mileage is state owned. Light railways ascend many of the peaks, such as that of the *Jungfrau*, which climbs nearly to the summit 11,342ft (3,456m). These and the narrow-gauge railways are usually privately owned and tariffs are often higher than on the Federal system.

On the Federal Railways, ther are progressive reductions for journeys of more than 100 kilometres and reductions for return tickets. Railway tickets can be used for corresponding steamer journeys on many of the lakes.

Swiss Card entitles the holder to free travel from any airport or border railway station to destinations in Switzerland, and back. It is also an entitlement to buy tickets for rail, boat or bus at half-price and at a reduced rate on mountain railways and for reductions on the cost of Regional Holiday Season Tickets.

Swiss Pass covers travel by rail (main line and private) post buses and lake steamers, plus trams and buses in twenty-four Swiss towns. In addition it offers 25 per cent discount on excursions on mountain railways and cable systems. Available for four days, eight days, fifteen days or one month.

Regional Holiday Season Tickets cost varying amounts (reduced by 20 per cent for holders of the Swiss Card) according to the size of the eight regions for which they are available. Most are valid fifteen days, on any five of which holders travel free over a large part of the region; on other days half fare is allowed on any number of journeys.

The Postal Services provide excellent motor coach facilities at about the same price as rail travel, and run trips over all the high passes in summer. Tickets for these journeys may be bought from the post office where the bus is boarded, well in advance if possible, though a few hours is often sufficient. Bus services rarely duplicate rail routes but start from terminal points of railways to reach otherwise inaccessible areas.

Money

The Swiss *franc* is divided into 100 *centimes* or *rappen*. There are coins for 5, 10, 20 and 50 *cts*, 1, 2 and 5 *franc* and notes for 10, 20, 50, 100, 500 and 1,000 *francs*.

There are no currency restrictions and at exchange offices (*Bureaux de Change* or *Geldwechsel*) you can buy and sell most foreign currency. Banks are open all day but close two hours for lunch; not open on Saturdays.

Clothing

For mountain regions take ordinary summer clothing with warm garments for evenings when the temperature often drops rapidly, a waterproof coat whatever the season, and boots for walking on mountain paths.

Restaurants and Meals

Restaurants are good but expensive, although *à la carte* dishes are generous and there is a choice of inexpensive local wines. Set meals at temperance restaurants (*Gemein-destube/Restaurants sans alcool*) can be appreciably cheaper.

Public Holidays

Federal holidays when banks, shops and offices are closed are 1 January, Good Friday, Ascension Day, 25 and 26 December, Easter Monday, Whit Monday, 1 August. The first four have Sunday transport services. Many of the cantons observe additional public holidays, notably Corpus Christi and 15 August in Catholic cantons.

Maps

The Swiss produce some of the finest maps in the world; all the country is mapped on the Landeskarte der Schweiz series on a scale of 1:50,000, ideal for walkers. There are also series at 1:100,000 and 1:25,000. For motorists and cyclists the Michelin series of four maps, on a scale of 1:200,000, is the most satisfactory.

Accommodation

There are about ninety youth hostels, some in the cities and well-known resorts and many in the countryside, often situated at lofty altitudes. Although visitors under 25 years enjoy priority, Swiss youth hostels are no longer restricted to 'youth' in its narrow sense; they are now open to those of more mature years.

Alpine Huts

The Swiss Alpine Club (*Schweizer Alpen Club/Club Alpin Suisse*) maintains many climbers' huts. Membership entitles one to reduced hut charges and priority at busy seasons. Membership is open to men and women, minimum age 18 years; annual subscription can be paid through the Association of British Members of the Swiss Alpine Club, c/o Swiss National Tourist Office, 1 New Coventry Street, London W1.

Camping

All the best sites are listed by the Fédération Suisse des Clubs de Camping, Lucerne, in a booklet complete with map, available from Swiss National Tourist Office, 1 New Coventry Street, London W1.

Motoring

Motorists should carry their registration certificate, insurance certificate (preferably International Green Card) driving licence, reflective warning triangle and country-of-origin sticker. International highway code applies; traffic coming from right has priority, so too do trams in cities and post-buses on mountain roads. Motorways, often impressively engineered, are free of tolls; speed limits of 130km/h (81mph). Other roads are limited to speeds of 100km/h (62mph) and, in towns, to 60km/h (37mph). On-the-spot fines can be imposed for speeding.

Cycling

In spite of the hilly nature of the country, cycling is popular and there are cycle shops in towns, in most large villages on the plateau and in main valleys. Main road surfaces are good and there are some cycle tracks. After a severe winter metalled surfaces on such passes as the *St Bernard* and *St Gotthard* are badly damaged by frost and snow. The best combination of scenery and not too strenuous riding is around the central lakes. Avoid the hot dusty trench of the *Rhône*, unless you intend to make steep ascents into the lateral valleys. Bicycles can be hired at many railway stations and handed in at any other station.

Touring Routes

R1 Basel to Chiasso via Lucerne and St Gotthard Pass (200 miles, 322km)
This is the main north-south route, both for railway and road, giving access to *Lucerne*, the Italian-speaking canton of *Ticino* and the lakes of northern Italy. Fast trains from *Basel* to *Lucerne*, 60 miles (96km) in 70 minutes; to *Lugano*, 185 miles (296km) in about 4 hours.

 Basel△, second largest city; near frontier with France and Germany, *Rhine*

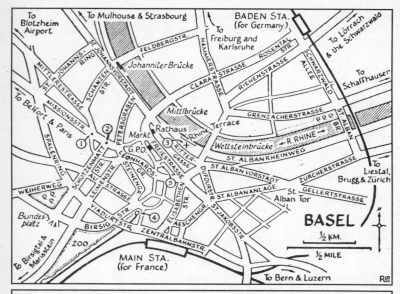

1 Spalentor. 2 Spalenbrunnen. 3 Minster. 4 Birsigtal Railway Station.
5 Barfüsser Platz.

port, international rail junction, commercial and industrial centre. Founded by the Romans; was one of the most important cities of Europe in the fifteenth century; university dates from 1460; joined Confederation in 1501. Red sandstone *Minster* on hill in old town, founded eleventh century, rebuilt in Gothic style after an earthquake; behind *Minster* is *Rhine terrace*, for view; *Marktplatz*, with six-teenth-century *Rathaus; Spalentor*, fourteenth-century gate; *Spalenbrunnen*, fountain with peasants dancing to bagpipes; eighteenth-century houses, espe-cially in *Rittergasse*; paintings by Holbein in *Fine Arts Museum*.

EXCURSIONS: (a) by steamer from the *Schifflände* (summer only, not every day) in 1¹/₂ hours to walled town of *Rheinfelden*. (b) by valley of *Birs* for 25 miles (40km) to *Delémont*Δ, approach to *Jura* mountains by fast train in 30 minutes. (c) by Birsig Valley Light Railway to *Flüh*, thence 1 mile (1¹/₂km) to *Mariastein*, picturesque church; another 1 mile (1¹/₂km) to *Rotberg*Δ overlooking French frontier.

From *Basel* road and rail pass through agricultural countryside, famed for cherry orchards, into hills of *Jura* and down to *Olten* on River *Aare*, small industrial town with old buildings, covered wooden bridge. Across fertile plateau to *Sursee*, old walled town, late Gothic town hall and baroque church. Along Lake *Sempacher*, *Rigi* and *Pilatus* come into view.

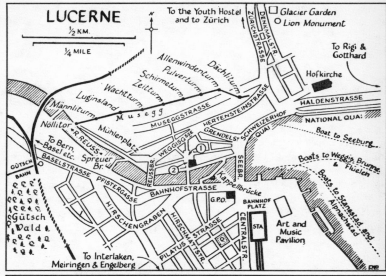

1 Kornmarkt. 2 Old Town Hall.

Lucerne△, on River *Reuss* where it quits lake, popular tourist resort; *Kappell-Brücke*, roofed wooden bridge crossing *Reuss* diagonally (1333), 112 paintings (sixteenth century) in roof depicting deeds of local heroes; *Spreuer-Brücke*, smaller covered bridge; thirteenth-century ramparts with nine towers (*Musegg Türme*); see *Glacier Garden* and nearby *Lion Monument*, to memory of Swiss Guards who died defending Louis XVI and Marie-Antoinette; old quarter round *Kormmarkt*, with sixteenth-century town hall; *Hofkirche*, sixteenth-seventeenth century cathedral. Town crowded every year for International Musical Festival, mid-August.

EXCURSION: **Pilatus**, long ridge south-west, to several peaks with impressive rocky outline: highest is *Tomlishorn*, 6,995ft (2,132m). Tradition that final resting place of Pilate's body was in small tarn on mountain and storm clouds are caused by his unquiet spirit. (*Pilatus* has highest rainfall in the country.) Lucerne municipal bus from station to *Hergiswil*, thence on foot via *Brunni* hotel, on marked track, 4½ hours; magnificent view. *Pilatus* may also be reached by steamer to *Alpnachstad* (1½ hours) then by world's steepest rack railway (3 miles, 5km, 30 minutes); alternatively by trolley bus to *Kreins* then by two cable railways, via *Fräkmuntegg*, in total 39 minutes, but note that the *Pilatus* mountain railways are expensive.

R1 (i) Lucerne to Engelberg (25 miles, 40km). Train in 1 hour, passes through farming country to *Stans*. Five hours' climb or mountain railway to *Stanserhorn*,

6,270ft (1,911m); fine view over several arms of Lake *Lucerne*; up valley of River *Aare*, narrow and steep at first, then widening to **Engelberg**Δ (3,300ft, 1,005m), summer and winter resort surrounded by mountains (snow-covered *Titlis*, 10,625ft, 3,238m). Famous Benedictine abbey, founded 1120, ruled whole valley until end of eighteenth century.

EXCURSION: (among many others) via *Trübsee* to *Jochpass* (7,267ft, 2,214m), 4¹/₂ hours on foot or by funicular to *Gerschnialp*, thence cable railway to *Trübsee* and chairlift to *Jochpass*; total journey 30 minutes. *Jochpass* provides good walker's approach to *Bernese Oberland* via *Meiringen* (see **R6**).

Lake Lucerne, cradle of the Swiss Confederation and scene of the exploits of William Tell. The area is influenced by the warm *Föhn* which shortens winter and gives mild summer climate; when blowing strongly it causes fierce storms on lake. Swiss Guard in Rome is mainly recruited here. Scenery becomes wilder eastwards; much of south shore consists of steep cliffs.

On 3 hours' trip from *Lucerne* to *Flüelen* the steamer calls first at *Weggis, Vitznau* and *Gersau*Δ; pleasant resorts on north shore, with sheltered southerly apsect.

EXCURSION: from each of above resorts, footpaths 2-3¹/₂ hours to ridge of **Rigi**, famous mountain with several peaks — highest, *Rigi-Kulm*, 5,742ft (1,750m). Also rack railway (steam operated on Sundays) from *Vitznau* to *Rigi-Kulm* in 35 minutes. Magnificent view from summit, extending 100 miles (160km). Excellent walks among alpine meadows and forest, eg *Rigi-Kaltbad-Scheidegg-Gäettrli* Pass-*Gersau*, 4 hours.

South of *Vitznau* two rocky points, the *Nasen*, jut out to reduce width of lake to barely half a mile (800m). Lake again narrows at *Brunnen*, small town at mouth of fertile *Muota* valley, where *St Gotthard* railway line rejoins road and lake.

EXCURSION: tram from *Brunnen* landing stage in 20 minutes to *Schwyz*, chief town of canton which gave name to Switzerland; interesting old churches and houses; strikingly modern Federal Archives building containing original document of Alliance of 1291. *Hoch-Ybrig*Δ is nearby.

South of *Brunnen* arm of lake is called *Urnersee*; steep banks, strange rock formations and waterfalls. Steamer crosses lake to the *Rütli,* a steeply sloping meadow famous in Swiss history, 15 minutes' walk from landing stage. Close to landing stage is natural rock monument, 80ft (25m) high called *Schillerstein* or *Mythenstein* with inscription dedicated to Schiller, German author of play of *Wilhelm Tell.*

Finely engineered road from *Brunnen* to *Flüelen*, with good views. Below road is rocky *Tellsplatte* ledge, where Tell leapt from boat in which Gessler was carrying him to prison; Tell's chapel with frescoes of events in his life.

At *Flüelen* rejoin *St Gotthard* railway for 2 miles (3km) journey to *Altdorf*, typical little central Swiss town, capital of canton of *Uri*, traditional scene of Tell's shooting apple from his son's head.

R1 (ii) Altdorf to Linthal via the Klausen Pass, 30 miles (48km) post bus in 3 hours. One of finest pass roads in country, reaching 6,400ft (1,950m), with impressive views of *Clariden* and *Tödi* mountains, passing *Bürglen*, supposed place of Tell's birth and death; old chapel with pictures of Tell story. Route can be pleasantly covered on foot, following old pass road which deviates from motor road. *Linthal*, railhead in canton *Glarus* (see **R2 [i]**).

St Gotthard railway and road ascend *Reuss* valley to *Amsteg*.

R1 (iii) Amsteg to Maderan Valley. Bus to *Bristen*, 3 miles (5km). Wild and beautiful valley, fine pine woods and many waterfalls. Road to *Bristen* thence mule tracks to SAC hotel, 4,377ft (1,334m), only habitation near head of valley, continue to *Hüfi* Hut at edge of glacier. Return via *Stäfel Alp* high level path and *Golzern Alp*, small village and pretty lake, bathing. Several SAC huts, climbs and glacier passes for the experienced.

Road crosses *Reuss* at *Pffaffensprung* waterfall; railway enters spiral tunnel, passes *Wassen*, doubles on its tracks and passes village twice more.

R1(iv) Wassen to Meiringen by the Susten Pass, 33 miles (53km) (post bus in 2¹/₄ hours), superbly engineered road with tunnels and viaducts. Up wild valley of *Meienreuss* into barren glacier country; through a tunnel, over 6,000ft (1,800m) above sea level, under *Susten Pass*, from Canton *Uri* into Canton *Bern*; on left is the *Steingletscher* (Stone Glacier), magnificent panorama; meals at *Steingletscher* hotel. Descent by the *Gadmen* valley into meadows and orchards, to *Meiringen* and *Bernese Oberland*.

At *Göschenen*Δ railway enters **St Gotthard Tunnel**, 9 miles (14km) long, 15 minutes transit, opened 1882. *Göschenen* cemetery has monument to Louis Favre, its builder, and the 277 workmen who were killed in its construction.

From *Göschenen*Δ road climbs *Schöllenen* gorge, between high rocky walls, over River *Reuss*, near splendid 100ft (30m) cascade; memorial to Russian troops who forced pass in 1799. Rack railway from *Göschenen* to *Andermatt*; left-hand side for best views.

Andermatt 4,760ft (1,451m) small fortified resort among hills, cooler than *Lucerne*; at junction of *St Gotthard, Furka* and *Oberalp* passes (see **R5**).

Road turns south-westwards to *Hospental*Δ, then south more steeply into wild scenery. *Lucendro* Lakes, lying a mile westwards of *Rodont* bridge merit diversion; top of pass at 6,395ft (2,114m).

This is the northern boundary of the Italian-speaking canton of **Ticino**, wrested from *Milan* between 1402 and 1512 and made an independent canton 300 years later; a land of sharp contrasts. Bleak precipices and rocky slopes rise from oak and chestnut forests, from valleys where maize, tobacco and vines are grown, and rivers, almost all swift-flowing streams, often with gorges. Summer here has long hours of brilliant sunshine, but rain, though of short duration, can be torrential. In the north are the usual alpine plants, pines and larches; near the lakes grow almonds, peaches, cypresses and palm trees; wild cyclamen can be found in autumn. *Ticino* is the principal wine-producing area; vines are draped on granite posts or wooden frames, often used to form a cool arbour in front of houses. Villages are picturesquely sited, often with a campanile rising above clustered roofs. The best time to visit the south is Easter to end of June, or in October when the chestnut trees are in their autumn colouring.

St Gotthard pass road descends by many zigzags, crosses River *Ticino* into rocky *Val Tremola*; short cuts by bridlepath. *Airolo*, first small town of Italian appearance, where railway emerges from tunnel, centre for exploring granite *Gotthard* massif.

EXCURSIONS: (a) west to *Val Bedretto* (upper valley of River *Ticino*) for mountain walking and climbing. On foot *Airolo* to *Bedretto* village in 2 hours, or by post bus in 35 minutes. Above *Bedretto* is *Pizzo Rotondo*, highest peak of *St Gotthard* group (10,500ft, 3,200m). On foot via *Madrano* and *Altanca* to Lake *Ritom* and *Piora* Valley.

Enter *Val Leventina* and descend through picturesque gorges and two spiral tunnels near *Dazio Grande* ravine. *Faido*, small resort, sixteenth-century wooden houses. Route bordered by steep cliffs, many waterfalls, *Biaschine* ravine with two more spiral tunnels; *Giornico*, in pretty position, surrounded by chestnut trees, vineyards, at foot of mountains rising 6,000ft (1,800m) above valley; fine twelfth-century Lombard-Gothic church. Valley widens towards *Biasca*, junction with *Val Blenio*.

R1 (v) Biasca to Disentis via Lukmanier Pass, 38 miles (61km). Beautiful *Blenio* valley (River *Brenno*), rising at northern end of *Lukmanier* Pass, 6,295ft (1,917m), giving access to Romansch-speaking upper Rhine valley (see **R5**) by steep descent with eleven tunnels. Light railway *Biasca* to *Acquarossa*, thence post bus in $2^3/_4$ hours to *Disentis/Mustér*.

Continue down valley, now level and here called *Riviera*, to **Bellinzona**, capital of *Ticino*, important strategic town; three castles built by Duke of Milan, taken by Swiss in 1508; view from *Castello Corbaro*: several old churches, old houses.

R1 (vi) Bellinzona to Thusis via San Bernardino Pass, 68 miles (109km). Light railway to *Mesocco*, then post bus; total journey $3^1/_2$ hours. Following *Valle Mesolcina*, enter canton of *Grisons*, still Italian-speaking; *Mesocco*, small resort, twelfth-century church; landscape becomes more alpine, *San Bernardino* (5,300ft, 1,614m), good centre for easy mountain excursions in beautiful surroundings; **San Bernardino Pass** (6,700ft, 2,041m), with little *Lago Moësola*, fine views; descend to valley of *Hinterrhein*, centre for climbs in *Rheinwald* group, view of *Zapport* Glacier. Continue through forests, gorges and meadows to *Andeer*, then through the *Via Mala* (Evil Road), a wild gorge with walls of 2,000ft (600m) to *Thusis*△ (see R2).

R1 (vii) Bellinzona to Locarno and Lake Maggiore, 12 miles (19km); rail in 30 minutes. Across broad plain of *Magadino* to **Locarno** on River *Maggia* and *Lake Maggiore*; old streets, interesting churches, bathing, lakeside walks; lake steamers — regular service to *Brissago*, special excursions to *Stresa* in *Italy*.

EXCURSIONS: (a) *Madonna del Sasso*, monastery and pilgrimage church, good viewpoint. On foot in 30 minutes by the *Via Crusis*, or by funicular railway in 6 minutes. (b) northwards into *Val Maggia*, broad valley between precipices, waterfalls; 17 miles (27km) to *Bignasco*, good centre for walks, junction of two valleys. Light railway from *Locarno* in 55 minutes. (c) up the *Centovalli*, gentle valley with luxuriant vegetation; light railway over Italian frontier to Domodossola, whence connection to *Simplon* (see R4).

On to **Lugano**△, largest town in canton, resort between *Monte San Salvatore* and *Monte Bre* on shore of beautiful and irregularly shaped lake; mild southern climate. Old part of town has streets with wide arcades, cobbled roadways with stone tracks for the cartwheels; churches of *San Lorenzo* and *Santa Maria degli Angioli*; Civic Museum with old Ticinese furniture.

EXCURSIONS: (a) by funicular to *Monte San Salvatore* (3,000ft, 914m, 10 minutes) or to *Monte Bre* by bus from *Piazza Giardino* to *Cassarate*, then funicular; total time 40 minutes. Both have fine views, but often obscured by heat haze in summer. (b) by boat east to *Gandria*, picturesque but tourist-conscious fishing village (20-30 minutes) or south to *Morcote*, lovely position, thirteenth-century church (1 hour).

Continue south along lakeside and cross *Melide* causeway, foundations built on natural rock bar, thence on eastern side of lake to *Capolago*, for rack railway up *Monte Generoso* (5,580ft, 1,710m, in 1 hour) and magnificent views over *Alps*. On through hilly but fertile district to frontier at *Chiasso*.

R2 Basel — Zürich — St Moritz (217 miles, 349km)

A route that crosses the northern plateau from west to east, with prosperous, well-tilled farm land, tidy towns and villages to begin with, but gaining height in the eastern part of the route among lofty mountains.

Express trains from *Basel* to *Zürich* $1^1/_4$ hours, to *Chur* in $3^1/_2$ hours, to *St Moritz* in 6 hours.

Basel (see R1) road and rail follow the *Rhine* to *Rheinfelden*, ancient town, spa and famous for its beer. Route ascends fruit-growing area of *Frick* valley, descends to old town of *Brugg*△ on River *Aare*; on to *Baden*△, spa on River *Limmat*.

Zürich△, between wooded hills at foot of lake of same name; largest city in the country, commercial, industrial and university centre, fine modern buildings as well as old quarters. *Kunsthaus*, distinguished art gallery; wonderful collection

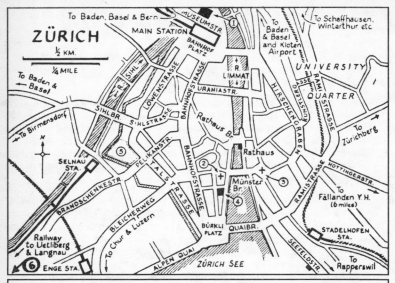

1 Landesmuseum (National Museum). 2 Fraumünster. 3 Grossmünster.
4 Post Office. 5 Botanic Garden. 6 Youth Hostel (Mutschellenstrasse).

— old masters to twentieth century. *Grossmünster,* Romanesque cathedral, founded by Charlemagne; became focus of Reformation under Zwingli; *Fraumünster*, severely Gothic, but has twentieth-century windows by Marc Chagall; old streets near River *Limmat*; *Landesmuseum* showing history and development of Switzerland (furniture and architecture, including complete rooms, local costumes); long lake promenade. Main shopping thoroughfare is *Bahnhofstrasse.*

EXCURSIONS: Pleasant walks with good views on *Zürichberg* (east) and *Uetliberg* (south-west); lake steamers; bathing and boating. *Fällanden*Δ on the *Greifensee*, 6 miles (10km) east of *Zürich.*

From *Zürich* follow Road No 4 through pleasantly wooded *Sihl* valley or by electric train from *Selnau* station to Uetliberg (2,863ft, 872m, 25 minutes) then excellent ridge walk via *Albis* peaks in 5 hours, to *Sihlbrugg*, rejoining Road No 4. From *Sihlbrugg*, choice of by-roads to *Einsiedeln*, small country town (2,900ft, 883m), important Catholic pilgrimage centre; Benedictine monastery founded 984, burnt down several times; splendid baroque church, containing shrine of miraculous 'tenth-century Black Virgin'; main pilgrimage 14 September.

From *Einsiedeln* return to lake and follow Road No 3 or main railway, across level tract of land reclaimed from River *Linth*, to *Ziegelbrücke*, junction for *Glarus*.

R2 (i) Ziegelbrücke to Glarus, 7 miles (11km). *Glarus*, at foot of *Glärnisch* mountain and in ravine of River *Linth*, is capital of canton of same name, cut off to south by high peaks and glaciers of *Tödi* (11,886ft, 3,623m) and *Clariden* groups. Little known to foreign tourists; many fine walks and climbs. Holds open-air 'parliament' on first Sunday in May. Chief resorts *Elm, Braunwald△*, and *Linthal*; Lake *Klöntal* surrounded by cliffs and forests. 400-year-old game sanctuary near *Kärpfstock* mountain, many chamois. For route to *Altdorf* on Lake *Lucerne*, via *Klausen* Pass, see **R1 (ii)**.

Weesen, small resort on *Walensee*, lying between chestnut woods and pasture terraces on south and steep cliffs of *Churfirsten* mountains on north. *Filzbach△* above southern shore. South-east to *Sargans*, junction for *Buchs* and Austria.

R2 (ii) Sargans to Feldkirch (Austria) via Liechtenstein. 21 miles (34km). Beyond *Buchs* rail and road cross *Rhine* and enter principality of **Liechtenstein**. This tiny independent state of about 60sq miles (150sq km) and 12,000 inhabitants is governed by a prince, with elected parliament of fifteen members. Army abolished in 1866. Customs, monetary and postal union with Switzerland, but issues its own stamps; Roman Catholic and German-speaking. Mainly mountainous, with fruit growing industry in valleys. Good walks in *Triesenberg* and *Samina* valley districts. Capital *Vaduz△*, can be reached by bus in 10 minutes, from railway station of *Schaan*; royal castle dates from tenth century, much restored.

From *Sargans* route follows *Rhine* southwards; *Bad Ragaz*, spa using water brought by conduit from *Pfäfers*. Scenery becomes more alpine, several ruined castles, shortly before *Landquart* enter the canton of the *Grisons*.

The largest and most sparsely settled canton, the **Grisons** is named after the grey clothing worn at a meeting in 1424 at which the 'grey league' was established to secure the independence of the region which stayed outside the Confederation until 1803. Much barren rock or ice; many valleys above 5,000ft (1,500m). Was Roman province of *Rhaetia*, a name still in use today, and on medieval trade route. *Romansch*, derived from Latin, is spoken by inhabitants of *Rhine* and *Inn* valleys; German is official language, but Italian is spoken in the southern valleys. *Rhaetian* railway, narrow gauge, affords most spectacular means of travel.

R2 (iii) Landquart to Davos. 43 miles (69km) by the *Rhaetian* railway, through picturesque *Prätigau* valley, several small villages, gorges, ruined castles; *Klosters△* resort, walking, skiing, climbing. Railway mounts through forests, then descends to **Davos**, fashionable ski and mountain resort in wide valley at about 5,000ft (1,500m); exceptionally sunny, particularly in winter, many sanatoria. Several mountain railways, including *Parsenn* funicular to *Weissfluhjoch* ($2\frac{1}{2}$ miles, 4km) where Swiss Federal Institute for Snow and Avalanche Research is situated. Continue by cable railway to summit of *Weissfluh* (9,344ft, 2,850m); fine ski-runs. *Wolfgang△*, north of *Davos*.

On to **Chur**Δ, capital of canton and terminus of *Federal, Rhaetian* and *Oberalp* railways; narrow streets, eleventh/twelfth-century cathedral, bishop's palace; cable car up to Brambrüesch sun terrace.

R2 (iv) Chur to Arosa, 22 miles (35km). Impressively constructed railway line with many tunnels and bridges, including *Langwies* viaduct; meadows, forests and forges. *Arosa*Δ, at 6,000ft (1,800m) is a summer and winter resort. Many walks and climbs. Chair-lifts to *Hörnli* (8,190ft, 2,496m, 15 minutes) and aerial cableway to *Weisshorn*).

EXCURSION: On foot via *Urdenfürkli* pass in 6 hours to *Lenzerheide-Valbella*Δ; attractive mountain valley.

At *Reichenau*, the *Vorderrhein* and *Hinterrhein* unite to form the *Rhine*, and route turns south through *Domleschg* valley; gentle slopes dotted with castles, villages and churches. *Thusis*Δ at junction of three valleys (2,370ft, 722m), small resort. *Hohen-Rhätien* castle for viewpoint; *Avers*Δ is nearby at 6,975ft, 2,126m. *Ehrenfels* castle at *Sils im Domleschg*Δ; see **R1(vi)** for *San Bernardino* route to *Bellinzona*.

Railway penetrates narrow *Schyn* gorges, road goes through *Pass Mall*. Near village of *Solis*, invisible at 1,000ft (300m) above route, road crosses River *Albula* by bridge 250ft (75m) high, railway bridge at 290ft (87m). *Tiefencastel*, on post bus route to *Chur* via *Lenzerheide* (see **R2 [iv]**) and to *St Moritz* via impressive *Julier Pass*. Valley widens, wooded country, distant lofty peaks in view. *Filisur* (3,500ft, 1,066m), village with typical local houses, impressive view of viaduct; line follows walls of narrow rocky valley, rising 1,000ft (300m) in $5^1/_2$ miles (9km), many tunnels and loops. *Bergün/Bravuogn* (4,475ft, 1,364m), pretty village, in sheltered position, twelfth-century church. A further $7^1/_2$ miles (12km) of track with impressive tunnels, loops and bridges achieves $3^1/_2$ miles ($5^1/_2$km) of distance and rise of 1,360ft (414m) before entering *Albula* tunnel, reaching *Inn* valley at *Bever*. The road over the pass (7,595ft, 2,315m) reaches valley at *La Punt* farther north.

The **Engadine**, or *Inn* valley, *En* in *Romansch*; extends from *Maloja* in west to *Tirol* frontier in east. Protected from west winds, the rainfall is low; high altitude, strong sunshine, cold nights; long winter, excellent skiing. Treeline at 7,000ft (2,100m), is about 1,000ft (300m) higher than in rest of country. Larches are common; alpine flowers best seen in June. Sturdily built stone houses, white-washed, often with scroll-like decorations; small square windows frequently have decorative wrought-iron grilles. Upper *Engadine* valley is at the same altitude as the *Rigi* summit.

R2 (v) Bever to Zernez (for Swiss National Park), 21 miles (34km). Rail and road down valley of *Inn, Zuoz*, has some fine old houses, small resort; 5 miles (8km) below *Zuoz* road crosses *Punt Ota* (high bridge) boundary between Upper and Lower *Engadine*; valley descends to *Zernez*, best approach to **Swiss National Park**, nature reserve since 1909, 50sq miles (130sq km) with about 100 peaks rising to 10,000ft

(3,000m), some most impressive scenery. Several cabins provide overnight accommodation and simple fare. Only the marked paths may be used and no plants or animals harmed. Fine show of flowers particularly in June, many chamois, ibex, golden eagles, marmots, foxes and other alpine animals and birds. But this is in no sense a zoo; the animals are completely wild, so do not expect to see them all; field-glasses are useful.

On to *Samedan*, chief village of *Upper Engadine* and to **St Moritz**Δ (5,990ft, 1,826m), spa, fashionable winter and summer resort, in beautiful position on small lake. Many walks, climbs and tours. Bus services in summer to Milan, Lugano, Landbeck/Tirol, Munich, Bolzano and Garmisch-Partenkirchen.

EXCURSION: cable railway in two stages to *Corviglia*, then chairlift to *Piz Nair* (10,040ft, 3,060m), total journey time 21 minutes.

R3 French Frontier — Bern — Lucerne (158 miles, 254km)

An attractive route, crossing the *Jura* mountains and the *Bernese Oberland*. Express trains from Paris to *Bern* cross Swiss frontier at *Delle* (via Belfort) or at Les Verrières (via Dijon). This route is from Les Verrières, by rail or road through *Jura* mountains by wooded *Val de Travers*, emerging at *Neuchâtel*.

NeuchâtelΔ, on lake of same name, capital of French-speaking Protestant district; educational centre, with university; abbey church and castle, fine patrician houses; museum in Hotel Peyron.

EXCURSIONS: (a) ridge walk of *Chasseral*. Tram to *La Coudre*, then funicular to *Chaumont* (3,870ft, 1,179m) or on foot from *Neuchâtel* in 1½ hours. From *Chaumont* fine ridge walk in 4 hours to *Chasseral* (5,300ft, 1,165m) view to Alps in clear weather. (b) by rail in 25 minutes. Righteen miles (29km) to *Bienne*Δ (*Biel*), bilingual town on lake of same name; centre of watchmaking industry; visits to watch factories can be arranged. (c) by steamer, on certain days only, by canal through to *Lake Morat*. *Morat* is scene of victory of Swiss over Charles the Bold in 1476, an unspoilt medieval town, with walls, gates, arcaded shops.

Ten miles (16km) beyond *Neuchâtel* is *Ins*, road and railway junction for *Fribourg*.

R3 (i) Ins to FribourgΔ, 26 miles (42km), rail in 1 hour, capital of canton, on River *Sarine* (German: *Saarne*) which forms language boundary from here southwards. Old City on rocky hill in bend of river, many attractive old houses, fourteenth/fifteenth-century cathedral with famous organ. Catholic educational centre, university. Local costumes may be seen at Wednesday and Saturday markets. Corpus Christi procession worth seeing.

Route enters German-speaking Switzerland, crosses central plateau to *Bern*. **Bern**Δ, in wooded, hilly country, with view of distant *Alps*, chief city of wide ranging canton. Joined Confederation in 1353 and quickly became the most powerful unit. Seat of Federal Government and administration. Headquarters of

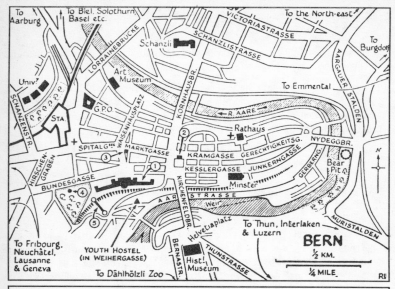

1 Bundeshaus (Federal Parliament). 2 Zeitglockenturm. 3 Käfigturm.
4 Universal Postal Union Monument. 5 Funicular.

Universal Postal Union. See the *Minster*, fifteenth/sixteenth century; *Bundeshaus*; Historical Museum; *Zeitglockenturm*, originally city gate, clock with puppets, performance starts 8 minutes before each hour, best at midday; *Käfigturm* (Prison Tower); baroque *Erlacher Hof* in *Junkerngasse*. Best views from *Bundeshaus* terrace, *Minster* terrace and *Schänzli*. Bear pit near *Nydegg* bridge; bears have been kept since 1513 and figure in arms of city. Many attractive old streets with arcades and fountains, espeically *Kramgasse*. Swimming pool near zoo.

> EXCURSION: by road or rail to *Langnau*△, 23 miles (37km). Centre of **Emmental**, sub-alpine region with characteristic fine wooden farmhouses, most cheese sold as Gruyère is made here.

South-east to *Thun* on lake of same name, with twelfth/fifteen-century castle and arcaded streets; gateway to the **Bernese Oberland**, sharply towering mountains, glaciers, waterfalls and alpine meadows, on the northern slopes of the *Bernese Alps; Finsteraarhorn* (14,026ft, 4,275m) is highest peak. Subalpine districts are characterised by neat villages, wooden chalets with wide eaves, verandas and window-boxes. Highly-developed tourist industry, resorts and youth hostels; crowded in summer and in winter sports season.

Steamer to *Interlaken* takes two hours and calls at *Oberhofen* on north shore,

Spiez, attractive town among orchards with medieval castle, junction for railway to *Montreux* (**R4 [i]**); and *Faulensee*△ on south shore.

R3 (ii) Spiez to Brigue by the Lötschberg Railway 63 miles (100km) 1$^1/_2$ hours by fast train. Yet another example of magnificent railway engineering (opened in 1913). *Reichenbach*, for beautiful little *Kiental*; mountain excursions. From *Kandergrund* (2,825ft, 861m) line mounts rapidly with loops and spiral tunnels, fine scenery, to **Kandersteg** (3,875ft, 1,181m) mountain and ski resort. *Blümlisalphorn, Balmhorn, Doldenhorn*, all about 12,000ft (3,600m).

EXCURSIONS: (a) on foot in 1$^1/_4$ hours or by chair-lift in 9 minutes to beautiful mountain-girt *Oeschinensee*, at foot of *Blümlisalphorn*. Nature reserve on south side; fine display of 'alpenrosen' — a kind of rhododendron. (b) on foot over the *Gemmi* pass (7,620ft, 2,302m) to *Leuk* in *Valais* (**R4**), 6 hours. Fine zigzag mountain path safe throughout; or by aerial cableway from *Kandersteg* to *Stock*, thence over *Gemmi* pass to *Leuk* (4 hours).

Railway runs through tunnel for 9 miles (14km) to *Goppenstein* in *Lötschental*. The valley has preserved its unspoiled nature, completely isolated until construction of railway. Characteristic old houses, black barns, small richly decorated churches. Road only part of way, then mule track; main peak is lovely pyramid of *Bietschhorn* (nearly 13,000ft, 4,000m), very difficult climb. At *Kippel*, impressive procession at Corpus Christi (2nd Thursday after Whitsun) and following Sunday; church dignitaries in colourful vestments, local costumes, the 'Grenadiers of God' in seventeenth-century uniform. Railway descends, with splendid views of *Rhône* valley, to *Brigue* (see **R4**).

Interlaken△ is a popular and expensive resort, very warm in summer, between Lakes *Thun* and *Brienz*, view of *Jungfrau*.

EXCURSIONS (amongst many others): by rail to *Wilderswil* then rack railway in 1 hour to *Schynige Platte*, 6,500ft (1,980m), one of finest views on Oberland; alpine garden. Easy path to summit of *Faulhorn* (8,803ft, 2,682m) in 4 hours. Descent from *Faulhorn* may be made via *First* (2 hours) and chair-lift to *Grindelwald*, whence train may be taken back to *Interlaken*. (b) by bus from *Interlaken* (West) station to *Beatushöhlen* (caves) on north side of Lake *Thun* 4 miles (6km); stalactite formations, admission charge.

R3 (iii) Interlaken to Grindelwald and Lauterbrunnen. This route visits the most famous mountain resorts of the *Bernese Oberland*, and can easily be done by railway (rack-and-pinion in steeper parts) either in sections or as a complete circuit, as described here.

From *Interlaken* (Ost) station, rail and road pass *Zweilütschinen* and enter valley of *Schwarze Lütschine*, beyond *Burglauenen* valley widens; 12 miles (19km) to **Grindelwald**△, a popular resort at 3,420ft (1,042m).

EXCURSIONS: (a) on foot via the *Kleine Scheidegg* (6,770ft, 2,064m) in 6-8 hours to *Lauterbrunnen*. (b) on foot to the *Grindelwald* glaciers; should not be missed; easy footpaths. (c) ascent of *Faulhorn* (8,803ft, 2,682m) by moderately easy marked track in 5$^1/_2$ hours, or by chair-lift to *First* in four sections (total 30 minutes) then on foot in 2 hours. (d) by *Grosse Scheidegg* (6,434ft, 1,961m) to *Meiringen* (see **R6**).

From *Grindelwald* the *Wengernalp* rack railway (accompanied by footpath but no road) climbs over to the **Kleine Scheidegg pass** (6,770ft, 2,064m), 5^1/$_2$ miles (9km) in 36 minutes.

EXCURSION: *Kleine Scheidegg* is starting point of famous **Jungfrau Railway**, highest in Europe and a spectacular feat of engineering. It climbs 4,500ft (1,370m) in less than 6 miles (10km) mostly by rack system. Railway runs first along crest of *Scheidegg*. *Eigergletscher* station (7,620ft, 2,322m) with views of *Eiger, Mönch* and *Jungfrau* glaciers. Rest of track ascends in remarkable tunnel cut through the *Rotstock* and the *Mönch* but viewpoints are arranged at stations (hewn out of rock) of *Eigerwand* (9,405ft, 2,866m) for magnificent view over mountains, glaciers and plains to Vosges and Black Forest; Eismeer station (10,370ft, 3,161m), *Joch* station (11,340ft, 3,456m) where view is even more magnificent, walks on glacier, skiing throughout year. Hotel, skating rink, tourist house with dormitories. Tunnels lead to viewpoints, observatory and meteorological research institute.

From *Kleine Scheidegg* railway descends via *Wengen* (4,200ft, 1,280m), winter and summer resort, linked to outer world only by railway to *Lauterbrunnen*, a resort hemmed in by precipices and many waterfalls, of which best are *Staubbach, Trümmelbach* and upper *Schmadribach*; falls are fed by glaciers on *Jungfrau* and other mountains.

EXCURSION: on foot in 2^1/$_2$ hours or by narrow-gauge railway in two stages in 30 minutes to *Mürren*, fashionable winter-sports resort at 5,400ft (1,646m) with wonderful view of *Eiger* (the Ogre), *Mönch* (the Monk), *Jungfrau* (the Virgin) and other peaks. *Gimmelwald*△. *Schilthorn* (9,754ft, 2,973m) is a fairly easy climb on a marked track; descent also to *Kiental*.

From *Lauterbrunnen* to *Interlaken* (7^1/$_2$ miles, 12km), down valley to *Weisse Lütschine*.

On to *Brienz* by road, rail or steamer (rail tickets interchangeable for steamer). Scenery more mountainous than around *Thun* and *Brienzersee* much deeper. Steamer in 80 minutes. *Brienz*△, attractive large village, centre of wood-carving industry.

EXCURSION: by rack railway (steam operated) in 35 minutes, to the *Rothorn* (7,714ft, 2,315m), with very fine views. Good mountain path in 4 hours to *Brünig* pass on road to Lake *Lucerne*.

Proceed from *Brienz* to *Brünig* pass, but a detour via *Meiringen* is recommended. *Meiringen*△ is chief village of *Hasli* valley, small mountain centre at junction of seven valleys, including *Grimsel, Susten* (see **R1 [iv]**), *Brünig, Grosse Scheidegg* and *Jochpass* (see **R6**).

EXCURSIONS: *Meiringen* is starting point for fine 'Three-Pass Tour' by postal motor coach; *Grimsel, Furka* and *Susten* (the first two are 7,000ft, 2,100m). Round trip in 9 hours (including lunch break).

Route turns northwards by road or narrow-gauge rack railway rising steeply with many good views to *Brünig* Pass (3,396ft, 1,035m), then down between rocky walls and dense pine woods to several small resorts, including *Sachseln*, with shrine of Switzerland's most recent saint, Nicholas von der Flüe, fifteenth-century hermit; along *Sarnersee*, below *Pilatus* to *Lucerne* (see **R1**).

R4 Geneva to Brigue (128 miles, 206km)

This route traverses the French-speaking cantons of *Geneva, Vaud* and *Valais*, a sunny, fertile region with many fashionable resorts and access to numerous mountain valleys. From *Lausanne* onward the route is that of the London/Venice International Express.

Fast train from *Geneva* to *Brigue* in 3 hours, main Road No 1 to *Lausanne*, thence No 9.

Geneva△, on River *Rhine* and *Arve*, at south-west tip of lake of same name; banking and commercial city, intellectual centre of French-speaking Switzerland, with university, watch and jewellery manufacture. Was headquarters of Calvin and his followers in the sixteenth century. Headquarters of International Red Cross, World Health Organisation, International Labour Office, a section of

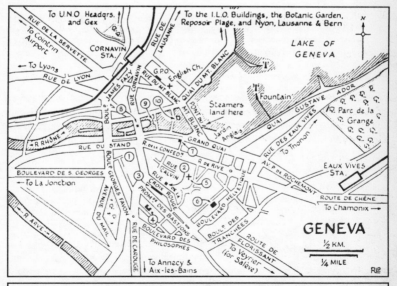

1 Grand Theatre. 2 Hôtel de Ville. 3 Reformation Monument. 4 University. 5 Cathédrale de Saint Pierre. 6 Museun of Art and Industry. 7 Tour Molard. 8 Tour de l'Ile. 9 Pont de la Machine. 10 Ile Rousseau.

the United Nations, and many religious and welfare organisations.

Renaissance *Hôtel de Ville* with ramp instead of steps. Imposing Reformation Monument in University Gardens, with statues of John Knox and Oliver Cromwell. *Tour de l'Ile* and *Tour Molard* gateways; hydro-electric works (*Forces Motrices*) and electricity station (*Pont de la Machine*) on River *Rhine*; Museum of Art and History. From *Quai du Mont Blanc, Mont Blanc*, 40 miles (64km) away, may be seen in clear weather. Fine promenades and parks; 400ft (122m) fountain at end of jetty. Best shopping street is *Rue de la Confédération*, continued under names of *Rue du Marché* and *Rue de la Croix d'Or* to south of lake. Walk along *Route de Lausanne* to *Reposoir*, pleasant bathing beach.

EXCURSIONS: Geneva is almost entirely surrounded by French territory, and for longer excursions a passport is necessary. (a) on foot to the *Jonction* (south-west corner of city), where blue *Rhône* meets grey *Arve*. (b) tram to *Veyrier* (20 minutes) and cross frontier to France, cable railway or rough footpath onto the *Salève*, limestone ridge of about 4,000ft (1,219m) with magnificent views of lake and *Alps*. (c) by lake steamer to Swiss or French resorts — eg to *Nyon* in $1^1/_4$ hours.

From *Geneva*, road and rail routes run north along lake, but much shore is priate property. *Coppet*, château of Mme de Staël; *Nyon*, old houses, sixteenth-century castle.

EXCURSION: by narrow-gauge railway to *St Cergue*Δ (3,400ft, 1,036m), small centre for *Jura* mountains. Chair-lift from *Archette* (15 minutes from *St Cergue*) to *La Barillete* (4,700ft, 1,432m); magnificent views across lake to *Alps*. From *St Cergue* ascent of *La Dôle* (5,540ft, 1,689m) on foot in $2^1/_2$ hours; descent may be made to Les Rousses Δ in France.

LausanneΔ, junction for *Bern*, also Paris via Vallorbe, in a steep situation on slopes of *Mont Jorat*, cleft by gorges formed by River *Flon* and *Louve*, above its port of *Ouchy*. University; seat of Supreme Federal Court of Justice, capital of canton of *Vaud*. Fine twelfth/thirteenth-century Gothic cathedral, approached by covered stairway; *St Maire* castle, fifteenth century, housing canton government offices; picturesque cobbled streets.

EXCURSIONS: (a) by road or rail (21 miles, 34km, rail in 40 minutes) to *Croy-Romainmôtier*, on line to Vallorbe. *Romainmôtier* is old town with one of the finest churches in Switzerland. (b) Steamer to Thonon (France) in 70 minutes for access to Savoy Alps.

Shores of lake grow steeper, many vineyards, attractive hill villages, views of Savoy mountains. *Vevey*, twelfth-century church, restored. The *Dents du Midi* are seen to south; lake now sheltered from the *Bise* for several miles. *Clarens, Montreux, Territet*Δ, fashionable resorts.

EXCURSIONS: By mountain railways to heights behind the towns such as *Les Pléiades, Rochers de Naye, Caux* and *Les Avants* (famous for wild narcissi late May to early June); all with splendid views across lake to *Alps*.

R4 (i) Montreux to Spiez (85 miles, 137km). Picturesque route by narrow gauge railway from *Montreux* to *Zweisimmen*Δ, then by standard gauge line to *Spiez*. Total journey 3 hours. Railway climbs from *Montreux*, many loops and fine views over lake, to *Les Avants* (3,200ft, 947m) and enters sub-alpine western (French speaking) extremity of *Bernese Oberland*. Railway keeps at or above 3,000ft (900m) level most of way, passing *Château-d'Oex* Δ (smart resort), *Saanen*Δ, where French language gives way to German, *Gstaad* (noted for winter sports); thence down *Simmental* valley to reach Lake *Thun* near *Spiez* (see **R3**). Journey *Montreux-Spiez-Interlaken* can also be made by Europabus service in 4 hours.

Chillon, fine twelfth/thirteenth-century fortress picturesquely situated. Long used as a state prison, and one Bonivard was subject of Byron's poem *Prisoner of Chillon*; Shelley, Dickens and others have cut their names on the walls of his cell.

At *Villeneuve* route leaves lake, and enters upper valley of *Rhône* between mountain groups of *Diablerets* to east and *Dents du Midi* to west. Beyond Bex enter canton *Valais*, the 90 miles (145km) trench of the upper *Rhône*. Inhabitants here work immensely hard to gain a living against many adversities — poor soil, extremes of climate, rock-falls, avalanches, flood and drought. Old traditions and customs are kept, local costumes worn on Sundays, church festivals and ceremonies such as blessing of fields and animals are devoutly observed. Some communities live near the *Rhône* during the winter and migrate in spring to the mountains, with schoolteacher and priest. Water is brought to the lower slopes by a centuries-old system of ditches and conduits, known as *bisses*. French, including several dialects, is spoken in the west, German in the east.

Northwards, foothills of the central mountains form sunny terraces with resorts and sanatoria; to south rise the *Pennine Alps*. These great snow-covered mountains lie at the head of long, wild valleys and also form high spurs which isolate the valleys from each other. Light railways, or postal motor coaches, connect with the main line, following a long straight course near the *Rhône*, through vineyards, orchards and maize fields.

St Maurice has oldest monastery in the *Alps*, founded fourth century, some work dating from tenth century; has one of richest ecclesiastical treasures in Christian world; open to view.

*Martigny*Δ, where valley turns north-east. Fine covered bridge over River *Dranse*.

R4 (ii) Martigny to Aosta (Italy) via the Great St Bernard Pass, 50 miles (80km). Coach in 3 hours. In winter the coaches use the *Great St Bernard Tunnel*, 4 miles (6km) long, for motor vehicles only (toll). *Orsières* is picturesque village at 3,000ft (900m). (*Champex*Δ is nearby). *Great St Bernard Pass* is at 8,111ft (2,472m) between *Grand Combin* 14,160ft (4,316m) and *Mont Blanc* ranges. Hospice founded in eleventh century, accommodates travellers in distress; monastery, chapel and library, post office; famous dogs trained to rescue travellers. Italian frontier. Finely-engineered road down *St Bernard* valley (largely French-speaking) to Aosta.

R4 (iii) Martigny to Chamonix, 23 miles (37km). Road and rail by impressive gorges of River *Trient* across frontier into France and skirting massif of *Mont Blanc*, with superb views. *Martigny* to *Le Châtelard* by rack railway in $1\frac{1}{2}$ hour or by postal bus in 1 hour. Railway continues to Vallorcine (France) whence connection by French National Railways to ChamonixΔ.

R4 (iv) Martigny to Mauvoisin (Val de Bagnes), 21 miles (34km). One of wildest of southern valleys; waterfalls, glaciers and snow-clad peaks; unusual alpine flora. Rail *Martigny* to *Le Chable* in 45 minutes. *Bruson*Δ is 2 miles (3km) south then bus via *Fionnay* (summer resort) to *Mauvoisin* (1 hour), centre for mountain and glacier tours.

Continuing up *Rhône* valley to *Sion*Δ, chief town of *Valais*, bishopric since sixth century, old quarters between *Tourbillon* hill, ruined castle, and *Valère* hill, fortress and thirteenth-century church. Cathedral, fifteenth century, tenth-century tower.

R4 (v) Sion to Arolla, 25 miles (40km). Motor bus into lovely *Hérens* valley via *Evolène* and *Les Haudères*, quiet summer resorts, then to *Arolla* (6,440ft, 1,963m) in 2 hours, small mountaineering centre amid larches and Arolla pines, surrounded by snowy peaks and glaciers.

Continue alongside *Rhône* past vineyards and orchards to small town of *Sierre*, interesting museums. *Sierre* is overlooked by tripartite health and winter sports resorts of *Montana-Vermala-Crans*; many sanatoria.

R4 (vi) Sierre to Zinal, 17 miles (27km) by *Val d'Anniviers*, perhaps most beautiful of tributary valleys of Upper *Rhône*. Bus $1\frac{1}{2}$ hours via *Vissoei* to *Zinal*, 5,505ft (1,678m), small mountain centre amid peaks and glaciers of *Dent Blanche, Gabelhorn* and *Weisshorn*.

Beyond *Sierre* German-speaking territory is entered. *Leuk*, interesting old town, fifteenth-century church, castle from which *Gemmi* Pass route leads to *Kandersteg* (see **R3 [ii]**). To north of road, *Lötschberg* railway to *Bern* may be seen climbing above *Rhône* valley. *Visp*Δ, village with medieval houses and old church.

R4 (vii) Visp to Zermatt, 22 miles (35km). Narrow-gauge railway in $1\frac{1}{4}$ hours. Road goes only as far as *St Nicklaus*. Railway climbs by gorges and tunnels to *Stalden*.

EXCURSION: 12 miles (19km) (bus in 70 minutes) up beautiful *Saas* valley to *Saas-Fee* (9,500ft, 2,895m), climbing and walking centre, surrounded by high peaks, notably *Mischable* group, easy ascent of *Mellig* (8,813ft, 2,686m) in 2 hours, or chairlift (to *Plattjen*) part of way.

Continue up *Nicolaital*, narrow picturesque valley, with restricted views, several small villages to **Zermatt**Δ (5,300ft, 1,615m), climbing, tourist and winter sports centre, overshadowed by *Matterhorn* (14,980ft, 4,565m). Alpine Museum, containing relics of accident to Whymper's party, first to ascend *Matterhorn* in 1865.

EXCURSIONS: (a) via *Riffelalp* and *Riffelsee* to rocky ridges of *Gornergrat* (10,290ft, 3,136m). Rack railway in 50 minutes. Magnificent views across glaciers to *Monte Rosa* group (15,200ft, 4,632m) and *Matterhorn*. Return by *Obere Kelle, Grünsee* (Green Tarn), warm enough for bathing, and foot of *Findelen* Glacier. (b) *Schwarzsee* and *Hörnli* Hut (9,494ft, 2,894m) at foot of *Matterhorn*; chairlift in two sections. (c) *Schönbiel* Hut, views of sheer north face of *Matterhorn* and *Dent d'Hérens*.

Road and rail continue to **Brigue**, junction for *Lötschberg* railway to *Bernese Oberland* (**R3[ii]**), *Furka-Oberalp* railway to *Andermatt* and *Chur* (**R5**). *Brigue* has seventeenth-century *Stockalper* castle, with gilded 'onion' domes, old houses, steep narrow streets.

EXCURSION: bus in 35 minutes to *Blatten*, 5 miles (8km), then on foot in 2 hours or by cable railway in 8 minutes to *Belalp*, 7,010ft (2,137m), for splendid view of *Aletsch* glacier, largest in Europe, stretching 16 miles (26km) from *Jungfraujoch* and edged by peaks exceeding 11,000ft (3,350m).

Brigue is at entrance to **Simplon Tunnel**, $12^1/_4$ miles (20km), longest in world, leading to Domodossola in Italy; road crosses the *Simplon* pass (6,590ft, 2,009m) with hospice kept by the St Bernard monks. *Brigue*-Domodossola bus in $3^1/_2$ hours.

R5 Brigue to Chur via Andermatt (138 miles, 222km)

Road and narrow-gauge railway. Fast train in about 5 hours. Also bus on central portion *Gletsch-Andermatt* (20 miles, 32km, $1^1/_2$ hours) with better views than train (via *Furka* pass, 7,992ft, 2,436m). An alternative route between western and eastern Switzerland; slower and more expensive than via *Zürich*, but with finer scenery; open early June to mid-October.

Road and rail ascend *Rhône* valley, flanked by mountain peaks; *Fiesch*Δ, small resort.

EXCURSIONS: (a) up remote *Binn* valley, noted for rare minerals and flowers. (b) *Eggishorn* (9,626ft, 2,934m), 4 hours' steep walk, magnificent prospect of *Aletsch* glacier and surrounding peaks.

Orchards and vineyards are left behind. Valley now known as *Goms*, alpine meadows and forests, many small villages suitable for walking centres, seldom visited by foreign tourists. At *Gletsch*, fine views of imposing 1,600ft (487m) ice-fall of *Rhône* glacier, hanging high above valley. Bus from *Gletsch* to *Andermatt* passes edge of glacier, and crosses desolate *Furka* pass. Rail descends lonely valley (road may be seen at higher level) to *Hospental*Δ at foot of *St Gotthard* road and *Andermatt* (see **R1**).

Beyond *Andermatt* route rises in loops and spirals, with views of *St Gotthard* mountains, to bare, stony *Oberalp* Pass (6,733ft, 2,052m) then descends into the *Grisons*. *Tschamut* (5,405ft, 1,648m), small climbing and walking centre, from which Lake *Toma*, source of River *Vorderrhein*, may be visited. *Sedrun*, climbing and skiing centre; *Disentis/Mustér*, junction of *Oberalp* and *Rhaetian* railways. small spa and market town, in broad green valley below 9,000ft (2,700m) peaks; Benedictine abbey, originally founded seventh century. Mountain excursions in the *Medel* group and along the *Lukmanier* Pass route.

The valley is now known as the *Bündner Oberland*; here, as in the *Engadine*, Romansch is spoken; many unspoilt villages in excellent walking country; *Ilanz*, with old houses, churches and gateways; *Miraniga*Δ, near *Meierhof*.

EXCURSIONS: (a) on foot to *Piz Mundaun* (6,780ft, 2,067m), by marked path, for fine view. (b) by road (7$^1/_2$ miles, 12km, bus in 40 minutes) to *Flims*, pleasant small resort with woods and lakes; thence chairlift, 2$^1/_2$ miles (4km) long (two sections) in 20 minutes to *Alp Naraus*, at 7,000ft (2,100m); thence aerial cableway to *Fil de Cassons*.

From *Ilanz* the line runs 10 miles (16km) through extraordinary limestone gorges to *Reichenau*, junction of *Vorderrhein* and *Hinterrhein*, and down *Rhine* to *Chur*Δ. (For *Thusis* and *Engadine*, see **R2**.)

R6 Lake Geneva to Lake Lucerne by Oberland Pass Route (14 days' walk)

A route for keen walkers experienced in fell or mountain walking; rough mountain paths and low temperatures on alpine passes make boots and adequate outdoor clothing essential. Passes marked (*) ought never to be attempted in unsettled weather.

By train or road from *Montreux*Δ along the eastern edge of the lake, then skirting the flood plain of the *Rhône* to *Aigle*, a little town in pleasant surroundings.

One hour railway journey up the *Ormonts* valley to *Les Aviolats*; thence on foot in a few minutes to *Vers l'Eglise*. From here an easy path follows the river for 2 miles (3km) up to *Les Diablerets*, winter sports resort almost surrounded by lofty mountains. Uphill road for 3 miles (5km) in 2 hours to *Col du Pillon* (5,086ft,1,550m) affording view of magnificent *Creus-de-Champ*, streaming with ice. Thence to *Gsteig*, a downhill walk of 5 miles (8km) between snowy peaks; alternatively, a bus goes from *Les Diablerets* to *Gsteig* in 45 minutes. A footpath of 4 miles (6km) goes across the *Krinnen* pass (5,446ft, 1,660m) to *Lauenen* (choice of easy ascents to surrounding peaks). From here the *Truttlisberg* pass (6,699ft, 2,042m) strikes eastwards for 8 miles (13km) (6 hours) to *Lenk*; mountaineering centre with sulphur springs. On to *Adelboden* via the *Hahnenmoos* pass (6,400ft, 1,950m), an easy walk in about 5 hours.

EXCURSION: *Engstligen Falls*, 1$^1/_2$ hours by footpath and on to the *Engstligenalp* (6,470ft, 1,972m) in a further hour.

From *Adelboden* to *Kandersteg* via the *Bonderschrinde* pass (7,830ft,

2,386m) is an 8 mile (13km) walk (6 hours). Take the chairlift from *Kandersteg* to *Oeschinen* (see **R3 [ii]**) and follow the path for 8 hours across the *Hohtürli pass to the hotel at *Griesalp*. Track and footpath up the valley on to the *Sefinenfurgge pass (8,583ft, 2,616m), a way between the topmost crags and affording view of *Jungfrau* to the east, *Blümlisalp* to the south-west; descend to *Gimmelwald*Δ (10 miles, 18km in 8 hours). Follow the high level path for 2 miles (3km) along the side of the *Lauterbrunnen* valley to *Mürren*, set on a mountain terrace.

EXCURSION: chairlift (longest in Europe) up to the *Schilthorn* (9,742ft, 2,969m).

From *Mürren* to *Grütsch Alp*, an easy walk in 1 hour, the track lies beside the railway but affords splendid views of the crests of the *Silberhorn, Jungfrau, Mönch* and *Eiger*. Descend by the rack railway to *Lauterbrunnen*, thence by footpath up the valley side eastward for $1^1/_2$ miles ($2^1/_2$km) to *Wengen*. Track for 3 miles (5km) up on to the *Wengern Alp* and sight of deep ravine of *Trummelbach*; on for $1^1/_2$ miles ($2^1/_2$km) to *Kleine Scheidegg* (6,772ft, 2,064m).

EXCURSION: walk for 45 minutes to snout of *Eiger* glacier (ice caves).

On for 6 miles (10km) on the *Kleine Scheidegg* pass to *Grindelwald*Δ (see **R3 [iii]**). By road and bridle path for 3 hours beneath the rock walls of the *Wetterhorn* to the *Grosse Scheidegg*, a col at 6,434ft (1,961m) in the shadow of the *Wetterhorn*. Path descends via *Schwarzwaldalp* to *Rosenlaui*, tiny summer resort, and on to *Meiringen*Δ by easy paths between meadows (4 hours from top of pass).

EXCURSIONS: *Reichenbach Waterfalls*; by tramway and funicular to *Upper Reichenbach Fall*. Here Sherlock Holmes made his seemingly final exit.

Road and path from *Meiringen* to *Innertkirchen*, via the *Aar* gorge (3 miles, 5km; small toll) thence easy track up the *Gental* valley to the *Engstlen Alp* (11 miles, 18km). From *Engstlen Alp* to *Jochpass* (7,267ft, 2,215m) is walk of $1^1/_2$ hours; varied scenery and near views of glaciers of Titlis. Descend in 3 hours via *Trübsee* and *Gerschnialp* to *Engelberg*Δ (see R1[i]).

From *Engelberg* the road ascends to the *Aar* valley, passing the *Tätschbach* waterfalls, then by track to the top of the *Surenen* pass (7,563ft, 2,305m) in $4^1/_2$ hours; fine retrospect of *Titlis*. Descend in 4 hours to *Altdorf* near end of southern arm of Lake *Lucerne* (see **R1**).

YUGOSLAVIA

Geographical Outline

Land

Yugoslavia lies south-easterly from the Alps, extends into south-east Europe and is as much Balkan as central European; bordered by Austria and Hungary to the north, Italy to the north-west, Albania and Greece to the south and Rumania and Bulgaria to the east.

Most of the country is mountainous; the *Julian Alps* lie to the north, the *Dinaric Alps* extend along the Dalmatian coast and include great areas of mountain country in the centre and south. Mountain limestone, dry and barren *karstland*, makes precipitous walls behind the narrow strip of the Adriatic coastline, more gentle to the north-east where the River *Sava* flows across the country through *Zagreb* and to *Belgrade* to join the *Danube*.

Narrow valleys lie parallel to the coast, making access difficult, but the River *Neretva* has cut through the western edge of the mountain mass and made a through route from the coast to the interior. The deeply indented Adriatic coastline has a shore-length of 1,300 miles (2,100km), with hundreds of islands lying between *Rijeka* and *Dubrovnik*, all rather barren with poor limestone soil, but the rocky Dalmatian coast is majestically beautiful and has many resorts, flourishing on tourism. This coastal area divides unequally into four regions; to the north is Istria, the peninsula between *Trieste* and *Rijeka* with a rocky indented coast and pebbly beaches. Then comes the Croatian coast between *Rijeka* and *Zadar*, where the barren mountain limestone makes steep rock faces, sheltering the coastal resorts from the *bora*, the harsh winter wind. From *Zadar* south-eastwards to *Cavtat* is the Dalmatian coast proper and, here again, the coastal strip is backed by the mountain limestone barrier; steep-sided inlets, bays and many islands make this the most beautiful sea-coast of Europe. To the south the Montenegrin littoral stretches to the Albanian frontier, nearly 100 miles (160km) of remote and mountainous coast with sandy beaches and the spectacular fjord of *Boka Kotorska*.

Yugoslavia comprises six republics and they are best described separately to give a better idea of the composition of the country.

Slovenia is closest to the West; almost entirely mountainous, bordered to the north by the *Julian* and *Karawanken Alps*, by Austria and Italy and, at various times, ruled by these two countries. *Ljubljana,* the capital, is on the international railway route. The people of Slovenia are Slavs, but they use the Latin alphabet and are European in outlook.

Croatia comprises almost all the coastal region of Yugoslavia, from Istria southwards to *Herceg-Novi*, beyond *Dubrovnik*, and inland to the Hungarian frontier. The *Plitvice Lakes National Park* lies equidistant between *Zagreb* and *Zadar*; the railway line of the *Venice/Athens* express runs through Croatia, so does the *Zagreb/Belgrade* motorway. Croatians use the Latin alphabet and, like the Slovenes, are Western in outlook, history and tradition.

Bosnia-Herzegovina, with its capital at *Sarajevo*, is mountainous too; forested mountains inland and barren limestone mountains along the coast cutting off access to the sea, except for the gap made by the River *Neretva*. Routes **R4(i)** and **R4** follow the main road from the north through *Jajce*, *Sarajevo* and *Mostar* to the sea. The people are Serbs and Croats, speaking Serbo-Croat and using the Latin alphabet.

Serbia is the largest of the Yugoslav republics, with *Belgrade* as its capital; it includes the autonomous regions of Vojvodina to the north and Kosmet to the south. Although land-locked and mountainous, often forested but with great tracts of mountain pasture, the relief of the country falls northwards to the plains of the River *Danube*. The Cyrillic alphabet is used, Serbo-Croat is spoken.

Montenegro is the smallest republic, its Slav name *Crna Gora* means Black Mountains. It lies at the southern end of Yugoslavia's coast; extremely mountainous country, adjoining Albania. Its remoteness has resisted the tourism of the Dalmatian coast, but its capital, *Titograd*, is connected by a wonderfully engineered railway to *Belgrade*. The people are Serbs and use the Cyrillic alphabet.

Macedonia, the most southerly and most remote of the republics is bordered by Albania, Bulgaria and Greece; mountainous and harshly dry in summer. A fast motorway from *Belgrade* to Athens via *Skopje* goes through Macedonia, together with the railway line of the *Venice/Athens* express. The people are very like the Serbs but their language and Cyrillic alphabet are a little different.

Climate

In Slovenia the climate is part Alpine, part central European; most favourable in summer until September. In the interior of the country — shut off from the sea by the mountains — wide variations in seasonal temperatures occur. In Bosnia and Serbia, most of Croatia, Montenegro and Macedonia it is very hot in summer; autumn is likely to be best for touring. The Montenegrin mountains have the

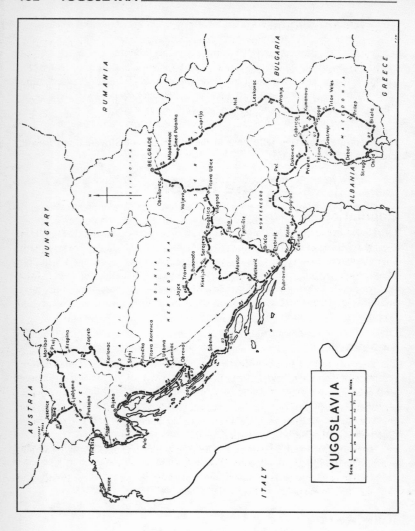

highest rainfall in Europe and remarkably severe winters. The Dalmatian coast enjoys the Mediterranean climate but mild winters can be spoiled by the icy wind off the mountains, the *bora*. Spring comes early on the Mediterranean coast, autumn is warm and sunny, even beyond October.

Plants and Animals

Large variations in climate and terrain are matched by a wide range of vegetation; from coniferous forests in the north and the inland mountain regions to sub-tropical plants — mimosa and bougainvillea and trees such as palms, figs, citrus fruits — on favoured sites on the islands and southern, sheltered parts of the coast.

Vines are grown in Dalmatia, tobacco in Macedonia. Much of the *karst* plateau is barren, but in the valleys and hollows in the limestone, where there is water, vines and other Mediterranean fruits flourish.

There are bears and wild boar in the mountains of Slovenia and Bosnia, chamois in the *Julian Alps*.

The People

Population

Official estimates, recently published, show a population of about 20 million. Nearly 8 million of this figure are in Serbia, another 8 million are almost equally shared between Bosnia and Croatia; almost 2 million live in Slovenia, $1^1/_2$ million in Macedonia and $^1/_2$ million in Montenegro. In addition to the five nationalities of Yugoslavia (Serbs, Croats, Slovenes, Macedonians and Montenegrins) there are minority groups of Turks, Rumanians, Albanians, Hungarians, Slovaks and Gypsies.

Language

The three official languages of Serbo-Croat, Slovenian and Macedonian closely resemble one another. Serbo-Croat, the first language of Yugoslavia, is written in the Latin alphabet in Croatia, but in Serbia and Montenegro the Cyrillic alphabet is used. The Latin alphabet is used for Slovenian and a form of Cyrillic for Macedonian, although both these are near enough to Serbo-Croat to be understood with a Serbo-Croat phrase book.

Most notices in tourist resorts are in the Latin alphabet and, even in Serbia and Macedonia, Cyrillic is supplemented by a Latin alphabet translation.

English is widely understood in towns and tourist resorts, so are French and German. Italian is spoken in Dalmatia.

Religion

Most Yugoslavs who practise a religion belong to the Orthodox faith, fewer are Roman Catholic; the remainder are Muslim. Roman Catholics predominate in Slovenia and Croatia, the Orthodox faith is followed in Serbia and Montenegro, while Bosnia and Macedonia are largely Muslim.

Church and state are quite separate; there is no religious teaching in schools and no public holidays at Christmas and Easter. Yugoslavia is, however, rich in religious monuments, as described in the touring routes that follow. Visitors to mosques should enquire whether non-Muslims can be admitted; shoes should be taken off before entering.

History

The name Yugoslavia means 'the country of the South Slavs'. The Slavs came here in the fifth century AD from what is now Poland and by the seventh century they predominated throughout the Balkan peninsula. Before this all the country south of the River *Danube* had been part of the Roman Empire and the inhabitants were Celts and Illyrians. The western part of this territory — what is now Slovenia, Croatia and Bosnia — was ruled from Rome, was Latin speaking and used the Latin alphabet; the eastern part — Serbia, Montenegro and Macedonia — was under the rule of Constantinople and the language was Greek. This division, marked by the east/west line of the *Danube* and *Sava* rivers and an imaginary north/south line through *Sarajevo* and *Dubrovnik*, was the fundamental boundary between Eastern and Western civilisations in Europe. Even before this there had been Greek settlements on the coast and traces of Stone Age settlements remain.

Slovenia originally belonged to the western Slavs (not the southern Slavs), or Slovenes. In the seventh and eighth centuries it was part of an independent principality named *Carantania* which included what is now southern Austria (Carinthia). In the ninth century *Carantania* became a German province and most of Slovenia remained German or Austrian for more than a thousand years, excepting a break early in the nineteenth century when Napoleon set up the Illyrian provinces, briefly uniting Slovenia with Croatia and Dalmatia.

Croatia, coming under Frankish rule, became independent under King Tomislav in the tenth century. Later Croatian kings extended their rule to the Dalmatian coastal towns which previously had been ruled by Constantinople, but in 1102 the Croatian Crown passed to the heir to the Hungarian throne and Croatia became part of the Hungarian kingdom. Istria, at various times under the authority of Franks, Germans and the Byzantine empire, came to be dominated by Venice.

Serbia became independent of the Byzantine empire in the twelfth century under Steven Nemanja, an enterprising ruler who resisted invasion by Hungarians and Bulgarians, gained the territory of Albania, Macedonia and northern parts of Greece, established the Serbian Church and promoted arts and commerce. In 1345 the Serbian King Duzan proclaimed himself Tsar of the Serbs and Greeks but his empire was short-lived and by the end of the century, marked by Serbian defeat at the historically significant battle of *Kosovo* on 28 June 1389, Serbia was entirely overrun by the Turks and remained under Muslim rule for nearly five hundred years.

Bosnia was under the authority of Hungary for much of its history; it gained independence in the thirteenth century under King Tvrtko who ruled Bosnia, Serbia, Croatia and Dalmatia but after his death the Hungarians again seized power, only to be overrun by the Turks in 1463. Bosnia embraced Islam with little difficulty, inasmuch as the Bosnian Church was out of favour and persecuted by the Orthodox Church; many Bosnian noblemen accepted Turkish rank, but one of them, Steven Vuksic, set up an independent dukedom in southern Bosnia and assumed the title of Herceg; this province called Hercegovina, is thus named after him.

Macedonia was, up to the end of the tenth century, under Byzantine or Bulgarian rule, and was then part of Serbia until, after a long period of Turkish dominance from 1371 to 1912, it joined again with Serbia.

Montenegro was in the ninth and tenth centuries the independent kingdom of Zeta but became part of the medieval Serbian empire. In the late fourteenth century the Turks assumed nominal rule but constant conflict ensued between the Montenegrins and the Turks and the country was never conquered. By the mid-nineteenth century Montenegro was recognised as an independent principality, becoming a kingdom in 1910, remaining so until World War I.

Most of the country had come under Turkish rule by the end of the nineteenth century; Dalmatia, apart from *Dubrovnik*, belonged to Venice for three hundred years up to the end of the eighteenth century when it passed to the Habsburgs, who already had Slovenia and Croatia.

Napoleon's armies took Dalmatia, Slovenia and Croatia in 1809 and set them up as a province named Illyria, with *Ljubljana* as capital; this, however, lasted only four years and then the Habsburgs resumed their authority.

By this time Serbia had gained a large measure of independence from its Turkish rulers and, with Montenegro, came to the assistance of Bosnia in bringing about a successful insurrection against the Turks in the 1870s. The Congress of Berlin in 1878, however, declared that Bosnia should be administered by the Habsburgs who, in 1908, arbitrarily seized complete power. Bosnia opposed such Austrian authority; nationalism flourished, encouraged by Serbia and the fact that the Turks had been driven out in the Balkan Wars of 1912-13.

On 28 June 1914, the anniversary of the Serbian defeat at *Kosovo*, the Austrian Archduke Franz Ferdinand was assassinated in *Sarajevo* by a young Bosnian nationalist; the spark that touched off the holocaust of World War I.

King Peter, a Serbian, became sovereign of the kingdom of Serbs, Croats and Slovenes, set up soon after the end of World War I; his son Alexander succeeded him in 1921 and, in 1929, the kingdom changed its name to Yugoslavia, but Istria and the ports of *Rijeka* and *Zadar* remained Italian. Alexander was assassinated in Marseille in 1934, his young son Peter succeeded him under a Regency but, early in 1941, Yugoslavia was invaded by Germany and King Peter and the Government escaped to London.

Slav resistance to Nazi occupation was established in guerrilla armies of partisans and nationalists; one of their leaders was Josip Broz, a Croat who became known as Marshal Tito. He was backed by the Allies, fought the Germans throughout the occupation and, by the end of World War II, his communist partisans had command of all the country. As early as November 1943 Tito had declared Yugoslavia to be a Federal Socialist Republic and, in the elections of 1945 he secured a great majority to confirm his leadership; thus he remained until his death in 1980 when a collective precidency was established.

Government

Yugoslavia is a Federal Socialist Republic of six countries — Serbia, Croatia, Slovenia, Bosnia-Herzegovina, Macedonia and Montenegro — each enjoying a large measure of internal self-government. The autonomous provinces of Vojvodina and Kosmet are associated with Serbia. The central government in *Belgrade* deals with foreign affairs and defence, but each republic administers its own affairs within the authority of the Federal constitution.

Resources

Yugoslavia's economy is based almost equally upon agriculture and industry. Maize, rye, potatoes, sugar beet, plums and apples are main crops; some are exported, together with tobacco and wines. Copper, lead, zinc and bauxite are exported; manufactured exports include textiles, footwear, ships, vehicles and machines of almost every description. Tourism is significant in the economy of the country, the government promotes and subsidises the industry and each republic has its own tourist offices.

Food and Drink

A variety of regional dishes and different ways of cooking make for interest. Meat dishes are highly flavoured, usually grilled. *Cevapcici*, small grilled fingers of minced meat and served with raw chopped onions, are popular. So too is *raznjici*, made of cubes of pork grilled on a skewers, similar to a kebab. *Cevapcici* and *raznjici* can make a cheap meal, for they can often be bought to take away. Pastry dishes named *burek*, with meat, cheese or vegetable fillings are often cheap; yoghurt, called *kisolo mljeko*, is served with them. Pancakes are almost a national dish; they are usually served with very sweet fillings. Turkish coffee is the national beverage, served thick and strong in very small cups. Mineral waters are excellent and in great variety. Wine is cheap, mostly light; *Riesling* and *Sylvaner* are everywhere popular. Plum brandy named *Slivovica* is Yugoslavia's best known drink, it comes in a range of quality, always strong and potent.

Sport

Sailing, fishing and hunting are popular sports. Sheltered waters along the coast afford excellent sailing and boats may be hired by the day in the seaside resorts. Sea fishing is free and there is no close season; fresh-water fishermen enjoy a splendid choice of fish but fishing permits must be obtained. Football is most popular throughout the country and Yugoslav teams match those of other countries in international events. Winter sports facilities are best in Slovenia but many mountain resorts in Bosnia and Croatia are also equipped to international standards.

Culture

Art and Architecture

A few relics of Stone and Iron Ages remain and traces of Greek occupation can be seen in Macedonia and on the Adriatic coast.

Roman architecture is evident, some as early as the third century BC, although most of it belongs to the first and second centuries AD contemporary with the empire-building campaigns of Tiberius and Trajan; the amphitheatre at *Pula* and Diocletian's palace at *Split* are leading examples. *Byzantium* retained remnants of Roman power against the Slav invasions of the fifth century and the basilica at *Porec* with its magnificent mosaics belongs to this era.

The ninth-century Slav churches of St Donat at *Zadar*, St Barbara at *Trogir* and St Cross at *Nin* all show Roman and Byzantine influence. St Sophia at *Ohrid*, an eleventh-century church, is a perfect example of Byzantine architecture.

Architecture in medieval times is shown at its best in the monastic buildings of Serbia and Macedonia, a composite style of Roman and Byzantine with stone and brick external decoration and Byzantine frescoes adorning vault and wall. Serbian mural painting flourished in the fourteenth century but declined with the coming of the Renaissance and the Turkish invasion.

Romanesque art and architecture flourished on the Adriatic coast in many churches and in the cathedrals at *Rab* and *Trogir*. *Zadar* became artistically important for its gold and silver work — now treasured in churches there. Enigmatically ornamented stone tombs belonging to the Bogomils, a heretical religious sect, made their appearance at this time; many thousand such memorials, decorated with geometric symbols or figures of soldiers, dancers or huntsmen, remain scattered, or grouped in remote cemeteries in Bosnia, Dalmatia and Montenegro.

Gothic architecture is restricted to Slovenia and Croatia where Gothic churches are everywhere evident, many of them decorated with endearingly naive frescoes. The cathedral at *Sibenik* is a beautiful example of Gothic architecture overtaken by the Renaissance.

Minarets everywhere give point to Turkish influence in architecture from the fifteenth century onwards; the mosques at *Sarajevo, Banja Luka* and *Tetova* are particularly fine, the bridges at *Mostar* and *Visegrad* stand as elegant examples of Turkish architectural skill.

Renaissance architecture, often Venetian, is evident along the Adriatic coast. *Dubrovnik* is particularly rich in styles of architecture; Gothic, Renaissance, Roman and Venetian baroque churches, palaces and monasteries all contained within the city walls.

Sculpture by Ivan Mestrovic (1883-1962) is best known. His work, in unmistakably heroic style, is seen at the *Mount Avala* war memorial near *Belgrade* and in churches throughout the country. Paintings by Paja Jovanovic (1859-1957), popular in Western Europe at the turn of the century, are on show in the National Museum in *Belgrade*.

Literature

Yugoslav literature in poem and ballad form, epic tales of Slav defiance of Turks, translated and published by Vuk Karadzic in the mid-nineteenth century, remain popular. Ivo Andric, a Bosnian (1892-1975), won the Nobel prize for literature in 1961. His famous novel *The Bridge on the Drina*, the story of life in *Visegrad* from the sixteenth century up to World War I, has been translated into English.

Folklore

Traditional dress is to be seen on special occasions and on market days in the country. Eastern modes of dress are worn in those parts of the country which have been subject to Byzantine and Turkish influence; the fez is evident.

Folk dancing and singing are everywhere popular. The Serbian national dance, the *kolo*, is the most common — danced in a group, hands linked — often accompanied by wind instruments.

Costume and dance are part of the way of life; many old wedding customs of dancing and feasting remain and festivals of folk dancing and singing are popular throughout the country.

Touring Information

Access

From London by rail (a) Tauern Express (afternoon departure), daily through service throughout the year to *Jesenice* (frontier), 26 hours; *Ljubljana*, 27 hours; *Zagreb*, 30 hours; *Split*, 40 hours. (b) Rijeka Express (morning departure) summer only, daily through service via *Ljubljana* to *Rijeka*, 30 hours. (c) Direct-Orient and Simplon Expresses, through service to *Ljubljana* (33 hours), *Zagreb*

(36 hours) and *Belgrade* (41 hours). By air; APEX return, must be booked 1 month in advance, valid 3 months.

Transport

The main railway route through Yugoslavia passes inland via *Zagreb, Vrpolje* (junction for *Sarajevo* and *Dubrovnik*), *Belgrade*, *Nis* and *Skopje*. There is no railway along the coast, and connections to *Dubrovnik* from the interior are slow.

Transport to many of the more remote places is provided by local buses, and there are special direct summer services between main centres and holiday resorts. Tickets are bought before boarding buses; they can usually be had a day in advance from the bus station or local tourist office.

The Adriatic coast can be pleasantly seen by using steamers of the *Jadranska Line*, linking *Rijeka, Split, Dubrovnik* and places between. Local services call at several small ports, including many on islands, whereas the more expensive express steamers, some of them making extended voyages between Venice or Trieste and Piraeus, make fewer calls.

Accommodation

There are about forty youth hostels; a few are tented and only open in the summer, but most others are open throughout the year. Many are situated on the coast, some others in less frequented places in the interior and there are large hostels in *Belgrade, Dubrovnik, Sarajevo, Skopje* and *Zagreb*.

Mountain huts of varying standards of amenities are maintained by Alpine Clubs in all the country's high mountains, notably those of Slovenia, Croatia and Bosnia. They are normally open to all so far as space allows. Prices, seasonal closing periods and other particulars should be checked with the local tourist office before setting out on a mountain tour.

Private houses will often put up tourists quite cheaply. In tourist resorts letting is arranged through the local tourist office, to whom also payment is made. Rooms are classified according to facilities. To book a room in advance write to the *Turisticki biro*, at the place where you wish to stay.

Visitors arriving in Yugoslavia without having booked accommodation are recommended to enquire at the local tourist office.

Camping

There are many tourist camping grounds throughout the country, where those bringing their own tents may make use of the facilities at small expense. Camping is also possible in certain open spaces on obtaining permission from the municipal or forest authority concerned. No special document is required. An annual survey of camping sites can be obtained from the Yugoslav National Tourist Office.

Information Services

Yugoslav National Tourist Office, 143 Regent Street, London W1R 8AE, supply general information about the country, and lists of addresses of the local tourist associations.

Public Holidays

National holidays are 1 and 2 January, 1 and 2 May, 4 July, 29 and 30 November. Republic holidays are 7 July in Serbia, 13 July in Montenegro, 22 July in Slovenia, 27 July in Bosnia and Croatia, 2 August and 11 October in Macedonia.

Clothing

The climate on the coast is generally similar to that of Italy, and light clothing is required. In the mountains it can be very cold, especially early and late in the day; be equipped with warm clothing and when exploring isolated areas, a down sleeping bag.

Maps

Large scale maps of Yugoslavia are not generally available, except these of the *Julian Alps* and *Kamnik Alps* in Freytag & Berndt's 1:100,000 series. Other maps are Freytag & Berndt's scale 1:600,000, two sheets, 'West Yugoslavia' and 'East Yugoslavia'. Kummerly & Frey publish a quite detailed road map, scale 1:1,000,000 on one sheet.

Walking

The Julian Alps and *Kamnik Alps* of Slovenia provide excellent walking of all degrees of strenuousness in magnificent country, and are not too uncomfortably hot in summer.

For walking tours in other parts the height of summer is best avoided. Subject to this, suitable areas of exceptional interest include the *Plitvice Lakes National Park*, the *Mount Tara National Park*, the mountains south-west of *Sarajevo*, and the neighborhood of *Lakes Ohrid* and *Prespa* in Macedonia.

Mountaineering

Triglav (9,400ft, 2,865m), the highest peak in Yugoslavia, is in the *Julian Alps* — a continuation at a somewhat lower level of the *Karawanken* range just north of the border. It is regarded by mountaineers as the foremost challenge in the country. The *Julian Alps* and *Kamnik Alps* are well provided with huts, with a warden in charge. Meals can be obtained at many of the huts and need not be booked in advance.

The mountains in the centre and south of the country — in Croatia, Bosnia,

Montenegro and Macedonia — often separate small communities with their own local traditions and customs. The mountains themselves are wild and desolate and, since good walking maps are practically unobtainable, it is essential to be well equipped with both information and supplies.

Motoring

Motorists belonging to their own national organisations can benefit from facilities and concessions (especially discounted prices at filling stations) offered them by corresponding organisations in Yugoslavia; they need to carry with them their own national documents — vehicle registration certificate, certificate of insurance, international driving licence, together with a red warning triangle and international identity sticker. Although not compulsory, an international Green Insurance Card is advisable. International traffic regulations apply with the addition of speed limits, beginning at 60km/h (37mph) in built-up areas.

Problems met with are inadequate and/or expensive parking in cities, the hazards presented by the fast and aggressive motoring favoured by the Yugoslavs and the relative narrowness of many main roads. Motorways connect the cities and big towns; many stretches of them have toll charges. Minor roads are often unmetalled but all main roads are adequately surfaced.

Yugoslav Automobile Association (AMSJ) headquarters is at Ruzveltova 18 in *Belgrade* and there are branch offices in *Zagreb, Sarajevo, Skopje, Titograd* and *Ljubljana*.

Cycling

Road surfaces in Slovenia and the north are mostly good and those roads linking the cities and resorts throughout the country are first class, but cyclists can expect rough going on unmetalled roads on less frequented routes. A low-range gear capability is essential. Most available spares are in metric dimensions; spares for British and American machines are hard to come by.

Canoeing and Boating

The spectacular gorges of the River *Danube* in Bosnia can be navigated by log-raft from *Foca* to *Visegrad* (see **R4**), and on the River *Tara* from *Durdevica Tara* to *Foca*. Approach is by rail from *Sarajevo* via *Ustipraca* to *Foca*, where rafts may be hired, through the Foca Tourist Association.

Touring Routes

R1 Jesenice — Ljubljana — Pula — Rijeka (270 miles, 434km)

Walkers, cyclists and motorists can enter from Austria by *Wurzner Pass* (3,400ft, 1,036m) across *Karawanken Alps* down to *Podkoren*, the first town in Yugoslavia. Nearby *Kranjska Gora* is suitable starting point for walking and climbing tours in **Julian Alps**. First stop for international express trains is *Jesenice*, from which return to *Kranjska Gora* can be made by local trains. Paths in *Julian Alps* are well marked, but hut tours involve a good deal of scrambling, with use of pitons and fixed wire ropes.

Jesenice, frontier station and factory town. **Bled**Δ, 7 miles (11km); popular tourist resort in idyllic setting; boating and swimming in warm waters of lake; walk to *Vintgar Gorge* and *Falls*. *Bohinj Bistrica* village, 13 miles (21km), near **Lake Bohinj**; remote and quiet; walks to *Savica Falls*; *Valley of the Seven Lakes*: climbs include *Triglav* (9,400ft, 2,865m). Return to *Bled*. *Radovljica*, 5 miles (8km); medieval town with fine view of Alps.

Ljubljana, 26 miles (42km); capital of Slovenia; university town; baroque architecture in attractive Old Town; Cathedral of St Nicholas and Golovatz Castle: National Museum and Art Gallery: Modern Gallery.

Postojna, 35 miles (56km); magnificent caves, largest in Europe; miniature railway takes visitors 2 miles (3km) into caves of enormous dimensions and perfect acoustics; symphony concerts here during season. Route then skirts Italian territory, keeping to limestone uplands enjoying fine views over *Trieste*, then descending steeply to sea level.

Koper, 35 miles (56km); fifteenth-century cathedral; palaces. *Piran*, 10 miles (16km), one of many picturesque bathing and fishing resorts on coast of **Istria**. At *Buje* leave main road for coast road. *Porec*, 32 miles (51km), village; *Basilica of Euphrasius* with famous mosaics in style of Ravenna.

Across eroded limestone to *Pula*Δ, 35 miles (56km); port, with remarkably well-preserved Roman amphitheatre, second century AD, and *Temple of Augustus*. Summer season of opera and films in amphitheatre.

Through popular resorts on east coast of Istria to **Rijeka**, 65 miles (105km), chief port of Yugoslavia.

EXCURSIONS: (a) islands of **Krk** (with walled town of same name; cathedral and castle) and **Cres**; (b) *Senj*, 45 miles (72km), on gulf once hide-out of Uskok pirates; *Ucka*, mountain with fine view over bay and islands, accessible by road.

R2 Ljubljana — Maribor — Zagreb — Plitvice Lakes — Zadar (385 miles, 620km)

From *Ljubljana* to *Kamnik*, 14 miles (22km); castles of *Mari Grad* and *Stari Grad*. Road over **Kamnik Alps** by *Stahovica* and *Crnilec Pass* (2,931ft, 893m) to *Gornji Grad*, 17 miles (27km), mountain resort. Through gorge to *Mozirje*, 12 miles (19km). *Celje*, 18 miles (29km); town of Roman foundation; medieval and Renaissance buildings. Mountain road to *Slovenska Bistrica*, 25 miles (40km), famous for its wines.

Maribor, on River *Drava*, 13 miles (21km), chief city of Slovenian Styria; in countryside of apple orchards; many Renaissance and Baroque buildings showing Austrian influence; museum in castle. *Ptuj*, 16 miles (26km); wine-making town on Roman site; *Temple of Mithras*, Wine Museum. South-west to *Ptujska Gora*, 8 miles (13km); fifteenth-century church with fine wood carvings. At *Rogatec* enter Croatia. *Krapina*, 31 miles (50km) from *Ptuj*.

ZagrebΔ, 39 miles (63km), capital of Croatia and second city of Yugoslavia; rich cultural centre; opera, theatres, concerts; several museums and galleries; parks.

EXCURSIONS: (a) **Mount Sljeme** (3,395ft, 1,053m), 5 miles (8km) north. (b) **Zelanjac Gorge** near *Klanjec* in *Sutla Valley*, 32 miles (51km). (c) *Samobor*, 15 miles (24km), picturesque village.

Karlovac, 35 miles (56km) south-west, fortified town up *Korana* valley; *Slunj*, 32 miles (51km); castle. **Plitvice Lakes National Park**, 27 miles (43km); series of sixteen beautiful lakes linked by waterfalls. Through forest country via *Titova Korencia*, 13 miles (21km); *Udbina*, 20 miles (32km); *Ploca*, 10 miles (16km); and across *Velebit* mountains at 3,427ft (1,044m), to coast road at *Jasenica*, 35 miles (51km). **Zadar**, 20 miles (32km) (see **R3**).

R3 Rijeka — Zadar — Split — Dubrovnik (405 miles, 652km)

From *Rijeka* (see **R1**) by steamer to **Zadar**Δ (or 141 miles, 227km by coast road, with many beaches); ancient town on peninsula; *Roman Forum* and many other Roman remains; associations with Fourth Crusade (1204); held by Venetians for almost 600 years, then by Habsburgs; Venetian walls and fortifications, narrow alleys; *Church of St Donat*, ninth century, now a museum.

EXCURSIONS: (a) **Nin**, 12 miles (19km), village near ruined Roman town. *Aenona Civitas*; capital of Croatia in ninth century, ninth-century *Church of St Croce* and ruined *Church of St Ambrogio*. (b) cruising by fishing boats among the many islands.

SibenikΔ, by steamer (or road, 45 miles, 72km); busy port on extraordinary island-studded inlet; town built steeply on hillside, dominated by *Castle of St Anne* (view); famous Gothic and Renaissance cathedral, built of local stone, including its remarkably wide roof.

EXCURSIONS: (a) *Skradin* (boat or bus) for **Krka Falls.** (b) island of **Zlarin**, known for corals and sponges; local costumes; bathing.

Trogir, 36 miles (58km), on small peninsula; originally Greek settlement (third century BC); now largely Venetian in appearance; Romanesque and Gothic cathedral with rich carvings; *Kamerlengo Castle; Church of St Barbara* (ninth century) and many other interesting buildings.

Road along Riviera of the Seven Castles; fortified villages among olive groves and vineyards. *Kastel Gomilica.*

Split (*Spalato*), 17 miles (27km); name means 'in the palace' and the city has grown in the vast fourth-century **Palace of Diocletian** (715ft x 577ft, 218m x 176m); Venetian and other buildings among the Roman columns; circular cathedral, designed as Emperor's mausoleum; general view of palace from cathedral tower; narrow Venetian streets; important archaeological and ethnographic museums; medieval churches. Direct journey by road to *Dubrovnik* is 145 miles (233km) with *Duce-Omis*Δ, *Baska Voda*Δ, *Makarska*Δ, *Zaostrog*Δ, and *Neum*Δ en route.

EXCURSIONS: **Mestrovic Museum** on route to *Solin*, near which are ruins of *Salona*, Roman capital of Dalmatia; museum. Medieval fortress of *Klis* in hills above.

Steamer to **Hvar**, ancient Greek *Pharos*, island noted for mild climate, subtropical vegetation, flowers and fruit. Steamer to **Korcula**Δ, home of Marco Polo, on well-wooded island of same name. Steamer to *Dubrovnik.*

Dubrovnik Δ, formerly *Ragusa*, with long tradition as independent republic trading by land and sea all over Europe. Splendid walls and towers entirely contain old town; walk around ramparts takes about half an hour and affords views across city, notably from *Minceta Tower*; main street built after earthquake (1667); *palazzi* in narrow streets; *Cathedral of St Biagio* with many treasures; *Rector's Palace; Franciscan Monastery*; Summer Festival; national costumes often worn. Busy resort, best visited out of season; mild winters.

EXCURSIONS: (a) *Mount Sergius* (1,350ft, 412m) with Napoleonic fort; on foot by winding path from *Minceta Tower* (about 1 hour) for panoramic view. (b) *Lokrum*, island where Richard Coeur de Lion was shipwrecked. (c) *Trsteno*, tropical botanical garden and *Falls of River Ombla*. (d) **Trebinje**, 15 miles (24km), small market town in Herzegovina with Turkish buildings and oriental atmosphere (see **R4**).

R4 Dubrovnik — Mostar — Sarajevo — Foca — Dubrovnik (387 miles, 623km)

Follow coast road north-west to *Metkovic*, 56 miles (90km), by hairpin bends up valley of River *Neretva*.

Mostar, 31 miles (50km), chief town of Herzegovina, named from its famous Turkish bridge (1566) over *Neretva*; gaunt surroundings of *karst* cliffs; many mosques, including sixteenth century *Karadjoz Bey's*.

Continue up spectacular *Neretva* valley; *Jablanica* 30 miles (48km); road follows barrage lake to *Konjic*, 15 miles (24km), and across *Mount Ivan* to *Sarajevo*, 38 miles (61km).

SarajevoΔ, capital of Bosnia-Herzegovina. Contrasts between oriental town of Turkish period, nineteenth-century town of Austro-Hungarian administration and modern industrial and residential town. Among many mosques, particularly fine are the *Gazi-Husref-Bey Mosque* (sixteenth century) and the *Medresa Seminary* near the famous souks. View from *Mount Trebevic*Δ (cable-car); rich National Museum; museum relating to assassination here of Archduke Franz Ferdinand, which sparked off World War I.

R4 (i) Sarajevo to Jajce. *Kiseljak*, 23 miles (37km) spa. *Busovaca*, 16 miles (26km). **Travnik,** 18 miles (29km), the 'green city', in beautiful countryside, once residence of Turkish Governor of Bosnia; **Suleiman Mosque;** *Mosque of Knoak*: tombs of Pashas and Turkish cemetery. Through wooded mountain country, road reaching 3,041ft (927m), and descending to *Donji Vakuf*, 23 miles (37km); market town on River *Vrbas*.

  Jajce, 22 miles (35km), historic town in delightful natural setting where River *Pliva* falls 100ft (30m) to join *Vrbas*. Reputed burial place of St Luke. Declaration of Republic made here in 1943. Fortress; Franciscan church; wooden Turkish water-mills.

Road eastwards climbing to 4,534ft (1,382m). Fork right at *Podromanija*, 29 miles (47km); *Rogatica*, 20 miles (32km); *Gorazde*, 23 miles (37km), on River *Drina*; fishing centre. At *Foca*, 21 miles (34km), begins the two-day passage of the **Drina Gorges** by log-raft to *Visegrad* through spectacular canyons. *Foca* is fishing centre; fine *Aladza Mosque*; town and district were scene of much fighting in World War II. *Tjentiste*, 19 miles (30km); War Memorial, focus of national patriotism. Road climbs *Sutjseka* valley and descends to *Gacko*, 26 miles (42km). *Bileca,* 30 miles (48km); where River *Trebisnjica* disappears underground. *Trebinje*, 17 miles (27km); *Mosque of Osman Pasha*; Bey's House. Westward by steeply engineered road, for 19 miles (30km) to *Dubrovnik*.

R5 Sarajevo — Visegrad — Mount Tara — Belgrade (228 miles, 367km)
Sarajevo (see **R4**). East of twisting mountain roads to *Podromanija*, 29 miles (47km), *Rogatica*, 20 miles (32km) and *Visegrad* 25 miles (40km); sixteenth-century bridge of eleven arches over River *Drina*, finest Turkish bridge in Yugoslavia.

At *Kremna*, 25 miles (40km), by-road leads into **Mount Tara National Park**; densely forested, with rich flora and fauna. *Titova Uzice*, 44 miles (71km); finely situated industrial town.

Road north to *Karan*, 13 miles (21km); fine Serbian Orthodox church with fourteenth-century frescoes. By winding road through *Kosjeric* and *Bukovi* to *Valjevo*, 36 miles (58km), famous for plums and other fruit. Road enters plain of River *Sava*. *Obrenovac*, 30 miles (48km), and thence to *Belgrade*, 20 miles (32km).

BelgradeΔ, capital of Serbia and of the Federal Republic, in historically fateful position on *Pannonian Plain* at confluence of *Sava* and *Danube*. Citadel of *Kalemegdan*: Mestrovic statue, the *Pobednik* (Victor); Cathedral of St *Sava*, now being rebuilt as the largest Orthodox cathedral in the world; National Museum; Fresco Art Gallery (copies of medieval frescoes in the monasteries).

EXCURSIONS: (a) **Mount Avala** (1,702ft, 518m), 12 miles (19km), with monument to Unknown Warrior by Mestrovic; view over *Belgrade*. (b) the **Iron Gates of the Danube**: steamer down river through *Djerdap Gorges (Iron Gates)* — one of the grandest natural features of Europe; night at *Kladovo*, returning upstream next day. (c) **Smederevo**, 30 miles (48km), huge fifteenth-century fortress on *Danube*. (d) **Fruska Gora**, wooded hills about 45 miles (72km) north-west, with several Orthodox monasteries built as refuge from Turks.

R6 Dubrovnik — Cetinje — Skopje (331 miles, 531km)

Road southwards along coast, *Cavtat* 9 miles (14km); agreeable little resort, *Gruda,* 11 miles (18km). *Herceg-Novi*, 11 miles (18km), built in tiers overlooking *Boka Kotorska*, extraordinary fjord-like inlet; lush, sub-tropical vegetation; Spanish, Turkish and Venetian fortresses.

EXCURSIONS: (a) *Savina Monastery* with valuable library. (b) *Mount Radostak* (4,700ft, 1,431m), view over the *Boka*.

Road skirts around *Boka Kotorska*, passing through *Zelenika*Δ and ancient, historic ports of *Risan* and *Perast* to **Kotor**, 30 miles (48km), at its head (also steamer from *Herzeg-Novi*); town famed (with *Perast*) for its seamanship; spectacular setting at foot of *Mount Lovcen* (5,770ft, 1,758m); Romanesque cathedral; Maritime Museum.

Steep zigzag road climbing 4,000ft (1,200m) up *Mount Lovcen* with magnificent views over the *Boka*. Road continues across arid *karst* to **Cetinje**, 26 miles (42km), former capital of Montenegro; museums. **Titograd**, 30 miles (48km), rebuilt town and new capital, on ancient site.

R6 (i) South Montenegrin Littoral. At *Budva,* 26 miles (42km) from *Kotor*, road begins to hug a coast more indented than Dalmatia, and without islands; good beaches. *Budva* can also be reached by steamer from Herceg-Novi; it has an eighth-century church with seventeenth-century Venetian paintings. Follow coast road via *Petrovac*Δ, *Buljarice*Δ and *Sutomore*Δ for 28 miles (45km), to *Bar*, near ruins of older town; railway inland to *Titograd, Ulcinj*Δ, 18 miles (29km), once haunt of pirates.

R6 (ii) Durmitor Mountains. From *Titograd* via *Niksic*, 35 miles (56km); mountain road to *Savnik*, 28 miles (45km) and *Zabljak*, 25 miles (40km); base for walks and climbs in mountains reaching 8,000ft (2,400m).

Mountain road to *Andrijevica*, 62 miles (100km). From *Murino*, 11 miles (18km), road climbs to *Cakor Pass* (6,067ft, 1,849m) on Serbian border, descending to Pec Δ, 38 miles (61km), centre of *Metohija* district (part of *Kosmet*, an autonomous area of Serbia, with an Albanian minority); town of oriental character.

At *Decani*, 10 miles (16km) south, detour 2 miles (3km) north-west through mountain scenery to fourteenth-century Romanesque-Byzantine monastery of *Visoki-Decani*, fine building with particularly interesting frescoes.

Djakovica, 13 miles (21km); town noted for gold and silver filigree work. *Prizren*, 23 miles (37km); similarly noted, picturesque town under fortress of *Kaljaja*; medieval frescoes in *Church of Our Lady of Ljeviska*, fourteenth century; *Mosque of Sinan Pasha*.

Road eastwards over **Sar Planina** mountains, *Gabrica*, 35 miles (56km). *Kacanik*, 6 miles (10km). South through gorge between *Black Mountains* of *Skopje* and *Sar Planina* mountains near peak of *Ljuboten* (8,189ft, 2,496m). At *Cucer*, 13 miles (21km), detour 1 mile (1^1/$_2$km) east to *Church of Sveti Nikita*: medieval frescoes.

SkopjeΔ (10 miles, 16km) on River *Vardar*; capital of Macedonia; scene of disastrous earthquake, July 1963; monuments of Roman and Ottoman empires remain, albeit restored. *Emperor Dusan Bridge* (fourteenth century); *Dhaut Pasha's Hammam* (Turkish bath, which now contains museum of Macedonian history and gallery of sixteenth-century icons); *Mosque of Mustapha Pasha*; *Mosque of Isa Beg*; *Kursumli Han* caravanserai; *Kale* fortress; *Orthodox Church* of *St Spas* with fine wood carving and paintings.

EXCURSIONS: (a) *Mount Vodno*, view of *Skopje* and *Vardar* valley. (b) **Nerezi**, 3 miles (5km); church with famous twelfth-century frescoes, important in art history. (c) through *Treska* gorges to monasteries of *Matka* and *Sveti Andrija* (St Andrew); frescoes.

R7 Skopje — Bitola — Lake Ohrid — Tetovo — Skopje (288 miles, 464km)

Skopje (see **R6**) to *Titov Veles*, 33 miles (53km); town finely situated on both sides of gorge of River *Vardar*, with many mosques, but crowned by modern Serbian Orthodox Church; junction of two routes into Greece. *Gradsko*, 16 miles (26km) where Roman *Via Egnatia* joins historic route through *Vardar* gap. *Stobi*, 3 miles (5km) south, excavated Greek and Roman town; impressive remains.

By *Via Egnatia* across mountains to *Prilep*, 36 miles (58km); modern market town, tobacco growing centre. *Vissovi*, 13 miles (21km), necropolis of 1,500BC. *Bitola*, 10 miles (16km) (near ancient *Heraclea*); *Church of St Dimitri* (wood carvings); many mosques. Mountain road westwards reaching 3,875ft (1,181m) to *Resen*, 21 miles (34km), and another pass, 3,872ft (1,180m), to *Ohrid*, 24 miles (39km).

OhridΔ, ancient and delightful town beautifully sited on *Lake Ohrid*; enjoys exceptionally mild climate although altitude of 2,300ft (700m), crystal clear waters, famous for trout, pebble beaches, important in history of Orthodox Church; Cyrillic script invented here. Many churches and monasteries with remarkable frescoes, notably *St Sophia*, where Turks white-washed walls to obliterate paintings and thus preserved them, *St Clement* higher up, has particularly fine fourteenth-century frescoes, recently restored and *St Jovan Kaneo* on castle hill and fine prospect of lake. At southern end of lake, reached by boat, or 19 miles (30km) by road, is *Monastery of St Naum* (tenth century) in lovely situation with sandy beach.

Lakeside road north-west to *Struga,* 10 miles (16km). *Velesta* 6 miles (10km); Albanian type village. Road skirts Albanian frontier. *Debar,* 27 miles (43km). At *Boletin,* 15 miles (24km), in *Radika* valley, track on right to *Monastery of St Jovan Bigorski,* impressively sited building, with famous Filipovski wood carvings. Return to *Boletin;* continue up *Radika* gorge between high mountains (*Korab,* 9,070ft, 2,764m), *Lake Mavrovo,* 12 miles (19km). Road climbs to 4,462ft (1,360m), and descends to *Gostivar,* 15 miles (24km). *Tetovo,* 16 miles (26km), at foot of *Sar Planina* mountains, for mountaineering and winter sports; famous *Coloured Mosque. Skopje,* 27 miles (43km).

R8 Skopje — Nis — Belgrade (294 miles, 473km)
Skopje (see **R6**) to *Kumanovo* (20 miles, 32km) (7 miles, 11km, westwards among mountains is remote *Matejic Monastery*). Near *Strezovce,* 11 miles (18km) enter Serbia. At *Bujanovac,* 12 miles (19km), join valley of River *Morava.* **Vranje** 10 miles (16km), town of district noted for flax and tobacco; Turkish bridge, Turkish baths, Derenka fountain; two residences of pashas. *Vladicin Han,* 15 miles (24km), small Turkish town. Road passes through *Grdelica Gorge* for 19 miles (30km) to *Grdelica. Leskovac,* 11 miles (18km), industrial town; two museums; traditional Balkan houses.

Nis, 28 miles (45km), rail and road centre at confluence of *Nisava* and *Morava*; birthplace of Constantine, first Christian Roman Emperor; a place much fought over throughout history; fortress originally Byzantine, now of Turkish appearance, seventeen sides and five bastions; notorious *Cele Kula (Tower of Skulls)* (1809), barbaric memorial of Ottoman rule; rebuilt *Monastery of Panteleimon; Archaeological Museum.*

Continue down fertile, populous valley of *Morava. Aleksinac,* 21 miles (34km); *Cuprija,* 36 miles (58km), a bridge town.

EXCURSION: valley and gorge of **River Ravanica**, many caves and water-sinks in limestone; fourteenth-century Ravanica monastery, 7 miles (11km).

Direct road to *Belgrade* is busy motorway, or route can be taken westwards across hills via *Kragujevac*Δ and *Topola.* An alternative route goes 15 miles (24km) northwards to remarkable fortified **Manasija Monastery**, fifteenth century, with moat and eleven towers; beautiful frescoes. Road north-west down fertile *Resava* valley. *Svilajnac,* 15 miles (24km). Turn westwards across motorway to *Raca,* 10 miles (16km); unusual eighteenth-century wooden church; *Topola,* 21 miles (34km).

Mladenovac, 15 miles (24km); *Mountt Avala* (see **R5**), 23 miles (37km); **Belgrade,** (see **R5**), 12 miles (19km).

Continental Measures

The metric system (based on multiples of 10) is used in all continental countries. Distances are measured in kilometres, length and heights in metres, weight in grams.

Length
30 centimetres = 1 foot.
1 metre = 39.37 inches.

Weight
10 grams = $\frac{1}{3}$ oz.
100 grams = $3\frac{1}{2}$ oz.
500 grams = $\frac{1}{2}$ kilo = just over 1 lb.
1,000 grams = 1 kilo = $2\frac{1}{5}$ lb.

Volume
1 litre = $1\frac{3}{4}$ pints.

Kilometres to Miles
For approximate conversions, divide by 8 and multiply by 5.

Km	Miles	Km	Miles
1.0	$\frac{5}{8}$	100	62
1.6	1	200	124
8	5	300	186
10	$6\frac{1}{4}$	400	249
16	10	500	311
50	31	1,000	621

Metres to Feet
Heights are measured in metres. One metre is 39.4in, or 3.28 ft, but for rough calculations multiply the figure in metres by 3.3.

Metres	Feet	Metres	Feet
100	328	500	1,640
200	656	1,000	3,280
300	984	2,000	6,560
400	1,312	3,000	9,840

International Rail Timetable Signs

 Sleeping car

 Dining car

 In train column = refreshments obtainable on train. In station column = refreshment room on station.

 Frontier station; customs and passport check

 Trains running on certain days only

 Couchette

 Train subject to special regulations stated in footnotes of the timetable concerned

 Sundays and public holidays only

 Except Sundays and public holidays

 Diesel rail car

 Through carriages, classes indicated by numbers

Index

Abbreviation used: Is = Island(s), L = Lake, Mon = Monastery, P = Peninsula, R = River, V = Valley.

For names beginning Bad, Col, La, Le, Les, Mont, etc, see under place name, eg Bad Aussee = Aussee, Bad.

AUSTRIA

BELGIUM

DENMARK

ENGLAND AND WALES

FINLAND

FRANCE

GERMANY

GREECE

ICELAND

IRELAND (REPUBLIC)

IRELAND (NORTHERN)

ITALY

LUXEMBOURG

NETHERLANDS

NORWAY

PORTUGAL

SCOTLAND

SPAIN

SWEDEN

SWITZERLAND

YUGOSLAVIA